The publisher gratefully acknowledges the
generous contribution to this book provided by
the Classical Literature Endowment Fund of
the University of California Press Foundation,
which is supported by a major gift
from Joan Palevsky.

# The Mother of the Gods, Athens, and the Tyranny of Asia

# The Mother
# of the Gods, Athens,
# and the Tyranny of Asia

*A Study of Sovereignty in Ancient Religion*

Mark Munn

UNIVERSITY OF CALIFORNIA PRESS

*Berkeley   Los Angeles   London*

Frontispiece. Attic funerary relief depicting husband and wife, with attributes of the Mother of the Gods—lion and tympanum—accompanying the wife, circa 350 B.C.E. (Ashmolean Museum, Oxford, inv. no. 1959.203).

*For Mary Lou*
*Loving wife, wise mother*

University of California Press, one of the most distinguished
university presses in the United States, enriches lives around the
world by advancing scholarship in the humanities, social sciences,
and natural sciences. Its activities are supported by the UC Press
Foundation and by philanthropic contributions from individuals
and institutions. For more information, visit www.ucpress.edu.

University of California Press
Berkeley and Los Angeles, California

University of California Press, Ltd.
London, England

Library of Congress Cataloging-in-Publication Data

Munn, Mark Henderson.
    The Mother of the Gods, Athens, and the tyranny of Asia : a study
of sovereignty in ancient religion / Mark Henderson Munn.
        p.      cm.
    Includes bibliographical references and index.
    ISBN 0-520-24349-8 (cloth : alk. paper)
        1. Cybele (Goddess)—Cult—Greece—Athens—History.
    2. Religion and politics—Greece—Athens—History.
    3. Sovereignty—Religious aspects—History of doctrines.
    4. Cybele (Goddess)—Cult—Turkey—Lydia (Kingdom).
    5. Religion and politics—Turkey—Lydia (Kingdom)—
    History.   6. Despotism—Religious aspects—History of
    doctrines.   I. Title.

    BL820.C8M86    2006
    292.2'114—dc22                                    2005013449

Manufactured in the United States of America
13   12   11   10   09   08   07   06
10   9   8   7   6   5   4   3   2   1

This book is printed on New Leaf EcoBook 60, containing 60%
post-consumer waste, processed chlorine-free; 30% de-inked
recycled fiber, elemental chlorine–free; and 10% FSC-certified
virgin fiber, totally chlorine-free. EcoBook 60 is acid-free and
meets the minimum requirements of ANSI/ASTM D5634–01
(Permanence of Paper).

# CONTENTS

# ILLUSTRATIONS

# PREFACE

This book has many origins. As the outgrowth of ideas formulated in *The School of History: Athens in the Age of Socrates,* I presented a paper entitled "The Mother of the Gods and Athenian Identity" in the colloquium "Reading Ancient Ritual," organized by Lisa Maurizio, Victoria Wohl, and Deborah Lyons, at the annual meeting of the American Philological Association, December 1998. That paper was refined through presentations at the Johns Hopkins University in September 2000, at the invitation of Alan Shapiro and the Department of Classics, and at Bryn Mawr College in April 2001, at the invitation of Leslie Lundeen and the graduate students of the Department of Greek, Latin and Ancient History. In light of discussions on those occasions, it seemed appropriate to transform the paper into a book. The project grew quickly, thanks to the experience of years of study around a topic that, I came to realize, has guided my approach to classical studies.

Like the subject of the present book, I came to Greece from the East. By virtue of my father's career in the diplomatic corps, I saw Babylon, Jerusalem, Gordium, and Sardis before I ever arrived in Athens. That experience led me to an undergraduate degree in classical studies at the University of California at San Diego in 1974, where I wrote an honors thesis entitled "Kybele" under the direction of Edward Lee. Later that year, in the Graduate Group in Ancient History at the University of Pennsylvania, my interest in this transcultural phenomenon of the eastern Mediterranean yielded my first graduate research paper, "The (Phrygian) Mother of the (Greek) Gods," written for Michael Jameson. Eventually, it led to my first dissertation proposal in 1977, "Kubaba: A Study of the Cultural Affinities of North Syria/Cappadocia, ca. 1900–500 B.C.," which was accepted by James Muhly. Then I arrived at Athens, where Tyche led me in other directions—fortunately. For though I had formulated most of the questions that underlie this book,

I did not yet have the experience that could yield productive insights on so large a topic.

Rediscovery has been key to progress. Good fortune has placed me among colleagues and students at the Pennsylvania State University whose interests, expertise, and advice have encouraged my work. Among these I especially thank Philip Baldi, Jonathan David, Baruch Halpern, and Gonzalo Rubio, who have all made helpful comments on portions of the manuscript. From outside Penn State, I thank J. David Hawkins and Craig Melchert, who have given valuable advice on linguistic matters, and Stephanie Lynn Budin, Keith DeVries, Crawford H. Greenewalt, Jr., Olga Palagia, and Alan Shapiro for references and other useful guidance. Most helpful have been those who have read and commented on the whole manuscript: Kurt Raaflaub, Lynn Roller, Henk Versnel, an anonymous reader for the University of California Press, and my wife, Mary Lou Zimmerman Munn. I thank them for their patience and perspectives, which have helped to improve many aspects of my thought and expression. Translations, unless otherwise noted, are my own. I thank the Department of History at Penn State and its donors for subvening the cost of photographs. Finally, I thank the editorial staff at the University of California Press, Julie Brand, Laura Cerruti, Cindy Fulton, Paul Psoinos, Kate Toll, and Lynne Withey, for seeing this book through.

# ABBREVIATIONS

| | |
|---|---|
| A²Hc | Artaxerxes II, Hamadan C: Old Persian text and translation (in Kent 1950, 155) |
| A²Sa | Artaxerxes II, Susa A: Old Persian text and translation (in Kent 1950, 154) |
| AA | *Archäologischer Anzeiger* |
| ABSA | *Annual of the British School at Athens* |
| AC | L'Antiquité Classique |
| AD | *Archaiologikon Deltion* |
| AfO | *Archiv für Orientforschung* |
| AJA | *American Journal of Archaeology* |
| AnatStud | *Anatolian Studies* |
| ANET | *Ancient Near Eastern Texts Relating to the Old Testament*, 3rd. ed., with Supplement, ed. J. B. Pritchard (Princeton, 1969) |
| AntK | *Antike Kunst* |
| AntW | *Antike Welt* |
| Bartoletti | V. Bartoletti, ed., *Hellenica Oxyrhynchia* (Leipzig, 1959) |
| BASOR | *Bulletin of the American Schools of Oriental Research* |
| BCH | *Bulletin de Correspondance Hellénique* |
| BICS | *Bulletin of the Institute of Classical Studies* |
| CA | *Classical Antiquity* |
| CAD | [*The Chicago*] *Assyrian Dictionary*, 21 vols. (Chicago, 1956–92) |
| CAH | *The Cambridge Ancient History*, 3 eds., 11 vols. (Cambridge, 1924–2000) |
| CHLI | J. D. Hawkins, ed., *Corpus of Hieroglyphic Luwian Inscriptions*, vol. 1, *Inscriptions of the Iron Age*, 3 parts (Berlin, 2000) |
| CJ | *Classical Journal* |
| CP | *Classical Philology* |

| | |
|---|---|
| *CQ* | *Classical Quarterly* |
| *CRAI* | *Comptes Rendus de l'Academie des Inscriptions et Belles-Lettres* |
| *CSCA* | *California Studies in Classical Antiquity* |
| Davies | M. Davies, ed., *Poetarum Melicorum Graecorum Fragmenta*, vol. 1, *Alcman, Stesichorus, Ibycus* (Oxford, 1991) |
| DB | Darius, Behistun: Old Persian text and translation (in Kent 1950, 116–34) |
| Dindorf | W. Dindorf, ed., *Aristides*, 3 vols. (Leipzig, 1829) |
| DK | H. Diels and W. Kranz, eds., *Die Fragmente der Vorsokratiker*, 6th ed., 3 vols. (Berlin, 1951–54; reprint: Zurich, 1996–98) |
| DNa | Darius, Naqsh-i-Rustam A: Old Persian text and translation (in Kent 1950, 137–38) |
| DPe | Darius, Persepolis E: Old Persian text and translation (in Kent 1950, 136) |
| DSm | Darius, Susa M: Old Persian text and translation (in Kent 1950, 145) |
| Edmonds *EI* | J. M. Edmonds, ed., *Greek Elegy and Iambus*, 2 vols., Loeb Classical Library (Cambridge, Mass., 1931) |
| Edmonds *LG* | J. M. Edmonds, ed., *Lyra Graeca*, 2nd ed., 3 vols., Loeb Classical Library (Cambridge, Mass., 1928) |
| *EG* | D. L. Page, ed., *Epigrammata Graeca* (Oxford, 1975) |
| Evelyn-White | H. G. Evelyn-White, ed., *Hesiod, the Homeric Hymns and Homerica*, Loeb Classical Library (Cambridge, Mass., 1914) |
| *FGrHist* | F. Jacoby, ed., *Die Fragmente der griechischen Historiker*, 3 vols. in 7 (Berlin, 1923–) |
| Fornara | C. Fornara, ed., *Translated Documents of Greece and Rome*, vol. 1, *Archaic Times to the End of the Peloponnesian War*, 2nd ed. (Cambridge, 1983) |
| *GRBS* | *Greek, Roman and Byzantine Studies* |
| Harding | P. Harding, ed., *Translated Documents of Greece and Rome*, vol. 2, *From the End of the Peloponnesian War to the Battle of Ipsus* (Cambridge, 1985) |
| *HSCP* | *Harvard Studies in Classical Philology* |
| *HTR* | *Harvard Theological Review* |
| *ICS* | *Illinois Classical Studies* |
| *IG* | *Inscriptiones Graecae* (Berlin, 1873–1981) |
| *IstMitt* | *Mitteilungen des Deutschen Archäologischen Instituts (Istanbul)* |
| *JANER* | *Journal of Ancient Near Eastern Religions* |
| *JAOS* | *Journal of the American Oriental Society* |
| *JHS* | *Journal of Hellenic Studies* |
| *JNES* | *Journal of Near Eastern Studies* |
| *JRS* | *Journal of Roman Studies* |

KA      R. Kassel and C. Austin, eds., *Poetae Comici Graeci* (Berlin, 1983–)

*LCM*    *Liverpool Classical Monthly*

*LIMC*   *Lexicon Iconographicum Mythologiae Classicae*, ed. L. Kahil, 8 vols.
        in 16 parts (Zurich, 1981–99)

LP      E. S. Lobel and D. Page, eds., *Poetarum Lesbiorum Fragmenta*
        (Oxford, 1955)

LSJ     H. G. Liddell, R. Scott, and H. S. Jones, eds., *A Greek-English
        Lexicon*, 9th ed. (Oxford, 1940; with Supplement, 1968)

*LW*     R. Gusmani, *Lydisches Wörterbuch* (Heidelberg, 1964)

*LWErg*  R. Gusmani, *Lydisches Wörterbuch: Ergänzungsband*, 3 fascicles
        (Heidelberg, 1980–86)

*MH*     *Museum Helveticum*

ML      R. Meiggs and D. Lewis, eds., *A Selection of Greek Historical Inscrip-
        tions to the End of the Fifth Century B.C.* (Oxford, 1969)

MW      R. Merkelbach and M. L. West, eds., *Fragmenta Hesiodea* (Oxford,
        1967)

Nauck   A. Nauck, ed., *Tragicorum Graecorum Fragmenta*, 2nd ed. (Leipzig,
        1889)

*OJA*    *Oxford Journal of Archaeology*

*PCPS*   *Proceedings of the Cambridge Philological Society*

*QUCC*   *Quaderni Urbinati di Cultura Classica*

*RA*     *Revue Archéologique*

Radt    S. L. Radt, ed., *Tragicorum Graecorum Fragmenta*, vol. 3, *Aeschylus*
        (Göttingen, 1985); vol. 4, *Sophocles* (Göttingen, 1977)

*RdA*    *Revue d'Assyriologie et d'Archéologie Orientale*

*RE*     *Real-Encyclopädie der Classischen Altertumswissenschaft*, ed. A. von
        Pauly, G. Wissowa, et al. (Stuttgart, 1839–)

*REA*    *Revue des Etudes Anciennes*

*RhM*    *Rheinisches Museum*

*RLA*    *Reallexikon der Assyriologie* [*und vorderasiatischen Archäologie*]
        (Berlin, 1932–)

Rose    V. Rose, ed., *Aristotelis Qui Ferebantur Librorum Fragmenta* (Berlin,
        1886; reprint: Stuttgart, 1967)

Sandys  J. Sandys, *The Odes of Pindar, Including the Principal Fragments*,
        Loeb Classical Library (Cambridge, Mass., 1946)

*SEG*    *Supplementum Epigraphicum Graecum* (Leiden, 1923–)

*SIG³*   *Sylloge Inscriptionum Graecarum*, ed. W. Dittenberger, 3rd ed.
        (Leipzig, 1915)

*SMEA*   *Studi Micinei ed Egeo-anatolici*

Snell   B. Snell, ed., *Pindari Carmina cum Fragmentis* (Leipzig, 1955)

*SV*     *Die Staatsverträge des Altertums*, ed. H. Bengtson, vol. 2, *Die Verträge
        der griechisch-römischen Welt* (Munich, 1962)

*TAPA*   *Transactions of the American Philological Society*

Thalheim *AO*   T. Thalheim, ed., *Antiphontis Orationes* (Leipzig, 1904)

Thalheim *LO*   T. Thalheim, ed., *Lysiae Orationes* (Leipzig, 1901)

Tod             M. N. Tod, ed., *A Selection of Greek Historical Inscriptions*, vol. 2, *From 403 to 323 B.C.* (Oxford, 1948)

West            M. L. West, ed., *Iambi et Elegi Graeci ante Alexandrum Cantati*, 2 vols., 2nd ed. (Oxford, 1989–92)

West *LH*       M. L. West, ed., *Lives of Homer*, in *Homeric Hymns, Homeric Apocrypha, Lives of Homer*, Loeb Classical Library (Cambridge, Mass., 2003)

Winiarczyk      M. Winiarczyk, *Diagorae Melii et Theodori Cyrenaei Reliquiae* (Leipzig, 1981)

Wyss            B. Wyss, ed., *Antimachi Colophonii Reliquae* (Berlin, 1936)

XPh             Xerxes, Persepolis H (Daiva Inscription): Old Persian text and translation (in Kent 1950, 150–52)

*ZPE*           *Zeitschrift für Papyrologie und Epigraphik*

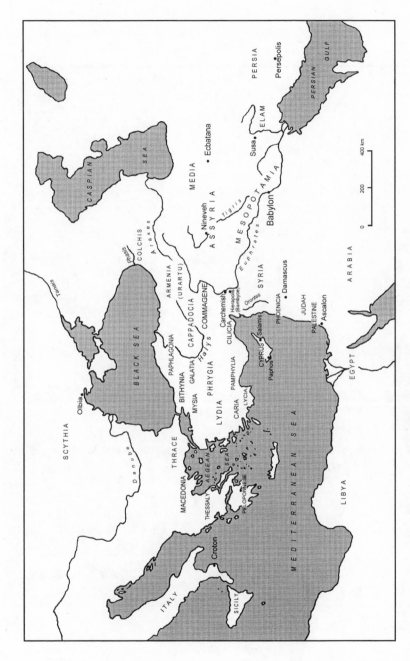

Map 1. The eastern Mediterranean and the Near East.

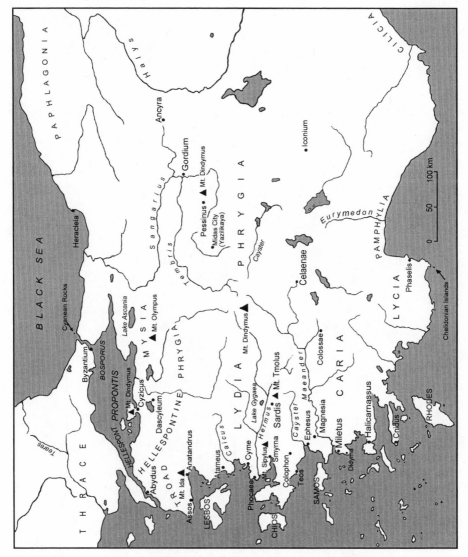

Map 2. Western Anatolia.

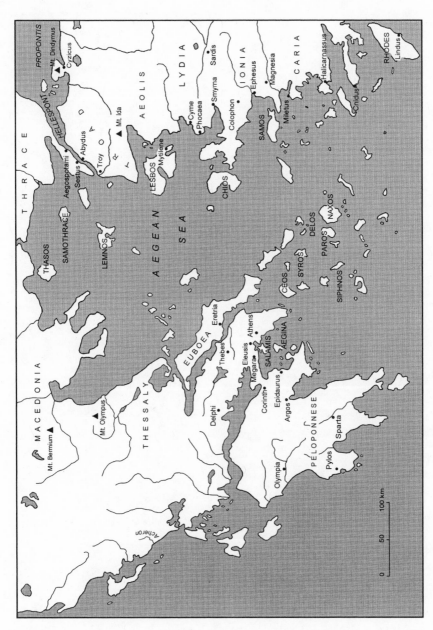

Map 3. Aegean Greece.

# Introduction

The present study originates in the question: How did the Mother of the Gods, a foreign deity, come to Athens? An answer to this question requires an understanding of the role of religion in classical Greek history, giving equal attention to the evidence of history and of religious ideology. To pursue such an understanding in the case of the Mother of the Gods and Athens, this study moves on two levels. One is the level of narrative, describing the background of the cult of the Mother of the Gods, and the circumstances under which it became established at Athens. Right away, however, the subject becomes complicated. Her story is the model of an etiological myth, describing the power of a deity through her manifest impact on a great city of men. Her arrival in that city is said to be historical, but the evidence is unclear about when this took place. As a result, all accounts of the Mother of the Gods and Athens, both in ancient sources and in modern scholarship, have left the historical side of the question vaguely defined, and historically inadequate.

In order to situate the story of the Mother of the Gods and Athens more firmly in the history of ancient religion, this investigation moves at a second and more general level. It examines the relationship between humanity and divinity, between human communities and the world, and the meanings of these relationships for the nature of sovereign power, especially as these issues were conceived by Greeks of classical antiquity. These are the concepts that underlay Herodotus' historical inquiries. As will be shown in the present study, Herodotus' work preserves elements of the story of the Mother of the Gods and Athens interwoven with insights into the nature of sovereign power and of the relationship of humanity to universal divinity. Herodotus' *Histo-*

*ries* further demonstrates that the Greek perspective on these concepts cannot be studied in Greek terms alone. From the beginning of the orientalizing era in the seventh century through Herodotus' day in the fifth, the Greeks were forming their ideas of sovereignty, humanity, and divinity with an awareness of the wider world, populated by others in addition to themselves. If we are curious, therefore, to understand the Greek quest for universal truths about the human condition, we need to consider in historical terms the manner in which the Greeks encountered and interacted with such high-order concepts among their neighbors. The story of the Mother of the Gods and Athens, as we will see, provides a suitable historical framework upon which to build such a larger understanding.

The Mother of the Gods, or simply the Mother, was the Asiatic deity also known to the Greeks as Kybebe or Kybele. Her cult was long established in Syria and Asia Minor before she appears in Greek sources, an earlier history that lies beyond the horizon of the present study.[1] She is not named by Homer or Hesiod, but in one form or another she was known and honored in cult among Greeks, especially among Asiatic Greeks, as early as those poets. Classical sources indicate that the cult of the Mother of the Gods was one among several foreign cults established at Athens in the fifth century. Sources from late antiquity indicate that the Mother did not, at first, find easy acceptance at Athens. The historical basis of the controversies surrounding the worship of the Mother of the Gods at Athens is itself a matter of scholarly debate. This book advances a new interpretation of the ancient controversy by expanding the scope of the modern debate over the worship of the Mother of the Gods, placing it in the context of the Greek perspective on the relationship between humanity and divinity, and of religion and sovereignty.

The early chapters of this book will consider the influences exerted over the Greeks chiefly by the kingdom of the Lydians. In the period covered in the second half of the book, Asiatic sovereignty is represented by the empire of the Persians. As the Athenians take the lead in Greek opposition to Persia, the influence of religion in shaping expressions of Athenian identity will be traced. Kingdoms, empires, and states, like Persia and Athens, that asserted various and sometimes conflicting claims to sovereignty or autonomy did so in reference to concepts of the relationship between human dominion and the principles that gave order to this world. We will therefore have occasion to consider the form in which the world was then understood, how notions of sovereign power over the world were expressed, and how these concepts related to ideas of divinity. We will also encounter the emergence

---

1. Lynn Roller 1999 provides a thorough and readable account of the Anatolian (Phrygian) cult of the Mother and its dissemination in the Greco-Roman world. My interpretation differs from hers on points of historical development, as will be noted below. On the Near Eastern background to the cult of Kybele, Laroche 1960 is still fundamental.

of the ideas of Europe and Asia. For among the Greeks, the dichotomy between Europe and Asia became the geographical expression of an order to the world that corresponded both to forms of sovereignty and to aspects of divinity. Did these expressions describe irreconcilable divisions, or parts of a greater unity? This is the question that animates the present study.

The scope of this book is admittedly ambitious, and so its limits should be acknowledged. It focuses on the relationship of divinity to sovereignty at a specific period of time (primarily the seventh through fifth centuries B.C.E.) and place (Athens, the Greek Aegean, and the lands of neighboring Asia). It does not examine the prehistoric origins of sovereignty, or of religion, or of any particular cult, nor does it adopt a comparative approach beyond the fairly wide regional scope it already embraces. The meanings pursued here are to be understood, as far as possible, from the standpoint of those whose lives and perceptions were shaped by the events described here. Therefore, although preexisting conditions will be acknowledged and the recollections of later sources will be consulted, the present book is primarily a study of the classical Greek experience of worldly power and its expression in the conceptual realm of the gods.

Composed of familiar elements, the interpretation that unfolds in the following pages is new, in that its elements have never before been connected in this manner. Readers should therefore be aware that much of the following account is the product of arguments that assert causal connections and suggest interpretations where our sources are not always explicit. Many well-known episodes from the pages of Herodotus and other familiar sources will be framed here by the evidence of texts and monuments that will be less familiar to many students of classical antiquity. As a result, much will be seen from new perspectives. Even if some readers are not immediately persuaded by every detail of the argument, all who attend to the evidence will recognize that most of the account here is told through the declarative statements of our ancient sources, who reflect views and attitudes often contemporary to the events under discussion. From such testimony and arguments about the connections between the Mother of the Gods, tyranny, and Athens, this study develops a coherent description of the relationship between sovereign power and religious ideology in classical Greek experience. The result is a thesis with profound implications for our understanding of archaic and classical Greek political and religious institutions.

## THE THESIS

Maternal deities are many to name, and even within the comparatively orderly classical Greek pantheon their roles often overlap. Multiplicity and diversity seem to be virtues in this system of conceptualizing divinity, although our own understanding of it tends to grow by emphasizing the separation of roles. Into the classical Greek system made known by Homer and Hesiod, later sources introduced a deity called the Mother of the Gods. Her roles overlap those of other deities in all directions: she is variously described as a devoted mother, a chaste wife, an impassioned lover, and a virgin daughter; in some stories she is even male, or androgynous in origin. She is vulnerable and she is powerful; she attacks and she protects; she drives mad and she makes wise; she dances and she contemplates; she loves the wilderness and she keeps cities. With so many valences, the Mother of the Gods became exceedingly popular in cult, yet at the same time she became almost transparent, and hard to separate from other divinities whose roles she shared.[2]

It is not the object of this study to examine the stories of the Mother of the Gods in all their variety, or to distill an essential meaning from her cult; her meanings are as many as are her stories. My intention is rather to focus on the implications connected with a specific aspect of her story, her origin as the Greeks understood it. For almost as soon as we can recognize her cult among the Greeks, we find the Mother identified as foreign, or Asiatic. This foreign aspect is the most intriguing feature of her identity, and one that is most conducive to a historical understanding.

The thesis of this book is that the Mother of the Gods impressed herself on the awareness of the Greeks particularly through her role in defining one of the most impressive experiences of worldly power, namely the dynasty of the Mermnad tyrants of Lydia, which ruled over western Asia Minor from the time of Gyges (ca. 680–645 B.C.E.) until the end of the reign of Croesus (ca. 560–547 B.C.E.). Just as Lydian rulership, which brought the word "tyranny" into the Greek language, was accepted by its subjects as the perfect embodiment of worldly power, so too was the deity who symbolized the divine legitimation of Lydian sovereignty, the goddess who was both divine mother and consort of the Lydian ruler. To the Lydians, she was Kybebe, to the Phrygians *Matar Kubeleya,* or Kybele (and hence later Cybele to the Romans); to the Greeks she was most commonly known as the Mother of the Gods.

Intimately identified, in this manner, with a sovereign power of Asia Minor, the Mother of the Gods had an ambiguous relevance to those Greeks who did not live under the sway of Lydia. Moreover, when Lydia and its splendid tyranny suddenly collapsed, overthrown by Cyrus the Great in 547 B.C.E., the relevance of the Mother of the Gods became problematic to all Greeks. Nearly all of our Greek sources mentioning the Mother of the Gods come

2. Vermaseren 1977, Borgeaud 1996, and Roller 1999 survey the cult of the Mother of the Gods over a broad historical scope; Roller 9–24 provides a good survey of earlier scholarship. Lancellotti 2002 examines the figure of Attis, consort of the Mother of the Gods, in classical and later times. Myths of the Mother of the Gods and Attis are related by Diodorus 3.58–59; Ovid *Fasti* 4.179–372; Pausanias 7.17.9–12; Arnobius *Adversus Nationes* 5.5–7. (The latter two give accounts of the androgynous origin of the Mother, also known as Agdistis.)

from after this event, and they often reflect the ambiguous relationship of the Greeks to a deity who represented a concept, the tyranny of Asia, that had been fundamentally transformed by the Persian conquest of Lydia. The Persians adopted much from the Lydians and others whom they conquered, and they encouraged their subjects to view Persian sovereignty through the symbolic systems that were familiar to them. The cult of the Mother in Asia, or specifically of Kybebe at Sardis, the Lydian capital, became a token of subservience to the more powerful monarchy of Persia, whose rule was contested by many Greeks, the Spartans and Athenians chief among them. It was in reaction to this token of power, once estimable and admirable to the Greeks, but under the Persians a token of subservience, that the cult of the Mother of the Gods became problematic to the Athenians. Consequently, it is in connection with the developing relationship between Athenians and Persians that the cult of the Mother of the Gods becomes historically grounded. The violent rupture of relations between Athens and Persia at the beginning of the fifth century marks the rejection of the Mother of the Gods at Athens, while the movement toward rapprochement between Athens and Persia in the later fifth century marks the transformation by which the cult of the Mother of the Gods eventually became fully accepted at Athens.

## METHODOLOGICAL ORIENTATION

This inquiry into the Mother of the Gods and Athens provides an exemplary case of a general definition of religion expounded by Clifford Geertz, namely that religion articulates a prevailing sense of order that belongs simultaneously to the apprehensible, physical world and to the intuitive, metaphysical nature of things.[3] The case of the Mother of the Gods, however, problematizes this understanding of religion in an interesting way by asking: To whose religion does she belong, and whose sense of order does she represent?

The predominant picture in our sources shows the Mother of the Gods moving from the boundaries and eventually into the mainstream of Greek religion. Typically, movement of this sort is understood in chronological terms, as a product of the widening boundaries of Hellenic into Hellenistic culture, when, after the conquests of Alexander, those boundaries became more permeable, even blurred, and Greeks more readily took as their own certain cultural features that were earlier considered foreign (or barbarian, in Greek terms). This, to put a name to it, is the story of Hellenistic syncretism.

3. In Geertz's words (1973, 90): "A religion is: (1) a system of symbols which acts to (2) establish powerful, pervasive, and long-lasting moods and motivations in men by (3) formulating conceptions of a general order of existence and (4) clothing these conceptions with such an aura of factuality that (5) the moods and motivations seem uniquely realistic."

But the story of how the Mother of the Gods came to Athens is not a story of the age of Alexander and after. The present study demonstrates conclusively that religious syncretism of the sort commonly accepted in the Hellenistic world had a much longer, earlier history.

By establishing some of the main lines of this earlier history of borrowings and cultural transformation, the present study provides the basis for a broad reappraisal of the nature of religious syncretism. Such a reappraisal is highly desirable, in view of the predominant tendencies of the past century of scholarship in this area.[4] Our understanding of the process by which foreign gods were adopted among the Greeks, and later among the Romans, has been straining under the weight of received notions about relations between West and East, or between Europe and Asia—what Edward Said has called "orientalism."[5] It is true that those notions originated in classical antiquity, in the very context under examination here, but the conditions generating them have not yet been sufficiently examined.[6] Here we must ask: What conditions could account for the adoption and integration of foreign elements into the religious practices of classical Greek antiquity?

One explanation sees exotic elements in Greek religion as the cumulative influence of those at the margins of a community's political identity (women and foreigners in particular). Under this model, the official adoption of a foreign deity is understood as an almost involuntary consequence of a growing search for spiritual meaning at the individual or personal level. So it has long been assumed that the cult of the Mother first gained popularity among the Athenians in private cult, where it gratified the desires of many individuals for a more intimate religious experience than, presumably, could be found in long-established cults. Only as a consequence of this growing informal popularity was the Mother given a place in official cult.[7]

Such a process seems plausible at first sight, especially inasmuch as it corresponds roughly to the pattern of behavior leading to the eventual acceptance of a notionally foreign deity, Dionysus, as his story was told in the *Bacchae* of Euripides. But it is hard to find objective evidence to support this picture. The evidence that relates to private cult, chiefly the material remains of minor votive offerings, is almost entirely later in date than the official adoption of the cult of the Mother of the Gods at Athens in the late fifth cen-

4. I take the overall message of Henrik Versnel's *Inconsistencies in Greek Religion* (1990) to be a call for such a reappraisal.

5. E. W. Said 1978, 6, where "orientalism" is defined as the "accepted grid for filtering through the Orient into Western consciousness."

6. Walter Burkert 1992 and M. L. West 1997 stand out among recent appraisals of this transformative period, but their works barely touch the realm of religious ideology.

7. So Roller 1999, 144–61, seeks to explain the personal appeal of private rituals of the Mother in the period during which her cult was becoming established on the Greek mainland, and particularly at Athens. See also the discussion by R. Parker 1996, 188–94.

tury.[8] As a historical explanation, this model lacks an account of how private enthusiasm had the force to change public policy. Such an account is surely required when we seek to understand an act of religious innovation in an age when charges of impiety drove many Athenians into exile, and when Socrates could be condemned for not respecting the deities respected by the Athenians.[9] If a hypothetical swell of private popularity does not suffice to explain the adoption of this foreign deity, what other model could take its place?

Martin Nilsson once advocated an approach that has had an abiding influence on our understanding of classical Greek religion. This was his model of popular or folk religion. Contrasting his own approach to those accounts of Greek religion based either on its supposed primitive origins (e.g., by J. G. Frazer or Jane Harrison), or on the refined expressions of classical poetic or philosophical literature (e.g., by U. von Wilamowitz–Moellendorff or W. Otto), Nilsson strove to discern a mainstream of popular beliefs and practices rooted, he argued, in the pastoral and agricultural lifestyle of the majority of ancient Greeks. From this perspective, the adoption of the Mother of the Gods, Nilsson's "Great Mother of Asia Minor," was comprehensible only when she became "thoroughly assimilated to the Greek Mother, Demeter," the paramount deity of agricultural fertility. Why the Greeks should pay attention to a Great Mother of Asia Minor in the first place was not a concern of Nilsson's, however.[10] His model is useful, therefore, for explaining the workings of a religion as a closed system, but it does not do well in accounting for change, or for the acceptance of foreign influence.[11] We return to where we started at the beginning of this section, with the problem posed by the Mother of the Gods: Whose sense of order does she represent?

A foreign deity who is accepted and enshrined in public cult in a new home, as the Mother of the Gods was at Athens, is a symbol of connection to a wider world. The ceremonial process of making that connection is, at a

---

8. Roller 1999, 121–44 (following Graf 1984 and 1985, 111–15) appeals to the evidence for the cult of the Mother among Ionian Greeks in the sixth century as evidence for the beginning of this wave of personal influence. In the pages that follow, however, it will be argued that the Ionian cult of the Mother reflects larger issues of sovereign authority, in which personal choice is secondary to matters of state and sovereignty.

9. On the relationship between religious orthodoxy and the trial of Socrates, see R. Parker 1996, 199–217; Munn 2000, 273–91. On questions of religious innovation and conformity in the late fifth century, see Yunis 1988.

10. Nilsson 1940, 3–6 (methodology), 91–92 (the Great Mother); cf. Nilsson 1955, 725–27.

11. Robertson 1996 has advocated an account of the cult of the Mother of the Gods that combines certain features of Nilsson's approach with the focus on primitive origins. Robertson explains the Mother as a pastoral deity known to Greeks since the Bronze Age who shared certain features with an Anatolian deity, and therefore became identified (or confused) with her in the archaic period. As with Nilsson's approach, Robertson's thesis effectively offers no explanation of the Asiatic aspect of the cult of the Mother of the Gods.

certain level, as much an act of public policy as the negotiation of a treaty of alliance with any foreign power. Even more than a treaty of alliance, which respects differences as well as shared interests between two parties, the adoption of a deity is an act of complete integration. It is a declaration of united purpose between community and deity that is meant to transcend civic or political boundaries in precisely the manner in which deities are believed to imbue the wider world with their power. If the adoption is successful—which means, if the deity is accepted without qualms and is widely honored in the new setting—then the foreign origin of the deity ceases to be a consideration; the deity is naturalized, at home; or better still, the deity is back home (as exemplified in the tale of Dionysus' eventual triumph at Thebes).

When we seek to explain the institution of a public cult in the ancient world, or a cult that has the explicit support of the sovereign authority of a state, then we must form our understanding in terms of issues of public policy, or sovereign interests, as they were expressed and affirmed in the state in question. This suggestion has much in common with the perspective described by W. Robert Connor in an influential article examining the relationship between leaders and followers revealed in narratives about festivals and civic ceremonies in archaic Greece. Where previous scholars had seen political leaders manipulating their followers by using religious symbols, Connor recognized that leaders like Solon or Peisistratus often used ceremonial events as a way of manifesting solidarity among all levels of the civic community, in effect minimizing the distinctions between leaders and followers. Connor describes this process as follows:[12]

> The leader seems not to stand at a great distance from the attitudes and the behaviour of his fellow countrymen. Rather both appear to be linked by shared patterns of thought and united in a communal drama. The citizens are not naive bumpkins taken in by their leader's manipulation, but participants in a theatricality whose rules and roles they understand and enjoy. These are alert, even sophisticated, actors in a ritual drama affirming the establishment of a new civic order, and a renewed rapport among people, leader and protecting divinity.

Connor's approach explains political change as a process in which all participate because all recognize a common set of symbols by which widely held beliefs and values are affirmed. A further implication of the examples considered by Connor, and reflected, as we will see, in the example of the cultic installation of the Mother of the Gods, is that such symbols do not arrive unannounced. The way has been prepared well in advance. The connections and purposes that they imply are already generally known, recognized, and approved by those who participate in the ceremony. The ceremonial event

12. Connor 1987, 46 (= 2000, 67).

itself, be it a procession, the foundation of an altar, or the dedication of a shrine or a cult image, is a ritual that serves to unite a community with these purposes through reserving a specific time and place for a communal focus on them. In this sense, as Geertz has remarked, "the dispositions which religious rituals induce thus have their most important impact . . . outside the boundaries of the ritual itself as they reflect back to color the individual's conception of the established world of bare fact."[13] The reception of a deity, in other words, must relate to real-world conditions as they are expressed, for example, in political terms.

This is a model that can account for the testimony of poetry, theological philosophy, and drama foreshadowing the coming of the Mother of the Gods to Athens, and the votive monuments and civic institutions that were established upon her arrival. It is also a model that allows us to seek the connection to political events that will enable us both to date the arrival of the Mother at Athens, and to explain the significance of the event. For, as we will see, our sources are either allusive on this subject, or interested in more enduring meanings than those that informed a political event at Athens in the late fifth century.

## THE ORDER OF THE ARGUMENT

The first concern of this study is to establish a framework for discussing the relationship between politics and religion in the classical Greek world. This is the goal of chapter 1, which continues the discussion initiated in this introduction. Chapter 1 introduces the concept of sovereignty as an idea that is projected into the notion of a sovereign divinity, and explores the manner in which this notion informs relations within human communities even in the absence of a human sovereign monarch. In this chapter, we will see how ideas about the kingship of Zeus, especially as depicted by Hesiod and Homer, correspond both to Asiatic notions of sovereignty and divinity, and to political and social customs and conditions among the Greeks of the archaic and classical eras.

With chapter 2 our focus turns to the Mother of the Gods as she was identified in classical Greek sources. Here we will find the paradoxical combination of a divinity who was both well known to the Greeks, and to the Athenians in particular, yet was undeniably foreign. Consideration of the specific identification of the Mother as both Lydian and Phrygian in origin directs our attention to the earliest horizon of the Greek memory of the Mother, associating her with the kingship of Midas. Midas, king of Phrygia, was a figure that made a deep impression on following generations, beginning most im-

13. Geertz 1973, 119.

mediately with the dynasty of the Mermnad tyrants of Lydia. Chapters 2, 3, and 4 describe the wider associations of Midas and Mermnad Lydia in Greek tradition, and place these associations into the context of the ideology of Lydian tyranny. Although native Lydian monuments and documents are comparatively few, their significance emerges clearly when they, along with the testimonia of Greek sources, are examined against the background of an older Asiatic tradition of kingship and its consummation in the rituals of Sacred Marriage with a divinity.

Chapter 5 considers how the metaphysics of Asiatic kingship, or the ideology of tyranny, related to concepts of the physical world. The earliest Ionian maps of the world, attributed to the Milesians Anaximander and Hecataeus, described physical relationships between continents and seas at a time when the centers of sovereign power in Asia and in the Greek world were in flux. Geography, at this early date, was never far from cosmology, and both were related to ideologies of power. This investigation of the conceptual underpinnings of Ionian geography elucidates a number of symbolic events that accompanied the contest for world sovereignty between Lydia and Persia and between Persia and the Greeks, and that accompanied the attempt by Polycrates of Samos to establish sovereignty over the seas.

The dominance of Persia, and tensions between Persia and the Greeks, are the focus of chapters 6 and 7. In these chapters, the case will be made for recognizing the symbolism of Lydian tyranny in the rhetoric of Persian sovereignty and in the counterclaims of the Greeks. The destruction of the shrine of Kybebe at Sardis in the course of the Ionian uprising against the Persians, as described by Herodotus, gains new significance according to this argument. As a result, the religious and symbolic dimensions of the ensuing Persian demands for Athenian submission are seen from a new and deeper perspective.

The testimony of Herodotus is central to our understanding of Greco-Persian relations in the late sixth and early fifth centuries. His *Histories* is also a strong indicator of the symbolic dimensions of events as they were understood by Herodotus' contemporaries in the later fifth century. The relationship of divinity to historical causation in Herodotus' thought is therefore the subject of chapter 8. Herodotus' concept of divinity, as revealed in several key passages, is shown to be closely related to his articulation of the concept of universal history. These concepts in turn are closely related to the universalizing thought guiding the Athenian venture to secure a sovereign empire.

Chapter 9 brings this story of the Mother of the Gods to its conclusion, with an account of the circumstances under which her cult was formally established at Athens in the late fifth century. This development is shown to be a consequence both of the evolving relationship between Athens and Persia, and of the desire to set a universal divinity at the center of Athenian sovereignty. Viewed in context, the establishment of the civic cult of the Mother of the Gods by the Athenians is seen not to be a radical step of assimilating a foreign concept. Instead, as a divinity with transcendent meanings, the Mother of the Gods was readily seen as another aspect of goddesses long recognized by the Athenians: Nemesis and Themis among those goddesses most closely identified with rightful sovereignty; Demeter, Aphrodite, and Artemis among those ancient goddesses who epitomized the all-encompassing goodness of maternal nurture, of impassioned affection, and of protecting wisdom.

So the Mother of the Gods, despite her Asiatic identity, is seen to be a figure familiar to the Athenians. Such simple equations efface paradoxical contradictions, yet both the equations and the contradictions continue to exist. The object of this study is not to reduce the Mother of the Gods to a single explanation, but to elucidate how both her equations and her contradictions were variously seen, and variously used, across a period when Greeks generally and Athenians especially sought ways of understanding and controlling sovereign power and tyranny.

# Chapter 1

# Sovereignty and Divinity
# in Classical Greek Thought

In the study of classical Greek religion and its relationship to Greek society, there is no equivalent to Henri Frankfort's *Kingship and the Gods: A Study of Ancient Near Eastern Religion as the Integration of Society and Nature* (1948).[1] The reason is not far to seek. By contrast to their neighbors in the Near East, Greeks of the classical era generally shunned the institution of kingship, and organized themselves according to various forms of collective government. The theme of kingship, therefore, has not seemed particularly appropriate for any study devoted to Greece of the classical era. Yet the imagery and the ideology of kingship were never far from the awareness of Greeks of the sixth, fifth, and fourth centuries B.C.E., particularly when they were assembled in political and religious gatherings. For the gods they honored on those occasions were conceived of as a community under the order of the divine kingship of Zeus, under whom, by extension, all mortal communities were also ordered. It stands to reason, therefore, that the ideological implications of kingship did have a bearing on classical Greek society, although the manner in which they may have done so is not immediately obvious.

Kingship and the gods has been a subject of study in Greek history for those looking outside the classical period, to the Mycenaean Bronze Age or to the era of Hellenistic monarchies.[2] In both of these chronological directions, scholars have looked to the institutions of kingship and religion in the

1. Works that do take up the subject of divinity and kingship in classical Greek sources (Oliver 1960, Auffarth 1991, e.g.) demonstrate the cogency of this observation.

2. For the Bronze Age Aegean and Mycenaean Greece, see Rose 1959; Walcot 1967; C. G. Thomas 1976; Burkert 1985, 46–50; Kilian 1988; N. Marinatos 1993; Wright 1994; Rehak 1995; M. L. West 1997, 14–19. On the deification of Hellenistic monarchs, see Nock 1928 and 1957; Balsdon 1950; Habicht 1970; Badian 1981; S. R. F. Price 1984.

Near East and Egypt to discover parallels and influences that could account for the institutions of kingship and its religious dimensions in the pre- or postclassical Greek world. But why is there a hiatus in the classical interlude? Did a powerful wave of secular egalitarianism sweep away all such influences from the archaic and classical Greek world? Did rational, political thought banish ideologies of kingship and the gods to the realms of myth and vestigial cultic institutions? Do the trappings of divine kingship in the age of Alexander and his successors mark the arrival of foreign ideas, or a resurgence of ideologies that were always embedded in the matrix of Greek thought about humankind, the world, and the gods?

This book argues that concepts of divinity were never far removed from ideologies of sovereignty among the Greeks, even in those periods when kingship and ruler cult were suppressed. Contests for political power and struggles over constitutional questions, most often analyzed in secular terms, can be seen to be shaped also by religious ideologies, and those ideologies respond to a wider range of historical and cultural influences than is apparent when the focus is on purely secular issues. To build the case for the validity of this wider view, this chapter will examine, in purely Greek terms, the connections between the divine kingship of Zeus and the social and political organization of the archaic and classical Greek world. The chapters that follow will examine the cultural and historical context that shaped classical Greek concepts about the relationship between humanity and divinity. Here we will discover how closely bound to the thought and experience of their Eastern neighbors the Greeks were, throughout the archaic and classical eras.

## THE STUDY OF RELIGION IN GREEK HISTORY

If the study of kingship seems out of place in the classical Greek world, then at least sovereignty, the abstraction of kingship, is a notion more congenial to discussions of Greek political history and ideology. Sovereign assemblies and sovereign laws are the stuff of Greek constitutional history. But even here, for a variety of reasons, scholars have been slow in seeking relationships between political ideology and the history of religious thought. In part this is because the historical developments of Greek political ideology are viewed in terms of progress and response to change, while religion is understood to be an inherently conservative expression of the influence of past tradition. Politics looks forward, to put the matter in simplistic terms, while religion looks backward. Modern interest in ancient religion, particularly in the classical world, has been profoundly influenced in this direction by the search for relics from the more distant past preserved in religious customs and institutions. This is the heritage especially of the quest for primitive beliefs by members of the Cambridge ritualist school of a century ago, James Frazer, Jane Harrison, and A. B. Cook chief among them. But it is an orientation that has survived, in other forms, even longer than did the coherence of the Cambridge school.[3] For all the merits of this approach in drawing attention to underlying continuities, it has generally retarded the search for progressive developments in the history of religion.

Some remedy to the extremes of the quest for origins has come from the structuralist approach to Greek myth and religion, chiefly represented in the works of Marcel Detienne, Jean-Pierre Vernant, Pierre Vidal-Naquet, Nicole Loraux, and Christiane Sourvinou-Inwood.[4] This approach has had the virtue of insisting on discovering the direct relationship between myths and those who told them, particularly in terms of the structure of their social institutions. Myth and ritual here are principally seen no longer as vestiges of a prehistoric past, but as expressions of contemporary living systems. The limitation of this approach, however, is that the structures and relationships it has described are, for the most part, ahistorical. That is, they are presented as paradigms of social order belonging generally to archaic or classical Greece (or to "Grèce ancienne"), but with little indication of how these paradigms behaved and changed historically, when they were animated by the course of events.

In recent decades scholarship in this field has demonstrated an increasing interest in the correlation between religious custom and specific historical settings: religion and Greek colonization, and Peisistratid Athens, and the Persian Wars, for examples.[5] Since the themes of these studies have been defined in historical terms, they signal the potential for the study of Greek religion to follow a narrative of historical development. A significant step in this direction is Robert Parker's *Athenian Religion: A History* (1996).

In studies of this recent generation, the evidence of religious imagery or cult practice appears more often to be organized chronologically, according to historical events, rather than analyzed as integral to our understanding of historical events. Historians, ancient and modern, have a marked tendency to relegate religious issues to the background of politics, and students of religion have largely accepted this disassociation. The few episodes where religion and political history seem inextricable—the scandals surrounding the profanation of the Mysteries at Athens, for instance, or the trial of Socrates— are usually understood on a local scale, within the context of the practices of a single city-state (Athens naturally predominates) examined over a compara-

3. For discussions of the influence and decline of the Cambridge school, see J. Z. Smith 1978, 208–39; Versnel 1993, 16–88; I. Morris 1993. For later examples of the quest for origins, see Burkert 1983; Simon 1983.

4. Noteworthy are Detienne 1977; Vernant 1988; Vidal-Naquet 1986; Loraux 1986; Sourvinou-Inwood 1991.

5. Examples cited elsewhere in the present work include Malkin 1987; Shapiro 1989; Mikalson 2003.

tively limited time span. As a result, the dividends of this recent interest in the historical basis of ancient religion have been modest.

The present chapter is an endeavor to initiate broader historical study of the relationship between notions of divinity and the forms of sovereignty articulated by the Greeks of the classical era. For religion was, arguably, the most essential medium through which the identity of each individual Greek city-state was expressed. To the widest audiences, both civic and Panhellenic, ideas of community and communal purpose were represented in terms of relationships between humanity and the gods. Notionally, these relationships had been established by ancestors and maintained ever since; in living practice, these relationships were constantly being shaped and renegotiated. The process, in effect, was an ongoing enactment of ideologies of sovereignty.

## SOVEREIGNTY AND TYRANNY

Sovereignty is the principle of rulership; it is highest authority, or that which commands obeisance. Among Greeks of the classical era, highest authority was expressed chiefly as an abstraction, as the rule of *nomos*, "custom" or "law," or as the collective rule of a sovereign people. Pindar gave famous expression to this principle in a statement quoted by Herodotus and Plato: "*Nomos* is king of all" (νόμος ὁ πάντων βασιλεύς).[6] Herodotus elsewhere expresses the supremacy of *nomos* among the Spartans by the phrase "*nomos* is master" (δεσπότης νόμος), while Plato recasts the maxim of Pindar in the form "*nomos*, which is tyrant over men" (ὁ δὲ νόμος, τύραννος ὢν τῶν ἀνθρώπων).[7] Among Athenians, the supremacy of *nomos* is equated with the verdicts of the demos, the assembled people, in various expressions of Pericles and his contemporaries.[8]

This concept of law or custom as sovereign authority is expressed through the metaphor of kingship, where authority emanates from a monarch who is king (*basileus*), master (*despotēs*), or tyrant (*tyrannos*). It is reasonable to assume that the experience of actual monarchy, in some form, preceded or accompanied the abstraction of the concept of sovereign *nomos*. But evidence for the institution of actual kingship among the forebears of the Greeks of the classical era is slight and generally ambiguous at best. With the qualified exception of the Spartan dual kingship, the sovereignty of kings was experienced by Greeks chiefly in the form of the circumscribed duties of religious

---

6. Pindar fr. 169 (Sandys), cited by Herodotus 3.38.4 and Plato *Gorgias* 484b.

7. Herodotus 7.104.4, reporting the speech of Demaratus to Xerxes; cf. Xenophon *Lacedaemonian Constitution* 4.6, 8.1–5. Plato *Protagoras* 337d reports the expression of Hippias of Elis.

8. Thucydides 2.37.1 and 3, reporting Pericles' funeral oration; Xenophon *Memorabilia* 1.2.41–42, reporting a conversation of Pericles and Alcibiades. Euripides *Suppliants* 403–8 explicitly juxtaposes the authority of a tyrant with the authority of the demos. Martin Ostwald 1969 and 1986 examines Athenian notions of *nomos* and popular sovereignty.

officials, or apprehended from a distance as an ill-defined remembrance of the heroic past.[9] Contemporary kingship was known to the Greeks as a feature of the barbarian (i.e., non-Greek, generally Asiatic) world. Barbarian kingship also went by the name of tyranny, and tyranny was a form of rulership that actually was experienced by many Greeks, both in its aboriginal, foreign form, and as a transplant onto Greek soil.

Tyranny had its earliest currency among the Greeks living near the coast of Asia, where it was preeminently identified with Lydian kingship.[10] For more than a century before the coming of the Persians, the Mermnad tyrants of Lydia dazzled the Greeks with their power and wealth. By the middle of the sixth century, all peoples living in Asia Minor west of the Halys River, Greeks and non-Greeks alike, were subjects of Croesus, and he counted the kings of Media, Babylon, Egypt, and Sparta as his allies. Here was the chief experience of sovereignty to which the Greeks reacted, and from which they abstracted their ideals of political power. The impact of Lydian tyranny is clearly imprinted in the vocabulary of Greek political thought.

Tyranny, epitomized by the rulers of Lydia and adopted from them as a model of autocratic power by a number of rulers of Greek cities, was fraught with ambiguous associations.[11] Tyranny, in theory, was irresistible. A tyrant came to power in a way that no man could stop, and in power a tyrant was accountable to no man. Popular approval and reverence accompanied the establishment of a tyrant who was a ruler both proud of and admired for his excellence. But the tyrant was also envied, feared, and detested for these very

9. Robert Drews 1983 has reviewed the evidence for kingship in Dark Age Greece, and has concluded that those who are called kings (*basileis*) in various sources, from Hesiod on, are no more than highborn peers, or the holders of a magistracy. Drews thus dismisses the view (represented, e.g., by Andrewes 1956, 9–11) that a strong tradition of hereditary kingship generally devolved into an annual magistracy. This conclusion is largely supported by Walter Donlan's analysis (1979) of the nature of leadership in the *Iliad*, where there is no strong institutional authority that could be recognized as kingship. For further discussions of Homeric kingship, see Taplin 1992; 47–58, McGlew 1993, 53–61; S. P. Morris 2003. On the possible origins of civic kingship at Sparta, see Oliver 1960, 3–46; for Athens, see R. Parker 1996, 10–28.

10. Archilochus fr. 19 (West; quoted and discussed further below, at note 116, and in chapter 3 at note 71), referring to the seventh-century tyranny of Gyges, is the earliest use of the word *tyrannis*, "tyranny." Herodotus, who affirms that Archilochus was the contemporary of Gyges (1.12.2) also states that Gyges established a *tyrannis* among the Lydians (1.14.1). *Suda* s.v. τύραννος cites Hippias "the sophist" (i.e., Hippias of Elis, a contemporary of Herodotus) for the information that the word *tyrannos*, "tyrant," not used by Homer, was adopted by the Greeks in the time of Archilochus. Jules Labarbe 1971 has collected the testimonia of Greek sources on the origin and meaning of tyranny. The origin of the word is discussed further in chapter 3 at notes 80–82.

11. Victor Parker 1998 reviews attitudes toward tyranny, as a concept and as a reality, attested by archaic and classical Greek sources. Volker Fadinger 1993, 263–93, reviews the evidence for the Near Eastern origin of the stereotypical aspects of tyranny as they are outlined by Aristotle *Politics* 1313a–1314b.

qualities. The negative connotation of tyranny came especially from the notion that an irreproachable ruler would, sooner or later, indulge in crimes of greed, passion, or sheer arrogance simply because he could do so with impunity. Exemplified by the reputation of notorious foreign monarchs and by the hateful memory of their own Greek tyrants, by Herodotus' day tyranny was frequently associated with the highest forms of hybris.[12] It was often seen as seductive, but containing the seeds of its own destruction. For by Herodotus' day the view of tyrannical regimes was chiefly a catalogue of spectacular failures.

Despite its aspect of being above the law and its history of tragic failures, tyranny as irresistible power could still be regarded as something admirable to audiences of Herodotus's day. If this power were wisely exercised, then tyranny could still describe the highest form of sovereign authority, whether it was exercised by a monarch or a collective body. In classical Athenian drama, the idealized kingdoms of the heroic age, even Athens itself, are often called tyrannies without implying any reproach.[13] In contemporary politics we find that it was acceptable for Pericles and other Athenian statesmen, as well as comic poets, to speak to their Athenian audiences about the tyranny that they collectively wielded. The context always serves to indicate the high calling of tyranny, and to urge Athenians to take the implications of their power seriously: "Your empire is a tyranny," Thucydides reports Pericles as

12. Herodotus often uses *tyrannos*, "tyrant," as an alternative to *basileus*, "king," in a generally neutral sense, although a negative impression more often emerges from the accounts of those he calls tyrants. The peculiarities of an important criticism of tyranny, in Herodotus 5.91, are discussed in chapter 4. For differing assessments of Herodotus' usage of the word "tyrant," see Ferrill 1978, who argues that the term always has a negative connotation in Herodotus, and V. Parker 1998, 161–64, who argues (more persuasively, in my view) that Herodotus can use the term with no sense of reproach. Carolyn Dewald 2003 strikes a judicious balance in her observation that Herodotus credits the "idiosyncratic personal achievement" of individual tyrants (26) within the larger, strongly negative evaluation of despotism conveyed by his *Histories*.

13. As James McGlew observes: "It is a commonplace of scholarship on classical Greece that *tyrannos* is a neutral word in tragedy" (1993, 204). The neutral use of *tyrannos* as a synonym for *basileus* in Attic tragedy is surveyed by V. Parker 1998, 153 and 158–61. As in Herodotus, Attic tragedies often characterize tyrants and tyranny negatively, as Richard Seaford 2003 emphasizes, but it is remarkable how often tyrants and tyranny appear with no such negative characterization (a feature that Seaford neglects in his selective survey). To the examples discussed by V. Parker (above) we may add Euripides *Hippolytus* 843, where Theseus refers to his own palace as the "tyrant house"; *Children of Heracles* 111–13, where Demophon, son of Theseus and like him ruler of a "free land," is called a tyrant; and *Ion* 235, 829, 1464, 1572, where Erechtheus and his descendants are called tyrants, occupy the halls of tyrants, and are seated, by the command of Athena, on tyrannical thrones. In Sophocles' *Oedipus Tyrannus*, aside from the tragic effect of uncovering the secret of his birth, there is no hint that the tyranny of Oedipus was in any way displeasing to the people of Thebes. Aristotle's categories of "lawful" tyranny, and tyranny that "acts the part of kingship," *Politics* 1285a16–b26, 1314a33–1315b10, seem designed to rationalize the tradition of benevolent tyranny in tragedy.

saying, "and if you suppose it was unjust to take it up, know that it is dangerous to let it go."[14] History showed that tyranny was dangerous to those who held it; but whether, in this case, it was just or not depended on the collective wisdom of the Athenian demos.

Only when the Athenian empire failed, shortly before the end of the fifth century, did the notion of tyranny finally harden into its completely negative aspect. At about this time we find tyranny clearly defined, for the first time, as the rule of an unconstitutional monarch distinguished from the legitimate kingship of a *basileus*, "king," whose rule was lawful and in accordance with the consent of his people.[15] In the fourth century, with Plato and Aristotle, we find this distinction developing into the essentialist categorization of true kingship as absolutely good and tyranny as absolutely bad.[16] The idea of tyranny that has thus come down to us is primarily a characterization of ruthless, lawless rule, and an unmitigated evil. It is important to realize, however, that before this meaning became fixed, tyranny simply represented the highest form of sovereignty.[17]

But is high sovereignty desirable? This question was raised by Greeks as

14. Thucydides 2.63.2, a passage whose subtleties are well appreciated by Lisa Kallet 2003, 119–20. Likewise, in Thucydides 3.37.2, Cleon reminds that Athenians that their empire is a tyranny over unwilling subjects, and at 6.85.1 an Athenian speaker admits to a Sicilian audience that the rule of Athens is like a tyranny. Contemporary comedy is even more unapologetic about celebrating the Athenian demos as a man whom "all men fear like a tyrant" (Aristophanes *Knights* 1114). As Jeffrey Henderson 2003, 159, observes, "Old Comedy confirms that the status of absolute and unaccountable ruler was one that most Athenians were happy to apply to themselves." With Kallet 2003 and Henderson 2003, I am persuaded by Connor 1977, who has argued that tyranny does not always convey a negative image when used by Athenians of the fifth century to characterize their own democracy and its empire. McGlew 1993, 183–90, suggests how democracy could embrace elements of tyranny. Against such appraisals, Kurt Raaflaub 1979 and 2003 argues that tyranny has an unambiguously negative meaning in all such self-descriptions, and could never have been embraced in any constructive sense. Raaflaub's argument imposes the long retrospective verdict of history on what was still, in the later fifth century, a complex and evolving set of meanings.

15. V. Parker 1998, 164, identifies Thucydides as the first writer who "distinguished with absolute consistency between tyrants and kings." The distinction is implicit in Thucydides, but it was explicitly defined soon after he wrote. So Xenophon *Memorabilia* 4.6.12 defines the difference between kingship and tyranny, attributing the distinction to Socrates. A similar definition of tyranny is found in Aristotle *Politics* 1295a, where it is identified as *pambasileia*, or absolute kingship.

16. Anthony Andrewes 1956, 20–30, traces the shifting meaning of "tyranny" in Greek sources, with conclusions similar to those outlined here. Plato *Gorgias* 466b–471a depicts a debate between Socrates and Polus about whether tyranny is desirable or not. By the arguments leading up to *Republic* 576d, Plato asserts that tyranny is opposed to kingship as evil is to good. Aristotle *Politics* 1310b–1311a attributes the distinction between the altruism of legitimate kings and the self-indulgence of tyrants to the inborn goodness of the former and the innate baseness of the latter.

17. Even in the age of Plato and Aristotle and afterward, tyranny was not always a term of reproach, as V. Parker 1998, 165–66, shows. In Hellenistic ideology, tyranny could still be a

soon as the word "tyranny" was used in their language. Even the most admirable examples of tyranny, as Herodotus' historical lessons taught, were to be contemplated with the awareness that such unparalleled rulership would find its downfall, sooner or later. This was the lesson of the pride and the fall of Croesus, as Herodotus tells it, and Herodotus emphasizes that this outcome was a consequence of the effect on human affairs of τὸ θεῖον, "the divine" or "the divinity."[18]

The same lesson that pride and great power must eventually be undone was also conveyed when the Greeks contemplated the paradigms of sovereignty among the gods. Not only were the reigns of Uranus and Cronus each overthrown in turn, but even the reign of Zeus would be undone. In the Aeschylean *Prometheus Bound,* for example, the oppressed titan, Prometheus, refers to Zeus throughout the play as a tyrant, and he does so in the context of his own prophecy that Zeus, king of gods, will eventually be overthrown.[19] Similarly, the comic enactment of the overthrow of Zeus, in the *Birds* of Aristophanes, is described as the surrender of Zeus' tyranny to a new tyrant.[20] Tyranny is supreme, but not everlasting sovereignty.

### SOVEREIGNTY AND GREEK RELIGION

The spectacle of the overthrow of Zeus may seem an exceptional figment of the Greek imagination until we reflect that the stability of the divine order was regularly figured in Greek poetry and art as the outcome of battle and contest. The outcome of these cosmic struggles was not thought to be preordained by some higher power (not, at least, outside of Orphic, Ionian, and later Neoplatonic cosmologies). The battles of the gods were events that unfolded, like the course of history, to shape what came after. Zeus had won kingship of the gods by overthrowing the previous king, his father, Cronus. Thereafter, with the support of other gods, Zeus won victories over Titans,

---

positive quality when it was an attribute of divinity—e.g., of Mēn Tyrannos, or of Isis; see Henrichs 1984, 351 and n. 76; Versnel 1990, 39–95.

18. See Herodotus 1.32.1 and 34.1. The nature and role of τὸ θεῖον in Herodotus' thought is examined in chapter 8.

19. In *Prometheus Bound,* Zeus is called tyrant not only by the resentful Prometheus, but by such elemental forces as Kratos, "Power," whose words open the play with an injunction to Prometheus to "learn to love the tyranny of Zeus" (10–11), and Oceanus, who refers to Zeus as "a new tyrant among gods" (310, where newness also hints at transience). Prometheus refers to Zeus' inevitable fall from tyranny at 756, 907–96.

20. Aristophanes *Birds* 1605, 1643, 1706–65, where the new tyrant, the Athenian Peisetaerus, assumes cosmic supremacy by marrying Βασίλεια, Zeus' own sovereignty personified. Similarly, Zeus, whose reign is denounced through the power of intellect in Aristophanes' *Clouds* 365–82, 816–28, is called "the mighty tyrant of gods" in lines 563–65.

Giants, and monsters, and had finally secured his reign; but a new contest could conceivably undo it. The gods of the Greeks were created beings who had parents, who had experienced birth, and who, even though they were immortal, were not invulnerable.

Such anthropomorphism is a sign of how the gods of the Greeks were projections of human experience. The conceptual interaction between reality and divinity is especially vivid in the case of the gods of the Greeks, as they were depicted under the influence of Homer and Hesiod. Ever since Xenophanes at the end of the sixth century, commentators have used anthropomorphism as a way to explore, sometimes to criticize, how divinity was conceived by the Greeks. Here, however, I propose reversing the terms of this analogy in order to consider how stories of the gods and of the mortals closest to them reflect the Greek understanding of the dynamics of power and authority in this world. Hesiod's observation "Kings are from Zeus," for example, invites us to examine the attributes of Zeus' kingship for clues about the principles of worldly sovereignty as it was understood by the Greeks in Hesiod's day and after.[21]

The dominion of Zeus, we have noted, was a dominion of vulnerable gods who existed in the presence of other, potentially hostile divine forces, and who endured by virtue of their mutual support of the leadership of Zeus. A world conceived in such terms paid heed to power in its elemental forms. For superior power was the key to sovereignty, and relations of power, among the gods as among communities of men, were established through victory in battle. For this reason, Zeus was not only the paramount signifier of sovereignty, but also the foremost patron of victory.[22]

Zeus was victory accomplished. The fray of battle itself was the domain not of Zeus, but of other gods: Zeus' children, siblings, and supporters. Zeus stood for the decisive outcome, when superior power had proven itself, and he stood for the order established by victory, and for the hope that it would endure as his rule endured. Men who reached for sovereignty invoked Zeus as a way of asserting their achievement, sometimes when it was secure, and sometimes when they only hoped it would be so. So we find that Cylon, an Olympic victor, attempted to seize the Acropolis and establish his tyranny at

21. Hesiod *Theogony* 96: ἐκ δὲ Διὸς βασιλῆες. (Cf. *Homeric Hymn* 25, *To Apollo* 4.) So also Terpander fr. 1 (Edmonds *LG*): Ζεῦ πάντων ἀρχά, πάντων ἀγῆτορ ("Zeus, the beginning of all, the leader of all"). Cf. *Iliad* 2.100–109, 203–6, where the kingship of Agamemnon is signified by his royal scepter, which came from Zeus. The consistent meaning of the depictions of Zeus in Greek literature and cult is summed up by Burkert 1985, 130: "All sovereignty among men proceeds from Zeus." See also Oliver 1960, 37; Lloyd-Jones 1971, 6–7; Vernant 1988, 105–9.

22. Hesiod *Theogony* 383–403 indicates the proprietary right of Zeus to command *Nikē* (Victory), *Zēlos* (Rivalry), *Biē* (Force), and *Kratos* (Superiority; for this meaning, see Benveniste 1973, 357–67).

Athens during the "great festival of Zeus."[23] Peisistratus and his sons commenced construction on a monumental temple of Olympian Zeus at Athens.[24] Later, Alexander signified his assumption of sovereignty in Asia by vowing to build a temple of Olympian Zeus on the site of the Lydian palace at Sardis and by sacrificing at the temple of Zeus the King on the site of the palace of Midas at Gordium.[25]

As the example of Cylon illustrates, like a victorious warrior, a victorious athlete might lay claim to sovereignty. Zeus presided over the accomplishments of both warriors and athletes alike, especially at Olympia, where trophies won in war adorned the field where athletic victory was achieved.[26] In a symbolic sense, the distinction between athletes and warriors effectively disappeared as they both partook of the status of victor. For a victorious athlete was potentially equivalent to an all-conquering tyrant.[27] A crowned athlete could lead troops into battle, and strike terror into his foes.[28] His power was greater than mere strength or speed; it was numinous, and commanded a special reverence even from his foes.[29] Although it was presumptuous and dangerous to do so, for an indefinable moment a victorious athlete could even be regarded as Zeus incarnate. Pindar demonstrates this possibility by warning against it, when he tells victors, "Do not strive to become Zeus" and "Do not strive to become a god."[30] Like a conqueror a victorious athlete sometimes had city walls thrown down to make way for his entry. Like a king he was crowned, paraded, feasted, and celebrated in monuments and songs. Like

23. Thucydides 1.126.3–6, explaining that Cylon took the "great festival" to be that of Olympian Zeus; cf. Herodotus 5.71.

24. Aristotle *Politics* 1313b23; cf. Thucydides 2.15.4, 6.54.5.

25. Arrian *Anabasis* 1.17.5–6; 2.3.1–8. Other sources are cited in chapter 2 note 107.

26. Mallwitz and Herrmann 1980 publish a selection of the many dedications of arms and armor found at Olympia, dating from the end of the eighth century to the fifth. Some of these trophies are inscribed with the names of the victor (who dedicates the prize of war to Zeus) and the vanquished. Similar dedications are described by Pausanias 5.10.4–5, 6.19.

27. The example of Alcibiades serves to illustrate how athletic victory was readily converted into political prowess and to fears of tyranny: see Thucydides 6.15–16; Isocrates 16, *On the Team of Horses*, esp. 32–38; [Andocides] 4, *Against Alcibiades* 25–31; Plutarch *Alcibiades* 11–12. The case of Alcibiades is discussed in chapter 9.

28. See, e.g., the examples of Milo of Croton (Diodorus 12.9.5–6); Phaÿllus of Croton (Herodotus 8.47; Plutarch *Alexander* 34.2); Eurybates of Argos (Herodotus 6.92). On the Spartan custom of arraying Olympic victors around the kings in battle, see Plutarch *Lycurgus* 22.2; Kurke 1993, 133.

29. See the reverent treatment of Philippus of Croton (Herodotus 5.47), Dorieus of Rhodes (Pausanias 6.7.4–5), and Lacrates of Sparta (Xenophon *Hellenica* 2.4.33) by their enemies. Leslie Kurke 1993 has discussed the transcendent quality of a victor as "talismanic," borrowing the term from Emile Benveniste's definition of the *kudos,* "renown," won by athletes (Benveniste 1973, 348).

30. Pindar *Isthmian* 5.14; *Olympian* 5.24; cf. *Pythian* 3.61–62. See also the dangerous example of Salmoneus, discussed below at note 38.

a king he could found colonies. And like a god after death his memory could be enshrined in cult as a divine and beneficent force.[31]

The assimilation of contest to conquest, linking victory to kingship, and linking kingship to divinity, all lie at the heart of the two most prevalent accounts of the origin of the Olympic Games, namely that they commemorated Zeus' overthrow of Cronus to become king of the gods, and Pelops' overthrow of Oenomaus to become king of Elis and the Peloponnese. The reenactment of victory through the athletic contests at Olympia, on the very spot of these great events of the past, seems to have been designed, in some sense, to recreate and participate in the effects of these archetypes of victory.

The seventh-century Spartan poet Tyrtaeus could name no higher example of kingliness among men than Pelops son of Tantalus.[32] In the fifth century, Pindar evoked the same archetype of kingship in his first *Olympian Ode* in praise of an equestrian victory of Hieron, tyrant of Syracuse. Pindar's song made the story of Pelops an explicit link in the chain of divine communion that began with Tantalus feasting the gods in Lydia, that came with his son, Pelops, to the kingship won at Olympia, and that finally arrived with Pindar's own song "at the rich and happy hearth of Hieron, who wields the scepter of justice in Sicily, rich in flocks."[33] Pindar's ode thus provides both a picture and a pedigree for sovereignty, designed to please the tyrant Hieron by depicting him as the living heir of the heritage of Pelops and ultimately of Olympian Zeus.

The kingliness of Pelops, and hence the legitimacy of his legacy, was based on more than just victory celebrated on the spot where Zeus had won kingship. The link between Pelops and the gods, as Pindar reminds his listeners, was as intimate as it could be: he had been rapt away by Poseidon to be his lover, as Pindar tells it; or as others say, he had been offered to the gods as a meal, and had been partially consumed by them before he was saved. In either case, Pelops had been presented to the gods by his father, Tantalus, king of Lydia (or Phrygia, in some versions), as a token of gratitude for the

31. Kurke 1993 discusses examples of all such honors associated with athletic victors. Further examples of men and women bearing the attributes of divinity and receiving reverent honors are noted by Connor 1987, 43–46. See also F. M. Cornford, following A. B. Cook: "In many cases [the victor] was worshipped after his death, as a hero; not because he was a successful athlete, but because he had been a god incarnate" (Cornford in J. E. Harrison 1927, 221). Fontenrose 1968 gathers testimony to the heroic status achieved by many victorious athletes; Bohringer 1979 suggests some of the political considerations that led to the heroization of athletes.

32. The praise of Pelops is conveyed in a negative conditional phrase: Tyrtaeus fr. 12.7 (Edmonds *EI*), "I would not give favorable mention to a man, not even if he were kinglier than Tantalid Pelops."

33. Pindar *Olympian* 1.10–13 and ff. Pindar's ode thus provides both a picture and a pedigree for sovereign tyranny. (Cf. Euripides *Orestes* 4–21.) On Hieron in Pindar's poetry, see further in note 44 below.

favors that the gods had shown him. But the offering of Pelops was said to be an abomination to the gods, and showed that Tantalus had gone too far, a transgression for which he was punished.[34] Despite, or because of, the outrage for which his father was eternally damned, Pelops had achieved an intimacy with divinity that assured his rise to sovereignty over the land that would bear his name, the Peloponnese. Vestiges of the kingship of Pelops were sufficiently potent, it was believed, that they could give power to those who possessed them. So, Pausanias tells us, possession of the shoulder blade of Pelops was a talisman that eventually enabled the Achaeans to capture Troy, and the very same bone was said to have been buried in the hero shrine of Pelops at Olympia.[35] Those who paid reverence to Pelops at Olympia might expect to share in the power of his talismanic presence, which probably explains why, according to Pausanias, the Eleans favored Pelops above other heroes with their honors just as they favored Zeus above other gods.[36] Pausanias also tells us that a ritual law firmly separated devotees of Pelops from devotees of Zeus. Those who partook of offerings made in the shrine of Pelops, he states, were forbidden from "entering the company of Zeus," which probably meant that they were forbidden from partaking also in sacrifices to Zeus until they had ritually purified themselves from their association with Pelops.[37] This ritual injunction appears to be intended to prevent the sort of transgression that Tantalus had committed, mixing human and divine elements in a common meal. If this understanding is correct, then the injunction served to reinforce the delicate boundary between mortal and divine kingship, lest a victor at Olympia arrogate to himself the attributes of both and, in violation of Pindar's warning, deem himself a kingly god.

Ritual prohibitions and poetic warnings should encourage us to consider what danger was foreseen when injunctions were transgressed and wise maxims ignored. In this instance, the danger was that of claiming a status that was too great, that was constrained by no man, and that rivaled even Zeus.

34. Pindar *Olympian* 1; cf. Euripides *Orestes* 4–21. Apollodorus *Epitome* 2.1 refers to a version of the story of Tantalus in which he was punished because "he told Mysteries of the gods to men, and shared ambrosia with his age mates." The earliest allusions to the punishment of Tantalus include *Odyssey* 11.582–92, and Archilochus fr. 53 (Edmonds *EI*). The variation in Tantalus' home, in Lydia or Phrygia, is discussed in chapter 2 note 44.

35. Pausanias 5.13.4–6 (cf. 6.22.1); Pliny *Historia Naturalis* 28.34. Pindar *Olympian* 1.26–27 evidently refers to this talisman when he mentions the "revered shoulder [of Pelops] gleaming with ivory" in the hands of the gods. Clement *Protrepticus* 4.42, claims that the bones of Pelops were used to make the Palladium, an image of Athena from Troy.

36. Pausanias 5.13.1.

37. Pausanias 5.13.3 specifies that "anyone, whether Elean or foreign, who eats the meat of victims sacrificed to Pelops is not allowed to enter the company of Zeus." Pausanias then compares this injunction to the terms imposed upon those who sacrifice to Telephus at Pergamum, where "they are forbidden from going up into the company of Asclepius until they have bathed."

This was precisely the folly committed by Salmoneus, the proud king who founded a city in the region of Olympia and who declared himself to be greater than Zeus. After appropriating to himself the offerings that were due to Zeus, he attracted the jealous eye of the god, who destroyed him and his city with a thunderbolt.[38] Here was the extreme to be avoided; but where in the quest for greatness was the recommended moderation of this extreme? For that there was no prescription. The sages' famous inscription at Delphi, Μηδὲν ἄγαν, "Nothing in excess," warns against only the extreme.

Greatness was to be won at Olympia; it went by the name of *kudos,* "renown," and it was a quality endowed by Zeus.[39] *Kudos* was a quality sought by victors, by kings, and by the assemblies that wielded collective sovereignty among the Greeks. So, for example, among the verses attributed to Solon we have the following invocation: "Let us first pray to King Zeus son of Cronus to bestow good fortune and *kudos* on these ordinances."[40] Because it was divine in nature, this greatness was a power that had the potential to overwhelm mundane conditions. But among those Greeks who abhorred the overwhelming power of tyranny, this power had to be controlled. So, although *kudos* was much sought after and universally admired, we find that myth, history, and ritual contain multiple warnings and guidelines for how to avert the dangerous consequences of producing and handling *kudos.*

Pindar's victory odes, as Leslie Kurke has demonstrated, served in one respect to civilize the godlike victor, making his numinous state safe to deal with, and enabling his reintegration into his civic community.[41] Many of the odes were composed to accompany the public homecoming of a champion, and the elevated status that he enjoyed on that occasion was often perpetuated through lifetime honors. So Xenophanes describes the customary honors awarded to Olympic victors by their fellow citizens: "Such a man will obtain renown in the citizens' sight [ἀστοῖσίν κ' εἴη κυδρότερος προσορᾶν], and be given a front seat and be on display at all civic occasions, and he would be

38. Apollodorus *Library* 1.9.7; Diodorus 4.68.1–2, 6.6.4–7.3; Strabo 8.3.31–33, who cites Euripides and Ephorus for elements of the traditions about Salmoneus; Pindar *Pythian* 4.143, notices Salmoneus "of bold intentions" (θρασυμήδης).

39. See Kurke 1993 on the *kudos* of athletes. On *kudos* as an endowment from Zeus, see Benveniste 1973, 349–55.

40. Plutarch *Solon* 3.4 (= Solon fr. 31 [Edmonds *EI*]). On the primacy of Zeus among the patron deities of deliberative bodies, note that Zeus Boulaios ("Counselor") and Athena Boulaia had a shrine in the Athenian Council House where the presidents of the council made offerings on behalf the democracy, according to Antiphon 6, *On the Choreutes* 45; Pausanias 1.3.5 mentions a wooden statue of Zeus Boulaios in the Council House. The foundation of a shrine of Zeus Syllanios and Athena Syllania is the first item named in the constitution of Sparta's deliberative body, according to the oracular *rhêtra* cited by Plutarch *Lycurgus* 6.1; on Sparta see further below, with note 51.

41. Kurke 1991, 257–62. See also the discussion of epinician poetry, victors, and tyrants by McGlew 1993, 35–51.

given his meals all at the public expense, and be given a gift from the city to take and store for safekeeping."[42] By these means, a quality that was essentially individual in nature, the supremacy of a victor, became distributed over his entire community. The ceremonial and institutional forms for distributing such honors, like the sharing of political power, are among the most distinctive characteristics of classical Hellenism.

These characteristics of classical Hellenism represent a self-conscious opposition to a different set of customs, where the glorification of the supreme individual, as victor, as king, possibly as a god, had no constraints. The characteristics of Hellenism were usually set in opposition to those of barbarism, meaning the customs of non-Greeks chiefly of Asia, a distinction that became sharply drawn only by the time of the Persian Wars, at the beginning of the classical era.[43] Were the Greeks developing their distinctive customs at a distance from the models that they opposed, or were they rather developing them as part of the process of differentiating themselves from institutions and customs in which the Greeks themselves were participants? I suggest the latter. As with the metaphoric kingship of *nomos* (law, custom) considered above, in *kudos* we see another example of the Greek endeavor to abstract a singular quality inherent to an ideal monarch into a collective quality that can be borne by an entire political community. And as with the concept of sovereignty and its relationship to tyranny discussed above, the abstraction of *kudos* suggests that the Greeks had some experience of, or belief in, the reality of sovereign, champion monarchs.

Were there instances of victors who were, by that very fact, kings, and possibly even divine? In Pindar's day, anyone who openly displayed and claimed these qualities would be violating the norms of Panhellenism. But the example of Hieron, the tyrant of Syracuse who was praised in Pindar's first *Olympian Ode*, shows how close below the surface of public display such claims could be. By Herodotus' account, Hieron's family held political power by virtue of their tenure of a hereditary priesthood of the Chthonian Goddesses, a privilege that assured them divine favor.[44] Homeric poetry presented examples of many champions who were kings by virtue of their excellence in war—by definition, as victors—and who were close to the gods, who in some cases were sons of gods, and who were looked upon by their

42. Xenophanes DK 21 B 2, modified translation of B. Knox. This passage is discussed further below at note 147. Documents attesting the Athenian custom of entertaining victors in the Panhellenic games with public meals at the Prytaneum include *IG* I³ 131.11–17; Plato *Apology* 36d

43. This is the central argument of Edith Hall's *Inventing the Barbarian* (1989); see also Lévy 1984 and Hartog 1988.

44. Herodotus 7.153, quoted in chapter 2 at note 128. On Hieron in Pindar's poetry, see McGlew 1993, 32–33, who observes that Pindar "comes very close to putting Hieron on a level with the gods."

people as gods.[45] The historical example of Cylon's attempted tyranny at Athens exemplifies sovereignty claimed by virtue of a victor's status, we have noted, and the claim involved the appropriation of sacred ground, the Acropolis of Athens. At the end of the archaic era, King Alexander I of Macedon asserted his Hellenic identity, as Herodotus reports, by proving his Argive (i.e., Heraclid) ancestry and then by competing in the stadium race at Olympia, where he won "an equal first." The victor's prize, in other words, appears to have been awarded to him by the judges in deference to his royal standing.[46] At the end of the classical era, Alexander III of Macedon made a similar display. Among the many ceremonies that attended his crossing into Asia, Alexander is said to have run a race with his companions at the tomb of Achilles by Troy.[47] That Alexander won the race is not stated, but by virtue of his unmatched kingship and eventual divine honors, it is self-evident that he must have done so.

Such examples of godlike kingly victors represent either the glorification of the heroic past or aberrations (tyranny, Macedonian kingship) from classical norms. They demonstrate nonetheless that such examples were never far from the awareness of the Greeks. A more mainstream example of the close conjunction of kingship, victory, and divinity can be found at Sparta, where political institutions preserved a distinctive balance between the ideals of collective excellence and their highest embodiment in the person of a king.

At Sparta, the institution of kingship had a prominence that was unique in Greece. True to the ideal type of traditional kingship, Spartan kings inherited their office and held it for life. The fact that there were two royal dynasties seems designed to assure that no individual king attained the unchallenged sway of a tyrant.[48] Both royal families claimed descent from Heracles, and through Heracles from Zeus. Heraclid lineage was a particularly potent link to divine kingship, since Heracles, besides being an unparalleled champion, was also a mortal who was taken by Zeus to live among

45. The speech of Sarpedon to Glaucus in *Iliad* 12.310–28 describes the privileges of kingship over the Lycians in terms comparable to the privileges accorded athletes, according to Xenophanes, and includes the observation that "all look upon us as gods" (312).

46. Herodotus 5.22. On the award of "an equal first" to Alexander by a decision of the judges, see How and Wells 1912, vol. 2, 8. The unrivaled championships in Panhellenic games won by the emperor Nero may be compared.

47. Plutarch *Alexander* 15.4.

48. Our sources usually specify that either the Council of Elders (the Gerusia) or the ephors were established by Lycurgus to check the tyrannical tendencies of the kings. (So Plutarch *Lycurgus* 5.6–7, 7.2–3; cf. Thucydides 1.18.1.) Drews 1983, 78–85, has argued that the dual kingship itself was instituted along with the ephorate, probably in the eighth century; Cartledge 1987, 102–4, 338–39, similarly argues that the customs of the dual kingship became established between the early eighth and mid-seventh centuries.

the gods.[49] The care with which the Spartans endeavored to assure the legitimacy of the heirs to their kingship came from the desire to keep this bloodline intact.[50] Spartan kings in office served as chief priests, above all to Zeus, and as war leaders.[51]

Many Spartan institutions were devoted to the production of victories.[52] Such was the case both in the custom of ambushing helots, against whom the Spartans were in a perpetual state of war, and in the vaunted prowess of Spartans in pitched battle, where yielding to the enemy was far worse than death.[53] Spartan prowess in Olympic competition was not far behind Spartan prowess in war. The lawgiver Lycurgus, credited with founding most of the institutions of the Spartan warrior state, was also credited with cosponsoring, along with Iphitus of Elis, the original Olympic truce.[54] Over half of the Olympic victors known by name from the late eighth until the early sixth century were Spartans, while from the mid-sixth until the early fourth cen-

49. Tyrtaeus frr. 2 and 3 (Edmonds *EI*) expresses the privileged link between the Heraclids of Sparta and Zeus. Herodotus 7.204 recites the lineage of King Leonidas back to Heracles; cf. 6.52.1. See also the Heraclid lineages of Sparta given by Apollodorus *Library* 2.8.1–5 and by Pausanias 3.1.5–10.5.

50. Xenophon *Lacedaemonian Constitution* 15.2 specifies that descent "from the god" justified the kings' roles in offering sacrifices and leading the army; cf. the ritualized reinstatement of Pleistoanax as king, in response to a Delphic oracle bidding Spartans to bring back "the seed of the demigod son of Zeus" (Διὸς υἱοῦ ἡμιθέου τὸ σπέρμα), reported by Thucydides 5.16.2–3. The history of Spartan kingship is replete with examples of controversial successions. See, e.g., the accounts of the accession of the sons of Aristodemus (Herodotus 6.52); of Charilaus (Plutarch *Lycurgus* 3.1–5); of the sons of Anaxandridas (Herodotus 5.39–41); of the sons of Ariston (Herodotus 6.61–70); of Agesilaus (Xenophon *Hellenica* 3.3.1–4; Plutarch *Agesilaus* 3.1–5; *Lysander* 22.3–6; Pausanias 3.8.8–10). See Cartledge 1987, 99–115, for a discussion of the exceptional nature of Spartan kingship.

51. The two priesthoods reserved for Spartan kings were of Zeus Lakedaimonios and Zeus Ouranios, according to Herodotus 6.56; the Spartan king offers sacrifice to Zeus Agetor (Leader) as his first duty in leading the Spartan army, according to Xenophon *Lacedaemonian Constitution* 13.2, 11; cf. 15.2–6.

52. Note that Xenophon *Lacedaemonian Constitution* 4.5 identifies competition, or "strife" (*eris*) among young Spartans as "dearest to the gods and to the highest degree political [πολιτικωτάτη], through which what is necessary to achieve—excellence—is revealed." The competitive aspect of the chief rituals of the rearing (*agōgē*) of Spartan warriors is clear from Burkert's summary (1985, 262–63).

53. Formal warfare against helots, and ambushes by young Spartan warriors, are described by Plutarch *Lycurgus* 28.1–4, citing Aristotle and Thucydides. The Spartan murder of some two thousand helots who had been crowned for their prowess in war on behalf of Sparta (Thucydides 4.80.3–4) may be understood to have had a ritual as well as a ruthlessly political purpose. Coming, as Thucydides reports, in the aftermath of the alarming defeat of Spartans at Pylos, this slaughter of crowned warriors was probably considered to be a mass sacrifice for the sake of restoring the Spartan claim to supremacy.

54. Plutarch *Lycurgus* 1.1 and 23.2, citing Aristotle's account of the inscribed discus at Olympia; cf. Pausanias 5.4.5.

tury Spartans dominated the prestigious four-horse chariot races.[55] Olympic victors enjoyed the honor of entering battle in the immediate company of the king, signifying the close conceptual bond between athletic victory, prowess in war, and the honors of kingship.[56] Even non-Spartan victors of great renown could be honored and courted by the Spartans as a bearers of divine favor. Teisamenus of Elis, an Olympic champion who was foreordained to achieve victory, was on that account embraced by the Spartans as a naturalized citizen and war leader.[57]

The talismanic power of victors was thus placed at the service of the kings of Sparta. By virtue of their leadership of a society devoted to victory, and by virtue of their own divinely endowed Heraclid lineage, the kings of Sparta stood at the threshold of divinity. Scrupulous attention to ritual and to the laws of Lycurgus enabled the Spartans to live with such sovereigns without descending into the more heinous forms of tyranny. The only unrestrained display allowed to Spartan kings was after death, when Spartan custom required the entire Laconian community, from Spartiates to helots, to participate in mass lamentations at their funerals.[58] Xenophon observes that the customs of Spartan royal funerals "show that the Lacedaemonians have honored [their kings] not as men, but as heroes."[59] Herodotus observes that the Spartans had this form of royal funeral in common with the barbarians of Asia.[60]

As we will see, the most impressive examples of royal Asiatic funerary custom were provided by the Lydians.[61] Likewise, Pelops, who was honored for

55. Hodkinson 1999 and 2000, 307–28, examines the relationship between wealth and the prestige of Olympic victory at Sparta.

56. Reported with an anecdote by Plutarch *Lycurgus* 22.4.

57. On Teisamenus, see Herodotus 9.33–35 and the discussion of Kurke 1993, 135–36. Note also the singular honors accorded to Themistocles at Sparta, according to Herodotus 8.124 and Plutarch *Themistocles* 17.1–2, where his achievement is said to have overawed everyone at the Olympic festival. For other accounts of foreigners honored for their value to the Spartans, see the story of Pherecydes, below, note 128.

58. Herodotus 6.58.2. See also Tyrtaeus fr. 7 (West; Edmonds *EI*), cited by Pausanias 4.14.4–5.

59. Xenophon *Lacedaemonian Constitution* 15.9; cf. Xenophon's comment on the funeral of Agis II, *Hellenica* 3.3.1: "He received a more worshipful burial than is due a man" (ἔτυχε σεμνοτέρας ἢ κατὰ ἄνθρωπον ταφῆς).

60. Herodotus 6.58.2. Cartledge 1987, 331–43, analyzes Spartan royal burial custom, and discusses its role in asserting the "exclusive linkage between superhuman descent and political function," and "the essential connection between the well-being of the Spartan state and the continued existence of the dual kingship" (337).

61. The significance of the ritualized mourning for Lydian kings is discussed below, in chapter 4. The famous tomb of the fourth-century king Mausolus of Caria (Pliny *Historia Naturalis* 36.30–31) exemplifies the continuation of this Asiatic tradition of heroic royal burial. Cartledge

his kingship at his funerary mound at Olympia, was believed to have brought his distinctive amalgamation of kingship and divinity with him from Asia, specifically from Lydia. As with the form of supremacy known as tyranny, here are reasons for suspecting that the chief models of sovereignty known to the Greeks were reflections of Asiatic kingship.

Did the Greeks have their own paradigms of sovereignty, independent of traditions that refer us to the royal courts of Asia? The oldest traditions available to the classical Greeks are represented in the poetry of Hesiod and Homer. There, besides the representation of kingship among men as the rivalry of heroic champions, we find a tradition of strong kingship depicted among the gods. In the following section, we will examine the conditions that generated and sustained divine sovereignty, according to Hesiod and Homer. We will then be better able to weigh the evidence for the historical development of worldly sovereignty and its ideological underpinnings among the Greeks. Eventually, we will return to the proposition that the Greeks, from the beginnings of their archaic literature, were tutored in the ways of kingship and the gods in the royal courts of Asia.

## THEOGONY; OR, THE CONDITIONS OF SOVEREIGNTY

The god-supported strength of a community, we have seen, was affirmed and reinforced by rituals and ceremonies that repeatedly brought it into contact with the archetypes of power. Living enactments of victory and heroic honors to the dead were reminders of, perhaps even direct links to, celebrated victors and kings of the past, both legendary and foreign. All of these, ultimately, referred in one way or another to the power of Zeus, and to the cosmic triumphs of the gods that secured his sovereignty.

But what could it mean to this symbolic system when one could envision a time before, and a time after, the reign of Zeus? What power might constrain Zeus himself? Here we reach ground less often trodden in Greek myth. The overthrow of Zeus is turned into a comic celebration in Aristophanes' *Birds*, is foretold in *Prometheus Bound*, and is even distantly hinted at in the *Iliad*, most clearly perhaps when Zeus acknowledges that even he cannot overturn the dictates of fate.[62] The cosmic conditions that might bring about Zeus' downfall are more directly brought before our mind's eye by Hesiod, who depicts the passage of aeons and the perilous course by which Zeus gained

---

1987, 333, following Hartog, draws attention to certain resemblances between Spartan and Scythian royal funerals, but this cannot be the comparison Herodotus had in mind; Scythians were not Asiatic according to Herodotus' geography, but inhabited the unexplored vastness of Europe west of the Tanaïs River and the boundary of Asia. (See Herodotus 4.1, 21, 44–45.)

62. This constraint is dramatized in the anxiety of Zeus witnessing the death of his son Sarpedon: *Iliad* 16.431–61; cf. *Odyssey* 3.236–38.

his sovereignty, and who also depicts, more clearly than Homer, abstract principles such as strife and justice that govern life in this world under Zeus. Could Zeus be constrained by the conditions of his own realm?

The question directs our attention again to the implications of the anthropomorphic paradigm that made Zeus such a compelling archetype for earthly sovereignty. Zeus, like every living king, rose to power by a combination of birthright and force, and secured his reign against rivals through wise rulership that gained the willing obedience of gods closest to him. But because he was not autonomous, because he relied on other deities to begin his rise to power, his reign was contingent, and open to challenge. Every manifestation of his sovereign power could, conceivably, be appropriated by others and used against him. Even mortals, from time to time, attempted to arrogate his privileges, although their stories were told to illustrate the disastrous consequences of such vainglory and high folly.[63] But Prometheus' theft of fire from Zeus, and gift of it to mankind, was a sign that not even Zeus himself could guard his own powers forever.

Sovereigns prior to Zeus, Uranus, or Heaven, and Cronus, father of Zeus, had been overthrown. Uranus, whose embrace once smothered his mate, Gaea, Earth, had been emasculated by his son, Cronus, and had withdrawn to his place high above the earth. The only remnants of Uranus' original dominion were the offspring of that bloody separation, chief among whom was Aphrodite who was called Urania, the Heavenly One. Cronus too had been overthrown by his son Zeus, and was either imprisoned beneath the earth in Tartarus, or removed to the ends of the earth, reigning in exile over the Isles of the Blessed. From his reign only lesser daemons remained on earth as guardian spirits, helpful to mankind. But once a year, in the festival called Kronia, the customary order of things was inverted, and slaves were free to scoff work and mock their masters—the polarity of sovereignty was reversed, and for a day Cronus reigned again.[64] With this single exception, Zeus' sovereignty prevailed; it did so in the negation of the powers of Uranus and Cronus.

It was otherwise, however, with the mates of Uranus and Cronus, who were Gaea, Earth herself, and Rhea. Both were very much present and honored within the dominion of Zeus. In concept, only Zeus could hold paramount sovereignty, but the very foundations of his sovereignty were his maternal

---

63. Tantalus (above, note 34) was said by some to have revealed secrets of the gods to mankind (Diodorus 4.74.2). Niobe daughter of Tantalus dared to boast of her children to Leto (Homer *Iliad* 24.602–17; Apollodorus *Library* 3.5.6). Ixion dared to seduce Hera (Pindar *Pythian* 2.40–89; Diodorus 4.69.3–5). Salmoneus dared to imitate Zeus and appropriate his offerings. (See note 38 above.)

64. Testimony to the Kronia in various cities, and to the month name Kronion, is gathered by Nilsson 1906, 37–39; Burkert 1985, 231–32; Trümpy 1997, 14 n. 55, 293, 295.

nurturers, Gaea and Rhea. They were responsible for bringing Zeus to power, in Hesiod's account, and we find that they were therefore given honors in cult, especially where Zeus' sovereignty was also celebrated. At Athens, the close relationship between Gaea, Rhea, Cronus, and Zeus was reflected by the clustering of their sanctuaries beside the Ilissus River at the edge of the city.[65] At Olympia too, Gaea enjoyed cult honors beside Zeus at the foot of the Hill of Cronus.[66] Likewise at Sparta, Gaea and Zeus shared a shrine in the agora.[67] According to the *Homeric Hymn to Demeter*, Rhea played a decisive role in reconciling her daughter Demeter to her place in the regime of Zeus. It was probably in connection with this role that Rhea received honors, as the Mother at Agrae, in the Lesser Mysteries at Athens.[68] Otherwise, Rhea was chiefly honored in cult at places associated with the deception of Cronus and the birth of Zeus.[69]

Gaea and her daughter Rhea are the center of a group of divinities, in the pantheon common to Homer and Hesiod, who did much more than nurture Zeus and raise him to power. These divinities, all of them goddesses, relate to Zeus as the sources and the personifications of qualities that Zeus must control in order for his sovereignty to endure. They include Rhea's sisters, Themis and Mnemosyne, her nieces, Metis, Eurynome, and Leto, and her daughters, Demeter and Hera. All of these goddesses coupled with Zeus to bring significant forces into the world. Beyond these goddesses were divinities who held powers that Zeus did not control, and who were capable of striking awe or fear into Zeus: Nyx, Night, and her children, and Aphrodite, and Gaea herself.

Gaea, "universal mother, eldest of all beings," was more manifest in this world even than Zeus. As the *Homeric Hymn to Earth, Mother of All* begins: "She

65. Thucydides 2.15.4 notes that the sanctuary of Earth was located close to the temple of Olympian Zeus at Athens; Pausanias 1.18.7 calls her "Olympian Earth" and says that her shrine was within the precinct of Zeus. Close by was also a temple of Cronus and Rhea (also within the precinct of Zeus: Pausanias 1.18.7). On the cult of Cronus and Rhea here, see Robertson 1992, 27–29; and see note 68 below.

66. There was an altar of Earth atop a monument called the *Gaion* at Olympia (Pausanias 5.14.10), near which Cronus received offerings and Rhea may have been honored (Pausanias 6.20.1; cf. 5.7.6).

67. Earth and Zeus Agoraios at Sparta: Pausanias 3.11.9.

68. *Homeric Hymn* 2, *To Demeter* 441–70. Simon 1983, 26–27, citing relevant vase paintings, identifies Rhea with the Mother at Agrae, whose cult place was beside the Ilissus near the Olympieum. Robertson 1992, 27–29, argues plausibly that Cronus too enjoyed cult here; R. Parker 1996, 188 n. 129, points out that this does not dissociate this shrine from the Lesser Mysteries, as Robertson argues.

69. Rhea is honored in the vicinity of Mount Lycaeum in Arcadia (Strabo 8.3.22; Pausanias 8.36.2–3, 41.2, 47.3); at Chaeronea in Boeotia (Pausanias 9.41.6); at Delphi (Pausanias 10.24.6). Strabo 10.3.12–14 and 19–20 testifies to a literary debate over the competing claims of Mount Ida on Crete and Mount Ida in the Troad as Rhea's hiding place for the infant Zeus.

feeds all creatures that are in the world; and all that go upon the bright land, all that go in the ways of the sea, and all that fly, these are fed from her bounty."[70] Because she is omnipresent to all living things, and because all depend on her, Gaea is often named first of all deities as witness and as enforcer of oaths.[71] She is rarely depicted as an active personality among divinities. Impregnated by various forces, she gives birth to Titans, to lesser daemons, ultimately to humankind, and also to monsters that challenge Zeus. Among communities of mortal men, Gaea gave birth to several lines of legendary kings, including Erechtheus or Erichthonius at Athens. Autochthony, or birth from the earth, was a warrant of local legitimacy and localized sovereignty for these ancestral kings and their descendants.[72]

Sovereignty among the gods too came from birth out of the earth.[73] But among the gods, where sovereignty was universal and sovereigns were immortal, succession implied a rupture of legitimacy. Hesiod describes the succession of Cronus over Uranus, and of Zeus over Cronus, as just retribution carried out by the son for the outrageous behavior of his father. Gaea is the one who knows when retribution is due, and can offer counsel to secure its effect or can warn and avert, or postpone, its effect. Gaea secures Zeus' rise to power and warns him of several threats to his sovereignty. Gaea is thus aware of forces that have the capacity to overthrow even a divine and immortal sovereign. This awareness makes Gaea the original source of prophecy, and she is so represented at Delphi, as Aeschylus describes her at the opening of the *Eumenides*. Gaea is also the mother of Prometheus, according to Aeschylus, and she is the source of his knowledge that Zeus himself will fall one day.

Nyx, Night, is the one divinity in the *Iliad* said to make even Zeus recoil in awe.[74] Like Gaea, Nyx was a primal being who came into existence after primordial Chaos. Among her many children are the various personifications of fate and death, forces affecting mortal beings in ways that Zeus might influence, but cannot control. Nemesis, Retribution herself, was a child of Nyx

---

70. *Homeric Hymn* 30, *To Earth, Mother of All* 1–4. Cf. Hesiod *Theogony* 104–19.

71. Homer *Iliad* 3.103, 15.36; Zeus is invoked first in 3.274, 19.258; cf. Aeschylus *Seven against Thebes* 5–19, 69–77; Euripides *Orestes* 1495. In some oath formulas, Gaea is replaced by representatives of her attributes—Demeter, Thallo, Auxo, etc.; see Burkert 1985, 250–51.

72. Earth bore, e.g., Erechtheus at Athens (*Iliad* 2.548; Herodotus 8.55); Erichthonius at Athens (Pausanias 1.2.6); Anax at Miletus (Pausanias 1.35.6); Hyllus in Lydia (Pausanias 1.35.8); Triptolemus at Eleusis, according to Musaeus (Pausanias 1.14.3). Nicole Loraux 1993 and 2000 has studied aspects of the theme of autochthony and its relationship to the concept of citizenship at Athens and elsewhere.

73. Uranus is born from Gaea before becoming her mate, according to Hesiod *Theogony* 126–27. Before overthrowing Uranus, Cronus is hidden within the body of Gaea (*Theogony* 157–59), much as the infant Zeus, borne by Rhea, was hidden by Gaea within herself (*Theogony* 482–83) before overthrowing Cronus.

74. *Iliad* 14.256–61.

who could conceivably mark the moment when the divine sovereign himself overstepped the bounds of rightful behavior. She certainly had the capacity of overturning the excessive pride of men, and was chief among the children of Nyx to receive reverential honors of cult worship among the Greeks, particularly in Attica and in Asia Minor.[75] Nemesis gave birth to Eris, Strife, who pitched the Apple of Discord into the banquet of the gods, resulting in the most famous conflict between Europe and Asia, if we grant the Trojan War pride of place over the historical conflict of Greeks and Persians. At Rhamnus in Attica, Nemesis was honored as the mate of Zeus who had given birth to the incomparable Helen, fated to be at the center of the Trojan War.

Aphrodite, born at sea out of the severed genitals of Uranus, had the power to beguile Zeus. Zeus could sometimes induce her to do his bidding, but their tit-for-tat was more often presented as the interplay of equals than the wrangling of a father and his sometimes obstreperous daughter.[76] Aphrodite played a decisive role in stimulating Zeus' involvement with mortal women, and thus was a key element in defining the relationship between gods and mortals in genealogical terms.[77] Aphrodite also played the decisive role in setting Greeks and Trojans at war with each other by offering Helen to Paris.

Aphrodite, as the power impelling sexual procreation, also underlay the generation of the divine offspring of Zeus who together formed the pantheon over which Zeus reigned. The very notion that Zeus participated in sexual and procreative unions was an essential condition of his sovereignty. For from these unions Zeus acquired most of the qualities that defined and sustained his sovereignty, qualities that in turn were the most important blessings that rightful sovereignty could bring to humankind. But they were not qualities of Zeus himself, his only by affiliation. So Themis, who was Rightful Order personified, bore Eunomia (Good Customs), Dike (Justice), and Eirene (Peace) among other daughters to Zeus; Mnemosyne (Memory) bore the Muses, to impart inspired words to kings and poets; Eurynome (Wide Dominion) bore the Charites (Graces); Leto bore Apollo and Artemis; Demeter bore Persephone to be bride of Zeus' brother and counterpart Hades; Hera bore Ares, Hebe (Youth), and Eileithyia, goddess of childbirth.[78] The most remarkable offspring of Zeus, however, was Athena. The story of her birth signifies vulnerabilities that were rarely spoken of in myth or cult, but were always latent in Zeus' condition.

75. References to the cult of Nemesis at Smyrna are given by Nilsson 1906, 441, and by Santoro 1973, 200–201, who also cites testimony to her cult at Nicaea; Head 1911, 952, indexes numerous late Hellenistic and imperial cults of Nemesis attested by numismatic evidence. Her cult at Rhamnus in Attica is discussed in chapter 9.

76. Aphrodite is sometimes called the daughter of Zeus and Dione (e.g., *Iliad* 5.311–430).

77. See *Homeric Hymn* 5, *To Aphrodite* 33–52; cf. *Iliad* 14.153–224.

78. Hesiod *Theogony* 901–29.

Athena was the product of the union of Zeus and Metis, his first wife, whose name means Cunning Intellect. In Hesiod's words, Metis was "wisest of the gods and of mortal men."[79] Zeus was warned by Gaea and Uranus that she was capable of bearing a child of great wisdom, who could wield a force more powerful than even Zeus' own thunderbolts and who could thus overmaster Zeus himself. Therefore, "so that no other one of the eternal gods should hold royal honor in place of Zeus," Zeus swallowed Metis.[80] From this remarkable union, in due course a daughter was born out of Zeus' head: Athena, "equal to her father in strength and wise understanding."[81] Thus in Hesiod's narrative we learn explicitly that Zeus was aware of the danger of being overthrown by his own offspring. He contained the threat by making his firstborn his own in a unique way, and by preventing Metis from bearing the child who could turn against him.

Yet even Athena herself, with powers equal to her father's, could have overthrown Zeus. Hesiod's text is curiously vague about how Athena was from the first completely loyal to him.[82] We infer what Aeschylus in the *Eumenides* later makes explicit, in the words of Athena herself: "Because no mother gave birth to me, I honor the male in all ways . . . and am with all my heart strongly on my father's side."[83] At the moment of her birth, however, her paternal allegiance was yet to be demonstrated. For after Zeus had labored in supreme discomfort, Athena appeared suddenly out of his head, brandishing her spear and in full armor, and might have struck down her father then and there, effecting another cosmic revolution, if she had been so minded. The fearful uncertainties around which the fate of the cosmic order revolved at the moment of her birth are clearly described in *Homeric Hymn* 28, *To Athena:*[84]

79. Hesiod *Theogony* 886–87. Note that Acusilaus made Metis along with Eros a primordial force created out of Erebus and Nyx, before the generation of gods: DK 9 B 1.

80. Hesiod *Theogony* 892–93.

81. Hesiod *Theogony* 896.

82. The duplication of the account of Athena's birth, with variations, in a Hesiodic passage quoted by Chrysippus (lines 929a–t in the Loeb edition; see the commentary by M. L. West 1966, 401–2) perhaps indicates that this story was told in more detail in other renditions of the *Theogony*.

83. Aeschylus *Eumenides* 736–38, cf. 658–66.

84. *Homeric Hymn* 28, *To Athena*. In the sentence "Then wise Zeus heaved a great sigh of relief" (γήθησε δὲ μητίετα Ζεύς), I translate γηθέω (commonly "to rejoice") by the more descriptive "to breath a sigh of relief." This is justified by Philostratus *Eikones* 2.27, who attests to the disorientation, fright, and resourcelessness of the gods at the first sight of Athena (οἱ μὲν ἐκπληττόμενοι θεοὶ καὶ θεαί... φρίττουσι.... καὶ ὁ Ἥφαιστος ἀπορεῖν ἔοικεν), followed by a great breath of pleasure, "like those who have accomplished a great struggle for a great reward," breathed by Zeus (ὁ δὲ Ζεὺς ἀσθμαίνει σὺν ἡδονῇ, καθάπερ οἱ μέγαν ἐπὶ μεγάλῳ καρπῷ διαπονήσαντες ἄθλον) when he realized that the event, which could have turned out badly, had turned out well.

I begin to sing of Pallas Athena, glorious goddess, shining-eyed, of great cunning, with a relentless heart, discreet maiden, savior of the city, courageous, Tritogeneia, whom wise Zeus himself, from his revered head, bore wearing warlike armor, golden, resplendent.

Awe seized all the immortals who beheld her. But she sprang quickly from the immortal head of aegis-bearing Zeus, brandishing her sharp spear. Great Olympus began to reel terribly at the mighty roar of the shining-eyed one; all around, the earth shrieked fearfully. Even the sea was moved, heaving with dark waves and bursting whitecaps. The gleaming son of Hyperion stayed his swift-footed horses for a what seemed like an eternity—until the girl removed the godlike armor from her immortal shoulders.

Then wise Zeus heaved a great sigh of relief.

And so hail to you, child of aegis-bearing Zeus! Now I will remember you and another song as well.

This was the drama depicted in the east pedimental sculpture of the Parthenon: it was the moment when Athena's powers were first manifest, when she might have overthrown Zeus, just before she signaled her allegiance. Athena's loyalty, once declared by her disarmament, was made steadfast to Zeus in a manner that, again, Hesiod does not explain. Her "affection for the male in all ways," in Aeschylus' formulation, had but one exception: sexual union. Athena would remain ever her father's unmarried daughter, always a *parthenos*. This meant that she would never bear the offspring that might yet fulfill the warning of Gaea and Uranus to Zeus.

The transcendent forever-after nature of the immortal gods thus fused two opposing qualities into the undying nature of Athena. She embodied both the threat of the offspring who could overthrow Zeus, and the promise that no such threat will be fulfilled (by a child of Metis, at any rate). Through the paradoxes of Athena, we gain our most direct view of the precarious condition of Zeus' sovereignty. As much as Zeus' powers were augmented through procreation, so too were they threatened by his unions. In this respect, Zeus is analogous to every earthly monarch who forms alliances through marriage, but who must confront his own eventual downfall and displacement, most likely by his own offspring aided by her who gave him birth. In the paradigm of immortal Olympians, Athena stood for procreation arrested, and sovereignty preserved.

In Hesiod's theogonic mythology, Zeus' sovereignty emerges from, is manifested through, and is defended by goddesses who bear him and raise him to kingship, who mate with him, and who are his offspring. Divine sovereignty therefore rests on a balance of sexual relationships, as it is depicted in the foundational texts of Greek theogony. Earthly sovereignty among Greek communities of the classical era invoked various forms of communion with this paradigm of divine sovereignty, but did not seek to replicate it. Tyranny among the Greeks and among the tyrants of Asia themselves, on the other hand, did tend to construct power through the manipulation of sexual relationships, and did attempt to replicate aspects of the Hesiodic paradigm. The contrast is illustrated when the role of Athena is compared to that of other goddesses, whose sexuality is dynamic.

Athena, innocent of sex and therefore the unchanging guardian of an immortal sovereign, was well suited to defend the collective and self-regenerating sovereignty of an assembled demos, as she did for both the Spartans and the Athenians. Athena was not, however, the ideal divine champion of a mortal monarch or tyrant, who required the powers of procreation to be at his personal service in order to perpetuate his sovereignty.[85] Either Hera, the chief consort of Zeus, or Aphrodite, the agent of procreation, was a much more suitable divine champion for kings and tyrants. This may account for the prominence of Hera at Argos, where Pheidon provided a strong example of early archaic kingship, and the prominence of Aphrodite at Corinth, where sovereignty early on was embodied in Bacchiad kingship and Cypselid tyranny. Sovereignty among tyrants, as we will see, was signified by sexual relationships, where the forces that generated, sustained, and perpetuated divine kingship were embodied in persons of the royal court. In such cases, the distinction between mortals and immortals is deliberately confused. We will see that this, too, is a feature of tyranny.

## HUMANITY AND DIVINE SOVEREIGNTY

Sexual generation, in the Hesiodic theogony, is the agency that produces sovereignty among the gods. The foregoing discussion also suggests that the sexual activity of some divinities and the asexuality of others defined significant conditions of the relationships between gods and mortals, particularly affecting those mortals who assume the trappings of sovereign power. In the popular understanding of Hesiod's day and after, the sexual unions of gods and mortals were accepted features of the heroic age, when Heracles was fathered by Zeus, for example, or Achilles was borne by Thetis. Hesiod's picture of the passing of the age of heroes encourages the view that such things had ceased to be by his day. But it would be a mistake to take this impression as an absolute rule, as scholars sometimes do, and to assume that, after Hesiod, Greeks did not believe that gods could ever interact with humanity in the same way.[86] There was no discontinuity between present re-

85. Athena's patronage by Peisistratus at Athens is a sign of the atypical quality of his tyranny, which came late in the historical development of tyranny and was a bridge to popular sovereignty. It is no accident that Herodotus accompanies his story of Peisistratus and Athena with an account of procreation arrested. See Herodotus 1.60–61, discussed below at notes 97–101.

86. Paul Veyne, in his *Did the Greeks Believe in Their Myths?* (translated in 1988), insists that Greeks of the historical era judged tales of the past "by means of what we would call the doc-

ality and the marvelous past; marvels could happen. As with the repudiation of tyranny, and the restraint imposed upon the quest for *kudos,* divine generation became a rare commodity among men in the classical world, but it was not extinguished.

The readiness of a wide public to accept the possibility of intercourse between a god and a human is attested in a story told by Plutarch, on the authority of an earlier source, who was probably the fourth-century historian Ephorus.[87] Lysander the Spartan, the man responsible for destroying the Athenian empire, conspired by various means to secure divine authorization for his revolutionary goal of transforming Spartan kingship. Lysander learned of a woman from Pontus, in Asia Minor, who claimed to be bearing Apollo's child. Her claim had wide popularity, and when a son was born to her, he attracted much attention. Lysander devised ways to spread her story through reputable sources, involving even the Delphic Oracle, so that not even Spartan authorities could discount it out of hand. Lysander's scheme, once this child was grown, was to have the boy summoned to Delphi in order that priests there (who were conspirators with Lysander) could test his claim to be the son of Apollo. For Lysander had prepared secret oracles in writing at Delphi, pertaining to the kings of Sparta, and these oracles were to be read only by a son of Apollo. Lysander died before the plot could be accomplished, and the conspiracy was revealed by one of Lysander's collaborators. But the fact that such a plot could be carried so far reveals just how strong conventional piety could be as a force in public opinion, having the potential of shaping official action regardless of the presence, as Plutarch notes, of skeptics, doubters, and calculating manipulators.

The marvelous possibility of a divine birth may have been given credence on this occasion in part because its premise, that gods could mate with mortals, was regularly enacted in ritual contexts. Ritualized intercourse of gods and mortals was not populating the world with demigods, however, but was

---

trine of present things. The past resembles the present, or, in other words, the marvelous does not exist" (14). Veyne must often admit, however, that this distinction was upheld only by those whom he calls "thinkers" (18, where he names Thucydides, Hecataeus, Pausanias the Periegete, and Saint Augustine as examples), while many "who were not thinkers" (e.g., Pindar) allowed their imaginative faculties to transgress this boundary of present reality. Even Veyne's "thinkers" allow themselves to slip into "popular credulity" from time to time. (See 31, 73–74, 95–102.) Jenny Strauss Clay, in her *Politics of Olympus* (1989), 166–201, interprets the *Homeric Hymn to Aphrodite* as a narrative whose message is that Zeus "aimed at putting an end to sexual relations between gods and humanity, thereby bringing a close to the age of heroes" (198). Reasons for interpreting this hymn otherwise are discussed in chapter 3.

87. Plutarch *Lysander* 26 tells the story of the boy called Seilenus "following the account of a historian and philosopher" (25.4). Immediately before this reference, and twice elsewhere, Plutarch cites Ephorus as his authority for details of Lysander's conspiracy and use of oracles (*Lysander* 20.6, 25.3, 30.3).

legitimizing civic institutions. Like other divine endowments still recognized in the classical era, the benefits of sexual communion with gods were disbursed over a community at large through rituals ministered by public and priestly officials. At Athens this was done in the Anthesteria festival, when the union of Dionysus with the "queen" of Athens (Basilinna, actually the wife of the archon basileus, "king archon") was celebrated in a Sacred Marriage (*hieros gamos*) on behalf of the city.[88] The Athenians also celebrated a Sacred Marriage in honor of Zeus and Hera in a festival called Theogamia, "Divine Marriage," and the union of Zeus and Demeter was said to play a part in the Greater Mysteries performed in the Anaktoron, or "House of the *Anax* [Sovereign Lord]," at Eleusis.[89] We have no clear indication how the significant act may have been represented in each of these ritual events (a mystery in the truest sense), but it is clear that, in all of them, sexual intercourse was accepted as the basis of communion between humanity and the divine. When a human participated in that intercourse, as the Basilinna did with Dionysus, he or she played the role of royalty.[90]

The comedies of Aristophanes often portray Athenian rituals in farcical contexts, with specific ritual acts and choral songs that parody those of festal occasions.[91] More than once he depicts a comic triumph as the marriage of a man and a divine being, and in one instance he appears to mimic the Sacred Marriage of Zeus and Hera in the Theogamia. In Aristophanes' *Birds,* an Athenian man, Peisetaerus, replaces Zeus as ruler of the universe. The revolution is consummated at the end of the play in the marriage of Peisetaerus to the divine Basileia, the personification of Sovereignty. She is

88. [Demosthenes] 59, *Against Neaera* 73–79, provides a detailed if elliptically discreet description of the consummation of the *hieros gamos* of the wife of the archon basileus and Dionysus. Further testimonia, including vase paintings, are discussed by Deubner 1932, 100–110, emended by Simon 1983, 96–99; also Parke 1977, 110–13.

89. The *hieros gamos* of Zeus and Hera celebrated in the Theogamia festival made the winter month Gamelion the most propitious for marriages; for Athens, see Deubner 1932, 177; Parke 1977, 104; Simon 1983, 16; Clark 1998, 17–20. For the same month in other Greek calendars, see Trümpy 1997, 132–34. For discussion of the *hieros gamos* of Zeus and Demeter in the Eleusinian Mysteries, see Deubner 1932, 84–87; Mylonas 1961, 311–16; Brumfield 1981, 202–7.

90. Strabo 14.1.3, citing Pherecydes, reports that descendants of Androclus, founder of Ephesus, who was "the legitimate son of Codrus, king of Athens," maintained the honorary title *basileis* at Ephesus, and enjoyed symbolic royal privileges, including conduct of the rites of Eleusinian Demeter. At Athens, Codrus and his son, Neleus, shared a shrine with a divinity named *Basilē* ("Queen," or perhaps "Royalty" or "Kingship" personified); see Shapiro 1986; Kearns 1989, 151, 178, 188. This shrine contained a grove, and probably the grave of Codrus, but the nature of its cult is virtually unknown; see Travlos 1971, 322–23. (R. Parker 1996 makes no mention of this cult.)

91. Aristophanes' *Acharnians,* e.g., depicts the rural Dionysia (Deubner 1932, 135–37; Cole 1993); his *Frogs* depicts processional songs of the Eleusinian Mysteries (Mylonas 1961, 250–55); his *Clouds* even parodies Eleusinian mystic rites (Burkert 1983, 268–69).

described as a "the most beautiful girl, guardian of Zeus' thunderbolts, and everything" and the "enthroned partner" of Zeus.[92] In the finale, a wedding procession commences when a messenger announces the splendid arrival of Peisetaerus with the words: "Welcome your tyrant to his happy halls!"[93] As Peisetaerus and his bride enter, probably on a chariot, the chorus sings his praises, sings of the blessings to come to their community, and sings: "You have made a most blessed marriage for this city!"[94] The chorus compares the occasion to the wedding of Zeus and Hera as they drove to their wedding in a chariot guided by Eros. As Peisetaerus and his bride approach the very marriage bed of Zeus, the chorus hails him, "O highest of gods!"[95] Whatever connection this scene may have had with the actual rites of the Theogamia at Athens, it represented sovereign power as the outcome of a relationship between a human being and a divinity. Similar enactments elsewhere are associated with real tyranny, and real kingship.[96]

A possible antecedent to the scene in Aristophanes' *Birds* is found in Herodotus' account of the installation of Peisistratus in his second tyranny at Athens. The event marked the resolution (for a time) of civil strife at Athens, and took place with popular approval and with the support of Peisistratus' most powerful rival, Megacles son of Alcmeon. Herodotus describes the occasion as follows:[97]

> In the village Paeania there was a woman name Phye, who was nearly six feet tall, and quite beautiful as well. They fitted this woman out in full armor and had her mount a chariot and pose in a most striking attitude, and then drove into the city, preceded by messengers who said, as they had been instructed, when they reached the city, "Athenians! Receive and welcome Peisistratus, since Athena herself has honored him especially of all men, and is bringing him to her own acropolis." They spread this account throughout the city, and soon word had reached the villages that Athena was bringing Peisistratus back, and

---

92. Aristophanes *Birds* 1537–39: τίς ἐστιν ἡ Βασίλεια;/ καλλίστη κόρη, ἥπερ ταμιεύει τὸν κεραυνὸν τοῦ Διὸς καὶ τἄλλ' ἀπαξάπαντα. 1753: καὶ πάρεδρον Βασίλειαν ἔχει Διός.

93. *Birds* 1708: δέχεσθε τὸν τύραννον ὀλβίοις δόμοις.

94. *Birds* 1725: ὦ μακαριστὸν σὺ γάμον τῇδε πόλει γήμας.

95. *Birds* 1732–43; 1757–58: ἐπὶ πέδον Διὸς καὶ λέχος γαμήλιον. 1764–65: ὦ δαιμόνων ὑπέρτατε. Lines 1737–40 refer to Eros as the charioteer of Zeus and Hera.

96. Clark 1998, 20, observes that this scene "could be the dramatisation of the myth of the divine *gamos*." Chapter 4 will discuss elements of Sacred Marriage texts from Mesopotamia that parallel certain elements of this scene. Chapter 9, at note 23, discusses the historical context of this play. Cf. also the Sacred Marriage rituals noted by Herodotus 1.181–82 as contemporary practice in Babylon, Egypt, and Lycia.

97. Herodotus 1.60.4–5, translated by Sinos (1993), with modifications. The story is repeated by Aristotle *Athenian Constitution* 14.4, who cites Herodotus and reports variant details, "as some say." The fourth-century Atthidographer Cleidemus *FGrHist* 323 F 15 also reported the story. This vignette is the centerpiece of Connor's study of the political role of processions and ceremonies (1987); see also Sinos 1993.

the city's inhabitants, convinced that the woman was the goddess herself, offered prayers to this mortal woman and welcomed Peisistratus back.

The creation of sovereignty through the communion of a divinity and a man was never more open and explicit than this. The drama was so simple, yet its premise—that a mortal man and an immortal divinity could be seen together in this manner—is so completely contrary to everyday experience that Herodotus cannot tell the story without pausing to tell his audience how remarkable he finds it. Yet he affirms without qualification that the Athenians on that occasion were convinced that the woman was the goddess herself.[98]

The event may have been believable because its conventions were familiar at the time, although they had become much less so to audiences of Herodotus' day. When we look for parallels to this story, we find suggestive echoes, but no perfect match. Chariot processions involving gods and heroes were relatively common in late sixth-century black-figure vase painting. John Boardman has drawn attention to chariot scenes depicting Athena escorting Heracles into the company of the gods of Olympus, and has suggested that the procession of Peisistratus and Athena was meant to connect Peisistratus with Heracles in the eyes of the Athenians.[99] Peisistratus is never explicitly compared to Heracles in any of our sources, however, and so Boardman's interpretation has not been accepted without reservations by scholars. Other vase paintings depict weddings where a couple rides a chariot with gods attending their progress.[100] As noted above, a chariot carried Zeus and Hera to their wedding, as the event was recalled by the Athenians, in song if not in ritual. In the procession of Athena and Peisistratus, however, the goddess was surely not accompanying Peisistratus to their wedding on the Acropolis. Yet, as Louis Gernet has pointed out, the occasion of Peisistratus' assumption of tyranny was also the occasion of his marriage. For he had arranged to marry the daughter of Megacles "for the tyranny," and, in a literal and possibly also symbolic sense, it was this marriage that made Peisistratus tyrant.[101] Similarly, Athena's escort of Heracles to Olympus culminated in a marriage—not to Athena, but to Hebe, daughter of Zeus and Hera—which effectively also signified the immortal status of Heracles.[102]

---

98. Herodotus' personal comments are discussed below. Among the strongest of modern skeptics, K. J. Beloch considered the entire story a fiction elaborated by popular imagination, perhaps aided by some commemorative monument depicting Athena and Peisistratus together. See the summary of scholarship by How and Wells 1912, vol. 1, 83; and more recently Connor 1987, and Sinos 1993, reflecting a current trend toward accepting Herodotus' account.

99. Boardman 1972 and 1989b; see the discussion of Sinos 1993, 81–82.

100. See Sinos 1993, 75–78, and Oakley and Sinos 1993, 28–30.

101. Gernet 1968, 358.

102. *Odyssey* 11.602–4. Oakley and Sinos 1993, 35 and figures 100–104, discuss and illustrate a black-figure vase depicting Athena conducting Heracles to a marriage bed, where Hebe is his bride.

From among these examples, processions leading to tyranny or deification consistently involve a marriage. In this case, it seems most likely that Peisistratus' procession to the Acropolis culminated in the marriage of Peisistratus and the daughter of Megacles, and that the marriage was seen as a living enactment of heroic weddings like that of Peleus and Thetis, or Heracles and Hebe. In the process, the actors assumed the status of heroes and gods. Sacred Marriage ceremonies, wherein mortals consorted with or even played the role of divinities, were certainly known to Athenians of Herodotus' day, as they are attested by Aristotle and mimicked by Aristophanes. What had become unfamiliar to Athenians of Herodotus' day was the notion that the public would join in the celebration of a divine marriage that actually elevated a man to sovereign power. But Aristophanes shows that even this was not completely unfamiliar. It was ludicrous, perhaps, but it was not inconceivable.[103] Such things had been within the ken of Greeks, and Athenians among them, in the not so distant past.

### THE PASSING OF AN AGE OF INNOCENCE

When Herodotus describes the plan formed by Megacles and Peisistratus to unite their families in a tyrannical dynasty at Athens, he describes it as "the most simpleminded trick that I have ever come across." He goes on: "The Greeks have long been distinguished from barbarian peoples by being more clever and less susceptible to foolish simplicity, and of all Greeks the Athenians are considered the most intelligent; yet it was at the Athenians' expense that this trick was played."[104] The contrast of present Athenian sophistication with barbarian simplicity is significant, for it implies that the simplicity characteristic of the Greeks of old, and even of the Athenians at the beginning of the Peisistratid era, was more closely akin to the attitudes—specifically attitudes of reverence for authority—prevailing among barbarian peoples. We do not have to look far to begin assembling further testimonia to this connection of archaic Greek and barbarian custom. Herodotus' comment about the resemblance of elaborate Spartan royal funerals to the royal funerals of barbarian Asia is a case in point. Thucydides, looking back from close to the time of Herodotus, also identifies several old-fashioned cultural habits that have survived from the time of Homer until his day, and he re-

---

103. The procession of a king to the Acropolis, where he enjoyed the intimacy of one or more women within the privacy of Athena's Parthenon, is attested at the end of the fourth century for Demetrius Poliorcetes, who was also honored as a god by the Athenians. See Plutarch *Demetrius* 10.3–13.2, 23.3, 24.1, 26.3; *Comparison of Demetrius and Antony* 4.2–3; Habicht 1970, 44–55.

104. Herodotus 1.60.3.

marks: "One could point to many other old-fashioned Hellenic habits that are similar to those still maintained by the barbarians."[105]

The tendency to be easily awed by pageantry and by symbols of sovereign power is one that classical writers readily associate with Lydians and Phrygians. In the *Birds*, for example, Aristophanes has Iris deliver an ultimatum to mortals from Zeus himself, with emphatic gestures to demonstrate the effects of fiery destruction by lightning bolts if it goes unheeded. Peisetaerus, the sophisticated Athenian, brushes off this warning with the words: "Do you think you're spooking some Lydian or Phrygian with talk like that?"[106] The same assumptions about barbarian nature are displayed by Euripides, in the *Orestes*, when he depicts at length the craven cowardice of a Phrygian who displays his obeisance to Orestes with the words: "I offer you reverence, my lord [*anax*], prostrating myself in barbarian manner!"[107] Such displays of reverential prostration (*proskynēsis*) were the customary gestures of obeisance to the Persian king, but Greeks had come to regard them as unbecoming for any free Greek, except in reverence to a god.[108] After Alexander's defeat of Darius III, when the propriety of such gestures became the subject of controversy among Alexander's courtiers, we find obeisance linked not only to the idea of divinity, but also to the idea of tyranny.[109]

Classical Greek thought associated the idea of a man as supreme sovereign with the distasteful memory of tyranny and with the unacceptable confusion of man and god. Such concepts and confusions were regarded as customary among the barbarians of Asia, particularly among Lydians and Phrygians, but alien to Greeks. In the scene from Euripides' play mentioned above, when the Phrygian falls at the feet of the Greek hero, Orestes replies: "This is not Ilium, but Argive land!"[110] The Phrygian's gesture is at home in

---

105. Thucydides 1.6.6. At 1.3.2–3, Thucydides describes the distinction between Hellenes and barbarians as a slow process that had not even been completed by the time of Homer. Cf. Herodotus 1.56–57 for indications that the inclusion of Athenians among Hellenes did not take place in the most distant past.

106. Aristophanes *Birds* 1243–45 (quoted in chapter 8, at note 58).

107. Euripides *Orestes* 1507, from the extended scene of the agitated Phrygian slave (1369–1526). Cf. the similar scene of supplication of a Phrygian depicted by Timotheus *Persians* 151–73 (Edmonds *LG*).

108. This is most explicitly stated in the speech of Xenophon in *Anabasis* 3.2.13, and at length in the speech of Callisthenes in Arrian *Anabasis* 4.11. Cf. Herodotus 7.136; Isocrates 4, *Panegyricus* 151. The meaning of *proskynēsis* performed before the Persian king is so thoroughly imbued with Greek ideology that it is difficult to assess, from Greek sources, its nature and significance in a Persian context; see T. Harrison 2000a, 87–89; and Briant 2002, 222–23.

109. Plutarch *Alexander* 55.1; Arrian *Anabasis* 4.10.3–4. Note that where Herodotus 1.60.5 says that the Athenians "offered prayers" (προσεύχοντο) in reverence to Phye as Athena, Aristotle *Athenian Constitution* 14.4 says "they performed gestures of obeisance" (προσκυνοῦντες).

110. Euripides *Orestes* 1508.

Asia, in other words, and does not belong in Hellas. This is why Herodotus felt the need to distance himself from the implications of the story of Phye and Peisistratus at Athens. It violated the strong conceptual boundaries that Greeks had erected between themselves and attitudes that they considered characteristic of the barbarians of Asia.

When was this boundary erected? When were Greeks less ashamed of participating in the ceremonies that they later claimed were unbecoming of free men? Between the time of Peisistratus and the time of Herodotus, the conflict with Persia marked a cultural horizon that was capable of defining major currents in Greek thought. As Kurt Raaflaub has shown, this was the experience that led to the identification of freedom as a fundamental quality of Hellenic identity.[111] This was also the experience, as Edith Hall has shown, that crystallized the distinction between Hellenes and barbarians in Greek thought.[112] Central to the present book is the identification of this same episode, the Greek conflict with Persia, as a watershed in Greek thought about the relationship between humanity and divinity.

But the confrontation between Greeks and Persians did not define the Greek experience of tyranny, nor did it focus attention on the issue of divine kingship. Other factors must have contributed to the consciousness that Hellenes did not revere the same symbols of power that the barbarians of Asia did. Although the details are scattered in clues that still need to be pieced together, the larger issues pertaining to the rejection of tyranny and the emergence of a distinctive Hellenic identity are set forth by Herodotus and Thucydides. Thucydides recognized that the Greeks did not yet distinguish themselves collectively from barbarians in Homer's day.[113] The circumstances that we seek, then, are to be found after the composition of the Homeric poems and before the great battles between Greeks and Persians of the early fifth century. If we rephrase the present question and ask what made the Greeks become ashamed of participating in the pageantry of tyranny, then we need to look for the most impressive failure of tyranny known to the Greeks. In his own terms, Herodotus has anticipated this line of inquiry and has arrived at the answer, which he sets forth in the first 94 chapters of his *Histories*. The unexpected fall of the greatest tyranny of its day, the rule of Croesus, was the event that encouraged the Greeks, collectively, to distance themselves from the veneration of sovereign monarchs, and to insist that the line between a man and a god should not be crossed.

111. Raaflaub 1985.

112. E. Hall 1989; see also Lévy 1984.

113. Thucydides 1.3.3, where Thucydides indicates his awareness that Homer "was born a long time after the Trojan War." Herodotus 2.53 similarly identifies Homer (and Hesiod) as defining the beginnings of a distinctively Hellenic self-awareness, in terms of their own pantheon, and places this awareness "not more than four hundred years ago."

Before the foundation of the Persian empire and the arrival of Cyrus at Sardis, the Mermnad dynasty of Lydia and the Phrygian kingdom of Midas gave the Greeks their most intimate experience of the power of a true sovereign monarch. Starting with Midas, these kings of Asia were the first barbarians to make dedications to Apollo at Delphi, Herodotus tells us.[114] Tyrtaeus, in the middle of the seventh century, names Midas as a paragon of wealth in the same sentence in which he names Tantalid Pelops as a paragon of kingliness.[115] As we have already observed, Tantalus, legendary king of Lydia or Phrygia, was closer to the gods than any man ever was, or ever should be, in Greek memory. At about the same time that Tyrtaeus was comparing the qualities of Asiatic kings and princes to the virtues of Spartan warriors, Archilochus was memorializing the splendor of Gyges, forebear of Croesus and founder of the Mermnad dynasty. In the verses that later Greek sources cite as the earliest use of the word "tyranny," Archilochus has a carpenter avert his eyes from such magnificence: "I am not interested in the wealth of golden Gyges, nor have I ever envied him, nor am I jealous of the doings of gods, nor do I desire great tyranny, for such things are far from my eyes."[116] Great wealth, great tyranny, and the doings of gods are listed as qualities that distinguish Gyges, the king of Lydia, from ordinary men. The disdain that Archilochus expresses for the power, splendor, and pretense of Lydian royalty made his verses especially memorable to Greeks centuries later, when the kingdom of Gyges was gone. But Archilochus' disdain did not define the prevailing view among his contemporaries. As Victor Parker has observed: "The point of these four lines is quite clearly that Archilochus expects that others will desire Gyges' wealth very much, will be duly impressed by great deeds, and will most certainly desire power such as that of the Lydian king."[117]

Before the middle of the sixth century, Phrygia and Lydia together were the immediate source of all that was magnificent and impressive to the Greeks. The most essential among many tokens of material prosperity, coinage, was an invention of the Lydians, or, some said, of the wife of Midas.[118] The most emotionally powerful music of ecstasy and of lamentation was taught to the

---

114. Herodotus 1.14.

115. Tyrtaeus 12.6 (Edmonds *EI*), cited above at note 32. The reputation of Midas is discussed further in chapter 2 at note 47.

116. Archilochus fr. 19 (West = [fr. 25 Edmonds *EI*]; quoted by Aristotle *Rhetoric* 3.17.16, where the character of Charon, a τέκτων, is named as the speaker). On the occurrence of τυραννίς in this passage, see above, note 10. For further discussion of the "doings of gods" (θεῶν ἔργα), see chapter 3 at notes 71–74.

117. V. Parker 1998, 151.

118. Xenophanes (DK 21 B 4) and Herodotus 1.94.1 attribute the invention of coinage to the Lydians; Pollux *Onomasticon* 9.83 adds Pheidon of Argos, Demodice of Cyme (the wife of Midas), and Erichthonius of Athens to the list of reputed inventors of coinage.

Greeks by Phrygians and Lydians.[119] The most impressive spectacles of massed military might were provided by the Phrygians and the Lydians.[120] The Cypselids of Corinth were ready custodians, and perhaps also the bearers, of Phrygian and Lydian dedications at Delphi.[121] The Spartans welcomed the poet Alcman as a man of Sparta and of Sardis, and were pleased to exchange gifts and pledges of friendship with Croesus.[122] A wealthy Athenian family named a son Croesus, and a wealthy Sicilian family named a son Midas.[123]

Only after the sudden collapse of the Mermnad dynasty in 547, when Cyrus overthrew Croesus and when the greatest monarch known to the Greeks was shown to be fallible, could the Greeks begin to describe the symbols and ceremonies of tyranny as fatuous. The foolish simplicity that Greeks now ascribed to Lydians and Phrygians lay not in the reverence of sovereignty, but in the idea that any living man could be its perfect embodiment. Phrygians and Lydians, as we will see, had revered their kings for their intimacies with gods, and had celebrated kingship as the highest medium of communion with the gods. The rites of kingship remained at the center of Lydian and Phrygian ritual forms, even after their own living kings were no more. They remained, after all, under the dominion of the Persian King of Kings. The Greeks were more used to envisioning perfect sovereignty from a distance, and were better able to separate their beliefs and their ritual forms from the persons of living rulers, and to attach them to the unseen Olympian immortals. In time, as the Greeks became more resentful and more fearful of the power of Persian kings, they also became more derisive of those who lived in Asia and who respected the sovereignty of its monarchs. The collapse of the Lydian tyranny, therefore, marked the decisive parting of the ways between those who called themselves Hellenes and those whom they called barbarians. With the fall of Croesus, the Greeks began to come of age.

## THE QUEST FOR TRANSCENDENT DIVINITY

Contemporaneously with the revolution in world sovereignty represented by the fall of the Mermnad dynasty, skepticism begins to color religious at-

119. See Thiemer 1979, and the authorities cited in chapter 4 note 125.

120. In *Iliad* 3.182–90, Priam describes the mass of Phrygian warriors as second only to the mass of Achaeans led by Agamemnon. Sappho 38.17–20 (Edmonds *LG*) describes "all the chariots and armored footsoldiers of the Lydians" as second only to the sight of her own beloved.

121. See Herodotus 1.14, 3.49.

122. On Alcman as both a Sardian and a Spartan, see *Palatine Anthology* 7.18 and 709 (cited in Edmonds *LG*, vol. 1, 44–46; see the comments of Page 1962, 29; and Lesky 1966, 149). On Spartan relations with Croesus, see Herodotus 1.69–70.

123. The statue of the Athenian Croesus, the Anavysos Kouros, with its inscribed base, is in the National Museum of Athens (no. 3851): see Boardman 1978, figure 107. Midas of Acragas was a victorious aulete for whom Pindar's *Pythian* 12 was composed.

titudes among the Greeks. Evidence of this skepticism is immediately at hand in the theological philosophies propounded by the Ionians Pherecydes, Pythagoras, and Xenophanes, all of whom lived in the generation that witnessed the fall of Sardis. Founded on a tradition of speculative thought that is more commonly referred to as the beginning of Ionian science, their writings represent a radical challenge to established religious traditions. The theological concepts of these Ionians were aimed precisely at the manner in which the link between humanity and divinity should be conceived.[124] Their challenge did not displace customary practices, however. We have already encountered enough examples of reverence for the heroism of victorious athletes, the divinity of Spartan kings, and the mystic powers of Sicilian tyrants to recognize that many customary expressions of the relationship between gods and men current in the seventh and early sixth century still had a long life ahead of them. But these Ionian theorists mark the beginning of the critical tradition within which Herodotus, among others, could later observe a pronounced difference in outlook between Greeks and barbarians.

The beginnings of the literary tradition of speculative thought among Ionian Greeks about the nature of divinity and its relationship to the tribes of humanity can be traced to the heyday of Lydian tyranny. The Lydian context is significant, because the ideas of the origin and nature of the physical world as understood by Thales and Anaximander were related to the ideological justification for Lydian kingship. (See chapter 5.) With the fall of Croesus, the king who had been the living embodiment of all such ideology was gone; no Persian king would fill this ideological role, for the Persian kingship did not directly participate in the same symbolic system as the Lydian. One consequence, within the former Lydian dominion of Asia now held by the Persians, was to abstract the sacramental role that kings had once played, and to invest this ideological system completely in the divinities with whom the king had formerly interacted. Evidence for this development will be found in the cult of the goddess Kybebe at Sardis as it was maintained under Persian suzerainty. (See chapter 6.) From the Greek perspective, however, and particularly from the perspective of those Greeks who did not live under Persian rule, the premises that had once provided a unified understanding of the world, of the world ruler, and of the gods, were completely overthrown. Now it was possible, and even necessary, for speculative thought to define the unity of humanity and divinity at a higher level, without the intermediation of living kings.

The first such theology to be based on a more abstract notion of sover-

124. The growth of influence of Orphic rites, discernible in roughly the same period, is testimony to the same interest in discovering ritualized access to underlying truths; see M. L. West 1971, 229–33; R. Parker 1995. Numerous connections have been observed between Orphic teachings and those of Pythagoras in particular (as observed already by Herodotus 2.81).

eignty was that expounded by Pherecydes of Syros.[125] Pherecydes is said to have been born in the reign of King Alyattes of Lydia (ca. 610–560), and his writings were probably produced after the midpoint of the reign of Darius (522–486).[126] Anecdotes of unknown reliability place Pherecydes on the island of Samos, in the Peloponnese, and at Ephesus in Asia Minor, where he is said to have been buried; another tradition claims that he was buried on Delos.[127] According to a more remarkable tradition, reported by Plutarch, Pherecydes was put to death by the Spartans, and his skin was preserved by their kings. However bizarre the story seems, it was told as a mark of highest respect on the part of the Spartans for the wisdom that Pherecydes embodied.[128] Influences on his writing are said to include "secret books of the Phoenicians" and "the prophecy of Ham," which, whatever they may refer to, should at least be taken as an indication that the cosmopolitan scope of Pherecydes' theological thought was recognized in antiquity.[129] Aside from his writing, Pherecydes is known for having made a sundial on the island of Syros.[130]

125. I am persuaded by the arguments of David Toye 1997, who identifies Pherecydes of Syros, the cosmographer, and Pherecydes of Athens, the genealogist, as one and the same person. Felix Jacoby (1947) argued for the separation of the two, supporting the segregation of the cosmographical fragments of Pherecydes by Diels and Kranz (DK 7; cf. Kirk et al. 1983, 50–71; M. L. West 1971, 1–75; Schibli 1990), and grouping the genealogical fragments as the work of a mythographer in *FGrHist* 3. (Cf. R. Thomas 1989, 161–73.)

126. *Suda* s.v. Φερεκύδης Βάβυος Σύριος (DK 7 A 2) reports his birth during the reign of Alyattes. His father's name, Babys, links his ancestry with western Asia Minor, perhaps Phrygia: see M. L. West 1971, 3; Schibli 1990, 1 n. 2. On the dating of his writing, see Toye 1997.

127. See Diogenes 1.116–21, Diodorus 10.4.3, and *Suda* s.v. Φερεκύδης Βάβυος Σύριος (these and other sources cited in DK 7 A 1–7), where Pherecydes is said to have been a teacher of Pythagoras. M. L. West 1971, 1–4, and Schibli 1990, 5–13, review of the traditions on the life of Pherecydes with circumspection.

128. Plutarch *Pelopidas* 21.2 tells the story of Pherecydes slain and skinned by the Spartans, and attributes this account to seers in the army of the Thebans at Leuctra deliberating on precedents for human sacrifice. Elsewhere, Plutarch *Agis and Cleomenes* 10.3 names Pherecydes along with Terpander and Thales as foreigners who had been held in high esteem and honored by the Spartans. Svenbro 1993 treats the very similar story related by Diogenes 1.115, of the body of the seer Epimenides preserved at Sparta, as an example of the Spartan fixation on appropriating the literal embodiment of laws, oracles, or wisdom. M. L. West 1971, 4, regards Plutarch's account of the skin of as "patently unhistorical." I see no reason to be so dismissive. The story of Pherecydes' skin, and probably also Epimenides' body, belongs close to the time when, in 508, King Cleomenes of Sparta removed from the Acropolis at Athens oracles collected by the Peisistratids (Herodotus 5.90), and when, sometime before the battle of Plataea in 479, the Spartans appropriated the endowment of victories vouched to Teisamenus of Elis by the Delphic Oracle (Herodotus 9.33, noticed above at note 57).

129. *Suda* s.v. Φερεκύδης Βάβυος Σύριος (DK 7 A 2); cf. Philo of Byblos *FGrHist* 790 F 4.50 (DK 7 B 4); Clement *Stromateis* 6.9 (DK 7 B 2). For discussion of these reported sources, see Kirk et al. 1983, 53–54, 65–66 n. 2; Edwards 1993, 67–68. M. L. West 1971, 28–68, suggests that Pherecydes' theology reflects Iranian and Indic along with Semitic influences.

130. Testimony to Pherecydes' sundial is given by Diogenes 1.119; Kirk et al. 1983, 54–56, relate this passage to *Odyssey* 15.403–4, with scholia, where the island of Syrië is said to mark

Theopompus named Pherecydes as "the first to write on nature and the gods," thus associating his work simultaneously with those many early philosophers who wrote works entitled *On Nature*, and with those later prose authors who wrote genealogies linking men with the gods.[131] The opening of Pherecydes' book is quoted for us by Diogenes, and it reveals the essential premise by which Pherecydes cut the conceptual ties with Hesiod and with living embodiments of divine sovereignty: "Zas and Chronus always existed, and Chthonië; and Chthonië got the name Ge [Earth] because Zas gave her earth as her prerogative."[132] Zas, or Zeus, was not a created being, and had no battles to win, according to Pherecydes, because he was one of three essential and eternal principles: Zas (the divine sovereign), Chronus (Time), and Chthonië (the fundament of Earth). The relationship between Chthonië and Ge is clarified in another fragment, where Pherecydes describes the marriage of Zas and Chthonië, and the gift of a decorated robe (*pharos*) that Zas presents to Chthonië. The robe, which becomes the bridal veil of Chthonië, is "decorated with Ge and Ogenos [Earth and Ocean]," and this endowment of Chthonië by Zas not only becomes the creation of Earth and Ocean, but also gives occasion for "the first unveiling [*anakalyptēria*] of the bride; and from this the custom was established for gods and for men."[133]

Pherecydes has deftly presented divine entities with names that are familiar yet different from those in Hesiod, participating in significantly different primal acts. At the center of creation is an archetypal Sacred Marriage, but one that establishes radically different relationships between the divine couple, Zas/Zeus and Chthonië/Ge, Sovereign and Earth, on the one hand, and all other gods and humanity. The generation of gods and men is not described in any surviving fragment, but it may in some sense be the fruit of this sin-

---

"the turnings of the sun." The significance of sundials and solar markers, in which Thales and Anaximander were also interested, is discussed below in chapter 5.

131. Diogenes 1.116, citing Theopompus (*FGrHist* 115 F 71), whose report is closely echoed by Josephus *Against Apion* 1.2. The unusual scope of Pherecydes' work has certainly contributed to the controversy, ancient as well as modern, over whether the fragments attributed to Pherecydes were the work of one or two individuals of that name.

132. Diogenes 1.119 (Pherecydes DK 7 B 1). See Kirk et al. 1983, 57, and M. L. West 1971, 50–53, for discussion of the distinctive nomenclature used by Pherecydes, and its possible etymological basis.

133. Pherecydes DK 7 B 2, col 1. This passage encourages the speculation that the *anakalyptēria*, the ceremonial unveiling, was the definitive act in every ritual Sacred Marriage. On this passage in its entirety, and the *pharos* (which has been likened to the Panathenaic peplos presented to Athena), see Kirk et al. 1983, 60–66; M. L. West 1971, 15–20, 52–55, who seeks Near Eastern parallels; also Edwards 1993, 65–72, who examines numerous points of contact between myths of Cybele and Pherecydes' theogony. Schibli 1990, 50–77, draws limited conclusions (chiefly that the marriage ritual is the divine prototype for human marriage ceremonies; so also Oakley and Sinos 1993, 25–26) from an extended discussion.

gle, archetypal union of Zas and Chthonië.[134] Battles of gods and monsters take place in Pherecydes' scheme, but these belong to the history of those generated after Zas and Chthonië. Thus strife, victory and defeat, and the procreation of diverse lineages all take place in Pherecydes' theogony, but Zas and Chthonië appear to remain above and uninvolved in these events. The eternal and timeless existence of Zas and Chthonië suggests that they are eternally monogamous, and not promiscuous with lesser divinities or with humankind. It appears that in Pherecydes' cosmos, all mortals stand in the same relationship to the divine sovereign and the earth. No mortal champion, king, or tyrant could ever claim a privileged link to divine sovereignty in this theological system.

Pythagoras of Samos is said in some sources to have been a student of Pherecydes, although the reliability of this tradition is unknown.[135] Pythagoras' teachings are generally connected with his residency at Croton and Metapontium in southern Italy, where he ended his life. The influences that shaped his thought, however, must have originated from his earlier years on Samos and abroad, for which Herodotus offers testimony.[136] Other sources report that Pythagoras was on Samos during the tyranny of Polycrates (ca. 535–522), that he traveled widely, particularly to Egypt (which Herodotus also supports), and that he handled correspondence between Polycrates and Amasis, king of Egypt (a correspondence that Herodotus attests, without mentioning Pythagoras).[137] All sources affirm that Pythagoras sought knowledge from rites of initiation wherever he might encounter them.

Out of his experience, Pythagoras distilled a profoundly unitarian philosophy based on number, and specifically on the potential of unity itself, oneness, to generate all relationships subject to quantity or measure of any sort. All is abstracted into number and numeric ratios, in the Pythagorean system, and ratios define all sensible features, such as music, and heavenly bodies, and significant relationships, such as justice and marriage. This system included the gods honored in conventional piety, but only as manifestations themselves of the higher, universal order of number. Mortals are an-

---

134. Chronus, coeval of Zas and Chthonië, plays a role in creating "fire, wind, and water," and "numerous other offspring of gods" (πολλὴν ἄλλην γενεάν... θεῶν) out of his own semen, "in five hollows" (ἐν πέντε μυχοῖς: in Earth?), according to DK 7 A 8, discussed by Kirk et al. 1983, 56–60; M. L. West 1971, 12–15, 36–40; and Schibli 1990, 14–49. But the nature and consequences of this generative act are far from clear.

135. Diogenes 1.119, 8.2; see also note 127 above.

136. Herodotus 4.95–96 describes the distinctive belief in immortality among the Thracians, and its connection with Salmoxis, whom some identify as a slave of Pythagoras on Samos.

137. See the sources collected in DK 14, and in particular Diogenes 8.2–3, and Porphyry, citing the fourth-century Aristoxenus (DK 14.8), cited by Kirk et al. 1983, 222–24. On Pythagoras and Egypt, see also Herodotus 2.81 (cf. 2.123.2); Isocrates 11, *Busiris* 28–29. On the correspondence of Amasis and Polycrates, see Herodotus 3.39–43; cf. Diogenes 8.3.

imated by immortal souls and thereby participate, through the cycles of life, death, and rebirth again, in the universal order of unity and proportion in which the gods also participate; but no god, in this system, has achieved supremacy by birth, strife, or violence, and no human stands, by birth, in a uniquely privileged relationship to the gods.

The object of Pythagorean understanding was to conduct one's life according to the principles of this higher order so as to purify one's soul, rendering it closer to the essence of the universal, sovereign unity. In practical terms, this meant avoidance of features and practices deemed to partake of lesser or impure customs, such as animal sacrifice. The ideal sacramental community engendered by Pythagoras therefore became constrained by practices that tended to divide it sharply from those participating in traditional rites. Devoted to political organization according to these principles, in the short term the strictures of diet, dress, and behavior generated a hostile reaction that proved fatal to the new order in Croton. But the ideas shared by Pythagoras and his followers, even when not put into rigorous practice, provided an abiding foundation for skepticism about the basis of conventional notions of piety.[138]

Even more radically than Pherecydes, then, Pythagoras rejected the structure of relationships between divinity and humanity that had been represented in the pantheon of Hesiod and Homer. His motives for doing so, however, we can deduce only from the time in which he lived and the circumstances of his travels. By the present line of argument, we may suggest that Pythagoras was working to fill an ideological void created after an older order of sovereignty had collapsed, and no new order, neither the Persian kingship that Darius was struggling to define, nor the likes of the lesser tyrannies of Peisistratus or Polycrates, had succeeded in replacing.

The evidence for such an explanation is somewhat better in the case of another contemporary, Xenophanes of Colophon. We know that Xenophanes despised the transformation of his own native Colophon by the habits of Lydian luxury, and that later in life, like Pythagoras, he moved to Italy and Sicily.[139] We also learn that he considered a fireside conversation over food and drink with a new acquaintance to begin most appropriately with the questions: "Who are you, sir, and where in the world of men do you come from? What is your age? And, pray, how old were you when the Mede arrived?"[140]

138. R. K. Hack 1931, 47–58, provides a concise account of Pythagorean cosmology and piety; see also Kirk et al. 1983, 214–38. Burkert 1985, 296–304, traces the close relationship of Pythagorean and Orphic mysticism; Detienne 1977, 40–59, 121–31, observes the symbolic relationships in Pythagorean dietary and sacrificial practices.

139. Testimonia for Xenophanes' biography and philosophy are collected in DK 21: see esp. B 3, 8; see also Hack 1931, 59–68; Kirk et al. 1983, 163–80.

140. Xenophanes DK 21 B 22. See also DK 21 B 3; Diogenes 9.18 (DK 21 A 1).

"The Mede" was Harpagus, the Median general of Cyrus who finally subdued Ionia in 545, decisively settling the unrest that came after the fall of Sardis over a year earlier.[141] His campaign was clearly the seminal moment of Xenophanes' life and times, and Xenophanes expected that the event would likewise shape the outlook of every thoughtful man.

In the words of Xenophanes we find the first explicit criticism of Homeric and Hesiodic notions of divinity, and the first explicit rejection of the physical, emotional, violent, and procreative acts that had traditionally bound divinity to humankind:[142]

> Homer and Hesiod attributed to the gods everything that is disgraceful and objectionable among men, thievery, adultery, and deceiving each other.

The basis of this criticism is the anthropomorphic conception of divinity, which, as we have observed, was the very foundation of the rites of communion between gods and men that were widely established in civic cults:[143]

> Mortals consider that the gods are born, and that they have clothes and speech and bodies like their own. . . . But if cattle and horses or lions had hands, or were able to draw with their hands and do the works that men can do, horses would draw the forms of the gods like horses, and cattle like cattle, and they would make their bodies such as they each had themselves.

By implication, the common conceptions of divinity are truly ridiculous, and must therefore be wrong. There is, according to Xenophanes:[144]

> One god, greatest among gods and men, similar to mortals neither in body nor in thought. . . . He is all sight, all thought, all hearing. . . . He always remains in the same place, moving not at all. . . . But with no effort at all he incites all things by thought of mind.

Such a transcendent divinity may be honored by libations, lustrations, incense, garlanded altars, offerings of bread, cheese, and honey, and by hymns and prayers, Xenophanes says, but such rites should avoid inauspicious speech, and should make no mention of[145]

> battles of Titans, Giants, and Centaurs—the fictions created by previous generations—or of violent factions, in which there is nothing honorable. One should always adhere to what is good, mindful of the gods.

---

141. On the Persian conquest of Ionia, see Herodotus 1.141–69.

142. Xenophanes DK 21 B 11.

143. Xenophanes DK 21 B 14–15, translated by Kirk et al. 1983, 169.

144. Xenophanes DK 21 B 23–26. See Versnel 2000, 91–112, for an appraisal of the tendency toward monotheism evident in Xenophanes' thought, and a review of scholarship on this subject.

145. Xenophanes DK 21 B 1.

By his standards of propriety and ritual purity, and above all by his efforts to define the transcendence of all being, Xenophanes had much in common with his contemporary and fellow Ionian and wanderer Pythagoras.[146] Both spoke as men of the world, more concerned with its overall coherence and the rightful place of humanity in it than they were with the privileges of a native city. They had broken that tie with the past, and were not bound by parochial loyalties to celebrate mythic deeds of violence, blood sacrifice, or divine procreation that traditionally endowed this or that community with a sense of exalted purpose. Nor were they bound to celebrate ritualized violence, the feats of strength by which athletes inspired their fellow citizens to believe that Zeus was among them. Xenophanes is famous as the first who leveled a well-aimed critique at this custom:[147]

> Now, supposing a man were to win the prize for the foot race at Olympia, there where the precinct of Zeus stands beside the river, at Pisa: or if he wins the five-contests, or the wrestling, or if he endures the pain of boxing and wins, or that new and terrible game they call the pankration, contest of all holds: why, such a man will obtain honor, in the citizens' sight, and be given a front seat and be on display at all civic occasions, and he would be given his meals all at the public expense, and be given a gift from the city to take and store for safekeeping. If he won with the chariot, too, all this would be granted to him, and yet he would not deserve it, as I do.
>
> Better than brute strength of men, or horses either, is the wisdom that is mine. But custom is careless in these matters, and there is no justice in putting strength on a level above wisdom which is sound. For if among the people there is one who is a good boxer, or one who excels in wrestling or in the five-contests, or else for speed of his feet, and this is prized beyond other feats of strength that men display in athletic games, the city will not, on account of this man, have better government. Small is the pleasure the city derives from one of its men if he happens to come in first in the games by the banks of Pisa. This does not make rich the treasure house of the state.

Cogent though this argument is, it flew in the face not only of Greek custom generally, but of the deep and emotional bond between patriotism and the unquestionable merit of victory that had been given a grounding in cult, ritual, theogonic myth, and civic identity over more than two centuries before Xenophanes. Thinking men, men with a wider vision of the world, might be convinced by this argument to temper their enthusiasm for the victorious athlete, but it could never have shaped popular ideology. The ideas of

146. Pythagoras and Xenophanes also differed in their views, as Diogenes 9.18 reports, and as comparisons of their cosmologies and theologies bear out. See Hack 1931, 47–68; Kirk et al. 1983, 216–38 (on Pythagoras); Burkert 1985, 296–311 (on Pythagoras and early Presocratics generally).

147. Xenophanes DK 21 B 2 (from Athenaeus 10.413f–414c), translated by Bernard Knox.

Xenophanes, like those of Pythagoras and Pherecydes, flowed largely outside of the mainstream of Greek civic history.

Nevertheless, the impact on later Greek philosophy of this generation of Ionian thought is a marker of the extraordinary in historical experience. Diverse as their ideas were, their visions were linked at their inception by revolutionary events that had transformed both civic identities and the nature of world sovereignty in their day. By the late sixth century, the sovereign lord of Asia was the Persian King of Kings, and he did not represent Greek ideals. This was new. In earlier generations, poetic expression had often allowed Greek identity to blend imperceptibly into Asiatic. No language barrier separated Homer's Achaeans from his Trojans. Hesiod's theogonic poetry bears the imprint of Asiatic mythology. Before "the Mede arrived," Alcman was at home at Sardis as much as at Sparta. Eros, for Sappho, drew all eyes toward Sardis, and all the great sophists of Greece, Herodotus tells us, paid court to its kings. But with the fall of Lydia to Persian rule, the separation of Greek from barbarian that Herodotus and Thucydides later spoke of was under way. By the end of the sixth century, there was as yet no strong center to Greek identity that could replace the dominating pull formerly exerted by the tyranny of Asia. In a new world of political pluralism among the Greeks, the writings of Pherecydes, Pythagoras, and Xenophanes reflect a new diversity in metaphysical ideology. Their quest for the universal nature of divinity, and scorn for the parochial, would gather adherents especially where their teachings found a community that was more ambitious than most, that possessed the resources to transform the balance of sovereign power in the world, and that was seeking to enlarge its ideological capital in the process of doing so, not merely to conserve it. Such a city was Athens in the fifth century, not Sparta.

Later chapters in this book examine the Athenian encounter with the transformative events of the sixth and fifth centuries, and consider how Athenians, bound by patriotism and emotion to their traditional and parochial symbols of divinity and sovereign independence, nevertheless struggled by public consensus to enlarge their ideological capital to suit an expanding vision of their place in the world. While philosophers grappled with questions about the transcendent nature of the world in increasingly abstract terms, the public constructed its understanding in terms of heroes and deities. By the end of the fifth century, as we will see, the Athenian public had embraced a universalizing deity, the Mother of the Gods, who seemed both familiar and eternal, and therefore a secure custodian of Athenian sovereignty. But gods have their myths, their personal histories, and the Mother of the Gods was widely acknowledged to be a deity whose earliest home was in Phrygia or Lydia. Like tyranny among the Greeks, she was a vestige of an archaic past when Greek identity was not sharply differentiated from the Asiatic. And like the concept of absolute sovereignty embodied in Asiatic tyranny, the Mother of the Gods was an idea that the Greeks, especially the Athenians, had had to dissociate themselves from before they could approach it in their own terms. In the next chapter, we begin tracing the evidence for the history of the Mother of the Gods among the Greeks of the classical era.

# Chapter 2

# The Mother of the Gods
# and the Sovereignty of Midas

Wherever we find the Mother of the Gods honored among the Greeks, she was a divinity whose powers over this world were manifest in many ways. To her devotees, her motherhood was her capacity as a nurturer, particularly of all animate creatures, animal and human. In this respect, the Mother of the Gods could be regarded as another name for Earth, Ge or Gaea, who was often invoked as Mother, Mother of All, and even Mother of the Gods.[1] Motherhood, as a description of her place in the pantheon of gods, was a quality by which she was most closely associated with Zeus, whose mother she was often said to be. In this respect, the Mother of the Gods was the same as Rhea in Homer and Hesiod.[2] In another sense, her motherhood was a quality pertaining to her role as a wife of Zeus, and in this respect we find her sometimes identified with Demeter, who is also sometimes called simply Mother.[3]

Such universal valences render the Mother of the Gods close to the uni-

---

1. All of these titles are used in *Homeric Hymn* 30, *To Earth, Mother of All;* cf. Hesiod *Works and Days* 563 and *Theogony* 117. Note that Sophocles *Philoctetes* 391–92 addresses Earth, ὀρεστέρα παμβῶτι Γᾶ, μᾶτερ αὐτοῦ Διός, "All-nourishing mountainous Earth, Mother of Zeus himself," in a Lydian context.

2. In Euripides *Bacchae*, the Mother of the Gods, called Μάτηρ μεγάλη Κυβέλα in lines 78–79, is identified as Rhea (Ῥέα Μάτηρ, lines 59 and 128), and is honored by Lydian and Phrygian rites (lines 55–165); see also Sophocles *Philoctetes* 391–92, cited above, note 1. Apollonius *Argonautica* 1.1125–51, identifies Μήτηρ Δινδυμίη πολυπότνια, "Dindymian Mother, Great Mistress," Μήτηρ Ἰδαίη, "Idaean Mother" (Dindymon and Ida being mountains), as Ῥείη πολυπότνια, "Great Mistress Rhea," who is also said to be the object of Phrygian worship.

3. Euripides *Helen* 1301–68, in a context that describes Demeter's search for Persephone, identifies ὀρεία μήτηρ θεῶν, "Mountain Mother of the Gods," as Δηώ, an epithet of Demeter. (Cf. *Homeric Hymn* 2, *To Demeter* 47, 211, 492.) Cf. Euripides *Phoenician Women* 683–87, and *Bacchae* 275–76: Δημήτηρ θεά, γῆ δ' ἐστίν, ὄνομα δ' ὁπότερον βούλει κάλει, "Divine Demeter, who is Earth,

tarian concepts of divinity articulated by Pherecydes, Xenophanes, and even Pythagoras. Chthonië, wife of Zas in Pherecydes' theogony, wears the mantle of Ge, or Earth; it would not be surprising if we were to find testimony to the effect that Chthonië was also called the Mother of the Gods.[4] Xenophanes is quoted as saying that "all things come from Earth, and into Earth all things are resolved."[5] More strikingly, the fifth-century Pythagorean Philolaus of Croton located the principle of universal governance ($\tau\grave{o}\ \dot{\eta}\gamma\epsilon\mu o\nu\iota\kappa\acute{o}\nu$) in "the fire around the center of the universe," which he refers to as the Universal Hearth, also calling it the House of Zeus and the Mother of the Gods.[6]

If we ask where among Greeks in classical antiquity did the Mother of the Gods receive cult honors befitting her cosmocentric status, the answer is: at Athens, in the Council House of the Athenians, just before the end of the fifth century B.C.E. (the very years in which Philolaus was active). For in that setting, as we will see, the image of the Mother of the Gods was enthroned at the very heart of the deliberative institution that guided the sovereignty of the Athenian people. The chamber in which her statue was erected was also the repository for the official texts of all laws, and all important public documents of Athens. As of the end of the fifth century, therefore, the state archives of Athens became known as the Metroön (Shrine of the Mother), after the Mother of the Gods.

When we ask how and under what circumstances was she enshrined there, the answer is not immediately obvious. Although Athens, by the middle of the fifth century, was becoming the center of progressive, speculative thought in the Greek world, and the Athenians were becoming famous for having more festivals and honoring more gods than any other Greek city, the Athenians were also quite jealous of the privileges of worship attached to their ancestral gods. There is no clear pedigree for the cult of the Mother of the Gods at Athens; no ancestral priesthood served it. It would be difficult to maintain that Pythagorean speculation could be so influential as to win a place for the Mother of the Gods in the heart of the city. In fact, this was the very era in which the Athenians were most notoriously suspicious of

---

call her whatever name you wish." See also the Hellenistic hymn to $M\acute{\eta}\tau\eta\rho\ \theta\epsilon\hat{\omega}\nu$ from Epidaurus, *IG* IV² 131; M. L. West 1970, 212–15.

4. Pherecydes' Chthonië ($X\theta o\nu\acute{\iota}\eta$) calls to mind the epithet $\chi\theta\acute{o}\nu\iota\alpha\iota\ \theta\epsilon\alpha\acute{\iota}$ used by Herodotus 6.134 and 7.153, to refer to Demeter and Persephone. Edwards 1993 traces nomenclature to the numerous parallels between Pherecydes' theology and the myths of Kybele, or the Mother of the Gods.

5. Xenophanes DK 21 B 27. On the concept of divinity expressed in the fragments of Xenophanes, see Hack 1931, 59–68; Kirk et al. 1983, 168–72; Versnel 2000, 91–112.

6. Philolaus DK 44 A 16: $\Phi\iota\lambda\acute{o}\lambda\alpha o\varsigma\ \pi\hat{\upsilon}\rho\ \dot{\epsilon}\nu\ \mu\acute{\epsilon}\sigma\omega\ \pi\epsilon\rho\grave{\iota}\ \tau\grave{o}\ \kappa\acute{\epsilon}\nu\tau\rho o\nu\ \ddot{o}\pi\epsilon\rho\ \dot{\epsilon}\sigma\tau\acute{\iota}\alpha\nu\ \tau o\hat{\upsilon}\ \pi\alpha\nu\tau\grave{o}\varsigma\ \kappa\alpha\lambda\epsilon\hat{\iota}\ \kappa\alpha\grave{\iota}\ \Delta\iota\grave{o}\varsigma\ o\hat{\iota}\kappa o\nu\ \kappa\alpha\grave{\iota}\ \mu\eta\tau\acute{\epsilon}\rho\alpha\ \theta\epsilon\hat{\omega}\nu$. See also DK 44 A 17, B 7, and the commentaries of Aristotle and Simplicius on Pythagorean cosmography, DK 58 B 37. For discussion of these passages, see Hack 1931, 49–52; Kirk et al. 1983, 342–45, and 322–24 on Philolaus' life.

philosophical speculation, especially where it involved the gods. It is, therefore, truly "a great puzzle," as Robert Parker has said, to find the Mother of
the Gods occupying so honored a place in the archive chamber of the Athenian council.[7]

In this chapter we will consider the evidence testifying to the arrival of
the Mother of the Gods at Athens, and to her establishment in the building
in the agora that became known after her as the Metroön. From the evidence
reviewed in the previous chapter, it should be clear that "arrival" in this context does not mean the earliest awareness of the deity on the part of the Athenians, but rather, their formal acknowledgment of her, and formal installation of her in public cult. The narratives that describe the installation of the
Mother at Athens indicate that the acceptance of this specifically foreign god
took place within the fifth century B.C.E. We now turn to those narratives,
and we will proceed from them to investigate the foreign, and specifically
Phrygian, associations of her cult.

### THE MOTHER OF THE GODS AND "THE PHRYGIAN MAN" AT ATHENS

Among tales of gods who go unrecognized or are rejected, who reveal their
power and finally win acceptance, the tale of the Mother of the Gods is surely
one of the most remarkable. Unlike Dionysus or Demeter, whose arrivals were
placed by classical sources in the legendary past, the most famous tale of the
Mother's arrival is set historically, in Athens of the fifth century. The story
of the annunciation, rejection, and ultimate acceptance of the Mother of
the Gods at Athens has been preserved in a variety of late sources, the most
distinguished of which is an essay by the last polytheist emperor, Julian.

In opening his fifth oration, *To the Mother of the Gods*, Julian asks: "Ought
I to say something on this subject also? . . . And shall I write about things not
to be spoken of and divulge what ought not to be divulged? . . . Who is the
Mother of the Gods?" Julian's deference to mystic custom here bears comparison to the discretion that reserved the secrets of the Eleusinian Mysteries to initiates, a secrecy not otherwise associated with the Mother of the
Gods.[8] Julian continues with his account of the cult of the Mother:[9]

> The rites of the Mother . . . were handed down by the Phrygians in very an-
> cient times, and were first taken over by the Greeks, and not by any ordinary
> Greeks, but by the Athenians who learned by experience that they did wrong
> to jeer at one who was celebrating the mysteries of the Mother. For it is said

7. R. Parker 1996, 188. For assessments of the attitudes toward speculative thought and the
gods in late fifth-century Athens, see Dover 1976, Yunis 1988, and Wallace 1994.

8. Myths of the Mother are openly expounded in Lucretius' *De Rerum Natura* 2.581–645,
and in the synopsis of Neoplatonic piety by Sallustius, *On the Gods and the Universe* 4.

9. Julian *Orationes* 5.159a–b, translated by W. C. Wright.

that they wantonly insulted and drove out the Gallus, on the ground that he was introducing a new cult, because they did not understand what sort of goddess they had to do with, and that she was the very Deo whom they worship, and Rhea and Demeter too. Then followed the wrath of the goddess and the propitiation of her wrath. For the priestess of the Pythian god who guided the Greeks in all noble conduct, bade them propitiate the wrath of the Mother of the gods. And so, we are told, the Metroön was built, where the Athenians used to keep all their state records.

As Julian reports, the arrival of the Mother of the Gods at Athens was precipitated by the rejection of the man whom he calls "the Gallus." *Gallus* was the title by which, as of the third century B.C.E., the Phrygian eunuch priests of the Mother of the Gods were commonly known.[10] Other sources refer to the priest who brought the rites of the Mother to Athens as "the Phrygian man" (ὁ Φρύξ). Most often, in the sources cited below, he is called "the *Mētragyrtēs*," the begging priest of the Mother. Julian states that this man was driven out by unsympathetic Athenians. Other accounts make the point that he was put to death by the Athenians, and also explain that the eventual atonement for this offensive behavior was somehow connected to the manner and place in which the Athenians had put the *Mētragyrtēs* to death. The fullest such account is found in the lexicon of Photius, under the lemma "Metroön":[11]

10. In classical sources, the title Gallus is associated earliest with the works of Callimachus; see Lane 1996b, 121. The title was used among the Galatians who settled in central Phrygia after 278 B.C.E., and who adopted the cult of the Phrygian Mother; see Polybius 21.6.7 and 21.37.5–7; Livy 38.18.9–10; cf. Welles 1934, nos. 55–61; Strabo 12.5.1–3; Pausanias 1.4.5 and 7.17.10. In addition to Lane 1996b, see discussions by Pachis 1996; Roller 1997 and 1999, 229–32; Lancellotti 2002, 96–105. The origin of the eunuch priesthood of the Mother is discussed in chapter 4, at notes 83–91.

11. Photius *Lexicon* s.v. Μητρῷον. My translation interprets an ambiguity in the meaning of the verb ἀνεῖλον (from ἀναιρέω) in the phrase "on the spot at which they had put the *Mētragyrtēs* to death" (ἐν ᾧ ἀνεῖλον τὸν μητραγύρτην). Ἀναιρέω has the essential meaning "take up," but also has a number of idiosyncratic meanings, the most common of which is "do away with," "kill." With many commentators (e.g., R. Parker 1996, 190 n. 137; Roller 1999, 164), I take the latter meaning. Wycherley (1957, 155 no. 487), Vermaseren (1977, 32), and Cerri (1983, 160 and 162) prefer the meaning "recovered [the body]," but to make sense of the phrase in this context they must add words to the effect of "and gave it proper burial," which is in no way supported by the Greek text. The whole debate could have been avoided if commentators had noticed the unambiguous use of ἀνεῖλον meaning "put to death" in the parallel description of this event given by the scholiast to Aristophanes *Wealth* 431: πρόσπολον γάρ τινα φρύγα τῆς Ῥέας ἐκεῖσε βαλόντες ἀνεῖλον ὥσπερ μαινόμενον ("For they put to death a certain Phrygian attendant of Rhea by throwing him there because he was insane"). The thing that was "fenced in" (περιφράττοντες αὐτόν) was thus the place within the Council House where the *Mētragyrtēs* was condemned to death (i.e., the altar on which votes were placed: see note 33 below), not his tomb. There is no independent evidence associating the Council House with a tomb of the *Mētragyrtēs*.

A certain *Mētragyrtēs* came to Attica and was initiating women in the rites of the Mother of the Gods, as they say. The Athenians killed him by throwing him head first into the *barathron* [executioner's pit]. When a plague broke out, the Athenians received an oracle commanding them to atone for the murdered man. On this account they built the Council House, on the spot at which they had put the *Mētragyrtēs* to death. Fencing the place in, they dedicated it to the Mother of the Gods, and they erected a statue of the *Mētragyrtēs*. They then made use of the Metroön as an archive building and repository for laws, and they filled in the *barathron*.

Here we learn the manner of death that the Athenians accorded to the *Mētragyrtēs*. We are also told that the Metroön and archive house is identical with the Council House (*bouleutērion*) of the Athenians. A variant of this account states that it was a law court (*dikastērion*) rather than the Council House that was built on the spot where the *Mētragyrtēs* was put to death.[12] Another account, explaining the word *barathron,* states the Phrygian origin of the priest, as does Julian, and adds details that call attention to the link between the Mother and Demeter, as does Julian:[13]

> *Barathron:* A dark, well-like chasm in Attica, into which they used to throw male-factors. . . . Here they threw the Phrygian devotee of the Mother of the Gods because he had gone mad, since he announced that the Mother was coming in search of her daughter. But the enraged goddess sent crop failure into the land; and when, through the advice of an oracle, they realized the reason for this, they filled in the chasm and offered propitiatory sacrifices to the goddess.

These accounts of the Mother's establishment at Athens are circumstantially detailed and consistent in all important respects. But could they be historically accurate? The fact that they are preserved only in late sources has raised suspicions. The manner in which the story of rejection and atonement so clearly conforms to a mythical paradigm has decided the matter for a number of scholars, who dismiss the entire account as a late invention.[14] The case for dismissal has been put succinctly by Robert Parker:[15]

---

12. This variant, in Apostolius 11.34, is not necessarily faulty, or contradicted by the usual version; see note 33 below.

13. *Suda* s.v. βάραθρον. See also scholion to Aristophanes *Wealth* 431, where the nearly the same account is given to explain the term βάραθρον, but where the offended deity is identified both as Rhea and as Demeter.

14. Skeptics include Henri Graillot (1912, 9–22), Edouard Will (1960, 101 n. 2), and more recently E. D. Francis (1990, 112–20), Angel Ruiz Pérez (1994), Philippe Borgeaud (1996, 129–30), Robert Parker (1996, 189–90), Noel Robertson (1996), and Maria Grazia Lancellotti (2002, 67–73). Lynn Roller (1999, 162–69) offers a detailed review of the evidence, and is cautiously noncommittal on this question.

15. R. Parker 1996, 190. Noel Robertson 1996, 259 n. 79, offers a similar assessment of the value of the story of the rejected priest: "Until these details are accounted for, it is rather

The account is obviously not true (to speak dogmatically)—or rather, even if it were true, we could not know it to be so, so closely would reality on this view have imitated an aetiological legend of a familiar type. And we may doubt whether it is ancient enough even to provide evidence for Athenian perceptions of the cult.

Parker's dogma is softened, slightly, by his admission that the tale might after all be true. In the absence of proof the matter can be viewed either way, and others have willingly stated their conviction that the story must have a historical basis.[16] The reason is the remarkable manner in which these late accounts coincide with evidence, both literary and archaeological, from the fifth century B.C.E.

Athenian drama of the last three decades of the fifth century repeatedly presents the Mother of the Gods to Athenian audiences, often challenging Athenians to see the Mother as somehow the same as Rhea, Demeter, and Ge, the Earth herself, and akin to Aphrodite and Artemis.[17] She is called "the Phrygian . . . Great Mother of gods and men, Mistress Kybele" by Aristophanes.[18] A chorus of Sophocles invokes her as "Mistress Mother, warder of the great gold-bearing Pactolus," at Sardis.[19] Also at Sardis, "Tmolus' Lydian stronghold," and at "the city of the Phrygians," the "rites of the Great Mother Kybele" are repeatedly proclaimed by the chorus of Euripides' *Bacchae*.[20] In the usage of Euripides, she is the "Idaean Mother" in the Troad and in Crete alike.[21]

While Athenian audiences were thus repeatedly reminded of the Asiatic

wishful thinking to hold up the story, and many do, as illustrating some dramatic turn in religious feeling."

16. Champions of the historicity of the tale of the *Mētragyrtēs*, as the priest of the Mother was most commonly called, include Maarten Vermaseren (1977, 32), Walter Burkert (1979a, 103–5), Dario Cosi (1980–81), Giovanni Cerri (1983), and Henrik Versnel (1990, 105–11). The foundations of this historicizing trend were laid chiefly by Homer Thompson's interpretation of the archaeological remains unearthed in the Athenian agora (1937, esp. 205–9), supported by the scholarship of E. R. Dodds (1940) on the influence of foreign cults at Athens, and of Martin Nilsson (1955, 725–27) on the history of the cult of the Mother.

17. On the testimony to the Mother of the Gods appearing in Attic drama of the late fifth century, see Henrichs 1976; Cerri 1983; Shear 1995, 171–77; Blomart 2002. Roller 1996 provides the most detailed review of sources. See also the references in notes 1–3 above.

18. Aristophanes *Birds*, after naming φρυγίλος Σαβάζιος as a pun for Φρύγιος Σαβάζιος (872), goes on to name μεγάλη μήτηρ θεῶν καὶ ἀνθρώπων δέσποινα Κυβέλη (873–75).

19. Sophocles *Philoctetes* 394–95: μᾶτερ πότνια... ἃ τὸν μέγαν Πακτολὸν εὔχρυσον νέμεις. (Cf. note 1 above.)

20. Euripides *Bacchae*: λιποῦσαι Τμῶλον ἔρυμα Λυδίας (55), ἐν πόλει Φρυγῶν (58), τά τε ματρὸς μεγάλας ὄργια Κυβέλας θεμιτεύων (78–79). Cf. *Bacchae* 64–65, Ἀσίας ἀπὸ γαίας ἱερὸν Τμῶλον ἀμείψασα ("From the land of Asia, departing holy Tmolus"); 85–87, κατάγουσαι Φρυγίων ἐξ ὀρέων Ἑλλάδος εὐροχόρους ἀγυιάς ("Bringing him down from Phrygian mountains to the wide ways of Hellas"); 141, ἱέμενος εἰς ὄρεα Φρύγια, Λύδια ("running to the Phrygian, the Lydian mountains").

21. See Euripides *Orestes* 1453, *Helen* 1324, *Bacchae* 120–34, *Palamedes* fr. 586 (Nauck), *Cretans* fr. 472.13 (Nauck). For the later debate about the primacy of the Trojan vs. the Cretan Ida as home for the Mother, see Strabo 10.3.12–14 and 19–20.

origin of the rites of the Mother, they were also reminded that it was customary to disparage her wandering priests. The comic poet Cratinus used two different appellations of the begging priest of the Mother: in his *Runaway Women* he used the term *agersikybēlis* (beggar of Kybele) to satirize the contemporary seer Lampon; in his *Thracian Women* he used the term *Kybēbos* (Kybebe-man), which Photius' lexicon cites as an Ionicism for *Mētragyrtēs*.[22] In Sophocles' *Oedipus Tyrannus*, Oedipus chides Teiresias, who speaks ill-omened words, as a *dolios agyrtēs* (deceitful beggar), alluding to the type of the unwelcome begging priest associated with the Asiatic Kybele.[23] In the realm of political rhetoric, Aristotle cites an exchange between Iphicrates and Callias son of Hipponicus in which Iphicrates refers derogatorily to Callias, who was a torch-bearing priest (*daidouchos*) of Demeter, as a *Mētragyrtēs*.[24]

These allusions to the Mother of the Gods, the Asiatic Kybele, and to her wandering priests were all part of the literary record of the late fifth century, and were therefore available to later generations, when devotees of the Mother might, just conceivably, have concocted the story of the *Mētragyrtēs* out of them. Likewise, the famous plague of the early Peloponnesian War, which struck Athens in the very period when this growing attention to the Mother is attested, was part of the historical record.[25] It would be hard to defend the historicity of the story on the basis of these elements alone. Other elements of the story, however, involve more obscure details that are less likely to have been common knowledge. For example, the *barathron* is attested as the executioners' pit from the beginning of the fifth century, but after the early fourth century it is remembered only as a relic of the past.[26] But the most remarkable set of details, which no source explains or even mentions outside of these stories about the *Mētragyrtēs* and the Mother, involves the conversion of the Council House in the Athenian agora simultaneously into an archive for state records and a shrine to the Mother.

Close to the end of the fifth century, a cult image of the Mother of the Gods was created by Agoracritus and installed in the building in the agora

22. Cratinus *Runaway Women* (Δραπέτιδες), fr. 66 (KA, from Photius s.v. Ἀγερσικύβηλις); Cratinus *Thracian Women* (Θρᾷτται), fr. 87 (KA, from Photius s.v. Κύβηβον).

23. Sophocles *Oedipus Tyrannus* 387–88, where Teiresias is also likened to a Persian magus.

24. Aristotle *Rhetoric* 1405a, who also cites Callias' retort that Iphicrates must not be an initiate to Demeter, or he would know the difference between a μητραγύρτης and a δᾳδοῦχος. The exchange between Callias and Iphicrates most likely took place early in the fourth century. (For their association, see Xenophon *Hellenica* 4.5.13–14.) The *Mētragyrtēs* was also a figure of fourth-century comedy: Antiphanes fr. 152 (KA). Cf. Athenaeus 12.541e; Demosthenes 18, *On the Crown* 259–60.

25. Earlier scholarship (e.g., Foucart 1873, 64) accepted the identification of the plague of 430 B.C.E. with the plague of the *Mētragyrtēs*. Nilsson 1955, 727, introduced a skeptical note by pointing out that we cannot assume that the plague of the story is historical. Cerri 1983, 168–69, is dismissive of the plague of 430.

26. See Cerri 1983, 161–62.

Figure 1. Typical naiskos of the Mother of the Gods, depicting
the enthroned statue of the Mother holding libation dish and
tympanum, with recumbent lion on her lap, flanked by attendant
figures, all in an architectural facade, from the Athenian agora,
fourth century B.C.E. (American School of Classical Studies at
Athens, Agora Excavations, inv. no. S922).

of Athens that became known after her as the Metroön.[27] The statue is known
to us through the many miniature replicas of it that were produced for house-
hold shrines, beginning in the fourth century. (See figure 1.) Literary and

27. Pausanias 1.3.5 and Arrian *Periplus* 9 attribute the statue to Pheidias; Pliny *Naturalis
Historia* 36.17 attributes it to his pupil Agoracritus, which is widely believed to be correct: see
Ridgway 1981, 171–73; Naumann 1983, 159–69; Palagia 2005, 125.

epigraphic sources confirm that the building called the Metroön was also the state archive building, and that it was organized as such by the end of the fifth century.[28] Archaeological investigation has revealed that this building actually was the old Council House, originally built in the time of Cleisthenes, which was replaced in the last decade of the fifth century by a new Council House built beside it, making way in the older building for the state archives, and for the Mother of the Gods.[29]

The coincidence of the story of the "Phrygian man," the *Mētragyrtēs*, with so many circumstantial details, and especially with the archaeologically documented history of the Athenian Council House, raises a strong suspicion that the story of the *Mētragyrtēs* bears some relation to historical events. The objection that the story is so late, coming to us from late antiquity, might even be eliminated by evidence indicating that the literary origin of the story of the *Mētragyrtēs* and the foundation of the Metroön was a historical work of the fourth century B.C.E. A scholiast, explaining a reference to archival documents "in the Metroön beside the Council House" in a speech of Aeschines, adds the following: "We know from the *Philippics* that the Athenians converted a portion of the Council House into the Metroön, which is the sanctuary of Rhea, on account of that Phrygian man [διὰ τὴν αἰτίαν ἐκεινοῦ Φρυγός]."[30] The story of "that Phrygian man" was evidently told in a work entitled *Philippics*, which was most likely the work of that title either by Theopompus or by Anaximenes, both of whom wrote in the second half of the fourth century.[31] Here, if only it were fully preserved, we could have found the story of the *Mētragyrtēs*, and of the foundation of the Metroön, set in its historical context.

28. On the evidence for the virtually simultaneous foundation of the Metroön as temple and as archive, see Shear 1995, 178–89, and most recently James Sickinger 1999, 105–13. Testimonia are collected by Wycherley 1957, 150–60.

29. This interpretation of archaeological remains by H. A. Thompson 1937 has been challenged in various ways (see most recently Francis 1990, 112–20; S. G. Miller 1995), but still represents the prevailing view. See the summaries by Camp 1986, 90–94; Sickinger 1999, 82–83 and 111; and especially the detailed rebuttal of Miller's radical reinterpretation by Shear 1995.

30. Scholion to Aeschines 3.187.1.

31. Wycherley 1957, 151–52 no. 467, identifies the author of the *Philippics* mentioned here as either Theopompus or Anaximenes; Wycherley's suggestion has been accepted by Cerri 1983, 164; Versnel 1990, 106 n. 37; Shear 1995, 178; Roller 1999, 163. Cerri suggests that Anaximenes is most likely the author cited, since he is elsewhere known to have discussed laws kept in the Council House (*FGrHist* 72 F 13). R. Parker 1996, 190 n. 137 (endorsed by Lancellotti 2002, 70), expresses skepticism about a fourth-century authority. He insists that this reference to the *Philippics* "without the citation of an author can surely only refer, as regularly in these and other scholia, to the *Philippics* of Demosthenes as read with a commentary; and since Demosthenes does not tell the story, we are back with a late commentary." Although such a misdirected reference—not to Demosthenes' *Philippics*, but to a late commentary on them—seems improbable, Parker's thesis cannot be refuted on its own terms; its foundation is removed by dem-

Some of the agnostic caution noted above has been prompted by apparent inconsistencies between the story of the *Mētragyrtēs* and the physical evidence. For one thing, archaeological investigation has found no trace of either a *barathron* or a tomb of the *Mētragyrtēs* (as understood by some) on the site of either the old or the new Council House in the agora.[32] But the story of the *Mētragyrtēs* actually requires neither of these features to be located on the site of the Council House or Metroön. The tomb of the *Mētragyrtēs* enters the account only by virtue of a misleading translation of the testimony. (See note 11 above.) The statement that the Council House and later Metroön contained "the spot at which they had put the *Mētragyrtēs* to death" can be understood as the spot on which the sentence of death was passed on the *Mētragyrtēs* by the Athenians.[33]

A more serious obstacle to accepting the main elements of this story as historical has been the indisputable evidence that the cult of the Mother of the Gods was widespread across the Greek-speaking world by at least the first half of the sixth century B.C.E.[34] Athenians were certainly aware of this deity, as references to her in drama attest, before the last decade of the fifth century, when her new cult place in the agora was established.[35] If this deity was so well known, then how could the establishment of her cult in classical Athens have been as controversial as Julian and other sources make it out to have been? Compounding this paradox is the following question: If the cult of the Mother of the Gods actually was in any sense foreign and controversial, then how did she become not merely accepted among the gods honored at Athens, as other foreign gods were in the later fifth century, but en-

onstrating other reasons for believing that the story of "the Phrygian man" likely was in fact an element of fourth-century historiography. (See chapter 9 at note 111.)

32. So R. Parker 1996, 190 n. 137, notes: "The argument that the story is based on good knowledge of Attic *Realien* appears to founder on the claim in Photius that the Metroön was built on the spot where 'they killed' (ἀνεῖλον) the *metragyrtes*, sc. over the quondam pit."

33. Ἀνεῖλον meaning "did away with" (see note 11) can also mean "voted for the sentence of death upon," as it does in Euripides *Andromache* 518. The spot on which the votes (ψῆφοι) for a death sentence are placed is emphasized in controversial executions carried out by the Thirty: Xenophon *Hellenica* 2.4.9; Lysias 13, *Against Agoratus* 37. The solemnity of taking votes (ψῆφοι) "from the altar" is attested on the decrees of the Demotionidae, *IG* II² 1237, A.29: φέρεν δὲ ψῆφον ἀπὸ τὸ βωμῦ (e.g.). On the altar in the (new) Council House (called both ἑστία and βωμός), see Xenophon *Hellenica* 2.3.52 and 55.

34. All surveys of the cult of Kybele or the Mother of the Gods acknowledge the antiquity of her cult in Anatolia and its early spread among the Greeks of Ionia and from them to European Greece and its colonies: so Will 1960; Vermaseren 1977, 16–37; Burkert 1979a, 102–5; 1985, 177–79; Naumann 1983, 136–55; Graf 1984 and 1985, 107–15; Borgeaud 1996, 23–26; Roller 1999, 119–44, 164. J. de la Genière 1986 assembles the evidence for the archaic cult of the Mother of the Gods in the Peloponnese.

35. Archaic figurines from Athens probably to be identified as the Mother of the Gods are noted by Naumann 1983, 145–46, with an example from the Acropolis (inv. 655) illustrated in plate 19 no. 3.

shrined in the old Council House and archives, and thereby intimately identified with the institutional seat of Athenian democracy?

Even if we were to dismiss as pure invention the story of the outlandish *Mētragyrtēs* and his role in the foundation of the Metroön, no commentator has yet offered a cogent explanation for why the Mother of the Gods, so openly recognized as an Asiatic deity, should preside over the state archives in the old Council House.[36] In view of this enigma especially, Parker introduces his discussion of the cult of the Mother of the Gods at Athens by calling her cult "a great puzzle and great paradox at the heart of religious and civic life."[37]

This puzzle can be solved, I will argue, only when all of its main pieces—the mission of the "Phrygian man," his identity as a eunuch priest of the Mother, his rejection, the eventual inauguration of the Metroön as an archive as well as a shrine, and, above all, the Phrygian origin of the rites of the Mother of the Gods—are successfully integrated into the explanation. To begin with, we must consider the meaning of the foreign origin of the Mother of the Gods and her *Mētragyrtēs*. In doing so, we cannot look only to the Mother as Other, as Not-Greek, or as Female occupying a seat of Male political authority; such perspectives help us visualize a variety of pertinent factors, but they do not explain the cult of the Mother at Athens.[38] The rites of the Mother are said to be Phrygian in origin, and they are said to have been brought to Athens by a "Phrygian man." Fifth-century sources agree with the later accounts of the *Mētragyrtēs* in associating the Mother with Phrygia, so we need to consider the significance of Phrygia, and what this association of the Mother of the Gods meant to an Athenian audience.

## THE LAND OF MIDAS

In the previous chapter we encountered Phrygians and Lydians depicted as paragons of cowardice, or more precisely, as men who knew how to cringe be-

---

36. So Shear 1995, 189, can suggest only that space for her cult was fortuitously available after the new Council House was built. Sickinger 1999, 122, leaves the question unresolved. S. G. Miller 1995 does not even ask the question. Roller 1999, 163, referring to the attested association of a Metroön with the public archives of Colophon from a century later than the establishment of the Metroön at Athens, suggests that familiarity with Ionian practice induced the Athenians to establish the Mother in this particular manner.

37. R. Parker 1996, 188.

38. With few exceptions (S. G. Miller 1995, Robertson 1996, Blomart 2002), the Mother has regularly been regarded as one among several foreign gods imported into Athens in the later fifth century: so Foucart 1873, 60–65; R. Parker 1996, 188–98; Roller 1999, 164–65 (with qualifications). Garland 1992 is silent on the subject. The Mother as foreign Other is considered by Hartog 1988, 70–75, 80–82, 110–11, 244–45. Loraux 1998, 67–79, considers the Mother as Female Other.

fore those who are powerful.[39] In the estimate of Athenians of the fifth and fourth century, such habits made these Asiatics fit for servitude. The explanation, we will find, lies in the logic that a land that produced men who knew how to abase themselves to power also produced the most awesome symbols of power. In the previous chapter, Lydian Sardis was described as the most impressive seat of power in the days of the Mermnad tyrants. But before the rise of Gyges, founder of the Mermnad dynasty, Lydia itself had been part of the greater dominion of King Midas. The Phrygian kingdom of Midas, as we will see, impressed itself on Greek memory as the prototype of Asiatic sovereignty.

Phrygia, to the Greeks, embraced not only the vast plateau of central Anatolia, where Gordium beside the Sangarius River was located, but also the region of mountains and coastal plains west of the Sangarius known as Hellespontine Phrygia.[40] While its heartland is well known, and its extension to the shores of the Hellespont is generally recognized, the overall boundaries of Phrygia are ill defined. In large part this is because our sources have tended to identify Phrygia with its most famous kings. The kingdom of Phrygia, in this sense, was therefore always something greater than the designation of a homogeneous linguistic or cultural zone.[41] Troy and its kings were regarded as Phrygian in this sense in classical, and especially Athenian sources.[42] Thus the Troad, which was the western extremity of Hellespontine Phrygia, was considered part of Phrygia.[43] In this sense too, Tantalus, whose home was gen-

39. See chapter 1 at notes 106–10. On the theme of barbarian—i.e., Asiatic character in general—as depicted in Attic drama, see E. Hall 1989. On developments in this stereotype by the end of the fifth century, see S. Saïd 1984.

40. Herodotus 5.52.1, 7.26–31, refers to defined boundaries of the Phrygian heartland, perhaps influenced by Persian administrative districts (cf. 3.90.2, 127) or Ionian maps (cf. 5.49.5); cf. Xenophon *Anabasis* 1.2.6–19, 1.9.7; *Cyropaedia* 2.1.5, 8.6.7. On the wider extent of Phrygia, see Strabo 2.5.31, where Phrygia comprises an indefinite portion of the land "inside the Halys," including "the part called Hellespontine, part of which is the Troad," and "the part in the interior of which a portion is the region of the Gallograeci called Galatia and Epictetus [the "Acquired" part]." See also Strabo 12.4.10–5.4 and 13.4.12.

41. See Strabo 14.5.16 on the ready conflation of the Troad, Lydia, and Phrygia in Attic tragedy. On the geography of Phrygia according to classical sources, see Laminger-Pascher 1989, 9–14 (who observes difficulties in reconciling sources); Muscarella 1989 and 1995; Innocente 1995, 216–18; and Cassola 1997, 141–49 (all of whom reconcile the traditions of a greater Phrygia).

42. In the *Iliad*, kinship between Trojans and Phrygians is close, but they are distinct. E. Hall 1988 examines the assimilation of Trojans to Phrygians, and argues that this took place first in the creative imagination of Aeschylus, only after which the identification became a commonplace of Attic drama and art; cf. E. Hall 1989, 38–39; M. C. Miller 1995; Erskine 2001, 73–74. In chapter 3 we will see that the premise for identifying Trojans with Phrygians is already set forth in *Homeric Hymn* 5, *To Aphrodite*.

43. Hellespontine Phrygia, Aeolis, and the Troad are named together as a unit in Xenophon *Anabasis* 5.6.24 (cf. *Cyropaedia* 8.6.7, *Hellenica* 1.1.4–6, 24–26, 3.1.10), indicating that these were all part of the Persian satrapy of Hellespontine Phrygia. Herodotus 3.90.2 indicates that this

erally placed in the vicinity of Mount Sipylus, was said to have been a king of Lydia or a king of Phrygia, indicating that Lydia, too, was part of a greater Phrygia.[44] The fact that all such legendary kings of Asia gravitated, in classical Greek sources, toward a Phrygian identity was likely due to the influence of a historical king of Phrygia, Midas.

Midas lived and ruled over Phrygians and neighboring peoples at the end of the eighth century, as records of the Assyrians prove.[45] Midas also left tangible evidence of his kingship among the Greeks, for he was the first barbarian king to make a dedication at Delphi, according to Herodotus.[46] Among the Greeks Midas was remembered as a great king and a figure of wonder. He was a man whose kingship had extended across wide reaches of the earth, who had acquired great wealth with ease, and who had conversed with gods. In all these ways, Midas had reached the farthest imaginable limits of human experience. Yet the tales that preserve his memory all convey a bittersweet picture of the life lived by Midas, as if to show that mortal existence imposes limits that no power, wealth, or wisdom can, in the end, overcome.

As early as Tyrtaeus in the mid-seventh century, Midas was remembered as king of enviable wealth.[47] Midas tamed the immortal half-human Seilenus and learned from him the meaning of life and the nature of the world.[48] Midas entered the company of Dionysus, or Bacchus, who gave him his golden touch.[49] Midas judged the musical competition of Marsyas and Apollo, and patronized the music of the *aulos,* or reed pipe, one of the legacies of Phry-

---

arrangement was recognized in the time of Darius I; see Carrington 1977, 122; Briant 2002, 697–700.

44. Tantalus and Pelops are variously described as Lydians (Pindar *Olympian* 1.24–38, 9.9; Strabo 1.3.17; Pausanias 5.1.6, 9.5.7) or Phrygians (Bacchylides 35.50 [Edmonds *LG*]; Herodotus 7.8c; Strabo 7.7.1 [citing Hecataeus], 2.8.2, 21, 14.5.28). Cassola 1997, 144, explains this ambiguity as the result of a tradition that Phrygia once dominated Lydia; see also Sakellariou 1958, 436–37, for a discussion of Phrygian place names in Lydia. On the other hand, Sakellariou (226–34) reviews the wide geographical associations of Tantalus and Pelops and uses them to suggest the diverse origins of the Greek founders of Smyrna. Note that Diodorus 4.74 calls Tantalus a king of Paphlagonia; cf. Herodotus 3.90.2 and 7.72–73, and Strabo 12.4.10 on the affinity of Phrygians and Paphlagonians.

45. The Assyriological evidence for Midas is noted below at notes 132–34. See Muscarella 1989 for a survey of classical and Near Eastern sources, and archaeological evidence, bearing on Midas. Roller 1983 surveys the classical Greek traditions of Midas.

46. Herodotus 1.14.3, discussed below at note 118.

47. Tyrtaeus 12.6 (Edmonds *EI*), cited in chapter 1, note 115. The celebrated wealth of Midas is also noted by Aristophanes *Wealth* 287; Plato *Republic* 3.408b, *Laws* 2.660e.

48. On the capture of Seilenus in archaic and classical vase painting, see Roller 1983, 303–6; M. C. Miller 1988. Bacchylides fr. 57A (Edmonds *LG*) describes Seilenus' education of Midas; the fullest account is given by Theopompus *FGrHist* 115 F 75 (from Aelian *Varia Historia* 3.18)); see also Xenophon *Anabasis* 1.2.13; Aristotle fr. 44 (Rose).

49. The golden touch was known to Aristotle (below, note 51), but the story of how Midas acquired it is not preserved until Ovid *Metamorphoses* 11.90–145 and Hyginus *Fabulae* 191.

gia to the Greeks.[50] To each of these legends, however, there is an outcome that renders this enviable man pitiful. His golden touch proved to be a curse that no mortal could live with.[51] From Seilenus he learned that it was best never to have been born, and, failing that, to reduce suffering by having a short life.[52] His very greatness deformed Midas, according to some accounts, giving him the ass' ears that enabled him to overhear all the was going on throughout his kingdom; other accounts say that he was given ass' ears for criticizing Dionysus, or for rendering judgment against Apollo in the contest with Marsyas.[53] The *aulos* music associated with Midas was devoted to the rites of mourning at his mother's funeral.[54]

The greatness of Midas, in many ways, was defined and memorialized through the conditions of mortality and the observances occasioned by death. Callisthenes, a contemporary of Alexander the Great, records a story of Midas and the wrath of Idaean Zeus wherein Midas was advised by an oracle to appease the god by sacrificing what was most precious to humanity. After his subjects had thrown their gold, silver, and women's adornments into a chasm in the earth, all to no effect, Midas' son Anchyrus realized what was necessary, and threw himself into the chasm.[55] A similar story was told of another son of Midas, Lityerses, who gave the gift of agriculture to mankind, but whose pride at his invention soon led to his death. The death of Lityerses was said to be the origin of a reaping song known to Theocritus, and it was also a funeral dirge first sung to console Midas for his loss.[56]

50. Athenian red-figure vase paintings depict the contest of Marsyas and Apollo (see Boardman 1989a, figures 310 and 389), and the contest is noticed by Herodotus 7.26.2 and Xenophon *Anabasis* 1.2.8. Xenophon refers to it as a contest "of wisdom" (περὶ σοφίας); see also Plato *Symposium* 215b–216a; Thiemer 1979, 57–59, on the musical basis of the wisdom of Marsyas; and M. L. West 1992, 330–31, on Marsyas and his reputation in connection with Phrygian music. Midas' role as judge is not described until Ovid (below, note 53), but Marsyas was identified with Seilenus as early as the fifth century (see notes 62 and 63 below), and Midas is named in the same context as Marsyas and his *aulos* music in Hellenistic sources (below, note 98).

51. Aristotle *Politics* 1257b cites the starvation of Midas as a sign that true wealth must suit actual needs.

52. The moral is reported by Bacchylides and Theopompus (above, note 48).

53. Midas is depicted with ass' ears on Attic vases of the mid-fifth century: see Roller 1983, 303–6; M. C. Miller 1988; Boardman 1989a, figure 139; see also Aristophanes *Wealth* 287. The mythographer Conon (*FGrHist* 26 F 1.1; in Photius *Library* 186.131a) describes the ass ears of Midas as a manifestation of his network of informants. (Cf. *Suda* s.v. Μίδας; scholion to Aristophanes *Wealth* 287.) Ass' ears were given to Midas in retribution by Apollo, according to Hyginus *Fabulae* 191 and Ovid *Metamorphoses* 11.146–93, or by Dionysus, according to another account recorded in the *Suda* s.v. Μίδας.

54. On the music of mourning for the mother of Midas, see below at notes 97–98.

55. Callisthenes *FGrHist* 124 F 56. On Callisthenes' interest in the lore of Asia Minor, especially in connection with Alexander's march, see below at note 105.

56. Theocritus 10, *The Reapers* 41, mentions the reaping song called "Lityerses," and the scholion on the passage summarizes the tale of Lityerses son of Midas, who was said to be the

Midas' greatest memorial, in the Greek tradition, was his own tumulus (τύμβος), which was remembered especially for his funerary epigram, said to have been composed by Homer. Some of its verses were known to Cleobulus of Lindus, one of the Seven Sages of the early sixth century, and to Simonides at the end of the sixth century, as a fragment of Simonides attests. Plato knew the epigram, and it is cited and discussed in several later sources:[57]

> A maiden of bronze am I, and on Midas' memorial I stand. As long as water
> flows and tall trees grow, and the rising sun shines, and the bright moon too,
> and rivers run and the sea waves break, standing here upon this tear-drenched
> mound I will announce to passersby that here Midas is buried.

Through repeated citation and discussion, this epigram became a literary artifact, yet its original form as an archaic inscription on stone is not seriously questioned. Its self-described form, on an inscribed stele or pillar bearing the statue of a maiden, or *korē*, standing atop a tumulus, would more likely belong to the time of Cleobulus than to an earlier period.[58] The location of this tumulus of Midas is not reported. The fact that modern scholarship generally regards Midas to have been buried in one of the tumuli at Gordium has little relevance to the Greek tradition of the burial place of Midas.[59] Reference to "the waves of the sea" in the epigram, and in Simonides' reference to it, suggests that it was not far from the Anatolian coast, and this inference is consistent with other clues. Homeric tradition associates the commemoration of Midas with Cyme in Aeolia, where Homer was said to be at the time when, at the request of Midas' grieving kinsmen, "he composed this epigram, which still today is inscribed on the stele of the memorial of the son of Gordius."[60]

---

inventor of agriculture (γεωργίας εὑρετής); see also Pollux *Onomasticon* 4.54–55 (cited by Edmonds *LG* vol. 3, 500–505). The tale of Lityerses was told by Sositheus, a tragedian of the third century B.C.E., in his satyr play *Daphnis; or, Lityerses:* see note 65 below.

57. The text is as given by Diogenes 1.89–90, who also cites Simonides (fr. 31 [Edmonds *LG*]; *PMG* 581); and Simonides refers the verses to Cleobulus of Lindus. The epigram appears with minor variations in the pseudo-Herodotean *Life of Homer* 135–40 (11 West *LH*), and in the *Contest of Homer and Hesiod* 324 (15 West *LH*); a shorter version, omitting the middle two lines, is recited by Plato *Phaedrus* 264c–d. See Pfohl 1967, no. 24.

58. See Raubitschek 1969, 13–15, for a discussion of the form of the epigram, and for the suggestion that the monument likely corresponds to a column with an Ionic capital, topped possibly by a sphinx (resembling the Naxian sphinx at Delphi), and that it probably dates to around 600 B.C.E.

59. On the tumuli at Gordium, see below, note 135. It is instructive to recall that, until the mid-twentieth century, the rock-cut facade now referred to as the Midas Monument (Phrygian Yazılıkaya, discussed below) was commonly identified as the Tomb of Midas; see Ramsay 1890, 29, 31; Haspels 1971, 3, 28, 99, 185–86 and n. 111.

60. Pseudo-Herodotean *Life of Homer* 131–34 (11 West *LH*). The epigram is also attributed to Homer in the *Contest of Homer and Hesiod* 324, where it is said to have been commissioned by

Pythagoras, according to a tradition known to Aristotle, suggested to one of his associates, Myllias of Croton, that he was the reincarnation of Midas son of Gordius. Myllias then went "to the continent" (εἰς τὴν ἤπειρον: i.e., to Asia) to perform rites prescribed to him by Pythagoras on the grave of Midas.[61] Here, too, a location familiar to the Greeks of Asia Minor and not far from the coast seems most likely.

Whatever its precise location, the Tumulus of Midas was but one point in a vast dominion associated with Midas by landmarks from southeastern Phrygia to western Macedonia. The most widespread tradition in the geography of Midas concerns the location of the spring where Midas captured Seilenus (or "the satyr," sometimes identified as Marsyas).[62] The most famous spring to be associated with Midas and the capture of Seilenus was at Celaenae (later Apamea), at the headwaters of the Maeander River, where both Xerxes and Cyrus the Younger paused on their marches across Phrygia[63] Callisthenes reports that Midas founded an altar to Zeus at Celaenae, for this was where his son Anchyrus had plunged into a chasm in the earth.[64] Sositheus, a tragedian of the third century B.C.E., describes Celaenae as Midas' capital, and as the place where the body of Midas' other son, Lityerses, was flung into the Maeander River.[65] Another spring of Midas and Seilenus was at Thymbrium, east of Celaenae, where it was visited by Xenophon on his way with Cyrus from Phrygia toward Cilicia.[66] Yet another was located at Ancyra (modern Ankara), a city said to have been founded by Midas and visited by Alexander.[67] Farthest from these central Anatolian sites was the spring in Macedonia at the foot of Mount Bermium, where the Macedonian royal dynasty

---

sons of Midas named Xanthus and Gorgus (Gordius?). For another tradition that associated Midas with Cyme, see below, note 72.

61. Aristotle fr. 191.72 (Rose, from Porphyry *Life of Pythagoras* 25; cf. DK 14, 7.7–8, from Aelian *Varia Historia* 4.17). Pythagoras' interest in the identity of reincarnated souls is among the earliest and best attested features of his philosophy, parodied by Xenophanes (DK 21 B 7, from Diogenes 8.36); see also Herodotus 2.123.2, 4.95; Kirk et al. 1983, 219–20. Pythagoras claimed that his own previous incarnations were Anatolians, as reported by Heracleides Ponticus (DK 14, 8.6–24, from Diogenes 8.4–5).

62. On Marsyas the Seilenus, see Herodotus 7.26.2; on Marsyas the Satyr, see Plato *Symposium* 215b, 221d. Marsyas is also identified with Pan in later sources: see Roller 1983, 308.

63. Herodotus 7.27–29 tells of the reception of Xerxes at Celaenae by Pythius son of Atys, and at 7.26.2 refers to Marsyas the Seilenus at the springs of Celaenae, combining elements of the story of the capture of Seilenus and the contest of Marsyas and Apollo. Xenophon *Anabasis* 1.2.7–8, mentioning the palace at Celaenae said to have been built by Xerxes, refers to the flaying of Marsyas by Apollo at Celaenae. (See note 50 above.)

64. Callisthenes *FGrHist* 124 F 56; see above at note 55.

65. Sositheus treated these themes in his satyr play *Daphnis; or, Lityerses* fr. 2 (Nauck, cited in part by Athenaeus 10.415b).

66. Xenophon *Anabasis* 1.2.13.

67. Pausanias 1.4.5; Arrian *Anabasis* 2.4.1.

originated, according to a tradition familiar to Herodotus.[68] This was very likely at the site of the Nymphaeum at Mieza, where Aristotle later tutored Alexander in the arts of rulership and in metaphysical matters, and where, as some have suggested, Aristotle made Alexander mindful that he was heir to a kingship that had once belonged to Midas.[69]

Ancient historians who recalled the landmarks of Midas, as the foregoing examples show, did so on occasions when these were visited by men seeking to establish or extend sovereignty. The most famous such pilgrimage of power was Alexander's encounter with the Gordian Knot. The knot itself belonged to the cart that Midas dedicated to Zeus the King, on what was reputed to be the site of Midas' palace at Gordium.[70] Whether by sword stroke or by more patient means, Alexander was reputed to have undone the knot that held the yoke onto the tongue of this cart, thereby fulfilling a local prophecy that he who undid the knot would rule Asia, or, according to the alternative version, would rule the inhabited world (*oikoumenē*).[71]

Midas, in this instance, was clearly the paradigm of worldly rulership. All of the monuments and landmarks associated with Midas were places for contemplation, and possibly ceremonial acknowledgment, for those who sought sovereignty. They betokened the outermost limits of greatness. They were also reminders that those with the greatest wealth and power owed the greatest sacrifices to assure the well-being of their dominions. They also signified, in a mythopoeic manner, the attributes of sovereignty as the personal attributes of Midas. Midas' kingship was thus the origin and basis of agriculture, according to the legend of Lityerses. And Midas' kingship was the source of the gold that the earth of Asia yielded, in the Pactolus River at Sardis. For Midas' personal attribute, the golden touch that was his gift or curse from the gods, was either washed off him by the Pactolus, or transferred to that stream after his death.[72]

68. Herodotus 8.138.2–3. A different location in northern Macedonia is reported by Bion in Athenaeus 2.45c. On the tradition of Phrygian origins in European Thrace and Macedonia, see Herodotus 7.73; Strabo epitome of book 7.25, 14.5.28; Justin 7.2.11; Diodorus 5.64.4; Conon *FGrHist* 26 F 1.1 (in Photius *Library* 186). The tradition is discussed and variously interpreted by Fredericksmeyer 1961; Carrington 1977; Drews 1993; Muscarella 1995.

69. Plutarch *Alexander* 7.2–5; cf. Pliny *Historia Naturalis* 31.30, and the discussion of Fredericksmeyer 1961, 163–64.

70. The accounts of Midas' dedication and the Gordian Knot are discussed below at note 107. Remains of a small building with a decorated facade discovered by the Körte brothers on the citadel at Gordium in the early twentieth century may well be those of the shrine of Zeus where the cart of Gordius was dedicated; see Körte and Körte 1904, 153–69; Van Loon 1991, 34 and figure 16.

71. Tarn 1948, 262–65, has established the standard interpretation of Alexander's encounter with the Gordian Knot; see also Fredericksmeyer 1961. The Phrygian legend narrated on this occasion is discussed below at notes 105–7. The significance of the alternatives Asia or the *oikoumenē* is discussed in chapter 5.

72. Midas' golden touch passes to the Pactolus after his death, according to the scholia to Aristophanes *Wealth* 287; the same outcome is implied by Aristotle *Politics* 1257b. Midas is de-

In sum, Midas was remembered as a man who had achieved everything men could dream of, and had won everlasting fame. Although certain elements of the legend of Midas, as told by the Greeks, made a farce of his grandeur, the farce was only a reminder that Midas, like every other human being, was mortal in the end. The epigram on his tomb described the forces of nature as reminders of his former greatness. Midas' more widespread monuments were springs and rivers, and even beds of reeds that whispered his name in the wind. One could say that the memory of Midas had become a feature of the natural landscape.

### THE HOME OF KYBELE, THE MOTHER OF THE GODS

The lands associated with Midas, specifically the Asiatic lands that were embraced by the widest definition of Phrygia, were also identified by the Greeks with the aboriginal home of the rites of the Mother of the Gods. It was the mountains of these lands in particular, the several mountains named Dindymus in Phrygia, Mount Tmolus at Sardis, and Mount Ida in the Troad, all of them famous for springs and the waters that flowed from them, that were particularly identified with this deity.[73] These mountains were the visible features of the Mother, or the Mountain Mother (μήτηρ ὀρεία), as she was often called,[74] and were reminders of her presence just as the sea evoked Poseidon or gathering storm clouds evoked Zeus.

Classical poets, beginning with Pindar, invoke the Phrygian Mother of the Gods also by the name of Kybele (Κυβέλη).[75] Strabo provides one of the more comprehensive lists of names and epithets that all refer to the Mother of the

---

livered from his curse by bathing in the Pactolus, according to Ovid *Metamorphoses* 11.127–45 and Hyginus *Fabulae* 191. Note that the wife of Midas, Demodice or Hermodice of Cyme, was said to have invented coinage: see Aristotle fr. 611 no. 37 (Rose); Pollux *Onomasticon* 9.83. His golden touch and his wife's invention thus place coinage among the remarkable firsts associated with the legendary Midas, an association that is not historically implausible, at least in the form of pre-coin dumps: see Balmuth 1971; Kraay 1976, 20–28; DeVries 1980, 34; Muscarella 1989, 335.

73. On the Mother associated with mountains named Dindymus (μήτηρ Δινδυμήνη), see Herodotus 1.80.1 (discussing the source of the Hermus River in central Phrygia) and Apollonius *Argonautica* 1.1125 (discussing Mount Dindymus above Cyzicus in Hellespontine Phrygia). On the Mother and Mount Ida ("Ιδαία μᾶτερ), see Euripides *Orestes* 1453; Apollonius *Argonautica* 1.1128; cf. the Homeric Ἴδη πολύπιδαξ, μήτηρ θηρῶν, *Iliad* 8.47, 14.283, 15.151. Mount Tmolus above Sardis, source of the Pactolus, is home to her rites: see Euripides *Bacchae* 55, 65, 141, 154; cf. Sophocles *Philoctetes* 391–402. For additional testimonia and discussion, see below at notes 76–82, and chapter 5, note 24.

74. E.g., Euripides *Hippolytus* 144; Aristophanes *Birds* 746; Timotheus *Persians* 135 (Edmonds *LG*); Xanthus *FGrHist* 765 F 28; cf. *Homeric Hymn* 14, *To the Mother of the Gods* 5.

75. Pindar invokes the Mother of the Gods as Μήτηρ ("Mother," *Pythian* 3.78), Μήτηρ μεγάλη ("Great Mother," fr. 95 Bergk in Sandys), and Δέσποινα Κυβέλη Μήτηρ ("Mistress Mother Kybele," fr. 80 Snell); cf. Philodemus *On Piety* 19 (Gomperz), who cites Pindar for the identification of

Gods, and offers an explanation for the variation in nomenclature. After describing the manner in which the Curetes celebrated Rhea's delivery of the infant Zeus, Strabo goes on:[76]

> The Berecyntian tribe of Phrygians, and the Phrygians as a whole, as well as the Trojans living in the vicinity of Ida honor Rhea themselves and perform the same orgiastic rites, calling her the Mother of the Gods, and Agdistis, and the Great Phrygian Mother, and also calling her, after the place, Idaea and Dindymene and Sipylene and Pessinountis and Kybele and Kybebe.

The name Kybele is thus said to derive from a toponym, just as the Mother is said to be known after her sacred mountains, Ida, Dindymus, and Sipylus, and her sacred city, Pessinus. But while these mountains and the city of Pessinus are places known independently of their association with the Mother of the Gods, the toponyms associated with Kybele are more or less ubiquitous, and are not clearly attested independently of their association with the deity Kybele.[77]

The tradition of identifying variations of the name of Kybele (usually Κυβέλη, sometimes Κύβελη or Κύβηλις) with place names can be traced back as far as the iambic poet Hipponax of Ephesus and the geographer Hecataeus of Miletus, both writing in the later sixth century. "Hipponax calls Rhea Kybelis, from the fact that she was worshipped at the city Kybella in Phrygia," writes the Byzantine scholar Ioannes Tzetzes.[78] The geographical lexicon of Stephanus of Byzantium affords a wider glimpse into the topography of Kybele:[79]

> *Kybeleia:* A city of Ionia, according to Hecataeus in his book on Asia. But Herodian says Kybele was a city of Phoenicia. There is also Kybela in Phrygia. There is also a sacred mountain Kybela, after which Rhea called Kybele, and Kybele-born, and Kybelis. So reports Peisander in his tenth book.

Another Byzantine lexicon quotes the first-century-B.C.E. author Alexander of Miletus (Polyhistor) in support of a similar explanation of the name Ky-

---

Kybele as the Mother of the Gods. Henrichs 1976 identifies Pindar's "Mistress Mother Kybele" with the Phrygian "great mother of gods and men, Mistress Kybele" named by Aristophanes (*Birds* 873–75) and the "great mother Kybele" of Euripides (*Bacchae* 78–79); on these and related passages, see above, notes 18 and 20.

76. Strabo 10.3.12; cf. 12.5.3.

77. The three Phrygian sites labeled "Cybele" on map 62 of the *Barrington Atlas* (Talbert 2000), e.g., are rock-cut monuments plausibly associated with the Phrygian Mother, but do not correspond to an independently known ancient toponym.

78. Hipponax fr. 156 (West, from Tzetzes, commentary on Lycophron *Alexandra* 1170): ὁ Ἱππῶναξ Κύβηλιν τὴν Ῥέαν λέγει, παρὰ τὸ ἐν Κυβέλλᾳ πόλει Φρυγίας τιμᾶσθαι.

79. Stephanus of Byzantium s.v. Κυβέλεια, citing Hecataeus of Miletus (sixth century B.C.E.) *FGrHist* 1 F 230, Herodian Grammaticus (second century C.E.), and Peisander of Laranda in book 10 of his Ἡρωϊκαὶ Θεογαμίαι (*Heroic Divine Marriages*, probably third century C.E.).

bele: "*Kybelon:* A mountain in Phrygia, where there is a pure shrine of Kybele the Mother. Alexander Polyhistor says in his book on Bithynia: 'It is probable that Kybele was named after the mountain.'"[80] Other lexicographers report that not only mountains, but caves, and simply "places" are named after this goddess: "*Kybela:* Mountains of Phrygia; also caves; also bedchambers."[81] "*In the Kybelioi:* In the places of Rhea, for Rhea is Kybele, . . . and Kybela are the mountains of Phrygia, where she is worshipped."[82]

This identification of the Mother of the Gods with distinctive features of the Phrygian landscape, attested as early as her names appear in Greek authors, echoes the manner in which the memory of Midas had become a feature of the natural landscape. Testimony to this identification of the Mother of the Gods, as the Mountain Mother and as Kybele, with features of the earth is even stronger than in the case of Midas, both in the number of literary attestations and in terms of physical evidence. For while the tomb of Midas with its inscribed monument, as it was known to the Greeks, is preserved only in literary memory, archaic rock-cut monuments in the highlands of Phrygia still exist to demonstrate that the deity known to the Greeks as the Mother of the Gods and as Kybele was manifest to her worshippers especially at prominent points in the natural landscape. In the most impressive of these archaic monuments, the Mother is explicitly connected with the memory of King Midas.

In the Phrygian highlands west of Gordium, where the headwaters of the Sangarius River rise, not far from the headwaters of the Hermus and the Maeander rivers, are many reliefs in the form of simple niches and more elaborate architectural facades cut into natural outcrops and rock faces.[83] The simple and the elaborate monuments alike are often located in the vicinity of water sources.[84] The oldest and most monumental of these reliefs are archaic,

---

80. Alexander Polyhistor *FGrHist* 273 F 12, from the *Etymologicum Magnum* 542, 54: Κύβελον, ὄρος ἐν Φρυγίᾳ. ἔνθα Μητρὸς τῆς Κυβέλης ἱερὸν ἅγιον ἐστίν. Ἀλέξανδρος δὲ ὁ Πολυΐστωρ ἐν τῷ Περὶ Βιθυνίας "ἔοικεν οὖν Κυβέλη ἀπὸ τοῦ ὄρους κληθῆναι."

81. Hesychius s.v. Κύβελα· ὄρη Φρυγίας. καὶ ἄντρα. καὶ θάλαμοι.

82. *Suda* s.v. Κυβελίοις· τοῖς τῆς Ῥέας. Κυβέλη γὰρ ἡ Ῥέα. . . . Κύβελα γὰρ ὄρη Φρυγίας, ἔνθα ἐτιμᾶτο. See also Diodorus 3.58.1 (the infant Kybele was exposed "on the mountain [in Phrygia] called Kybelon"); and scholion to Aristophanes *Birds* 876: "He calls Rhea Kybele from the Kybela Mountains; for she is a mountain goddess."

83. On the monuments of the Phrygian highlands generally, see Gabriel 1965, 51–90; Haspels 1971, 73–93; Roller 1999, 84–105. Barnett 1953 interprets the archaic monuments; Akurgal 1961, 86–110, offers stylistic analysis; Sams 2000, 1156, discusses them in the context of a survey of Phrygian culture. Other recent studies and interpretations include Özkaya 1997, Berndt-Ersöz 1998, and Vassileva 2001.

84. Barnett 1953, 80–82, recognizes the significance of the proximity of most Phrygian rock-cut facades of western Phrygia to water sources. See also Haspels 1971, 99 n. 140, who argues that proximity to water cannot be the sole significance of the Phrygian facades; and Roller 1999, 43 (and nn. 10, 11), 138, 211, who notes several monuments near water sources.

Figure 2. Arslankaya, a rock-cut architectural facade in the Phrygian high-lands with a relief in the doorway depicting the Phrygian Mother standing between two lions, seventh or sixth century B.C.E. (Photo: C. H. Emilie Haspels, The Highlands of Phrygia [© 1971, Princeton University Press; renewed PUP 1999], reprinted by permission of Princeton University Press).

seventh or sixth century in date, and generally take the form of the ornamental facade of a building with a gabled pediment. The chief architectural feature of these facades is a monumental doorway form of a central niche. In a few instances, a standing human form, identifiable as an image of the Phrygian Mother, is carved from the bedrock in the center of the niche. (See figure 2.) In other cases, it is clear from rock-cut dowel holes that portable or perishable images were erected in these niches. Imitating the form of freestanding buildings yet formed out of living rock, these facades are generally considered to be cult monuments of the Phrygian Mother, appropriate to her identification in Greek sources as the mistress of mountains and springs. The precise nature of and occasions for their cultic use remain obscure.

Inscriptions in Old Phrygian sometimes accompany these elaborate facades, and are present on some of the simpler rock-cut monuments in the Phrygian highlands as well. Some of the inscriptions invoke the goddess known to Greeks as the Mother of the Gods by calling her, most often, simply *Matar* (Mother), occasionally *Matar Kubileya* or *Kubeleya,* whence her Greek name Kybele.[85] The most famous archaic Phrygian inscription, on the so-called Midas Monument (Yazılıkaya, figure 3), a rock-cut facade below the archaic Phrygian citadel known today as Midas City, bears the dedication of one Ates to Midas (*Midai,* in the dative) with the titles *Lavagtaei* (Leader of the Host) and *Vanaktei* (Lord.)[86] The inscription tops the most famous and elaborate gabled facade in the Phrygian highlands, which is known from it as the Midas Monument. The central niche in the facade accommodated a movable statue of the Mother, whose name, *Matar,* occurs in Phrygian graffiti in several places within the niche, along with Midas' name. The Midas Monument most likely dates to the late seventh or early sixth century B.C.E., and is a posthumous dedication to Midas as a heroized or deified king.[87]

85. On the identification of Phrygian *Matar* as *Matar Kubileya/Kubeleya,* or Kybele, see Brixhe 1979. The derivation of the name Kybele is discussed further in chapter 3.

86. On the Midas Monument, see Akurgal 1961, 110 and plate 67; Gabriel 1965, 51–72 and plates 24–33; Haspels 1971, 73–76 and 289–91, and plates 1, 7–13, 510, 598–99; Van Loon 1991, plate 35; Roller 1999, 69 and figure 64. On the Midas Inscription see Lejeune 1969; Brixhe and Lejeune 1984, M-01, pages 6–17 and plates I–VII. On the titles of Midas, see note 88 below. The possible identity of the dedicator, Ates, is discussed in chapter 4 at note 40.

87. Criteria for dating the Midas Monument are subjective, and opinions are divided between an early date close to the beginning of the seventh century, in the time of the historical King Midas (see below, with notes 132–34), and a date in the first half of the sixth century. Gabriel (1965, 71), Haspels (1971, 104, 108–9, 143–46), and Mellink (1993, 154) favor the earlier date, partly on the strength of the resemblance of the decorative scheme to the decorations on wooden furniture in the Great Tumulus at Gordium. Akurgal (1961, 86, 108, 110) compares the Phrygian motifs to elements found in Greek art and dates the Midas Monument and similar rock-cut facades no earlier than the sixth century. Brixhe and Lejeune (1984, 6) summarize the various datings that have been suggested; epigraphic criteria allow an early date, in their view, but are ultimately indecisive. My opinion is closest to Akurgal's. (See chapter 4,

Figure 3. Midas Monument (Yazılıkaya), a rock-cut architectural facade at Midas City in the Phrygian highlands, with Old
Phrygian inscription recording dedication by Ates to Midas
above the pediment to left, seventh or sixth century B.C.E.
(Photo: C. H. Emilie Haspels, The Highlands of Phrygia
[© 1971, Princeton University Press; renewed PUP 1999],
reprinted by permission of Princeton University Press).

at note 40, for possible historical considerations.) Roller (1999, 100–102) analyzes the criteria for dating the Midas Monument; she believes that the Midas Inscription is most likely posthumous (and Mellink 1991, 641, allows this possibility), and provides evidence consistent with
a date at almost any time within the seventh or first half of the sixth century. (She prefers a seventh-century date.) The Midas Monument appears to be among the earliest such Phrygian
facades, the majority of which were probably carved in the sixth century; a few are probably

From the titles inscribed on this monument, Midas is clearly invoked as an archetype of sovereignty.[88] The association here of a heroized or deified Midas with the divinity *Matar* attests that Midas' sovereign authority was in some way associated with the Phrygian Mother of the Gods. It appears that the Phrygian Mother of the Gods, the personification of nurturing forces in nature, and Phrygian Midas, the personification of ideal kingship, were envisioned as attributes of each other. The ideal king, in other words, is seen as the one who evokes the beneficial forces of nature, and the divine forces of nature in turn sustain the ideal king. The Midas Monument, by this hypothesis, would be a monument to sovereignty and divinity intertwined. This would indeed be an awesome symbol of power whose native home would be identified by posterity with Phrygia.

## THE MOTHER OF MIDAS

Midas' kingship was identified, by Phrygian legend reported in Greek sources, with the riches that the earth yields to humanity, both in agriculture and in gold. In both cases, Midas' kingship was described as the aboriginal source of these foundations of civilized life. Such origins are manifestly ahistorical, in that they ignore evidence that kingship and agriculture, if not also the extraction of Pactolan gold, were far more ancient than Midas. Greeks were aware that rival claims were made by other peoples, but alternative traditions could not supplant the archetypal image of kingship provided by Midas, and the more powerful archetype underlying the kingship of Midas, that of his mother, the divine Mother.

Herodotus bears witness to the strength of ahistorical Phrygian traditions in the strange tale that he tells at the opening of his second book, devoted to the antiquities of Egypt. Ever since the reign of Psammetichus I (ca. 664–610), he relates, the Egyptians have acknowledged that the Phrygians were "the first of mankind," older even than the Egyptians, and it was in the Phrygian language that the first articulate human voice spoke, and that *bekos*, the Phrygian word for bread, was the first word spoken.[89] Herodotus states that Psammetichus himself established the fundamental priority of Phrygia by his famous experiment, isolating two infants from all human speech until they

---

fifth-century. (See Haspels 1971, 104–8, and the reviews of scholarship by Naumann 1983, 56–62; Borgeaud 1996, 22–24; Roller 1999, 98–102.)

88. The Homeric and Mycenaean resonances of the titles of Midas, *Lavagtaei* and *Vanaktei* (cf. Mycenaean Greek *Lawagetas* and *Wanax*), are much discussed. Huxley 1959 and de Graaf 1989 emphasize the possible Bronze Age ancestry to Phrygian kingship implied by these titles. Cassola 1997, 146, links these distinctively Greek titles with the influence of Homeric tradition in archaic Phrygia. Börker-Klähn 1997, 259 points out that *Lavagtaei* denotes Midas' unique position as "Heerführer" over all lesser kings within his domain.

89. Herodotus 2.2; cf. 2.15.3.

spontaneously uttered a primal plea for sustenance in what proved to be the Phrygian language. The story of Psammetichus' discovery was told in several versions, Herodotus affirms, by Egyptians and by Greeks.[90] Bread, language, and humankind itself were thus elements in a strong tradition of aboriginal generation from the land of Phrygia, deserving of wide respect, as Herodotus' relation of Psammetichus' experiment implies.[91] Whether or not Psammetichus actually conducted such an experiment is not a concern here; what is significant is the fact that such a discovery was widely reported and attributed to Psammetichus well before Herodotus' day.[92] Although neither Midas nor his mother appears in this story, the story attests to the wide recognition of Phrygia as the place where agriculture was discovered, a discovery that other accounts attribute to the son of Midas, and it attests to the fame of Phrygia spreading abroad during the period in which Phrygian monuments to the Mother, along with Midas himself, were being carved.

Later Greek and Latin sources make the association of Midas and the divine Phrygian Mother explicit. The Mother was Midas' mother. The Roman mythographer Hyginus states that Midas was the son of the Mater Dea, the Divine Mother, whom he also names as Cybele.[93] Lactantius Placidus' commentary on Ovid's *Metamorphoses* reports that Midas was regarded as the son of Magna Mater, the Great Mother, and cites Hesiod as an authority for this tradition.[94] The value of the citation of Hesiod in this context is uncertain, and these authors might be dismissed as late and unreliable witnesses to earlier beliefs were it not for an accumulation of testimony to the same effect, agreeing with better-attested Phrygian traditions, and consistent with the interpretation of the archaic Phrygian monuments suggested above.

Plutarch notes that the deity known to the Romans as Bona Dea, the Good Goddess, was regarded by the Phrygians as their own, "and they say she was

90. Herodotus 2.2.5. How and Wells 1912, vol. 1, 156, suggest that Hecataeus of Miletus, writing in the late sixth century, might have been one of the Greeks known to Herodotus who related this story. It was known to Hecataeus' contemporary Hipponax (fr. 125 [West]), and is alluded to in a parody of science by Aristophanes *Clouds* 398. *Bekos* appears in the maledictions of several Neo-Phrygian funerary inscriptions: see Lubotsky 1997, 124, 126; Brixhe and Drew-Bear 1997, 87, 90–91, no. III.

91. Vannicelli 1997 explains the story in terms of Herodotus' narrative strategies; Drews 1993 cites the story as evidence of a Phrygian tradition of autochthony.

92. Note that Pausanias 1.14.2, reporting rival Greek claims to being the most ancient recipients of the gifts of Demeter, attests that "among barbarians, the Egyptians compete with the Phrygians" for this claim; cf. Pollux *Onomasticon* 4.54–55. Lucretius *De Rerum Natura* 2.611 assigns the first cultivation of grain to Phrygia.

93. Hyginus *Fabulae* 191.1 and 274.6.

94. Hesiod fr. 352 (MW). This passage may derive from the Hesiodic *Catalogue of Women,* which was probably compiled within the sixth century.

the mother of King Midas."[95] Under the heading "Goddess of Midas" (ἡ Μίδα θεός), Hesychius relates the following: "The subjects of Midas revered the goddess of Midas and pledged oaths by her, who some say was his mother, who was honored highly."[96] According to the *Suda* lexicon, these honors included mournful music accompanied by the *aulos*, which "they say Midas later performed as a funerary dirge around the altar, wishing to deify his mother when she had died."[97]

Hellenistic mythographers were familiar with the Phrygian tradition describing the Mother, or Kybele, as a mortal woman whose wisdom and nurturing love earned her divine honors as the Mother of the Gods. This tradition was irreconcilable with theogonic narratives that traced the descent of all gods from primordially divine origins, so the encyclopedic scholarship of the Hellenistic world had to treat the Phrygian tradition as an excursus from more universalizing narratives. So, for example, Diodorus introduces the story of Phrygian Kybele as an aside. She was an unwanted daughter born to Meion, the king of Lydia and Phrygia, and his wife, Dindyme, according to Diodorus. The infant was abandoned on a mountain called Kybelon, where she was raised by wild beasts and grew to become a beautiful and wise woman who taught rites of healing, purification, and initiation through music. Marsyas was attracted into her following, and eventually, after Kybele (as she became known) had passed away, King Midas took the lead in establishing divine rites in her honor.[98]

In this account, Kybele was a woman who wandered the earth teaching rites of purification and attracting an enthusiastic following through the inspiration of her music. These are exactly the attributes of Kybele as depicted by Euripides in his *Bacchae*.[99] There Kybele is also called Rhea, and the story of her mortal origin and subsequent deification is left out of the account. (Euripides focuses the theme of ambiguous divinity on Dionysus.) But the

---

95. Plutarch *Caesar* 9.3, referring to Ἀγαθή (Latin *Bona Dea*), "whom the Greeks call Γυναικεία, 'the Women's Goddess,'" adding that "the Greeks call her the unnamable one [τὴν ἄρρητον] among the mothers of Dionysus." On the identity of Bona Dea with the Magna Mater, see Brouwer 1978; on the resemblance of her cult to the Thesmophoria, see Versnel 1993, 228–88.

96. Hesychius s.v. Μίδα θεός · οἱ ὑπὸ Μίδα βασιλευθέντες ἐσέβοντο καὶ ὤμνυον τὴν Μίδα θεόν, ἥν τινες λέγουσιν μητέρα αὐτοῦ, ἣν ἐκτετιμῆσθαι.

97. *Suda* s.v. Ἔλεγος θρῆνος ... τὸν δὲ αὐλὸν ὕστερον ἐπικήδειον Μίδαν, φασί, τὸν Γορδίου βασιλεύοντα περιβώμιον ποιῆσαι βουλόμενον τὴν ἑαυτοῦ μητέρα ἀποθεῶσαι τελευτήσασαν. Cf. Pollux *Onomasticon* 4.53–55 on the θρῆνος that originated with the death of Lityerses son of Midas (above, note 56).

98. Diodorus 3.58–59. Cf. Clement *Protrepticus* 2.12, and Justin 11.7.14 (discussed below) on the role of Midas. Diodorus 5.48–49 offers a variant theogony of Kybele associated with the Samothracian Mysteries. (Cf. Apollodorus *Library* 3.12.1.)

99. Euripides *Bacchae*, esp. 12–87, 120–69; cf. Apollodorus *Library* 3.5.1.

idea of gods who had once been mortals was certainly known to Euripides and his contemporaries. Prodicus of Ceos advanced an account of Demeter and Dionysus as mortals who taught agriculture and viticulture, and who were accorded divine honors after their deaths in recognition of their gifts to humanity.[100] The argument that the gods familiar to the Greeks were once mortals was a key element in the suspicion that sophists like Prodicus were atheists.[101] The cosmogonic ideas of Prodicus are ridiculed by Aristophanes in his *Birds,* the very play in which Aristophanes also ridicules superstitious Phrygians and Lydians, but also honors the divinity of "Mistress Kybele, . . . mother of gods and men" (perhaps with comic irony).[102] Diagoras of Melos, who is also made fun of in the *Birds* and who was remembered centuries later as "the Atheist," offended against the Mysteries of Demeter at this time through his writings in a book known by the title *Phrygian Stories* (Φρύγιοι Λόγοι).[103] It is highly likely that the sophistic tradition, which included treatises on Phrygian lore, took up the question of the identification of the Mother of the Gods with the mother of Midas.

Men of learning like Herodotus, Euripides, Aristophanes, Prodicus, and Diagoras were well aware of the contradictions inherent in the juxtaposition of Greek and Phrygian theologies. In view of the prominence of Midas in archaic and classical Greek lore about Phrygia, the connection of the great Phrygian king with the deification of the woman who gave fundamental gifts to humanity must have been known to them as it was to later Hellenistic mythographers. But Diagoras' example demonstrates that, in the political climate

100. Prodicus DK 84 B 5, discussed by Guthrie 1969, 238–42 and 279; and by Henrichs 1984. Guthrie and Henrichs both draw attention to the reflection of Prodicus' thought in Euripides' reference to Demeter and Dionysus in *Bacchae* 274–85. See note 3, above, where testimony to the assimilation of the Mother of the Gods to Demeter is cited.

101. Guthrie 1969, 235–47, surveys the ancient testimony concerning the nature of the atheism alleged of Diagoras, Prodicus, and Critias, and its relationship to Plato's views on atheism. On the intellectual and political context of these allegations, see Dover 1976; Ostwald 1986, 274–90.

102. At the opening of a cosmogonic hymn tracing the origin of the gods in the manner of Hesiod, Aristophanes *Birds* 692 pointedly ridicules Prodicus. On superstitious Phrygians and Lydians, see chapter 1, note 106. On "Mistress Kybele," see notes 18 and 75 above.

103. The nature and contents of Diagoras' Φρύγιοι Λόγοι are unknown (as is the meaning of its alternative title, Ἀποπυργίζοντες Λόγοι): see Jacoby 1959, 24–31; Woodbury 1965; Guthrie 1969, 236 n. 2. The title is attested by Tatian *Oratio ad Graecos* 27 (= Winiarczyk T 68 [cf. T 10 and T 93–96]; *FGrHist* 800 F 6). Note that a Φρύγιος Λόγος is listed among the works of Democritus of Abdera (Diogenes 9.49), who is said, in a late tradition, to have been a teacher of Diagoras (*Suda* s.v. Διαγόρας = Winiarczyk T 9). Jacoby (28 n. 231) and Woodbury (201), repeating the commentary in DK 68 B 299e, regard the Φρύγιος Λόγος of Democritus as an anonymous work, probably of the third century B.C.E.; both express doubts, therefore, that Φρύγιοι Λόγοι could be a title contemporary to Diagoras (so too Rives 2005). The present discussion obviates objections to Φρύγιοι Λόγοι as a description, if not a title, of a genuine work of the late fifth century. Aristophanes *Birds* 1072–73 parodies a decree condemning Diagoras; Lysias 6, *Against Andocides* 17–18, describes Diagoras' offense against the Eleusinian Mysteries as "by words" (λόγῳ: i.e., probably in writing).

of Athens of the late fifth century, a bold theological exposition, especially one that gave a privileged place to an Asiatic tyrant, might lead to a charge of impiety.[104] Phrygian theology had to be treated with discretion, and it should come as no surprise, therefore, that no exposition of the deification of the mother of Midas survives from a fifth-century Greek source.

An old Phrygian story accounting for the deification of the mother of Midas first appears in Greek sources that relate the cutting of the Gordian Knot by Alexander of Macedon. The existing accounts of this episode, like the histories of Alexander generally, were all written in the Roman imperial period, but it is widely recognized that they derive from accounts written in the lifetime of Alexander or soon thereafter. The recording of the Phrygian legend of the Gordian Knot, in particular, owes much to Callisthenes' history of Alexander's march.[105] Callisthenes, whom we have already met as the source of the legend of Midas and the sacrifice of Anchyrus at Celaenae, is known from other references to his work to have been interested in the lore of Lydia and Phrygia, and of Midas in particular.[106] The story of the Gordian Knot, related by Callisthenes and his near contemporaries as an old Phrygian legend, is narrated in greatest detail by Arrian:[107]

> When Alexander arrived at Gordium, he was seized with a desire to go up into the citadel, where the palace of Gordius and his son Midas was located, in order to see the cart of Gordius and the knot tying the yoke of the cart. There was an elaborate story about this cart current among the inhabitants of the area, to the effect that Gordius was a poor man among the Phrygians long ago, and he had a small piece of land to till, and two yoke of oxen. Gordius used one of these for plowing and the other to draw the cart. One day, while he was plowing, an eagle flew down onto the yoke and remained sitting there until the time came for the unyoking of the oxen at the end of the day. Being alarmed at what he saw, he went to the Telmessian soothsayers to consult them about

104. Note that the condemnation of Diagoras parodied by Aristophanes *Birds* 1072–73 is directly juxtaposed with a condemnation of tyranny. On the political dangers of theological speculation at this time, see Dover 1976 and Ostwald 1986, 274–90; and see chapter 8 at note 50.

105. On Callisthenes as primary source, see Pearson 1960, 38–39; Prandi 1985, 73, 88, 91–93. The variant accounts of what Alexander actually did with the knot are examined by Tarn 1948, 262–65; Pearson 157, 160. Frei 1972 and Roller 1984 consider the relation of these accounts to Phrygian tradition. Burke 2002 proposes that elements of the Phrygian tradition of the Gordian Knot can be found in Hittite ritual texts.

106. See Pearson 1960, 39–42; Prandi 1985, 87–93, 106.

107. Arrian *Anabasis* 2.3.1–6, translated E. J. Chinnock, with modifications. Plutarch *Alexander* 18.1–2 reports that Alexander "listened to the account that the barbarians place their faith in," which promised "kingship of the inhabited world" (βασιλεῖ γενέσθαι τῆς οἰκουμένης) to him who undoes the knot. (This theme is discussed further in chapter 5.) Variants of the story of the Gordian Knot are related by Justin 11.7.4–15 and Curtius 3.1.14–18; abbreviated versions are related by Aelian *De Natura Animalium* 13.1 and by a scholion to Euripides *Hippolytus* 671. Their accounts are compared by Frei 1972 and Roller 1984.

the sign from the deity; for the Telmessians were skillful in interpreting the meaning of divine manifestations, and the power of divination has been bestowed not only upon the men, but also upon their wives and children from generation to generation. When Gordius was driving his cart near a certain village of the Telmessians, he met a maiden fetching water from a spring, and he told her how the sign of the eagle had appeared to him. Since she herself was of the prophetic race, she instructed him to return to the very spot and offer sacrifice to Zeus the King. Gordius asked her to accompany him and instruct him how to perform the sacrifice. He offered the sacrifice in the way the girl suggested, and afterwards married her. A son was born to them named Midas. When Midas was grown to be a man, handsome and valiant, at that time factional strife was troubling the Phrygians, who received an oracle telling them that a cart would bring them a king who would put an end to their factional strife. While they were still deliberating about this very matter, Midas arrived with his father and mother, and stopped near the assembly, cart and all. They, comparing the oracular response with this occurrence, decided that this was the person whom the god meant that the cart would bring. They therefore appointed Midas king; and he, putting an end to their factional strife, dedicated his father's cart in the citadel as a thank-offering to Zeus the King for sending the eagle. In addition to this the following saying was current concerning the cart, that whoever could untie the knot of the yoke of this cart was destined to rule over Asia.

The "elaborate story" ($\lambda\acute{o}\gamma o\varsigma$ ... $\pi o\lambda\acute{v}\varsigma$) told by the locals of Gordium thus explains not just the cart dedicated in the shrine of Zeus the King, but also the portents that foretold Midas' kingship over the Phrygians. The story assigns a decisive role in the creation of the kingship of Midas to an unnamed Telmessian girl, a *parthenos,* who was on her way to draw water. She had the inspired wisdom to know the meaning of the portents that appeared to Gordius, she knew the appropriate measures to take, she united with Gordius in marriage, she gave birth to Midas, and she rode with her son on the day he was acclaimed king of the Phrygians. This story not only provides the background for all of the Greek references to the Mother of the Gods as the mother of Midas, but, more significantly, it also explains the iconography and chief attributes of the Mother as she appears in archaic Phrygian art.

Sculpted reliefs from central Phrygia depict the Mother standing in a niche or doorway, clothed in a long garment and wearing a tall *polos,* or headdress, holding a bird of prey in one hand and either a bowl or a pitcher in the other.[108] (See figure 4.) It is possible that sculptures of this type were

108. Examples of central Phrygian sculptures and reliefs of the Mother are illustrated in Akurgal 1961, plates 60–62; Naumann 1983, plates 5.2–4 and 6.1; Mellink 1983, plates 70, 71.1, 72.1–3 (taken to be a male figure by Mellink, female by Naumann), 73.1–2; DeVries 1990, figure 38; Van Loon 1991, plate 39a, b; Roller 1999, figures 7–9 and 12. Roller (81–83) reviews the evidence for dating these sculptures.

Figure 4. Relief of the Phrygian Mother standing in the doorway of an architectural facade holding a water pitcher and a bird of prey, seventh or sixth century B.C.E., from Ankara.

produced as early as the eighth century, but they are more certainly established by the later seventh or early sixth century, contemporaneous to the rock-cut facades of the Phrygian highlands, where images of this type were carved or installed in the monumental doorways of the facades. The attributes found on the better-preserved sculptures of the Phrygian Mother can be directly related to the story of the mother of Midas told at Gordium, and can be paralleled in other accounts related by Greek sources.

The bird of prey, either an eagle or a hawk, was a sign of sovereignty according to an iconographic tradition that was widespread around the eastern Mediterranean in the first millennium B.C.E. Among Greeks the eagle was regarded as a sign of Zeus and a royal portent; among Egyptians, and among those, like the Phoenicians, who adopted elements of Egyptian iconography, the hawk or falcon was the symbol of Horus, son of Isis, and a sign of kingship; Xenophon states that a golden eagle was a royal standard in the army of the Persians.[109] In an Anatolian context, Aelian states that the eagle was the signifier of the future kingship of Midas, and elsewhere he reports that a hawk of a variety called *mermnos* was sacred to the Mother of the Gods.[110] The *mermnos* hawk evidently gave its name to the Mermnad dynasty founded by Gyges in Lydia. Relating the story of the foundation of the Mermnad dynasty, Nicolaus of Damascus tells of two giant eagles that appeared as portents over the bedchamber of a princess of Mysia, indicating that she would couple with two kings.[111] The mother of Midas in the story told to Alexander was one who knew the meaning of such birds. The bird of prey held by the archaic images of the Mother was thus a symbol of the sovereignty that she conveyed.

Water vessels signify the connection of the Mother with springs and the flowing, life-giving waters of the earth. It was in the act of bearing water that the mother-to-be of Midas foretold his kingship, and the conjunction of these activities probably alludes to an ideological link between sanctified kingship and water as a life-sustaining force of the earth. The deity who holds a water vessel in Phrygian reliefs is depicted standing in a doorway, and this feature too alludes to the legend of the mother of Midas. In the version of the story of the knot told by Justin, Gordius encounters the prophetic maiden when she is standing in a gateway.[112] The Phrygian rock-cut facades depict monumental doorways in the vicinity of water sources, therefore suggesting that

109. On the eagle as a sign of Zeus displayed especially to kings and their sons, see, e.g., Homer *Iliad* 8.245–51, 24.306–21; Pindar *Pythian* 1.6. Hesiod *Works and Days* 202–12 describes the hawk as a portent for kings. On the falcon of Horus and its adoption in Phoenician and Levantine art, see Keel and Uehlinger 1998, 205–6, 351–52, 377–78. On the Persian standard, see Xenophon *Cyropaedia* 7.1.4.

110. The eagle of Midas: Aelian *De Natura Animalium* 13.1. The hawk (μέρμνος) of the Mother of the Gods: Aelian *De Natura Animalium* 12.4. On the hawk and the Mermnads, see Fauth 1968.

111. Nicolaus of Damascus *FGrHist* 90 F 47.6, relating an alternative version of the story of Gyges and the wife of King Candaules told by Herodotus 1.7–12.

112. Justin 11.7.6, where Gordius encounters the beautiful maiden standing *obviam in porta*. Roller 1984, 266, recognizes the connection between this motif and the standing images of the goddess in the doorway of her western Phrygian rock-cut facades. Rein 1993, 38, summarizes this characteristic well: "An affinity for entrances and city boundaries emerges as a meaningful element of the iconography of the Phrygian Mother." Among the examples that Rein lists, note especially the presence of a statue of the Mother in a naiskos within a sixth-century gateway of Hattusa-Boğazköy: Bittel 1970, 150–52. Compare also the setting and the sovereign-sustaining attributes of Wisdom (Sophia) described in *Proverbs* 8.

the two versions of the meeting of Gordius and his bride-to-be are identical in their essential points. An encounter with an image of a beautiful maiden standing in a great doorway in such a setting could be understood as a recreation of Gordius' meeting with the wise maiden, the future mother of Midas, according to either version of the story.

Springs and running water are often mentioned in Greek sources when the Mother of the Gods is involved, especially as Mountain Mother.[113] The Mother is also associated with the young women who draw water from springs. Pindar invokes the Mother of the Gods in a context that places her by a doorway (*prothyron*) and near the spring of Dirce at Thebes, where "maidens often sing to the Mother."[114] Plutarch gives an account of a "bronze statue of a maiden called 'the water bearer,'" a statue taken from Athens by Xerxes that was later seen by Themistocles in the Temple of the Mother at Sardis, where it had been dedicated by the Persians.[115] The classical Greek depictions of the Mother of the Gods enthroned regularly show her holding a *phialē*, or libation bowl, just as she does in some of her Phrygian images. In all cases, the vessel probably alludes to the beneficent giving of water by the goddess.[116]

The Phrygian legend related to Alexander at Gordium depicts the mother of Midas as she who possesses the wisdom, the fertility, and the nurturing ability to engender the ideal king. The Phrygian rock-cut facades and reliefs depicting the Mother, and in one case invoking Midas, represent these personal attributes as the universal qualities of a deity and associate them with natural features, mountains and water sources, of the earth. At the center of this nexus of attributes is the mother of Midas, the matrix of sovereignty, who is the Phrygian *Matar*, or *Matar Kubeleya*, and who is known to the Greeks as the Mountain Mother, Kybele, and the Mother of the Gods. Herein lie the traits of Phrygian legend that deal with men and women who were born and died in the past, and yet who are honored as the source of gifts that civilize humanity, and who are regarded, in effect, as divinities. This is what some Greeks condemned as the godless (*atheos*) quality of Phrygian

113. See above, notes 73 and 74.

114. Pindar *Pythian* 3.77–79 refers to singing the sort of "invocation that maidens often sing to the Mother together with Pan before my door [παρ' ἐμὸν πρόθυρον]." Most commentators take ἐμὸν πρόθυρον simply as the door to Pindar's own house. Robertson 1996, 265–66, suggests that it might refer to a gate of Thebes. The frequent songs of maidens by this πρόθυρον would be better explained, however, if we understand the πρόθυρον to be the doorway of a naiskos by the spring of Dirce, where Pausanias 9.25.3 identifies Pindar's shrine of the Mother Dindymene. Such a shrine would therefore resemble the facades of the Mother in Phrygia.

115. Plutarch *Themistocles* 31.1. This late archaic bronze kore calls to mind the bronze kore of the Midas epigram, where flowing waters are mentioned (above, at note 57).

116. Simon 1953 studies depictions of deities pouring libations from a phiale, particularly as an attribute of the Mother of the Gods (79–87), although she does not bring Phrygian evidence into consideration.

religion, while others, like Prodicus and Diagoras, and possibly Pythagore-
ans like Philolaus, appear to have found such notions to be expressive of
fundamental truths.[117]

SOVEREIGNTY AND THE GODS OF PHRYGIA

From the earliest evidence for the recognition of Midas among the Greeks,
possibly from his own lifetime, the accomplishments of Midas were closely
associated with the favor of the gods. Midas' prosperity and the fame of his
royal judgment were honored among Greeks who came to Delphi in the seventh century, for, as Herodotus notes, "Midas dedicated the royal throne on
which he used to sit when he rendered judgments, and it is a sight worth seeing."[118] Wise judgment was an essential quality of Midas' kingship, according to the story told at Gordium, since he first exhibited his kingly authority by resolving factional strife in the assembly of the Phrygians. Hesiod, a
close contemporary of Midas and of his dedication at Delphi, describes the
qualities of just leadership as the attributes of "god-nurtured kings" ($\delta\iota o\tau\rho\epsilon$-
$\phi\acute{\epsilon}\epsilon\varsigma$ $\beta\alpha\sigma\iota\lambda\tilde{\eta}\epsilon\varsigma$), by which he was referring both to living kings, of the sort who
might appreciate his poetry, and to legendary kings who were, he tells us,
actually born from gods.[119] The associations of divinity and sovereignty that
Hesiod describes are given concrete expression in the Midas Monument. This
union of sovereignty and divinity, in monuments, legends, and cult practices
after Midas' lifetime, has distinctive implications for the motives behind the
cult of the Phrygian Mother.

Sovereignty and divinity are inextricable, according to the cult of kingship born in Phrygia. To a remarkable degree, sacred knowledge (the prophetic gift of the mother of Midas, and her instructions to Gordius) and ritual practice (the rites and ceremonies established by Midas, and especially
their distinctive music) are in essence sovereignty itself. This is implicit in
the story of the kingship of Midas as told by Arrian, and it is explicit in the
conclusion to the same tale in Justin's account, where Midas "filled Phrygia

117. On the original meaning of *atheos*, "atheist," as "godless" rather than "denier of gods,"
see Woodbury 1965, 208. Woodbury (179, 197–99) also notices that the fragments of Diagoras' poetry give no hint of radical atheism, but seem rather to attest a conventional piety. On
Prodicus as a forerunner of the Euhemerism later expounded by Euhemerus of Messene and
Hecataeus of Abdera, see Henrichs 1984. On Philolaus and the Mother of the Gods, see note
6 above, and note Pythagoras' alleged interest in Midas: above, note 61.

118. Herodotus 1.14.3. The throne of Midas is still worth seeing at Delphi today. Keith
DeVries (2002) has made the plausible suggestion that the oriental ivory figure of a young warrior with a lion at his side found at Delphi (illustrated in Boardman 1980, figure 39, e.g.), a
figure that is in fact a furniture attachment, is Phrygian work dating to the late eighth or the
seventh century and may be part of the throne of Midas seen by Herodotus.

119. Hesiod *Theogony* 81–96.

with religious cults, and this, throughout his life, protected him more effectively than could an armed guard."[120]

Cult practice and the exercise of sovereignty are still more graphically linked in an account of the means by which Midas extended his dominion. The story is related among the military stratagems collected by Polyaenus:[121]

> Midas, pretending that he was going to perform rites for the Great Gods, led out the Phrygians in the night with *auloi*, tympana, and cymbals, and with hidden swords. Townspeople came out of their houses to see the procession; those who were playing the tympana and cymbals slew the spectators as they came into the streets, took possession of their houses, which lay open, and proclaimed Midas tyrant.

This tale has no specific setting, and therefore describes no particular historical event of the reign of Midas. Rather, it describes a concept underlying his kingship, or irresistible tyranny: his ritual procession is conquest. Opening one's door to the spectacle of the Mother's rites is prelude to subjection to the king who celebrates those rites. The result is the appropriation of conquered land, and the tyranny of Midas.

Implicit in this tradition is the idea that the rituals that made Midas great could be adopted by others to their benefit, but always with a sense that the resulting strength or prosperity was due to ritual practices that originated in the cult of the Phrygian Mother. Polyaenus tells a similar story of Artemisia, queen of Caria in the time of Xerxes, who captured the city of Latmus by deploying the musical and enthusiastic rites of a procession of the Mother of the Gods.[122] Nicolaus of Damascus tells a story of dynastic rivalry among the Neleid rulers of Miletus, in which Phrygian rites play a similar role. The ruling king, Leodamas, was slain by a rival, and Leodamas' children and supporters fled from Miletus to Assesus, where they were besieged by their enemies. Appealing to an oracle for advice, they were told to await the arrival of "helpers from Phrygia, who would exact vengeance for the murder of Leodamas and deliver the Milesians from their troubles." In due course two young Phrygian men arrived bringing a "covered basket containing sacred objects of the Cabeiri." They declared that they had been sent by a god's command to convey sacred objects from Phrygia for the benefit of the people at Assesus and Miletus. The Phrygians were welcomed at Assesus by the Milesians, who "vowed to institute the sacred objects among themselves and grant them

---

120. Justin 11.7.14.

121. Polyaenus *Stratagems* 7.5. The "Great Gods" ($\mu\epsilon\gamma\acute{\alpha}\lambda o\iota\ \theta\epsilon o\acute{\iota}$) in the passage are related to the Cabeiri of Samothrace, and their rites were identified with those of the Phrygian Mother. (See Diodorus 5.49.1–4, Strabo 10.3.7, and the passage from Nicolaus of Damascus discussed below.)

122. Polyaenus 8.53.4.

honors" if they achieved success. Thereupon the Phrygians performed their customary rituals, and ordered the Milesians "to arm themselves, and to march en masse against their enemies, while the sacred objects were conveyed in front of their phalanx." Upon their doing these things, a "god-sent terror" (δείματος θείου) fell on their foes, who were routed and slaughtered, and strife was brought to an end at Miletus.[123]

A march of conquest, once again, is depicted as a ritual procession, and the story, moreover, legitimizes the foundation of a Phrygian cult at Miletus. In Nicolaus' day, in the reign of Augustus, the province of Asia had adopted on its coinage the *cista mystica,* the "mystic basket" alluded to in this story of early Miletus, as the symbol of its unity and prosperity under the hand of divine providence.[124] This was the container of the mystic sacred objects that were both from Phrygia and of the Cabeiri, uniting the rites of the Mother of the Gods with those observed on Samothrace. Among neighboring peoples as well, conveyance of such a revered ritual talisman at the head of an army, accompanied by enthusiastic music, was an ancient manner of displaying sovereign power.[125]

Rituals of sovereignty and conquest like those depicted by Polyaenus and Nicolaus are attested in two stories that Herodotus tells about power originating in Asia Minor. Herodotus illustrates the ritual basis of Lydian sovereignty over the Greeks of Asia in his central story of the Lydian war to dominate Ionia. For twelve years, the Lydian kings Sadyattes and Alyattes made war on Miletus, marching through the broad valley of the Maeander River and into Milesian territory. Each year, the Lydian king[126]

> would invade at the time when the crops were ripe, with his troops marching to the sound of pipes, harps, and treble and bass reed pipes. When they reached Milesian land, they left all the houses in the countryside standing, throughout the territory, without razing or burning them or breaking into them; instead, they would destroy all the fruit trees and crops, and then return home.

---

123. Nicolaus of Damascus *FGrHist* 90 F 52. Another version of this dynastic rivalry, omitting the intervention of the Phrygians, is given by Conon *FGrHist* 26 F 1.44. Drews 1983, 17–20, attempts to assess the historical value of these accounts, and concludes that they "belong not to history but to myth" (19–20).

124. On the cistophoric tetradrachms of Asia, see Seltman 1933, 239; Woodward 1956. See also below, chapter 5, at note 96.

125. Compare Joshua's conquest of Jericho in Joshua 6, where musicians march before the shrine of the deity (the Ark). Similarly, in 2 Samuel 6:1–5, David assembles his army and places the Ark at its head, while the army danced "with all their might to the sound of singing, of lyres, lutes, tambourines, castanets, and cymbals"; and note Numbers 10:1–10, where the music of trumpets inaugurates both battle and sacrifice. Psalms 68:1–7 invokes God to lead the army of his followers and to disperse their foes, while 68:24–25 describes singers and tambourine players leading the procession of God.

126. Herodotus 1.17.

By the time of Sadyattes and Alyattes, the Mermnad kings of Lydia held sovereignty over lands that were formerly ruled by Midas. The march of the Lydian army to the accompaniment of ritual music, unopposed by any foe, was an enactment of rituals of appropriation similar to those of Midas and to those performed by the Phrygians in the same Milesian countryside. The music described by Herodotus is not incidental, or merely martial in character, and cannot be separated from the rites of the Phrygian Mother. The Spartans, who were best known among Greeks for marching to *aulos* (reed pipe) music, were believed to have received their musical tutelage from Lydia and Phrygia, and from the rites of the Mother of the Gods in particular, while violent elements of their warlike rituals in honor of Artemis Orthia were regarded as Lydian in nature.[127] It follows, a fortiori, that the music of war performed by the Lydians themselves, as Herodotus describes it, had all of the cultic associations that the Greeks recalled when they traced the musical inspiration of the Spartans to its source.

Herodotus bears witness to another instance of sovereign power based on the rites of deities of the earth in the story he tells to explain the origin of the tyranny of Gelon at Syracuse:[128]

> Gelon's ancestor, who first settled at Gela, came from the island of Telos, off Triopium, and when the settlement at Gela was made by Antiphemus and the Lindians of Rhodes, he took part in the expedition. In the course of time his descendants became priests of the Earth Goddesses [ἱροφάνται τῶν χθονίων θεῶν], an office that they have continued to hold ever since Telines came into possession of it. Telines got it in the following manner: as a result of civil strife in Gela, a number of men had been compelled to leave the town and to seek refuge in Mactorium on the neighboring hills. These people were reinstated by Telines, who accomplished the feat not by armed force, but simply by vir-

127. See Plutarch *Lycurgus* 21 on Spartans as "most musical and at the same time most warlike," and on the *aulos* as the most warlike musical instrument. Plutarch *Aristides* 17.8 mentions a violent "Procession of the Lydians" in the rites of Artemis at Sparta, noting that "some say" that the rite arose from an incident at the battle of Plataea. The association of Artemis Orthia and Lydia is part of the lore of the Asiatic origin of her statue at Sparta: see Pausanias 3.16.8. On the warlike or Pyrrhic dances of the Curetes associated with the Phrygian music of the Mother of the Gods, see the discussion of Thiemer 1979, 42–47. On the archaic cult of the Mother of the Gods in Laconia, see de la Genière 1986. The assertion by Thucydides 5.70 that the Spartans marched into battle to the sound of many *aulos* players "not for religious reasons, but in order that they might advance in unison with the rhythm," reveals that a religious explanation of this practice was in fact current in his day.

128. Herodotus 7.153, translated by A. de Sélincourt, with modifications. The χθόνιαι θεαί here are Demeter and Persephone (or Kore), as Herodotus 6.134 and testimony in the following notes unambiguously demonstrate. On the "soft and effeminate" (θηλυδρίης τε καὶ μαλακώτερος) appearance of Telines, compare the effeminacy of Dionysus described in Euripides' *Bacchae* 233–38, and note the prominence of eunuchs in the service of Ephesian Artemis, Kybele, and Anatolian goddesses generally (above, note 10, and chapter 4 at notes 83–88).

tue of the sacred objects of the goddesses. How or whence he came by these things I do not know; but it was upon them, and them only, that he relied; and he brought back the exiles on condition that he and his descendants after him should be priests of the goddesses. In view of what I have heard, it is a marvel that Telines should have been capable of such a feat. I have always imagined that it is by no means everybody who is equal to things like that, which usually call for both strength and courage; yet people in Sicily maintain that Telines was neither strong nor brave, but, on the contrary, a rather soft and effeminate person. In any case, that was how he obtained his office.

This account has clear affinities with the story of the victory of the exiles at Assesus over their fellow citizens of Miletus. The basis of tyranny in the cult of Demeter and her daughter attested here by Herodotus is confirmed by Pindar,[129] and is linked with the rites adopted at Miletus not just by similar actions, but also by common Asiatic origin. Herodotus hints, and a scholiast later states, that the sacred objects of the Earth Goddesses came from the Triopium peninsula, where a cult of Demeter was maintained at Cnidus.[130] Apparently, the ritual basis of sovereignty identified with the earth of Asia could be exported as sacred objects in the name of the goddesses of the earth, the Mother and her daughter, in order to establish a new sovereign foundation on other soil.[131]

The myth-historical context underlying all of these accounts is the endowment of sovereign tyranny to Midas by the Mother, his mother. Midas was the prototypical conqueror, invoked as Lord and Leader of the Host in the archaic Midas Monument. The same monument indicates what later Greek and Latin sources affirm, namely that the rites of the Phrygian Mother were both the means and the justification for his irresistible tyranny. As a cult place dedicated to the memory of Midas and the Mother, the Midas Monument represented one of several places where tyranny was evoked by those who sought to exercise it. As opposed to the portable sacred objects that could be used to transplant the power of tyranny, as was done at Miletus or in Sicily, the rock-cut Midas Monument displayed the basis of sovereign power as a feature of the Phrygian landscape, in the highlands where the chief rivers of western Asia arose, in the native land of Midas' tyranny. Like the story Herodotus tells attesting the power of the claim that the Phry-

129. Pindar *Olympian* 6.92–96 attests that Hieron, brother of Gelon, kept the cult of Demeter, her daughter, and Zeus at Syracuse. Diodorus 11.26.7 states that Gelon built a temple of Demeter and Kore at Syracuse.

130. The scholiast to Pindar *Pythian* 2.27 names Deinomenes as the founder of the cult, and states that he brought "the sacred objects" (τὰ ἱερά) from Triopium. Nilsson 1906, 319–20, assembles evidence for the cult of Demeter Thesmophoros at Cnidus. See Diodorus 5.5.1–3 on the cult of Demeter at Syracuse.

131. The Asiatic pedigree of the Deinomenid tyranny is also affirmed by Pindar in *Olympian* 1, as discussed in chapter 1 at note 33.

gians were "the first of mankind," that the word for bread was first spoken in Phrygia, and, as other sources attest, that Lityerses invented agriculture in that land, the lore of Phrygia asserted that this land was the native home to the greatest king the world had ever known. Anyone who sought sovereign power after Midas' day, according to this ideology, had to acquire it from the source.

## THE LEGACY OF MIDAS

With King Midas we are on the threshold of history. As surely as he was a figure of Greek folktale and myth, Midas was also a historical figure. Eusebius reports the dates of Midas' reign as 738–696/5, according to the Greek chronographic tradition, which agrees well with the evidence of contemporary Assyrian records. Midas appears in the records of Sargon II of Assyria as Mita of Mushki (biblical Meshech, later the Μόσχοι of classical sources).[132] During the reign of Sargon (721–705), Midas was at the head of an empire based in central Anatolia that extended its influence across the Neo-Hittite states of Cappadocia (Assyrian Tabal, biblical Tubal, Greek Τιβαρηνοί) and Cilicia, to the kingdom of Urartu in eastern Anatolia and to the state of Carchemish in northern Syria. After a long period of warfare, during which the Assyrians gained a foothold in Cilicia, Assyrian texts record a reconciliation between Sargon and Midas.[133] The Assyrians clearly felt that an old adversary had been humbled by this agreement. From the side of the Phrygians and their allies, this reconciliation could well have been seen as evidence that Midas had made Assyria bow down to him. In 705, Sargon died in battle in Cappadocia, fighting in support of Midas against their common enemies. Following the death of Sargon, the Assyrians lost their hold on Cilicia

132. The identity of Midas with Mita of Mushki is widely recognized: e.g., by Bittel 1970, 135–37; Barnett 1975, 425–26; Roller 1983, 330–31; Muscarella 1989 and 1995; Mellink 1991, 622–26; Hawkins 1994a; Cassola 1997, 139–41; Sams 2000, 1149; Bryce 2003, 98–100. Laminger-Pascher 1989, 17–40, casts doubt on the identification of Mita and Midas; her arguments are accepted by Burkert 1992, 13, but are rightly dismissed by Muscarella 1995, Cassola 1997, and Starke 1997b, 383 n. 8. Mita was evidently a dynastic title, for a regional ruler of this name is attested in Hittite records of the Late Bronze Age: see Barnett 420; Bryce 1998, 155–56 and 415. Burke 2002 suggests that the name Mita may be explained by a Hittite royal ritual containing elements also found in the story of the Gordian Knot. On the Mushki, known from Assyrian records as early as the twelfth century as a powerful people in the region of the upper Euphrates, see Börker-Klähn 1997. Biblical Meshech is one of the seven sons of Japheth in the Table of Nations (Genesis 10:2, 1 Chronicles 1:5), named along with Tubal and Javan (cf. Assyrian *Iawanu*, Persian *Yauna*, Greek Ἰάονες = Ionians = "Greeks"). In Herodotus 3.94.2 Μόσχοι are listed with Τιβαρηνοί and other tribes of northeastern Anatolia in the nineteenth satrapy of Darius; and in 7.78 they are brigaded together in Xerxes' army.

133. For summaries of the Assyrian texts, see Hawkins 1982, 417–22, and 1994a; Grayson 1991, 90–92; Bryce 2003, 98–100, 105.

for nearly a decade, and Midas lived out his last years without a serious threat from Assyria.[134]

Assyrian sources and the archaeological remains of Midas' capital at Gordium attest to the actual greatness of Midas, but the picture of Midas conveyed by Greek sources seems to belong more to the realm of myth or folklore than to history. This unreal quality to the Greek perception of this historical figure can be explained as a consequence of his actual greatness and its immediate aftermath. Midas made such a strong impression on his contemporaries in Anatolia that, after he was dead, they longed to emulate and recreate his kingship. They did so, however, by elevating him to the status of a semidivine king whose power could be invoked by appealing to the deities that were thought to have sustained him. So we find, within the dominion of the Lydian empire, that the memory of Midas' sovereign greatness was enshrined in a cult monument to the Phrygian Mother, while archaic Greek sources attest that a tumulus of Midas was place of reflection, and even, if the Pythagorean tradition is reliable, of ritual communion.

Later Greek sources recall that the Phrygian Mother was Midas' own mother, honored as a divinity by Midas at her funeral. Impressive funerals were evidently a real feature of the reign of Midas, to judge by the tumulus field at Gordium and especially the Great Tumulus, which contained an elderly male dating from the time of Midas.[135] Ritualization of the memory of Midas' own family thus very likely began in his own lifetime, in the context of royal funerals at Gordium. The tradition, also recalled by Greek sources, that Phrygian gods and their ritual music were potent escorts to an army of conquest also probably reflected actual practice by the armies of Midas on the march. Tales of the magnificence of Midas must have originated with those who had been a part of the great hosts assembled for war and likewise for royal funerals in the lifetime of Midas. The memory of Midas afterwards was associated especially with the Phrygian music of marching and the music of mourning.

The image of Midas as he was known to the Greeks, and certain qualities of the divinities associated with his kingship, are thus features of memories preserved, with the aid of ritual and music, over the generations that im-

---

134. Strabo 1.3.21 associates the death of Midas with the invasion of the Cimmerians, and Assyrian sources attest to warfare between Cimmerians (Akkadian *Gimirrai*) and Urartians at the end of the eighth century. It has therefore seemed reasonable to assume that the Cimmerians brought an end to the kingdom of Midas. The so-called Cimmerian destruction level at the citadel of Gordium, however, has now been conclusively redated to the second half of the ninth century (DeVries et al. 2003), and cannot be used as evidence for the end of Midas' reign.

135. On the tumuli of Gordium and their excavation, see Körte and Körte 1904; Kohler 1980 and 1995; Young et al. 1981; a brief summary is provided by Sams 2000 1152–53. On the identity of the sixty-year-old man buried in the Great Tumulus (Midas or Gordius?), see Mellink in Young et al. 1981, 271–72; Prag 1989; Muscarella 1995.

mediately followed the lifetime of Midas. The image of the divine *Matar*, the Phrygian Mother herself, was shaped by the memory of Midas. The Phrygian monuments that clearly depict or explicitly name *Matar* date from the seventh or sixth century. By this time, Midas had become a talisman of sovereignty, and his mother, the divine Mother, had become identified as the natural source of sovereignty, identified with landmarks, mountains and water sources, across the landscape west of the river Halys. By the second quarter of the seventh century, this had become the domain of the kingdom of Lydia under the Mermnad dynasty founded by Gyges.[136] These circumstances explain why the Athenian playwrights of the fifth century knew the Mother of the Gods as a Phrygian deity of mountains and springs, whose most famous center of worship was below Mount Tmolus, at the Lydian capital, Sardis.[137]

The following chapter will consider the aspects of the Mother of the Gods that were associated with Lydia, its tyrants, and their capital at Sardis. At Sardis we will find this deity to be known as Kybebe, a name that identifies her with Kubaba, divine protectress of sovereigns in the time of Midas and earlier. In the cult of Kybebe at Sardis we will also find evidence that the goddess who was the divine mother of the king was also the divine lover of the king. Through the evidence that converges to explain the cult of Kybebe at Sardis, in the next and in subsequent chapters, we will also find the circumstances that suggest that "the Phrygian man" who announced the Mother to the Athenians came from Sardis.

136. Sardis (Saparda) is mentioned in the records of the Assyrian king Esarhaddon (681–669), and Gyges king of Lydia (Gugu of Ludu) is mentioned in Assyrian records early in the reign of Assurbanipal (668–627) as a dependent ally who later became hostile; see Mellink 1991, 643–47. Pedley 1968, 44–50, reviews Greek and Assyrian textual evidence for the reign of Gyges.

137. See Baldriga 1997 on the conflation of Phrygia and Lydia; see also Beekes 2002, cols. 205–19, on the probable relationship between Maeonia (the older name of Lydia) and what later became western Phrygia.

# Chapter 3

# The Mother of the Gods and the Ideals of Lydian Tyranny

The story told to Alexander during his visit to Gordium about how Midas became king preserves, I believe, the earliest account of the Mother of the Gods as she became known to the Greeks.[1] This conclusion emerges from the close correspondences, observed in the previous chapter, between the symbols and imagery described in that story and those depicted in the Phrygian relief sculptures and archaic monuments to Phrygian *Matar,* the Mother, which probably began to be carved in the seventh century and became most widespread in the sixth.[2] *Homeric Hymn* 14, *To the Mother of the Gods,* is probably sixth-century in date, and is therefore contemporary to the majority of the Phrygian monuments.[3] The hymn sings of the din of rattles, drums, and pipes celebrating the Mother, as well as the calls of wolves and lions echoing through mountains and glens, all of which would appropriately describe celebrations of the Mother in the vicinity of the archaic rock-cut monuments in the Phrygian highlands. All other references to the Mother of the Gods in Greek literature, describing either her cult or her cosmological role, are likely to be later than this. It was specifically in her guise as the Phrygian Mother, then, that the Mother of the Gods became familiar to the Greeks.

But what was Phrygia, in the seventh and sixth centuries? Why should a Phrygian divinity be so prominently recognized? After the reign of the great Midas there was no powerful king of Phrygia. It is true, as Herodotus records, that a royal Phrygian lineage passed on the names of Gordius and

---

1. The Phrygian story as told by Arrian is quoted in chapter 2 at note 107, where variants are cited.

2. See chapter 2, with notes 83–87 and 108.

3. See Roller 1999, 122–23.

Midas to succeeding generations, but they were nonentities.[4] An answer emerges when we consider the time and place in which the fame of the Phrygian Mother grew. Phrygia, in the seventh and sixth centuries, evoked the memory of the great Midas in a land that was now ruled by the tyrants of Lydia. The heart of Phrygia lay within the bounds of the Lydian empire, west of the great bend of the Halys River. Early in the sixth century, Alyattes the Lydian was fighting the Medes along the Halys River, and there is no indication that this represented a recent enlargement of his dominion.[5] Before the middle of the seventh century, Assyrian sources took note of the power and influence of Gyges of Lydia.[6] In the absence of any Phrygian ruler of note in this period, it is most probable that Gyges became overlord of the former dominion of Midas, on the Anatolian plateau, not long after the death of the great Midas. Any explanation of the significance of Phrygia and its native Mother in the seventh and sixth centuries must take account of the interests of the rulers of Lydian Sardis.[7]

"Phrygian," in the context of the archaic cult of the Mother, should not be understood as a simple identification of ethnic origin. The Phrygian identity of the Mother of the Gods was an ideological construct, signifying the essential divinity of the primeval land of Phrygia. Like the legacies of Phrygian Midas, who engendered the discovery of agriculture and who endowed the Pactolus River with its charge of gold, the gifts to humanity of the Phrygian Mother were in the custody of the rulers of her land. And those rulers were the Mermnad tyrants of Lydia. The elaborate rock-carved shrines and cult places of the Phrygian Mother were monuments of the heartland of the Lydian empire, created during the seventh- and sixth-century era of Mermnad rule. Inscriptions on these monuments in the Phrygian language, far from signifying a cultural distinction between Phrygia and Lydia, represent the Lydian appropriation of Phrygia as a signifier of ancient authenticity.

A reflection of this appropriation of Phrygian tradition is found in Herodotus' story about *bekos*, the Phrygian word for bread.[8] The discovery that

4. Herodotus 1.35.1 and 45.3, giving the ancestry of Adrastus, slayer of Atys son of Croesus. Snodgrass (1971, 349–50), Jeffery (1976, 238), and Drews (1983, 32–35) all suggest that a later Midas might have contributed to the reputation of the famous Midas. The name Midas (Mita) may well have been a dynastic or ritual title (see chapter 2, note 132), but there is no evidence for any Midas of note later than the great Midas of the eighth century.

5. Herodotus 1.73–74.

6. See chapter 2, note 136.

7. Talamo 1979, 16–31 and 57–63, followed by Baldriga 1997, traces the close associations between Lydia and Phrygia indicated in the Lydian genealogies reported by Greek sources from Herodotus to Nicolaus of Damascus, and likewise sees Gyges as the heir to the dominion of Midas.

8. See chapter 2 at notes 89–92.

this Phrygian word was the first articulate sound uttered by a human voice was announced in the name of Psammetichus I of Egypt, the contemporary of Gyges of Lydia. Shortly before the middle of the seventh century, Psammetichus had secured his rule in Egypt with the assistance of Ionian and Carian mercenaries, as Herodotus attests, who were sent on the authority of Gyges, as contemporary Assyrian records indicate.[9] In affirming the primacy of Phrygia, Psammetichus was acknowledging that his kingship depended upon the true source of sovereignty, centered in Phrygia and controlled by the tyrant of Lydia. The truth about the origins of human life that Psammetichus allegedly discovered was in fact a reflection of contemporary realities. Although Herodotus does not explicitly say so, the Phrygian story that he tells at the beginning of his account of Egypt reflected the power and influence of Gyges and of the dynasty of Lydian tyrants that he founded.

The present chapter examines the characteristics that made the Phrygian Mother of the Gods an appropriate manifestation of Lydian sovereignty. Like the figure of Midas, a real person whose memory generated an ahistorical archetype, we will find that the divine Mother in Lydia was, paradoxically, both a mortal woman and mother of a king-to-be, and a divinity whose communion with tyrants assured their supremacy. As in the case of Midas, this paradox was achieved through the perspective of time. Real individuals of the past were enshrined through rituals and monuments to become the idealized foundations of present conditions. In this process, the mothers of kings tended to lose their individual identities and become assimilated to the ideal of the divine Mother.

The ideal of a divine woman who engenders tyrants was not the invention of the Mermnads. Although the Greeks (and evidently the Saïte kings of Egypt) regarded Phrygia as the original home of this divine bearer of sovereignty, in fact she was a type long familiar among the rulers of the eastern Mediterranean. In this chapter we will encounter the goddess known to the Lydians as Kybebe, and familiar to the contemporaries of Midas as Kubaba. This ancient deity of northern Syria and central Anatolia was the archetype on whom the Phrygian Mother was formed, and after whom, as we shall see, she became known as Kybele.

---

9. Herodotus 2.152 reports that prior to his rise to power, Psammetichus had spent time in exile in Syria (which, to Herodotus, might include Cappadocia; see 1.72 and 76), and that he secured his power with the support of armed Ionians and Carians. An alliance of Gyges and Psammetichus I is attested in the records of Assurbanipal of Assyria, and it is widely accepted that these Carians and Ionians were sent to Psammetichus, ca. 655 B.C.E., as a result of this alliance (Kienitz 1953, 12; Mellink 1991, 645; Redford 1992, 406, 431). Kaplan 2002 discusses the circumstances of Ionian and Carian mercenary service under Psammetichus

### THE LOVER OF GORDIUS

The story of the mother of Midas embedded in the account of the Gordian knot is an etiological legend. It identifies the mother of the king-to-be as the figure depicted in the doorways of the archaic shrines and rock-cut facades of Phrygia, as we saw in the previous chapter. She is the Phrygian *Matar Kubeleya,* or to the Greeks the Mother of the Gods. In her story we have a template that can be transferred to a number of figures in archaic art, lore, and poetry, and that can inform us about the potency that each of these figures symbolized to Greeks and non-Greeks living in western Asia Minor in the seventh and sixth centuries.

The most significant understanding gained by acknowledging the mother of Midas as an archetype in archaic iconography and ideology comes from her narrative. For the mother of Midas is a figure who has a life history, although, remarkably, she has no name. The anonymous woman of the story of Gordius and the kingship of Midas is, first of all, a woman who comes from a clan possessing prophetic wisdom (the Telmessians);[10] she is, second of all, a *parthenos,* a virgin girl eligible for marriage, and said to be of great beauty; she is next a bride, *nymphē,* who mates with the man who will be father to the great king; then she becomes the mother, *mētēr,* of the young king; and finally, when she dies and is given honors by the great king, Midas, she is ἡ Μίδα θεός, "the goddess of Midas," or the divine Mother.[11] All of these elements are understood to be present in the Mother whenever she is evoked in image or by name, although not all of these stages can be described or depicted simultaneously. Envisioned at each stage, as virgin, as bride, or as mother in a work of art, a poem, or a votive prayer, she stands for the completion of all these stages of life.

In this respect, the Mother of the Gods represents potentiality. She is the sign of good things to come rather than a presence herself. (Hence she has no personal name.) When Greek sources attempt to look directly at her and describe her personal qualities, she immediately becomes transcendent; she becomes the Mountain Mother, giver of water, nurturer of animals and mankind, and in effect she becomes the world. For this reason, too, the story of the mother of Midas always mentions her as she is in the process of effecting a transition, and bringing about something good in the world. (As

---

10. The Telmessian origin of the mother of Midas, as the story is reported by Arrian *Anabasis* 2.3.3, is difficult to account for in a Phrygian legend, as Roller 1984, 262 and 268, has noted, but is a strong indicator of the Lydian origin of this account. The seers of Telmessus prophesied at the foundation of Sardis by Meles, and to Croesus at its fall, according to Herodotus 1.78 and 84.

11. See chapter 2, with the sources cited in notes 93–98.

Plutarch tells us, she is also called ἡ Ἀγαθὴ Θεός, "the Good Goddess," or *Bona Dea* in Latin.)[12]

Among the qualities of the woman who becomes the mother of Midas is her ability to inspire "love at first sight." She has the power of Aphrodite about her, and this was a feature associated with women who consorted with the tyrants of Lydia, as we will see below. The archetypal lover of the Lydian tyrant, the woman who became the mother of his successor, was a great beauty who was otherwise an anonymous *pallakē*, or concubine. But from her comes sovereignty itself.

## SOVEREIGNS AND THEIR CONCUBINES

The polygamy of sovereigns had two general purposes, each served by a distinct class of royal consort. Because a sovereign ruler was most deserving of things gratifying and good, he possessed a great harem of choice concubines to please him. And because his possession of sovereignty should not be open to question, a ruler was expected to take wives from the most noble families, so that he could control the generation of significant offspring. This distinction between concubines and wives of sovereigns corresponds to the classic distinction between concubines and wives in Greek usage: "we keep . . . concubines [*pallakai*] for the daily care of our persons, but wives [*gynaikes*] for the procreation of legitimate children."[13] Herodotus indicates that the same distinction was made by the Persians and Macedonians between their legitimate wives (*kouridiai gynaikes*) and their concubines (*pallakides*).[14] In the case of sovereign rulers, however, the difference between a wife and a concubine was not always clear-cut. Because connubial relations could affect the nature and perpetuity of sovereign power itself, sovereign concerns could determine the status of connubial relations; according to circumstances, a sovereign's consort might shift between the status of concubine and legitimate wife.

Concubines were not expected to produce offspring, and when they did,

12. Plutarch *Caesar* 9.3.

13. [Demosthenes] *Against Neaera* 122, where the ellipsis in the quotation is a reference to the keeping of courtesans for pleasure. Courtesans (*hetairai*) represent an aspect of the services more anciently provided by concubines that have become a commodity in a monetary economy. On the relationship between concubinage and legal marriage at Athens, see Sealey 1984, and, more concisely, Blundell 1995, 124–25.

14. Herodotus 1.135 states of the Persians that "each one of them marries many *kouridias* wives, and possesses an even greater number of concubines." From context, *kouridias gynaikas* clearly means something like "legitimate" or "lawfully wedded wives," and so κουρίδιος is assigned the meaning "wedded" in LSJ. The essential quality of *kouridiai gynaikes* is probably that they bear sons (*kouroi*) capable of succeeding their fathers, distinguishing them from *pallakai*, who serve and attend to needs other than procreation. For the Macedonians, see Herodotus 5.18.2. Xenophon *Cyropaedia* 4.3.1 describes how some of the Medes accompanying Cyrus' army "drove

their offspring were incidentals, or illegitimate (*nothoi*). Under rare circumstances, the son of a royal concubine could usurp the standing of a legitimate heir, but his questionable birth was not soon forgotten.[15] Legitimate wives, by contrast, were expected to produce offspring, and when they did not, their status was in jeopardy. When Peisistratus, in his second entry into power at Athens, refused to have procreative intercourse with his new bride, the daughter of Megacles, the marriage and dynastic alliance of their families broke down.[16] Amasis, king of Egypt, foresaw a similar outcome when Cambyses, king of Persia, requested his daughter in marriage, "because he knew full well that Cambyses did not intend to make her his wife, but to keep her as a concubine."[17] In both cases, the actual or perceived treatment of a consort as a concubine instead of a favored wife contributed to the characterization of each of these rulers, Peisistratus and Cambyses, as tyrants.

As a ruler whose supremacy depended more on popular acclamation than on his esteem within a network of noble families, the stereotypical tyrant had no need to seek legitimacy through dynastic marriage alliances. The archetypal tyrant, therefore, reduced all of his consorts to the status of concubines. Herodotus and other classical authors clearly recognize this as one of the abominations of tyranny.[18] As opposed to the wives of kings, whose names and family connections are remembered, the consorts of tyrants were typically women who were anonymous and whose ancestry was effaced.[19] But in keeping with tyranny's ambition to embody the highest form of sovereignty, the tyrant's choice concubine could be taken as the embodiment of the greatest attributes of sovereignty.

The concubine who commands the affections of a man appears to him as

---

wagons of the most beautiful legitimate wives, and of concubines [γυναικῶν τῶν βελτίστων τῶν δὲ καὶ παλλακίδων] accompanying the army on account of their attractiveness." Additional passages giving similar testimony are cited by Briant 2002, 277–78.

15. Darius II was remembered as Nothus ("the Bastard"), because he was the son of a concubine of Artaxerxes I, whose legitimate son had been killed; see Pausanias 6.5.7 and Ctesias *Persica* (epitome) 44–48, discussed by Lewis 1977, 73–75; Brosius 1996, 33; Briant 2002, 278 and 588–90. Similarly, the invidious description of Plato *Gorgias* 471a–c and Aelian *Varia Historia* 12.43 of King Archelaus of Macedon as the son of a slave must indicate that his mother was the concubine of Perdiccas; see Carney 2000, 17. Biblical accounts of the connubial relations of patriarchs and kings, beginning with Abraham in Genesis 16, provide several examples of contested status among wives and concubines over the issue of offspring; see the discussion of de Vaux 1961, 24–26 and 115–19.

16. Herodotus 1.61.1–2.

17. Herodotus 3.1.

18. In addition to the passages cited in notes 16 and 17 above, see Herodotus 3.80.5; cf. 5.18–20; Euripides *Suppliants* 452–55. The reduction of all consorts to concubines accords with the observation by Aristotle *Politics* 1311a4: "The object of tyranny is pleasure" (ἔστι δὲ σκοπὸς τυραννικὸς μὲν τὸ ἡδύ).

19. In those few instances where the consort of the tyrant is named, her reputation lies chiefly in her amorous relationship to the tyrant and not in the prestige of her own personal ancestry.

the embodiment of Aphrodite herself.[20] Such a scenario describes not only the union of Gordius and the wise Telmessian maiden who became the mother of Midas, but also the ideal union of any powerful ruler, or ruler-to-be, and his choice concubine. Her past, her family, her identity, are all incidental. Her beauty and her wisdom, manifested at the moment of their meeting, is everything. As a manifestation of Aphrodite, such a concubine transcends the status of all other women. The power of Aphrodite present in the moment of significant encounter is, in a sense, the measure of tyranny.

The sovereign tyrant and his choice concubine were thus paradigms of both power and love. Wherever a ruler and his consort held such a high place in popular esteem, they were seen as sacral actors, and their sexual union was, ideally, a *hieros gamos,* a Sacred Marriage performed for the benefit of sovereignty. In classical Greek sources, such a symbolic union is attested in the rites of Sacred Marriage, such as that at Athens, said to be performed between the god, Dionysus, and the Basilinna, the (usually anonymous) wife of the archon basileus.[21] At Athens these roles were played by civic office-holders as an obligation and an honor. In states where monarchs or tyrants exercised sovereignty, the ruler and his consort who assumed such sacral roles could not be treated as ordinary mortals. They assumed a godlike standing in the eyes of their subjects for life, and after life as well.[22]

Men who demonstrated supremacy in rulership, as tyrants, monarchs, or even as successful statesmen, tended to be assimilated in popular imagination to the paradigm of the tyrant, and their consorts to the paradigm of the tyrant's concubine. The reputation of Aspasia, wife of Pericles, is colored by the stereotype of the choice concubine of the tyrant, and her fame reflects both the abnegation of personal identity and the sacral attributes that accompanied this status. Tradition describes Aspasia as the concubine (*pallakē*) rather than the legitimate wife of the great Pericles, and characterizes their son, the younger Pericles, as illegitimate (*nothos*). These characterizations almost certainly derive from the satires of contemporary comedy, and from the reputation of the great Pericles as a man of such power that he resembled a tyrant.[23] The contemporary comedies that called Aspasia a concubine

20. Note that prized captive women, like Briseïs or Cassandra, can share with the desirable *pallakē* this quality of having the "likeness of golden Aphrodite" (ἰκέλη χρυσέῃ Ἀφροδίτῃ): *Iliad* 19.282, 24.699. Carney 2000, 210 and 218–25, discusses many examples of wives and courtesans of Hellenistic monarchs and powerful men who were honored in cult as the likeness of Aphrodite.

21. Louis Gernet 1968, 344–59, has similarly characterized the marriages of tyrants as Sacred Marriages. On the *hieros gamos* in the Anthesteria at Athens, see chapter 1 at note 88.

22. Theocritus' encomium to Ptolemy Philadelphus and Arsinoë (*Idyll* 17) most clearly attests the godlike status of king and consort. (See Hunter 2003.) The same is indicated by the epithets Aeschylus uses of Atossa and Darius in the *Persians* (discussed in chapter 6 at notes 39–42).

23. See Plutarch *Pericles* 24.3–6, where Plutarch quotes Cratinus *Cheirones* fr. 259 (KA) and Eupolis *Demes* fr. 110 (KA). Note also *Pericles* 7.1 and 8.2–3 on the alleged resemblance of Per-

also named her Hera, Deïaneira, and the New Omphale.[24] Aspasia, in other words, was likened to the archetypal divine consort whose coupling with Zeus was celebrated in the Theogamia, as well as to the princess of Calydon whose passions inflamed Heracles, and to the queen of Lydia who enslaved the same great hero. These mythical archetypes described a bond between Aspasia and Pericles that their contemporaries found to be one of exceptional, erotic attraction, displayed, as Plutarch remarks, by a kiss of love that Pericles gave her every time he left or returned home.[25]

Aspasia's beauty had a political edge to it. Aspasia was likened to a famous Milesian courtesan named Thargelia who had drawn her lovers into allegiance to the king of Persia; likewise Aspasia drew prominent Athenians into the circle of Pericles and into allegiance to his vision of Athens.[26] Aspasia's charm lay not merely in her grace and beauty, as Socrates affirmed (according to Plato), but in her conversation and intellect as well. Plato's *Menexenus* makes much of Aspasia's eloquence, and even makes Socrates claim that she instructed Pericles in rhetoric and composed many of his speeches.[27] In fact, in all of these respects—her grace, intelligence, and political influence, as well as her erotic attraction—Aspasia was being described by her contemporaries as the embodiment of the wise maiden who becomes the bride of a man of power, and who together engender sovereignty. Her type was that of the bride of Gordius in the Phrygian story of Midas. Aspasia's own Milesian ancestry points to the native home of her archetype, in Asia Minor. At Miletus in particular, Herodotus reports, it was the custom of Milesian wives to remember their ancient Carian ancestry in a manner that suggests a ceremony of ritual concubinage.[28] Aspasia at Athens, as the choice consort of Pericles, was clearly thought of as the archetypal Anatolian concubine.

The testimony of Herodotus, the comments of sophists, and the satires of

icles to Peisistratus and to "Olympian [Zeus]," and Thucydides' famous saying (2.65.9) that the administration of Athens under Pericles was a democracy in name, but in fact the rule of one man.

24. See Plutarch *Pericles* 24.6.

25. Plutarch *Pericles* 24.5 and 6. The authority for these impressions and anecdotes goes back to Antisthenes and Stesimbrotus, both of them younger contemporaries to Aspasia herself: see Athenaeus 13.589d–e.

26. On Thargelia, see Plutarch *Pericles* 24.2 and Athenaeus 13.608e–609a, where a work by the fifth-century sophist Hippias is cited as an authority.

27. Plato *Menexenus* 235e–236d, 249d–e. Hermesianax, a Colophonian poet of the third century B.C.E. (quoted by Athenaeus 13.599a–b), identifies the wisdom that Socrates derives from Aspasia as originating in the fire of Aphrodite.

28. See Herodotus 1.146.3, describing the custom passed from Milesian mother to daughter of not eating together with their husbands or addressing them by name. The custom corresponds to the services performed by a concubine. Note the evidence from later inscriptions for ritual concubinage performed by Carian women in the service of Zeus (Poljakov 1989, 11–13, nos. 6 and 7; the texts are discussed by Budin 2003b).

the comic poets all indicate that educated Athenians of the fifth century, and probably much of the public at large as well, were aware of this Anatolian paradigm of the semidivine concubine who signifies and conveys sovereignty. The type was identified especially with the dominion of the tyrants of Lydia. Herodotus traces the Heraclid dynasty of Lydian tyrants that came to an end with Candaules back to Heracles and the "slave of Iardanus" (Omphale), a description that likens Omphale to a concubine. (Other sources call Omphale the daughter of Iardanus, queen, and the woman tyrant of Lydia.)[29] Another significant Lydian royal concubine (called a *pallakē* by Herodotus) was the anonymous woman who bore a lion to King Meles.[30] She who gives birth to a lion gives birth to a future king or tyrant, as the Greeks knew this metaphor.[31]

Viewed through the storybook window of popular beliefs, the concubine of a tyrant could be no ordinary woman, for a tyrant naturally chooses only that which is exceptional. And the woman who, above all others, commands the special affection of the tyrant or man of great power must therefore be regarded as a paragon of feminine charm. Popular stories give us vignettes of "a love like no other," where the end of the story defies all mundane experience. The most memorable stories of this sort, like the love of Paris for Helen, are set in Asia Minor. Another such a story with a more historical setting recounts the fame of a poor Greek woman of Phocaea named Milto, who later took the name Aspasia.

Born to poverty, the young Milto found herself in the hands of a procurer who offered her, among other concubines (*pallakides*), to the Persian prince Cyrus the Younger when he held sway over Ionia.[32] Because of her beauty and modesty, Aspasia (Plutarch says she was given this name after the famous wife of Pericles)[33] immediately attracted Cyrus' attention. Because she refused to be treated like merchandise, Cyrus favored her company, respected her virginity, and called her "the wise one" (*sophē*).[34] Between them, Aelian relates, "a love gradually developed into something close to mutual respect, not dissimilar from the meeting of minds and dignity of Hellenic marriage."[35]

---

29. Herodotus 1.7. See Apollodorus *Library* 2.6.3 and 2.7.8; Diodorus 4.31.6–8; Clearchus in Athenaeus 12.515f; Sophocles *Trachiniae* 248–57.

30. Herodotus 1.84.3.

31. Pericles himself was thought of as such a "lion": Herodotus 6.131.2. The symbolism of lions and sovereignty is discussed further below; see notes 123 and 125.

32. Aelian *Varia Historia* 12.1 describes how Aspasia (the former Milto) was offered along with other virgins to Cyrus by one of his satraps. The satrap is later called a procurer (*agorastēs*), while the virgins (*parthenoi*) are called *pallakides*.

33. Plutarch *Pericles* 24.7.

34. Aelian 12.1 reports that, unlike Aspasia, the other girls behaved *kapēlikōs* (prostituted themselves) before Cyrus. Plutarch 26.5 reports that Cyrus called Aspasia *sophē*.

35. Aelian *Varia Historia* 12.1: ἡ φιλία προῆλθεν, ὡς ἐγγὺς ἰσοτιμίας εἶναι καὶ μὴ ἀπᾴδειν Ἑλληνικοῦ γάμου ὁμονοίας τε καὶ σωφροσύνης. The transition is one from servile concubine to respected

After Cyrus was killed in battle, the fame of Aspasia was such that she soon became a favorite also of Artaxerxes II. Eventually, Artaxerxes consecrated Aspasia as a priestess of Artemis (or Persian Anahita), we are told by Plutarch, so as to preserve her chastity from the affections of his own son.[36]

The love of Cyrus the Younger for his concubine Aspasia became "famous in Ionia and throughout all Hellas," according to Aelian. It is no accident that Sardis in Lydia was the seat of power that Cyrus occupied when he encountered the marvelous Aspasia, for the story follows a pattern familiar to the Greeks from the legends and monuments associated with the most famous consorts of the rulers of Lydia. So, for example, Xenophon, in his *Cyropaedia*, tells a tale of the love of the elder Cyrus for a woman named Pantheia ("All-divinity," surely a significant name) whose beauty "burns like fire." Pantheia was the wife of the king of Susa who fought in the army of Cyrus; in her husband's absence she was kept in Cyrus' company. A chaste love developed between them, and ended in her noble suicide on the battlefield at Sardis, where her husband had just died fighting to secure the kingship of Cyrus. Befitting his deep affection, Xenophon reports, Cyrus heaped up a monumental burial mound for the couple, "so they say."[37]

The stories of Pantheia and Aspasia and their lovers, the lords of Persia, are examples out of a long history of erotic tales set at Sardis and in the realm of Lydia. Ever since the time of Sappho, Lydia has been known in Greek literature as a land that inspired stories of "love like no other."[38] The court at Sardis continually drew to it the most beautiful of women, as Sappho lamented. Whether they went with their families' blessings, or through the arrangements of pimps and procurers, they were brought to both embellish and justify tyranny. Among such beauties, by divinely ordained chance, the tyrant would encounter the woman who would seize his fancy and bear his progeny, just as Gordius had encountered the mother of Midas. The anonymous concubine who thus became the paramount consort of the Lydian

---

wife, the reverse of the transition that Megacles and Amasis feared for their daughters (above at notes 16 and 17).

36. Plutarch *Artaxerxes* 27.3.

37. Xenophon *Cyropaedia* 5.1.2–18 describes the beauty of Pantheia (beauty that burns like fire: 5.1.10 and 5.1.16). *Cyropaedia* 6.1.31–51 describes the mutual respect of Cyrus and Pantheia; 7.3.8–16 describes her death at Sardis (discussed in chapter 4 at notes 71–72).

38. For the erotic attractions of Lydia and Sardis in the poetry of Sappho and her contemporaries Alcaeus and Alcman, see below, with notes 67–69, and chapter 4, note 122. Another seventh-century poet, Mimnermus, wrote elegies of love to Nanno (a Lydian name: *LW* 169–70). Hipponax of Ephesus, in the sixth century, has a woman administering a remedy for impotence lapse into Lydian speech (ηὖδα δὲ λυδίζουσα, 92.1 [Edmonds; West]). Antimachus of Colophon, a contemporary of Cyrus the Younger, composed a famous elegy to love under the name *Lydē*, and his countryman Hermesianax carried on the tradition a century later in his *Leontion*.

tyrant was regarded to be a woman of unparalleled beauty and supernatural power, an embodiment of Aphrodite. Through their Sacred Marriage, the most desirable goddess proves the supremacy of the man who is her consort.

APHRODITE AND LYDIAN TYRANNY

Just as the mother of Midas was the mother of his tyranny, and came to be honored as a divinity, so too was the woman who signified the foundation of Lydian sovereignty. Her story is preserved in *Homeric Hymn 5, To Aphrodite.* This Greek hymn describes the sexual union of a goddess, who proves to be Aphrodite herself, and the father of a future lord of an Asian land. Although the hymn makes no mention of Sardis or Lydia, its specific references to geography and lineage all point in the direction of the Mermnad tyrants of Sardis. So too do the circumstances of its composition.

The *Homeric Hymn to Aphrodite* stands out among other Homeric hymns in several respects that are significant to our inquiry. It is probably the earliest of the hymns, arguably contemporary to the principal poems attributed to Hesiod and Homer in the first half of the seventh century.[39] Both its dialect and its geographical references indicate that it was probably composed within the sphere of greater Lydia.[40] Above all, the image of Aphrodite it presents has been widely recognized as Asiatic in character, and likens Aphrodite in several respects to the image elsewhere associated with Phrygian Kybele.[41]

Just as Zeus sent a sign of kingship to Gordius, which was fulfilled through his encounter with a woman who was more than merely mortal, so too does

39. Janko 1982, 169 and 228–31, places the composition of the hymn to Aphrodite between *Theogony* and *Works and Days,* and regards a date in the first half of the seventh century to be most likely for all three poems.

40. The poem's principal geographic references are to the Troad and to Phrygia; the connection of these to Lydia is discussed further below. On the basis of the form of its epic diction, Janko 1982, 151–80, has concluded that the hymn to Aphrodite was probably composed in northern Ionia or Aeolis.

41. Wilamowitz 1920, 83 n. 1, was in no doubt about the debt of *Homeric Hymn 5, To Aphrodite,* to Asiatic myth: "Hier dürfte es aber Umbildung des asiatischen Kultmythus sein, denn diese Aphrodite ist keine andere als die Kybele, zu der Attis gehört." Rose 1924 and Nilsson 1955, 522–23, approve this association. Ferri 1960 reviews earlier interpretations, and strongly supports the equation of Aphrodite in the hymn with Anatolian Kubaba. Boedeker 1974 argues that Aphrodite in the hymn, and in epic poetry generally, reflects an earlier Indo-European dawn goddess. Friedrich 1978, stressing the syncretic nature of Aphrodite, recognizes (68–69) the likely connection to Phrygian legend in this hymn. Among more recent studies, Crane 1988, 64–70, discerns the Near Eastern background to Aphrodite in the hymn, while P. M. Smith 1981a, and Clay 1989, 152–201 (with a review of scholarship on pp. 152–54, nn. 2–6), have sought to understand the hymn in its own terms, without adopting a strong position regarding origin and influences.

Zeus, in the *Homeric Hymn to Aphrodite,* bring about the birth of a child, Aeneas, "who is destined to be lord over the Trojans" (ὃς ἐν Τρώεσσιν ἀνάξει).[42] Zeus does so by impelling Aphrodite to couple in secret with a humble mortal, the herdsman Anchises. After anointing herself with perfumed oil and dressing in elaborately decorated clothing and rich jewelry in her temple at Paphos on Cyprus, Aphrodite comes to Anchises on Mount Ida "of the many springs, mother of wild beasts [μήτηρ θηρῶν]."[43] As the goddess approaches, "gray wolves and fierce-eyed lions fawn on her, and bears, and swift leopards ravenous for deer."[44] Making her unannounced appearance to Anchises, "like a matchless maiden [παρθένος ἀδμήτη] in height and form," Aphrodite is hailed by him as a sovereign deity (ἄνασσα).[45] Perhaps, he says, she is "Artemis, or Leto, or golden Aphrodite, or well-bred Themis or gray-eyed Athena, or perhaps one of the Graces . . . or else one of the nymphs who inhabit this lovely mountain and its river springs and grassy meadows."[46]

The encounter of a man with an unknown woman who might prove to be a powerful goddess is a familiar Homeric scene.[47] Such encounters mark moments when the woman has the power to change the destiny of a man. Like the unforeseeable path that she opens to a man at such a moment, the divine identity suggested by the providential woman is fundamentally am-

42. *Homeric Hymn* 5, *To Aphrodite* 196.

43. *Homeric Hymn* 5, *To Aphrodite* 68. This and several of the features of the hymn to Aphrodite discussed below are also noted by Ferri 1960 and Crane 1988, 68, as indicators of the identity of Aphrodite with Kybele or Kubaba.

44. *Homeric Hymn* 5, *To Aphrodite* 69–72. Note the assembly of fawning beasts around the Idaean Mother's mountain spring in Apollonius *Argonautica* 1.1123–45. *Homeric Hymn* 14, *To the Mother of the Gods* 4–5, speaks of the affinity of the Mother for "wolves and fierce-eyed lions, echoing mountains, and wooded glens." Note also the "bull-devouring lions" of the Mother in Sophocles *Philoctetes* 400–401 (below, note 122); beasts serve her in Euripides *Helen* 1310–11; leopards and ferocious beasts protect and suckle the infant Kybele, and Midas honors her with the statues of leopards and lions in Diodorus 3.59.1 and 8; rock-carved lions fawn around the image of the Mother in the sixth-century Phrygian monument at Arslankaya (shown here in figure 2).

45. *Homeric Hymn* 5, *To Aphrodite* 81–82 and 92. This passage and the associated descriptions of Aphrodite's elaborate attire (60–65, 85–90, 161–65) recollect Justin's description (11.7.6) of the appearance to Gordius of the Telmessian woman of extraordinary beauty, and the appearance of the standing goddess in Phrygian reliefs (see figure 4 in chapter 2), in Sardian reliefs (see figure 7 below), and in Neo-Hittite reliefs, where she is elaborately dressed and regularly holds a mirror as a symbol of her artful beauty. (See figure 5 below; see also Bittel 1980–83; Van Loon 1991, 8–13, figure 4, and plates 9, 12b, 13a, 15b, and 16b; Roller 1999, 47–49 and figures 3 and 4.) M. L. West 1997, 204, draws a comparison between this passage in the hymn to Aphrodite and the appearance of Sumerian Inanna to her lover Dumuzi; see Leick 1994, 64–129, and note that later Akkadian hymns praising Ishtar and other divine consorts, Nana and Tašmetu (Leick 180–92), also bear comparison to the *Homeric Hymn To Aphrodite,* which is contemporary to Neo-Assyrian and Neo-Babylonian examples.

46. *Homeric Hymn* 5, *To Aphrodite* 91–99.

47. Compare especially Odysseus' encounter with Nausicaä, *Odyssey* 6.149–85.

biguous in nature. Not only is it unclear whether the woman is a goddess or a mere mortal, but it is also unclear which goddess she might be. Furthermore, the very range of alternative divine identities enumerated on such an occasion describes a quality characteristic of each of those deities. When, on other occasions, goddesses such as Artemis, or Themis, or Demeter are separately invoked, they are often hailed as "you who have many names" (πολυώνυμε).[48] This might suggest that the roll call of names like that found in the hymn to Aphrodite should be understood as an endeavor of the hymnist to name each and every manifestation of divinity that might be united in the striking appearance of an unknown woman, without implying that only one of the several alternatives could be correct.[49] The ambiguity or uncertainty conveyed by the narrative reflects the admission of the knowing singer, and hearer, of this story that in the presence of a divine force human comprehension has its limits.

Indications that the cult of this goddess is especially appropriate to a Phrygian setting soon follow in the hymn. Anchises ends his address with the promise of founding a conspicuous altar to her, and offering sacrifices in every season in exchange for the prominence, prosperity, and progeny that she might grant him. Such a vow made on Mount Ida must have called to mind the Mountain Mother, as she was known to classical audiences.[50] In the hymn, the disingenuous goddess introduces herself as the daughter of Otreus, lord of all Phrygia. She claims to have been seized by Hermes and brought to Anchises from her place among the nymphs and marriageable

48. For expressions of the polyonymous or ambiguous identity of goddesses, see the Aeschylean *Prometheus Bound* 209–10: "My mother [who is] Themis and Earth, many names for one form"; Aristophanes *Thesmophoriazusae* 320: "O many-named huntress" (Artemis); Euripides *Bacchae* 275–76: "divine Demeter, she is Ge, call her by whichever name you wish." Note the recitation of possible sources of divine possession in Euripides *Hippolytus* 141–50, where Hecate, the Mountain Mother, and Dictynna are among those named for an affliction caused by Aphrodite. *Homeric Hymns* 9, *To Artemis,* and 14, *To the Mother of the Gods,* both refer to honors paid simultaneously to these goddesses and "to all goddesses" (θεαί πᾶσαι; see chapter 4 at note 117).

49. The unification of diverse identities is characteristic of the Hellenistic aretalogies of Isis: see Henrichs 1984, 349–53, and Versnel 1990, 39–67, who discusses the description of Isis as "tyrant of all lands." For this as a characteristic of Neoplatonic thought, see Proclus *Hymn to Hecate and Janus* 6.1–2, where Hecate is identified with the Mother of the Gods, and Julian *Orationes* 5, *To the Mother of the Gods* 166a–b. Note the dedicatory epigram of the second century C.E. addressed to the patron goddess of Hierapolis Castabala in Cilicia: "Whether you are Selene, or Artemis, or whether you, divine one, are torch-bearing Hecate, whom we honor at crossroads, or Cypris [Aphrodite] of Thebe, whom the people honor in sacrificial gatherings, or Deo, mother of Kore Persephone, hear ye! and keep your leader safe and sound, and convey the famous consul to Italy" (after the text as edited by L. Robert, in Dupont-Sommer and Robert 1964, 51). The epichoric name of this deity, attested in an Aramaic text also published by Dupont-Sommer and Robert 1964, is Kubaba.

50. Compare *Homeric Hymn* 5, *To Aphrodite,* 99–101, to Diodorus 3.59.8: "As for Kybele, in ancient times they erected altars and performed sacrifices to her yearly."

maidens at the dance of Artemis,[51] and she promises rich gifts and a propitious wedding granted by her father to legitimize their destined union.[52] After her perfect seduction of Anchises, she reveals her divine identity to him, justifies her passion by referring to his godlike appearance, and foretells sovereignty for their son.[53] Their child, the future lord of the Trojans, Aeneas, is to be reared by woodland nymphs.[54] Finally, Aphrodite returns her identity to the ambiguity with which it began by warning Anchises never to reveal the true name of the mother of his child.[55]

The *Homeric Hymn to Aphrodite* lays the foundation to a claim of divine ancestry for sovereignty—but whose sovereignty? Aeneas, the favored child of the union of goddess and mortal man, is destined to be lord over the Trojans. But Troy was destroyed in the lifetime of Aeneas and the aged Anchises, as all who heard this hymn would know. The rulership bestowed to Aeneas by Aphrodite was a destiny that Romans and especially the house of the Julii would later lay claim to, but one could hardly claim that legitimization of the Roman empire was the immediate object of this archaic hymn.[56] The immediate beneficiary, I suggest, was the Mermnad dynasty of Lydia.

51. *Homeric Hymn* 5, *To Aphrodite* 107–21. The theme of a lost daughter, central to the *Homeric Hymn* 2, *To Demeter,* is often associated with the Mother of the Gods. In Euripides *Helen* 1312–18, the Mother of the Gods, also named Deo, searches in the company of Artemis and Athena for her own daughter, who has been "seized from the circle of maiden dances"; Aphrodite is the first to placate the grieving mother (1346–52). The "Phrygian man" who was put to death by the Athenians reported that the Mother was searching for her daughter. (See chapter 2 at note 13.) In Diodorus 3.58–59, Kybele, also called Mountain Mother, is herself the lost daughter; her own mother, Dindymene, is another name for the Mother of the Gods. (See chapter 2, with notes 73 and 76.)

52. *Homeric Hymn* 5, *To Aphrodite* 126–42. The love of a divine daughter of the king of Phrygia for a humble herdsman is a prominent feature in the later mythology of Phrygian Kybele and her beloved Attis: Diodorus 3.58.1–4; Theocritus 20.40. Following a late classical convention for depicting the Trojan Paris in a Phrygian herdsman's garb, Attis is regularly depicted as a shepherd in Hellenistic art: see Roller 1999, 180, 212. The story of the ring of Gyges, as told by Plato *Republic* 359d–60b, speaks of a herdsman who usurps kingship by marrying the queen.

53. *Homeric Hymn* 5, *To Aphrodite* 192–255. Note the adaptation of the motif of divine motherhood and kingship in *Homeric Hymn* 2, *To Demeter,* 225–300, where the goddess nurses Demophon, son of the ruler of Eleusis, and makes him grow like a god (235 and 300: δαίμονι ἶσος).

54. *Homeric Hymn* 5, *To Aphrodite* 256–85. A woodland nymph, or naiad, conceived and bore Attis after being impregnated by the severed genitals of Agdistis, according to the Phrygian legend related by Pausanias 7.17.10–11; cf. Ovid *Fasti* 4.223–44; Arnobius *Adversus Nationes* 5.5–7.

55. *Homeric Hymn* 5, *To Aphrodite* 286–90. The principle of anonymous motherhood is found in the stories of Gordius and the birth of Midas, where the bride and mother is not named, and in the story of Meles and the lion that signifies kingship, where the consort who bore the lion is not named. The names Kybele and Mother, moreover, are epithets. Naming is consistently an ambiguous or even deliberately obscured feature in these traditions.

56. Several recent commentators have remarked on the surprising "vacuum in which this admirable poem stands" (Clay 1989, 152; see also P. M. Smith 1981a, 8). Janko 1982, 151, finds the *Homeric Hymn to Aphrodite* to be "remarkably obscure in terms of date, place of origin and

Anchises and Aeneas are descendants of Dardanus, and it is as a Dardanid that Aphrodite hails Anchises when she reveals her identity and their mutual accomplishment to him.[57] By tradition vouched in the *Iliad,* the Dardanids were favorites of Zeus, and had occupied the land around Mount Ida before Troy was even built.[58] Later sources affirm that Dardanus once ruled over many nations in Asia, and that, as a token of his honored kingship, Dardanus had established the rites of the Mother of the Gods in Phrygia.[59] The Dardanid connection to Aphrodite on Mount Ida and in Phrygia thus appears to be part of the amalgamation of the Trojan and Phrygian identity that is accepted as fact by classical Attic playwrights.[60] Dardanid identity was also one of the links through which the Mermnad rulers of Lydia legitimized their appropriation of Phrygian sovereignty.

Strabo describes Abydus on the Hellespont as a Milesian foundation made under the authority of Gyges, and goes on to note that Gyges was king of "the entire Troad, and a peninsula toward Dardanus was named Gygas [after him]."[61] Other traditions reinforce this connection between the region of the Hellespont and Gyges, the founder of the Mermnad dynasty. The father of Gyges, according to Herodotus and other sources, was named Dascylus.[62] The name of Dascylus has long suggested to scholars that Gyges was native to the region known as Dascylitis in Hellespontine Phrygia, where Das-

---

relation to other poetry." Janko's subsequent conclusions about the date and place of its composition (cited above, notes 39 and 40) therefore have the virtue of being deduced without the prejudice of a particular theory about its connections. The vacuum observed by Clay and Smith exists only, as both indirectly acknowledge, if one dismisses a priori the connection to "Anatolian Great Mother cults" (Clay 152) that many other scholars have defended. (See above, note 41.) Erskine 2001, 47, 93–112, 126, reviews the comparatively few and obscure claimants specifically to the legacy of Aeneas among archaic and classical communities (chiefly Aeneia in the Chalcidice, and communities in the Troad itself); see also P. M. Smith 1981b, who finds such connections so inconsequential that, rightly, he dismisses them as a significant consideration in the transmission of the *Homeric Hymn to Aphrodite.*

57. *Homeric Hymn* 5, *To Aphrodite* 177: Ὄρσεο, Δαρδανίδη ("Rise, Dardanid!"), perhaps as much a prophecy as a command.

58. Aeneas describes his heritage in *Iliad* 20.213–43.

59. Diodorus 5.48–49; cf. Apollodorus *Library* 3.12.1–3; Conon *FGrHist* 26 F 1.21.

60. Edith Hall 1988 asks, "When did the Trojans turn into Phrygians?" and concludes that Aeschylus probably originated this conflation. (See also Hall 1989, 38–39.) The *Homeric Hymn To Aphrodite,* however, clearly shows that the foundation for such conflation already existed in the seventh century.

61. Strabo 13.1.22. See also Aristotle fr. 484 (Rose) for testimony that the Mermnad dynasty founded Adramyttium, below Mount Ida. Talamo 1979, 65–98, examines the traditional association of the Maeonians (ancestral Lydians) with the region around Mount Ida.

62. Herodotus 1.8.1 reports that Gyges was the son of Dascylus; at 1.12–14, Herodotus cites the authority of Archilochus and the Delphic Oracle for his account of the foundation of Gyges' dynasty. Nicolaus of Damascus *FGrHist* 90 F 47.10–11 also names Gyges son of Dascylus. (See Nicolaus F 44.11, 45–47, for testimony that Dascylus was a dynastic name in the

cyleum near Cyzicus was later a satrapal capital second only to Sardis in prestige.[63] A tradition traceable to Hellanicus of Lesbos at the end of the fifth
century, with a probable origin in archaic epic, relates that Aeneas was father to Ascanius, who became king in Dascylitis, a region of Hellespontine
Phrygia.[64] The essential links between divinity, sovereignty, and the lands
along the shores of the Hellespont and in the Troad are clearly present within
the *Iliad* and the Homeric hymn to Aphrodite, and they describe the ancestry
of the Mermnads. Later, after the fall of the Mermnad dynasty, there was little incentive among the Greeks to recall this ancient claim to kingship held
by the men from Dascylitis. But during the heyday of the Mermnads, from
the first half of the seventh until the middle of the sixth centuries, it supported the legitimacy of a splendid dynasty. Among those who shared the
Homeric tradition, this memory of the Dardanid lineage justified Mermnad
tyranny in Lydia and over many nations in Asia.

The silence that Aphrodite enjoins on Anchises about the divine maternity of Aeneas has seemed an odd feature of the *Homeric Hymn to Aphrodite*
in view of the fact that the *Iliad* depicts Aeneas openly declaring his parentage.[65] But the oddity of this feature disappears when we see that the hymn
presents Aeneas as an archetype of a semidivine king. Until he was grown,

---

Mermnad line.) It is highly probable that Gyges was called the son of Dascylus either by Archi-
ochus or by the Delphic Oracle, or both, in the seventh century. Parke and Wormell 1956 omit
the oracles to Gyges from their inventory of Delphic oracles, evidently because they regard the
story surrounding them as "too improbable for belief" (vol. 1, 128). The oracle to Gyges comes
with better credentials than many that they do include, however, and they even observe indications (139 n. 5) that Herodotus has paraphrased a genuine oracular text.

63. Dascyleum near Cyzicus: Strabo 12.8.10, 13.1.3. On Dascylus as a man from Dascyleum,
see How and Wells 1912, vol. 1, 58; Pedley 1968, 46; Baldriga 1997, 283–84. On the possible
Hittite etymology for the name Dascylus, see Neumann 1999, 17 and n. 7. On the Lydo-Phry-
gian culture of Dascyleum, see Bakir and Gusmani 1993 for the evidence of epichoric graffiti,
and Gürtekin-Demir 2002 for the evidence of Lydian pottery. For funerary monuments from
the Persian period at Dascyleum, see Nollé 1992.

64. Ascanius son of Aeneas, eponym of the Ascanian lake, becomes king in Dascylitis according
to Dionysius of Halicarnassus *Roman Antiquities* 1.47.5–6, citing the *Troica* of Hellanicus (*FGrHist*
4 F 31). Elsewhere, Ascanius is a Phrygian arrayed at Troy beside the chieftains of Maeonia (Lydia): *Iliad* 2.862–66; Apollodorus *Epitome* 3.35; cf. Strabo 12.4.5–8, 14.5.29, citing Xanthus of Lydia (*FGrHist* 765 F 14) on Phrygians coming from Ascania after the fall of Troy. Conon *FGrHist*
26 F 1.46 relates a tradition that Priam sent Oxynius and Scamandrus, sons of Hector, to safety
in Lydia upon the fall of Troy, and that they were later received by Aeneas on Mount Ida, all by
the grace of Aphrodite. On the historical relationship of Trojans to Lydians, see Neumann 1999
and Beekes 2002, who draw on a variety of evidence to argue that the ancestors of the historical
Lydians occupied the region of Hellespontine Phrygia and the Troad in the Bronze Age.

65. *Iliad* 20.208–9. See P. M. Smith 1981a, 98: "What are we intended to make of this (ultimately ineffective) prohibition and threat?" Smith (98–99) suggests that the audience's awareness that Aphrodite's command was eventually violated served to make this passage foreshadow
the eventual punishment of Anchises. Clay 1989, 198: "The injunction is puzzling."

Aeneas was vulnerable and his maternity had to remain concealed. But once he asserted his divinely ordained status, his secret had to be known. His heroic deeds and his claim to divine maternity each validated and explained the other. To all who later heard the tale of his conception, the story of Aeneas represented the possibility that a living king, who might appear godlike in deeds and appearance, might yet be the nursling of a goddess.[66]

In historical terms, any man who encouraged the notion that he was the son of a goddess asserted not only his own preeminence, but that of his father and his lineage as well. For Aphrodite did not consort with any but her most treasured darling among men, as the Homeric hymn makes clear. The reputation of divine parentage was a status that could be indulged by only the proudest of men from the proudest of families. The Greek lyric poets of the Anatolian coast attest that the godlike maidens of Lydia often brought Aphrodite to the minds of their beholders. But they also reminded their audiences that the intimate company of a woman who might be the goddess was not for ordinary men, but for tyrants, and the tyrants of Lydia above all others.

Alcman, the poet of Sardis and of Sparta, invites the spectators of his chorus of marriageable girls to yearn for what they cannot have: "Let no man soar to heaven nor yearn to mate Aphrodite, Mistress of Paphos."[67] Sappho of Lesbos praises the object of her desiring especially as she is highlighted in a Lydian setting: "Like a glorious goddess . . . now she shines among the women of Lydia." Elsewhere, Sappho juxtaposes surpassing beauty and Lydian martial might: "I would rather the sweet sound of her footfall and the sight of the brightness of her beaming face than all the chariots and armored footmen of Lydia."[68] Alcaeus, also of Lesbos, thinks of Lydian tyrants when he imagines the most enviable coupling: "Why when a distinguished man weds a woman who is all things to all, why, tell me, does he like to have a bodyguard like the king of the Lydians whenever he desires her sweetly?"[69] Similarly, Se-

---

66. For this reason, I cannot agree with Clay 1989, 166–201, where she argues that "Zeus' plan [in compelling Aphrodite to seduce Anchises] aimed at putting an end to sexual relations between gods and humans, thereby bringing a close to the age of heroes" (p. 198). The hymn nowhere indicates that this was a terminal act. Rather, it shows how such a rare event could take place in the most unlikely of circumstances, and only become known long after, when the glory of the resulting offspring was manifest. The alleged divine paternity of Alexander the Great (foretold by a Telmessian seer: Plutarch *Alexander* 2.3) illustrates how the potential for reenactment was always present.

67. Alcman *Partheneion* 1.16–21 (Edmonds *LG*). M. L. West 1997, 121 and 524, calls attention to the Near Eastern resonances in this passage of the imagery of soaring up to heaven. On Alcman's Sardian and Spartan identity, see chapter 1, note 122.

68. Sappho 86.5–9 (Edmonds *LG;* = 96 LP), and 38.17–20 (Edmonds *LG;* = 16 LP).

69. Alcaeus 37b (Edmonds *LG*, appendix; = A5 LP), where "Lydian" is a probable restoration to the text: [ὡς Λύδων βα]σίλευς ἔχην. Despite the many lacunae in this passage (restored *exempli gratia* by Edmonds, on which my translation is based), its general sense of drawing attention to the singular nature of royal marriages is clear.

monides, poet of Samos or Amorgos, warns against taking a dainty bride: "Such a woman is a beautiful sight for other men, but she becomes a bane for the one who has her, unless he be some tyrant or sceptered ruler, who takes pride in such adornments."[70]

The injunctions of Alcman and Semonides for ordinary men to guard themselves against yearning for what they cannot, or should not have, are reminiscent of the disavowal of tyranny voiced a generation earlier by Archilochus, when he wrote: "I am not interested in the wealth of golden Gyges, nor have I ever envied him, nor am I jealous of the doings of gods, nor do I desire great tyranny, for such things are far from my eyes."[71] Having the wealth and the great tyranny of Gyges, by implication, would involve a man in "the doings of gods" (θεῶν ἔργα). From the foregoing, we should understand that the most desirable such doings were those of Aphrodite, which, like gold itself, were so alluring.

But the doings of Aphrodite were the very essence of Lydian kingship, as the tale of Gyges and his encounter with the wife of Candaules illustrates. At the opening of his *Histories* (1.8–12), Herodotus tells the story of the folly of a king (Candaules) who was so infatuated with his own wife that he believed her to be the most beautiful woman in the world. The king felt that his impassioned conviction required affirmation, however, and so he commanded his trusted bodyguard, Gyges, to spy on her as she disrobed in her bedchamber at night, so that he, too, might see the truth that only Candaules knew. Gyges, loyal to his master but wiser than he, warned Candaules of the impropriety of this scheme, adding that "when a woman sheds her robe she also sheds her modesty." In shedding her clothing, the consort of the king reveals her true power, a divine and all-pervading power over the beholder.[72] But Candaules insisted, and Gyges obeyed and saw the queen naked in her bedchamber that night. But she saw Gyges as he was leaving, and realizing what her husband had done, the next day she summoned Gyges and gave

---

70. Semonides 7.67–70.

71. Archilochus fr. 19 (West; = 25 Edmonds *EI*), discussed in chapter 1 at note 116.

72. The warning of Gyges evokes the striking aspect of the Naked Goddess, Asiatic Aphrodite (Inanna, Ishtar, Astarte, Anat, or Asherah among other possible names), who demonstrates her power by revealing her nakedness. (For an example, see figure 6 below.) On the type in general, see U. Winter 1983, esp. 192–99; and Budin 2003a, 199–271, for the widespread Bronze Age type whose center of dissemination appears to be in Syria. Keel and Uehlinger (1998, 97–108, 154–67, 198–204, 323–49) trace the evolution of the type in Palestine; see also Hadley 2000, 156–205. Striking representations of the Naked Goddess come from Syria and Cyprus from the tenth through the fifth century, and examples are found on Samos within this period; see Orthmann 1971, plate 24b; J. Karageorghis 1977, plates 25, 33b, and 34; Burkert 1992, 18–20 and figure 2; Kyrieleis 1993, 146–48 and figure 7.15; V. Karageorghis 2000, 202–4 no. 330; Budin figures 8a, d, f; 9a–g. N. Marinatos 2000, 1–45, examines the marginal presence of the type in Greek orientalizing art.

him a choice: "Either you slay Candaules and take me and the kingship of the Lydians, or you yourself must die immediately!" Gyges made the necessary choice, and became ruler of the Lydians. "And so," Herodotus says at the conclusion of the story, "the Mermnads gained the tyranny, having deposed the Heraclids" (1.14.1).

Although no mention is made of Aphrodite in this story, the transfer of sovereignty here clearly involved her doings. The story was a popular one, told in several versions both before and after Herodotus.[73] The earliest of them, Herodotus affirms, was told by Archilochus, a contemporary of Gyges.[74] The story was one of many reminders familiar to the Greeks that it is presumptuous for any but a tyrant to consort directly with Aphrodite, or her likeness as the most beautiful woman in the world. And intimacy with Aphrodite was the prerogative of the tyrants of Lydia. Their claim to rulership both justified and depended upon it.

### APHRODITE, KYBEBE, AND KUBABA

Among the Phrygians and Lydians, Aphrodite had her own name, we are told by Charon of Lampsacus: she was called Kybebe ($Kυβήβη$).[75] Charon's contemporary Herodotus also tells us that Kybebe was a local deity ($\dot{\epsilon}πιχωρίη$ $θεός$) with a shrine of some importance at Sardis.[76] The local deity of Sardis, as Herodotus calls her, was a goddess with a long history in central Anatolia and northern Syria, where cuneiform, hieroglyphic Luwian, and Aramaic sources uniformly name her Kubaba.[77] Kubaba was also the paradigm for

73. The so-called Gyges Tragedy, known from papyrus fragments, gives an alternative version that might predate Herodotus; see Clay 1986, 12 and n. 20, for scholarship. Among later versions, the most famous is the story of the ring of Gyges told by Plato *Republic* 2.359d–360b; see Fauth 1970. Nicolaus of Damascus *FGrHist* 90 F 47.6 relates a version where the consort is actually the bride-to-be of Candaules, who first takes Gyges into her bed.

74. Herodotus 1.12.2, a reference bracketed by some editors as suspicious, but unnecessarily so. The reference is accepted as genuine, e.g., by Labarbe 1971, 491, and by Clay 1986, who argues persuasively that Archilochus fr. 23 (West) is a fragment of Archilochus' poem depicting the fateful encounter of Gyges and the wife of Candaules.

75. Charon of Lampsacus *FGrHist* 262 F 5 (= Photius s.v. $Kύβηβος$): $Χάρων$ $δὲ$ $ὁ$ $Λαμψακηνὸς$ $\dot{\epsilon}ν$ $τῇ$ $πρώτῃ$ $τὴν$ $Ἀφροδίτην$ $ὑπὸ$ $Φρυγῶν$ $καὶ$ $Λυδῶν$ $Κυβήβην$ $λέγεσθαι$. The same identification is made by Hesychius s.v. $Κυβήβη$ $ἡ$ $μήτηρ$ $τῶν$ $θεῶν.$ $καὶ$ $ἡ$ $Ἀφροδίτη$. Empedocles' praise of Aphrodite as a primal cosmic force bears comparison to the identification of Aphrodite with Kybebe (DK 31 B 17.24, 98.3, 128.4, 151; Kirk et al. 1983, 289, 302, 318); cf. also the fertility-engendering powers of Aphrodite described by Aeschylus *Danaids* fr. 44 (Radt; = Athenaeus 13.600a).

76. Herodotus 5.102.1: $\dot{\epsilon}ν$ $δὲ$ $αὐτῇσι$ [sc. $\dot{\epsilon}ν$ $Σάρδισι$] $καὶ$ $ἱρὸν$ $\dot{\epsilon}πιχωρίης$ $θεοῦ$ $Κυβήβης$. It is mentioned because it was burned in the Ionian Revolt, and became the Persians' justification for burning Greek shrines; these historical circumstances are discussed in chapter 6.

77. On the identification of Kybebe with Kubaba, see Laroche 1960. For a thorough survey of the textual sources for the cult of Kubaba in cuneiform and hieroglyphic Luwian texts, see Hawkins 1980–83; Hutter 2003, 221 and 271–73, discusses Kubaba in the Luwian pantheon.

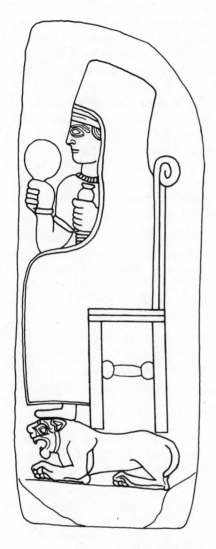

Figure 5. Relief of Kubaba enthroned
atop a lion, holding a mirror and scepter,
ninth or early eighth century B.C.E.,
from Carchemish.

the mother of Midas, or the Phrygian Mother, who became better known to
posterity as Kybele.

Kubaba's chief cult place was at Carchemish on the Euphrates, where hieroglyphic Luwian inscriptions hail her as "Queen of Carchemish." Reliefs
from Carchemish and elsewhere depict Kubaba in jewels and elaborate dress,
wearing a tall headpiece and a veil, and holding a mirror. The mirror suggests that Kubaba was famous for her beauty, while the elaborate ornaments
she wears are reminiscent of the jewelry donned by Aphrodite in her Cypriot

shrine, according to the Homeric hymn. Kubaba is usually depicted enthroned, sometimes with a lion below her feet.[78] (See figure 5.) In monumental inscriptions from Carchemish dating from the tenth through the eighth centuries, Kubaba is described as a deity of processions and of war, marching in the company of her male divine counterparts at the head of the armies of her favored rulers. Reliefs at Carchemish depict musicians beating drums and playing pipes near the enthroned image of Kubaba. In all these attributes, we find Kubaba anticipating the Phrygian Mother of the Gods, and Kybebe whose seat of sovereignty was at Sardis.

From the mid-eighth century, a stele with a dedicatory inscription by the ruler of Carchemish, Kamanis, bears a relief of Kubaba standing in a frontal pose. The inscription gives an elaborate picture of the veneration owed to this deity by every rightful ruler:[79]

> Kubaba's temple . . . I built, I myself set up my statue in front. . . . for Kubaba, Queen of Carchemish, I, Kamanis the Ruler, made an honored precinct. Kings and . . . lords will come in to pray to her, . . . He who shall come against this divinity with malice, . . . and shall not do [good to the house] of Kamanis, or who shall not listen to these words, against him may Kubaba of the hundred KISTARAs litigate, and for him [may she . . . ]

The hieroglyphic Luwian texts from Carchemish and elsewhere also reveal the origin of the word tyrant, Greek *tyrannos*, in the title *tarwanis*.[80] Phonologically, *tarwan-* was pronounced *\*trun-* in Luwian. (*Tροία*, "Troy," from Hittite *taruisa* › *\*truisa*, is a parallel.) Luwian *\*trun-* could have yielded the

---

78. The Carchemish monuments are published in Woolley and Barnett 1952, and Orthmann 1971, plates 20–37 (see pp. 274–79); selections in Bittel 1980–83; Roller 1999, figures 3 and 4; Aro 2003, 320–21. A mirror is a feminine attribute in late Neo-Hittite funerary reliefs from Maraş, depicting a couple (mirror held by the wife), and a couple with daughter (mirror held by the daughter): see Akurgal 1968, plates 26–28; Orthmann 374, plates 43h and 47d; Aro 326 and plate XXIIa.

79. *CHLI* vol. i.1, no. II.26 (Carchemish A31/32), sections 3–4, 7–8, 10–16, translated (with modifications) by J. D. Hawkins; cf. Woolley and Barnett 1952, 262; Hawkins 1981, 155–57 no. 6. The text is inscribed on the back of a basalt stele depicting a frontal standing image of Kubaba (now in the British Museum): see Bittel 1980–83; Rein 1996, figure 1; Roller 1999, figure 3. According to Hawkins 2000, 143, the reference to 100 KISTARAs is probably to "some type of temple of Kubaba's." The verb translated as "litigate" is represented by a logogram, transcribed LIS, whose meaning appears to be the opposite of "advocate," i.e., "contradict" or "oppose" (see Hawkins 2000, 418); context elsewhere indicates that this figurative term can describe the outbreak of war (*CHLI* vol. i.1, no. II.1, line 3). The last line appears to contain "an imprecation . . . directed against the malefactor's food" (Hawkins 2000, 143).

80. The derivation of Greek *tyrannos* from Luwian *tarwanis* has wide support among comparative linguists and specialists in Anatolian languages. It is advocated by Meriggi 1953, 44–46; Heubeck 1961, 69; Chantraine 1968, vol. 4.1, 1146; Gusmani 1969b, 511–12; Pintore 1983; Cornil 1995. Classicists look to Anatolia for the origin of this word (see especially Labarbe 1971), but are generally agnostic about its specific origin; Victor Parker 1998, 146, is an exception.

pronunciation *turan-, and hence τύραννος in Greek. Rulers in northern Syria, Cilicia, and Cappadocia in the early Iron Age commonly identified themselves in their monumental inscriptions by the title *tarwanis,* often in the same context in which they invoked Kubaba and her divine consorts. (E.g., "I am Katuwas, *tarwanis,* beloved by the gods. . . . Tarhunzas, Karhuhas, and Kubaba loved me because of my *tarwanati.*")[81] The etymology of *tarwanis* is not known, but a general meaning of "ruler," as J. D. Hawkins translates it, is clear from the context. The rulers who claim this title often also describe their leadership as *tarwanati* (ablative), usually translated "by [*or:* with] justice." The administration of justice was a distinctive attribute of Midas' kingship, as Herodotus and other sources attest, and it was generally a fundamental positive attribute of tyranny.[82] It is certainly significant that this form or attribute of rulership, *tarwanati,* appears prominently alongside the favor of Kubaba in monuments justifying the authority of Anatolian rulers.

Kubaba at Carchemish, like Kybebe at Sardis, was the protectress of tyrants. Kubaba's likeness to Aphrodite, with whom the Greeks identified Kybebe, is subtly indicated by the jewelry and the mirror she holds. Evidence of her irresistible sexuality is revealed, significantly, only when the sovereign consort, or wife of the ruler, is also represented, suggesting that the consort herself possessed this divine quality.

Among the tenth-century reliefs of the so-called Long Wall of Sculpture at Carchemish, the wife of the ruler Suhis II is depicted enthroned and wearing a veiled headpiece in a pose strikingly reminiscent of depictions of the goddess Kubaba (figure 6). A hieroglyphic text identifies her, and claims honors on a par with her husband. Immediately in front of her figure, at the same scale, is a standing frontal image of the Naked Goddess, winged and wearing a horned helmet, and offering her breasts.[83] No inscription names the goddess or explains the connection between her and the queen, but their juxtaposition leaves no doubt, even to the illiterate viewer, that the wife of

81.  Jasink 1998 reviews the geographic, chronological, and semantic contexts of the attested occurrences of the title *tarwanis,* concluding that the term "came in use in a new political situation occurring after the fall of the Hittite empire" (352). The text of Katuwas from Carchemish is translated by J. D. Hawkins, *CHLI* vol. i.1, no. II.11+12 (Carchemish nos. A11b, c).

82.  Herodotus 1.14.3 identifies the Throne of Midas at Delphi as a seat of judgment, and the resolution of factional strife was the quality that Midas first displayed as king, according to Arrian *Anabasis* 2.3.6. Note also that Deioces the Mede was "enamored of tyranny" (ἐρασθεὶς τυραννίδος) and rose to kingship over the Medes by virtue of his administration of justice, according to Herodotus 1.96–98.

83.  Hawkins 2000, 77, describes the monuments of Suhis II and his wife. The Long Wall of Sculpture is described by Woolley, in Woolley and Barnett 1952, 164–67. The relief of the wife of Suhis and the Naked Goddess, shown here in figure 6, is described by Woolley, 165–66; and Hawkins, 91, with illustrations of the wife of Suhis shown in plate 8; the full relief is illustrated by Woolley and Barnett, plates B 37a and B 40a, b; and by Orthmann 1971, plate 24b. The hieroglyphic text is presented in *CHLI* vol. i.1, no. II.7.

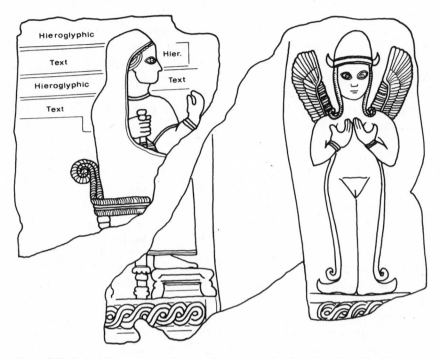

Figure 6. Relief of the enthroned wife of a ruler of Carchemish, identified by the hieroglyphic Luwian inscription, facing the standing Naked Goddess, who is not identified by any inscription, tenth century B.C.E., from Carchemish.

the ruler was intimately associated with the divine archetype of erotic love. As in the stories of the seduction of Anchises and the covert display of Candaules' wife, the revelation of supreme feminine sexuality signifies the imminence of irresistible sovereignty. Together with the deeds of Suhis, narrated on the adjacent wall, this scene of wife enthroned and goddess revealed presented a striking icon of the power of the ruler of Carchemish.[84]

The wide influence of Kubaba's cult in the early Iron Age is explained in

84. A monumental dedication to Kubaba by Panamuwatis, wife of the ruler of Kummuh (Commagene) in the early eighth century, reinforces the association of sovereignty with the goddess Kubaba through the mediation of the ruler's consort. In the text accompanying this dedication, Kubaba bears an unusual title rendered by the logogram FEMINA, meaning "woman" (also "wife") or "mother," suggesting that the goddess was assimilated to the role of the consort herself, or of the queen mother: *CHLI* vol. i.1, no. VI.1–2 (Boybeypınarı 1–2). On the title, see Hawkins 1981, 169; and 2000, 338. The same title appears on *CHLI* vol. i.1, no. VI.5 (Ancoz 1). The wife of a king from the region of the Orontes River in Syria bears the name of the goddess, Kupapiyas (Kubabiyas): *CHLI* vol. i.2, no. IX.14 (Sheizar).

part by the pivotal role of Carchemish among peoples and kingdoms around the eastern end of the Mediterranean.[85] Testimony to the wide connections maintained by rulers of Carchemish in the early eighth century is found in the texts of Yariris, a eunuch and devotee of Kubaba, and regent of Carchemish.[86] A relief bearing the image of Yariris reads, in part:[87]

> I am Yariris, the Ruler, . . . the Prince[?] far reputed from the West to the East, beloved by the gods. . . . my name on account of my justice Tarhunzas and the Sun caused to pass to heaven, and my name the gods caused to pass abroad, and men heard it for me on the one hand in Egypt [*Mizra*], and on the other hand they heard it [for me] in Babylon[?], and on the other hand they heard [it for me] among the Musa, the Muska and the Sura.

Musa, by the consensus of scholars commenting on this text, is what the Greeks call Mysia, and refers to the speakers of the Lydian language.[88] Muska is what Assyrian sources refer to as Mushki, the people ruled later in the eighth century by Mita, or Midas, and are therefore the Phrygians.[89] The fame of Yariris that the "the gods caused to pass abroad," as he claims, extended from the Hellespont to Egypt. This fame was spread through personal contact at Carchemish with people from these lands and through written correspondence in several languages, as Yariris claims in an inscription on a base that once supported his statue:[90]

> I am Yariris the Ruler, the Prince beloved by Tarhunzas, Kubaba, Karhuhas, and the Sun. Me the gods made strong and exalted over Carchemish. . . . Me the gods [ . . . ] in the city's writing, in the Suraean writing, in the Assyrian writing, and in the Taimani writing, and I knew twelve languages. My lord gathered every country's son to me by wayfaring concerning language, and he caused me to know every skill.

85. On the history of Carchemish, see Hawkins 1976–80 and 2000, 73–79. On the dominant influence of Carchemish in northern Syria during the ninth and eighth centuries, and its reflection in material culture, see I. J. Winter 1983.

86. Yariris' name was formerly read as Araras (Woolley and Barnett 1952, 240, e.g.). On Yariris' identity as a eunuch, see Hawkins 2000, 78 and n. 64, 128, and cf. 266, 349. Both of the following texts invoke Kubaba.

87. *CHLI* vol. i.1, no. II.22 (Carchemish A6), lines 1–6, translated (with modifications) by J. D. Hawkins. The logogram that Hawkins 2000, 126, identifies as "*Babylon*(?)" is a conjecture; Starke 1997a, 383–84, suggests that it signifies Urartu.

88. See Starke 1997a, 383–84; Hawkins 2000, 126. Neumann 1999, 19, and Beekes 2002, cols. 205–13, discuss the identification of the region of Mysia as Maeonia, said to be the earlier name for Lydia.

89. See chapter 2, notes 132–33.

90. *CHLI* vol. i.1, no. II.24 (Carchemish A15b), lines 1–2 and 18–22, translated (with modifications) by J. D. Hawkins. "The city's writing" is hieroglyphic Luwian. "Suraean writing" would either be an Urartian script (Hawkins) or Phoenician (Starke 1997a, 383–84). "Taimani writing" is probably Aramaic (Hawkins 2000, 133).

The statue of Yariris identified by this inscription was placed by Yariris "at the foot" of Kubaba, as the inscription states. Kubaba's name was never far from such monuments to the influence of Carchemish and its rulers. Kamanis, who ruled in the eighth century after Yariris and who erected the stele of Kubaba quoted above, proclaimed that even foreign rulers owed reverence to Kubaba: "Kings and . . . lords will come in to pray to her." Later in the eighth century, Pisiris of Carchemish became the ally of Midas (Mita of Mushki) against their common enemy Assyria. It is not unreasonable to suppose that Midas, like Hittite kings of the Bronze Age before him, honored the goddess of Carchemish, and may even have recognized her as a leader of armies and a.divine patron of all those allied to him.[91]

During the lifetime of Midas, Kubaba was the most influential goddess among rulers along the southeastern border of Midas' dominion; after Midas, she appears as a divinity honored especially at Sardis. The Greeks, as we have noted, knew her as a goddess of Lydians and Phrygians, and called her Kybebe ($Kυβήβη$), while the Lydians pronounced her name *Kuvavs* or *Kuvavas*.[92] Herodotus' reference to the shrine of Kybebe at Sardis (5.102) demonstrates that she was still held in high regard by the Persians after the fall of the Mermnad dynasty. When her shrine was burned by the Greeks at the beginning of the Ionian Revolt, Herodotus states, the Persians made this fact the justification for their retaliation against the shrines and temples of the gods of the Greeks. The vengeance of Kybebe, exacted as a demonstration of sovereignty, was a role that the rulers of Carchemish more than two centuries earlier would have understood: "He who shall come against this divinity with malice . . . against him may Kubaba of the hundred KISTARAs litigate!" As the sovereign lords of Lydia, the Persians were exacting divine justice in the name of Kubaba.

### KUBABA, KYBEBE, AND KYBELE

By the time Greek sources take note of Kubaba, in the sixth and fifth centuries, they call her Kybebe ($Kυβήβη$) and identify her with Aphrodite as she was known among the Phrygians and Lydians. At practically the same time that Kybebe appears, references to Kybele ($Kυβέλη$) appear in Greek sources, and there are indications that the two names were alternative appellations of the same divinity.[93] Later Greek and Latin authors explicitly treat the

---

91. A fragmentary inscription of Pisiris, the ally of Midas, declares reverence for Kubaba at some length, *CHLI* vol. i.1, no. II.31–32.

92. Gusmani 1969a publishes a graffito that preserves the root of Kybebe's name in Lydian as *Kuvav-*.

93. The forms Kybebe ($Kυβήβη$) and Kybelis ($Kύβελις$) are both attributed to Hipponax in the sixth century, frs. 127 and 156 (West). The naming of Kybele in early Greek sources is discussed by Roller 1999, 123–25.

names of Kybebe and Kybele (*Cybebe* and *Cybele* in Latin) as interchangeable, and equate both with the Mother of the Gods, Rhea, and Magna Mater.[94] The classical tradition, then, regarded these names as references to the same divinity, and many historians of religion have concurred with the judgment of classical sources on this point.[95] But not all scholars are confident that this equation provides an accurate picture of origins.

Scholars of Anatolian languages have expressed divergent views on the equation of Kybebe and Kybele.[96] In the absence of a plausible explanation of the phonological transformation of Kybebe into Kybele (or Kubaba into Kubeleya), the center of this debate has been taken by an analytic hypothesis, arguing for separate origins of these two names and of the deities they designate. Claude Brixhe has established the critical consensus on this question by observing that the Phrygian *Kubeleya* (also attested as *Kubileya*) is an attributive adjective modifying *Matar,* so *Matar Kubeleya* in Phrygian must mean "Kybeleyan Mother."[97] Unlike the proper name Kubaba, *Kubeleya* in Phrygian (the origin of the Greek *Κυβέλη*) is an epithet. As to the meaning of *Kubeleya,* Brixhe follows a tradition of comparative linguists who have observed that natural features in the Phrygian countryside, according to Greek sources, bore the name Kybela or Kybelon (*Κύβελα* or *Κύβελον*), suggesting that a Phrygian word underlies the name.[98] Brixhe has postulated that Greek *κύβελα* or *κύβελον* derives from the Phrygian word for "mountain," and that *Matar Kubeleya* is therefore identical in meaning to the Greek *μήτηρ ὀρεία*, "Mountain Mother," which is a well-attested appellation of the Mother of the Gods.[99]

The most significant conclusion that Brixhe deduces from this line of analy-

94. So Strabo 10.3.12 (quoted in chapter 2 at note 76). Virgil *Aeneid* 3.111 refers to *Mater Cybeli,* using Cybelus as a place name (cf. 11.768); at 10.220–33 Virgil names the goddess *Cybebe . . . Genetrix.* Catullus 63 alternates between Cybebe (63.9, 20, 35, 84, and 91: *Dea magna, dea Cybebe, dea domina Dindymi*) and Cybele (63.12, 68, 76). Lexicographers make the equation explicit: see Hesychius s.vv. *Κυβήβη, Κύβηβος*; Photius *Lexicon* s.v. *Κύβηβος*; *Etymologicum Gudianum* s.v. *Κυβήβη.*

95. So, for instance, Laroche 1960, Fauth 1969, col. 383, Diakonoff 1977, Vermaseren 1977, 21–24, and Burkert 1979a, 102–5, and 1985, 177–78, and Blomart 2002, 23–24, all consider that the names *Κυβήβη* and *Κυβέλη* both refer to the same deity.

96. Laroche 1960 offered no linguistic solution to "l'énigme de Cybèle" (128), although he felt that the historical evidence indicated that the link between Kubaba and Kybele would eventually be found. Diakonoff 1977 suggested that dissimilation could account for the development *Kubebe › Kubele,* but his explanation has not been taken up by others. Doubts about the equation were voiced by Gusmani 1969a, 160, and reinforced by Brixhe 1979.

97. Brixhe 1979 clarifies the readings of the relevant Old Phrygian texts and establishes the relationship between *Κυβέλη* in Greek and *Kubeleya* in Phrygian. See also Brixhe and Lejeune 1984, vol. 1, 45–47 no. W-04, and 62–68 no. B-01.

98. See Fauth 1969, 384, for references to earlier scholarship, and see Gusmani 1971, 314. For the Greek sources, see chapter 2 at notes 73–82.

99. Brixhe 1979, 43–45, supported by Zgusta 1982; Gusmani *LWErg* 68–69; and Innocente 1995, 216. (See also note 103 below.) It should be noted that, outside of this hypothesis, the Phrygian word for "mountain" is not attested.

sis is that the name Kybele is a Phrygian development, which can have nothing to do with the name Kubaba and its north Syrian origins.[100] At about the same time that Brixhe reached this conclusion, Fritz Graf presented a similar argument regarding the relationship between Phrygian Kybele and Lydian Kybebe. Based on iconography, the distribution of monuments, and testimonia to the names of these deities, Graf concluded that Lydian Kybebe "is clearly distinct from Cybele, whatever the relationship between the two names might be."[101] Supporting this hypothesis of separate origins, Mary Rein and Lynn Roller have drawn attention to distinctions between the Lydian and Phrygian deities, especially in iconographic details and in the settings of their monuments.[102] The apparent resemblance between the names Kybebe and Kybele, they conclude, is accidental, and the fact that the Greeks appear to have regarded them as one and the same is a sign of their insensitivity to distinct native origins. According to Roller: "The words Κυβήβη (Kybebe) and Κυβέλη (Kybele), while distinctive in their Anatolian languages, are only slightly different in Greek, and the Greeks may well have conflated them."[103]

This analytic hypothesis rests on the premise that the resemblance between Κυβήβη and Κυβέλη is only superficial, and has no legitimate linguistic explanation. Here I propose to dissolve the core of this analytic argument by showing that, on the contrary, the present understanding of Anatolian languages allows Κυβέλη to be explained as a development, via Phrygian *Kubeleya*, from the older name of Kubaba. This explanation respects Brixhe's demonstration that *Kubeleya* is an epithet, and his argument that it refers to topographical features (although not to mountains alone). The Phrygian epithet was formed out of the name of a deity long familiar to speakers of Hittite and Luwian, following patterns attested among related Anatolian languages, like Lydian, Lycian, and Carian, and only secondarily showing features imposed on it by speakers of Phrygian, which was a relative newcomer to Anatolia.[104]

---

100. Brixhe 1979, 45, concludes that his deductions "excluent que *Kubaba* et *Κυβέλη* dérivent d'un même thème ou que le second soit issu d'une altération du premier."

101. Graf 1984, 119 (from a paper delivered in 1979).

102. Rein 1993, 10–18, and 1996; Roller 1994b and 1999, 66–68 and 121–41.

103. Roller 1999, 124. Brixhe 1979, 44, put the matter differently, suggesting that the linguistic conflation corresponded to an ideological syncretism: "Ne serait-il pas préférable de voir dans la forme grecque [i.e., *Κυβέλη*] la contrepartie linguistique du syncrétisme culturel observé entre la déesse-mère phrygienne [i.e., *Matar Kubeleya*] et *Kybaba* (*Κυβήβη*)? *Κυβέλη* serait alors un compromis entre l'adjectif (phrygien) et *Κυβήβη*" (quoted with approval by Borgeaud 1996, 25). More recently, Manfred Hutter has expressed the relationship by suggesting that "among the Phrygians some external features of the Phrygian Mother were influenced by Kubaba, but such influences remained on a superficial level and did not really touch the character or symbolism of the Phrygian goddess" (2003, 272–73, citing Roller).

104. On Phrygian and its Balkan connections, see Neumann 1988, 4–8; Brixhe 1994, 175–76. On the close relationship among the Anatolian languages named above, to the exclusion of Phrygian, see Oettinger 1977; Melchert 1994, 121–22; and 2003, 11–23.

The name of Kubaba/Κυβήβη occurs in two Lydian inscriptions preserving the root form of her name: *Kuvav-*.[105] The attested vocalizations indicate that where Lydians pronounced the fricative *(v)*, others pronounced the labial stop *(b)* in the name of Kubaba/Κυβήβη.[106] Inflections in Lydian and related Anatolian languages will have altered the ending of this name according to its grammatical use. The genitive in Lydian is formed by an adjectival/genitive suffix, *-li-*, and a similar suffix, *-(ē)li*, is found in other Anatolian languages.[107] The adjectival or genitive form of the name of Kubaba in Lydian would thus, hypothetically, be *\*Kuvavli-*, pronounced by some as *\*Kubabli-*.

Both Lydian and Lycian show examples of this suffix attached to the names of divinities to create theophoric names. So from the name of Artemis (Lydian *Artimuś*, Lycian *Ertemi*) *Artimalis* is attested as a personal name in Lydian, and *Erttimeli* in Lycian, meaning "The One of Artemis."[108] Likewise, *Bakillis* is attested as the name of a Lydian month, formed from the name of a Lydian god *Baki-*.[109] The formation *\*Kuvavli-*, or *\*Kubabli-*, would accordingly fit a well-attested pattern for designating a person, place, or thing of or pertaining to Kubaba.

The consonant cluster at the end of *\*Kubabli-* was probably simplified to *\*Kuballi-* among speakers of Phrygian, and through an attested shift in vowels, *\*Kuballi-* became *\*Kubelli-*.[110] *\*Kubelli-* is probably the source of the Greek

---

105. One text, *LW* 252, no. 4a, line 4, names Kybebe as one of three deities protecting a tomb from desecration. (For corrected readings see Gusmani 1975, 266–67; uncorrected translation in Dusinberre 2003, 229–30, no. 11.) The second text, *LWErg* no. 72 (see Gusmani 1969a), is a graffito on a potsherd partially preserving her name. (On the findspot of this sherd, see note 120 below.) For the most likely readings of these texts, see Gusmani 1969a, and in *LWErg* 68 (revising an earlier reading in *LW* 156).

106. Gusmani *LW* 31–32 demonstrates the not infrequent alternation of the labials *b*, *v*, and *f* in Lydian.

107. On Lydian nominal declensions, see Gusmani *LW* 35–36 and Heubeck 1969, 405–9. On Lydian *-li-*, See Gusmani *LW* 36, *LWErg* 71; Heubeck 1969, 416–17; Georgiev 1981, 209; 1984, 9–10, and 34 n. 13. The possessive suffix *-(ē)li* is common to Carian, Lycian, Lydian, and Luwian; see Georgiev 1981, 211, and 1984, 8–9; Melchert 2003, 195.

108. Lydian *Artimalis*: Gusmani *LW* 63. Lycian *Erttimeli* and Ἀρτεμηλις: Laroche, in Metzger 1979, 58 and 114. Cf. Heubeck 1959, 21–23; Georgiev 1984, 9–10.

109. Gusmani *LW* 74. Cf. Greek Βάχχιος as a personal name, and the Ionian month Βακχιών: see Trümpy 1997, 57, 60, 64–65.

110. The consonant clusters *-vl-* and *-bl-* are not attested in surviving Old Phrygian texts, and may have been avoided in Phrygian. Brixhe 1994, 175–76, notices the tendency for Phrygian to adopt personal names from the Hittite and Luwian languages that Phrygian speakers came into contact with, yielding irregular nominal morphologies. Gusmani 1976, 79, discusses the vocalic phonology in the shift *ā* › *η*. The Lydian vocalic phonology is preserved in the earliest Greek text to name Kybele, a graffito on a sherd from Epizephyrian Locri, in southern Italy, probably dating to the early sixth century. It reads: [τᾶ]ς Ϙυβάλας ("of Kubala," using the Doric koppa instead of kappa); see Guarducci 1970 (the sherd is illustrated in a line drawing in Vermaseren 1977, 23, figure 12).

form *Κύβηλις*, said to be an epithet or a name for Rhea, the mother of Zeus, used by Hipponax of Ephesus at the end of the sixth century. Ioannes Tzetzes, who preserves this information, goes on to say that the name comes from the worship of this goddess in a Phrygian town called *Κυβέλλα*.[111] According to the derivation described here, this Phrygian *Κυβέλλα* can be understood as "Place of Kubaba."

Phrygian *Kubeleya* is a further formation from the same derivation. Like the Lydian suffix *-li-*, the Phrygian suffix *-eya* is used to form attributive adjectives.[112] The Phrygian *Kubeleya*, as an epithet modifying *Matar*, "Mother," can therefore be recognized as a Phrygian adjectival formation on *\*Kubelli-*, itself an adjectival formation from the name of Kubaba. *Matar Kubeleya* in the Phrygian inscriptions therefore designates "the Mother of the place of Kubaba," or "the Mother who is identified with the place of Kubaba." The name of Kubaba thus entered Phrygian as an attributive adjective in a form used in Lydian and in other Anatolian languages. The name was used to designate places that were especially associated with Kubaba.

The name *Κυβέλη* may have entered Greek, then, through the form *\*Kubelli-*, the probable origin of a Phrygian place name, *Κυβέλλα*, as noted above, and through the better-attested form *Kubeleya*. This last is identical to Greek *Κυβέλεια*, a place name (*πόλις*) in Ionia recorded by Hecataeus of Miletus at the end of the sixth century.[113] Phrygian *Kubeleya* and Greek *Κυβέλεια* alike were the names of places, and they were also divine epithets that characterized those places as dear to Kubaba. Greek *Κυβέλη* can be recognized as the nominalization of an attributive name, *Κυβέλεια*, just as the deity *Βασίλη*, attested at Athens and associated with the Ionian heroes Codrus and Neleus, can be understood as a personification of *βασιλεία*, "sovereignty," the attribute of a *βασιλεύς*.[114]

The somewhat odd tautology conveyed by the Phrygian *Matar Kubeleya*, "the Mother of the Place of Kybebe," is understandable as an invocation of the maternal aspect of a goddess of love in a place of erotic encounter. In her most ancient cult settings, the shrines of seventh- or sixth-century Phrygia, she was depicted as the beautiful bride who would become the mother of Midas. In the context of contemporary Lydia, such shrines in their natural settings demonstrated the opulence of the land under the rule of a

---

111. Hipponax fr. 156 (West), quoted in chapter 2 at note 78.

112. On the Phrygian adjectival or attributive suffix *-eyo/-eya* used in name formations, see Brixhe 1979, 43 n. 32; Neumann 1988, 7–8, 21.

113. Hecataeus *FGrHist* 1 F 230 (from Stephanus of Byzantium s.v. *Κυβέλεια*), cited in chapter 2 at note 79. Strabo 14.1.33 identifies Kybeleia as a village (*κώμη*) in the territory of Erythrae. A fourth-century dedication to *Μήτηρ Κυβέλεια* has been found on Chios: Forrest 1963, 59–60, no. 11.

114. On *Βασίλη*, see Shapiro 1986, and Kearns 1989, 151, where her relation to a figure named *βασιλεία* is noted. Note also the figure *Βασίλεια* in Aristophanes *Birds* 1537.

tyrant, who was the living consort of the goddess herself. Known also from her conspicuous mountains and their sheltering glens and secret caves that were nature's "bedchambers" (*thalamoi*), she was the divine Mother who, in the secret communion of Aphrodite and Anchises, had engendered the sovereign-lord-to-be. Her veneration in such places, beginning during the Lydian tyranny and continuing for centuries afterwards, was a demonstration of the faith of those who continued to invoke her beneficence in the land that tradition had established as her native home.

Although Kybele in Greek became treated as a personal name, its origin as an epithet that applied particularly to places sacred to Kybebe was never forgotten. The name Kybele was regularly conjoined with titles like Mistress (*Δέσποινα*) and Mother (*Μήτηρ*) by classical authors,[115] and Kybele was frequently invoked in connection with specific places. Hellenistic sources are more explicit; they claim that Kybele was named after one or another mountain or place called Kybelis or Kybelon.[116] Virgil's differentiation between Cybebe and Cybelus preserves the original distinction between the goddess named Kybebe and the places named after her.[117] The lexicographers summarize all of this by specifying that Kybele's name came from her mountains, her towns, her pure shrines, her places sacred to Rhea, from caves, and from hidden chambers.[118]

The classical tradition thus accurately preserves the tradition of her names and the complex relationships that they imply. The concept of divinity underlying this range of identifications is not comprehended by a simple lexical equation that selects one meaning (a hypothetical Phrygian word for "mountain" or "cave," e.g.) to the exclusion of all the rest. It is conveyed through the stories of Kybele, who was the mistress of sovereignty long known as Kubaba and Kybebe, who became known to posterity as the mother of Midas, and who was identified with the mother of Zeus, Rhea, and also with Demeter, with Earth, and with Aphrodite.

## MISTRESS OF LIONS AND CONSORT OF THE KING

Within western Phrygia, in monuments of the late seventh and sixth centuries, and in Lydia at Sardis, we find the Mother of the Gods associated with what became her most famous attribute, the lion.[119] At Sardis, an early sixth-

---

115. See chapter 2, notes 18, 20, 75.

116. See chapter 2 at notes 76, 79, and 80.

117. See note 94 above.

118. See chapter 2, notes 79–82.

119. Roller 1999, 130–31, recognizes the role of Lydia in fixing the lion as a regular attribute of the Mother of the Gods among the Greeks. Roller (49) notes that the lion "is a comparatively rare symbol in Phrygian religious iconography," but lions do occur as an attribute of the Mother in Phrygian art of the Lydian period: see the Arslankaya monument (figure 2, in

century monumental altar of Kybebe has been found in the vicinity of gold refineries beside the Pactolus stream, and it is surmounted by lions.[120] A marble temple model of the second half of the sixth century from Sardis (figure 7), thought to represent a local temple of Kybebe and presenting a standing image of the goddess on its facade, bears lions among its figured decorations.[121] When a chorus in the *Philoctetes* of Sophocles prays for arrogant behavior to be punished, it calls upon the Mother of the Gods at Sardis, whose fearsome power is embodied in this attribute: "Mountain goddess, all-nourishing Earth, Mother of Zeus himself, who dwells by the great gold-bearing Pactolus: there we call upon you, Mistress Mother, . . . O blessed one, enthroned on bull-devouring lions!"[122]

The lion is the most distinctive attribute of kingship in Lydia, and Kybele, or Kybebe, is depicted in sculpture at Sardis holding this emblem.[123] A legend of Lydian kingship demonstrates the significance of the lion at Sardis, and alludes to the importance of the anonymous woman who provides this token of power to the king. In narrating the end of Lydian sovereignty at the capture of Sardis by Cyrus, Herodotus tells the story of an earlier king of Lydia, Meles, who carried a lion most of the way around the walls of the citadel at Sardis at the advice of Telmessian seers, to make the citadel all but

---

chapter 2); Van Loon 1991, 32, notes "dowel holes containing traces of bronze," which "must have once held two separately carved lions, fixed with bronze dowels" on either side of the standing image of the Mother in the niche at Büyük Kapıkaya (Van Loon, plate 33b; Roller figure 22). Lions are an attribute of Kubaba in northern Syria. (See figure 5 above.)

120. The altar is described by Ramage in Hanfmann 1983a, 36–37 and figure 49; in Ramage and Craddock 2000, 72–80, with figures 4.2–17; and in Dusinberre 2003, 64–68; see also Hanfmann and Ramage 1978, 66–67, nos. 27–29, and figures 105–17; Hanfmann 1980, 105–6 and figure 20; Van Loon 1991, figure 18 and plate 44c. A sherd bearing the Lydian form of the name of the goddess, *Kuvav-* (Gusmani 1969a, discussed above at note 105), was found in the vicinity of this altar.

121. Hanfmann and Waldbaum 1969, 268; Hanfmann and Ramage 1978, 43–51, no. 7, and figures 20–50; Hanfmann 1980, figures 23–25; Hanfmann 1983b, 224, figure 3 and plate 43; Naumann 1983, 110–13, no. 34, plate 12.3; Rein 1993, 75–112 and figures 6–30; Roller 1999, figure 38; Dusinberre 2003, 104–6, 218, and figure 45.

122. Sophocles *Philoctetes* 392–402: ὀρεστέρα παμβῶτι Γᾶ, μᾶτερ αὐτοῦ Διός, ἃ τὸν μέγαν Πακτωλὸν εὔχρυσον νέμεις, σὲ κἀκεῖ, μᾶτερ πότνι᾽, ἐπηυδώμαν, . . . ἰὼ μάκαιρα ταυροκτόνων λεόντων ἔφεδρε.

123. The Lydian lion is best known as a coin type, where it is considered a royal emblem; see Kraay 1976, 24; note also observations by Cahn 1950 and Wallace 1988. Ratté 1989 catalogues and discusses sculpted Lydian lions from Sardis; see also Hanfmann 1980, 105–6; Dusinberre 2003, 100–103 and 224–26. A relief of ca. 400 B.C.E. from Sardis (illustrated here in chapter 4, figure 11) depicting figures of Artemis and Kybele/Kybebe standing side by side shows Kybele/Kybebe holding a lion. (See chapter 4, note 119.) The standing figure of Kybebe on the archaic temple model (illustrated here in figure 7; see note 121 above) holds a lion in her left arm according to Hanfmann, but damage to the figure makes this attribute uncertain to other observers (Rein 1993, 78–79).

impregnable.[124] The lion signified the future king or tyrant, whose power would become irresistible.[125] This lion was born to Meles, Herodotus reports, by his *pallakē,* his unnamed concubine. The favored concubine of the Lydian king, we have already noted, was regarded as the incarnation of the goddess of love, and her extraordinary status is demonstrated here by the nature of her offspring. It follows, therefore, that she was taken to be the incarnation of Kybebe, mistress of lions.

Kybebe, nurturer of lions and mother of sovereignty, was honored in a cult found both at Sardis and among the Greeks of Asia in the very period when the Lydian kings established their tyranny in Asia. A link with the Phrygian origin of this emblem of sovereignty is recognizable in the sculpted image of the beautiful maiden standing in a doorway. This Phrygian motif is found at Sardis beginning in the first half of the sixth century, in the form of sculpted naiskoi of Kybebe.[126] This is Kybebe as marriageable maiden, the likeness of Aphrodite as brought to life in the Homeric hymn, whose image is often evoked in the praise of beautiful maidens of Lydia in the poetry of Alcman and Sappho.

Simultaneously with their appearance at Sardis, naiskoi of the standing goddess become widespread among the Ionian, Aeolian, and Dorian Greek

124. Herodotus 1.84.3. The story of Meles and the lion appears to describe the iconographic type of a king or hero carrying a lion cub, represented in several examples from the eighth or seventh century. It appears in Phrygian art on a seal (Masson 1987), and in the ivory figure that may have been part of the Throne of Midas at Delphi (see DeVries 2002; and above, chapter 2, note 118); it appears in Neo-Hittite art on reliefs from Carchemish and Pancarli (Orthmann 1971, plates 35e and 48h), and on bronze horse-trappings (Orthmann, plate 70a, b); it appears in Neo-Assyrian art in a relief from the palace of Sargon II at Khorsabad, now in the Louvre.

125. Herodotus 5.56 reports a dream of Hipparchus son of Peisistratus that calls him a lion. Herodotus 6.131.2 reports the dream of Pericles' mother that she would give birth to a lion. (See above at note 31.) Callicles, in Plato *Gorgias* 483d–484a, likens the power of Darius or Xerxes to that of a lion, and the potential of any natural-born leader to that of a lion cub waiting to burst into violent action. See the prophetic parodies of Aristophanes *Knights* 1037, referring to a demagogue, and *Frogs* 1431–33, referring to Alcibiades; also the dream of Philip of Macedon of the sign of a lion on his wife's womb: Plutarch *Alexander* 2.2. Most striking in this context, because it combines the Phrygian and Lydian attributes portending sovereignty, is the oracle reported by Herodotus 5.92b foretelling the birth of Cypselus, tyrant of Corinth: "An eagle in the rocks has conceived, and shall bring forth a lion." The eagle alludes to the name given to Cypselus' father, Eëtion, which means "Eagle-man." Like the name of Cypselus himself ("Grain Bin"), these may be nicknames by which the tyrant and his father were known to posterity.

126. Fragments of archaic naiskoi and their standing images from Sardis are described and illustrated by Hanfmann and Ramage 1978, 41–53, nos. 4–7 and 9, and figures 11–50, 58–60; Dusinberre 2003, 108, 219–20, and figures 48 and 49. Hanfmann 1983b, 231, tentatively identifies relief no. 9 as Aphrodite, and notes Charon's identification of Kybebe with Aphrodite (above, note 75). The identity of the archaic sculpted images from Sardis is based on comparative iconography, for they are not inscribed.

Figure 7. Relief from Sardis depicting the goddess Kybele-Aphrodite standing in the facade of an Ionic shrine, with smaller attendant figures in low relief on the sides and back, second half of sixth century B.C.E. (© Archaeological Exploration of Sardis, Harvard University, photo no. 63.112:17).

cities of Asia.[127] An even more common image of the goddess also makes its appearance for the first time among the Greeks of Asia in the middle of the sixth century: naiskoi depicting the Mother seated, often with a lion on her lap. This type has no known precedent in either Lydian or Phrygian sculpture, but all indications point to a Lydian context for its development, in continuation of an older Luwian or Neo-Hittite tradition.[128]

The goddess enthroned is no longer a maiden, but is the goddess as

127. The types are illustrated and discussed by Naumann 1983, plates 12.4–14.2; Rein 1996, 230–33 and figures 2 and 3; and Roller 1999, 126–29 and figure 37.

128. Naumann 1983, 117–18, and Roller 1999, 131–34, summarize the evidence for the appearance and rapid diffusion of this type; see also Graf 1985, 107–15. The only western Anatolian precedent is the Hittite-period enthroned goddess cut into a rock face on Mount Sipy-

Mother in the fullness of her powers. The lion on her lap—a diminutive and docile lion—calls to mind both her status as the consort who has borne the king a lion, and the power of sovereignty itself. The goddess enthroned with lions is the image of the Mother that Sophocles places at Sardis. The image of the Mother in this form makes its appearance among the Greeks of Asia precisely when, as Herodotus reports, Lydian tyranny was achieved in the reigns of Alyattes and Croesus, when all the Greeks of Asia paid tribute to Sardis.[129] It should be recognized as both a consequence and an expression of Lydian tyranny over the Greeks of Asia.

### THE IDEALS OF LYDIAN TYRANNY: A SUMMARY SO FAR

The customs associated with Lydian tyranny and its appropriation of Phrygian heritage unite seemingly disparate elements, namely the legend of Midas' birth, the legend of Aeneas' birth, the royal custom of keeping concubines, and the naming of the goddess who sustains tyranny. The story of how Gordius founded kingship in Phrygia and became the father of Midas tells how a simple man met a beautiful woman who became the mother of his child, the future king. The woman who became the mother of Midas, in this story, has the attributes displayed by the archaic images of the divine Phrygian Mother, demonstrating that by the heyday of the Lydian empire the mother of the archetypal ruler had become the archetype of the divine Mother. The story of Anchises tells a similar tale of an encounter with a beautiful woman, this time identified as Aphrodite herself, who became the mother of his child, Aeneas, the future ruler. The Dardanid lineage of Anchises and Aeneas was the foundation of rulership in the Hellespontine lands that were the ancestral home to the Mermnad tyrants of Lydia. It is not unreasonable to assume, then, that the birth of Aeneas to Aphrodite was a legend promoted by the Mermnads, to justify a sovereignty that they renewed and perpetuated by consorting with Aphrodite and her likenesses, the beautiful women assembled at Sardis.

The Lydian custom of keeping a royal harem of choice concubines provided the conditions in which the tyrant could reenact the foundational encounter by finding the beautiful woman who would become the mother of the future tyrant. Marriage customs in Asia Minor may have drawn upon the symbolism of this encounter with irresistible beauty by enacting a period of ritualized concubinage. Such practice could account for Herodotus' description of the customs of Milesian brides (1.146.3), and could possibly also explain the Lydian practice of prostituting their daughters before marriage

---

lus above Magnesia, between Smyrna and Sardis: see Laroche 1960, 127; this may be the shrine of the Mother Plastene of Pausanias 5.13.7. The goddess enthroned, associated with lions, is a regular type of Neo-Hittite Kubaba. (See figure 5 here.)

129. Herodotus 1.6, 15.4–28.

(1.93.4–94.1). The numinous status of the Lydian tyrant's choice consort, as she who engenders sovereignty, is clear in several of Herodotus' stories. It lies behind the story of King Meles and the lion born to him by his concubine (1.84.3). It is central to the tale of Gyges and his encounter with the wife of Candaules, whose unmatched beauty bestows sovereignty on him who beholds it (1.8–12). In the following chapter, we will see that this paradigm lies behind the story of the marriage of Atys, the son of Croesus (1.39–44).

Marriage was the tyrant's most intimate communion with the divine forces that sustained his sovereignty. The tyrant's marriage was a Sacred Marriage. In a manner that ultimately defies rational exposition, the mate of the tyrant was taken to be a perfect woman who therefore must be the goddess, who loved her consort and bore his child to perpetuate sovereignty. The mate of the tyrant therefore took on the role of the goddess, who was Kybebe at Sardis, or Aphrodite among the Greeks. Like the intercourse between Aphrodite and Anchises, this was a private communion, a mystery veiled in a form of ritualized secrecy that, nevertheless, had to be widely known for its potency to be realized. When the generation of sovereignty was realized in the person of the new tyrant, the former tyrant's consort took on the identity of the divine Mother. Once established, this role was transcendent and enduring. The divine archetype of this role was the goddess known as the Mother of the Gods, mother of Zeus himself. Those who worshipped the Mother of the Gods embraced the ideals of tyranny by honoring its very source.

Aphrodite, the divine paradigm of matchless and irresistible beauty, was the mistress of sovereignty in this Anatolian context. Among the Lydians and Phrygians, Charon of Lampsacus reports, Aphrodite was known as Kybebe, and Kybebe, according to Herodotus, was especially venerated at Sardis. Kybebe, as Greek sources call her, was Kubaba, mistress of the land and consort of the chief gods among the Neo-Hittite states of southeastern Anatolia and northern Syria. The domain of Kubaba's worship thus extended from the Euphrates to the Pactolus, and it included Phrygia in its center. In Phrygia during the era of Lydian dominion, Kubaba was amalgamated into the figure of the mother of Midas, the maternal source of sovereignty, and she was invoked as *Matar Kubeleya*. The Phrygian epithet *Kubeleya* is an adjectival form derived from the name of Kubaba, and it describes the Mother who is "of the Place of Kubaba." As scholars have long noted, the Phrygian Mother or, to the Greeks, the Mother of the Gods was strongly associated with landmarks, often mountains and the headwaters of rivers. The peculiar circumlocution implied by naming her *Matar Kubeleya* appropriately describes a specific aspect and instance—this divine Mother, at this place—of a universal goddess, Kubaba. As her nomenclature was received by the Greeks, Kybele eventually became treated as a personal name. But classical sources never completely lost sight of the fact that properly her name was Kybebe (Κυβήβη in Greek, *Cybebe* in Latin)—the ancient Anatolian goddess Kubaba.

# Chapter 4

# The Mother of the Gods and the Practices of Lydian Tyranny

Mortality is the undoing of every scheme of worldly perfection. For this reason perfection belongs to immortal gods alone. The previous two chapters have traced the outlines of an ideology of rulership based on the premise that perfection on earth can be found where rulership comes closest to divinity, and actually participates in it through the coupling of kings and their godlike consorts. The present chapter will demonstrate how the inescapability of death for the men and women who lived and performed in these archetypal roles, in Lydia, was articulated through ritual, monument, and myth into a vindication of tyranny. In the process we will see that the Lydian ideology of sovereignty had much in common with better-attested Mesopotamian traditions linking kingship and the gods. In these older traditions we find the lovemaking of the king and the goddess glorified, and the mortality of the king lamented. Both of these elements were clearly present in Lydian rituals of celebration and lamentation, and were also reflected in the relationships between gods and humanity depicted in the Greek poetic traditions born on the shores of Asia.

In addition to treating the ideology of the Mermnad court at Sardis, this chapter begins to examine the historical interaction of Greek communities with Sardis, chiefly as narrated by Herodotus. Writing of a bygone era for Greeks of a later age, Herodotus had reason to find new meanings in old stories. Here I will argue that Herodotus has reshaped the core meanings of certain famous encounters between Greeks and the tyrants of Asia. Some of the interpretations I will suggest for such traditional tales as the lesson in tyranny taught by Thrasybulus of Miletus to Periander of Corinth indicate a strong revisionism at work in Herodotus' narrative. The meanings found in other tales, like the strange story of the nature of Periander's tyranny at Corinth, are meanings that Herodotus never disguised, but that have lain unrecognized because the conditions of tyranny itself were no longer understood in the same manner after his day.

One of the meanings implicit in Herodotus' account, and central to its message, is the greatest horror of tyranny: the tribute of youths and maidens that it exacts. I will argue that the collection of boys for castration and girls for concubinage, all in submission to the demands of sovereign tyranny, are at the center of the "wrongs" (*adika erga*) committed by the rulers of Asia against the Greeks, noted by Herodotus at the beginning of his *Histories*. I will also suggest that these ancient customs of enforced castration and concubinage are fundamentally connected to the traditions of ritualized prostitution and eunuch priesthood devoted to the service of the great goddess of Asia. As we follow the testimony to these practices especially from the perspective of Greek sources, we will come to appreciate how the ideals of tyranny founded a strange reality.

### TYRANNY AND FERTILITY

The Lydian tyrant was the notional lover of the goddess Aphrodite, or Kybebe, as the previous chapter has shown, marking their offspring as uniquely qualified for rulership. The sexual communion of tyrant and goddess also justified tyranny in a larger sense by assuring the well-being of all humanity. For this was the deepest meaning of the *hieros gamos,* or Sacred Marriage, as it has been recognized in Mesopotamian and classical Greek sources, and beyond.[1] In Mesopotamian poetry, the vital force of life in the world is identified with the intensity of erotic attachment expressed by the goddess of love and Queen of Heaven (Inanna in Sumerian, Ishtar in Akkadian) for her mortal lover, who might be the herdsman Dumuzi (or Tammuz), or a

---

1. The chief authority for the Sacred Marriage at Athens, [Demosthenes] 59, *Against Neaera,* says that it was performed "for the benefit of the city" (ὑπὲρ τῆς πόλεως, repeated in 73, 75, 81) and in the name of kingship (βασιλεία, 74). On the Sacred Marriage in Sumerian poetry, see Frankfort 1948, 295–99; Kramer 1969, esp. 49–66; Renger 1975, 255–59; Jacobsen 1976, 25–47; Cooper 1993; Steinkeller 1999; and Lapinkivi 2003, 81–90; for more skeptical assessments of the Sumerian evidence, see Sweet 1994 and Rubio 2001. On the continuity of Sacred Marriage, or the marriage of divinities, into the Neo-Assyrian, Neo-Babylonian, and Seleucid periods, see S. Smith 1958, 42–71; Renger 1975, 254–55; Matsushima 1987; Nissinen 2001; and Lapinkivi 2003, 81–90. U. Winter 1983, 311–68, examines the relationship of the Mesopotamian tradition of the Sacred Marriage to textual and iconographic evidence in Syria and Palestine, chiefly of the second millennium. On the Sacred Marriage in Ugaritic literature, see Walls 1992, 197–206; and Wyatt 1996, 219–307. The Sacred Marriage in Jewish tradition is discussed by Kramer 1969, 85–106; J. Z. Smith 1978, 104–28; Patai 1990, 135–54; Hadley 2000, 33–53; Nissinen 2001, 121–23; Lapinkivi 2003, 91–98. For Thracian parallels, see Marazov, in Fol and Marazov 1977, 37–38, 40 and 52; and Vassileva 2001 on the Thracian elements present in Phrygian cult. A speculative interpretation of the relationship of the Near Eastern tradition to Greek tyranny is offered by Fadinger 1993, 293–311.

great king such as Ur-Nammu, founder of the Third Dynasty of Ur.[2] Not only were good things brought about for humankind by this means, but it was also the most essential means by which the subjects of the ruler were able to command the affections of the goddess and, through her mediation, find favor among all the great gods.

In stories common to cultures from Mesopotamia to Greece, the gods are said to have turned away from humanity and inflicted pain and suffering, even mass destruction, upon these lesser beings. Such disaffection was the cause of the Great Flood in the time of Atrahasis, Noah, or Deucalion. It brought famine when the gods, Telepinus, Ishtar, or Demeter, disappeared or turned away from the rest of creation. Divine disaffection was also recalled, among the Greeks, as the root cause of the Trojan War.[3] Ritualized means of attracting the affection of divinity in its most potent, erotic form were therefore understood as appropriate means of assuring that such neglect or disaffection would never recur. The followers of the tyrant, in other words, had a compelling interest in assuring that he remained the choice one in the eyes of the goddess.

Love made by the Queen of Heaven with her beloved king was a wellspring for fertility, both of the fruits of the earth and of the progeny of animals and humankind. The meaning of this communion is utterly explicit in the Sumerian texts that describe the love made by Inanna to Dumuzi, or to others of her beloved kings. For example, a Sumerian hymn to Inanna praises the lovemaking of Iddin-Dagan, who was king of Isin early in the second millennium. In this passage, excerpted from a translation by Thorkild Jacobsen, a handmaiden of the goddess leads the king to the goddess' bed, and as she does so she praises the good things to be expected from this sexual union:[4]

> May the lord, the choice of your heart,
> may the king, your beloved bridegroom,
>     pass long days in your sweet thing, the pure loins!
> Grant him a pleasant reign to come!
> Grant him a royal throne, firm in its foundations;

2. Dumuzi (known in West Semitic languages as Tammuz: Ezekiel 8:14) was the most famous of the goddess' lovers. He was often described as a simple shepherd, although "shepherd" was an epithet for a king (just as it is in Homer), and Dumuzi was also known in the Sumerian tradition as a king of the city of Uruk (Erech), and one among several such early kings celebrated as enjoying the love of the goddess; see Gurney 1962; Kramer 1969, 57–66; Renger 1975, 255–56; Sefati 1998; Lapinkivi 2003, 29–80. On Ur-Nammu in this role, see Kramer 1991, 196–97 and 208–11 lines 203–15; Lapinkivi 2003, 61. Dumuzi is still well known in his role as the lover of Ishtar in Akkadian texts of the first millennium: see Lapinkivi 2003, 82.

3. Myths of destruction or distress visited on humanity by willful gods are surveyed by Güterbock 1961, 143–50; Richardson 1974, 258–60; Burkert 1992, 100–104; M. L. West 1997, 166–67, 377–80, 480–82.

4. Jacobsen 1976, 41–42. The same text is discussed in summary by Frankfort 1948, 295–97, and edited and translated by Sefati 1998, 301–11, no. 21.

grant him a sceptre righting [wrongs in] the land,
  all shepherds' crooks;
grant him the good crown, the turban that
  makes a head distinguished.

From sunrise to sunset,
from south to north,
from the Upper Sea to the Lower Sea,
from [where grows] the *huluppu* tree, from
  [where grows] the cedar tree,
and in Sumer and Akkad,
  grant him all shepherds' crooks,
and may he perform the shepherdship
  over their dark-headed people.

May he like a farmer till the fields,
may he like a good shepherd make the folds teem,
may there be vines under him,
  may there be barley under him,
may there be carp-floods in the river under him.
may there be mottled barley in the fields under him,
may fishes and birds sound off in the marshes under him.
. . .
may grass grow on [the rivers'] banks,
  may vegetables fill the commons,
may the holy lady [of the grains], Nidaba,
  gather grainpiles there!
O milady, queen of heaven and earth,
  queen of all heaven and earth,
may he live long in your embrace!

The lovemaking of king and goddess described in this hymn was cele-brated in a sacred structure called the *gipar* (Akkadian *gipāru*).[5] The *gipar* was an architectural feature associated with the chief temples of several Meso-potamian cities. It was a place of sovereignty identified with the forces of fer-tility in the world, as is clear from the combination of functions associated with the *gipar*. At Uruk, the most ancient home to the Sacred Marriage of Inanna and her "shepherd," Dumuzi, the *gipar* was the residence and admin-istrative center, in effect the palace of a ruler. The ruler who was the inti-mate consort of the goddess by implication shared in her dominion. In this context, like Iddin-Dagan above, he exercised an idealized rulership "from sunrise to sunset, from south to north, from the Upper Sea to the Lower Sea, . . . and in Sumer and Akkad"—that is, over the world. In the context of

5. On the *gipar* of Uruk, as it is named in the marriage of Dumuzi and Inanna, see Kramer 1969, 73, 76; Jacobsen 1970, 374 n. 32; 1976, 35–36; Steinkeller 1999, 105. On the functions of the *gipar*, and the physical remains of the *gipar* at Ur, see Harris 1971.

the Sacred Marriage, the *gipar* was also "the storehouse," which was said to be filled with all the good things that the earth produces; the bounty of the earth was described specifically as the product of the sexual potency of the king and the fertility of the body of Inanna. By metaphorical extension, the word *giparu* in Akkadian also meant "pasture" or "meadow," the sustenance that the earth yields voluntarily for the benefit of the creatures living on it.[6] The "shepherd" who tended these creatures was the steward of divinity's blessings, and the human being most responsible for assuring the continuing bounty of the land.

One of the distinctive features of the Mesopotamian *gipāru* most clearly attested by the Neo-Babylonian period is its garden, or orchard of fruit-bearing and exotic trees.[7] These gardens symbolized the remote corners of the earth, "from [where grows] the *huluppu* tree, from [where grows] the cedar tree," which also defined the extension of the king's sovereignty over such remote but fruitful lands by virtue of divine affection. Such gardens of transcendent existence were an ancient and long-lived custom in the kingdoms of the Near East. They were the paradigm for the biblical Garden of Eden, and their pattern was perpetuated in the Persian gardens or pleasure parks known by the name "paradise," *paradeisos* in Greek.[8] Like the Garden of Eden, the gardens of Assyrian, Babylonian, and Persian kings and grandees were also places where streams flowed from natural or artificial sources, symbolizing the flowing waters of the earth. The Hanging Garden of Babylon, with its terraced landscape and streams, was the most famous example of this tradition in Mesopotamia.[9] At Celaenae in Phrygia, Xenophon describes a "palace and large paradise full of wild beasts" built on the headwaters of the Maeander River, where King Midas was said to have had his capital, and where Xerxes and later Cyrus the Younger were said to have been entertained in royal manner.[10] Such parks were prominent features of the satrapal capitals

6. See *CAD* vol. 5, 83–84, *gipāru*.

7. S. Smith 1958, 47–48 and 71–73, discusses the *gipar* at Ur and the textual evidence that, before the time of Nabonidus (mid-sixth century), it was a plantation filled with fruit trees and palm trees.

8. On the Garden of Eden as a symbol of kingship over the earth, see Wyatt 1996, 302–7; and Goodwin 2000. On the Iranian derivation of Greek *paradeisos*, "paradise," see Chantraine 1968–80, vol. 3, 857. The nature and symbolism of Persian paradises are discussed by Briant 2002, 86, 201–3, 233–39.

9. On the royal gardens of Mesopotamia, particularly those of the first millennium, see Oppenheim 1965; Wiseman 1983 and 1984. On the Hanging Garden of Babylon in particular, see Wiseman 1985, 55–60; Dalley 1994. Diodorus 2.10.1–6 describes the construction, the abundance of "all kinds of trees," and the elaborate watering facilities of "the garden called 'hanging' beside the acropolis" at Babylon, built "by a later Syrian king for the sake of a concubine wife [γυναικὸς παλλακῆς]."

10. On Celaenae and its natural spring, palace, and park, see Herodotus 7.26–29 and Xenophon *Anabasis* 1.2.7–9. During the march of Cyrus the Younger, Xenophon states that

of Lydia and Hellespontine Phrygia, at Sardis and at Dascyleum, and we will see that they were also present at Sardis under the Mermnad dynasty.[11] Animal parks were also frequent features of these arrangements. In Mesopotamia, the sacred garden associated with palace or temple rituals was sometimes adjacent to an animal park, the *ambassu,* where both kings and gods were said to hunt wild game.[12]

Stocked with plants, animals, and flowing waters symbolizing life on earth, these royal parks and gardens and the rituals performed within them were a manner of establishing a claim to a wider realm of power. He who brought order and nurture to these good things of nature, and who demonstrated mastery over the most powerful animals, was accordingly close to the divine forces that ordered, nurtured, and mastered the world. Thus these parks and gardens were places of communion with divinity, sacred precincts within which, in bowered pavilions, rituals of Sacred Marriage were performed to signify the intimacy of the bond between humanity and divinity. Not only the king alone but also his son and heir designate, and also his daughter acting as a high priestess, could perform these rituals.[13] The garden and its marriage bed, and closely related to it, the grounds for the noble hunt, were paramount symbols of the union of sovereignty and divinity.

---

Cyrus stayed in his paradise at Celaenae for thirty days, and held a muster of thirteen thousand troops inside its grounds. On Midas at Celaenae, see chapter 2, with notes 63–65. See also Xenophon *Anabasis* 1.4.10 on the paradise at the palace of Belesys, ruler of Syria.

11. Xenophon *Oeconomicus* 4.8–5.20 discusses the relationship between kingship and agriculture, exemplified by Cyrus the Younger and his paradise at Sardis. This was probably the same as "the most beautiful of paradises," filled with running waters, meadows, and "retreats fitted out luxuriously and in royal manner" that the satrap Tissaphernes had named after Alcibiades: Plutarch *Alcibiades* 24.5. On the paradises of Pharnabazus at Dascyleum, see Xenophon *Hellenica* 4.1.15, 33.

12. The Mesopotamian *gipar* was regularly located beside or within the precinct of the sanctuary of the chief deity of a city. The Sacred Marriage of the deities Nabu and Tašmetu at Calah in Assyria was followed by an animal hunt in a game park, the *ambassu;* see Matsushima 1987, 139–43; Nissinen 2001, 99; Lapinkivi 2003, 84 n. 289; *CAD* vol. 1, part 2, 44, *ambassu.* S. Smith 1958, 43–44 and 43 n. 2, adduces this ritual as evidence that "a ritual in which a marriage was enacted, followed by a hunt, implies that both male and female parts were played by human beings." The same evidence is reviewed by Oppenheim 1965, 333, who suggests, less persuasively, that the descriptions might be merely figurative.

13. On the ministry of either a male, as *en* ("lord" or high priest), or a female, as *entu* ("lady" or high priestess), to the divinity in a *gipar* or comparable sacred enclosure, see S. Smith 1958, 45–53; Jacobsen 1970, 374 n. 32; Harris 1971; and Steinkeller 1999, 134. Herodotus 1.181–82 describes this custom still observed by a priestess serving Bel-Marduk at Babylon, and similar practices elsewhere. Smith (44–52, 72–73) discusses several examples of kings' sons or daughters performing this function. Xenophon *Cyropaedia* 1.3.14 depicts Astyages the Mede offering his young grandson, Cyrus, the privilege of hunting in his paradise as a gesture to recognize the legitimacy of this boy, who is destined to be king.

In Mesopotamia, the bowered shrine in which these rites took place, the *gipāru,* is described as a "pure place."[14] Scrupulous attention to ritual purity, like the hyperbolic praise of the lovemaking that went on in the "pure place" in ritual poetry, expressed the ecstasies of divine communion that all peoples, ideally, should celebrate, just as all peoples, ideally, should approve the sovereignty of the most perfect king.[15] But such praise was easily transposed into condemnation by those who did not share that vision of sovereignty and divinity. It is in this form that we find a Greek allusion to the Sacred Marriage rites of the Lydian tyrants as they were once celebrated in the parks and arbors of Sardis. This is what Clearchus of Soli, a student of Aristotle, had to say about the lifestyle of the Lydians generally and their tyrants in particular:[16]

> The Lydians in their luxury laid out parks [παράδεισοι], making them like gardens [κηπαῖοι], and so lived in the shade, because they thought it more luxurious not to have the rays of the sun fall upon them at all. And proceeding further in their insolence they would gather the wives and daughters of other men into the place called, because of this action, the Place of Purity [Ἁγνεών], and there violate them.

Clearchus concludes this vignette by describing the perverse form of sovereignty that issued from such rites, namely that one of these debauched women of Lydia became tyrant herself, Omphale. The hostile tradition, then, describes the place of royal lovemaking as a place of outrageous perversions. Most significant, for present purposes, is the fact that this condemnation works not by slanderous inventions, but by reappraising actual symbols and rituals of sovereignty.[17]

The shady parks and gardens of Sardis were no figment of Clearchus' imagination, or projection of later Persian custom into an earlier Lydian tradition. Herodotus records that the groves and shrines (τά τε ἄλσεα καὶ τὰ ἱρά) of Sardis were burned by the Ionians in their attack on Sardis in 498, and

14. S. Smith 1958, 72, quotes the Sumerian text of a dedication by the daughter of Nabonidus who declares: "I who made a *gipāru* for the *enutu*-office in a pure place" (*lu gi.par nam.en.bi.še ki.sikil.la du.a*). See also the quotation from *The Death of Ur-Nammu* below, note 23.

15. On the popular appeal and public celebrations accompanying these rituals in the Sumerian tradition, see Cooper 1993, 92–95. On the euphemisms and conventions of hyperbole used in speaking of such ceremonies, cf. the biblical title Song of Songs ("a veritable 'Holy of Holies,' to be read and studied and cherished," as Kramer 1969, 86, describes rabbinical respect for the book) for a hymn of praise to King Solomon's lovemaking.

16. From Clearchus *Lives* book 4, as quoted by Athenaeus 12.515e–f, translated by C. B. Gulick, with modifications.

17. Likewise, while the garden as a scene of royal lovemaking is extolled in the Solomonic Song of Songs (above, note 15), when kingship was in peril the prophet could warn the kings of Judah that "the sacred oaks in which you delight will play you false, the garden-shrines of your fancy will fail you" (Isaiah 1:29, Oxford Study Bible translation).

elsewhere he notes that the Persians considered the burning of the shrine of Kybebe on that occasion as the height of the outrage.[18] This shrine was uniquely important to Sardis, for its deity, Kybebe, was local (*epichōriē,* Herodotus notes). Her cult at Sardis, as we saw in the previous chapter, was part of a centuries-old Anatolian tradition. Recognizing the nature of that tradition, and the significance of Herodotus' words describing the offense committed by the Ionians at Sardis, we can now see that the Ionian Revolt was epitomized by the destruction of the very place, a garden sanctuary, where the sacred lovemaking of Kybebe and her darling tyrants had taken place.

## THE GRIEF OF THE GODDESS

Clearchus presents his disapproving perspective on Lydian love parks in an age when the Lydian paradigm had long since fallen into disrepute. A different perspective on the Asiatic tradition of the Sacred Marriage survives from the height of the Mermnad rulership at Sardis, in Greek poetry recounting the various legendary couplings of mortal men and goddesses, beginning with Iasion and Demeter. Their union is mentioned as the first coupling of a divinity and a mortal in Hesiod's *Theogony,* where "Demeter, radiant among gods, gave birth to Ploutos [Wealth] after coupling in sweet love with the hero Iasion, in the thrice-plowed fallow field."[19] This, in concise form, is the nature and the function of the Sacred Marriage of a man and a goddess: to engender wealth in the world. The same event is noticed in the *Odyssey* by the nymph Calypso, who recalls "when Demeter of the beautiful tresses yielded to her desire and lay down with Iasion in sweet lovemaking on a bed of a thrice-plowed field."[20] An erotic Demeter is uncharacteristic of her matronly manner later portrayed in the *Homeric Hymn to Demeter,* and later tellings specify that Iasion had sexual intercourse with Kybele instead of Demeter.[21] The eroticism of Demeter likely comes from an early period when the functions of the giver of grain and sexual gratification overlapped, as they clearly did in the case of Inanna.

The occasion for telling this and other such erotic tales in the narrative of the *Odyssey* reveals a familiarity of the Homeric poet with the Asiatic poetry sung in honor of the goddess of the Sacred Marriage. The occasion is the disruption of Calypso's lovemaking with a mortal man, Odysseus. Odys-

18. See Herodotus 7.8b on groves and shrines identified with the shrine of Kybebe burned in the Ionian Revolt (5.102.1).

19. Hesiod *Theogony* 969–71.

20. *Odyssey* 5.125–27.

21. Diodorus 5.49.1–4 recasts the communion of Iasion and Demeter as an act of gift giving on the occasion of the marriage of Cadmus and Harmonia, after which Iasion couples with Cybele, who gives birth to Corybas. Conon *FGrHist* 26 F 1.21 states that Iasion was struck by lightning after attempting to mate with the phantom of Demeter.

seus has been invited by the nymph to remain with her forever in her island paradise. Calypso and her island are at the center of the world, and her island, with its trees, birds, waters, meadows, and flowers, is a picture of the ideal *gipāru*.[22] All of the elements for the most perfect union of goddess and mortal man are present but for one factor: there is no city of humankind to benefit from Odysseus' lovemaking, and the blessings of the goddess' love are entirely contained within her island paradise. Into this place of inchoate bliss comes Hermes with a command from Zeus to let Odysseus go. Calypso is heartbroken and indignant at the other gods, who have never, she says, allowed a goddess to indulge her passion for a man without taking him away— usually by death. Demeter's love for Iasion is but one example on Calypso's list of grievances.

The grief of the goddess at the inevitable loss of her mortal lover was an integral element of the emotional bond between divinity and humanity as it was told in hymns describing the Sacred Marriage in Mesopotamia. This is strikingly the case, for example, in a lamentation uttered by Inanna herself at the death of her beloved king and lover Ur-Nammu. The goddess is both grief-stricken and enraged at the other gods who allowed Ur-Nammu to die; she will make all suffer the deprivation that she feels:[23]

> As for the place where the sun rises, there is no abundance
>     for the gods!
> [And so] they [i.e., the gods] have now returned [begging] to
>     the *gipar,* the pure shrine of my Eanna ["House of Heaven,"
>     the Temple of Inanna], which is like a mountain!
> But unless my shepherd enters there for me with his sexual
>     vigor, I will not enter into it!
> Unless my strong [*or:* virile] one is able to grow for me like herbs
>     in the steppe, unless he is able to be moored for me like a
>     riverboat in its appointed harbor [I will not enter
>     into it!]

Calypso, in the Homeric epic, is not a great goddess like Inanna, and cannot inflict widespread suffering out of her grief and frustration (although she can summon winds). She must obey Zeus, and therefore allows Odysseus to set sail and depart her island. Odysseus, in consorting with a divine bride,

---

22. Calypso's island, Ogygia, is the navel of the sea (ὀμφαλὸς θαλάσσης, *Odyssey* 1.50), and Calypso herself is the daughter of Atlas, "who knows the depth of the entire sea, and who holds the towering columns that separate earth and heaven" (*Odyssey* 1.52–54). On her island four springs give rise to bright waters that flow in different directions, a feature that has been compared to the four rivers emanating from the Garden of Eden (Genesis 2:10–14; see M. L. West 1997, 422).

23. *Death of Ur-Nammu* 211–15, translated by P. Steinkeller 1999, 132. Cf. Kramer 1991, 208–11.

is playing a role that Asiatic kings played. But unlike those kings, Odysseus willingly withdraws from the arms of a goddess in order to resume his rightful place within the community of mortals. In this respect, the *Odyssey* is implicitly criticizing a strong Asiatic tradition, and developing a teleology that serves a world that is not ruled by all-powerful sovereigns.[24]

Other such couplings of the Greek tradition—Eos with her several men, Circe with hers, and Thetis with Peleus—all ended in grief for the immortal nymph or goddess.[25] The wedding of the last couple in particular saw the presentation of the ill-fated Apple of Discord that would cause widespread grief for humanity along the boundary of Asia and Europe. These tales all acknowledge the power of the goddess of sexual desire or her avatars, whose relationships with mortal men have long been held to engender warriors and kings in the lands of Asia. But in these tellings, we find Greek epic poetry reworking this tradition of the Sacred Marriage by accepting the goddess while rejecting the form of rulership she engendered.

Perhaps the most telling episode to reveal both the familiarity and the contempt of the Greeks for the Asiatic tradition of glorifying godlike kings and their divine nativity occurs in the *Iliad*. Diomedes and his fellow Argives rampage through the Trojans, wounding even Aphrodite as she intervenes to save her own beloved son, Aeneas. The tide of battle swings back and forth, and when the onslaught against the Trojans resumes, among the first to go down to Argive spears are the brothers Aesepus and Pedasus, "whom the naiad nymph Abarbarea once bore to blameless Bucolion. Bucolion himself was the eldest son of proud Laomedon, but his mother bore him in a dark place. While shepherding his flocks he lay down with the nymph in a bed of sweet lovemaking, and she conceived and bore him twin sons."[26] Here we find Abarbarea, the "Barbarian Nymph," who bore twin sons, one of whom, Aesepus, bears the name of a river of the Troad; the other, Pedasus, is a place name in Asia.[27] She bears these sons to "The Herdsman" (which is what the

24. The *Epic of Gilgamesh* already contains key elements of this criticism of the Sacred Marriage. For comparisons of the rejection of Calypso by Odysseus and the rejection of Ishtar by Gilgamesh, and further observations on the thematic links between these epics, see Crane 1988, 63–70; Auffarth 1991, 138; M. L. West 1997, 410–12, 418, and 422.

25. Compare Odysseus' encounter and lovemaking with the enchantress Circe in her island home (*Odyssey* 10.210–574) with his time with Calypso (5.55–268). Eos (Dawn) and her mortal lovers Tithonus and Orion are all mentioned in *Odyssey* 5.1 and 120–24. See *Homeric Hymn* 5, *To Aphrodite* 218–38, for the unhappy outcome of the union of Eos and Tithonus. Hesiod *Theogony* 984–91 mentions the union of Eos with both Tithonus and Cephalus, the latter lover also shared with Aphrodite herself; see also *Theogony* 1006–20 for Thetis, Cytherea (Aphrodite), Circe, and Calypso concluding the list of significant couplings of men and goddesses that began with Demeter and Iasion.

26. *Iliad* 6.21–26.

27. On the river Aesepus, flowing from Mount Ida through Hellespontine Phrygia: *Iliad* 2.825, 4.91, 12.21; Hesiod *Theogony* 342; Strabo 12.4.6, 12.8.11, 13.1.4; see Demetrius of Scep-

name Βουκολίων means), as Aphrodite bore Aeneas to the herdsman Anchises. "Proud Laomedon" was a Dardanid who had other sons as well: Tithonus, a lover of Eos, and Priam, king of Troy.[28] "Shepherd" and "herdsman" are, of course, titles of Dumuzi and all kings beloved of the goddess in Sumerian poetry, and Dumuzi's vital role as lover of Ishtar was still observed in Mesopotamian texts of the first millennium. Kingship and the love of the goddess were clearly the birthright of this family.

At Athens, the "Herdsman's House," the Bucoleum (Βουκολεῖον), was the name of the place that "once belonged to the king," Aristotle tells us, but "now" was where the Sacred Marriage of Dionysus and the Basilinna took place.[29] These features demonstrate that the Greeks were well aware of the traditional Asiatic significance of the "herdsman" in the royal rituals of love-making with a divinity. The appearance at Athens of ancient Asiatic customs, best attested in Mesopotamian poetry, is elucidated by the maintenance of these customs by the Lydians. Asia Minor was the land in which these traditions were maintained, probably since the Bronze Age, and were still a prominent part of ritual custom in the seventh century.[30] The Greeks clearly had respect for the communion with a deity achieved through such rites, and the Athenian ritual established a means of bringing about its benefits through a representative of popular sovereignty. But as for flesh-and-blood princes and hereditary rulers, by unceremoniously adding the bodies of Aesepus and Pedasus to the carnage piled up at Troy, the Greek epic showed what Greeks should make of men who vaunted their divine birth.

## GRIEVING FOR ATYS

Grief for the departure or death of the darling of the goddess was a ritual obligation for all who accepted the dynamic relationship between fertility and sovereignty. Only by massive displays of sympathetic lamentation could the grief of the goddess be soothed and her blessings be restored to humanity.

---

sis on the rivers of the Troad, quoted by Strabo 13.1.43–45. On Pedasus as a place in the Troad: *Iliad* 6.35, 20.92, 21.87; on Pedasus, also Pedasa or Pedasis, in Caria, see Herodotus 5.121, 8.104; Strabo 13.1.59.

28. The Dardanid lineage and its main branches are recited by Aeneas in *Iliad* 20.214–41.

29. Aristotle *Constitution of Athens* 3.5. See note 1 above, and chapter 1, note 88.

30. Sidney Smith 1958, 64, observed the resemblance of the marriage of Dionysus and the Basilinna to Babylonian ritual, but could not explain the mechanism by which Babylonian custom reached Athens. Lydian dynastic traditions, however, attest contact with Babylon. (See Talamo 1979, 40–41 and 53–56, on Bel and Ninus, and on the sojourn of Meles in Babylon.) Such a link between Mesopotamian custom and classical Greek practice makes it likely that the poetry of bucolic love, made famous anew by Theocritus in the third century B.C.E., actually does descend from Sumerian prototypes, as has been hesitantly suggested by D. M. Halperin 1983, 99–123. Cf. the themes of sovereignty and fertility in the context of royal Sacred Marriage in Theocritus' praise of Ptolemy Philadelphus, *Idyll* 17.

Through elaborate ceremonial grieving, moreover, humankind was inter-
ceding on behalf of the bereaved goddess to entreat the gods to allow her
lover to return (in another incarnation).[31] This was a custom well known to
the Greeks of Asia. It was institutionalized in the massive royal funerals common to Asia and to the Spartans, according to Herodotus.[32] It was the essence
of the ritualized mourning for Adonis, beloved of Aphrodite, attested as early
as the poems of Sappho.[33] Sardis was a focal point for this practice on a grand
scale, as Herodotus reveals in his account of the two years of ritual mourning by Croesus for the death of his son, Atys.[34]

Atys, as Herodotus relates, was "by far and in all respects the most excellent young man of his generation." Shortly before Atys met his death in a
hunting accident on the slopes of Mount Olympus, in Mysia, Croesus had
"brought a wife to his son," and devoted considerable time to their wedding.
Croesus used the obligations of Atys as a newlywed (*neogamos*) as an excuse
to keep his son cloistered and away from any warlike activity. Finally, and (as
Herodotus tells it) unwillingly, Croesus allowed his son to recover his reputation for manly action by sending him on the hunt where he lost his life.[35]

This story has long been recognized as a parallel to the tale of Aphrodite
and her beloved Adonis, who leaves the bed of the goddess to go on a fateful hunt. Influence of this mythic paradigm on Herodotus' story is undeniable, but it does not make Herodotus the purveyor of colorful fictions in the
guise of history.[36] Herodotus has described precisely the sequence of events
that are attested as ritualized practice in the courts of Assyrian and Babylonian kings, and that are depicted in Anatolian funerary art of the Persian
period.[37] (See figure 8.) The son of the ruler is presented with a bride, who

31. Ritual lamentation was the institutional concern of temples and cult personnel who
composed, compiled, and performed formal lamentations and dirges across three millennia
of Mesopotamian history; see Cohen 1988, 11–44.

32. Herodotus 6.58.2: see the discussion in chapter 1 at notes 58–61.

33. Lamentations for Adonis are mentioned several times in the fragments of Sappho: frs.
25, 103, 136 (Edmonds *LG*), and *Palatine Anthology* 7.407. See Detienne 1977, esp. 133–45, for
a consideration of the Asiatic contribution to the picture of Adonis in Greek poetry; see also
Burkert 1985, 176–77.

34. Herodotus 1.46.1.

35. Herodotus 1.34–45.

36. Burkert 1979a, 104 and 108, notices Herodotus' "novella" as a reflection of the cult of
Attis and Adonis. Fontenrose 1978, 111, calls it "the myth of Attis and Kybele historicized." Stern
1989, 13–14, introduces the story of Atys as an example of the "historicizing of archaic myth"
by Herodotus. By contrast, How and Wells 1912, vol. 1, 70–71, suggest that there was "fact underlying this story." (Atys died young.)

37. On the setting of Mesopotamian Sacred Marriages and succession rituals, see above at
notes 5–14. On the wedding banquet as a theme in Anatolian funerary iconography, accompanied in some instances by hunting scenes, see Nollé 1992; cf. Pfuhl and Möbius 1977, nos.
2–6, 73–75, 111b, 687, 1399, 1402, 1403, 1410.

signifies the goddess of love and who will, ideally, bear his child. Their communion is a Sacred Marriage ritual that transpires over many days (the wedding and the honeymoon being part of the same ceremony, all taking place in the paradise of a *gipāru*).[38] All other obligations take second place to this ritual to assure the continuity of sovereignty. The ceremony comes to an end in a hunt of dangerous beasts, mentioned in Assyrian sources, where the bridegroom and heir apparent displays his manly vigor (precisely the reason why Atys wished to go on the hunt, according to Herodotus).[39] In Mesopotamian rites, the prince, king, or god emerges from this ceremony revitalized, to enjoy a prosperous reign. But the eventual outcome of this ritualized sequence of events was the inescapable fate of a mortal king and lover of the goddess in the Mesopotamian tradition: the lover dies, always too soon, and a display of profound grief or yearning for the deceased follows. Herodotus tells the story of Atys and his death specifically to demonstrate the depth of grief into which even the most prosperous of men could descend. This is precisely the teleology of the Mesopotamian tales of ritualized love and lament: the best things are the cause of boundless joy, but their loss means unrestrained anguish and torment. The reassurance that such a cycle of joy and grief is a universal human experience, and that even divinities participate in it, was so compelling that this sequence of ritualized events generated a rich and enduring repertoire of lamentation songs, and, by the Persian period at least, made scenes of the wedding banquet and hunt into icons of funerary art.

From the evidence assembled here, we can see that Herodotus has been faithful to an informed account of events that transpired at Sardis in the reign of Croesus. If they seem fabulous because they resonate with the legends of Adonis, Tammuz, or Dumuzi, it is because all such narratives came from a common tradition of legitimizing rulership through a ritual of communion with the goddess of love. There is every reason to believe that Atys the son of Croesus was a historical figure. The son of Atys, according to Herodotus, entertained Xerxes at Celaenae on his march to Sardis, and offered tokens of kingship to Darius before him; someone named Ates (an alternative spelling of Atys) dedicated the Midas Monument, and the son of Croesus would be

38. Cyrus the Younger's stay of thirty days at his palace and paradise at Celaenae (above, note 10) while on the march toward the battle for kingship very likely was occupied with rituals of royal succession, consorting with one or more women who represented the favor of the Queen of Heaven. (If we trust the story of Aspasia, the favored concubine of Cyrus, as told in chapter 3 at notes 32–36, then she accompanied Cyrus on this march.) Ritual lovemaking clearly played a role in Cyrus' attempt to claim kingship in an incident narrated by Xenophon *Anabasis* 1.2.12: a few days after leaving Celaenae, Cyrus received Epuaxa, wife of the king of Cilicia; "and it is said that Cyrus made love with the Cilician queen."

39. On the Assyrian evidence, see Wiseman 1983 and 1984; and note 12 above. Xenophon *Cyropaedia* 4.6.3–6 tells the story of an Assyrian, Gobryas, whose most excellent and only son was given to be wed to the daughter of the king of Assyria, and who was then killed in a hunt.

Figure 8. Persian-period funerary relief showing the deceased
in a hunting scene above, and in a wedding banquet below,
from Dascyleum, fifth century B.C.E.

an appropriate sponsor of such a monument to sovereignty.[40] The biography
of Atys son of Croesus has been distorted into a ritual archetype, to be sure,

40. Herodotus 7.27–30, referring to Pythius son of Atys as the wealthiest man in Lydia. How
and Wells 1912, vol. 2, 138, suppose reasonably that he was "probably a son of the unfortunate

but that in itself is a characteristic of his royal station. The transcendent significance of these rituals required their descriptions to follow an archetypal pattern, endlessly retold in hymns praising and then lamenting one lover of the goddess after another. Herodotus was very likely informed by a knowledgeable person (possibly one of the Persian *logioi*, since Persians controlled the rituals of kingship in Herodotus' day) who might even have had the text of a ritualized lament for Atys as his source. The woman who was the bride of this Atys was, of course, the embodiment of Kybebe for the purposes of their marriage ritual. The later cult of the dying Attis, beloved of Kybele, was merely the crystallization of this ancient narrative of essential grief in a later age, when living and dying Asiatic princes and kings no longer served as the focus of the ritualized lament that was still conducted for the benefit of the fertility of the earth and the well-being of all the creatures living on it.[41]

## THE TRIBUTE OF TYRANNY

Lydian tyranny was based on the premise that rulership included responsibility for the productivity of the earth. Those who derived their livelihood from the earth within the tyrant's domain, as a consequence, owed allegiance to the tyrant as a religious obligation. For it was through the cultic offices of the tyrant and his attendant cult functionaries that the highest rites of sacrifice and obeisance were performed to maintain the favor of the deity who embodied the life-sustaining forces of the earth.

This deity was known at Sardis as Kybebe, who, in her capacity as the consort of tyrants, was known to Greeks as Aphrodite. As the foundation of agricultural prosperity, Kybebe was also recognizable as Demeter, or Earth herself. Sophocles refers to this aspect of the goddess at Sardis when he describes her as enthroned with lions and calls her "all-nourishing Earth."[42] Euripides calls to mind the same associations, in the *Bacchae*, when he names "divine Demeter—she is Earth, or whatever name you wish to call her; she nourishes mortals with dry food."[43] Sardis, in the Roman period, could even be referred

---

son of Croesus . . . who had inherited the colossal wealth of the Mermnad kings." On the Midas Monument, a monument to the divine origin of kingship and the most splendid example of its kind, see chapter 2 at notes 86–88, and figure 3. On the attested variants of the Lydian name, Atas, Ates, Atis, and Atys, see Zgusta 1964, 105; Gusmani 1988, 191. Gusmani *LW* 30 discusses the alternation of the vowels *i, e,* and *y* in Lydian, noting evidence that "*y* eine Art Übergangslaute zwischen *i* und *e* war."

41. On the post-Lydian formalization of ritual lament over the death of Atys/Attis, see Roller 1999, 238–41, 304–7; and most recently Lancellotti 2002, esp. 25–96, who recognizes the importance of the royal and sacral role played by Atys/Attis.

42. Sophocles *Philoctetes* 392, cited in chapter 3 at note 122.

43. Euripides *Bacchae* 275–77, in a context where Kybele also has been named. (See chapter 2, notes 2, 3, and 20.)

to as a city of Demeter.[44] During the period of Mermnad rule, the goddess who was the giver of bread was also the giver of rulership. The golden statue of a woman dedicated by Croesus at Delphi, said by the Delphians to be Croesus' breadmaker, probably represented Kybebe in this capacity.[45]

The earth at Sardis was especially generous to him who ruled over it, for the Pactolus stream that flowed through Sardis was famous as a source of gold. This remarkable boon may be the chief reason why Sardis became the seat of Lydian tyranny. Coinage came into being at Sardis from the gold of the Pactolus, and from the first it was associated with the rites of Kybebe.[46] The only securely identified archaic cult place of Kybebe at Sardis is her altar in the midst of the gold refineries by the Pactolus, indicating that the Lydians recognized that this most exquisite gift of the earth came to them by her generosity. An etiological myth linked this bounty with the rites of Aphrodite at Sardis. The pseudo-Plutarchean treatise *On Rivers* tells the story of Pactolus the son of Leucothea, who unwittingly had intercourse with his own sister, Demodice, while practicing the Mysteries of Aphrodite. When Pactolus realized what he had done, he committed suicide by plunging into the river Chrysorrhoas (Goldenstream), which afterward bore his name.[47] Here we find elements of a tradition that once linked ritual marriage and ritual lament to the divine gift of gold at Sardis.

As chief beneficiary of the favors of the divine Earth, the tyrant owed sacrifice to her, particularly on those occasions when he sought some special relief or benefit. Sacrifice for the purposes of attracting the sympathies of the deity was not an emotionally neutral transaction. It had to entail the pain of loss, so as to gain the attention of the deity through a bond of emotional sym-

---

44. So Apollonius of Tyana refers to Sardis (Philostratus, *Letters of Apollonius* 75). Demeter is invoked (as *Lamētrus*) on a fourth-century Lydian funerary inscription: Hanfmann and Ramage 1978, 162–63, no. 242 (= *LW* 261–62, no. 26). On testimony to the cult of Demeter and Kore at Sardis, see Hanfmann 1983b, 226–28. Note the draped cult image of a goddess accompanied by standing ears of grain depicted on gems and coins of the Roman period from Sardis: Fleischer 1973, 187–201 and plates 78–83.

45. Herodotus 1.51.5. Plutarch *Moralia* 401e says that the dedication honored the woman who saved Croesus' life at the time of his accession, thus explaining the breadmaker as a kingmaker. Kurke, in Garret and Kurke 1994, 82–83, suggests that "Croesus' breadmaker" was a euphemism for his sexual partner, or courtesan; in view of the significance of royal concubines, as discussed in chapter 3, this suggestion points to the same conclusion as argued here.

46. On the attribution of the invention of coinage to the Lydians, see Herodotus 1.94.1 and Xenophanes DK 21 B 4 (= Pollux *Onomasticon* 9.83). On the archaeological evidence for gold extraction along the Pactolus at Sardis in the sixth century, see Ramage and Craddock 2000.

47. [Plutarch] *De Fluviis* 7.2. Pliny *Naturalis Historia* 5.30.110 also refers to the alternative name, Chrysorrhoas, for the Pactolus River. Demodice elsewhere is said to be the name of the bride of Midas, who was responsible for the invention of coinage; see chapter 2, note 72.

pathy. This was the essence of the advice of King Amasis to Polycrates of Samos, that he should devise a painful sacrifice in order to secure other benefits of his tyranny.[48] This was the rationale behind the sacrifice of all precious possessions made by the subjects of Midas, capped by the sacrifice of Midas' own son Anchyrus, according to the story told by Callisthenes.[49] This was also the rationale behind the sacrifices made by Croesus before seeking to enlarge his empire by war with the Persians, as told by Herodotus.

Croesus' decision to go to war, and the famous consultation and propitiation of the oracles that accompanied the decision, immediately followed the two years of mourning for the loss of his son, Atys, in Herodotus' account. The sequence is surely significant. After suffering supreme personal loss, and after ordering phenomenal sacrifices, Croesus could expect compensation. Herodotus reports that Croesus made his offerings out of respect for the prescience of the oracles, particularly the oracle at Delphi. But more than respect for Delphi was at stake in the spectacle staged by Croesus. As Herodotus also relates, his sacrifices, begun at Sardis, were also made for the sake of enlarging his worldly dominion:[50]

> Of every kind of appropriate animal he slaughtered three thousand; he burnt in a huge pile a number of precious objects—couches overlaid with gold or silver, golden cups, tunics, and other richly coloured garments—in the hope of binding the god more closely to his interest; and he issued a command that every Lydian was also to offer sacrifice according to his means. After this ceremony he melted down an enormous quantity of gold into one hundred and seventeen ingots about eighteen inches long, nine inches wide, and three inches thick; four of the ingots were of refined gold weighing approximately a hundred and forty-two pounds each; the rest were alloyed and weighed about a hundred and fourteen pounds. He also caused the image of a lion to be made of refined gold, in weight some five hundred and seventy pounds. The statue, when the temple at Delphi was burnt down, fell from the gold bricks that formed its base and lies today in the Corinthian Treasury. It has lost about two hundred pounds' weight in the fire, and now weighs only three hundred and seventy pounds.
>
> This was by no means all that Croesus sent to Delphi. . . .

Many precious articles could be sacrificed to the gods by burning them. Animals could be slaughtered, and a loved one could be consigned, in death, to Earth herself. But how could gold be dissipated, or returned to the earth from which it came, in an act of sacrifice? In such huge quantities, gold could be sacrificed only by sending it far away and entrusting it to the secure keeping of a god, such as Apollo at Delphi, who held a shrine founded by the *pro-*

---

48. Herodotus 3.40–43, where Polycrates throws his most precious ring into the sea.

49. See chapter 2 at note 55.

50. Herodotus 1.50–51.1, translated by A. de Sélincourt.

*tomantis,* Earth herself.[51] Apollo, the agent of divine sovereignty at Delphi, was but a trustee for the divine Earth who was the ultimate source of the wisdom that sustained sovereignty. Croesus' massive sacrifice that began at Sardis and ended at Delphi was made in order to entreat the divine Earth, and through her Apollo and all the gods, to favor Croesus' fortune. The devotion of gold in particular also served to impress the Greeks not only with the magnitude of the wealth at Croesus' disposal, but also with the generosity to Croesus of the Earth herself, a generosity that might yield still greater boons to Croesus and his followers in the coming venture.

The sacrifice of gold to the divine sustainer of sovereignty was an act performed not just by Croesus, but by all Lydians according to their means, as Herodotus tells us. The same communal sacrifice for sovereignty is attested in Herodotus' account of the Tumulus of Alyattes, "far the greatest work of human hands, outside of the works of the Egyptians and the Babylonians."[52] (See figure 9.) In addition to its great size, its most remarkable feature, according to Herodotus, was the commemoration of the classes of Lydians who contributed it, as recorded on five inscribed markers standing on top of the tumulus. These classes were the merchants, the craftsmen, and the working girls. Each of these classes generated wealth through transactions that earned payment in coinage. When one reckons the respective contributions of each class of revenue generators, Herodotus notes, the girls gave the largest share. This he explains as the proceeds from their custom of prostitution. The Lydian custom of prostituting their daughters before marriage, which Herodotus identifies as the single most obvious difference between the Lydian and the Greek way of life, is another example of the manner in which the rites of Aphrodite commanded a prominent place in the lives of the Lydians. Sexual initiation and the golden tokens that the Lydian girls received through the grace of Aphrodite all signified their participation in the rituals that justified sovereign tyranny at Sardis. Their contribution from the largesse of Aphrodite to the memorial of Alyattes should be understood as a record of their devotion to the goddess of tyranny and their sacrifice on the occasion of Alyattes' death, performed in order to gain divine support for the tyranny of Alyattes' successor, Croesus.

Herodotus' most famous story about the nature of tyranny also demonstrates that a tyrant's sovereignty depended on his control of the rites of sacrifice to the earth. In book 5 of his *Histories,* Herodotus presents the speech

51. On Gaea and the relationship between Apollo and the earth at Delphi, see Aeschylus *Eumenides* 1–20, and the discussions of J. E. Harrison 1927, 385–444; Fontenrose 1959, 365–433; and the more simplified outline of Parke and Wormell 1956, vol. 1, 3–16.

52. Herodotus 1.93.2. On the conspicuous mound at Bin Tepe, in the Hermus plain before Sardis, identified as the Tumulus of Alyattes, see the summary of Pedley 1968, 58–62, and the discussion of McLaughlin 1985, 43–48, 171–74 (where earlier bibliography is cited).

Figure 9. View of Alyattes' tumulus and the Gygaean lake looking north from Sardis (Photo courtesy of Crawford H. Greenewalt, Jr.).

of Socles the Corinthian to the Spartans and their allies, describing the terrors of tyranny and urging them to oppose its practices. The climax of his argument comes with the description of the deeds of Periander son of Cypselus, tyrant of Corinth, and what he learned from Thrasybulus, tyrant of Miletus in the time of Alyattes. Periander sent a messenger to inquire of Thrasybulus about the best way to secure power and administer the city. Thrasybulus responded by taking the messenger on a walk through the grain fields outside Miletus, cutting off the tallest ears of grain and discarding them as he went. The meaning of this behavior, as the story is explained in Herodotus' account, was that the tyrant should remove threats to his power by cutting down the most prominent of his own people.[53] An alternative meaning, better supported by the aftermath of this episode, is that Thrasybulus' silent demonstration was meant to show that the bounty yielded by the earth under a tyrant's wardenship was the chief justification for tyranny; and further, that in consideration of his custody of this gift of divine grace, it was the tyrant's obligation to sacrifice back to the earth the choicest portions of that bounty.

Herodotus reveals the cultic implications of this lesson in tyranny when he tells what Periander actually did when he realized the meaning of the lesson. After stating tersely that Periander left undone no wicked deed of murder or banishment—deeds that we might expect to learn more about, if cutting down potential rivals was the chief lesson—Herodotus goes on at far greater length to describe an elaborate funerary sacrifice. Periander commanded all the women of Corinth, free women and their attendants, to contribute their most costly garments and jewelry to a burnt offering to his deceased wife, Melissa.[54] Both the background that Herodotus gives to this story and the manner in which he concludes this narrative emphasize the significance of the sacrifice to Melissa as an insight into the essence of tyranny.

After describing the sacrifice to Melissa, Socles concludes: "This is what tyranny means, men of Lacedaemon, and what kind of deeds it entails!" To most modern readers the conclusion to Socles' account of tyranny seems peculiar; it gives an example of the presumptuous madness of tyrants, but the example seems to be more a testimony to the peculiar fixation of Pe-

53. Herodotus 5.92f. Herodotus' interpretation of this story has been better remembered than its details; Aristotle *Politics* 1284a reverses the roles of Periander and Thrasybulus in his telling.

54. Herodotus 5.92f–g, where the offering is said to have been exacted by deception and force on the occasion of a festival to Hera. Cf. the elaborate offerings made to "Hera" on behalf of his most beloved wife by Artaxerxes II, according to Plutarch *Artaxerxes* 23.5; cf. also the lavish sacrifice to the deceased beloved of Cyrus the Great in the story of Pantheia told by Xenophon *Cyropaedia*, 7.3.7, 11, 15–16 (cited in chapter 3 at note 37). These customs call to mind Herodotus' reference to the Asiatic style of the funerals of the kings Sparta (6.58; discussed in chapter 1, with notes 58–61).

riander on his dead wife than a general account of the nature of tyranny. Once we introduce the Lydian evidence for the status of the tyrant's consort and her funerary cult, the general picture of "what tyranny means, and what kind of deeds it entails," becomes clear.

Melissa, whose name was a cult title, was the choicest of the consorts of Periander the tyrant; she was herself the daughter of a tyrant, Procles of Epidaurus, and was the mother of the son who became Periander's favored heir.[55] Periander killed Melissa, Herodotus states, and copulated with her corpse (deeds that Herodotus states as facts but does not explain).[56] After her burial, Periander consulted the Oracle of the Dead on the Acheron River to learn from Melissa where to find a certain (unspecified) foreign thing held in trust (παρακαταθήκη ξεινική). This charge might have been a valuable deposit held on trust for a foreign friend, but as the object of the elaborate public sacrifice to Melissa its significance was probably greater. It probably signified what Periander hoped to gain by going through the public ritual of placating his wife's ghost: the security of his own sovereignty and through it the beneficence of the earth.[57]

Melissa, I suggest, was herself a sacrificial victim. She was the choicest possession of Periander, and by doing away with her, just as Thrasybulus had destroyed the best portions of his crop and as Polycrates made a sacrifice of his cherished ring, Periander sought to activate a deep and powerful bond of grief with the forces of nature that sustained his tyranny.[58] As the tyrant's

55. Herodotus 3.50 reports the kinship of Melissa, as does Diogenes Laertius 1.94, who also reports that her true name was Lysida, and that she was called Melissa by Periander. Pindar *Pythian* 4.60 speaks of the Melissa of Delphi who proclaimed kingship for Battus of Cyrene; scholia to the passage identify Melissa as the title of a priestess of Demeter; see also Callimachus *Hymn* 2.110; scholion to Theocritus 15.94. The association of Periander's Melissa and the Delphic priestess is also observed by Stern 1989, 17; and Ogden 2001, 56 and n. 52. The name certainly derived from Mylitta, attested by Herodotus 1.131.3 and 199.3 as the Assyrian name for Aphrodite and known from Neo-Assyrian texts as Mullissu, divine consort of the god Assur, in whose Sacred Marriage ritual the Assyrian king and queen participated at the city Assur; on Assyrian Mullissu, see Dalley 1979; Nissinen 2001, 95–97, 104.

56. Herodotus 3.50, 5.92g, whose account is repeated by Nicolaus of Damascus *FGrHist* 90 F 58.2; Diogenes Laertius 1.94 and 100 introduces the notion that Melissa's death was accidental. Stern 1989 finds the story too implausible to have any historical basis, and suggests that it represents Herodotus' historicization of the Mesopotamian story of the descent of Inanna-Ishtar into the underworld.

57. Stern 1989, 16–18, plausibly suggests that the παρακαταθήκη ξεινική signified the wealth of the earth itself, "entrusted" to humankind. Cf. the παρακαταθήκη received by Leto from Isis (which was the infant Apollo), according to the Egyptian account reported by Herodotus 2.156.4; cf. also the Phrygian "sacred objects . . . covered in a basket" (ἱερὰ . . . ἐν κίστει κεκαλυμμένα) received by the Milesians at Assesus, according to Nicolaus *FGrHist* 90 F 52, which became the basis of political stability at Miletus (discussed in chapter 2 at note 123).

58. Ogden 2001 observes several instances in which necromantic rites were said to involve the sacrifice of a human who was specifically an object of erotic affection (Ogden 196–201).

chief consort, Melissa embodied the goddess of love. Bearing within her Periander's offering of fertility (his "loaves in a cold oven," as the oracle put it), Melissa was the tyrant's personal emissary to the underworld, the fundament of earthly fertility. With the ghost of Melissa, Periander had a direct link to the wisdom of the earth that sustained sovereignty.

The bond of bereavement between consorts provided access to the metaphysical basis of sovereignty, much as it did between Atossa and her deceased husband, King Darius, as Aeschylus depicts their necromantic encounter in his *Persians*. An even closer parallel to the story of Periander and Melissa is the story of the Spartan regent and would-be-tyrant Pausanias, as told by Plutarch and, according to him, "attested to by many." Plutarch states that, while presiding at Byzantium over the Greek forces that had repelled Xerxes, Pausanias summoned to his bed a well-born young woman of Byzantium and slew her in the darkness of his bedchamber. After her murder, Pausanias consulted her ghost in the Oracle of the Dead at Heracleia, where she foretold his impending death.[59] As with Melissa and Periander, this unexpiated death of an intimate person was the basis of a strong link to the forces of the underworld.[60]

The sacrifice of Melissa by Periander was followed, in Herodotus' account, by the mass offerings of all Corinthian women, and by the accompanying sacrifice of other concubines (*pallakides*), burnt alive, according to other sources.[61] Only a tyrant could perform such an outlandish rite to assure the fertility of the earth, and to secure his own rulership. Although Periander of Corinth, Thrasybulus of Miletus, and the would-be tyrant Pausanias of Sparta were all Greeks, the most horrifying aspect of their tyrannical behavior—human sacrifice—derived directly from the model of Lydian tyranny, and was justified by an Asiatic concept of divinity. This was why, at the close of his tale of tyranny, Socles appealed to the Spartans in the name of "the gods of the Greeks" not to set up tyrannies in Greek cities.[62]

---

The most famous example is the alleged self-sacrifice of Antinous on behalf of the emperor Hadrian: Ogden 153–54.

59. Plutarch *Cimon* 6.4–6, where the Spartan regent Pausanias consults the Oracle of the Dead at Heracleia; Pausanias *periēgētēs* 3.17.8–9, where the regent Pausanias is said to have consulted *psychagōgoi* at Phigaleia in Arcadia. In both accounts the murder of the girl is reported as an accident, although the alleged accident happens in the course of an erotic encounter. On Pausanias' tyrannical behavior, see also Thucydides 1.95.3–7, 128.3–133.

60. See Crane 1988, 94–96, and Ogden 2001, esp. 30–32, for a discussion of this and other passages describing necromancy. Ogden (39–42, 100–107) points out the strong association of the Spartan regent Pausanias, in life and after his death, with stories of necromancy and exorcism in which the security and sovereignty of the Spartan state were at risk.

61. Diogenes Laertius 1.94, who cites Heracleides of Pontus and other classical and Hellenistic authors in his sketch of Periander.

62. Herodotus 5.92g: ἐπιμαρτυρόμεθά τε ἐπικαλεόμενοι ὑμῖν θεοὺς τοὺς Ἑλληνίους. The implication of this imprecation is that the divinities attending the sacrificial offerings made by Periander were something other than "the gods of the Greeks."

## DEIFYING THE MOTHER OF TYRANNY

The ideology of tyranny transformed death into a link between humanity and the gods, and defined the tyrant as chief officiant of the rites of the gods by virtue of his personal relationship, through nativity, marriage, and paternity, to those who have passed from life into the realm of the divine. The funerary rites of the tyrannical dead may be compared to the heroizing funerary cult of the kin and ancestors of affluent families of classical antiquity.[63] The difference between these and tyrannical rites was chiefly one of degree, measurable in size of funerary monument, number of mourners, and the like. But degree was everything, for the tyrant's assertion of sovereign supremacy had the effect of collapsing the distinction between heroized mortals and sovereign divinities. We have already noticed various expressions of this assimilation of humanity into divinity. It was characteristic of Spartan royal funerals, which Herodotus likened to Asiatic funerals, as was noted in chapter 1. It appears in the alleged deification of the mother of Midas as the Mother of the Gods, and in the so-called *Phrygian Stories* told by Prodicus of Ceos about the original nature of Demeter and Dionysus, as was noted in chapter 2. And it appears especially in the Sacred Marriage, where the chosen concubine of the Lydian tyrant is identified with Aphrodite, or Kybebe, as described above and in the previous chapter.

In the Mysteries of Aphrodite, only the tyrant could recognize the goddess by her irresistible splendor. The choicest consort of the tyrant, therefore, was always a woman whose true identity was overlain by her divine role, and by the need for her offspring to be accepted as the progeny of a Sacred Marriage. This conventional ambiguity gave space for Clearchus' innuendos about the tyrannical abuses of other men's daughters and wives in the grove at Sardis known as the "Place of Purity." Likewise it yielded the tale of incest that gave the Pactolus River its name. Above all, it was the basis of tales of the incestuous relations between the tyrant and his own mother.

The tyranny of Periander is the subject of another tale of sexual perversion, related in Hellenistic sources.[64] Periander's own mother became so enamored of her son, after he became ruler of Corinth, that she contrived to seduce him. She told Periander that a woman of great beauty was in love with him and wished to have intercourse with him, on condition that her identity would remain unknown. Although Periander demurred at first,

---

63. On classical funerary cult, Garland 1985 describes normative customs; Burkert 1985, 190–215, discusses the continuum from common cult to the heroic and deified dead; I. Morris 1992 discusses the variability of burial practices in terms of social structure. Note the reflection of royal ritual in the funerary art discussed above, and cited in note 37.

64. It is related by Parthenius *Erotica Pathemata* 17. Diogenes Laertius 1.96 refers to the story, and cites Aristippus of Cyrene *On the Luxuries of the Ancients* as his source.

eventually he was persuaded to meet his secret admirer in a darkened room, without speaking, and to gratify her desires. The silent encounter proved so pleasurable that, afterwards, Periander agreed to his mother's suggestion that it be repeated, again and again. As Periander's attachment to his anonymous lover grew, so did his desire to converse with her and to look upon her. So he told his mother, but she insisted that modesty prevented the woman from allowing this to happen. But Periander was determined to know who she was. At their next meeting, he took a lamp out of hiding and revealed her face, and when he recognized his own mother he lost his mind. The event so transformed Periander that he became cruel and murderous, a tyrant in the conventional sense; and his mother, tortured by the discovery, killed herself.

This story has echoes of the tale of Gyges and the wife of Candaules. In both cases, as a result of the passions of others, a man sees what he should not see—the wife of the previous ruler—and the outcome is his tyranny. The story also echoes the tale of Oedipus of Thebes, which Sophocles' play has made famous. Oedipus is the tyrant who unwittingly fulfills his destined fate by slaying his father and marrying his mother, whom at first he did not recognize. These crimes undermine his otherwise perfect rulership, and when they are revealed to him—as a result of his own insistence on knowing the truth—the effect is much like the outcome of the story of Periander.

These plot lines all derive their compelling twists from an authentic ideological premise of tyranny: the woman who gives birth to the tyrant is in some sense identical with the woman who bears the tyrant's own children. This paradoxical notion arises from the fact that tyrants are mortal men, and from the understanding that their consorts represent a divinity, the goddess of love herself, the source of tyranny. The name given to Periander's mother, Crateia (Power), affirms this: power created the tyrant, and is irresistibly drawn to him.

Still more remarkable is the fact that such incest was sometimes acknowledged as a positive sign of sovereign tyranny. Herodotus recounts a dream of Hippias son of Peisistratus in which "he thought that he slept with his own mother," and this dream gave him confidence that he would regain his tyranny over Athens.[65] Suetonius attributes the same omen to a dream of Julius Caesar, explaining that the image of sexual appropriation of one's own mother was believed to portend rulership over the earth.[66] The book of dream interpretation by Artemidorus of Daldis (a Lydian of the second century C.E.) provides a lengthy discussion of the symbolism of dreaming about sexual intercourse with one's own mother. Among its many positive meanings, he observes that "one's mother means one's native land," and "one's mother resembles the earth, since the earth is the nurse and progenitor of

65. Herodotus 6.107.1.
66. Suetonius *Caesar* 7.2.

all."[67] The mother of tyranny is the mother and mate of the tyrant, symbolically, and is Earth herself. Only a divinity could play such a transitive role, for when she is identified as a mortal woman, the incestuous implications are unavoidable.

The metaphysics of dreams could meld the identities of mother, lover, and earth into a potent symbol of sovereign legitimacy. But could the mortal mother of the tyrant ever be identified in person as such a symbol? Death made this possible. After death her mortal nature would not conflict with that of any living consort of the tyrant, and her identity could be assimilated to the divine—she could be deified, as we are told that the mother of Midas was.[68] Moreover, the tomb of the mother of the tyrant could become a shrine of the personified Earth. It should be remarked, however, that tradition preserves no memory of the tomb of any tyrant's mother. This may be because, as was suggested in chapter 2, monuments of the tyrant's mother were features of the earth itself. She became "The Mother," and mountains were her monuments, eternally yielding life-giving waters, nurturing flocks and wild beasts, and, to her devotees, eternally justifying tyranny.

Matters were different with the tyrant's lover. As a lover she represented evanescence: the bloom of desire and the ecstasy of its consummation. Like life itself, these were moments that would pass, and whose passings would be lamented. Anguish and lamentation over the death of the tyrant's lover, just as much as over the death of his son or of the tyrant himself, served to unite his people in an emotional bond with the heavenly Queen of Love, that she might be moved to restore the conditions of happiness on earth. For these purposes, a conspicuous tomb as a focal point of lamentation and its memory was most appropriate.

So it is that we find several traditions linking the great burial mounds of Lydia with lovers of the tyrant, or with love and the tyrant. The most explicit of these is related, once again, by Clearchus of Soli:[69]

> Gyges the king of the Lydians became all the talk not only for his erotic attachment to his mistress while she was alive, entrusting himself and his entire rulership to her, but especially because when she died he assembled all Lydians from the countryside and heaped up what is now called "The Courtesan's Monument" [τὸ νῦν ἔτι καλούμενον τῆς Ἑταίρας μνῆμα], raising it to such a height that, from wherever he traveled within the countryside of Tmolus, he could turn and see the monument, and it was visible to all the inhabitants of Lydia.

The woman called here the mistress (ἐρωμένη) of Gyges is surely the woman also known as the former wife of Candaules, whose bedchamber meant

67. Artemidorus *Onirocriticon* 1.79.
68. See chapter 2 at notes 95–97.
69. Clearchus, from book 2 of his *Erotica*, cited by Athenaeus 13.573a–b.

rulership for the man who entered it. The story of the Courtesan's Monument associates the memory of this woman with a funerary monument that was, in effect, a symbol of Mermnad sovereignty. Clearchus' story could well be an alternative account of the most famous monument to Mermnad sovereignty known to Herodotus, the Tumulus of Alyattes (figure 9 above), which was also a work of love, although of a different nature.[70] On the other hand, it is possible that several of the most conspicuous tumuli in the funerary field in the plain north of Sardis were linked to tales of love, death, and sovereignty. Such associations are found in Xenophon's tale of Pantheia, reputed to be the most beautiful woman in Asia, and the object of the chaste affections of Cyrus the Great.[71] The love and respect in which Cyrus held Pantheia was instrumental in motivating her husband, the king of Susa, to give his all for Cyrus in battle at Sardis against the army of Croesus. When Cyrus encountered Pantheia mourning over the body of her fallen husband, he offered to honor his memory with a tomb and a massive sacrifice of animals and precious ornaments, and to convey Pantheia herself wherever she wished to go. When Cyrus left her to mourn in private, Pantheia slew herself over her husband's body. So Xenophon's tale transformed the horror of human sacrifice into the pathos of a lover's suicide. When Cyrus learned of her deed, he marveled and mourned the woman whose devotion had served his rise to power so well. As Cyrus had promised, Xenophon concludes, "an exceedingly large burial mound was heaped up, so they say."[72]

Such stories and the monuments associated with them affirmed that sovereign power was truly founded on a love supreme. Their poignancy was deepened, as the tale of Pantheia exemplifies, if the love in question was unfulfilled. According to the paradigm of sacrifice advanced in this chapter, painful loss provokes grief, which encourages divine redress, and nothing is more painful than the premature loss of a loved one. The embodiment of grief in a funerary monument, therefore, is an enduring appeal for divine redress. This explanation surely underlies the account, related in chapter 2, of the funerary monument of Midas. In the much-quoted funerary epigram of Midas, the bronze statue of a maiden (*korē*) introduces herself to passersby and identifies the "tear-drenched mound" on which she stood as the tomb of Midas. The image signified all such marriageable girls who could have fallen in love with Midas, but who now, like her, will grieve for the perfect king that they can never have, so that through grieving they might yet bring to pass some new good thing in the world. Like the immortal women of

70. Herodotus 1.93.2. Pedley 1968, 62–63, also suggests that Clearchus may be referring to the Tumulus of Alyattes.

71. Xenophon *Cyropaedia* 4.6.11 (cf. 6.1.7), discussed also in chapter 3 at note 37.

72. Xenophon *Cyropaedia* 7.3.16.

myth—Calypso, Circe, Eos, Thetis, and even Demeter—who mourn the loss of their beloved, the mourning maiden is an avatar of the goddess of love herself. As one who might have become the lover of the tyrant and mother of his heir, she is an aspect of the one who did become those things, the Mother of the Gods.

### EUNUCHS, TYRANNY, AND THE MOTHER OF THE GODS

Even before Cyrus learned of the death of his beloved Pantheia, in the tale told by Xenophon, her eunuchs went into mourning. Three of them, who were charged with attending their mistress at all times, slew themselves on the spot. For their uncompromising loyalty they were given the honor of a burial mound, which, Xenophon says, "still today they call the Mound of the Eunuchs."[73] This vignette brings momentarily to the fore members of a class of servants who must always have been in attendance in scenes of courtly and ritualized love. In the course of time, as the principal royal actors receded from the historical stage of ritualized drama, the eunuch attendants assumed more central roles as devotees of the great goddesses of Asia. It is well to remember that their role was an extension of the ancient Asiatic custom of using eunuchs as servants and ministers in all great houses, especially in royal courts.

Eunuchs were the mainstay of the staff of the royal households of Assyria and Babylonia and surrounding kingdoms.[74] Not only domestic staff, eunuchs also filled a significant number of high offices in the administration of the Assyrian empire.[75] In chapter 3 we encountered Yariris of Carchemish, a eunuch who ruled this important north Syrian state in the early eighth century.[76] Among the Medes and Persians, Herodotus and other Greek sources note the service of eunuchs as royal bodyguards, as guardians of the king's wives and children, and as trusted emissaries.[77] Ctesias likewise reports

---

73. Xenophon *Cyropaedia* 7.3.15, where Xenophon describes the stelae that marked the burial places.

74. On the widespread employment of eunuchs in Neo-Assyrian administration, see Grayson 1995; Deller 1999; and Watanabe 1999b, 319. Diakonoff 1977, 338–39, offers impressive statistics on the number of eunuchs (3,892, or some 70% of all personnel) employed in the palace of the Urartian king Rusa II, a contemporary of Gyges in Lydia and Esarhaddon in Assyria. Grottanelli 1998 discusses Eastern court eunuchs primarily on the basis of the Greek sources.

75. Grayson 1995, 93–94 and 98, where other scholarship is cited.

76. See chapter 3, with notes 86–90. Hawkins 2000, 78, summarizes the status of Yariris as ruler, regent, and eunuch.

77. Herodotus speaks of eunuchs serving as royal bodyguards in 3.77 (cf. 1.113.3); as guardians of the royal harem (3.130.4–5, 8.104); as trusted emissaries (1.117.5, 8.106.1). Xenophon (cited below at note 82) approves the many valuable services performed by eunuchs. Plato *Laws* 3.694d–696b discusses the effects of rearing royal sons among the women and eunuchs of the harem in the Persian court.

the deeds and misdeeds of several powerful eunuchs at the Persian court, some of them kingmakers in the struggles of dynastic succession.[78] In his comprehensive study of the Persian empire, Pierre Briant has reviewed the numerous Greek accounts of eunuchs in the Persian court, but, considering the generally negative attitude of Greeks toward eunuchs, Briant regards many of these accounts to be unreliable, invidious stereotypes.[79] Briant also expresses doubts about whether so many castrated men actually had the influence or high office attributed to them, and suggests that Greek εὐνοῦχος, "eunuch" (literally, "bed keeper"), need not always refer to castrated men. But the Assyriological evidence is compelling: men referred to as eunuchs (ša rēš šarri or ša rēši in Akkadian) are described as sexually dysfunctional and are depicted as beardless, and these men are found serving at all levels of domestic and imperial administration.[80] The Greek sources merely affirm that the Persians continued this practice.

As guardians of their master's most prized possessions, eunuchs are commonly found as custodians of great harems.[81] The custody of the ruler's wives and concubines, however, was merely one facet of the trust placed by a ruler in his eunuchs. The basis of the use of eunuchs for all manner of service where loyalty is a paramount concern is clearly set forth by Xenophon, in his fictionalized history of Cyrus the Great, founder of the Persian empire, and (in Xenophon's eyes) paragon of every great tradition of Asiatic kingship:[82]

> Realizing that men are nowhere more vulnerable than when they are taking their food, their drink, their baths, in bed, or asleep, Cyrus considered who would be most dependable for him in such circumstances. He calculated that no man would ever be reliable who loved anything more than his duty as a guard. He knew, however, that men who had children or women to their likings, or boy loves, were compelled by nature to love these more; but seeing that eunuchs were deprived of all such things, he reckoned that these men would do anything for those who were able to enrich them and assist them if they were suffering any injury, and who could invest them with honors. On these men, Cyrus reckoned, he could never go too far in heaping benefactions.

The loyalty of eunuchs, as Xenophon observes, came from the ability of a great lord to grant them unsurpassed material and honorific rewards,

78. See D. M. Lewis 1977, 20–21, on Artoxares the Paphlagonian eunuch in the time of Artaxerxes I and Darius II, in Ctesias *Persica* (epitome) 39–40, 47, 49, and 53.

79. Briant 2002, 268–77.

80. Grayson 1995 is definitive on meaning of *ša rēši* as "eunuch; castrated male." For a comparative review of the custom of keeping court eunuchs, see Tougher 2002b.

81. On harem eunuchs in the Persian empire, see Briant (above, note 79) and Llewellyn-Jones 2002.

82. Xenophon *Cyropaedia* 7.5.59–60.

knowing that no other form of personal affection could have greater influence over them. By this model we see precisely why such important offices—generalships, governorships, high embassies—were entrusted to eunuchs. We also see more clearly why eunuchs were the custodians of royal harems. The trustworthiness of harem eunuchs consisted not so much in their inability to engage in generative intercourse as it did in their lack of any emotional attachment based on sex. In the presence of innumerable incarnations of the goddess of love, they could not be swayed by her powers. They were therefore perfect ministers to the rites of Aphrodite performed by others.

Within the traditions of Anatolia and the Near East, wherever custom treated the bride, consort, or mother of a sovereign ruler as a goddess or her likeness, we may expect to find eunuchs in her attendance. These are the circumstances that explain why we find eunuchs in honorable priestly offices, as in the cult of Ephesian Artemis. Strabo, writing at the beginning of the Roman imperial period about the older customs at the sanctuary of Ephesian Artemis, reports: "They had eunuch priests whom they called *Megabyzoi*, always seeking abroad for those who were worthy of this office, and holding them in great honor. It was obligatory, also, for unmarried girls to assist them in their priestly duties."[83] Priests or chief intendants ( *neōkoroi* ) of the cult of Artemis at Ephesus called Megabyzus are attested as early as the late fifth century, and their status as eunuchs is verified by the habit of using the Persian name Megabyzus to refer to a eunuch.[84] Although the hereditary name of these priestly eunuchs was Persian, there is every reason to believe that the custom of eunuch cult attendants was established at Ephesus, and elsewhere in Asia Minor, well before the Persians arrived.

Yariris, the eighth-century ruler of Carchemish, made monuments of his devotion to Kubaba. Yariris is the most prominent of many eunuchs attested in Neo-Hittite monuments, and together they dispel the notion, occasionally stated as a fact, that eunuch priests are not attested in any context be-

83.  Strabo 14.1.23.

84.  See Xenophon *Anabasis* 5.3.6–7 for Megabyzus, *neōkoros* of Artemis of Ephesus; *SIG*[3] 282, an inscription of 333 B.C.E., in which the people of Priene honor Μεγάβυξος Μεγαβύξου νεωκόρος τῆς Ἀρτέμιδος τῆς ἐν Ἐφέσῳ; Pliny *Naturalis Historia* 35.93 and 132, describing paintings of two different Megabyzi, priests of Artemis of Ephesus, by fourth-century artists; cf. Quintilian 5.12.21, describing the painted image of a Megabyzus as an obvious depiction of a eunuch. The personal name Megabyzus ( *Bagabuxša* in Persian) may have a meaning appropriate to a eunuch: "Freed by God" (Kent 1950, 53, 199; LSJ s.v. μεγάβυξος); an alternative meaning, "Who Serves God," has also been proposed (Benveniste 1966, 108–13; see Burkert 1999, 62–63 and n. 32). The tradition of eunuch priesthood at Ephesus is reviewed and accepted as ancient by Picard 1922, 169–73 and 222–28; by Burkert 1999, 62–63 and 67–68; and by Fleischer 1999, 609; J. O. Smith 1996 doubts that the Megabyzi were eunuchs, but with insufficient reason.

tween Mesopotamia in the second millennium and Anatolia in the Hellenistic era.[85] Yariris boasted that the gods made his name known far and wide, including in Phrygian and Mysian lands, so we may assume that the peoples of these lands were familiar with eunuchs who exercised sacerdotal offices. Influential eunuchs are attested at Sardis under Persian rule, as the example of Hermotimus (discussed below) shows. It is therefore reasonable to suppose that eunuchs regularly served as attendants to the cult of Kybebe at Sardis under Mermnad and Persian rule. In nearby Caria, eunuchs served in the priestly staff of the cult of Hecate, whose ancient cult was identified with that of Diana (Artemis) and the Mother of the Gods.[86] Eunuch priests are best known, from Hellenistic and later sources, as attendants to the rites of the Mother of the Gods, particularly at Pessinus in Galatian Phrygia,[87] and to the cult of the Syrian Goddess, Atargatis at Bambyce-Hierapolis, not far from Carchemish.[88]

Scholarship treating the origin of the eunuch priests and cult attendants who served the goddesses of Asia has been badly misled by the assumption that this manner of devotion was normally elective, and was fulfilled by men who chose to castrate themselves.[89] The drama of self-castration, it is true, provides the emotional apex of devotion to the goddess in the story of Attis'

85. On Yariris, see note 76 above. Azamis is another named eunuch who performed priestly functions in service to a ruler of Malatya in the eleventh or tenth century; see *CHLI* V.15, Izgin 1–2. For the assumptions that are disproved by this evidence, see Laroche 1960, 127–28; Gusmani 1971, 313; Roller 1997, 543; and 1999, 19–21; Grottanelli 1998, 414–15.

86. On the cult of Hecate at Lagina, near Stratonicea, see Strabo 14.2.25; Laumonier 1958, 344–425; Kraus 1960, 25–56; D. R. West 1995, 228–31. Tacitus *Annals* 3.62 refers to the Carian cult as that of Diana of the Crossroads. Authors from classical to late antiquity identify Hecate with other goddesses, including the Mother of the Gods: Euripides *Hippolytus* 141–44; Polyaenus *Strategems* 8.53.4; Proclus *Hymn to Hecate and Janus* 6.1–2. On Hecate as the attendant of royalty, see Aeschylus fr. 388 (Radt). On the remarkable prominence of Hecate in Hesiod's *Theogony* 411–52 and the probable Carian origin of the cult known to Hesiod, see M. L. West 1966, 277; Burkert 1985, 171; Johnston 1990, 20–21.

87. On the well-attested eunuch Galli (γάλλοι) of the Mother of the Gods, see Vermaseren 1977, 84–100; Lane 1996b; Borgeaud 1996, 56–88; Roller 1997, and 1999, 229–32; Lancellotti 2002, 96–105l; see also chapter 2, note 10.

88. See Lucian *On the Syrian Goddess* and the discussions of Grottanelli 1998 and Lightfoot 2002.

89. Nock 1925 and Roller 1997 exemplify the assumptions that have misguided the study of eunuch priests as the products of self-mutilation or self-castration. In his inquiry into the religious significance of castration, Nock notes that "we do not find inscriptions in which eunuchs assert that they have sacrificed their manhood or that they have given their *vires* to the goddess; there is no clear parallel to the *taurobolium* records, as we should expect if the castration was regarded as an act of value in itself" (30–31), and he observes that it was the castrated condition, not the act of entering that state, that had religious value. Roller notes the consistency with which eunuch priests and cult attendants were treated as outcasts, the equivalent of slaves, in Greco-Roman culture, yet assumes that their condition was always the result of their own deliberate choice.

self-sacrifice to the Mother, as Hellenistic and later sources relate.[90] I do not doubt that some men actually did choose to set this seal upon their lives, in emulation of what had become a symbol of uncompromising piety.[91] But that symbol, I suggest, was in origin a fiction expounded by those whose fates had been sealed for them, in order to make a virtue of what in fact was a hard reality for men who had been turned into castrated chattel for the profit and service of others.

There is no better picture of the reality that gave rise to this confusion of virtues and vices than the story that Herodotus tells of Hermotimus of Pedasa, a native of Herodotus' Carian homeland. Hermotimus was taken captive as a youth, perhaps at the time of the Ionian Revolt during the reign of Darius. He was purchased by a Chian slave trader with the ominous name of Panionius, "who made his living in the most atrocious way imaginable. He would acquire good-looking boys, castrate them, take them to Sardis and Ephesus, and sell them for a great deal of money; for among the barbarians eunuchs are more highly valued on account of their complete trustworthiness than men with testicles."[92] Becoming part of this trade in value-added human chattel, Hermotimus was sold at Sardis. From there, in due course, he was sent among other gifts to the court of Xerxes, where he won favor and eventually became Xerxes' most trusted eunuch. At the time of Xerxes' expedition against Athens, Hermotimus returned with his master to Sardis and was sent on business to Atarneus on the coast, where he ran into his former handler, Panionius.

Hermotimus next devised what Herodotus calls "the greatest retribution for the wrong done to him of any that we know of." He gulled Panionius with a display of friendship and even gratitude for the many good things that he had acquired since Panionius had set him on his new path in life, and promised to share his good fortune if Panionius would only bring his whole family with him to Atarneus. When Panionius with his wife and four sons fell into this trap, Hermotimus denounced his horrendous livelihood, praised the gods who had delivered his enemy into his hands, and forced Panionius

---

90. Lancellotti 2002, 96–105, discusses the manner in which the mythical self-castration of Attis has been taken as the paradigm of devotion followed by the eunuch Galli, but draws attention to the dichotomy between the mythic paradigm Attis, who dies by this act, and the Galli, who, after establishing their credentials by this alleged act, live to bear witness to their devotion.

91. Stevenson 2002 discusses the evidence for elective castration as an act of piety in early Christianity. Examples of elective castration practiced in other periods of history are surveyed by Bullough 2002, who describes the variety of clinical procedures used, emphasizing the risks involved, especially for men who were past adolescence. All such operations are performed by experienced practitioners under controlled conditions, and no example of self-castration, after the example of Attis, is attested as a regular practice.

92. Herodotus 8.105.1–2.

to castrate each of his own sons, and then forced the sons to do the same to their father.[93]

The story of Hermotimus illustrates the transformations that could lead from enslavement and involuntary castration to the highest ranks of royal service.[94] It also illustrates the fact that not even the highest such honors could efface the outrage of servitude and castration. The horror of castration for men and enforced concubinage for women is perhaps the epitome of the wrongs (ἄδικα) committed against the Greeks on those occasions when, as Herodotus notes, the Greeks of Asia were enslaved by the barbarian rulers of Asia.

Herodotus reports the third such enslavement on the occasion of the suppression of the Ionian Revolt in 494. On that occasion, he notes, the Persian commanders carried out their threats against Greek cities that had resisted by "selecting all of the good-looking boys for castration, making them eunuchs instead of men with testicles, and sending all of the fairest young girls [*parthenous*] to the king's court."[95] The taking of such human booty was customary practice. Other sources report that it occurred "by force, as often was the case, when cities were sacked or when tyrants or satraps used force."[96] The trade in captives and human castoffs was lucrative, as the story of Panionius indicates, and its volume was substantial, as is indicated by the tribute received by the Persian court. Herodotus reports that Darius received an annual tribute of a thousand talents of silver and five hundred castrated boys from Babylon, and that every four years the tribes of the Caucasus contributed a hundred boys and a hundred girls.[97]

As for the Greeks of Asia, their second enslavement, by Herodotus' account, was the original Persian conquest carried out under Harpagus in 545 (the "coming of the Mede" that was such a traumatic event in the memory of Xenophanes of Colophon).[98] The first such enslavement, and the beginning of the wrongs (ἄδικα ἔργα) committed against Greeks by the rulers of

93. Herodotus 8.105–6.

94. Like a harem eunuch, and like the Ephesian Megabyzus, Hermotimus had the honor of escorting Queen Artemisia of Caria and the children of Xerxes' concubines from Athens to Ephesus: Herodotus 8.103–4, 107.1.

95. Herodotus 6.32. This passage concludes: "Thus the Ionians were enslaved for the third time, the first being under the Lydians, and the two following occasions being under the Persians."

96. Aelian *Varia Historia* 12.1, describing the conditions under which Aspasia, the girl from Phocaea, became a concubine of Cyrus the Younger (chapter 3, note 32).

97. Herodotus 3.92, 97.4.

98. Herodotus 1.169.2; cf. the suppression of the Samian uprising by trawling this island (3.149), using the same method employed in 494: Herodotus 6.31. On Xenophanes and the coming of the Mede, see chapter 1, with notes 140 and 141.

Asia, took place under the Mermnad rulers of Lydia, from Gyges to Croe-sus.[99] Here, I suggest, with the tyrants of Lydia, was the historical injury and the fundamental reason why Greeks and barbarians went to war with one another, according to Herodotus: that injury was the form of submission that allowed the abomination of taking boys for eunuchs and girls for concubines.

The custom of collecting eunuchs for royal service was certainly an es-tablished practice among the Lydians before the arrival of the Medes and Persians. Herodotus relates the story of how Periander, the tyrant of Corinth, once sent three hundred boys, taken by him from the leading families of Cor-cyra, to Alyattes at Sardis, for castration.[100] Xanthus of Lydia, a contempo-rary of Herodotus, reported that the kings of Lydia even "began the custom of turning women into eunuchs, to use them instead of men as chamber-lains," or, by another version, "in order to enjoy them always in the bloom of youth."[101] These practices that were so detestable to the Greeks were the perquisites of tyranny among the Lydians.

### ARTEMIS AND THE MOTHER

There was another paradigm for a goddess of sovereignty in Asia that did not have quite the same relationship to the tyrant as did his divine mother or his consort. This was Artemis of Ephesus, the maiden who was forever un-married but who signified imminent marriageability.[102] She is best known from her archaizing cult images representing the beautiful goddess stand-ing, tightly clad and decorated with emblems of burgeoning life and vitality (figure 10).[103] In all of the many variants of her image, wild flora and fauna,

---

99. Herodotus 1.5.3 marks the beginning of his account of the historical offenses between barbarians and Greeks by "indicating the one whom I know to have been the first to commit wrongs against the Greeks." Croesus is the first person named after this passage, at the begin-ning of 1.6.1, but rather ambiguously Herodotus immediately thereafter begins his story of the rise of Gyges and the foundation of the Mermnad dynasty (1.7–14), and the commencement of Lydian wars against Greeks under Gyges and his successors (1.14–28).

100. Herodotus 3.48–49, where the story of how these boys were rescued by the interven-tion of the Samians is told.

101. Xanthus *FGrHist* 765 F 4 (from Athenaeus 12.515d–e and *Suda* s.v. Ξάνθος Κανδαύλου).

102. Odysseus' address to Nausicaä (*Odyssey* 6.149–60) treats Artemis as the vision of a de-sirable bride; so does the appearance of Helen in the halls of Menelaus (4.120–22) and of Pene-lope in the halls of Odysseus (17.37, 19.54). In *Homeric Hymn* 5, *To Aphrodite* 91, Anchises names Artemis first of all the goddesses who may have come to seduce him. The *Ephesiaca* of Xenophon of Ephesus depicts the eroticism of Anthia, a girl who is the likeness of Artemis herself at the goddess' Ephesian festival.

103. The characteristic image of Artemis of Ephesus is known from sculpture and coins of the Hellenistic and Roman eras: see Fleischer 1973. On its archaic origins, see Fleischer 386–90; Radner 2001.

Figure 10. Artemis of Ephesus, richly ornamented
statue of traditional type flanked by deer, second
century C.E., from Ephesus (Photo: Nicolas Gail,
© Österreichisches Archäologisches Institut, Vienna).

natural and supernatural, surround her form in orderly patterns. It is this
orderliness around the body of the goddess, displayed by creatures least given
to order—lions, panthers, bulls, stags, griffins, and winged sprites—that is
striking. The presence among these creatures of bees, wild creatures who are
the most orderly, signifies the principle of overarching purpose that the goddess represents. She renders the forces of nature amenable to human culture.

A similar message is conveyed by the breastlike pendants on her images, if these can now be correctly interpreted. The supposed breasts of Artemis were almost certainly the seasonal festoons of bulls' testes, gathered from the geldings of the year, whose submission to the domesticating knife rendered these powerful beasts useful to humanity.[104] Such sacrifice in the name of Artemis also validated the castrated status of her own attendant priests in this Asian land, where eunuchs were part of the accepted order of civilization.[105] Ephesian Artemis, and the closely related variants of her cult type across southwestern Asia Minor identified by the Greeks also with Aphrodite and by the Persians with Anahita, signified the foundations of the relationship of divinity to humanity as it was understood in this land.[106] The goddess truly is the ordering principle according to which all that is powerful and potentially dangerous in nature is rendered serviceable to humanity. The fact that she is a marriageable maiden, herself tightly constrained by the literal and figurative role she plays, signifies her own subordination to the imminent bridegroom, the godlike tyrant.

In its historically attested context, the cult of Artemis of Ephesus was not exclusively a royal prerogative. As opposed to the semianonymous Mother, Artemis was known by name to all, and her popularity was great as a result. Ephesian Artemis was celebrated in processions and in public banquets.[107] The annual celebration of the Ephesia, moreover, was famous as the occasion for Ionians from far and wide to come together in a massive display of

104. Gérard Seiterle 1979 has demonstrated that Artemis' breastlike pendants were, in origin, bulls' testes. His demonstration is approved, e.g., by Burkert 1979a, 130; 1999, 70; Fleischer 1983, 82 and 86; 1999, 605 and 609; Portefaix 1999, 612. It is rejected, e.g., by LiDonnici 1992, 393, and S. P. Morris 2001a, 142, both of whom mistakenly cite Fleischer as disapproving of the identification of the "breasts" as bulls' testes. Fleischer, in fact, gives Seiterle high praise for his solution to this problem (1983, 82, "Seiterle hat eine alte, oft gestellte Frage gelöst"; and 86, "Zusammenfassend kann man sagen, daß Seiterle mit dem Nachweis, daß es sich bei den 'Brüsten' der Artemis Ephesia um Stierbeutel handelt, eine glänzende Entdeckung gelungen ist"). What Fleischer criticizes, however, and what the archaeozoological evidence appears to contradict, is Seiterle's further suggestion that these testes were taken from sacrificial victims (Fleischer 1983, 87; 1999, 605 n. 5). Fleischer goes on to suggest what must be the correct explanation, namely that the source of these testes was the castration, or gelding, that transformed bulls into oxen. On this routine annual practice, applied to cattle, sheep, and goats, see Isager and Skydsgaard 1992, 89–91; Aristotle *Historia Animalium* 632a.

105. On the eunuch priests of Artemis of Ephesus and of related Asiatic cults, see above, with notes 83–88.

106. On Anatolian Aphrodite, best represented at Aphrodisias, see Fleischer 1973, 146–84 and plates 64–74. On Persian Anahita and her identification as either Artemis or Aphrodite, see chapter 6, notes 24 and 25.

107. The foundation of a procession and banquet for Artemis of Ephesus is attributed to Clymene, daughter of a king of Ephesus, in *Etymologicum Magnum* s.v. Δαιτίς. See Nilsson 1906, 243–47, on the several festivals of Ephesian Artemis, and 245–46 nn. 2 and 3 on the Δαιτίς; see also Picard 1922, 312–53. For the procession of Artemis attested in the Antonine period, see Knibbe 1995.

finery.[108] Croesus, before he became king, is said to have appealed to Artemis of Ephesus to grant him power over his enemies and rivals, and so to secure his kingship.[109] His conspicuous generosity toward Artemis and the people of Ephesus later in his reign was an acknowledgment that Croesus owed his tyranny in some measure to popular Ionian support. The historical relationship between the cult of this Ionian city and the Lydian tyrant contributed greatly to the fame of Artemis of Ephesus.

Herodotus reports that Croesus began his reign by laying siege to Ephesus. A fuller account of this campaign preserved by Aelian reveals that Croesus' goal was to drive out the tyrant of Ephesus, Pindar, who was the son of Croesus' own sister and therefore a potential rival.[110] As the siege was making progress, Pindar advised the Ephesians to save themselves by joining their city to the Temple of Artemis by a rope, thereby dedicating it to the goddess. The dedication was the basis of a settlement, and thereafter Croesus made conspicuous contributions to the building of the Temple of Artemis at Ephesus, increasing both his own fame and that of Artemis, and forming a close link between Ephesian Artemis and Sardis.[111]

From the reign of Croesus, Artemis of Ephesus assumed a significant and generally more conspicuous role than that of Kybebe as upholder of Sardian sovereignty. The relationship continued to grow even after the transfer of power in Lydia to the Persians. By the late sixth century, a monumental altar of Artemis was constructed at Sardis on a site later elaborated by the great Hellenistic temple.[112] From the late sixth through the fourth centuries, Lydian inscriptions record dedications to Artemis, *Artimuś* in Lydian, once with the epithet "of Sardis" and several times "of Ephesus," and sometimes paired with *Qldānś,* the Lydian Apollo, while Lydian and bilingual Lydian-Aramaic

108. Thucydides 3.104 compares the Delian festival to the Ephesian gathering of Ionians. Democritus of Ephesus *On the Temple of Ephesus* (quoted by Athenaeus 12.525c–e) describes the luxurious finery displayed by the Ephesians. Xenophon *Hellenica* 1.2.6 reports that Tissaphernes appealed to Ionian solidarity in war by invoking the name of Artemis of Ephesus; cf. Thucydides 8.109.1.

109. Nicolaus of Damascus *FGrHist* 90 F 65 (summarized in Pedley 1968, 56) reports Croesus' vow to dedicate an enemy's property to Artemis at Ephesus when he became king. See Georges 1994, 29–32, on the history of intermarriage between the Mermnads and the Basilids of Ephesus.

110. Herodotus 1.26; Aelian *Varia Historia* 3.26.

111. Herodotus 1.92.1. Schaber 1982 and Bammer 1984, 74–78 and 212–29, review the textual sources and physical remains of the Temple of Artemis at Ephesus in the time of Croesus. Hanfmann 1975, 10–13, and 1983b, 221–22 (= 1983a, 91), discusses the connection between Ephesian Artemis and Artemis at Sardis beginning in the time of Croesus; see also Hanfmann and Waldbaum 1969.

112. On the altar of Artemis at Sardis, see Hanfmann 1980, 105 and figures 21 and 22; W. E. Mierse, in Hanfmann 1983a, 51–52; Van Loon 1991, 35, figure 17, and plate 45a; Dusinberre 2003, 60–64.

funerary inscriptions invoke Ephesian Artemis, among other deities, as protector of graves.[113] A fourth-century Greek inscription from Ephesus attests the customary practice of sending a procession from the Artemisium at Ephesus to the shrine of Artemis at Sardis.[114] Greek literary sources meanwhile claimed that, for as long as Artemis had been honored at Ephesus, Lydians had maintained a close involvement in her cult.[115]

Artemis of Ephesus and Kybebe were like two poles to the axis of Lydian sovereignty. They were distinctive manifestations of a divine concept that, at its core, was a single unifying force justifying Lydian tyranny. Artemis, the beautiful maiden, was the goddess of the procession and the public spectacle in the Greek city; she was the ultimate embodiment of good things to come. Kybebe was the woman of the inner chamber, the tyrant's own lover, or mother; she represented the fulfillment of perfection in the person of the tyrant himself. They both had seats at Sardis, where their relationship may have been conceived as that of Mother (Kybebe) and Daughter (Artemis). Herodotus tells us that Aeschylus depicted Artemis as the daughter of Demeter in one of his plays, and makes the point that no Greek tradition supported this affiliation.[116]

Artemis and Kybebe, or the Mother at Sardis, are distinctively linked in Greek poetry and cult monuments. Philippe Borgeaud has drawn attention to the fact that *Homeric Hymns* 9 and 14, the former to Artemis and the latter to the Mother of the Gods, are the only ones that close with the dedication of song "to you and to all goddesses together."[117] The brief hymn to

113. Gusmani *LW* 63–65 discusses the numerous contexts, including theophoric names, in which *Artimuś* is named in Lydian inscriptions. On Artemis of Ephesus (*Artimuś Ibśimsis*), see *LW* 130–31; on Artemis of Sardis (*Artimuś Śfardan*) see *LW* 202–3. On Artemis and other deities named in Lydian funerary texts, see Dusinberre 115–16, and the discussion below in chapter 6 at notes 5–13. On Artemis' relation to funerary cult and the cult of Kybele at Ephesus, see Knibbe 1995, 142–44.

114. This document is sometimes referred to as the Sacrilege Inscription: see Hanfmann 1987; Dusinberre 2003, 120–22. For the text, see Wankel 1977; the inscription is translated by Dusinberre, 235–37, no. 54.

115. Aristophanes *Clouds* 598–99; cf. *Lysistrata* 1314; Callimachus *Hymns* 3.242–47; Aelian *De Natura Animalium* 12.9; Pausanias 7.2.8; Athenaeus 14.636a, quoting Diogenes Tragicus.

116. Herodotus 2.156.6 remarks upon this innovation by Aeschylus, which he believes Aeschylus "swiped" (ἥρπασε, an unusual use of this term: see How and Wells 1912, vol. 1, 245) from the Egyptian identification of Horus and Bubastis (Apollo and Artemis) as children of Isis and Osiris (Demeter and Dionysus). Herodotus' insistence on an Egyptian inspiration does not rule out the possibility that Aeschylus could have found the idea in Lydia, where Dionysus-Bacchus was also prominent. Note the number of Asiatic plays attested among Aeschylus' works (*Phrygians, Phrygian Women, Mysians, Carians*, e.g.). Note also that Hipponax fr. 127 (West) associates Kybebe with a daughter of Zeus, identified either as Thracian Bendis or Artemis.

117. Borgeaud 1996, 28. To Borgeaud's observation we may add the multiple names—Artemis is first of them—by which Aphrodite is addressed in *Homeric Hymn* 5, *To Aphrodite* 92–105; see chapter 3, notes 47–49.

Figure 11. Relief from Sardis depicting Artemis, holding a
deer on left, and Kybele, holding a lion on right, approached
by worshippers, with tympanum above, circa 400 B.C.E. (©
Archaeological Exploration of Sardis, Harvard University,
photo no. 68.94:33).

Artemis, as Borgeaud notes, invokes her specifically in an Ionian setting, while
the hymn to the Mother associates her with her many mountain haunts in
greater Phrygia. The open-ended nature of the closing invocation of these
two hymns is most appropriate to the image of transcendence encouraged
by the imperial cults of Lydia under Croesus, in light of which, most likely,
these hymns were composed.

Artemis of Ephesus and the Mother at Sardis are more directly linked in Timotheus' *Persians,* composed close to the end of the fifth century. In that ode on the defeat of Xerxes, Timotheus depicts the prayers of a shipwrecked Mysian sailor who appeals to the Mountain Mother (μάτηρ οὐρεία) and divine Mother (θεὰ μάτηρ) to rescue him from the ill-fated expedition that set out from Lydian Sardis; Timotheus then characterizes a Phrygian who prays to Artemis of Ephesus (Ἄρτιμις ἐμὸς μέγας θεὸς παρ' Ἔφεσον) to allow a safe return to Sardis, Susa, and Ecbatana.[118] From approximately the same time as Timotheus' poem, a votive relief from Sardis depicts both Artemis and the Mother standing side by side, Artemis holding a deer and the Mother a lion (figure 11).[119] Under Persian rule, especially from the time of Artaxerxes II, the fame of Artemis at Sardis seems to have benefited from her identification with Persian Anahita.[120] Centuries later, when the bipolarity of a Sardian tyrant or satrap and an Ionian populace no longer defined the axis of power in this part of the world, Artemis and the Mother of the Gods became indistinguishable from one another.[121]

## THE LEGACY OF LYDIA

Lydia played a pivotal role in the relationship between Greeks and the older civilizations of Asia. From the perspective of later Greek historiography, Lydia appears as the first chapter of the struggle by Greeks to free themselves from the domineering power of Eastern empires, a story that was prelude to the struggle against Persia. But from another perspective the height of Lydian power can be seen as the final chapter of an older tradition of Greek participation in the customs of Asiatic civilization. This tradition was already

118. Timotheus *Persians* 97–173 (Edmonds *LG*). The prayer of the Phrygian for a safe return to Sardis, Susa, and Ecbatana almost certainly indicates that he is understood to be an attendant of the royal court, and probably a eunuch; for discussion of the relevant passages, see Llewellyn-Jones 2002, 34; Witt 2002, 241–42.

119. Hanfmann and Waldbaum 1969, 265–66; Hanfmann and Ramage 1978, 58–60, no. 20, figures 78–83; Hanfmann 1983b, 221 and figure 1; Naumann 1983, plate 31.3; Vermaseren 1987, no. 460; Roller 1999, 196 and figure 52; Dusinberre 2003, 106–7, 218–19, and figure 46.

120. Tacitus *Annals* 3.62 reports that "Persian Diana" (Artemis Anaïtis) had been honored in Lydia since the time of Cyrus (whether Cyrus the Great, in the sixth century, or Cyrus the Younger, brother of Artaxerxes II, is uncertain; P. Briant 2002, 703, argues for Cyrus the Great). Persian Anahita and the fusion of Persian and Lydian cult under the name of Artemis Anaïtis are discussed in chapter 6 at note 24.

121. A Lydian relief of the Roman imperial period names Artemis and depicts her enthroned and flanked by lions, in the manner of Kybele or the Mother, with Demeter and Nike standing on either side (Vermaseren 1977, plate 16; Vermaseren 1987, no. 485; Horsley 1992, 136–40). In Cilicia, the cult of Kubaba at Hierapolis-Castabala, attested in an Aramaic text of the fifth or fourth century B.C.E., is identified with Artemis by Strabo 12.2.7: see Dupont-Sommer and Robert 1964, 12–13, 50.

strong in the heyday of Midas and the Phrygian empire, at the end of the eighth century, and may well have had its roots centuries earlier. Here we will consider some of the elements of Asiatic custom, nurtured under Lydian influence, that were variously preserved in Greek literature and in Greek religious and social practices, or recalled by later Greek sources as anomalies of their earliest cultural memories.

At Lydian Sardis, sovereignty was identified with divinity through a ritualized relationship of the tyrant to the goddess of love. Famous among Greeks for its pleasure gardens and extravagant displays of wealth and feminine beauty, the Lydian court at Sardis was a living tableau of the ancient customs of the royal Sacred Marriage. The evidence is too sparse to say exactly how and when such rituals may have been enacted, but we may deduce that the roles of goddess and her mortal lover were played by the tyrant or his son and a favored consort or bride. Signifying the relationship between ruler and divinity as a royal marriage, such occasions assured the well-being of all peoples under the sway of tyranny.

In the absence of a surviving body of Lydian literature we must look to the eastern neighbors of Lydia and to the cuneiform literature of Mesopotamia for a fuller picture of the ideology of such rituals. Across three millennia, from Sumerian to Seleucid times, an evolving tradition of ritual and poetry glorified the sacred and fructifying marriage of an all-powerful king, or the god he served and stood for, and a goddess who was the Queen of Heaven. Along with glorification, tales of lamentation in this tradition repeatedly affirmed that the union of mortal and deity was destined to end in grief. The death of a king put well-being itself in peril, and performances of ritualized grieving were essential to restoring and sustaining the bond between humanity and divinity represented by kingship. In the early first millennium B.C.E., the cycles of ecstatic joy and all-encompassing grief expressed in this Mesopotamian tradition are also found in myth, poetry, and ritual across the Levant and Anatolia, where they had become what may be regarded as the common mythology of sovereignty.

Lydia's place in this tradition is clearly reflected in contemporary Greek poetry composed within the sphere of Lydia. The poetry of Alcman, Sappho, and Alcaeus bears witness to the notion that Sardis was a place of supremely beautiful young women.[122] Underlying this community of beauty was the notion that every Sardian girl was a potential bride, or *pallakē*, of the king.[123]

122. Alcman *Partheneion* 1.64–72 evokes a Lydian setting in the midst of an extended praise of feminine beauty. So too do Sappho frs. 20, 38 *To Anactoria,* 45 *To Gongyla,* 86 *To Atthis,* 130 *To Cleïs;* likewise Alcaeus fr. 37b. See chapter 3, with notes 67–69. (Passages cited according to Edmonds *LG,*)

123. The supposition is explicit in Alcaeus fr. 37b (Edmonds *LG,* appendix; = A5 LP), see chapter 3 with note 69.

Participation in this community of beauty evidently involved ceremonies of public display. Alcman's *Partheneia* (Maidens' Songs) suggest that this may have taken place at Sardis as it did at Sparta, in the form of choral lyric performances in which the praises of beautiful girls were sung for the approval of all.[124] Standing close to the beginnings of this tradition, Archilochus expressed a combination of admiration and disdain for the wealth, power, and godlike doings of Lydian tyrants. He spoke for many Greeks who stood partly within this Asiatic culture of excellence, but who were aware that it overreached the bounds of humanity in its quest for perfection, in ways that the Greeks learned to abhor.

The musical modes of early Greek poetry reveal still more clearly the dependency of distinctive aspects of early Greek culture on the customs of Asia. Classical and later sources affirm that the foundations of Greek music were Lydian and Phrygian: the music of processions, of dancing, and of marching; the music of storytelling, of singing praise, and of celebration; and especially the music of lamentation.[125] In chapter 2 we noticed the traditions that connected specifically the music of the *aulos,* and forms of funeral dirges, with the cult of the mother of Midas. In this and the preceding chapter we have observed that from the Greek perspective, and perhaps from the perspective of the Lydians themselves, Phrygian cultural heritage was so generally overlaid and absorbed by Lydian that to name the one was to call to mind the other.[126] So too in music. Thus we find the Sicilian poet Telestes, contemporary of the tyrant Dionysius I of Syracuse and of the Spartan ascendancy over Greece at the beginning of the fourth century, juxtaposing Phrygian music with the ritual strains of the Lydian court in his account of the ancestry of Peloponnesian music: "The companions of Pelops were the first to sing, at the wine bowls of the Greeks and to the accompaniment of *auloi,* the Phrygian tune of the Mountain Mother. They struck up the Lydian hymn with the sharp twangs of the lyre."[127] Here the foundation of rulership in the Peloponnese is associated with the legacy of Lydia and the influence of the Mother of the Gods, and these associations were preserved in music and poetry.

124. Alcman's *Partheneia* are commonly envisioned in their performance at Sparta (so, e.g., Calame 1997), but almost never thought of in a Lydian, or Sardian context. The testimonia indicating that Alcman was as much a Sardian as a Spartan and the references to Lydia in his poetry (*Palatine Anthology* 7.18 and 709, cited in Edmonds *LG* vol. 1, 44–46) demonstrate that the culture of Sardis and Lydia accounts for at least half of the context of his poetry.

125. Hannelore Thiemer 1979 has examined the traditions of Asiatic, and specifically Phrygian, origins for Greek music; see also Borthwick 1988, 1505–10; M. L. West 1992, 329–36; 1997, 31–32; and see E. Hall 1989, 129–32, for the consistency of this tradition in Attic tragedy.

126. In art as well, it is often difficult to distinguish Lydian from Phrygian: see Muscarella 1971.

127. Telestes fr. 5 (Edmonds *LG,* from Athenaeus 14.625e).

The epic poetry of Hesiod and Homer stands at the beginnings not just of the Greek poetic tradition, but also of Mermnad tyranny in Lydia, drawing inspiration from many of the same sources as did tyranny.[128] In Greek epic we see the theological underpinnings of tyranny accepted, but reworked to show that competitive excellence can overpower even divinely endowed rulership. Hesiod articulates an elaborate pantheon, with stories of the generations of gods and their struggles for supremacy, of a type that was familiar to the traditions of northern Syria, of the Hittites, and of Mesopotamia, as is widely recognized.[129] But unlike, for example, the story of Marduk's rise to cosmic supremacy told in the Babylonian *Enuma Elish*, Hesiod's *Theogony* describes a pantheon with no preeminent worldly seat, no great temple, and no living king at its center and focus. The attributes of sovereignty that elsewhere came to a ruler from his unique relationship to a god, or a divine Mother, or a divine lover are distributed among many divinities, and through them to many deserving mortals. The acknowledged sovereignty of Zeus was not the proprietary interest of any one man.

Homer, or the poet of the *Iliad*, achieved a similar effect. The *Iliad* is far more ambitious and even more remarkable than Hesiod's achievement in its reckoning of the nature of humanity in relation to transcendent divinity. For the *Iliad* treats, with irresistible verisimilitude, the experience of great kings, Agamemnon and Priam, and their heroic followers, who are all alike bound by the limitations of their mortal condition. In depicting the convulsive war between the Achaean followers of Agamemnon and the forces assembled by Priam, Homeric epic remorselessly dissected the ironies implicit in the relationships between gods and the mortals who were closest to them. Even the children of gods must die, the *Iliad* shows, and no kingship was so sacred as to be proof against destruction. Not even Aphrodite herself, nor her greatest flatterer, Paris, could save the kingdom of Priam from the fatal consequences of its embrace of a love supreme. In the *Odyssey*, Odysseus achieved undying fame precisely by embracing mortality, by rejecting everlasting divine love in a garden paradise, and by honoring his steadfast wife. In all of these ways, Greek epic was criticizing the paradigm on which

128. On the date of the composition of the Hesiodic and Homeric epics, I favor the view of M. L. West 1966, 46: "The *Theogony* may well be the oldest Greek poem we have. The *Iliad* and *Odyssey* are both later, at least in their present form; for they both admit elements that archaeology shows to be not older than *c.* 700, and not only admit them, but attribute them to the Heroic Age." See also Burkert 1987, 44: "I, for one, imagine the first written *Iliad* as a set of leather scrolls in the first half of the seventh century, emerging from an oral tradition that had been flourishing mainly in the eighth." Burkert 1976 develops the argument in favor of this chronology; Taplin 1992, 33–35, agrees with Burkert and West.

129. For discussions of the relationship between the Hesiodic *Theogony* and the theogonic myths of northern Syria and Phoenicia, the Hittites, and Mesopotamia, see Walcot 1966; M. L. West 1966, 18–31; 1997, 276–303; Mondi 1990; Penglase 1994, 239–45.

Lydian sovereignty was founded without actually denying its major premise, namely that the gods engender greatness among men.

Other distinctively Greek customs can be seen to emerge out of a process of separation from the customs of Lydia. An example is the adoption by Greeks of coinage, acknowledged to be a Lydian invention, accompanied by the rejection of the sexual transactions that were tied to its use. Because their paradigm for sovereignty and order in the world was so intimately bound to venerating the forces of sexuality (the literal meaning of "veneration"), honoring the bloom of sexual attraction became a universal custom among the Lydians, as Herodotus reports. The signifier of this act of veneration was a precious gift given to mark the occasion. The gift of a coin, the token of "golden" Aphrodite, from a man to an unmarried Lydian girl was the basis of the customary prostitution of Lydian girls. For the essence of prostitution (*porneia*) was the taking of payment (*porneia* being cognate with περνάναι, "to sell").[130] The partners to such a transaction mutually surrendered to the will of Aphrodite, and the symbolic effect of their intercourse was to involve the attention of Aphrodite herself, the upholder of sovereign tyranny. In this respect, the act of *porneia* at Sardis was an act of devotion to tyranny.

The emerging distinction between Lydian and Greek custom comes into focus when Herodotus' testimony on Lydia is compared to the legislation on prostitution attributed to Solon. We are told that Athenian law regarded the surrender to an act of *porneia* (on the part of the one purchased) as tantamount to surrendering the interests of the community of the city (τὰ κοινὰ τῆς πόλεως).[131] Therefore any woman who had been sold in this manner was barred from participating in legal marriage and engendering legitimate children.[132] Likewise, and no doubt as an outgrowth of the original injunction against heterosexual prostitution, Athenian orators claimed that the law barred any man who sold himself in this manner from exercising the rights

130. See Chantraine 1968–80, vol. 3, 880 s.v. πέρνημι; Dover 1978, 20.

131. Aeschines 1, *Against Timarchus* 29.

132. Plutarch *Solon* 23.2 speaks of Solon's law forbidding a man from "selling his daughters or his sisters, unless he discovers that she, as a *parthenos*, has had intercourse with a man" (ἔτι δ' οὔτε θυγατέρας πωλεῖν οὔτ' ἀδελφὰς δίδωσι, πλὴν ἂν μὴ λάβῃ παρθένον ἀνδρὶ συγγεγενημένην). This is widely taken to mean that Solon permitted the sale of daughters or sisters into slavery if their virginity was compromised. (See, e.g., MacDowell 1978, 80 and 125.) The context, however, reveals that πωλεῖν means "offer for prostitution," for the same verb has just been used of *hetairai* offering themselves "for sale" (ὅσαι πεφασμένως πωλοῦνται, λέγων δὴ τὰς ἑταίρας), "for these are women who openly consort with those who give" (αὗται γὰρ ἐμφανῶς φοιτῶσι πρὸς τοὺς διδόντας [sc. payment for services]). The law essentially states that if a man prostitutes his daughters or sisters (i.e., engages in the custom that Herodotus says is common among the Lydians), he forfeits the right to offer them for marriage, hence for the procreation of legitimate children. Cf. Aeschines 1, *Against Timarchus* 14, for the injunction against anyone who procures for a freeborn child or a freeborn woman (τὰ μέγιστα ἐπιτίμια ἐπιγράψας, ἐάν τις ἐλεύθερον παῖδα ἢ γυναῖκα προαγωγεύῃ).

of citizenship.[133] Those who were habituated to receiving payment to surrender to Aphrodite, by this logic, were habituated to devoting their whole beings to the service of tyranny.

Not every law attributed to Solon by the Attic orators or by Plutarch should be accepted as a genuine archaic ordinance. But in this case the attribution is believable. As a contemporary of Alyattes, Solon was surely familiar with the symbolic behavior appropriate to tyranny. For this reason, between members of a community of free citizens he forbade transactions that paid homage to tyranny. According to Solon, prostitution was a suitable trade only for noncitizens. We are also told that Solon founded a temple of Aphrodite Pandemos (Of All the People) from the proceeds of a tax on brothels.[134] This sounds like an odd form of public service by the father of Athenian democracy, and not quite believable, until one recognizes that Aphrodite Pandemos is the exact inverse of Kybebe, the Aphrodite of tyranny.[135] Solon could not deny the power of the goddess of love, but he could direct her favor to the citizenry of Athens as a whole, so as not to encourage any one man from fancying himself as her special darling. With the same political implications in mind, Solon forbade lavish funerary sacrifices, and the excessive lamentations of women at the funerals of the wealthy and powerful.[136] These practices, too, upheld the ideology of tyranny, as Herodotus attests and the foregoing discussion illustrates.

The most notorious tyrannical custom, as discussed above, was that of de-

133. Demosthenes 22, *Against Androtion* 30–31; Aeschines 1, *Against Timarchus* 29 (cf. 13 and 137). As J. J. Winkler 1990, 60, observes: "The crucial point seems to be not sexual behavior in itself but rather some notion of preserving the political order by restrictions placed on its directors at the top." The notion in this case was to restrict the symbolic expressions of tyranny.

134. Athenaeus 13.569d, citing the third book of the *Colophoniaca* by Nicander of Colophon. (Cf. Harpocration s.v. Πάνδημος Ἀφροδίτη.) The occurrence of this reference in a book on the history and customs of Colophon suggests that, as here, Nicander contrasted Solon's legislation with the Asiatic customs practiced by the subjects of Lydia. Oliver 1960, 116–17, finds the law on prostitution improbable, but has useful suggestions about the meaning of Aphrodite Pandemos in Solon's day.

135. Solon's regulation of brothels is declared to be an anachronism by Rosivach 1995; R. Parker 1996, 49 n. 26; Dillon 1999, 69; and Frost 2002. But Graham 1998, discussing a Thasian text of the early fifth century regulating brothels, is more circumspect: "We may be hesitant to believe that Solon established prostitutes at Athens, but the state's interest in prostitution is clear." Scholtz 2003 reviews the evidence for the cult of Aphrodite Pandemos at Naucratis, as early as the seventh century. On the archaic cult of Aphrodite Pandemos at Athens, see Simon 1970 and 1983, 48–51; Shapiro 1989, 118–22; R. Parker 1996, 48–49; Stafford 2000, 121–29.

136. Plutarch *Solon* 21.4–5; Demosthenes 43, *Against Macartatus* 62. Cf. Plutarch *Solon* 12.5 on the attenuation of "harsh, barbaric behavior" among women at funerals. Contrast the noisy behavior of women described by Herodotus (6.58.1) on the occasion of Spartan royal funerals, "just as the barbarians do in Asia." This aspect of Solon's legislation is accepted as historical by R. Parker 1996, 49–50 and 133–34, where additional scholarship is cited.

voting boys and girls to the service of tyranny for life, as eunuchs and concubines. Herodotus attests the former practice, the appropriation of boys sent to Sardis for castration, as a vindictive measure taken by Periander against his enemies in Corcyra. Sappho may allude to the latter practice in her expressions of aching desire for the company of girls gone from Lesbos to Sardis. The appropriation of youths and maidens recalls the hated tribute that King Minos is said to have exacted from the Athenians until they were released from this oppression by Theseus. Does this celebrated story represent some past Athenian experience of this odious feature of tyranny? It seems reasonable to assume so, even if we cannot say exactly how or when this may have happened. The Thesean legend contains too much specific ritualized detail connected with the rites of tyranny for the story to be pure fantasy.

Rituals that commemorated the end of this hated tribute of youths and maidens are described in Plutarch's *Life of Theseus* and by other sources relying on the mythographers and Atthidographers of the fifth and fourth centuries B.C.E. The most distinctive of these rituals was that of the annual Oschophoria, when two feminized boys were selected to carry the *oschoi*, grape-bearing vine branches, in a procession marking the return of Theseus, according to some at the time of the vintage.[137] These boys, in Plutarch's words, were "changed in outward appearance almost entirely by giving them warm baths and keeping them out of the sun, by arranging their hair, and by smoothing their skin and beautifying their complexions with unguents . . . [and they were] taught to imitate maidens as closely as possible in their speech, their dress, and their gait."[138] The perfect disguise of these youths as maidens is explained as a ruse of Theseus on his mission to Crete, designed to hide the force at his service. But this explanation is almost certainly a reinterpretation of the boys who appear as girls, and the branches that they carry indicate the original nature of this ritual.

The *oschoi* (variously spelled in our sources: in the singular, ὠσχός, ὄσχος, ὤσχη, ὄσχη) are treated by our sources as unfamiliar items that must be explained as grape-bearing vine branches. No doubt, grape clusters were carried in the Oschophoria as it was celebrated in classical times; but the term betrays its origin as another sort of fruit. *Osche* (ὄσχη or ὀσχέα) is the regular word for "scrotum," and *oschis* (ὄσχις) is a synonym for *orchis* (ὄρχις), the reg-

---

137. Plutarch *Theseus* 23.2–3 (citing Demon *FGrHist* 327 F 6). At *Theseus* 22.4–5, Plutarch appears to synchronize this observance with the Pyanepsia, a festival of Apollo; but see Robertson 1992, 123 and n. 8; and R. Parker 1996, 315–16. See also Athenaeus 11.495f (citing Philochorus *FGrHist* 328 F 183 and Aristodemus' commentary *On Pindar*), who describes the Oschophoria as a race of ephebes from a shrine of Dionysus to the shrine of Athena Skiras in Phalerum. Further sources are cited and discussed by Deubner 1932, 142–47; Parke 1977, 77–81; Simon 1983, 89–92; Robertson 1992, 120–33.

138. Plutarch *Theseus* 23.2, translated by B. Perrin.

ular word for "testicle," which in turn is occasionally used to identify a similarly shaped fruit, such as an olive.[139] This term, together with the complete feminization of the boys who carry the *oschoi*, plainly reveals the original relation of this ritual to the practice of castrating boys and devoting them to servitude at a powerful seat of tyranny, all for the well-being of the community.

Plutarch's account of the Oschophoria at Athens has specific points of comparison with elements of a festival of Artemis on Samos that Herodotus says were maintained in commemoration of the rescue by the Samians of the three hundred Corcyraean boys who had been sent by Periander to the court of Alyattes to be castrated.[140] At both Samos and Athens, then, we find a memory of rites originally devoted to the propitiation of tyranny through the castration of boys, and we may suspect that similar rites were practiced at other Ionian cities. Artemis at Ephesus was accustomed to receive the service of eunuchs, as we have noted, and Ephesus, along with Sardis, was the regular outlet for Panionius' profitable trade in castrated boys still in the fifth century. At Athens, this custom was transformed at some point into a less drastic ritual of cross-dressing boys who carried symbols of fertility that were not excised from their own bodies. Through this process of ritual transformation, the Athenians were striving to deliver themselves from the odious obligations of tyranny. But the perceived importance of these rites for the well-being of the community was too great to abandon them outright.

When sovereign tyrants somewhere across the sea (in Crete? in Asia Minor? in Cyprus?) were no longer served by a tribute of Athenian youths and maidens, the rites of tyranny were still observed at Athens. For the celebrations of the deeds of Theseus, as Plutarch describes them, were observances of sovereignty and the Sacred Marriage patterned on the rites of tyranny. Plutarch explains the Oschophoria at Athens as an act of propitiation of Dionysus and Ariadne.[141] He also describes Theseus in the role of Dionysus as the consort of Ariadne, and draws attention to customs that equated Ariadne with Aphrodite.[142] Theseus, throughout this account, is the son of the king (Aegeus) who is about to become king himself. Across a maritime realm,

---

139. See LSJ s.vv. ὀρχάς (B), ὄρχις, ὄσχη, ὄσχις, ὄσχος, ὤσχη, ὠσχός. Under this last lexical item, LSJ notes the irregular orthography of this and the related ὠσχοφόρια, κτλ. Note the discussion of ὀσχέα in the procedures for castrating livestock, in Aristotle *Historia Animalium* 632a.

140. Compare Plutarch *Theseus* 23.3 and Herodotus 3.48. Sourvinou-Inwood 1988, 169–71, cites these parallels in support of her argument that Herodotus' account of events in the time of Periander is "'myth' in which any historical 'raw material' that might have gone into its making has been drastically manipulated and reshaped" (167). The present discussion does not contradict her argument, but, as with the tale of Atys (above, with notes 36–40), it does demonstrate a more complex interweaving of myth and history than has generally been recognized.

141. Plutarch *Theseus* 23.3.

142. Plutarch *Theseus* 20, esp. 20.3–4, where the foundation of the cult of Ariadne Aphrodite at Amathus on Cyprus is described.

from Crete to Athens and Naxos to Cyprus, and especially focusing on Delos, Theseus performed the acts of a Sacred Marriage in which he assumed
the role of a god (Dionysus) with a consort (Ariadne) who is identified with
Aphrodite. In the name of their own champion and king, Theseus, the Athenians thus maintained the observance of all of the significant associations
between sovereignty and divinity that we have found to be associated with
the tyrants of Lydia. The same is true of the Sacred Marriage of Dionysus
and Basilinna (Queen), the wife of the archon basileus, performed annually
in the Anthesteria festival at Athens. In all of these instances, we find Athenian myth and custom patterned after the rituals of power and sovereignty
that were celebrated in Lydia.

Athenian tradition is but one window into this legacy. Greek identity as a
whole, like the poetry of Hesiod and Homer, was born out of the tyranny of
Asia. In classical sources, we find the central symbols of Lydian sovereignty,
especially the Sacred Marriage of king or prince and goddess, attached to
heroes of legend, like Theseus, and confined to ritual reenactments, like the
Anthesteria, that rendered them safe and useful for a democratic community. When such rites were associated with tyrants, Greek authors describe
them in derogatory terms, either as the unrestrained sexual indulgences that
transpired in the bowered gardens euphemistically named Place of Purity,
or in the secretive and incestuous Mysteries of Aphrodite. The tyrant, when
depicted as a hateful stereotype, was always a man involved in perverse sexual relationships. So Periander the tyrant of Corinth was remembered as a
necrophiliac. So Oedipus the tyrant of Thebes was the man who murdered
his father and married his mother. It was the purpose of Herodotus and the
special genius of Sophocles to depict the twisted consequences of the ideological system that these Greek tyrants represented. Their stories, Greek stories, demonstrate how closely intertwined the heritage of Hellenism was with
the ideals and practices of Asiatic tyranny.

# Chapter 5

# Asia, the *Oikoumenē,*
# and the Map of the World

The Mermnad empire created under Gyges was a powerful peer to the empires of Assyria, of the Medes, of Babylon, and of Saïte Egypt. The Greeks, in this world of empires, were subordinate to the Lydians. By the time of Alyattes and Croesus, Greek communities were either among the many subject peoples of Asia under Lydian rule, or among Lydia's partners and allies across the Aegean. Among Greeks across the Aegean, unity with Lydia was represented by those who, like the Spartans, upheld kingship and a wide range of customs in common with the Lydians, and those who embraced Lydian-style tyranny, like the Cypselids of Corinth. From the Mermnad viewpoint, represented in the attested ambitions of Croesus, Lydian sovereignty had the potential to embrace the whole of the inhabited earth. In the previous chapter we encountered the idea that Sardis, the center of this conceptual empire, was a place where sovereignty was born and reborn with every generation. It was also the place where primal creation was believed to have taken place, as we will see in this chapter. The Mother of the Gods, who endowed both kingship and life on earth, was the metaphysical concept at the center of this ideology.

Out of this nursery of Lydian imperial ideology emerged Ionian cosmology. For among the Greek-speaking subjects of the Lydian empire, men like Thales and Anaximander began to describe the metaphysics of Lydian sovereignty in terms of the form and substance of the earth and the cosmos in which it was situated. In this chapter we will examine in particular the concept of the form of the earth and the earliest maps of its surface; we will consider the principles according to which human settlement on the face of the earth was understood; and we will observe the manner in which these conceptual schemes related to the metaphysics of Lydian sovereignty.

Born under the tyranny of Lydia, Ionian cosmology matured in succeeding generations under different political regimes. The transformation of political context had a subtle but significant influence on the trajectory of this intellectual development. In chapter 1 the fall of Lydian tyranny was described as the passing of an age of innocence, inasmuch as it forced the Greeks to reassess aspects of their notions about the relationship between humanity and divinity. So the goddess of sovereignty under the Mermnad tyrants remained important even after the collapse of the Mermnad empire, but her guise was transformed. So too, changes in the metaphysics of empire influenced speculation about the shape of the world, its relationship to centers of sovereign power, and to the nature of sovereignty itself.

Perhaps the most distinctive feature of early Ionian maps was the division of the face of the earth into two continents, Europe and Asia. The differentiation of these two continents was an innovation whose objective basis lay in the relationship between the Greeks and the Lydian empire, and in the transformation of the latter into the Persian empire. Underlying this differentiation was a question very much in contention at this time: Could there be such a thing as a unified sovereignty over a differentiated world? Closely related to this was the question: Did a universal divinity justify universal sovereignty? The remaining chapters of this book examine aspects of these contentious questions over the first century and a half of the history of the Persian empire and its dealings with the Greeks. This chapter begins the investigation by considering the origin and early development of the idea of Asia in Greek thought.

### THE IDEA OF ASIA

Asia is not attested as name of a continent until it appears in this sense in Greek sources beginning in the latter part of the sixth century. Its first certain use in this sense was in the world map drawn by Hecataeus of Miletus, where the world was divided into two continents, Europe (also so designated for the first time) and Asia (which included Africa, or "Libya").[1] The names Asia and Europe are older than this, to be sure, but they were not applied

---

1. *Asia* and *Europe* were the titles of the two books that comprised Hecataeus' geographical treatise; see Jacoby 1912, cols. 2672–73; Pearson 1939, 31–34. The commonplace division of the earth into two continents is attested by Herodotus 4.36.2 (quoted below, at note 33). Elsewhere, Herodotus 2.16 states that "the Ionians . . . say that all the earth consists of three parts: Europe, Asia, and Libya." On this basis, Jacoby (cols. 2703–4) assumes that Hecataeus' map distinguished three continents. ( Jacoby is followed on this point by, e.g., Gehrke 1998, 180; see also Naddaf 2003, in note 34, below.) This assumption clashes with the testimony to the division of Hecataeus' geographical writings into two books, *Asia* and *Europe*. Jacoby therefore assumes that this division of books was not Hecataeus' own and had no relationship to his division of continents. (Gehrke [178], however, accepts that the books *Asia* and *Europe* were Hecataeus' own divisions.) I find the balance of the evidence that Jacoby himself cites (e.g., the geography implied by Aeschylus' *Persians* and by the Hippocratic *Airs, Waters, Places* 12–24) inclines against his argument, and I agree with Pearson (31): "Hecataeus belonged to the school

to continents drawn on maps until the sixth century.[2] Scholarship generally treats the origin of the application of these names to two continents as obscure.[3] This is inevitably the case when our understanding of maps and mapmaking is reduced to the depiction of landforms based on empirical observations. Before the accumulation of any sizable body of systematic empirical observations, ideology must have played a large part in how the earth was depicted. Recognizing the role of contemporary ideology, and recognizing that the map of Hecataeus divided the world into two equal continents, are sufficient to orient us toward the origin of the idea of Asia.[4]

The very concept of a continent called Asia distinguished from a continent called Europe could emerge only among peoples aware of some physical division between lands, and more importantly, impressed by the apparent fact that this division corresponded to a significant principle of order in the world.[5] The only self-evident physical division between the continents of Asia and Europe is that formed by the waters of the Bosporus, Propontis (Sea of Marmara), Hellespont (Dardanelles), and the Aegean Sea. Every other notion of the extent and confines of Asia and of Europe proceeds by extension from this primary zone of demarcation.[6] For over a century prior

---

of thought which believed in two, not three continents." Herodotus' reference to the views of the Ionians therefore describes a contemporary debate, later than the time of Hecataeus.

2. Europa (Εὐρώπη) and Asia (Ἀσίη) are named by Hesiod *Theogony* 357 and 359 in the list of the daughters of Tethys and Oceanus, identified as rivers of the earth. (See the commentary of M. L. West 1966, 266–67.) Europa is more famous as the daughter of Phoenix ("The Phoenician") taken by Zeus from Phoenicia across the sea westward to Crete (*Iliad* 14.321–22; Herodotus 4.45.4). Her name comes from the Semitic root *'rb*, "to enter," the root of several West Semitic words referring to sunset (Hebrew *'ereb*, "sunset"; Akkadian *māt erēb šamši*, "land of the setting sun," meaning "western land"; cf. Greek Ἔρεβος, Erebus, land of darkness and way down into the underworld in the West: *Odyssey* 10.528; cf. 11.37). Astour 1965, 129–30, discusses the phonology; M. L. West 1997, 451, offers criticisms that do not seem substantial enough to dismiss this etymology. "Europe" is used to designate a continental shore for the first time in *Homeric Hymn* 3, *To Apollo* 251 and 291, approximately contemporary to Hecataeus (second half of the sixth century).

3. So, e.g., Thomson 1948, 21 and n. 3; cf. M. L. West 1966, 266–67. Jacoby 1912, cols. 2718–26, avoids the question of origins by reconstructing his understanding of the confines of Asia on the basis of Herodotus and Scylax, and attributing the reconstruction to Hecataeus' geography (a procedure that, he admits, is "fraglich," 2725).

4. No ancient rendering of Hecataeus' map survives, but enough is known about it to encourage efforts at reconstruction. Bunbury 1883, 149 figure II, has set the standard; cf. Thomson 1948, 99 figure 11.

5. Cf. the perceptive observation of Edward Said 1978, 11, that awareness of a distinction between Europe and Asia among Europeans and Americans (the "orientalism" of his study) "meant and means being aware . . . that one belongs to a part of the earth with a definite history of involvement in the Orient almost since the time of Homer." (See Said's further comments [56–57] on the classical foundations of modern orientalism.)

6. Note, for example, that Herodotus 4.45.2 has already recognized how arbitrary the designation of separate continents was, and that the division between Europe and Asia on the far-

to the appearance of the first maps distinguishing Asia and Europe, the most important principle of order in this part of the world was the Lydian empire. "Asia," as we will see, originally referred to the Lydian homeland. Accordingly, the idea of opposing land masses called Asia and Europe was born among peoples living around the Aegean Sea and the Propontis whose outlook on the world was shaped by their awareness of Lydian sovereignty. Asia as a continent was almost certainly a Greek idea conceived in a Lydian context. The idea of Asia reached this form in the lifetime of Hecataeus and under the influence of the Persian empire during the reign of Darius I.[7]

Before the name Asia came to be applied to a wider continent, it belonged to western Anatolia, and in particular to Lydia and adjacent regions. The application of the name Asia in this more limited sense is most clearly represented in the geographical entity that the Romans later identified as their province of Asia.[8] As to origins, the name Asia is probably related to Bronze Age *Assuwa,* the designation for a coalition of western Anatolian states opposing Hittite interests in the fifteenth century[9] The name has also been plausibly identified in Linear B texts from Mycenae, Pylos, and Cnossus as an ethnic in personal names, and in the name of a deity, *Potnia Aswiya.*[10] The probable locale for this Bronze Age toponym corresponds with the attested used of "Asia" in archaic Greek sources, and in the traditions of Lydia recorded by Herodotus.

According to Herodotus, the Lydians claimed that Asia was named after Asies (Ἀσίης, a masculine form), the eponymous founder of a Sardian tribe.[11]

---

ther side of the Black Sea was set by some at the river Phasis in Colchis (modern Georgia), at the east end of the Black Sea, and by others at the river Tanaïs (Don), beyond the Cimmerian Bosporus and the Maeotic lake (Sea of Azov).

7. The concept of continental Asia, implying also the opposing continent of Europe, corresponds closely to the concept of *barbaroi,* "barbarians," as distinguished from *Hellēnes,* "Greeks." See M. L. West 1966, 266; E. Hall 1989, esp. 75–76.

8. See Talbert 2000, maps 100 and 101, for the Roman province of Asia in the early second century C.E., and the diocese of Asiana in the early fourth century C.E.; Jones 1940, 54, summarizes the extent of the province of Asia created in 133 B.C.E. On the cultic community defined by the self-proclaimed cities of Asia, especially as indicated by their long-lived cistophoric coinage, see below at note 96.

9. This identification was made by Forrer 1932, and defended by Garstang and Gurney 1959, 105–7. Bryce 1998, 136, reports it as a widely held opinion. Starke 1997b, 456, connects *Assuwa* with the name and region of Assos, in the southern Troad (see note 14 below), and is not convinced that it is related to the name Asia. Heubeck 1961, 71–73, derives *Assuwa* from the Hittite *aššuš* (genitive *aššuwaš, aššawaš,* meaning "agreeable, pleasant." (Cf. ἱμερτὴν Ἀσίην, "lovely Asia" of Mimnermus [below, note 16]; cf. also the Hippocratic *Airs, Waters, Places* 12; Herodotus 1.142.1.)

10. Heubeck 1961, 71, discusses the relationship to Hittite *Assuwa* of the personal name Aswios (*a-si-wi-jo*), an ethnic applied to women, Aswia (*a-swi-ja*), and the divinity *Potnia Aswia* (*po-ti-ni-ja a-si-wi-ja*) in Linear B texts. S. P. Morris 2001b suggests that *Potnia Aswiya* may be the forerunner of Ephesian Artemis.

11. Herodotus 4.45.3; cf. Stephanus of Byzantium s.v. Ἀσία· πόλις Λυδίας παρὰ τῷ Τμώλῳ. On the tradition of the autochthony specifically of the people of Sardis, see Herodotus 1.78.3.

But the story told by most Greeks, Herodotus states, was that Asia (Ἀσίη, in the feminine) was an autochthonous woman (i.e., a native of the land that later bore her name) and that she was the wife of Prometheus; another version made Prometheus the son of Asia.[12] Regardless of the eponym, Greeks and Lydians were in agreement that "Asia" was a name to be localized in the realm of Sardis. A fragment of Archilochus refers to Asia in a phrase that appears to describe the dominion of his contemporary, Gyges: "He is master of sheep-rearing Asia."[13] Callinus of Ephesus, also writing in the seventh century, refers to a Cimmerian attack on Sardis coming "against the Esiones" (ἐπὶ τοὺς Ἠσιονεῖς), which Strabo, on the authority of Demetrius of Scepsis, declares to be an Ionic form of "Asiones" (Ἀσιονεῖς) and to refer to the people of the Lydian land of Asia (Ἀσία).[14] Homer, in the *Iliad*, refers to "the Asian meadow beside the Caÿstrian stream," associating Asia with a river and placing it in the part of Lydia that lies between Sardis, Smyrna, and Ephesus.[15] Mimnermus, another poet of the seventh century, refers to the foundation of Colophon, which lies in the same region, in "lovely Asia" (ἱμερτὴν Ἀσίην).[16] Mount Sipylus, also in this region, was the home of Tantalus and of Pelops, who was said to have come to Greece from Asia.[17] In later literature, Arrian indulges in a little scholarly exegesis while describing greater Asia. He states that "the names by which countries are called were attached in ancient times to rivers," and points out that Asia anciently was the land through which the river Hermus flows, from the mountain of the Mother Dindymene past Smyrna to the sea; he goes on to add the rivers Caïcus and Maeander to "the

12. Herodotus 4.45.3. Apollodorus *Library* 1.2.3 makes Prometheus the son of Asia and Iapetus.

13. Archilochus fr. 26 (Edmonds *EI;* = 227 West): ὁ δ' Ἀσίης καρτερὸς μηλοτρόφου.

14. Callinus fr. 5b (West, from Strabo 13.4.8, quoted in Edmonds *EI* vol. 1, 41). Heubeck 1954, 477–78, and 1961, 72, connects Ἠσιονεῖς to the epichoric form of the name Assos (Ἄσσός, the ethnic form of which is ΗΕΣΣΙΟΙ in the Athenian tribute lists), to Ἀσσάων, the name of the father of Niobe (and father of her children), according to Xanthus of Lydia *FGrHist* 765 F 20, and probably to the Trojan Hesione (Ἡσιόνη), daughter of Laomedon and sister of Priam (Apollodorus *Library* 2.5.9 and 2.6.4; Diodorus 4.42.3–7). Although Heubeck suggests that this derivation casts doubt on the connection between Ἠσιονεῖς, Ἀσιονεῖς, and Ἀσία, it is possible that the names are actually all related, and that Hesione might have been the eponym of the Lydian Esioneis (Ἡσιονεῖς); note the evidence for the Dardanid connection of the Mermnad dynasty discussed in chapter 3 at notes 56–64.

15. *Iliad* 2.461: Ἀσίῳ ἐν λειμῶνι, Καϋστρίου ἀμφὶ ῥέεθρα. See also Strabo 14.1.45 and Hesiod *Theogony* 359 for Asia as the eponym of a river. Arrian *Anabasis* 5.6.4 notes that the "Lydian plain of the Caÿster is named after a Lydian river." See also J. M. Cook 1967, 105–9, who argues that the Homeric catalog of Trojan allies (which 2.461 precedes) reflects the geography of the eighth century.

16. Mimnermus fr. 10.2 (Edmonds *EI;* = 9.2 West).

17. For Mount Sipylus in the native land of Pelops, see Pindar *Olympian* 1.38; further sources are cited in chapter 2, note 44; see also Sakellariou 1958, 407–9. On his arrival from Asia, see Thucydides 1.9.2.

rivers of Asia."[18] Asia, in this sense, has the Hermus River in its heart, and also gives rise to the Maeander, Caÿster, and Caïcus rivers. All of these references identify Asia with the domain of Lydia centered on Sardis, and with the Ionian and Aeolian coast to the west.

"Asian" personal names in Homer occur among the Trojan allies in the *Iliad,* where they are associated particularly with the Hellespont and with Phrygia. Asius, "who held Sestus and Abydus," on both sides of the Hellespont, was arrayed beside Pelasgians, Thracians, and Paeonians among the Trojan allies, who came from as far away as the Axius River in Macedonia.[19] Another Asius, "who made his home in Phrygia by the Sangarius stream," was the brother of Hecabe, therefore uncle to Hector.[20] The associations here echo the connections between Phrygians, Trojans, and ultimately Lydians that we have noted previously in connection with Midas, Aeneas, and the Mermnad homeland in Hellespontine Phrygia.[21] It is noteworthy that this set of associations does not respect the waters of the Hellespont as a boundary, but embraces both shores. The Lydian identity of Asia may imply this same wide embrace, since Sardian Asies is said to be the son of Cotys, according to Herodotus, and Cotys is a name with strong Thracian associations.[22]

This early use of "Asia" does not clearly correspond to a single ethnic or linguistic group. "Asia," rather, seems to describe a constellation of associated peoples and places with a center (roughly Lydia) but no definite boundaries.[23] The physical expanse of Asia seems to have been conceived in terms of the watershed of rivers. Hesiod knew Asia as the name of a river, and Arrian explains the origin of the name in these terms. It is possible, therefore,

---

18. Arrian *Anabasis* 5.6.4; cf. Herodotus 1.80.1 for a similar description of the river Hermus. On the Caïcus and Maeander, see Arrian *Anabasis* 5.6.7, and note the reference by Thucydides 1.138.5 to the monument to Themistocles "that is in the marketplace in Asian Magnesia" (ἐν Μαγνησίᾳ ἐστὶ τῇ Ἀσιανῇ ἐν τῇ ἀγορᾷ): i.e., at Magnesia on the Maeander.

19. Asius son of Hyrtacus is named in *Iliad* 2.835–39, with allies to the west listed in 840–50; he is in battle at 12.95–178, and dies at 13.384–416. Another Asius, from Abydus, is named at 17.583–84.

20. Asius son of Dymas: *Iliad* 16.717–19.

21. On the associations of Midas with Macedonia, see chapter 2, with notes 68 and 69. On the Mermnad heritage in the Troad and Hellespontine Phrygia, see chapter 3, with notes 56–64, and above, note 14. Note that the Paeonians were deported by Darius from Macedonia and settled in Phrygia, where they remained until the time of the Ionian Revolt: Herodotus 5.12–23, 98.

22. Herodotus 4.45.3. Note also the association of Kybebe with Thracian Bendis, attributed to Hipponax (fr. 127 West; Hesychius s.v. *Κυβήβη*). On the rites of Cotys and Bendis, and their resemblance to Phrygian rites, see Aeschylus *Edonians* fr. 57 (Radt), Strabo 10.3.16, and the discussions of Baldriga 1997, 282–83; Marazov, in Fol and Marazov 1977, 20–24 and 48–54; Vassileva 2001.

23. Compare this quality of Asia to the identity of Phrygia as discussed in chapter 2, with notes 40–44; and note also the associations of Midas, chapter 2, notes 57–69.

that the concept of Asia was related to rivers, and that it referred to a notional source of life-sustaining fresh waters from the earth.

Herodotus, in describing the Lydian homeland, and Arrian, in describing the ancient concept of Asia, both name Mount Dindymus, sacred to the Mother Dindymene, as the source of the Hermus River. Mount Dindymus was the largest mountain in the Phrygian highlands. In addition to being the source of the Hermus, Mount Dindymus gave rise to the Tembris River, a tributary of the Sangarius, and to one of the sources of the Maeander River. (See map 2.) All together, these watercourses traverse a wide region of western Anatolia within which there were several other mountains named Dindymus, or Dindymon, also associated with the worship of the Mother of the Gods, or the Mountain Mother, as she was also known.[24] The link between the early idea of Asia and lands that were watered through the beneficence of the Mountain Mother, from her several sacred mountains, corresponds also with the greater dominion of the Phrygian Mother, Kybele, and the land of Midas, as it was remembered by the Greeks. As we will see, the name Asia among the Greeks had a strong association with a form of sovereignty connected with the Mother of the Gods and with the life-sustaining waters that she bestowed upon humanity.

## ANAXIMANDER'S MAP

The application of the name Asia to a wider continent beyond Lydia is a product of the early history of world maps among the Greeks. For no such idea of a continent called Asia existed before the earliest Greek maps. The name Asia is not attested among the Assyrians, Babylonians, Persians, or in any other Near Eastern documents until the fifth century, when it appears in treaties between Greeks and Persians drafted in Greek. In these instances, "Asia" is used to refer to the portion of the Persian king's land in which Greek cities are established, which is effectively identical with the coastal regions of the former Lydian empire.[25] When Greek sources apply the name Asia to the wider continent, its original application to the dominion of Lydia is some-

24. In addition to Mount Dindymus and the Mother Dindymene at the headwaters of the Hermus and Maeander in the Phrygian highlands (above, note 19; and chapter 2, note 73), Dindymus and the Mother Dindymene are found above Cyzicus in Hellespontine Phrygia, and above Pessinus, near the Sangarius River in central Phrygia (Strabo 12.5.3). Roller 1999, 66–67 and n. 22, reports that "no fewer than seven separate mountains in Anatolia were called Dindymon." On the relationship between the Mother of the Gods, especially under the name Kybele, and the features of the natural landscape associated with her worship, see Strabo 10.3.12, quoted in chapter 2 at note 76, and the discussion of the origin of Kybele's name in chapter 3.

25. Asia as the king's land where Greeks live: Diodorus 12.4.5 (the Peace of Callias); Thucydides 8.58.2 (Spartan treaty with Darius II); Xenophon *Hellenica* 5.1.31 (King's Peace, treaty

times maintained in the designation "lower Asia," leaving "upper Asia" to designate all lands further to the east.[26] When Herodotus specifies a boundary between upper and lower Asia, it is the Halys River, which had been the frontier of the Lydian empire under Croesus.[27]

The first Greek map said to be of the οἰκουμένη (*oikoumenē*, "the settled world," a concept that will be examined more closely below) was drawn by a Lydian subject, Anaximander of Miletus, a contemporary and reportedly a student of Thales.[28] Thales of Miletus was remembered by Herodotus for his services to two Lydian kings, Alyattes and Croesus, both in the context of campaigns on the eastern frontier of the Lydian empire. Thales was best remembered for predicting the solar eclipse of 585 B.C.E., said to have occurred at the end of five years of warfare between the armies of Alyattes and Cyaxares the Mede on the Halys River.[29] This conflict ended in an agreement negotiated with the participation of the kings of Cilicia and Babylon, as Herodotus reports, and was cemented by a dynastic marriage between the rulers of Lydia and Media.[30] Marked by its association with the solar eclipse, the treaty on the Halys was certainly noticed by literate scholars throughout the Near East, particularly because it defined a new order to the post-Assyrian

with Artaxerxes II). See also Xenophon *Cyropaedia* 6.2.10 (Asiatic Greek allies of Croesus) and *Hellenica* 3.1.3, 3.4.5, and 3.8.27 (Greeks subject to Persian demands for tribute).

26. So Herodotus 1.96.1, 177. Xenophon never refers to "upper" or "lower" Asia, but he preserves the distinction described by Herodotus in his description of the march "up" by Cyrus from Lydia to Mesopotamia: *Hellenica* 3.1.2; *Anabasis* 1.1.2, 1.2.1, etc. (See also the discussion below at notes 64–65.) The supposed Letter of Darius I (ML no. 12, = Fornara no. 35), referring to the region of the Maeander as "in lower Asia" (line 12), provides the earliest example of this distinction, if the letter is genuine and if the term was not introduced into the Greek text at some point prior to its inscription in the Hadrianic era.

27. So Herodotus 1.72.2–3, 103.2, 130.1.

28. On Anaximander, his map, and his relation to Thales, see Agathemerus 1.1 (= DK 12 A 6): "Anaximander of Miletus, the pupil of Thales, was the first who ventured to draw the inhabited world on a tablet [πρῶτος ἐτόλμησε τὴν οἰκουμένην ἐν πίνακι γράψαι]." See also Strabo 14.1.7; Diogenes Laertius 2.1–2; *Suda* s.v. Ἀναξίμανδρος Πραξιάδου Μιλήσιος (quoted in part in note 59, below). These and further sources are quoted in DK 12 A, and discussed by Kahn 1960, 28–29; Kirk et al. 1983, 99–105; and Naddaf 2003, 32–33; see also Heidel 1921, 252–55; Mosshammer 1979, 274–76; and Gorman 2001, 75–80.

29. Herodotus 1.75 (Thales and Croesus); 1.74.2 and 103.2 (Thales and the eclipse; see also Diogenes 1.23 = DK 11 A 1). On Thales' alleged prediction, Neugebauer 1951, 136, argues that it has no reliable basis in attested contemporary astronomical science; Kirk et al. 1983, 82, argue that Babylonian science was sufficient for an informed guess; see also Halpern 2003.

30. Herodotus 1.74.3 reports the participation of Syennesis of Cilicia and Labynetus of Babylon in the treaty on the Halys. Herodotus' Labynetus is Nabonidus, later king of Babylon (556–539 B.C.E.), and representative of the reigning Nebuchadnezzar (605–562 B.C.E.) on this occasion, as demonstrated by Beaulieu 1989, 80–81. Aryenis daughter of Alyattes was given in marriage to Astyages son of Cyaxares (Herodotus 1.73.2, 74.4.). On this and other dynastic marriage alliances of this period, see Brosius 1996, 21 and 35–47.

world.[31] From the point of view of Lydia, and Lydia's Greek subjects, the emergence of this new world order was the appropriate occasion for Anaximander to prepare his map of the settled world.

Little is known and much is conjectured about Anaximander's map.[32] As the first in a tradition of Greek maps of the world, Anaximander's map certainly displayed the geometric simplicity that Herodotus so strongly criticized. "I laugh when I see all those who draw such nonsensical maps of the world," he says. "They picture Ocean flowing around the earth, which is circular as if drawn with the compass; and they make Asia equal to Europe."[33] The symmetrical division of a circular world into two continents is characteristic of the geometric simplicity and cosmogonic oppositions found in Anaximander's thought.[34] We can imagine, then, that Anaximander's map displayed a circular earth symmetrically divided into two semicircular continents, separated from each other by the waters of the Mediterranean, dotted with islands, all framed by the circle of Ocean. To call Anaximander's scheme a map encourages us to envision it as the earliest stage in the creation of the more recognizable representation of the world depicted in Ptolemy's *Geography;* but we should not expect much of this earliest depiction to appear familiar to us. Later geography developed according to principles and an accumulation of observations not yet available to Anaximander. As with the contemporary Babylonian map of the world, the schematic depiction of ideological relationships was more important on Anaximander's map than accurate spatial relationships.[35]

Anaximander probably did not consider Asia to be the name of an entire continent. As discussed above, Greek sources of the seventh century use "Asia" only to describe the Lydo-Ionian heartland between the Caïcus and the Maeander rivers, so it is most reasonable to suppose that Anaximander

31. On the literary and scholarly interest in astronomy, astrology, and prophecy especially in this period, see Grayson 1975, 12–14; J. Z. Smith 1978, 67–87; Wiseman 1985, 88–98; Halpern 2003.

32. For testimony, see note 28 above. For discussions of the form of the earth according to Anaximander, see Heidel 1937; Kahn 1960, 55–56, 81–84; Kirk et al. 1983, 104–5; Gehrke 1998, 171–77; Hahn 2001, 200–210; Couprie 2003, 194–201; Naddaf 2003, 32–55.

33. Herodotus 4.36.2.

34. On Anaximander's concept of cosmogonic opposites (τὰς ἐναντιότητας) see Aristotle *Physics* 1.4, 187a (cited in DK 12 A 9); see also the discussion of Kirk et al. 1983, 119–20 and 128–30. Naddaf 2003, 34–36, likewise recognizes that schematic simplification characterized Anaximander's cosmological and geographical thought. But rather than bilateral symmetry, Naddaf argues that Anaximander propounded a tripartite scheme, and that he should be understood as among the Ionians who divided the world into three parts (Herodotus 2.16; see note 1 above on the difference of opinions on this subject). Heidel 1937, 12, and Couprie 2003, 196, are among those who view Anaximander's and Hecataeus' maps as bilaterally divided into two continents.

35. The Babylonian map is discussed below at note 62.

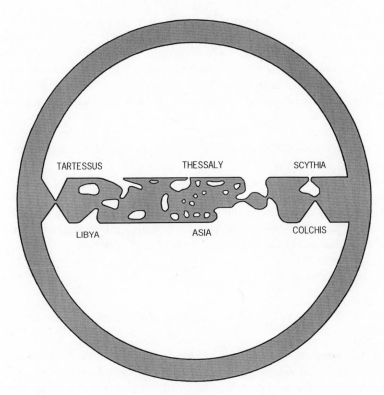

Figure 12. Conjectural rendering of the map of Anaximander.

understood "Asia" in this same limited sense. If Anaximander's map placed the name Asia at the center of a coastal region with no obvious delimitation from the greater continent on which it was located, then his map could have encouraged the wider definition of Asia that Hecataeus later endorsed. Herodotus later was at pains to counteract such an imprecise distinction between the coastal region Asia and the greater continent of which it was a part by describing "lower Asia" (essentially the peninsula familiar to us as Asia Minor or Anatolia) as a peninsula with a neck at its base.[36] This was one of many features about the configuration of the sea and the continents that later mapmakers and geographers could wrangle over.

36. Herodotus 1.72.3 greatly underestimates the distance across the neck (αὐχήν) of land between the coast opposite Cyprus and the coast of the Black Sea. (His "five-day walk for a man traveling light" is in fact more than three hundred miles; he repeats this underestimate at 2.34.2.)

Later sources never consulted Anaximander for the sort of geographic detail that was so richly represented on the map of Hecataeus. Instead, ancient and modern commentators have recognized balance and symmetry to be hallmarks of Anaximander's thought, and have discussed these concepts in the context of the Anaximander's contribution to the beginnings of Greek cosmology, where the progress of science could not reveal the inaccuracies of his conceptual scheme as quickly as it could in the field of geography. As a result, Anaximander's map has languished in obscurity, to be noticed only as the first step toward Hecataeus' better (but, by Herodotus' standards, still inadequate) map of the world.

Even knowing as little as we do, we know enough to realize that Anaximander's map had significant cultural and even historical implications. For it was drawn not only in accordance with principles of cosmological balance and a rudimentary sense of geography, but also according to an understanding of the principles of earthly sovereignty. This fact is conveyed in the single datum attributed specifically to Anaximander's map, namely that it displayed the *oikoumenē*.[37]

## KINGSHIP AND THE *OIKOUMENĒ*

The term *oikoumenē* (οἰκουμένη) is commonly translated as simply "the world," and is sometimes identified as an expression of Hellenistic thought, and therefore regarded as an anachronism when applied to Anaximander's map.[38] In fact, the term was in use as early as the earliest Ionic prose, and the context of its use by Herodotus reveals its established meaning. *Oikoumenē* means "settled," in the sense "possessing established communities" and, by extension, "possessing productive communities." *Oikoumenē* as a description of *gē*, earth, therefore refers to that part of the earth that is settled and cultivated from towns, and by extension, it describes all the lands of the earth under the regime of settled agriculture.[39]

The word *oikoumenē* is used in this sense by Herodotus (οἰκεομένη in Herodotus' Ionic) to describe Greek towns in Ionia and on the settled islands of

37. See Agathemerus 1.1, quoted in note 28 above. Gisinger 1937, cols. 2128–30, offers a useful appraisal of the significance of *oikoumenē* in this context. Heidel 1921 (esp. 271) and Naddaf 2003 recognize the integral connection of geographical and historical thought to Anaximander's cosmological concepts.

38. W. W. Tarn mistakenly claims that the term *oikoumenē* is anachronistic when applied to ideas as early as the age of Alexander the Great (1948, 79 n. 5). On the concept of *oikoumenē* in Hellenistic historiography, see Sacks 1981, 96–112; on the wider Hellenistic context of this concept and its legacy in early Christian historiography, see Mortley 1996.

39. On the history of the term *oikoumenē*, see Gisinger 1937, col. 2124: "In seinem einschränkenden Sinn [as a participial modifier of γῆ or χώρα] ist das Wort wohl zuerst verwendet worden in der Zeit der Entwicklung der altionischen Erdkunde."

the Aegean, to characterize India as the most distant settled land, to describe the frontier of settlement in Libya, Scythia, or among distant settled Thracians, and to describe Athens.[40] Settled land, as understood by Herodotus and by Thucydides as well, was desirable land, and was therefore vulnerable to appropriation by anyone who was strong enough to seize it.[41] Herodotus and Thucydides both recognized that the relationship between sovereign power and the productive lands that sustained sovereignty was the central problem facing the leading actors in their histories.[42] Anaximander was certainly aware of the importance of this relationship as well. As an Asiatic Greek whose city, Miletus, had submitted to the power exercised by the tyrants of Lydia over their agricultural land, Anaximander knew that the settled land of the earth was the foundation of sovereignty. The concepts were inextricably linked.

The *oikoumenē* was the proper domain of sovereign kings who possessed that domain in order to assure both its prosperity and their own. Xenophon, who always sought meaning in archaic paradigms, presents just such a definition of *oikoumenē* in his *Cyropaedia,* an idealized account of Cyrus the Great and his creation of the Persian empire. When Cyrus and his forces had invaded a land formerly controlled by the Assyrians, Cyrus inquired of some captured enemy cavalrymen "how long a way they had ridden, and if the country was inhabited":[43]

They said that they had ridden a great distance, and that the entire country was inhabited and full of sheep and goats and cattle and horses and grain and all good things. "There are two things," Cyrus said, "that we must make sure

40. Land οἰκεομένη (or people οἰκημένοι) in Herodotus: 1.27.4, 1.170.3 (Ionian settlements); 1.28 (lands subjugated by Croesus); 2.32.5 (parts of Libya); 3.106.1 (India); 4.110.2 (parts of Scythia); 5.73 (Athens); 8.115.4 (certain Thracians). In Herodotus' almost consistent usage, sedentary agriculturalists "inhabit" the land (οἰκέουσι), while nomads "use" or "graze" it (νέμονται), and, with rare exceptions, do "not sow" (οὐ σπείρουσι) the land; see his description of the practices of various Scythian tribes (4.17–25).

41. Herodotus' "inhabited land" (οἰκεομένη) is populated by agriculturalists who are the proper subjects of the sovereign of Asia (1.28, 5.13, 5.49, 5.73.2, 9.122, e.g.). Because of the insecurity of agriculture, Thucydides places "what is now called Hellas" originally outside the *oikoumenē* (1.2.1: φαίνεται γὰρ ἡ νῦν Ἑλλὰς καλουμένη οὐ πάλαι βεβαίως οἰκουμένη).

42. Adumbrated already in Herodotus' opening chapters on Lydia, this key problem is directly addressed in the closing passage of his *Histories* (9.122), where Cyrus advises the Persians, to whom "Zeus has given hegemony" and who now "rule over many men and all of Asia," to maintain their sovereignty by remaining stronger than those who inhabit cultivated lands. The relationship of power (δύναμις) to surplus or material resources (περιουσία χρημάτων or παρασκευή), ultimately resting on the quality of the land (ἀρετὴ γῆς), is likewise explicitly addressed in Thucydides' opening chapters (1.2–17).

43. Xenophon *Cyropaedia* 4.4.4–5. (Cf. the value of ἡ οἰκουμένη σπειρομένη in Xenophon *Agesilaus* 1.20.) The χώρα οἰκουμένη here is closely allied to the significance of χώρα, "countryside," alone as the term that refers to the specific locus of the Persian king's authority in the portions of Asia settled by Greek cities, as described in the three Persian-Spartan treaties of 411 B.C.E. quoted by Thucydides 8.18, 37, and 58; see D. M. Lewis 1977, 105.

of: that we are more powerful than those who possess these things, and that they stay where they are. For an inhabited land [χώρα οἰκουμένη] is a possession of great value; but when it is deserted, it becomes worthless."

Cyrus' formulation of the relationship between sovereign power and the subjugation of the cultivated *oikoumenē* was precisely the meaning of the sign that appeared to Gordius father of Midas, as Arrian tells it: "One day, while he was plowing, an eagle flew down onto the yoke and remained sitting there until the time came for the unyoking of the oxen at the end of the day."[44] The unshakable grip of the eagle on the yoke of the plowman's team, an alarming sight to Gordius the farmer, was the sign that a true king must always be "more powerful than those who possess these [fruits of the χώρα οἰκουμένη]." This was the relationship of tyrant to subject demonstrated in the ritual march of Midas through lands neighboring Phrygia, and of Alyattes through the land of Miletus; and the relationship of sovereign to subject was commonly signified by the yoke of submission and the power of an eagle or a hawk.[45]

Order in the settled world, therefore, depended on the orderly yet forceful relationship between sovereign and subjects. Force was demonstrated by indomitable prowess in war, exemplified by the conquests of Cyrus, and of Alyattes and Midas before him. The legitimacy of the resulting order was signified by reverence to the divinities who upheld order. While the prosperity of the settled, cultivated *oikoumenē* was generally associated with the beneficence of a maternal deity, such as Demeter or the Phrygian Mother, the divinity who most actively and forcefully extended the conditions for settled life was the young warrior usually identified as the son of the divine Mother. To the Greeks and their Asiatic neighbors, this was Apollo.

Apollo was the champion of sovereignty in a divinely ordered system. He was the archer and warrior whose power could threaten the gods, but whose loyalty to his father, Zeus the King, was steadfast.[46] With his sister, Artemis, he was also known as the offspring of the divine Mother, Leto, called the Mother of the Gods in Lycian texts, possibly appearing as the Mother in Ly-

---

44. Arrian *Anabasis* 2.3.3. (See chapter 2 at note 107.)

45. On Midas and Alyattes, see chapter 2, with notes 121 and 126. On the yoke of submission, e.g., note Aeschylus *Persians* 50. On the symbolism of the eagle or the hawk, see chapter 2, with notes 109–11. Note Hesiod's parable about the irresistible grip of the hawk on the nightingale (*Works and Days* 202–12), and the parody by Aristophanes *Knights* 1186–87 of the oracles of Bacis to the effect that Demos "will become an eagle and will be king of all lands."

46. Jenny Strauss Clay 1994 convincingly underscores the tension present at the opening of *Homeric Hymn* 3, *To Apollo*, and recurrent throughout, between Apollo's terrifying and threatening aspect (27: "the awesome god . . . appears as the potential violator of the Olympian order and usurper of Zeus' dominion") and his actual beneficence (35: "far from posing a challenge to his father's authority, Apollo proposes to propagate it among mankind by transmitting his father's ordinances to men").

dian inscriptions.[47] Greeks acknowledged that Apollo had ancient and venerable seats in Asia Minor, in Lycia and Lydia as well as at Miletus.[48] Among the Lydians, he was honored as *Qldãnś,* sometimes called the "great" or "powerful" god, and partner of *Artimuś.*[49] Apollo's birthplace on the island of Delos (according to the Greeks) and his many oracular shrines made him especially accessible as a link between gods and men. Through Apollo, kingship on earth was established, and order within the *oikoumenē* was maintained and extended.

Among Greeks, Apollo championed kingship and the expansion of the *oikoumenē* chiefly by instigating or legitimizing the foundation of colonies.[50] The oracle exercised that role by designating or instructing a founder, the *oikistēs,* whose role as leader of the new community was analogous, in several respects, to that of a conquering king. Through the god-supported oikist, a new orderly and prospering community was brought into existence. The identity of the oikist as a king or tyrant is even explicit in numerous instances early in the history of Greek colonization, when founders came from royal or tyrannical houses.[51] In the case of Battus, founder of Cyrene, Apollo's oracle calls him *basileus,* "king," and Battus' leadership resulted in the estab-

47. On *Eni Mahanahi,* "the Mother of the Gods," as Leto in Lycian cult, see Metzger and Laroche, in Metzger 1979, 5–28, 114; Bryce 1983; Burkert 1985, 171–72; Keen 1998, 194–96. Bryce argues that her cult did not arrive in Lycia until the late fifth century B.C.E.; Keen finds reason to believe the cult is older. "Mother" (*Enaś*) occurs in Lydian inscriptions, but is not certainly a deity: see Gusmani *LW* 106 and 258 no. 17 (= Hanfmann and Ramage 1978, 157 no. 233, dating to ca. 450–425 B.C.E.), and 264 no. 42 line 7 ( = Dusinberre 2003, 235 no. 48; fourth century).

48. *Homeric Hymn* 3, *To Apollo* 179–83, acknowledges the veneration of this god in Lycia, in Maeonia (i.e., Lydia), at Miletus (i.e., Didyma), at Delos, and at Pytho (Delphi); Pindar *Pythian* 1.39 calls Phoebus Apollo "lord of Lycia and Delos." See Burkert 1985, 143–49, and 1994, on the early history of the cult of Apollo, and its connections among non-Greek peoples in Asia Minor, Cyprus, and Syria. Wilamowitz 1903 and others have championed the view that Apollo was originally an Asiatic deity. Burkert 1975 challenged this view, but the linguistic basis of Burkert's argument has been recently challenged by Beekes 2003.

49. Hanfmann 1983b, 230, surveys the evidence for the Lydian cult of Apollo, and for the identification of *Qldãnś* as an Apollo-like figure. Gusmani *LW* 188 endorses the identification of Lydian *Qldãnś* as Apollo, noting that his name is sometimes coupled with Artemis (Lydian *Artimuś;* see Dusinberre 2003, 228 no. 1 and 230 no. 13). Heubeck 1959, 15–30, argues that *Qldãnś* should be identified with the Lydian moon god, Mēn, rather than Apollo. In *LWErg* 85, 137, Gusmani acknowledges Heubeck's identification with Mēn, but does not rule out the association with Apollo. It seems best to adopt Hanfmann's expression that *Qldãnś* is "an Apollo-like figure," in the same sense that Kybebe can be said to be a Demeter-like figure and also an Aphrodite-like figure.

50. On the Delphic Oracle and colonization, see Parke and Wormell 1956, vol. 1, 49–79; Forrest 1957; Graham 1983, 25–27; Burkert 1985, 116; Malkin 1987, 17–91; 1989.

51. On the role of the *oikistēs* and the relationship to tyrannical dynasties, see Graham 1983, 29–39, and Malkin 1989, 142–50, who draw attention especially to the foundations of the Cypselids of Corinth and the Philaïds and Peisistratids of Athens.

lishment of a royal dynasty.[52] The role of the founder approached that of the god himself by the fact that both were addressed as *archēgetēs,* "first leader," and by the heroic cult accorded to the founder after death.[53]

Such heroic honors after death recall the funerary honors accorded to the kings of Sparta and, as Herodotus notes, to kings in Asia.[54] They also recall the honors accorded to the memory of King Midas. In the dedication of the Midas Monument, inscribed in the seventh or sixth century, Midas is addressed as *wanax,* "lord," a title commonly used of Apollo. Midas is also called *lawag<e>tas,* "leader of the host," a title close to *archēgetēs.*[55] Kingship was assimilated to divine leadership here, and Apollo provided the paradigm of leadership that drew every rightful ruler to him. So it is that sovereign rulers, including colonial founders, the kings of Sparta, and the tyrants of Lydia, all sought guidance and justification from Apollo, especially through his oracular shrine at Delphi.

Gyges legitimized his usurpation of the throne by Apollo's oracle, Herodotus reports (1.14), and memorialized the event by gifts to Apollo at Delphi that bore his name thereafter. Alyattes reached a settlement in his war against Miletus through the mediation of Apollo at Delphi (1.19–21, 25). Croesus sought divine support for the expansion of his empire from Apollo's oracles, and displayed his reverence to the god's shrine at Delphi especially through his fabulously rich dedications (1.46–55, 87, 90–92; 8.35). A generous gift to Apollo in Laconia was an important gesture in Croesus' formation of an alliance with the Spartans (1.69.4). In all of these instances, we see the Mermnad rulers acting not as outsiders making deferential gestures to Greek customs, but as partners with Greeks in a shared cult.[56] In their day,

---

52. For the oracle given to Battus, see ML 5; Graham 1983, 224–26; and the account of Battus' role, and the history of his dynasty, in Herodotus 4.154–63; cf. Diodorus 8.29–3. These sources are reviewed by Malkin 1987, 60–69.

53. Thucydides 6.3.1 reports the foundation of the altar of Apollo Archegetes at Naxos, the first Greek colony on Sicily. Xenophon *Hellenica* 6.3.6 names Heracles Archegetes at Sparta. Pindar *Pythian* 5.60 names Apollo Archagetas of Cyrene, and the same title is given to Battus in the foundation decree of Cyrene (note 52 above). See Malkin 1989, 146–47, on the relationship of the *archēgetēs* to the *oikistēs,* and 189–260 on founder cults. Malkin 2002, 208–6, convincingly defends the traditional understanding of archaic founders and their memorials in cult against an effort by Osborne 1996, 4–17, to show that founder cults were invented to meet later propagandistic needs.

54. On Spartan royal funerals, see chapter 1, with notes 58–60.

55. On the Midas Monument (Yazılıkaya), its date, and the titles it gives to Midas (rendered here in Hellenized form), see chapter 2, with notes 86–88. Note that Lycurgus, the heroized Spartan lawgiver, was said to have been instructed by the Delphic Oracle to "lead the host on the way" (λαοῖς ἡγεῖσθε κέλευθον, Diodorus 7.12.2 = Parke and Wormell 1956, vol. 2, no. 218), which is close to addressing him as *Lawagetas.*

56. Pericles Georges 1994, 25–29, 34–37, proposes a similar understanding of Lydian offerings; contrast Kaplan 2005, who sees the Lydians as outsiders.

Lydia was home to indomitable prowess in war, and to the most magnificent kingship. By Apollo's authorization, the Mermnad tyrants of Lydia could be seen as the preeminent champions of order within the *oikoumenē*.

## THE ITINERARY OF THE *OIKOUMENĒ*

The concept of a world order established through the actions of kings and founders guided by divinity is an idea that implies a historical geography of the *oikoumenē*. That is, it implies a place of historical (or myth-historical) origin for this order, and it suggests that, with divine guidance, this order can be renewed or perpetuated, and even more widely extended. It thus becomes relevant to consider how such a historical geography might have been represented on Anaximander's map of the *oikoumenē*.

A place of origin for a cultural system would most appropriately be the center of a circular map. In deference to the strong tradition, attested by Pindar, Aeschylus, Euripides, and later sources, that the omphalos beside the Pythia's oracular seat at Delphi marked the center of the world, it is often assumed that Anaximander's map placed Delphi at its center.[57] In view of the importance of Apollo's oracle at Delphi by the time Anaximander composed his map, this is not an unreasonable supposition. But there are plausible alternatives. Apollo's birthplace, the island of Delos, also has a strong claim for consideration as the midpoint of Anaximander's map, especially if we accept that it depicted the earth as two continents separated by the waters of the Aegean and greater Mediterranean.[58] There is no way of knowing if any single place was identified as precisely the center of Anaximander's map, although it is a reasonable assumption that the Aegean and its shores were depicted as the central region of the *oikoumenē*.

The dissemination of a cultural system could be represented on a circular map in some manner other than radiation from an exact central point. Both the terminology used to describe Anaximander's map and the only surviving example of a world map contemporary to Anaximander, the Baby-

---

57. On the central omphalos at Delphi, see Pindar *Pythian* 4.74 (μέσον ὀμφαλόν); Aeschylus *Eumenides* 166 (γᾶς ὀμφαλόν); Euripides *Orestes* 331 (μεσόμφαλοι μυχοί), *Ion* 224 (μέσον ὀμφαλὸν γᾶς); Plato *Republic* 427c (γῆς ὀμφαλός). Agathemerus *Geography* 1.1.2 (= DK 68 B 15) says that "the ancients" (before Democritus) depicted a circular *oikoumenē* with Delphi and its omphalos at its center. It is widely assumed that Delphi as the midmost point of the earth was a most ancient concept, and that Anaximander depicted it; so, e.g., Thomson 1948, 98; Parke and Wormell 1956, vol. 1, 1; Couprie 2003, 94–96. Homer, however, shows no awareness of this feature of Apollo's shrine at Delphi (Pytho), but describes Calypso's island as the location of the "omphalos of the sea" (*Odyssey* 1.50: ὅθι τ᾽ ὀμφαλὸς θαλάσσης).

58. Gerard Naddaf 2003, 34–35 and 52–55, criticizes the readiness of scholars to assume that Anaximander placed Delphi at the center of his map, and suggests that either Miletus or the Nile Delta would more likely have been at its center.

Ionian map of the world, suggest how this may have been achieved. "Itinerary of the earth," *periodos gēs* (περίοδος γῆς), was one of the names by which Anaximander's map was known. *Periodos gēs* is usually taken to mean simply "map of the world," but its literal meaning, "itinerary of the earth," is also an appropriate description for a written treatise accompanying a map, as was the case in Hecataeus' geographical work and almost certainly for Anaximander as well.[59] It is probable that Anaximander described the *oikoumenē* shown on his map in some manner of a written itinerary.

The record of an itinerary, describing a march through the land and the places of importance encountered along the way, was often a symbol of appropriation in both ritual and military terms. Such topographical lists have a long history in cuneiform literature, especially among the Hittites, where historical annals, treaties, and ritual texts alike include itineraries of conquest and appropriation.[60] In a Mesopotamian tradition known to the Hittites, the third-millennium empire of Sargon of Akkad was represented in stories of conquest. By the late eighth century, in the time of Sargon II of Assyria, these stories were arranged into a more or less canonical series of itineraries embracing lands from the "Upper Sea" (Mediterranean) to the "Lower Sea" (Persian Gulf), establishing a pattern of conquest that the contemporary kings of Assyria sought to emulate.[61] A fragmentary version of Sargon's legendary conquests survives on the cuneiform tablet of the seventh or sixth century B.C.E. that also preserves the Babylonian map of the world.[62] This schematic map depicts the world as a circle, surrounded by the sea. The circle of the earth is divided in two by the Euphrates River, with Babylon placed prominently astride the river, but not at the center of the map, which is marked by a compass point. Other lands, such as Assyria and Urartu, are dis-

59. *Suda* s.v. Ἀναξίμανδρος (= DK 12 A 2) says that Anaximander "wrote *On Nature, Itinerary of the Earth, On the Fixed Stars,* and *The Sphere,* and other works" (ἔγραψε Περὶ φύσεως, Γῆς περίοδον καὶ Περὶ τῶν ἀπλανῶν καὶ Σφαῖραν καὶ ἄλλα τινά). It is likely that several of the titles here attributed to Anaximander are spurious and anachronistic (see Kirk et al. 1983, 102–3; Couprie 2003, 178–79), but a treatise known as *Gēs Periodos* is not implausible. Heidel 1921 makes a strong case that Anaximander's geographical ideas were represented in his writing as well as on a map. See also the discussions of Jacoby 1912, cols. 2690–2733; Gehrke 1998, 171–77; Naddaf 2003, 32–55.

60. Such itineraries are the foundation for the study of Hittite geography: see Garstang and Gurney 1959, esp. 5–31. Examples of ritual itineraries include the *evocatio* ritual (*ANET* 351–53), and the *nuntarriyasas* ceremony (Gurney 1958, 109–10; Garstang and Gurney 10–13; Haas 1994, 827–47).

61. On Sargon of Akkad (and his descendant Naram-Sin), who established the hallmarks of world empire, see in general Speiser 1955, 54–56, 69–70; Oppenheim 1964, 124–25, 151, 154, 205. On the geography and symbolism of his conquests see Weidner 1952; Grayson 1974; Jonker 1995, 41–68; Horowitz 1998, 67–95; Pongratz-Leisten 2001. On cultic implications of Sargon's kingship, see Grayson 1975, 43–48, on the Weidner Chronicle and Chronicle of Early Kings.

62. On the Babylonian map and accompanying texts, see Horowitz 1988 and 1998, 20–42.

persed around Babylon within the circle of the surrounding sea. Geography merges with legend and mythology in the texts that accompany this map.

The principles that established the configuration of the known world, from this Babylonian perspective, are the relative centricity of Babylon and the historical example of the conquests of Sargon of Akkad, who came not from Babylon itself, but from the land of "Sumer and Akkad" that the Babylonians claimed as their own. It is likely that Anaximander adapted the principles of Mesopotamian geography to an Anatolian context in his depiction of the *oikoumenē* and description of its extent, just as he is known to have utilized other aspects of Babylonian science.[63] Anaximander's map probably displayed the framework for an itinerary of appropriation emanating from Lydian Asia, possibly from Sardis itself. A written itinerary (*periodos*) through the settled communities of the earth was probably the manner by which Anaximander defined the extent of the *oikoumenē*.

The identification, among Greeks, of the *oikoumenē* with the Asiatic dominion of Lydia is indicated in a distinctive use of this term by Xenophon. In his *Anabasis* of the younger Cyrus, Xenophon applies the description οἰκουμένη to towns visited by Cyrus on his march from Sardis to Cilicia, on his way to the Euphrates.[64] Xenophon's usage has a specific geographical boundary: no city beyond the Syrian Gates is described as οἰκουμένη, even though several flourishing towns there would deserve such a description as much as the Phrygian and Cilician towns he passed through. The implied distinction suggests that Xenophon's usage derives from a Sardocentric itinerary listing the settled regions within an idealized Lydian empire. This itinerary embraces regions beyond the Halys River, corresponding better with the eastern extent of territory actually controlled by the historical Midas, at the turn of the eighth to seventh centuries B.C.E., than with the region within the Halys controlled by Alyattes after his treaty with Cyaxares in 585. Xenophon's notice of a landmark associated with Midas along his way may indicate that this Sardocentric itinerary described the Mermnad view of the empire of Midas, the ideal template for their own empire.[65]

---

63. Herodotus 2.109.3 mentions sundials as a Babylonian invention, and other sources identify Anaximander as the first Greek to employ such devices. (See below at notes 80 and 89.) The relationship of the Babylonian map to contemporary Ionian thought was recognized by Meissner 1925.

64. Xenophon *Anabasis* 1.2.6–20 (Sardis–Colossae–Celaenae–Peltae–Ceramon Agora–Caÿstrou Pedion–Thymbrium–Tyriaeum–Dana), and 1.4.1, 6 (Issus-Myriandus). No town is described as οἰκουμένη thereafter until the army of the Ten Thousand has crossed the Araxes River on its northward march across Armenia (at Gymnias, 4.7.19) and reaches Hellenic settlements along the Black Sea (e.g., Trapezus, 4.8.22).

65. At Thymbrium, Xenophon notices the "spring of Midas, where Midas caught the satyr" (*Anabasis* 1.2.13). At 1.2.8 Xenophon also calls attention to the cave at the headwaters of the Marsyas River, at Celaenae, where Apollo hung up the skin of Marsyas—an episode narrated

Midas was for Lydian Asia what Sargon of Akkad was for contemporary Babylonia, and Sesostris was for Egypt—the model world conqueror. An ancient Mesopotamian literary tradition provided the authority for Sargon's wide conquests. A pastiche of Egyptian records and misappropriated Hittite monuments documented Sesostris' itinerary.[66] Compared with Midas, these traditions were vastly different in the nature and antiquity of their origins, yet the traditions of Sargon, Sesostris, and Midas appear to have matured into their most familiar forms contemporaneously, in the seventh and early sixth centuries. Anaximander's map and the commentary that accompanied it appear to have been an outgrowth of the Asiatic tradition of Midas, for they represented the itineraries that defined Midas' kingdom, and suggested the ways along which it could be extended by his heirs. The *oikoumenē,* as described and depicted by Anaximander, represented the natural domain of the world tyrant.

## THE BALANCE OF JUSTICE IN THE WORLD

Scholars commenting on Anaximander's cosmological ideas have always been struck by the manner in which he conceived of the elements of the natural world as governed by a moral principle, in which justice is rendered for wrongs committed.[67] Such is the concept at the core of the single surviving passage of Anaximander's writings, as quoted by Simplicius:[68]

> Anaximander . . . says that the "first principle" [or "rule," ἀρχή] was neither water nor any of the other so-called elements, but some other "boundless nature [φύσις ἄπειρος], out of which all the heavens [οὐρανοί] and all the orders [κόσμοι] within them arise. Out of these comes the generation of existing things, and back to them by necessity things disintegrate, for these things render justice and retribution to each other for wrongdoing according to the ordering of time."

It seems likely that the idea of cosmic balance and symmetry also informed Anaximander's image of the rightful domain of sovereignty conveyed by his

---

by Diodorus 3.59.1–6 in the context of the story of Cybele and her veneration by Midas. Celaenae and the Cave of Marsyas were also points of note on Xerxes' march to Sardis, according to Herodotus 7.26.3.

66. On Sesostris see A. B. Lloyd 1982, 37–40; S. West, 1992. For the suggestion that "Sesostris" is a corruption of an epithet of Ramesses II, *Ssy-r'*, see Redford 1992, 257–58 n. 2. On Midas, see chapter 2.

67. See, e.g., Kahn 1960, 166–96; Kirk et al. 1983, 117–22; Naddaf 2003, 31.

68. From Simplicius' commentary on Aristotle's *Physics* 24.13 ( = DK 12 A 9, B 1). Other ancient authorities paraphrase this passage; these versions are collected in DK 12 A 10 and 11, and are compared by Kahn 1960, 28–39; by Kirk et al. 1983, 106–8; and by M. L. West 1971, 81–83.

map and description of the *oikoumenē*, in an abstract as well as a graphic way. Like all paradigms of "the heavens and all the orders [that arise] within them," worldly sovereignty, too, grew and declined in accordance with justice and in retribution for wrongdoing.[69] Among the Mermnads of Lydia as well as among other long-suffering neighbors of the Assyrians, belief in such a world order was a powerful incentive to establish their own just sovereignty over the world.

So we find that the concept of world dominion expressed in terms of cosmic justice, supported by omens, and symbolized by a map of the world was also at the forefront of scholarship in the Babylonian court of Nebuchadnezzar II and his successors, the contemporaries and allies of Alyattes and Croesus.[70] Acts of piety and devotion to traditional cults are prominent among the measures taken by Babylonian rulers to demonstrate their worthiness. Neo-Babylonian Sargonic texts emphasize these same devotions as the basis for Sargon's legendary success, and their neglect as the reason for the dissolution of his empire under his successors.[71] Other texts describe the divine sanction by which a new world empire now was deemed to belong to King Nebuchadnezzar. Among these are references to the inhabited world (Akkadian *dadmū*)[72] in terms that echo the concepts embedded in the story of the Gordian knot and Anaximander's map of the *oikoumenē*. So Nebuchadnezzar is proclaimed as king of[73]

> all the lands [*mātātu*], the entire inhabited world [*dadmū*] from the Upper Sea to the Lower Sea, distant lands, the people of vast territories, kings of faraway mountains and remote *nagū* ["regions" or "islands"] in the Upper and Lower Sea, whose lead-rope Marduk, my lord, placed in my hand in order to pull his yoke.

69. Kahn 1960, 169–70, 179, has recognized that one of the closest parallels to the language used by Anaximander is found in Herodotus' description of the origins of wrongdoing and the cycles of retribution in wars between Europe and Asia at the opening of his *Histories*.

70. Vanderhooft 1999, 33–51, summarizes the tenor of Nebuchadnezzar's imperial rhetoric, which emphasizes the beneficence and justice of his leadership. On Babylonian scholarship and prophecy, see note 31 above.

71. Note the views of early kingship found in the Weidner Chronicle and the Chronicle of Early Kings, discussed by Grayson 1975, 43–49. Note also the critical view of Nabonidus' religious innovations taken by the Nabonidus Chronicle, Grayson 21–22, 106–11; see also Beaulieu 1989.

72. On *dadmū* meaning ' the inhabited world (settlements and inhabitants)" see *CAD* vol. 3, 18–20. *Mātu*, "land" (plural *mātātu*, "lands") is also a close equivalent to the Greek *oikoumenē*; see *CAD* vol. 10, part i, 415–17, "country (as a political unit)"; 420–21, "the population of a country," often "in relationship to the ruler of the country." See also note 105 below.

73. Text of Nebuchadnezzar quoted from Horowitz 1998, 31. Horowitz (295–301) discusses various Akkadian terms (*dadmū, kibrātu, mātātu,* and *kiššatu*) for earth or land. This text is close in tone and content to another composed at Babylon and referring to the advent of Cyrus (after 539 B.C.E.), Isaiah 41:1–5: "Listen in silence to me, all you coasts and islands; let the peoples come to meet me. . . . Who has raised up from the east one greeted by victory wherever he goes,

Babylon in the time of Nebuchadnezzar II (605–562 B.C.E.) was very much a city of the world. By the time of the treaty on the Halys in 585, Nebuchadnezzar had established his undisputed sway "from the Upper Sea to the Lower Sea" (from the Mediterranean to the Persian Gulf). His claim to wider suzerainty over "kings of faraway *nagū*" was more wishful than actual, but it was based on the reality that men of every station, from royal emissaries and high-ranking exiles to skilled and unskilled laborers from Greece, Lydia, Egypt, Media, Elam, and Arabia, were to be found in Babylon.[74]

The reign of Nebuchadnezzar was the acme of Babylon's worldly dominion. But the prosperity it enjoyed as a result of the collapse of Assyria might have been lost even more rapidly than it had been gained if the war between the Lydians and the Medes along the Halys had resulted in a clear victory for either of those two powers. Lands to the south, from Cilicia to Palestine and Mesopotamia, would surely have suffered if a single superpower had emerged. For that reason, Nabonidus (Herodotus' Labynetus), representing Nebuchadnezzar, and Syennesis the king of Cilicia were keen to resolve the war of the Lydians and the Medes along the Halys, and to establish a rough equilibrium among all neighboring powers. Thereafter, each side looked for subtle signs in omens and oracles, and to the insights gained from ancient wisdom and world knowledge, indicating that the balance of worldly power and of divine justice had shifted in its favor.

The first half of the sixth century, and particularly the era between the treaty on the Halys in 585 and the fall of Sardis to Cyrus in 547, was remembered in Greek tradition as the era of the Seven Sages.[75] Including in their number such prominent men as Thales of Miletus, Solon of Athens,

---

making nations his subjects and overthrowing their kings? . . . Who has summoned the generations from the beginning? I, the Lord, was with the first of them, and I am with those who come after. Coasts and islands saw it and were afraid, the world trembled from end to end" (Oxford Study Bible).

74. Vanderhooft 1999 characterizes the centripetal focus of imperial policy and ideology under Nebuchadnezzar, in which glory was manifested more by the works accomplished in Babylon (as in the construction of the Ziggurat of Marduk) and by the foreign kings who contributed to them, rather than by the establishment of provincial administrations on the Assyrian model. On foreigners in Babylon under Nebuchadnezzar, see Wiseman 1985, 76–86 (evidence for Lydians, 75–76, 83; Greeks, 77–78; Medes, 83; Egyptians, 78, 83).

75. Herodotus 1.29.1 notes the court of Croesus as a regular resort of the wise men of Greece. On the tradition of the Seven Sages, see Plutarch *Solon* 4–6 and Diogenes Laertius book 1; Snell 1938 collects all testimonia. Diogenes 1.22 notes that Thales was "the first to be named *sophos*, in the archonship of Damasias at Athens, as a result of which all seven were called *sophoi*, as Demetrius of Phalerum says in his treatise on the archons." The date 582 B.C.E. corresponds to the inaugural celebration of the Pythian Games. On the chronographic tradition, see Mosshammer 1976, who prefers a tradition supporting a date of ca. 580 for the naming of the Seven Sages. Fehling 1985 doubts that the Seven were so called before the time of Plato; R. P. Martin 1993 answers his skepticism. A Mesopotamian tradition of seven wise men, primordial

Chilon of Sparta, and Periander of Corinth, the fame of the Seven came in part from their travels to the courts of Sardis and Egypt, if not also to Babylon. Their collective reputation, and the favor with which several among them were received in the courts of the powerful, reflect the keen interest of this era in an understanding of the world and its relationship to orderly society, and ultimately to world sovereignty.

The Seven were reputed to have formed their association in the name of Apollo after settling the disposition of a prize that was to be awarded "to the wisest." Unlike the legendary Apple of Discord, which was to be given "to the fairest," and which, by the will of Aphrodite, led to the war between Asiatics and Achaeans at Troy, a tripod said to have been pulled from the sea bearing the inscription *To the Wisest* produced gestures of deference among these men, who passed it from hand to hand until they agreed to dedicate it in common to Apollo.[76] The Sages were certainly aware of the fall of Assyria, and were witnesses to the competing claims to supremacy of Sardis, Egypt, Babylon, and Media. They were therefore aware of the fragility of the actual supremacy of any one of these powers, and their peaceful association may reflect their awareness that true world power could come only from collaborative harmony. Here was a significant conceptual development in the relationship between world knowledge and world power.

Such a notion, on a small scale, had been the heart of a plan that Herodotus attributes to Thales for preserving Ionian independence by forming a league of Ionian cities participating in a common council at a central location.[77] Anaximander expressed the same notion on a larger scale, as the balance of cosmic justice, and on his map he displayed its practical implications for the benefit of Croesus' understanding of Lydia's place in the balance of power in the world. If, according to Anaximander, "boundless nature" ($\phi \acute{v} \sigma \iota \varsigma$ $\ddot{\alpha} \pi \epsilon \iota \rho o \varsigma$) was the origin of "all the orders [$\kappa \acute{o} \sigma \mu o \iota$]" that might arise in this world, then the only limitations on the physical extent of a sovereign power were, first, its ability to conform to justice and to benefit more than to suffer from retribution, and second, the physical extent of the *oikoumenē* that it would dominate. Human understanding could best grasp the

---

scholars, may have prompted the Greek adoption of this notion at this time of international contact: see Reiner 1961.

76. The wisdom of the Seven is associated with Delphi as early as they are attested as a group (Plato *Protagoras* 343a–b). The dedication of the tripod to Apollo at Delphi (or at Thebes, or Didyma) is related by Plutarch *Solon* 4; Diogenes Laertius 1.28–33, 82–83. Diogenes 1.32 reports a tradition that linked the tripod to the Apple of Discord, alleging that it was originally a wedding gift from Hephaestus to Pelops, and was later taken from his descendant Menelaus by Paris, and was thrown into the sea by Helen.

77. Herodotus 1.170.3 reports Thales' advice, before Alyattes had forced Miletus into submission, "to establish a single council house [*bouleutērion*] of Ionia, and for it to be at Teos, because Teos was in the middle of Ionia."

first of these conditions through some manner of consultative and deliberative process, and the second through a map of the world.

Sardis lay close to the center of the world map, as it was drawn by Anaximander, but not at the precise center, for the world was divided by waters into two great continents. Across those waters from Sardis lay Sparta, then the most powerful state in Greece. Balance across this cosmic fulcrum was symbolized by alliance between Sardis and Sparta. The harmony of their names—Greek Sardis (Attic Σάρδεις, Ionic Σάρδις or Σάρδιες) was Sfar[da-] in Lydian, Sapardu in Akkadian, Sprd in Aramaic, Sepharad in Hebrew, and Sparda in Persian—may have suggested the harmony of their interests.[78] To gain an alliance with Sparta, Croesus pursued a long-term policy of courting Spartan favor by making impressive gifts to Apollo at Delphi and to the Spartans on behalf of Apollo. Croesus intensified his efforts in this undertaking especially after the world order established under Alyattes was upset by the overthrow of the Median dynasty by Cyrus in 550.[79] As has been suggested above, Croesus' piety was probably motivated by more than a simple desire to gain the support of the strongest military power in Greece. Through Apollo Croesus was seeking an affirmation that his ambitions were consistent with just order in the world. Croesus may also have acted in accordance with a sense of cosmic balance in this union of two powers poised on either side of the center of the earth. This notion derives support from one of the few items of information left to us about the life of Anaximander.

We are told that Anaximander paid a visit to Sparta for the purpose of establishing a "solar indicator on 'The Sundials.'"[80] A solar indicator, a gnomon, was a device that could signify the relationship of the place where it was erected to the orbit of the sun through the path traced by the gnomon's shadow. Anaximander's gnomon and the monument called The Sundials were almost certainly related to the building near the agora of Sparta called The Sunshade (Skias) according to Pausanias, "where even today the Spar-

78. No ancient testimony draws attention to the harmony of names, although the ambiguity of the Spartan-Sardian identity of the poet Alcman (Alcman TA1–3, TA5–9, TA12 [Davies]; fr. 2a Edmonds LG; Suda s.v. Ἀλκμάν; Palatine Anthology 7.18, 709; Aelian Varia Historia 12.50) suggests that this connection was not neglected. The names of Sardis are given by Kent 1950, 210, s.v. Sparda-; and Gusmani LW, 201–2.

79. On Croesus' gifts to Delphi, see chapter 4 at note 50, and above at note 56. Croesus' Spartan alliance is reported by Herodotus 1.69; cf. 1.56, 65–70, 82.1, 3.47; Pausanias 4.5.3.

80. Diogenes Laertius 2.1 states that Anaximander "was the first to invent the gnomon, and he set one up on The Sundials (ἐπὶ τῶν σκιοθήρων]) in Sparta, as Favorinus says in the Miscellaneous History, to mark solstices and equinoxes; he also constructed hour-watches [or "season-watches," ὡροσκοπεῖα]" (= DK 12 A 1; cf. A 2 and A 4). The description γνώμονα . . . ἐπὶ τῶν σκιοθήρων is tautological, since both gnomon and skiothērēs refer to a sundial, or shadow caster (see Gibbs, 1976, 6); therefore it is likely that ta skiothēra, "The Sundials," is the name of a place (Kirk et al. 1983, 103), or, as argued here, a monument. On this passage see also Heidel 1921, 243–46; Hahn 2001, 207–9; Couprie 2003, 188.

tans meet in assembly; they say this *Skias* was the work of Theodorus the Samian."[81] Theodorus of Samos was a distinguished contemporary and intellectual peer of Anaximander, and was known to have worked for Croesus.[82] It is entirely plausible, therefore, that these two men came to Sparta together as representatives of Croesus and, in consummation of the Spartan alliance with him, participated in the founding of a house of assembly that included on it a conspicuous solar indicator, a gnomon (a device that the Greeks learned about from the Babylonians, according to Herodotus).[83]

A sundial and a building called the *Skias* were associated with sovereign deliberative bodies at Athens as well, in the century after Anaximander and Theodorus' visit to Sparta. The tholos (round building) built in the agora of Athens as a meeting place for the fifty *prytaneis*, the presiding board of the Athenian council, was also called the *Skias;* the meeting place of the Athenian assembly on the Pnyx was marked by the sundial erected by the astronomer Meton.[84] Before the construction of these Greek "sunshades" as meeting places for deliberative bodies, the *skias* was known in its original form as a portable royal sunshade, which was a conspicuous sign of the presence of sovereign authority in Assyrian and, later, Persian royal ceremony.[85] With the visit of Anaximander to Sparta, this symbol of sovereignty was brought

81. Pausanias 3.12.10: ἡ καλουμένη Σκιάς, ἔνθα καὶ νῦν ἔτι ἐκκλησιάζουσι. The reference by Xenophon *Hellenica* 3.3.8 to ἡ μικρὰ καλουμένη ἐκκλησία at Sparta indicates a small sovereign body that could assemble in such a building. (See Cartledge 1987, 130–31, for discussion.) The *hōrologion* of Andronicus beside the Roman agora at Athens (better known as the Tower of the Winds; see Travlos 1971, 281–88) is an elaborate Hellenistic example of a building with solar indicators that might have accommodated some body of public officials. It also illustrates how a single monument could be designated by the plural, "Sundials" (*ta skiothēra*).

82. Theodorus of Samos was the master craftsman and architect who made the silver cauldron dedicated by Croesus at Delphi (Herodotus 1.51.3), made the famous ring of Polycrates (Herodotus 3.41.1), devised the foundations for the Temple of Artemis at Ephesus (Diogenes Laertius 2.103), and wrote about the design of the Temple of Hera at Samos (Vitruvius *De Architectura* 7, preface 12). Among other achievements, Theodorus is also said to have invented (or first written about?) such tools as the architect's square (*norma*), the plumb line or level (*libella*), and the lathe (*tornus* [or compass?]: Pliny *Naturalis Historia* 7.198). Theodorus' well-attested concern for representing geometric precision in spatial form links him to the concepts embodied in Anaximander's map. (Note also that the *tornos* was allegedly the device used to draw maps like Anaximander's, according to Herodotus 4.36.2.) The intellectual kinship of Anaximander and Theodorus, among other contemporary Ionian architects, is discussed at length by Hahn 2001, 62, 72–83.

83. Heidel 1921, 246 n. 23, and Naddaf 2003, 33, also suggest that Anaximander came to Sparta as an ambassador of Croesus.

84. On the sundial of Meton, see Travlos 1971, 466. On *skias* as a name for the Athenian tholos, see *IG* II² 1013.39, 45; Harpocration s.v. θόλος; Travlos 553; Camp 1986, 76–77.

85. A decorated sunshade is sometimes held above the Assyrian king when he is on foot, and more often when he is mounted on his chariot, in reliefs of Assur-nasirpal II, Shalmaneser III, Tiglath-pileser III, Sennacherib, and Assurbanipal (ninth through seventh centuries B.C.E.). *Skias* is the term for the golden parasol under which Xerxes sat to watch his troops give battle

from the East to signify the seat of deliberative sovereignty at Sparta, the counterpart to the seat of Lydian sovereignty at Sardis, and a visible token of the cosmic relationships depicted theoretically on Anaximander's map.[86]

A gnomon, in theory, could demonstrate the relationship of a place to a map of the earth. To an observer like Anaximander, who assumed a flat earth over which the sun rose everywhere at the same time, a gnomon (a vertical rod) was a means of calculating proximity to the apparent center of the earth. The shadow cast by a gnomon at midday, its shortest shadow, indicates the local meridian (north-south line). If the sun rose over a flat earth, only the meridian actually crossing the center point of the earth would exactly bisect the angle between sunrise and sunset. By comparing readings at different points, at substantial distances across the earth, early observers like Anaximander could hope to determine which points were closer to, and which points were farther from, the apparent center of the earth. In fact, because of the sphericity of the earth, every observable meridian lies exactly midway between sunrise and sunset, a fact that would initially encourage observers to believe that they were close to the mark. Only after a long accumulation of observations at many points, however, would the futility of seeking the center of the flat earth become evident. But by the time empirical science had proceeded this far, the tradition connecting monumental solar indicators with the center of the earth was well established as a symbol of sovereignty.[87]

On the present hypothesis, the solar indicator at Sparta designed by Anaximander, installed on a structure designed by Theodorus, was a means of demonstrating how close Sparta was to the center of the earth. But this was not done in support of any claim that Sparta was exactly at the center; rather, it was done to show that, according to the premises of flat-earth astronomy, Sparta was equally as close to the center of the earth as Sardis was. This dis-

---

(Plutarch *Themistocles* 16.2). M. C. Miller 1992, 93–95, cites textual and iconographic evidence of sunshades as especially appropriate to royalty or people of high status from the Neo-Assyrian to the Persian period; M. L. West 1997, 572, cites passages from Babylonian and Assyrian texts likening the king himself to "the sun-canopy of the land," or "shade of the world-quarters."

86. Interest at this time in cosmic symbolism at Sparta is demonstrated in the Laconian cup attributed to the Arkesilas Painter depicting Atlas and Prometheus. See Yalouris 1980, 313–14; Naddaf 2003, 33–34.

87. The implications of Anaximander's flat-earth hypothesis are well appreciated by Hahn 2001, 205–10; and by Couprie 2003, 183–97. By contrast, Dicks 1966 and Gibbs 1976 are so focused on the evolution of astronomical science and the technology of later sundials that they do not recognize the implications of these early solar indicators. Regarding the symbolism of solar indicators, note that the obelisk of Psammetichus II (contemporary of Alyattes) was moved from Egypt to Rome by Augustus and placed near the Mausoleum Augusti (a funerary tumulus comparable to the Lydian tumuli) and used as the gnomon of his *horologium solare* (Pliny *Naturalis Historia* 36.72–73).

position was apparent on Anaximander's map, where the sea crossed the middle of the earth. It was implicit in this configuration that the collaboration of these two sovereign powers together, Sparta and Sardis, constituted the achievement of a cosmic balance across the center of the earth.

## THE LANDSCAPE OF CREATION AT SARDIS

Measured solar observations were something new to the Greek world in the time of Anaximander, according to later Greek recollections. Thales may have been first in this regard, as he was in other respects, since he is said to have measured the height of the Pyramids in Egypt by measuring their shadows against a standard (in effect a gnomon).[88] Both Thales and Anaximander served the Lydian tyrants of their day, so it is possible that they also employed the technology of solar indicators at Sardis, providing a basis for comparative observations made elsewhere. No explicit testimony places a sundial or solar indicator at Sardis, although a tradition ascribed to Xanthus of Lydia, a contemporary of Herodotus, records an unusual relationship between Sardis and the solar year, suggesting that there was in fact a long tradition of solar observation there.[89]

In a world where divine power was geographically situated—at a god's birthplace, an oracle, or a hero's tomb, for example—solar observations could demonstrate empirically what was already believed to be unique about the cosmic position of a significant place. At Sardis, in addition to Zeus' sacred Mount Tmolus, to the gold of the Pactolus, and to the sacred grove and shrine of Kybebe, a conjunction of features in the Hermus Plain in front of the city marked this as a special place. Below Sardis and across the Hermus Plain was the sacred Gygaean lake, and beside it a tumulus field containing the most conspicuous funerary monuments of the Lydians, first among them the Tumulus of Alyattes, "far the greatest work of human hands, outside the works of the Egyptians and the Babylonians," according to Herodotus. (See figure 9 above.) Atop the Tumulus of Alyattes stood five inscribed pillars

---

88. Reported by Diogenes Laertius 1.27, citing Hieronymus of Rhodes (= DK 11 A 1.27), and Pliny *Naturalis Historia* 36.82 (= DK 11 A 21). Thales' interest in solstices and equinoxes (Diogenes 1.23; cf. DK 11 A 2, 3) likewise implies that Thales used a *gnōmōn* to mark solar movements; see Hahn 2001, 56.

89. Ioannes Lydus *De Mensibus* 3.20, citing Xanthus of Lydia (*FGrHist* 765 F 23), reports that "it is clear from [the name of] the royal city of the Lydians that they honored the year as a god." He reports the curious fact that the name Σάρδιν (accusative of Sardis) rendered as a Greek numeral yields the number 365; he goes on, "from which it is clear, then, that from the number of days in a year the city was named 'Sardin' in honor of Helios. Even now it is agreed by most people that to say 'new Sardin' means 'new year.' There are those who say that, in the ancient Lydian language, the year is called 'Sardin.'"

(οὖροι) giving testimony, Herodotus reports, to the diverse classes of people who had contributed to the building of the monument.[90] In view of Thales' interest in Egyptian pyramids as solar indicators, it is possible that the pillars atop Alyattes' tumulus were also regarded as solar indicators marking the seasonal movements of the sun.[91]

Like the sun that is reborn each day, and whose intensity waxes and wanes with the seasons, the Tumulus of Alyattes and the other tumuli of this burial field also signified the perpetual renewal of life, and with it sovereignty. This regenerative power was signified not only by the cycles of the eternal sun, but also by the seasonal cycles of life-giving waters. Like the Pyramids beside the floodplain of the Nile, the Tumulus of Alyattes lay between the waters of the Hermus River, "which flows from the sacred mountain of Mother Dindymene,"[92] and the Gygaean lake, "said by the Lydians to be never dry."[93] The Gygaean lake was a special manifestation of waters issuing from Asian earth through the beneficence of the Mountain Mother, for it had generative properties, and even gave birth to several Maeonian (i.e., Lydian) warriors, according to the *Iliad*.[94]

The creative force identified with Lake Gygaea made it a place of special reverence. Strabo cites both Homer and Herodotus on Lake Gygaea, and reports that the lake was later renamed Koloë, where Artemis Koloëne (attested as *Artimuś Kulumsis* in Lydian inscriptions) had a shrine where rites of great sanctity (μεγάλη ἁγιστεία) were celebrated. Strabo goes on: "They say that the baskets [*kalathoi*] dance in the festivals there [or, "They say they do the basket dance in the festivals there"]; I do not understand why they speak in riddles rather than the plain truth."[95] The *kalathoi* of the basket dance of Koloë

---

90. Herodotus 1.93.2, discussed in chapter 4 at note 52. On the pillarlike funerary markers commonly referred to in modern literature as phallos markers, see McLaughlin 1985, 126–39. Although these are believed to represent the sort of οὖροι described by Herodotus, none have been found bearing inscriptions.

91. Hipponax fr. 42 (West) refers to the Tumulus of Alyattes ("Attales") marking the road "through Lydia . . . toward the setting sun" (διὰ Λυδῶν . . . πρὸς ἥλιον δύνοντα), suggesting that the royal Lydian tumulus had solar associations. J. E. Harrison 1927, 396–415, illustrates and discusses pillars atop tumuli, omphali (tombs as well as navel stones), and obelisks akin to the pillars on the Monument of Alyattes.

92. Herodotus 1.80.1. On the significance of Mount Dindymus and the Hermus River, see above, at notes 18–24.

93. Herodotus 1.93.5.

94. On the Gygaean lake as mother to two Maeonian warriors, allies of the Trojans, see *Iliad* 2.865. Note especially 20.382–92, where Achilles slays Iphition, "whom a naiad nymph bore to Otrynteus, sacker of cities, beneath snowy Tmolus in the wealthy *dēmos* of Hyde"; Achilles vaunts over him: "Lie here. . . . Here is your death, though your birth was by the lake Gygaea, where your ancestral precinct is, by the fish-filled Hyllus and swirling Hermus."

95. Strabo 13.4.5–7 (at 5: φασὶ δ' ἐνταῦθα χορεύειν τοὺς καλάθους κατὰ τὰς ἑορτάς, οὐκ οἶδ' ὅπως ποτὲ παραδοξολογοῦντες μᾶλλον ἢ ἀληθεύοντες ). Nilsson 1906, 253–55, suggests that the bas-

are probably to be identified the with mystic *cistae* depicted on the popular cistophoric coins of Asia, minted at Pergamum, Ephesus, and Sardis among other towns of Ionia, Lydia, and Phrygia, from the late third century B.C.E. well into the Roman era. The types, a serpent crawling out of a half-open basket (*cista*, or *kalathos*) surrounded by an ivy wreath, and two serpents coiled around a bow case, represent the chthonic symbols of life generated from the earth associated with the royal weapon of Asia, all evocative of the royal burials near Koloë, at the Gygaean lake.[96]

The fresh waters of the Gygaean lake, which were said to have never dried up may be recognized as a vestige of the primordial moisture that Thales is said to have posited as the first principle ($\dot{\alpha}\rho\chi\dot{\eta}$), source of generation ($\sigma\pi\dot{\epsilon}\rho\mu\alpha$), and nourishment ($\tau\rho\phi\dot{\eta}$) for all things.[97] A report that Thales considered burial (as opposed to cremation) as the appropriate way to resolve a body back to its watery origin suggests that the tumulus field by the Gygaean lake was a place where the regenerative cycles of water and life would have seemed evident to Thales.[98] The primacy of water in the cosmogony of Thales was developed by Anaximander into an account of the emergence of earth from water in a process of gradual drying, and the emergence of living creatures from aqueous into terrestrial forms.[99] Primeval slime ($\dot{\iota}\lambda\dot{\upsilon}_S$) was thus the medium of creation in Ionian philosophical thought.[100] This concept is expressed most directly at the end of the sixth century by Xenophanes of Colophon, who wrote that "all things that come into existence and

---

ket dancers of Koloë are connected with the cult of Bendis, and with Caryatids in the Peloponnesian cult of Artemis (p. 197). Hanfmann 1983b, 222, compares Artemis of Koloë to Syrian Atargatis, whose cult is also associated with sacred lakes. On *Artimuś Kulumsis*, who is named along with Artemis of Ephesus (*Artimuś Ibśimsis*) in two Lydian funerary inscriptions, see *LW* 63, 156–57; the texts are translated in Dusinberre 2003, 229 nos. 9 and 10.

96. On the mystic *cistae*, see the story of the sacred objects brought by Phrygians to Miletus: chapter 2 at notes 123–24. On the cistophoric coins of Asia see Seltman 1933, 239 and plate LVII nos. 7 and 9; Noe 1950; Woodward 1956. Jane Harrison (1927, 261–67) aptly compares the symbolism of this Asiatic coinage to the Athenian imagery of their autochthonous serpent-kings, Cecrops and Erechtheus/Erichthonius, on the Acropolis.

97. On water as a first principle to Thales, see Aristotle *Metaphysics* 1.3, 983b and Plutarch *On Isis and Osiris* 364d (see DK 11 A 11–13), where Thales is said to have learned this in Egypt. See also note 88 above.

98. Servius *ad Aen.* 11.186 (DK 11 A 13, 23–26).

99. Aristotle *Metaphysics* 1.3, 983b (DK 11 A 12) and Aetius 3.16.1 (cited under DK 12 A 27) and 5.19.4 (DK 12 A 30) describe the aqueous origins of earth and life according to the cosmogonies of Thales and Anaximander. Additional sources and commentary are provided by Kahn 1960, 63–71, 100–114; Kirk et al. 1983, 88–95 and 138–42; Naddaf 2003, 13–17.

100. The generative qualities of slime ($\dot{\iota}\lambda\dot{\upsilon}_S$) are associated with the thought of Anaximander by Kirk et al. 1983, 139–40. Archelaus of Miletus, a contemporary of Anaxagoras, "speaks of life generated from warm earth that yields milklike, nutritive slime" (Diogenes Laertius 2.17 = DK 60 A 1). The same medium of genesis is found in the Orphic cosmogony attributed to Hieronymus and Hellanicus by Damascius (DK 1 B 13).

grow are earth and water."[101] The same concept of elemental creation is reflected in the myth that mankind had been formed out of water and earth by Prometheus. Asia herself was either mother or wife of Prometheus, according to Greek sources; so it is clear that Prometheus was commonly understood to have performed his act of creation on Asian soil.[102]

The conjunction of tumulus mound and water signifying a place of primeval creation was an ancient and widespread concept. The primeval mound rising above floodwaters was both the center of the cosmos and the place of the first city, according to a Sumerian tradition known also to the Hittites. The mound as tomb rising above floodwaters, signifying both creation and the perpetual regeneration of life, was likewise characteristic of the Egyptian pyramids; such monuments marked a notional beginning or center of the earth.[103] At Babylon, the same symbolic renewal was associated with the Ziggurat (temple tower) of Bel-Marduk, which represented the temporary tomb of Marduk as a mountain, and which was the setting for the New Year festival celebrated by the king.[104] The Tower of Bel, the Ziggurat of Marduk, which was rebuilt in the time of Nebuchadnezzar (and Alyattes), was known to the Babylonians as *Etemenanki*, "the Building That Is the Foundation of Heaven and Earth," and it was built "on the heart of the *kigallu*," a word that denotes the netherworld, but which may also mean "fallow ground."[105] *Kigallu* in this context is thus another Akkadian synonym for the

---

101. Xenophanes DK 21 B 29 (from Simplicius' commentary on Aristotle's *Physics* 189.1): γῆ καὶ ὕδωρ πάντ᾽ ἐσθ᾽ ὅσα γίνοντ(αι) ἠδὲ φύονται. This and related passages are discussed in Kirk et al. 1983, 175–78.

102. Apollodorus *Library* 1.7.1 relates that Prometheus created mankind out of water and earth. On the relationship of Prometheus to Asia, see above, with note 12. Stephanus of Byzantium s.v. Ἰκόνιον relates a Phrygian story of how Zeus, after the flood of Deucalion, commanded Prometheus and Athena to fashion idols (or icons: εἴδωλα or εἰκόνας) of human beings out of clay, and caused life to be breathed into them, from which the place, Iconium, took its name. Iconium (modern Konya) is located beside a seasonal floodplain in Lycaonia or southern Phrygia. The account is cited by Jacoby *FGrHist* 800 F 3, and is possibly derived from the *Phrygiaca* of Hermogenes *FGrHist* 795 F 2.

103. On the Pure Mound of creation in Sumerian and Hittite ritual, see Haas 1994, 108. On the Egyptian pyramids representing the Primeval Hill arising from primeval waters at "the center of the earth, or at least the place round which the earth solidified," and combining solar with chthonic symbolism, see Frankfort 1948, 151–54.

104. On the tower temple of Bel-Marduk as mountain and tomb of the god, see Frankfort 1948, 321–24. On the symbolism of creation in the New Year (*Akītu*) festival, see also Jacobsen 1970, 35–37; 1976, 225–26, 230–39; J. Z. Smith 1978, 72–74; Grayson 1975, 35–36 and 131–32 on Chronicle 16, the *Akītu* Chronicle.

105. Wiseman 1985, 68, discusses these names for the Ziggurat of Marduk. On the meanings of *kigallu*, see *CAD* vol. 8, 348–49: "1. Raised platform for cultic purposes. 2. Pedestal, base (for a statue, cult object, an architectural feature made of stone, metal, brick, precious stones etc.). 3. A poetic term for the underworld." The unifying concept is that of the foundation on which an object of reverence, awe, or power (such as civilized life, and kingship) rests. The syn-

*oikoumenē,* meaning the fundament of life in this world, infused with the fertility of regenerating life and rendered beneficial to humanity through the agency of legitimate sovereignty. To the Babylonians, then, the tower of Bel-Marduk was the link between underworld and heaven, the center of the inhabited earth, and thus the balancing point of the world.

Among the Lydians, the Tumulus of Alyattes was the symbolic anchor of their sovereign's beneficent power in much the same manner as were the ancient pyramids in Egypt and the contemporary Ziggurat of Marduk at Babylon. In an era when Lydia was a peer to both Egypt and Babylon, we may also imagine that there was a certain amount of ideological rivalry invested in the interpretation of these monuments. There can be no doubt that the far greater antiquity of the traditions of Babylon and Egypt weighed against Sardis as a claimant to be the seat of cosmic centering. Opposing the weight of these traditions, therefore, the combination of a treatise on cosmology and an exposition of the form of world in the map of Anaximander provided a powerful rhetorical tool. On the map, it could be seen that neither Egypt nor Babylon stood in the center of the world as it was known, but rather that the balancing point lay closer to Sardis.

In 550, the overthrow of Astyages the Mede by Cyrus the Persian upset the balance established in 585, and marked a shift in the balance of justice and retribution that Croesus, brother-in-law of Astyages, interpreted as an opportunity in his favor. Cyrus and the Persians were outsiders, on the fringes of the *oikoumenē* at best, and were therefore pretenders when it came to the exercise of legitimate sovereignty over those settled lands whose rightful rule had been established by the Medes. Croesus and the Lydians, at this time, were at the height of their powers, with all of Ionia subservient, and with bonds of friendship and obligation tying the kings of Sparta, Egypt, and Babylon to them.[106] Croesus had good reason, therefore, to expect that the "ordering of time" (to quote Anaximander) now pointed to him as the agent of cosmic stability. Anaximander's map, as much as Apollo's ambiguous oracle about the fate of a great

---

onym *kikallū* (also *kigallū, CAD* vol. 8, 351), meaning "fallow land" (i.e., potential farmland), fits within the same semantic field. Cf. Latin *fundus* ("bottom," "foundation," and "land" or "farm") and *fundamentum* ("bottom," "foundation," "basis"). Note also Greek κρηπίς ("foundation": e.g., Herodotus 1.93.2, referring to the Tumulus of Alyattes), used figuratively of any deep foundation or beginning (e.g., Aeschylus *Persians* 815; Pindar *Pythian* 4.138; Xenophon *Memorabilia* 1.5.4); likewise βάθρον ("base," "platform": e.g., Herodotus 1.183.1, referring to the base of the statue of Bel-Marduk at Babylon; also used figuratively, Pindar *Olympian* 13.6), whence βόθρος ("pit," especially one giving access to the underworld, as in *Odyssey* 10.517, 11.25). M. L. West 1997, 584, compares *kigallu* to the use of πυθμήν ("base") and θέμεθλα (or θεμείλια, "foundation") in Greek poetry; cf. also Benveniste 1973, 381, who relates θέμεθλα and θεμείλια to θέμις and θεσμός, "that which is laid down (as custom)."

106. On the empire of Croesus and the extent of his alliances, see Herodotus 1.77; Xenophon *Cyropaedia* 6.2.9–11. On the questionable status of the Persians within the *oikoumenē,* see the warning of Sandanis to Croesus, Herodotus 1.71.2–4.

empire, must have encouraged Croesus to set in motion the forces that he expected would make him the rightful ruler of the entire *oikoumenē*.[107]

## THE PURIFICATION OF DELOS

The unexpected defeat of Croesus at the hands of Cyrus and the fall of Sardis to the Persians are the centerpiece of book 1 of Herodotus' *Histories,* dramatizing its lesson on the transience of human greatness. In chapter 1 of the present work, the fall of Lydia was identified as the passing of an age of innocence for the Greeks. The Mermnad tyrants had been widely admired for their wealth, power, and godlike doings, and the collapse of their rulership challenged traditional understandings of all these constituents of tyranny. After the fall of Croesus, tyranny found new modes of expression, reflected particularly in new ways of expressing the relationship between sovereignty and the gods. Historical developments surrounding the cult of Delian Apollo provide a case in point.

The earliest explicit testimony to a relationship between tyranny and the cult of Delian Apollo belongs to the aftermath of the fall of Lydia. Peisistratus of Athens and Polycrates of Samos are both remembered for their attention to Apollo's birthplace on the island of Delos. In the developing framework of Ionian geography, Delos, lying midway between Europe and Asia, appeared to be at the center of the world. Anaximander's map may have suggested that Delos occupied this special place, and the spectacular fall of Sardis seems to have encouraged belief that this actually was the case. The few facts reported to us about the symbolic acts undertaken in turn by Peisistratus and Polycrates at Delos lend support to the notion that the fall of Sardis gave rise to a new age for Delos, emphasizing the unique significance of the island in the cosmos.

Peisistratus established his tyranny for the third and final time probably in the year 546/5, the year following the capture of Sardis in the fall of 547.[108] After describing the events that returned Peisistratus to power, Herodotus states that he "gave firm roots to his tyranny" (ἐρρίζωσε τὴν τυραννίδα) by hiring mercenaries, by taking hostages from the families of his rivals, and by purifying the sanctuary of Apollo on Delos (1.64). The first two, the more

107. Apollo's oracles to Croesus: Herodotus 1.53–56, 71.1, 90–91. Measured by the standards of legitimate power and influence over the *oikoumenē*, Croesus' empire should have been readily identified as the only truly "great empire" (μεγάλη ἀρχή) in existence, and accordingly the only one that could be destroyed.

108. On the chronology of the Peisistratid tyranny I accept the conclusions of P. J. Rhodes 1981, 191–99. On the date of the fall of Sardis, I favor the view that the fragmentary passage in year nine (autumn 547) of the Nabonidus Chronicle (col. 2, lines 16–18) refers to the defeat and capture of Croesus by Cyrus; see Grayson 1975, 21 and 107; notwithstanding the strong cautions of Cargill 1977.

practical measures, can be clearly understood in political and military terms. The third, a more symbolic action, has seemed opaque. Scholars have been able to do little more than state the self-evident by explaining the action as an effort by Peisistratus to show himself to be a good Ionian, or to foster cults for political ends, or to engage in the competitive sport of powerful men in the display of piety.[109] Why should a display of piety for the purpose of giving "firm roots to tyranny" take this particular form?

Herodotus explains that what Peisistratus did was to "purify the island of Delos in accordance with oracular utterances" by removing burials "within sight of the shrine" to another part of the island.[110] The removal of human burials from the area of Apollo's birth thus disrupted an older custom that associated death and burial with divine birth. This is the pattern we have noted at Sardis, where the most famous burial ground for Lydian nobility and kings was set in a landscape of creation.

The sacred topography of Delos replicated landmarks of Sardis in a manner strongly suggesting that the archaic cult on Delos was shaped by Asiatic custom. Leto gave birth to Apollo on Delos by the side of a marshy lake, reminiscent of the life-giving waters of the Gygaean lake; and like the mound of Alyattes near the lake at Sardis, the site on Delos was overlooked by a tumuluslike mound, Mount Cynthus, associated with Zeus.[111] Like Artemis Koloëne at Sardis, Artemis on Delos had a celebrated cult, despite the fact that traditions vary about whether or not Artemis was born with her brother on Delos.[112] On Delos as at Sardis, the divine Mother gave birth and nurture to the young warrior god; a community of worshippers gathered to honor

---

109. To be "a good Ionian": Laidlaw 1933, 58. A "policy of fostering cults for political ends": Shapiro 1989, 48. "Competitive sport": R. Parker 1996, 88. On the date of the purification of Delos (ca. 545–540) see Shapiro (48); for the archaic temple to Apollo on Delos possibly associated with Peisistratus, see Bruneau and Ducat 1966, 82 no. 11; Boersma 1970, 17–18 and 169 no. 34.

110. Herodotus 1.64.2; see also Thucydides 3.104.1, reporting the second purification of Delos by the Athenians in 426/5.

111. Theognis 8 describes the birth of Apollo on Delos "beside the wheellike [i.e., round] lake" (ἐπὶ τροχοειδέϊ λίμνῃ). *Homeric Hymn* 3, *To Apollo* 16–18, describes the birth of Apollo on Delos "by the long hill and Cynthian mound, nearest the palm tree, by the streams of Inopus" (πρὸς μακρὸν ὄρος καὶ Κύνθιον ὄχθον ἀγχοτάτω φοίνικος, ἐπ' Ἰνωποῖο ῥεέθροις). Euripides *Iphigeneia in Taurus* 1097–1104 refers to Artemis "who dwells by the Cynthian mound and the rich-bowered palm tree . . . and the lake with circling waters" (ἃ παρὰ Κύνθιον ὄχθον οἰκεῖ φοίνικά θ' ἀβροκόμαν . . . λίμναν θ' εἰλίσσουσαν ὕδωρ κύκλιον). See also Herodotus 2.170.2 for the comparison of the lake on Delos to an Egyptian lake in a sanctuary of Athena (Neith) associated with the (unmentionable) rites of Osiris. On Mount Cynthus as a cult place of Zeus, see sources collected by Laidlaw 1933, 154, 158–59, and 165; see also Bruneau and Ducat 1966, 148–53. This tumuluslike mountain is reminiscent of the Ziggurat of Marduk, which represented the temporary tomb of Marduk as a mountain. See note 104 above.

112. On the early archaic cult of Artemis and her cult place at Delos, see Bruneau and Ducat 1966, 16–17, 27, and 100–101; Coldstream 1977, 215, 330. Artemis is said to have been born

the event and the place most famously in choral dances; and the community memorialized its eternal bond with these symbols by placing its burial ground there. Before Peisistratus, burial on Delos signified participation in an ideology that celebrated a unique link between humanity and divinity, and especially with the divine paradigm of sovereignty.

According to Thucydides, the burials removed from Delos were Carian, recognizable as such because of the manner of burial and the style of the weapons found in them.[113] Herodotus and Thucydides both attest a tradition that associated the early settlement of the Cycladic Islands with Carians under the leadership of Cretan Minos, another celebrated archetype of sovereignty.[114] Herodotus also reports that the Carians themselves celebrated close kinship with the Lydians and Mysians, sharing with them the cult of Carian Zeus.[115] Regardless, therefore, of the accuracy of Thucydides' identification of the graves on Delos as Carian, and of the association of these Carians with the legendary rulership of Minos, it is clear that the Greeks remembered what Peisistratus did as the effacement of an Asiatic tradition at Delos.

By uprooting the dead, Peisistratus assured that no people of this earth could appropriate this sacred spot to legitimize their own dynastic tyranny. No living ruler could claim descent from the god, or from the god's divine Mother, by appealing to the monuments of his ancestors surrounding the god's own birthplace. In the aftermath of the fall of Lydia, Peisistratus was dismantling a key part of the Lydian paradigm for divinely engendered tyranny. His own leadership was strengthened by removing the opportunity for any rival to lay claim to power through this traditional means.[116] In the process, Delian Apollo was being transformed from the divine image of a living tyrant into a more abstract advocate of communal sovereignty.

---

on Ortygia as distinct from Delos in *Homeric Hymn* 3, *To Apollo* 15; Artemis is said to have been born with Apollo on Delos by Pindar (*Prosodion to Delos* fr. 87 [Sandys], quoted by Strabo 10.5.2) and by Herodotus 6.97.2 (reporting the words of Datis). Strabo records the various traditions about the location of Ortygia, from a sacred grove near Ephesus (14.1.20), to the island of Rheneia near Delos (10.5.5), to the island acropolis of Syracuse (6.3.4). Ortygia became Delos, and was the birthplace of both Artemis and Apollo, according to Apollodorus *Library* 1.4.1.

113. Thucydides 1.8.1. Archaeological evidence from the so-called purification pit on Rheneia has revealed that the burial goods removed from graves on Delos are chiefly late Geometric and archaic in date, and are Cycladic in character. See R. M. Cook 1955, 267–70; Bruneau and Ducat 1966, 61–63; Coldstream 1977, 213–16.

114. Herodotus 1.171.1–3. Thucydides 1.4.1 and 1.8.1–2 associates the thalassocracy of Minos with the expulsion or subjugation of Carian islanders.

115. Herodotus 1.171.5. On the cult of Carian Zeus in Lydia, see Bengisu 1996.

116. Peisistratus' interest in the symbolism of Delos was no doubt influenced by his alliance with Lygdamis, whom he installed in power on Naxos, an island that had a long history of patronage to Delian Apollo. On Lygdamis, see Herodotus 1.61.4, 64.2, and Aristotle *Politics* 1305a40–42. On Naxian connections with Delos, see Bruneau and Ducat 1966, 17, 40–43; 77–81; Coldstream 1977, 213–15; note also the connection between Naxos and Delos in the

## THE RULERSHIP OF THE SEA

Not long after Peisistratus, Polycrates of Samos laid claim to this symbol in a more ambitious manner. While the tokens of cosmogonic creation at Sardis were the basis for extending a claim of sovereignty over the *oikoumenē* on earth, Delos was maritime, not of the continental earth. In fact, according to an account endorsed by Pindar, Delos was a heavenly body set on the face of the sea—it had, therefore, a genesis independent of the one that saw land emerge from the water of the Gygaean lake.[117] This notion that Delos was an astral body come to earth was surely the origin of the notion that it was a floating island.[118] By ceremonially tying Delos to the nearby island of Rheneia, Polycrates himself assumed a role in completing the cosmic order, giving astral Delos a terrestrial anchor.[119] This was also the occasion on which Polycrates disseminated a newly articulated theogony of the god, in what we know as the *Homeric Hymn 3, To Apollo*.

*Homeric Hymn 3* tells of the birth of Apollo on Delos and the foundation of his sanctuary, and then, in a discrete second part, tells of his arrival in and appropriation of Pytho (Delphi), and of the foundation of his most famous temple and oracular shrine. In this manner, the composite hymn celebrates the renown of Pythian Apollo, but makes it secondary to Apollo's Delian origin. The essential unity of the *Homeric Hymn to Apollo* is widely recognized,

---

legend of Theseus: Plutarch *Theseus* 20–21. It is probably relevant that the family of Isagoras, a chief contender for power after the fall of the Peisistratid dynasty at Athens, was known to maintain the cult of Carian Zeus (Herodotus 5.66.1).

117. Pindar *Paean* 5, *For the Athenians to Delos*, strophe 7, says that Apollo gave the Ionians Delos, "the body of Asteria, to inhabit" (δᾶκεν... Ἀστερίας δέμας οἰκεῖν). Known to Hesiod *Theogony* 409 as a sister of Leto, Asteria is said by Callimachus *Hymn* 4, *To Delos* 36–38, to have plunged from heaven into the sea "like a star," while Apollodorus *Library* 1.4.1 says that Asteria dove into the sea and became the polis known first as Asteria, later Delos. Pindar reflects this tradition of a heavenly origin for the island in his *Prosodion to Delos*, strophe 1 (fr. 87 Sandys), where he hails the island as "god-built . . . daughter of the sea, unmoved marvel of the wide earth that mortals call Delos, but that the blessed gods of Olympus call the far-seen star of dark-blue earth" (τηλέφατον κυανέας χθονὸς ἄστρον). See Laidlaw 1933, 4 and 20 n. 5, summarizing the interpretations of this passage favored by Wilamowitz and Farnell.

118. The earliest reference to Delos as floating is Pindar *Prosodion to Delos*, strophe 2 (fr. 88 Sandys), where the island is "borne by waves and wind" (φορητὰ κυμάτεσσιν παντοδαπῶν ἀνέμων ῥιπαῖσιν) until the arrival of Leto gives the island secure foundations in the form of "four columns rising from the roots of the earth" (τέσσαρες ὀρθαὶ πρέμνων ὄρουσαν χθονίων); cf. Callimachus *Hymn* 4, *To Delos* 51–54. The notion that Delos was a floating island is echoed in Herodotus' account (2.156) of the floating island of Chemmis in Egypt, where Leto saved Apollo, and where a temple of Apollo (Horus) stood.

119. Thucydides 3.104.2 reports that Polycrates had dedicated Rheneia to Apollo by joining Delos to Rheneia with a chain (cf. 1.13.6). Similarly, when Nicias reinaugurated the Delian festival, probably in 426, he landed first on Rheneia, and entered Apollo's shrine by ceremoniously crossing from Rheneia to Delos on a bridge of boats (Plutarch *Nicias* 3.5).

and the most likely occasion for its original performance was the joint celebration of the Pythian and Delian festivals of Apollo by Polycrates of Samos,
probably in 522.[120] The original performance of this double hymn may well
have mimicked the itinerary of the god himself, starting from Delos and ending at Delphi.

The deeds of Polycrates at Delos are famous, but if the consensus that he
also honored Pythian Apollo in the hymn is correct, then it is remarkable
that his devotion to Apollo at Delphi is otherwise obscure. An explanation
emerges when the connection between Polycrates and the Treasury of the
Siphnians at Delphi is recognized. This elaborate Cycladic monument was
built in the 520s, at very the time when Polycrates was reaching the height
of his influence, and when the Siphnians were among the islanders under
his sway.[121] By all accounts, ancient and modern, the treasury was an extraordinary dedication for such a minor island. The quality and iconographic
richness of its elaborate friezes have made it a major landmark in archaic
Greek art.[122] If, however, it was promoted by Polycrates, it would have
demonstrated his Panionian leadership and its Panhellenic pretensions,
echoing, in this regard, the implications of the *Homeric Hymn to Apollo*. The
sudden decline of Siphnian fortunes would correspond with the demise of
Polycrates himself.[123] The personal ambitions of Polycrates came to nothing
in the end, but the Siphnian monument remained to amaze visitors to Delphi for centuries thereafter. Polycrates' Panhellenism, ironically, may have

120. The unity of the *Homeric Hymn to Apollo* is defended on historical grounds by Burkert
1979b and 1987, 54; and on thematic grounds by A. M. Miller 1985 and Clay 1989, 17–92.
Burkert 1979b, 58–62, advances strong arguments for dating the composition to the celebration of the Pythia and Delia by Polycrates in 522; see also Parke 1946; R. Parker 1996, 88 n.
86. Janko 1982, 99–132, defends the independent composition of the Delian and Pythian hymns
(he relies heavily on historical deductions that I find much less convincing than the arguments
of Burkert; see 112–14, 127–28), but he sees both "cobbled together" probably at the time of
Polycrates' celebration on Delos (113–14).

121. Herodotus 3.57.2 is key testimony on the Siphnian Treasury; on the importance of
this evidence for archaic stylistic chronology, see Ridgway 1977, 8–9; Sparkes 1991, 3–6; Biers
1992, 100 n. 9. Herodotus 3.57–58 shows that the Siphnians who dedicated this treasury to
Apollo were enemies of the enemies of Polycrates (i.e., most likely his allies); Siphnos is surely
to be included among the "other islands" (in addition to Rheneia) over which Polycrates exercised some form of rulership, according to Thucydides 1.13.6 and 3.104.2.

122. The cosmogonic significance of the Gigantomachy on the north frieze of the treasury
is discussed in chapter 9. L. Vance Watrous (1982, 162–66) has interpreted imagery of the Siphnian frieze as indicative of an anti-Athenian outlook, yet these images work equally well as pro-
Samian tokens. (Among the giants battling against the gods are those with helmet emblems associating them with Naxos, Paros, and Eretria, all of them rivals to Samos.)

123. Herodotus 3.57.3 follows his account of Siphnian wealth with an oracle warning of its
imminent end. Pausanias 10.11.2 attributes the end of Siphnian prosperity to the flooding of
their mines, brought on by divine retribution for greed. Both stories echo the fate of Polycrates,
as told by Herodotus.

succeeded in obscuring even his own memory. For after the time of Poly-crates it was more appropriate to honor the glory of a prospering commu-nity than that of a prospering tyrant. It was no longer the age of the throne of Midas, the treasures of Gyges, or the gold of Croesus.

Herodotus and Thucydides both draw attention to Polycrates' grandiose ambitions. As Herodotus puts it: "Polycrates was the first of the Greeks whom we know of who had designs to be ruler of the sea, with the exception of Mi-nos of Cnossus."[124] The reference to Minos as predecessor to Polycrates was surely influenced by the propaganda put on by Polycrates in 522, and is reflected in the *Homeric Hymn to Apollo,* where the cult of Pythian Apollo at Delphi is said to have been instituted, under Apollo's guidance, by Cretan sailors come "from Cnossus, city of Minos."[125] By this account, even the Pythian cult was by its very origin beholden to a maritime patron. Although he himself is not named in the public displays he sponsored, Polycrates left no doubt among his contemporaries and to posterity that he was the heir and champion of that maritime heritage.

The grandiose nature of Polycrates' schemes surely made him suscepti-ble to the idea of an alliance with the lord of Sardis at that time, the Persian Oroetes.[126] Such an alliance, joining the Lydian heritage of lordship on earth with Polycrates' claim to dominion of the sea, had a cosmic logic similar to the one that had earlier drawn the Spartans, the champions of European Hellas, into alliance with Croesus, the champion of Asia. Herodotus' story of the ominous dream of Polycrates' daughter and of warnings from friends against this alliance reflects the widespread awareness of how high the stakes were.[127] The horror of Polycrates' death by crucifixion at the hands of Oroetes, within a year of this celebration on Delos, was a measure both of his megalomania and of his nearly unparalleled magnificence among Greek tyrants, according to Herodotus.[128] The fate of Polycrates provided a lesson in how the mighty fall that is second only to the story of Croesus in its the-matic importance to Herodotus' narrative, each story foreshadowing the greater drama that spanned the reigns of Darius and Xerxes.

## HECATAEUS' MAP

The Persian conquest of the "great empire" of Croesus in 547, followed by the capture of Babylon in 539, elevated Cyrus to the position of world ruler

124. Herodotus 3.122.2. Cf. Thucydides 1.13.6, 3.104.2.

125. *Homeric Hymn 3, To Apollo* 393.

126. On Oroetes, see Herodotus 3.120–26 (also discussed below at notes 134–36).

127. Herodotus 3.124–25, where the dream follows "many warnings from prophecies and from friends" against the venture.

128. Herodotus 3.125.2–3 calls the death of Polycrates an end "unworthy of his ambitions [φρονήματα)]" and his nearly unrivaled magnificence (μεγαλοπρεπείη).

and bringer of order that Nebuchadnezzar had once coveted, and that Croesus had tried to grasp.[129] At Sardis and at Babylon, Cyrus brought the two great centers of the *oikoumenē* under his sole sovereignty, and his son Cambyses added Egypt. Under the reign of Darius I (522–486 B.C.E.), this new world order was consolidated, organized, and described in lists that manifested the power of Darius, king of kings.[130] Darius was also responsible for sending his agents by sea to the east and west of his domains, gathering information about the nature of the world beyond.[131] These acts of description, in Herodotus' account, were prelude to Darius' endeavors to bring those parts of the world within his dominion.

At the same time that Darius was working to bring the *oikoumenē* under one sovereign king of kings, Hecataeus of Miletus was preparing a new Greek map of the world.[132] Compared to the map of Anaximander, Hecataeus' work is said to have been a marvel of detail, and it gave him the reputation of being widely traveled.[133] Most notable is the fact, observed at the beginning of this chapter, that the map of Hecataeus and the written commentary that ac-

129. At Babylon, the swift canonization of Cyrus as restorer of order, supported by Marduk, is a notable feature of both the Babylonian records (Beaulieu 1989, 224–32; Chronicle 7, the Nabonidus Chronicle, col. 3, lines 12–28, Grayson 1975, 109–11 [= *ANET* 306–7]), and likewise of biblical accounts, where Cyrus is "God's shepherd" and even "messiah" (Isaiah 44:28, 45:1). In both cases, Cyrus was accepted and praised as divinity's agent of retribution.

130. Herodotus 3.89–95 describes the regularization of satrapies and their revenues among the first acts of Darius after securing the kingship. Monumental lists of satrapies and subject peoples were displayed beginning under Darius, most famously in the Behistun Inscription (1.6), as well as in the Persepolis inscriptions of Darius and his successors. (For texts and translations, see Kent 1950, 116–56.) The manifestation of power through lists was also graphically displayed in the sculpted reliefs of throne bearers and tribute bearers at Persepolis and at Naqsh-i-Rustam, to which even the inscriptions call attention: DNa, section 4: "If thou now shall think that 'How many are the countries which King Darius held?' look at the sculptures (of those) who bear the throne, then shalt thou know, then shall it become known to thee" (Kent 138). Briant 2002, 172–83, describes the characteristics of this form of imperial display.

131. Herodotus 3.134–38 (expedition of Democedes and Persians to the West); 4.44 (expedition of Scylax in the Indian Ocean).

132. Herodotus 5.36.2 refers to the occasion, ca. 500, when Hecataeus "enumerated all the nations that Darius ruled, and the power at his disposal," indicating Hecataeus' close familiarity with the documents published by Darius (above, note 130). On this basis, Jacoby 1912, cols. 2670–71, concludes that Hecataeus' geographical treatise was composed after 516 and before 500. On Hecataeus' geographical writing generally, see Pearson 1939, 25–96; Gehrke 1998, 178–86.

133. Agathemerus 1.1 (= Hecataeus *FGrHist* 1 T 12a; quoted by Kirk et al. 1983, 104), cited above in note 28, where the quotation continues: "after whom [i.e., after Anaximander] Hecataeus the Milesian, a widely traveled man, refined [the map], so that it was a marvelous thing." On Hecataeus as successor to Anaximander, see also Strabo 1.1.1 (= *FGrHist* 1 T 11a), and see Jacoby 1912, col. 2690; Heidel 1937, 51; Pearson 1939, 18 and 28; Lesky 1966, 164, 220; Gehrke 1998, 177–78; Gorman 2001, 83–85.

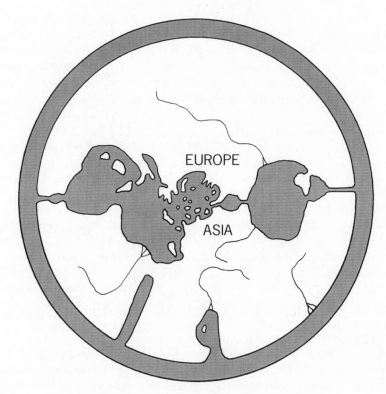

Figure 13. Conjectural rendering of the map of Hecataeus.

companied it provide the earliest certain instance of the name Asia applied to the entire continental mass across the sea from Greece. And this, in turn, corresponds to the earliest evidence for the designation of the continent facing Asia as Europe. (For a hypothetical rendering, see figure 13.)

By applying the Lydian name Asia to the entire continental mass, the bulk of which was now dominated by the Persian empire, Hecataeus was affirming the Lydo-Ionian worldview that Anaximander had begun to depict. This was a worldview that saw Sardis as the true capital of an Asiatic empire. The Persians were well aware of the symbolism of Sardis, and there are indications that they were interested in utilizing its symbolism for their own imperial designs, rather than replacing or effacing it.

Oroetes, satrap of Sardis from the reign of Cyrus until the beginning of Darius' reign, seems to have had designs to make Sardis the capital of his own empire. In the waning of Cambyses' short reign, Oroetes began murdering his closest rivals, Mitrobates the satrap of Dascyleum and Polycrates the tyrant of Samos.[134] By the time Darius had emerged victorious in Media and Persia against other contenders for the throne, Oroetes was well established at Sardis, where he "held the Phrygian, Lydian, and Ionian sway."[135] Darius now recognized Oroetes as his most serious rival, according to Herodotus, and only after putting their closest supporters to a perilous test of loyalty did Darius prevail and have him put to death.[136]

Had Oroetes prevailed, as lord of Sardis he would not only have become ruler of the domains previously won by Cyrus, but he would also have been well positioned to bring the settled lands to the west under his rule. The idea of wider conquest in Europe that Darius later put in motion, according to Herodotus, came to him from a Greek at the court of Oroetes, Democedes of Croton. Democedes had originally been a companion of Polycrates of Samos, and after he came to the attention of Darius, Democedes was sent by the king to carry out a coastal reconnaissance in the West, as far as southern Italy.[137] It thus becomes clear that, in the reign of Darius, leading men of Sardis and Ionia were still articulating the vision of an empire of the *oikoumenē* as it had been seen by the Mermnad tyrants of Lydia. This vision was centered not at Median Ecbatana, Elamite Susa, or the newly created capital of Darius at Persepolis, but either at Sardis itself, or in the waters that divided Europe from Asia, among the Cycladic Islands of the Aegean.

The influence of the Lydo-Ionian worldview, first articulated by Anaximander and displayed in greater detail by Hecataeus, must explain why it was relatively easy for Aristagoras, ruler of Miletus, to persuade Artaphernes, the satrap of Sardis, that the conquest of Naxos was the key to the subjugation of the surrounding islands and why, above all, this was a worthy invest-

---

134. Herodotus 3.120–26.

135. Herodotus 3.127: Oroetes εἶχε δὲ νομὸν τόν τε Φρύγιον καὶ Λύδιον καὶ Ἰωνικόν. Although *nomos* is sometimes used as a synonym for "satrapy" or "province" (so 3.89–90), it is also used as a synonym for *archē* "[place of] rule," "dominion." Oroetes' *nomos* was more than a Persian administrative district, for it comprised at least the first three, possibly also the fourth and the nineteenth, of the *nomoi* listed by Herodotus 3.90–94, and at least three, possibly five, of the provinces listed by Darius, Behistun 1.6 ("those of the Sea, Sparda [Sardis], Ionia," and possibly "Armenia, Cappadocia": Kent 1950, 117, 119).

136. Herodotus 3.127–28. Although Darius exalted himself by showing his triumph over rivals, the challenge posed by Oroetes was never mentioned by Darius in the Behistun Inscription or in any other monument (as noted by Olmstead 1948, 110–11; Briant 2002, 115). Perhaps it was too damaging to Darius' authority to admit that Sardis and the provinces of western Asia had not been loyal.

137. Herodotus 3.129–37. Griffiths 1987 argues that the "picaresque" aspects of Democedes' story reveal Herodotus' account of him to be "largely fictitious" (37), although he concedes that "the residual *curriculum vitae* is very probably accurate" (40). The present study demonstrates the plausibility of what Griffiths refuses to believe (and Briant 2002, 139, 143, doubts), namely that an educated Greek like Democedes could have brought grandiose ideas of world conquest with him to Darius' court.

ment of the king's resources.[138] Likewise, a decade after the failure of that enterprise, the same considerations of cosmic geography must explain why Artaphernes and Datis were so solicitous about the sanctity of the island of Delos. On their way to subdue Eretria and Athens in 490, they landed on Delos, declared their reverence for the birthplace of Apollo and Artemis, and "burned an offering of three hundred talents of frankincense heaped on the altar."[139] Control of the symbolic center, through ritual appropriation, was key to securing sovereignty over the balance of the world, through an itinerary of conquest.

The earliest historically attested use of a map of the world, which almost certainly was Hecataeus' map, was to show the way to conquer the world. In the year 501 or 500 B.C.E., Aristagoras traveled from Miletus to Sparta bringing with him a "bronze tablet [πίναξ] on which the itinerary of the entire earth [γῆς ἁπάσης περίοδος] was inscribed."[140] *Periodos gēs*, "itinerary of the earth," is the name by which Hecataeus' map and two geographical books, *Europe* and *Asia*, were generally known.[141] A descriptive itinerary, illustrated by the map drawn on the bronze tablet, was the centerpiece of Herodotus' account of Aristagoras at Sparta.

Aristagoras' proposal opened with an appeal to the Spartan king Cleomenes to "rescue your Ionian kinsmen from slavery [to the Persians] in the name of the gods of the Greeks." Aristagoras then went on to describe the nature of the undertaking:[142]

> "The barbarians are not warlike, while you have reached the peak of proficiency in war. . . . And those who inhabit that continent have more good things than all other peoples put together, starting with gold, silver, and bronze, embroidered clothing, beasts of burden, and slaves—whatever your hearts desire, you can have! I will demonstrate how they are situated in relation to each other.
>
> "From the Ionians the Lydians lie here; they inhabit good land and have more money than anyone." So saying, he pointed to the itinerary of the earth that he had brought, inscribed on a bronze tablet. "Now from the Lydians,"

---

138. Herodotus 5.30–32. On Naxian influence at Delos, see above, note 116.

139. Herodotus 6.97–99, 118. Herodotus 6.98 underscores the significance of this occasion by mentioning a unique earthquake that afterward shook Delos and the oracle predicting it. (The earthquake is also mentioned by Thucydides 2.8.3.) Briant 2002, 158–59, recognizes that the capture of Naxos and the offerings of Datis on Delos were elements in the systematic execution of "Persian ideological strategy."

140. Herodotus 5.49.1. Jacoby 1912, col. 2669, concurs that the map displayed by Aristagoras was "höchst wahrscheinlich die Erdkarte des H[ekataios]."

141. On the divisions of Hecataeus book and map, see note 1 above. Jacoby 1912, cols. 2670–72, collects and discusses the sources bearing on the title of Hecataeus' geographical work; he believes that the name *Periodos Gēs* originated with Herodotus, although he offers no compelling reason why the name cannot be older. Pearson 1939, 25–96, provides a clear review of the fragmentary remains of Hecataeus' writings.

142. Herodotus 5.49.3–7.

Aristagoras explained, "the Phrygians live here, toward the dawn; they are the richest in cattle and crops of all people that I know. Next after the Phrygians come the Cappadocians, whom we call Syrians. Sharing a border with them are the Cilicians, who live here, beside the sea, in which the island of Cyprus lies; they pay an annual tribute of five hundred talents to the king. After the Cilicians come the Armenians, here, and they are rich in cattle, and after the Armenians are the Matieni, in this country. After them comes this land, Cissia, in which Susa lies beside this river, the Choaspes; here the Great King usually stays, and keeps his money and treasure. Once you have taken this city, nothing will keep you from rivaling Zeus himself for wealth!"

No other episode in Herodotus' account so clearly shows the meaning of a map of the world in this age of empire building. The descriptions that Herodotus gives elsewhere of the benefits of conquest often echo this passage in ways suggesting that, whenever world conquest was under discussion, a map of the *oikoumenē* was close at hand. Such is the case, for example, when Herodotus reports the deliberations of Xerxes and the speeches of his advisors, as they contemplated the prospect of a war of conquest against Greece.[143] So too, in the comedies of Aristophanes, we find descriptions of the world, and in one case a map, presented as the opening argument to show a would-be sovereign, in comic manner, the whole world that he is to tyrannize.[144] In the most famous case, maps of Sicily, the sea around it, and all the lands bordering the sea as far as the Pillars of Heracles were produced in abundance as the Athenians became captivated by the idea of conquering Sicily.[145]

A map showing a *periodos* of the *oikoumenē*, by its very nature, displayed lands suitable for conquest. But to shift the balance of sovereign power in the world one had to act in accordance with the order (*kosmos*) of the world, and the will of the gods. In the terms laid out by Anaximander, conquest had to proceed in accordance with the natural movement of the forces of justice and retribution, and with the ordering of time, the forces that brought balance to the world. These terms were laid out in Anaximander's writings, displayed graphically on his map, and intended for the reflection of deliberative bodies like Thales' hypothetical council of Ionian cities, or the Spartans who met in the *Skias,* or later the *prytaneis* of Athens. To disseminate the same mes-

144. Aristophanes presents descriptions of the world as prelude to tyranny in *Knights* 168–78; *Wasps* 700–702, 707–11; *Birds* 175–86. The display of a diagram of the *periodos gēs* in Aristophanes *Clouds* 206–17 immediately turns the pseudoscientific discussion into a distinctly militaristic vein. Gehrke 1998, 187, observes the significance of such maps to the audience: "Er denkt an die Weltherrschaft."

145. Plutarch *Nicias* 12.1–2; *Alcibiades* 17.1–3. Curiously, although he recognizes the imperial ambitions implicit in the display of maps in comedy (above, note 144), Gehrke does not regard the interest in geography to be a serious intellectual pursuit, but rather to be "müßige Tätigkeit einer die Muße pflegenden Elite, einer 'leisure class'" (187).

sage across a wider segment of the public required visible tokens of cosmic order and divine will. And so, to array Greek and especially Spartan opinion to support his vision of sovereignty, Croesus had consulted the oracles of Greece, had rewarded their cooperation by his astonishingly lavish gifts, and had established in the *Sundials* at Sparta conspicuous tokens of the cosmic balance that he envisioned in harmonious relations between Sparta and Sardis. For similar reasons, Peisistratus, Polycrates, and Datis the Mede all later made public displays of their devotion to Apollo and Artemis at Delos.

When Aristagoras appealed to Cleomenes at Sparta, the map he displayed in support of his argument served to illustrate both geographical realities and an ideological justification. He must have been aware that he was addressing men who had learned to think of the world in terms of the Lydo-Ionian model, and he would therefore have assumed that the Spartans could envision themselves fulfilling a role that earlier had been the vision of Croesus. Aristagoras miscalculated, however. Instead of viewing the fall of Lydia as an opportunity to challenge Persia for the leadership of the *oikoumenē* (as Croesus had viewed the fall of the Medes), the Spartans saw the fall of Lydia as a warning against disturbing balance in the world.[146] The Spartans had been able to understand the balance inherent in their cooperation with the lords of Sardis, whose seat lay just three days' march from the coast of Ionia; it is conceivable that they could envision a role in which they would assume power on both sides of the fulcrum of the world, around the Aegean. But the idea of extending their power as far as Susa was manifestly at odds with the balance of the world. For these are the terms in which Aristagoras' appeal was rejected by Cleomenes: "Begone from Sparta, Milesian stranger, before the sun sets; for you speak no harmonious reason to the Lacedaemonians when you propose to lead them on a three-month march from the sea!"[147] Although unexpressed practical considerations may have influenced his decision, Cleomenes rejected Aristagoras in terms that were immediately comprehensible in terms of the map of the world.

Aristagoras had made his appeal to the Spartans in the name of the gods of the Greeks (πρὸς θεῶν τῶν Ἑλληνίων).[148] But the Spartans may have con-

---

146. Spartan sensibility about limits is already revealed in the Spartan command presented at Sardis, "forbidding Cyrus, by decree of the Spartans, from harming any city on Greek soil" (Herodotus 1.152).

147. Herodotus 5.50.3. "No harmonious reason" is οὐδένα λόγον εὐπέα. The word εὐπής, "well-spoken," consistently conveys the sense "melodious," "harmonious," "balanced": see the examples cited in LSJ s.v.

148. Herodotus 5.49.3. For the phrase θεοὶ οἱ Ἑλλήνιοι, see 5.92g (the appeal of Socles the Corinthian to the Spartans to reject tyranny, discussed above, chapter 4, with note 62); cf. the similar expressions at 2.178.2, 4.108, 8.144, 9.7a, and 9.90.2. On the emerging concept of gods of the Greeks as counterposed to gods of sovereignty (θεοὶ βασιλήιοι), see the discussions of Oliver 1960 (associating the opposition with the replacement of Greek monarchies by early constitu-

strued the gods of the Greeks as another of the factors that limited their action to Greek soil (γῆ τῆς ῾Ελλάδος).[149] Without a partner who could lay claim to Asiatic sovereignty, in the name of Asiatic divinities, the Spartans felt incapable of mobilizing their forces in the name of sovereignty over the entire *oikoumenē*.

When Aristagoras had previously invited Artaphernes to subdue the islands of the Aegean, he was addressing the satrap who represented a tradition committed to world sovereignty, and his appeal had succeeded. In making his appeal at Sardis, Aristagoras probably displayed the same map to show the itinerary of conquest open to the west. From the perspective of the lords of Asia, the imperative to extend their sovereignty to the other half of the world was clearly in accord with the nature of the world and the nature of Asiatic sovereignty itself. In making the appeal, and in accepting it, Aristagoras and Artaphernes must also have invoked the gods of sovereignty. Who were these gods?

In the present chapter we have examined how the ideology of sovereignty was reflected in the earliest Ionian maps of the world. We have also observed that the maps of Anaximander and Hecataeus described the *oikoumenē* as the rightful extent of sovereignty on earth. And we have observed that this concept, from the perspective of the Greeks, was developed with the sovereignty of Lydia specifically in mind. At the Lydian capital, Sardis, we have noted symbols of cosmic creation at a point of mediation between divinity and humanity, where the Mother of the Gods, or Kybebe at Sardis, embodied the concept of the all-sustaining earth and basis of sovereignty. The fall of Sardis to the Persians encouraged the Greeks to dissociate themselves from the cultic trappings of Lydian sovereignty. The Persians, on the other hand, found it useful to embrace those trappings, and to utilize them in constructing their own ideology of sovereignty. In the following chapter we will trace the historical significance, in relations between Greeks and Persians, of this ideological struggle, epitomized by the Phrygian deity honored at the Lydian capital who became a symbol of Persian sovereignty.

---

tional governments) and Raaflaub 1985, 125, 141 (identifying the development with the outcome of the Persian Wars); see further below, chapter 6 at note 108.

149. Herodotus 1.152, cited above, note 146.

# Chapter 6

# The Mother of the Gods and Persian Sovereignty

According to Herodotus, when Sardis fell to the Persians, the possessions of Croesus became the possessions of Cyrus.[1] Perhaps even more important than the transfer of the material wealth of Sardis was the acquisition by the Persians of the symbolic capital of Lydia. In the eyes of the former subjects and neighbors of the Lydians, by seizing Sardis Cyrus and the Persians won the rulership of Asia.[2] When Darius began to assert Persian sovereignty across the waters from Asia, we find him utilizing the symbols that had previously justified Lydian sovereignty. The most distinctive token of dominion and submission associated with Darius and his expansion into Europe was the demand for earth and water.

In this chapter we will review the evidence for the Persian appropriation of symbols of Lydian sovereignty, beginning with earth and water. These elemental symbols of the basis of life prove to be part of the complex of symbols related to the ideology of Asiatic sovereignty centered at Sardis. Earth and water were abstractions of the Lydo-Ionian cosmogony that also found expression in divinity, most directly in Kybebe, Herodotus' "local deity" of the Sardians. She was the Asiatic Mother of the Gods, and the same emissaries from Darius who demanded earth and water of the Athenians in 491 also demanded recognition for this deity among the Athenians. The rejec-

---

1. Herodotus 1.88. Other indications of imperial continuity include the tribute paid to Persia by the Ionian Greeks, "much the same as it had previously been" (Herodotus 6.42.2), and the continued issue of Lydian coinage at the standard set by Croesus for some thirty years after the fall of Sardis to Cyrus; see Olmstead 1948, 188; Kraay 1976, 31–32; Briant 2002, 70.

2. See Herodotus 1.141 and 169. On Lydian Asia, and Persian claims to Asia in Greek texts, see chapter 5, with notes 25–27. Old Persian texts, following Darius, Behistun 1.6, refer to the region of Lydian Asia as the province of Sparda (the domain of Sardis), which is listed between "Those of the Sea" and "Ionia." See Briant 2002, 173.

tion of both by the Athenians was a decisive moment, arguably the single most decisive moment in determining the course of political, intellectual, and religious history in classical antiquity.

### EARTH AND WATER

Outside of the demands for earth and water described in Herodotus' *Histories,* these tokens are not attested as a sign of submission to Persian rule.[3] No Persian text describes submission to the king, or to any form of sovereignty or divinity, in terms of rendering earth and water; native Persian or Zoroastrian custom does not account for the practice.[4] Nor do the customs of Assyria or Babylonia provide an example of this particular expression of submission. In fact, no direct precedent for the demand for earth and water as it appears in Herodotus has yet been discovered. In Lydia, however, earth and water occur in a conjunction that accounts for the origin of these tokens of sovereignty.

In an early fourth-century bilingual Lydian-Aramaic funerary inscription at Sardis, Artemis is said to exercise control over the beneficence of earth and water: "Now whosoever damages this stele or this grave chamber, . . . to him, to his court and house, to earth and water, to whatever may be his possession, Artemis of Ephesus and Artemis of Koloë shall bring destruction."[5] The funerary context at Sardis, where Artemis of Koloë is invoked alongside

---

3. Kuhrt 1988, 88–89, lists the instances of the demand for or submission of earth and water in Herodotus. All classical references to earth and water in a political context refer to these same occasions. See Aeschines 3, *Against Ctesiphon* 132; Lycurgus *Against Leocrates* 71; Aristotle *Rhetoric* 2.23.18 (1339b); Polybius 9.38.2; Diodorus 11.2.3, 6, 11.3.5, 11.4.6, 11.15.1; Plutarch *Themistocles* 6.3; Pausanias 3.4.2, 3.12.7.

4. As Amélie Kuhrt (1988, 87) has noted, "the concept of earth and water . . . appears to be entirely self-explanatory," and therefore there has been little effort to explain this particular form of symbolic behavior. (So, e.g., Olmstead 1948, 149, simply accounts for earth and water as "the usual signs of submission.") Kuhrt's investigation of this customary behavior elucidates the nature of the vassalage it signifies, but fails to reveal its origin, and ends with no convincing answer to the question, "Why should any part of this process have been characterized as 'giving earth and water'?" (98). In his otherwise full study of Persian history, institutions, and ideology, Pierre Briant 2002 has nothing to say on the subject of earth and water except to remark in a brief bibliographical note (960) that the subject is attended by "persistent uncertainties." Greek and Persian sources attest Persian reverence for the earth and its waters among other natural forces or elements, but earth and water are never described as tokens of submission in any Persian text. There is no justification for Balcer's description (1995, 155) of "'earth and water,' the sacred Zoroastrian symbols of vassalage."

5. Gusmani gives the Lydian text in *LW* 250 no. 1, lines 4–7 (= Hanfmann and Ramage 1978, 162 no. 241; Dusinberre 2003, 229 no. 1); translation modified from Hanfmann and Ramage, following Gusmani. The text is on a funerary stele of Manes son of Kumlis, dated by the Aramaic text: "on the fifth of Marhesuan, of year 10 of Artaxerxes the King, in Sardis, the fortress" (cited in *LW* 250); Artaxerxes is presumed to be Artaxerxes II, based on Hanfmann's

Artemis of Ephesus, associates this reference to earth and water with the ideology of the birth and death of kings that we have encountered at the Tumulus of Alyattes beside the Gygaean lake.[6] Other Lydian funerary inscriptions from Sardis invoke the protection of Artemis of Ephesus alone, or
Demeter and Artemis, or Kybebe in the company of other deities, and probably a deity called Mother (although the contexts are fragmentary).[7]

It is not accidental that funerary inscriptions are our chief native source
of information on Lydian deities, and that one among them happens to mention earth and water as a domain of divine power. As we have observed in
the two preceding chapters, funerary ritual was a primary locus for Lydian
religious symbolism, focused especially on the funerary monuments of kings,
their consorts, their mothers, and their sons. The upper echelons of the Sardian populace also participated in the same symbolic system by employing
the likeness of royal ritual, at a smaller scale, in their own funerary practices.[8]
It is to be expected, therefore, that these funerary texts of the Lydian upper
class would reflect the ideology of divinity and sovereignty that was at home
in Lydian Asia.

Tombs, in a Lydian context, were places of numinous power where the
threshold of death was also seen as the doorway through which the forces
of life could reenter the world. This metaphorical symbolism became prominent in later Hellenistic funerary iconography centered in Phrygia, where
funerary monuments often took the form of carved doorways.[9] The ideology underlying later funerary cult and its iconography was already present
in the archaic rock-carved facades of the Phrygian highlands that we have

---

judgment that the accompanying relief is early fourth-century, and therefore the stele dates to
394 B.C.E. On the Lydian words for earth (*klida-*) and water (*kofu-*) see *LW* 152–53.

6. On the royal tumuli by the Gygaean lake, the regeneration of sovereignty, and the cult
of Artemis in that setting, see chapter 5 above, at notes 91–96.

7. Dusinberre 2003, 115–16, provides an overview of the deities that appear in funerary
inscriptions of the Persian period at Sardis, to which we may add Demeter (*Lamẽtruś:* see *LW*
158), and Kybebe (*\*Kuvav[a]ś*), along with *Śãntaś* and *Marvidas.* (See chapter 3, with note 105.)
On "Mother" (*Enaś*) in Lydian inscriptions, see chapter 5 note 47. Artemis of Koloё probably
became identified with the "Mother of the Gods of Lydia" attested in an inscription of the Roman imperial period from the north side of Lake Gygaea (Koloё): see Robert 1980. Hanfmann
1983b, 221–22, rejects this identification of Artemis and the Mother, but see chapter 4, note
121, for the conflation of Artemis and the Mother in Lydia by the imperial period.

8. McLaughlin 1985 provides a comprehensive study of Lydian burial customs; see also
Dusinberre 2003, 128–57, reviewing evidence from the Persian period. See also the discussion
in chapter 4 at note 63. Metcalf and Huntington 1991, 133–61, provide a series of instructive
comparative cases (including pharaonic Egypt) of royalty and nobility participating in a system
of funerary ritual with "identical religious significance," where the chief variable is "the scale,
elaboration, and drama of the rites" (142, speaking of Balinese rites).

9. See Waelkens 1986 for a full collection and study of Anatolian "Türsteine" as funerary
monuments, which begin to appear as a distinctive type during the Persian period. The precise meaning of these funerary doorways is debated, as Waelkens recognizes (17–19).

encountered as monuments of *Matar Kubeleya,* or Kybebe. Standing at a doorway into the earth, the goddess embodies the power of the earth in her several guises.[10] As Artemis, she was the goddess who presides over birth, nurtures young, and protects life-sustaining waters, particularly in their natural settings.[11] Artemis of Koloë did so for Lydians at the source of life itself, the Gygaean lake; Artemis of Ephesus did so for Ionians at an effluence of Asiatic waters into the sea of the world.[12] As Demeter (*Lamētruś* of the Lydian inscriptions), she was particularly concerned with the sustenance of humanity on earth, and was also a mediator, with the assistance of her daughter, Greek Kore, of the cycles of life and death.[13] Kybebe and Mother, in her various guises as Mountain Mother, the source of waters, the mother of kings, the mother of Zeus, and as Earth herself, embraced all of these functions.

Funerary practices and the cult of the Mother represent only part of the conceptual system encompassed by earth and water. Among the Lydians and Ionian Greeks of Asia, earth and water signified the source of life, the foundation of the *oikoumenē,* and the basis of sovereignty. The interweaving of these concepts, as we have seen above and in the preceding chapters, is represented in myth and cult, in Ionian cosmology, and in the rituals of tyranny. The thought of Thales and Anaximander is imbued with these concepts, and it is no mere coincidence that Xenophanes, in the time of Darius, identified earth and water as the elemental basis of all generation and growth.[14] Those who understood this Lydo-Ionian conceptual system could see it as the ordering principle of settled, productive communities. Those who accepted this as the basis of order in the world could see the justification for extending sovereignty from Sardis across the face of the earth, just as life itself had spread from its Asiatic source, to take hold wherever fertile soil and flowing waters sustained human communities. Ionian maps of the world encouraged the extension of this concept of sovereignty throughout the inhabited earth.

10. On the archaic Phrygian facades, see chapter 2, with note 83; see also Roller 1999, 53–62 and 84–104.

11. The main elements of the Greek image of Artemis are present in Homeric poetry, which, as has been observed in chapters 3 and 4, originated in close relation to Lydian cult and tradition. For a summary of the traits of Artemis, with notice of her Homeric aspect and close ties to Lydia, see Burkert 1985, 149–52; see also Cole 1998.

12. A great marsh at the mouth of the Caÿster River (fed by the "Asian meadow" of Homer *Iliad* 2.461) was the natural setting of Artemis' famous temple at Ephesus: Xenophon *Hellenica* 1.2.6–9; *Anabasis* 5.3.8; Pliny *Naturalis Historia* 36.95; see Kraft et al. 2001 on the geomorphology. Note also the lake of drinkable water by the shrine of Artemis Leucophrys, at Magnesia on the Maeander: Xenophon *Hellenica* 3.2.19. Artemis in the Peloponnese is frequently invoked as Limnaia or Limnatis, "She of the Lake" (e.g., Pausanias 2.7.6, 3.14.2, 3.23.10, 4.4.2, 4.31.3, 7.20.7–8, 8.53.11; the shrine of Artemis Orthia at Sparta is the Limnaion: Pausanias 3.16.7).

13. On Demeter and her daughter at Sardis, see chapter 4, with notes 42–45, 113, and 116; and above, note 7.

14. See chapter 5 at notes 98–102.

After Persian sovereignty had replaced Lydian in the continent of Asia, Persian sovereignty became that ordering principle.

But the Ionian maps also displayed a dichotomy, a division of the face of the earth into two discrete continents. Under Mermnad rule, the cultural affinities of Greeks and Lydians had been strong, and the sea in their midst did not represent an unbridgeable divide. But by the time Hecataeus drew his map, in the reign of Darius, circumstances had changed. Persian sovereignty was not familiar to the Greeks, and the physical division between Europe and Asia, now so labeled by Hecataeus, appeared to Greeks to have an undeniable metaphysical significance.

From the Persian point of view, the waters that separated Europe from Asia were but one among several features of the earth that separated outlying lands from the central continent, their own native land and home to settled life.[15] To the Persians, the extension of their sovereignty westward, beyond the shores of Asia, was part of the divinely ordained process of spreading rightful order, the order of the *oikoumenē*, across the entire face of the earth. To signify the rightful order of Persian rule, the Persians embraced symbols that were readily understood by the peoples living along the division between Europe and Asia. The Persians, therefore, became proponents of an ideology of Asiatic primacy that the Lydians had previously embraced. By demanding the submission of earth and water the Persians were asserting that they themselves were the rightful custodians of the basis of human life everywhere on the face of the earth.

According to the hypothesis advanced here, the Persians openly embraced the conceptual basis of Lydian sovereignty in the West. As outlined in the previous chapter, this was an ideology that had much in common with—perhaps even originated from—an older Mesopotamian ideology that justified kingship. But under the Persians, in the time of Darius, the demand for earth and water was seen to emanate from the lords of Asia who controlled Sardis, and the Persians demanded earth and water specifically from peoples who lived across the sea that defined the shores of Asia. Submission of these tokens was an acknowledgment of the unity of the entire earth and its life-sustaining waters, and an acceptance of the notion that the Persian king was, as he claimed to be, "lord over all men from the rising to the setting of the sun."[16]

15. Persian cosmography divided the world into seven *karshwars*, or continents. At the center was the Aryan homeland, "that splendid continent Xwaniratha, (the land of) village settlements and (of) healthy village habitation" (Yasht 10, to Mithra, stanza 15, translated by Malandra 1983, 60); the other six were arrayed around it, separated by water or thick forests; see Boyce 1979, 7; Malandra 187 s.v. *karshwar*.

16. This Persian claim of universal sovereignty from the rising to the setting of the sun is connected with the demand for earth and water by Aeschines 3, *Against Ctesiphon* 132. For other forms of the assertion of world dominion by Persian kings, according to Greek sources and in their own inscriptions; see note 63 below.

## THE PERSIANS AND THE GODS OF LYDIA

The tokens of earth and water were derived, I argue, from the religious and cosmological principles that underlay Lydian tyranny. The facts that the two elements earth and water are mentioned together in a religious context only in Lydia, and that they are also named together as the basis of life on earth in Ionian cosmography, and further, that these tokens are attested as demands made only of peoples living beyond the shores of Asia (i.e., western Asia Minor) are all indicators that Persian practice had a Lydian origin. But are there any more direct indications that the ideological basis of Lydian tyranny was taken up by the Persians? To what extent did the Persian kings or their satraps and ministers maintain the cult practices and symbols associated with Lydian sovereignty?

At first sight, indications are somewhat ambiguous. Starting with the testimony of Herodotus and proceeding to the evidence of Persian texts and monuments that speak of the Persian concept of sovereignty and its relationship to Zoroastrian religion, scholars have observed distinctions that seem to separate Persian beliefs and practices from those that were shared among the Greeks, Lydians, and other peoples of western Asia Minor.[17] More important to the present inquiry than the nature of native Iranian religion in the time of Darius, however, is the interplay between the symbols of Persian rulership and the religious beliefs and practices of Persian subjects in Asia Minor. It is appropriate, therefore, to draw attention to several indications of the manner in which the Persians upheld the cultic traditions of Lydia and Ionia, and to recognize the manner in which the Greeks readily understood the Persians as participating in these religious traditions, particularly as they affected the symbols of sovereignty.[18]

The first and most important of these indications is the plain statement

17. Herodotus 1.131–32 and 140 is the locus classicus for the distinctions between Persian and Greek cult and burial practices (e.g., the Persians erect no statues, temples, or altars; they worship the sun, moon, earth, fire, water, and winds in addition to Zeus and Aphrodite). The Daiva Inscription of Xerxes at Persepolis (Kent 1950, XPh; Boyce 1979, 56; Malandra 1983, 51) proclaims the king's hostility to certain daivas (lesser gods) of foreign lands. Herodotus depicts the Persians, on the one hand, as tolerating and even adopting foreign customs and religious practices (1.87–90, 145; 3.15, 38; 6.97; 8.54, 133–36; 9.42), and, on the other hand, as intolerant and insensitive to foreign customs, particularly in matters of religion (1.183, 187; 3.16, 25, 27–29; 8.35–39, 53; 9.65, 116). On Persian religion of the Achaemenid period generally, see Olmstead 1948, 195–99; Boyce 1979, 50–77; 1988; Malandra 1983, 3–27; Briant 2002, 240–54.

18. In her recent study of Sardis under Persian rule, Elspeth Dusinberre (2003) describes a process of cultural syncretism of Lydian and Achaemenid elements, yielding "a newly composed and socially symbolic art of empire" (171). She observes: "Elite society [at Sardis] represented a fusion of cultural traditions, not differentiated on the basis of cultural origin but serving to unite the elite as a more or less cohesive whole" (157).

by Herodotus that the Persians under Darius and Xerxes made the burning of the shrine of Kybebe at Sardis by the Ionians their justification for burning the shrines of the Greeks.[19] The incident provides strong prima facie testimony to the readiness of the Persians to assert sovereignty in the name of a cult localized specifically at Sardis.[20] A second indication is the high regard paid by Persians to the cult of Artemis of Ephesus, also closely associated with Lydian sovereignty, as discussed in chapter 4.[21] By the later fifth century we find the high priesthood of Artemis of Ephesus held by a man with the Persian name Megabyzus, reflecting what later sources describe as an established custom.[22] At the same time, in the late fifth century, we find the Persian satrap of Sardis rallying his Ionian allies in the name of Artemis of Ephesus to fight off the Athenians.[23] Within the Lydo-Ionian heartland, then, Persian power and sovereignty were clearly aligned with cults that had been closely identified with Lydian tyranny.

A distinctive fusion of Persian and Lydo-Ionian religion in the name of sovereign ideology emerges on a much broader scale within the Persian empire in royal sponsorship of the cult of Anahita. Anahita, whose name means "Pure" or "Untainted," was most often identified by the Greeks as "Artemis . . . who bears the name Anaïtis."[24] But she was also identified as Aphrodite, par-

---

19. Herodotus 5.102.1. The retributive burning of Greek temples in the time of Xerxes resonates with the zealous temper expressed in the name of right religion by Xerxes in the Daiva Inscription at Persepolis: "By the will of Ahuramazda I smote that country and set it in its (proper) place. And among these countries was (one) where formerly the daiwas were worshipped. Then by the will of Ahuramazda I destroyed the daiwa-temple. And I decreed, 'Let the daiwas not be worshipped!'" (XPh 36–40, translated by Malandra 1983, 51). The country "where formerly the daiwas were worshipped" was probably not Greece or Babylon: Olmstead 1948, 231–32, identifies it as Bactria; Briant 2002, 550–54, believes that the text is deliberately vague, and more ideological than historical; see also Kuhrt and Sherwin-White 1987.

20. The case is prejudged in a most unhelpful manner by How and Wells 1912, vol. 1, 59, who comment: "The Persians needed no excuse for destroying Hellenic shrines . . . , and the accidental destruction of a Lydian temple was clearly not the reason." Most commentators seem, tacitly, to have accepted this position, which has had the effect of suppressing inquiry into the significance of the burning of Kybebe's shrine.

21. See chapter 4 at notes 112–20. See also Briant 2002, 701–5, 1009–10.

22. See chapter 4 at notes 83 and 84.

23. Xenophon Hellenica 1.2.6. The alliance of Ephesian Artemis with the Persian cause is attributed to the time of Xerxes in the Persians by Timotheus of Miletus: see chapter 4 at note 118.

24. Plutarch Artaxerxes 27.3: τῆς Ἀρτέμιδος τῆς ἐν Ἐκβατάνοις, ἣν Ἀναΐτιν καλοῦσιν (discussed further below at note 33). Xenophon Anabasis 1.6.7 describes an oath of allegiance taken by the Persian Orontas to Cyrus the Younger at the altar of Artemis at Sardis (possibly Artemis Anaïtis, though she is not so called). Pausanias 7.6.6 refers to the fourth-century cult of "Persian Artemis" at Sardis, and at 3.16.8 refers to the cult of Artemis Anaïtis in Lydia. Tacitus Annals 3.62 refers to the establishment of the cult of "Persian Diana" at Hierocaesarea in Lydia in the time of Cyrus. (Briant 2002, 703 and 1010, identifies this as Cyrus the Great.) Rose Lou Bengisu 1996, 9–10, discusses the fusion of the imagery of Artemis and Anahita at Sardis. Maria Brosius 1998 attempts to distinguish Persian from Greek elements in this cult. On the cult in Lydia

ticularly from a Babylonian perspective, where Ishtar was the goddess whose power was most manifest in the world. Berossus, priest of Bel-Marduk at Babylon in the third century B.C.E., states that Artaxerxes II "was the first to set up the statue of Aphrodite Anaïtis in Babylon, and encouraged her worship also in Susa, Ecbatana, Persepolis, Bactria, Damascus, and Sardis."[25] The conjunction of Artemis and Aphrodite in the identification of Anahita by Greek speakers places her in the company of the Mother of the Gods or Kybebe at Sardis, who, like Inanna or Ishtar in Mesopotamia, was the consort of kings whose reciprocal love and devotion were the foundation of sovereignty.[26] The systematic royal sponsorship of the cult of Anahita by Artaxerxes II, a century after the reign of Darius I, marks a particularly demonstrative phase in the alignment of Persian sovereignty with this ancient paradigm, but it should not be taken for its beginning.[27] The nature of religious institutions encourages us to understand the promotion of Anahita by Artaxerxes as an elaboration of a preexisting tradition or ideology rather than a radical innovation.[28] Persian regard for Kybebe at Sardis bears witness to the identifi-

---

see also Mierse, in Hanfmann 1983a, 104; Hanfmann 1983a, 129–30; Fleischer 1973, 185–87; further scholarship cited by Briant 2002, 1009–10. On Persian Anahita see Malandra 1983, 117–30.

25. Berossus *FGrHist* 680 F 11 (from Clement *Protrepticus* 5.65.3).

26. On the iconographic resemblances between depictions of Anahita and the goddess of sovereignty in Urartian and Mesopotamian art, Briant 2002, 254, observes: "It seems clear . . . that Anāhitā owes much to Mesopotamian Ištar. Because of this, it is reasonable to suppose that syncretism was at work at least as early as the arrival of the Persians in these regions. This is probably what Herodotus meant when he wrote that the Persians 'learned from the Assyrians and the Arabians the cult of Uranian Aphrodite' (I.131)." Briant (678–79 and 1000–1001) adduces additional sources and scholarship into a discussion of the variety of assimilations and syncretisms associating Anahita with Babylonian Ishtar and Lydian Artemis (but omits any mention of Kybebe).

27. Malandra 1983, 117–19, suggests that "the Avestan Arədwī Sūrā Anāhitā is a syncretistic goddess composed of two major and independent elements. On the one hand, she manifests the ancient Indo-Iranian idea of the Heavenly River who brings the waters to the rivers and streams of the earth. On the other hand, she is a goddess of uncertain origin, who, though maintaining many of her original traits, came to be associated with the cult of Inanna-Ishtar. The merging of the two in the Avesta must be a late syncretistic effort on the part of Zoroastrians anxious to bring Anāhitā into the fold" (119). Boyce 1979, 61–63, speaks of Artaxerxes' promotion of Anahita as a "break with tradition" accompanied by "striking innovations" (iconic images and temple worship), but acknowledges that it could only have been with "co-operation from the [Zoroastrian] priesthood" and the "willing promotion of the cult by some of their order." Briant 2002, 253, observes: "Devotion to the goddess did not result simply from a sudden change; worship of her must have evolved over a long period of time." Briant (254, 703, and 1010) interprets the testimony of Tacitus *Annals* 3.62 to mean that the cult of Anahita was established in Lydia in the time of Cyrus the Great.

28. Yasna 38, quoted by Olmstead 1948, 233, in the context of religious reforms in the time of Xerxes, speaks of worshipping "this Earth which bears us" and "the Waters, outpouring and running together . . . with the names which Ahura-Mazda has given you, . . . you life-

cation of Persian sovereignty with the cult symbols of Lydian sovereignty already in the time of Darius I.

Persian hymns give strong support to the identification of Anahita with the Mother of the Gods in her various guises in Lydia and Phrygia. An Avestan hymn addressing the goddess by the full form of her names, *Arədwī Sūrā Anāhitā* (Moist Strong Untainted), praises her in the words of Ahuramazda spoken to Zoroaster:[29]

> On my account, worship her, O Zarathustra Spitama, *Arədwī Sūrā Anāhitā* who spreads abroad, who is healing, . . . who is worthy to be worshipped by the material world and worthy to be praised by the material world, who is a crop-increasing *ashawan* [manifestation of truth], a herd-increasing *ashawan,* an *ashawan* who makes the country prosper, who purifies the semen of all males, who purifies for conception the womb of all females, who gives easy delivery to all females, who gives milk to all females regularly and at the proper time; [worship her,] the vast, famed from afar, who is as great as all these waters which flow forth upon the earth, who forcefully flows forth from Mount Hukairya [the cosmic mountain] to the *Wouru.kasha* sea [the cosmic sea]. . . . She is strong, regal, tall, beautiful, in whom flow down by day and by night as many falling waters as all the waters which flow forth on the earth. She who is strong flows forth! On account of her *rayi* [opulence, might] and glory, I shall worship her with audible prayer, I shall worship her with well-recited prayer, *Arədwī Sūrā Anāhitā,* with libations. Thus may you be directed by this invocation, thus may you be better worshipped, O *Arədwī Sūrā Anāhitā.*

The attributes of Anahita in this hymn present a description exemplary of the features of the Mother of the Gods as she was known at Sardis, as she was worshipped according to what Greek sources describe as Phrygian and Lydian custom, and akin as well to Ishtar as she is known from Mesopotamian texts. In response to appropriate veneration, she makes crops and herds prosper, and she promotes human fertility. She is even worshipped by the supreme god himself ("He who is the Creator, Ahuramazda, worshipped her"),[30] thereby showing the king on earth the role that he too must play. Like the Phrygian Mother, who was associated with rivers and whose cult was observed at rock-cut shrines near springs in the Phrygian highlands, the beneficence of Anahita is closely linked with the flow of life-sustaining water from the earth.

We do not find rites of a Sacred Marriage to the king celebrated explicitly in the name of Anahita. But neither do any of our sources explicitly name

---

giving Mothers." In this hymn, Olmstead observes (234): "Instead of the stern, aloof Ahura-Mazda of Zoroaster, we detect the oriental King of Kings whose harem is full of mother goddesses." In all respects, these concepts harmonize with the ideology of divinity and kingship attending Lydian tyranny, as discussed in chapters 3 and 4.

29. Yasht 5, to *Arədwī Sūrā Anāhitā,* stanzas 1–3 and 15, translated by W. Malandra 1983, 120.

30. Yasht 5, stanza 17, translated by Malandra 1983, 121.

Kybebe as the partner of the king in the garden paradise at Sardis called the Place of Purity, or in other such gardens, where "the Mysteries of Aphrodite" were performed. Indirect evidence, however, suggests that Anahita was the paradigmatic consort of the king among the Persians just as Kybebe was among the Lydians.

Artaxerxes II, the most famous devotee of Anahita, assumed the throne after a period of ritual seclusion suggestive of a Sacred Marriage probably involving Anahita. Plutarch describes the royal rites of initiation (ἡ βασιλικὴ τελετή) undertaken by Artaxerxes at Pasargadae upon his accession. They took place in "the shrine of a warlike goddess, whom one might compare to Athena," and involved investiture in royal garments and a ritual meal. Plutarch concludes: "If anything else is done besides, it is unknown to outsiders."[31] Anahita, the only goddess named in the royal inscriptions of Artaxerxes II, is the only plausible candidate for the Persian identity of this goddess, "whom one might compare to Athena."[32]

Plutarch later relates the cult of Anahita to the story of a prized concubine in the court of Artaxerxes II named Aspasia, who was formerly the favorite of his brother, Cyrus the Younger, and who was revered by both men for her beauty and her wisdom. When Artaxerxes' son expressed his wish to have her for his own, Artaxerxes placed her beyond his reach by making her "the priestess of Artemis at Ecbatana, who bears the name Anaïtis, so that she would remain chaste [ἁγνή] for the rest of her life."[33] Chastity in such a setting was a ritualized notion, and was subject to the high calling of the rituals of sovereignty.[34] We do not know whether the duties of the chaste priestess of Anahita obliged her to participate in some rite of Sacred Marriage to the king, but we may be sure that her status reserved intimate contact with her person to Artaxerxes alone, among uncastrated males, as king and chief officiant of the cult of Anahita.

Another story told by Plutarch strongly suggests that Artaxerxes found outlet for the full range of intimacies associated with the rituals of Lydian tyranny. Artaxerxes fell deeply in love with his own daughter, named Atossa, and eventually decided that it suited his royal prerogative to take her openly as a wife. With that decision, his love for his daughter assumed ritual proportions:[35]

---

31. Plutarch *Artaxerxes* 3.1–2.

32. Olmstead 1948, 372, and Briant 2002, 523 and 677, identify this ceremony as a ritual of Anahita, lending support to the inference that the cult of Anahita was already well established before the reign of Artaxerxes II.

33. Plutarch *Artaxerxes* 26.3–27.3. The story of this same Aspasia is told in greater detail in Aelian *Varia Historia* 12.1. (See chapter 3 at notes 32–36.)

34. Note how the language of purity or chastity is attached to the temples, gardens, and cult figures who participate in rituals of the Sacred Marriage in Lydia and Mesopotamia; see chapter 4 at notes 14–16 and 23.

35. Plutarch *Artaxerxes* 23.4–5.

Atossa was so beloved by her father as his consort, that when her body was covered with leprosy he was not offended at this in the least, but offered prayers to Hera on her behalf, making obeisance and touching the ground with his hands before this goddess alone; and he ordered his friends and satraps to send so many gifts to this goddess that the entire distance of sixteen stades between the palace and the temple was filled with gold and silver and purple and horses.

We are not told what Persian deity was known by the Greek name Hera, but given the singular acts of devotion displayed and commanded by Artaxerxes, whose devotion to Anahita was well known, and in the absence of any other likely candidate, in all probability this was another identification by Greek sources of the cult of Anahita. In this case, the cult of the goddess is observed in honor of the favored wife and consort of the king, and so in Greek eyes she is assimilated to Hera, wife and consort (and sister) of Zeus.[36]

The divinity conceived as a single entity under the name Anahita, the "Pure One," was essentially the same as the concept evoked in multiple manifestations, according to an Avestan hymn, as the life-giving Mothers, identified with Earth and with Waters, whom Ahuramazda himself honored.[37] It is no surprise that Greek sources could recognize Anahita as Artemis, as Athena, as Aphrodite, or as Hera, depending on the context and occasion of her manifestation. Anahita, the "Pure One," seems to be the assimilation into Zoroastrian Persian theology of the nurturing and maternal force that represented sovereignty over the *oikoumenē*, the inhabitable world; she was the goddess of many names who had long been associated with sovereign power by the kings of Mesopotamia, Anatolia, and the Levant. The customary rituals of sovereign kingship common to all these lands virtually obliged the Persians to take her up and make her their own. The strength of these customs accounts for the protective attitude adopted by the Persians on behalf of the shrine of Kybebe at Sardis.

Because kingship in the lands of Anatolia, Mesopotamia, and the Levant was so intimately linked to the procreative intercourse of a goddess and a king (or the god he stood for), the mother of the king was regarded as the mother of sovereignty and an embodiment of the goddess of sovereignty. As

36. Briant 2002, 998, expresses doubts about the identification of Hera in this passage with Anahita, "for never in Classical texts is Anāhita so designated." Neither is Anahita ever explicitly equated with Athena, although Briant accepts without hesitation that she is the anonymous goddess of Plutarch *Artaxerxes* 3.1, "whom one might compare to Athena" (above, note 32). In the present passage, "Hera" can be recognized in her orientalizing form, best represented in the iconography of the Sacred Marriage in her cult on Samos (where she is akin to Ishtar; see Burkert 1985, 108 and 132–33), and in her nearness to both Aphrodite and Athena, as represented in the Judgment of Paris. See Clark 1998 for a discussion of the Sacred Marriage in the cults of Hera on the Greek mainland; Kyrieleis 1993, 145–49, summarizes the abundance of Eastern imports of the archaic era found in the Heraeum on Samos.

37. Yasna 38. (See note 28 above.)

was observed in chapter 3, the divinity of sovereigns and of the mother of sovereignty was honored most directly in a funerary context. Persian regard for such funerary symbolism is not directly attested, but a perceived connection between Persian royal power and funerary cult, particularly in its Lydian form, informs the thematic core of Aeschylus' *Persians*.

Throughout the *Persians*, prosperity (*ploutos, olbos*) for the realm, which is repeatedly described as "all of Asia," is signified by the stability of divine kingship.[38] The Persians of the play repeatedly refer both to Xerxes and to his deceased father, Darius, as divinities; nowhere else in extant fifth-century Attic tragedy is a king called a god (*theos*).[39] Atossa, the wife of Darius and mother of Xerxes, is referred to as the "consort of a god," "mother of a god," and "mistress of this land."[40] Commentators have remarked on the manner in which the royal consort and mother, godlike in status, is assimilated in the play to a personification of kingship, or even to the land of Asia itself.[41] Most striking is the central scene of the play, the summoning of the ghost of Darius from his tomb, to speak to his living wife about the portents of recent events for the sovereignty of Persia. All of these elements echo the language and symbolism of Lydian kingship through divine motherhood, Lydian royal funerary cult, and tyrannical necromancy.[42]

Even though the scene is putatively set at Susa, the paradigm for sover-

---

38. Wealth and prosperity (πλοῦτος and ὄλβος, lines 163–64, 250–52, 751) are recurrent concerns in Aeschylus' *Persians*. Prosperity depends both on the warlike forces "from all of Asia" (ἐκ πάσης Ἀσίας, lines 56–57; πᾶσα χθὼν Ἀσιῆτις, line 61; γῆς ἁπάσης Ἀσιάδος πολίσματα, line 249; cf. lines 12, 73, 270, 549, 584, 763, 929), and also on the stable succession of kingship (lines 762–86).

39. Divinity is attributed to Darius, who is dead but who appears as a ghost (*Persians* 157, 643, 711, θεός [god]; 620, 641–42, δαίμων [daemon, or god]; 856, ἰσόθεος [equal to a god]; 634: ἰσοδαίμων [equal to a daemon]; 651: ἄναξ [lord]), and to Xerxes, who is alive (157: θεός [god]; ἰσόθεος [equal to a god]). E. Hall 1989, 91–93, discusses the unique assertion of divinity in the *Persians*, and how it has variously been explained; see also T. Harrison 2000a, 87–89.

40. Atossa, the queen (βασίλεια γύνη, line 623), is called θεοῦ μὲν εὐνάτειρα Περσῶν, θεοῦ δὲ καὶ μήτηρ ἔφυς (line 157) and γῆς ἄνασσα τῆσδε (line 173). See T. Harrison 2000a, 44–47 and 132–33 n. 34, on the unusual status ascribed to Atossa.

41. Edward Said offers a striking formulation of Atossa's nature in the *Persians* (1978, 57): "Aeschylus *represents* Asia, makes her speak in the person of the aged Persian queen, Xerxes' mother." Mark Griffith 1998, 56, observes: "The emphasis in the play on the Queen's role as mother is obviously crucial in determining our attitude to this royal family, and to Xerxes in particular." Thomas Harrison 2000a, 45, notes: "It is the Queen, Atossa, who is the real representative of the monarchy." Harrison also draws attention to the manner in which Herodotus depicts Atossa, especially at 7.3.4, where he states that Xerxes was able to become king because "Atossa held all power" (ἡ γὰρ Ἄτοσσα εἶχε τὸ πᾶν κράτος).

42. Atossa pours libations to the earth and to the chthonic gods, to the dead, and particularly to the dead king: *Persians* 219–23, 228–29, 523–24, 609–80. On the necromancy of tyrants, its relation to sovereignty and the prosperity of the realm, and the role of bereaved lovers in the rites, see the discussion in chapter 4 at notes 53–62.

eignty depicted in the play is native to Sardis. The divine sovereign of Asia summoned from his grave, Darius, is even invoked under the title βαλλήν, which Greek lexicographers identify as the Phrygian word for "king."[43] To Greek ears, this was a potent invocation of sovereignty, and one most naturally accompanied by lamentation on a massive scale. To the Greeks, the rites of invocation and lamentation depicted by Aeschylus were simultaneously Lydian, Phrygian, and Persian.[44]

Aeschylus' *Persians* is recognized as a landmark in the articulation of Western perceptions of a fundamental distinction between the world inhabited by the majority of Greeks on the one hand and barbarian Asia on the other. Edward Said, for example, has identified Aeschylus' *Persians* as the earliest example of "a highly artificial enactment of what a non-Oriental has made into a symbol for the whole Orient." The "correctness of the representation," Said suggests, is not as important as the nature of the representation itself.[45] Other commentators, following Said's lead—among them Edith Hall and, more recently, Thomas Harrison—have concurred in judging the play to be more an indicator of the prevailing Greek or, more specifically, Athenian preconceptions about Persian customs than a reliable witness to them.[46]

These judgments are sound as far as they take us, but we are left to wonder precisely where the specific imagery conjured up by Aeschylus came from. We can now answer that question. Aeschylus' *Persians* is an elaboration of the distinction between Europe and Asia that was born in the realm of Lydia, in the cosmography of Anaximander, and brought to maturity in the geography of Hecataeus, as discussed in chapter 5. Like the name Asia itself, the imagery of the *Persians* was projected from Lydia onto the dominion of the new lords of this land. We may further conclude, based on the evidence for the Persian regard of Kybebe and Artemis of Ephesus, and on the evidence for the emergent cult of Anahita, that the Persian lords of Sardis

43. *Persians* 657–58: βαλλήν, ἀρχαῖος βαλλήν, ἴθι, ἱκοῦ. Cf. Sophocles *Herdsmen* (Ποιμένες) fr. 515 (Radt), where the chorus chants ἰὼ Βαλλήν, meaning ἰὼ βασιλεῦ in Phrygian, according to Sextus Empiricus *Against the Mathematicians* 1.313. See Hesychius s.v. βαλ[λ]ήν· βασιλεὺς Φρυγιστί.

44. The same identification of Lydian custom with Persian follows from Xenophon's depiction of the reverence of Cyrus the Great for the unparalleled beauty of Pantheia in *Cyropaedia;* see chapter 4 with notes 71 and 72.

45. E. W. Said 1978, 21; see also 56–67.

46. E. Hall 1989, 86: "It is more important to remember that Aeschylus is creating a poetic discourse by which to define the difference between barbarian and Greek." See also T. Harrison 2000a, 43, 44, and 87: "As we have seen, there is a danger of being distracted by the question of the veracity of Aeschylus' picture of Persian religious practice or belief. It should be stated at the outset that there is no evidence that the Persians believed that their kings were gods, or that the *proskynēsis* expected by a Persian king constituted worship. The Greeks, however, persisted in believing otherwise." See also Griffith 1998 (cited in note 41 above) and Briant 2002, 516–17, who comments on how the Greek, particularly Aeschylean, view of Xerxes has colored modern historiography.

gave the Greeks every indication that they embraced Lydian sovereignty, in all of its symbolic dimensions. It was from Sardis, in Lydia, that demands were issued for peoples living beyond the shores of Asia to submit tokens of earth and water. It was at Sardis, above all, that the Greeks envisioned the power of Persia that so enthralled them.

## SCYTHIA AND THE *OIKOUMENĒ*

Herodotus first attests the demand for earth and water in the course of Darius' expedition into Europe, his campaign against the Scythians. The Scythian campaign put the Lydo-Ionian geography of sovereignty to the test, and revealed its limits, as Herodotus' account makes clear. The account of Darius' campaign against the Scythians provided Herodotus with the occasion for his most systematic criticisms of Greek notions about the shape of the world, and some of his most revealing comments on the relationship between Asia and Europe.[47] The effect of Herodotus' account is to show that the world is composed of more complicated relationships than the simple binary oppositions displayed on Ionian maps and enacted in Persian imperial designs.

Herodotus invites his audience to consider the place of the Greeks within the relationships established by Darius' encounter with the Scythians. He does so before he describes the Persian expedition, in book 4, when he tells two stories to illustrate how strongly the Scythians reject "foreign customs, not least of all Greek customs."[48] From this statement and from similar comments on Scythian customs, François Hartog has recognized that Herodotus' entire account of the Scythians can be read as an implicit commentary, through contrasts, on Greek customs.[49] Hartog also recognizes a point that deserves greater emphasis here, namely that the Scythian account has yet another dimension to its commentary on Greekness: it raises implicit questions about the relationship between the Greeks and Persian sovereignty. Here too, the world is shown to be a more complicated place than the Persians knew, and possibly also more than Herodotus' Greek audience was generally aware. The Scythian campaign, and the Ionian Revolt that followed just over a decade later, called into question the Greek understanding of the relationship between Asia and Europe. This was an issue that remained unresolved in Herodotus' day.

47. Herodotus interrupts an extended description of the geography of northern lands (4.13–58) to criticize existing maps (4.36), and to comment: "Let me spend a few words in giving a proper notion of the size and shape of these two continents," whereafter a significant discussion of the relationship between Europe, Asia, and Libya follows, including an account of the circumnavigation of Libya (4.42) and his excursus on the origin of the name Asia (4.45).

48. Herodotus 4.76.1.

49. Hartog 1988.

One of the stories Herodotus tells to illustrate the Scythian aversion to Greek ways is the story of Scyles, son of a Scythian king and a Greek woman. Scyles attempted to live two lives, one as a Scythian king, and one as an inhabitant of the Greek town of the Borysthenites (Olbia, a Milesian colony) on the Black Sea. His Scythian kin tolerated his ways, even to the extent that Scyles enjoyed a Greek wife and a kept a Greek house during his visits to the Greek town. But his Hellenization finally became too much for his Scythian followers when Scyles became an initiate of Dionysus Baccheius. Scyles was deposed and eventually paid with his life.[50] The Hellenic custom that provoked this rejection of Scyles was a cult shared by Greeks (in this case, Milesian Greeks) and Lydians. For Baccheius, or Bacchus, was *Baki*, the name of Dionysus at Sardis.[51] The loss of identity experienced by an ecstatic throng of initiates to Bacchus, the particular feature of this ritual that so alarmed and offended the Scythians, was a cultic analogue to the loss of ethnic identity implied by submission to the tyranny of Sardis.[52] The Scythians, tolerant of Scyles' idiosyncrasies up to a point, could tolerate no such surrender by their own king.

The other story related by Herodotus also involves a worldly-wise Scythian, Anacharsis, who comes to grief as a result of his adoption of a ritual with disquieting implications for the Scythians. Again, although Herodotus does not draw attention to the fact, the ritual links its practitioners to the symbols of the sovereign power of Sardis. Herodotus tells how Anacharsis the Scythian traveled to Greece, became acquainted with its customs, and visited Cyzicus (another Milesian foundation) on his homeward voyage through the Hellespont. There, Herodotus reports:[53]

50. Herodotus 4.78–80; see Hartog 1988, 62–84.

51. The identity of Lydian *Baki* with Greek Dionysus is assured by the theophoric name *Bakivalis* = *Dionysikleos* in a bilingual Lydian-Greek dedication to Artemis of the mid-fourth century: Hanfmann and Ramage 1978, 177–78 no. 274 (= *LW* 259 no. 20, translated in Dusinberre 2003, 235 no. 49). On *Baki*- in a Lydian month name and in theophoric personal names, see Gusmani *LW* 74–75. On the Baccheius as a musical form originating in the circles of Lydian and Phrygian music, see [Plutarch] *On Music* 1141b. On the strong association of Dionysus, or Bacchus, with Lydia and Phrygia, see Nilsson 1955, 578–82; Hanfmann 1983a, 93 (= 1983b, 229) and 86; Burkert 1985, 163. On the early history of Bacchus and Baccheius in Greek sources, see Cole 1980, 226–31.

52. On tyranny as rule over many nations, see Herodotus 1.6 and 1.53.2 on the empire of Croesus over various ἔθνη, Diodorus 5.48.3 on the dominion of Dardanus (cited in chapter 3, note 59), and the section "Kingship and the *Oikoumenē*" in chapter 5. The surrender of identity involved in the cult of Dionysus, or Bacchus, coming from Lydia is the theme of Euripides' *Bacchae*. On the rites and initiations of Dionysus/Bacchus promoting prosperity, piety, and justice among mankind throughout the *oikoumenē*, see Diodorus 3.64.6–65.1, 4.3.4–5. On Dionysus as the leader of an army of conquest throughout the *oikoumenē*, see Diodorus 3.63.1–5, 65.2–8, 4.4.3–5.2. On Dionysus as son of Gaea, bearer of the vine and other forms of cultivation, see Diodorus 3.62.3–64.2, 4.1.6–2.6.

53. Herodotus 4.76, translated by R. Waterfield.

He found the inhabitants in the middle of an extremely impressive festival sacred to the Mother of the Gods. Anacharsis himself prayed to the Mother that if he got back home safe and sound, he would offer the same sacrifices to her that he had seen the Cyzicans offering, and would keep a night vigil in her honour. So after his return to Scythia, he slipped into Hylaea (a thickly wooded region, filled with all kinds of trees . . . ) and performed all the rites to the goddess, since he had a drum and had tied images of the goddess on to himself. However, his actions were spotted by a certain Scythian, who reported him to King Saulius. The king came in person, saw Anacharsis performing the rites, and shot him dead with bow and arrow.

It has often been remarked that the cult of the Mother of the Gods serves here as a peculiar illustration of Greekness.[54] But we may now see that the slaying of Anacharsis by Saulius demonstrates not merely the xenophobia of the Scythians, but the fact that the Scythians rejected the symbols of attachment to the Asiatic *oikoumenē*. This was also the message conveyed later when the son of Saulius, Idanthyrsus, rejected Darius' more explicit demand for submission by tokens of earth and water.

When Darius brought his army across the Bosporus and into Europe, he found the Thracians compliant to his rule. At least we hear of no resistance when Darius arrived, and only isolated resistance after he left, when Thrace became the satrapy of Skudra. At springs around the headwaters of the Teares River, where the streams divided into those flowing north to the Black Sea and south to the Aegean, Darius erected a monument praising the waters of the river and declaring his own kingship over the whole continent.[55] Thus far Darius found a land and a people amenable to the paradigm of Asiatic sovereignty, no doubt because the coastal Thracians had long been within the orbit and influence of the Mermnad kings of Lydia.[56]

But after crossing the Danube and entering Scythian lands, Darius encountered conditions that defied his sense of order. The Scythian army gave way before him at every turn and refused to give battle, blocking up wells and

---

54. See Hartog 1988, 70–75, 80–82, 110–11. Roller 1999, 156–57, speaking of Greek initiates, discusses this passage as a reliable indicator of "the impact of the Meter cult, simultaneously appealing and frightening, on a non-initiate."

55. On Darius' crossing into Europe, and on the remarkable springs of the Teares, see Herodotus 4.89–91; cf. 118. How and Wells 1912, vol. 1, 334, assert that the continent ($\mathring{\eta}\pi\epsilon\iota\rho\sigma$) Darius claimed was Asia, which is counterintuitive, especially in the context of a monument marking significant headwaters of European rivers. (Note the Scythian complaint [4.118.1–2] that Darius wants to make "this continent" his own, like "the other continent," which he came from.)

56. Herodotus 6.37 describes an incident at Lampsacus during the reign of Croesus illustrating the sway of Lydia over affairs on both sides of the Hellespont. On Cotys, Thracian Bendis, and cultic connections between Thrace and Lydia, see chapter 5, note 22. On Thracians within the *oikoumenē*, see chapter 5, note 40.

springs and spoiling pasturage as they went.[57] Darius interpreted their withdrawal as a sign of his supremacy, but requiring an acknowledgment of submission from the Scythians, he sent a messenger with the demand for earth
and water.[58] The Scythian king, Idanthyrsus, sent back an instructive reply.
After informing Darius that the Scythians have no towns or cultivated lands
to defend, and therefore no reason to risk battle, he went on: "As for your being my master, I acknowledge no masters but Zeus from whom I sprang, and
Hestia the Scythian queen. I will send you no gifts of earth and water!"[59]

The Scythians, by this account, owed obeisance to no condition of nature
over which the Persian king could claim authority. They were descendants
of Zeus, the sky, over whom no mortal could claim dominion, and they venerated Hestia, their hearths, which they moved with them as they migrated
from camp to camp.[60] By contrast, those who honored the deities of earth
and water patronized by the Persians were sedentary people who depended
for life upon the god-given fertility of the land they cultivated and the god-
given waters that flowed from the earth to sustain them in their fixed abodes.
These were the inhabitants of the oikoumenē, over whom Darius had extended
his sovereignty. Now Darius discovers, according to Herodotus, that the extent of the oikoumenē itself places a limit on his sovereignty. For only those
who give obeisance to the same forces of nature will give obeisance to the
same earthly sovereign.

Darius himself attests to the relationship between rulership and religion,
and to the problem that the Scythians posed to his image of sovereignty. In
the Behistun inscription Darius repeatedly attributes his sovereignty to divine agency: "Darius the king says: By the will of Ahuramazda I am king. . . .
Ahuramazda bore me aid, as did also the other gods who exist." Darius' own
kingship, overcoming all challengers, is the proof that "the other gods who
exist" cooperate with Ahuramazda in legitimizing Darius' sovereignty. With
the Scythians, however, Darius attests to religious dissonance: "Darius the king
says: Those Scythians were unruly and did not worship Ahuramazda."[61] By
implication, every other land brought firmly under the rulership of Darius
is viewed, from the Persian perspective, as participating in a harmonious system of deities supportive of, and embraced by, the will of Ahuramazda. Deities
identified with the common Asiatic tradition of ritualized kingship represented the highest concerns of human well-being in practically all the lands

57. Herodotus 4.120.
58. Herodotus 4.126.
59. Herodotus 4.127.4, translated by A. de Sélincourt.
60. Herodotus 4.5 and 59 gives more details of the Scythian pantheon. On the significance
of Hestia to the Scythians, see the discussion of Hartog 1988, 119–25.
61. DB 5.75, lines 30–31 (Kent 1950, 133–34, translated by Malandra 1983, 48–49). Note
Herodotus' final comments on the Massagetae, who slew Cyrus when he attacked them (1.216):
"They have no agriculture . . . ; the only god they worship is the sun."

ruled by Darius. These deities, above all, must have been understood from the Persian perspective as sustaining the will of Ahuramazda. Darius' rhetoric of divine legitimacy thus gives further support to the hypothesis we have been testing, namely that the Persians had made the conceptual basis of Lydian sovereignty their own.

The Scythian rejection of the demand for earth and water, then, is analogous to their rejection of the surrender to Bacchus, and their rejection of obeisance to the Mother of the Gods. Each of these actions signified their rejection of the paradigm of sovereign power associated with Sardis and the *oikoumenē*. Herodotus was aware of these connections, even if he did not spell them out. His Greek readers—or listeners, his intended audience—must certainly have been aware of where they themselves were situated within the *oikoumenē*, and which deities they themselves honored, and they could ponder the consequences indicated by Herodotus' testimony. Herodotus' audience would certainly also recognize that his account of the slaying of Anacharsis, devotee of the Mother, foreshadowed other rejections of the tyranny of Asia to follow in Herodotus' narrative, and that the ensuing incidents unambiguously placed the Athenians at the heart of the question: Where did Athens stand in relation to those who claimed to be sovereign lords of Asia and the *oikoumenē*?

### ATHENS, TYRANNY, AND PERSIA

Remorseless logic dictated the policy of empire during the reign of Darius. Tribute was regularized; coinage was instituted; a new royal capital was built; the power of the king was displayed in monuments.[62] By words and deeds, Darius showed that he perceived no natural boundaries to the extension of his sovereignty across the face of the earth. His inscriptions declared: "I am Darius the Great King, King of Kings, King of countries containing all kinds of men, King in this great earth far and wide."[63] Prowess in battle made these claims manifest, but their highest justification was the assertion that Darius

---

62. On the scope of Darius' administrative reforms and his monumental displays, see Olmstead 1948, 119–94; Briant 2002, 62–70, 165–83, and 210–25. On Persian coinage, see Kraay 1976, 31–34; Briant 408–10. Herodotus 3.89.3 reflects a Greek perspective on Darius, who ran his empire "like a shopkeeper"; see Kurke 1999, 68–89.

63. DNa 2, lines 8–12, in Kent 1950, 138. According to Herodotus 7.8c, Xerxes proposed to establish Persian rulership "bordered by the aether of Zeus; for the sun will not look down upon any land bordering our own, but by traversing Europe I will make them all one land for you." Cf. 7.19.1, 54.2; 8.109.3; and the dream of Cyrus portending rulership over Asia and Europe for the son of Hystaspes (Darius), 1.209.1. Diodorus 10.19.5 describes Darius' "boundless ambition" to bring the entire *oikoumenē* under Persian rule, and Xenophon *Anabasis* 1.7.6 reports the claim of Cyrus the Younger to ancestral rulership over all habitable lands between the uninhabitable south and north.

was fulfilling the will of the supreme deity, Ahuramazda. Persian texts, beginning in the reign of Darius, liken the king to a good husbandman, chosen by Ahuramazda to tend and cultivate the earth.[64] These were essentially the same terms that had justified Lydian tyranny.

As Darius was seeking to extend the tyranny of Asia into Europe, the Athenians were struggling within their own community to establish a form of sovereignty that explicitly rejected tyranny. This was an issue around which powerful public images and slogans were manufactured. Within the last decade of the sixth century, the martyred tyrannicides Harmodius and Aristogeiton were publicly honored, as no Athenians had yet been, by having their statues erected in the agora.[65] At the same time, Harmodius and Aristogeiton were celebrated in drinking songs as men who had "slain the tyrant and brought equality to Athens."[66] Athenian ideology clearly emphasized the elimination of tyranny, by legal measures if possible, and by violence if necessary.[67] In the last decade of the sixth century, then, a combination of chance and purpose, both set in motion by the world-transforming defeat of Croesus by Cyrus, found Athenian identity and Persian sovereignty on a direct collision course.

The intensity of antityrannical feeling at Athens was to a large extent an indication of how precarious the independence of Athens was. Sparta, the power actually responsible for expelling Hippias, the last tyrant of Athens, in 510, posed the most immediate threat to Athenian independence. The political reforms proposed by Cleisthenes, measures that we recognize as the foundations of Athenian democracy, were widely embraced by Athenians out of the desire to give their community the solidarity and strength in manpower to resist the Spartans, their allies, and their oligarchic friends at Athens.[68] So great was this fear of Sparta, Herodotus tells us, that the sup-

---

64. The husbandry of the earth is eloquently depicted in "The Cow's Lament" (Yasna 29: see Malandra 1983, 35–39), a Zoroastrian hymn in which a cow appeals to Ahuramazda to set a worthy husbandman over her. Xenophon *Oeconomicus* 4.4–25 states that it is the custom of the Persian king to value both the agricultural and the martial arts ($\gamma\epsilon\omega\rho\gamma\acute{\iota}\alpha$ $\tau\epsilon$ $\kappa\alpha\grave{\iota}$ $\dot{\eta}$ $\pi o\lambda\epsilon\mu\iota\kappa\grave{\eta}$ $\tau\acute{\epsilon}\chi\nu\eta$), both of which he promotes throughout his dominion in various ways; Briant 2002, 232–40, discusses this passage, and the authenticity of the Persian image of king as husbandman whose piety sustains the fruitfulness of the earth.

65. Pliny *Naturalis Historia* 34.17 places the dedication of the first statues of Harmodius and Aristogeiton in 509. On the traditions and monuments associated with the tyrannicides, see Brunnsåker 1971 and Taylor 1991.

66. For the Attic drinking songs, or skolia, see Athenaeus 15.695a–b. For discussion of the skolia, and of the meaning of $\grave{\iota}\sigma o\nu\acute{o}\mu o\nu s$ $\tau$' $\grave{A}\theta\acute{\eta}\nu\alpha s$ $\grave{\epsilon}\pi o\iota\eta\sigma\acute{a}\tau\eta\nu$ found in two of them, see Ostwald 1969, 121–36; Taylor 1991, 22–32.

67. The institution of ostracism, described by our sources an antityrannical measure of the Cleisthenic reforms, was the principal legal measure; see Thomsen 1972, 109–42, who defends a date as early as 508/7 for the institution despite the fact that it was not put to use until 487.

68. See Herodotus 5.74–78.

porters of Cleisthenes actually sought an alliance with the most powerful rival of Sparta—the Persians. Facing the threat of a Spartan attack against their city, the Athenians sent messengers to Sardis to negotiate an alliance with the Persians through Artaphernes, brother of Darius and satrap of Sardis. Artaphernes, in turn,[69]

> asked them what people they were who wished to become allies of the Persians, and where was the land they inhabited [κοῦ γῆς οἰκημένοι]; when he learned these things he told the representatives that it all came down to this: if the Athenians gave earth and water to King Darius, he would form an alliance with them; if they did not give these things, he bade them begone. The representatives, on their own initiative, said that they would make the gift, since they wanted the alliance. But when these individuals returned home they were severely censured.

This exchange took place in or shortly before the year 506, when the Athenians managed to beat off the so-called triple invasion of Attica organized by the Spartans.[70] Given the dangers confronting the Athenians on all sides, the Athenian populace must have been as attentive to the religious and symbolic dimensions of their situation as they were to strategic realities. Spartan intervention in Athens just two years earlier had been justified in religious terms, when the Spartans had declared Cleisthenes and his followers to be under a curse (ἐναγέες). In response, the opponents of the Spartans declared that the Spartan king Cleomenes had trespassed on sacred ground by entering Athena's shrine on the Acropolis.[71] Given this sensitivity to the claims of religion, we can assume that the censure of their emissaries to Sardis and the repudiation of the commitments they had made to Artaphernes involved the Athenians in a public discussion of the meaning of submitting earth and water to the king. In both practical and symbolic terms, to render earth and water to the Great King would have meant surrendering to the very forces the Athenians were resisting—tyranny, with all its attendant rituals of submission to the paradigm of Asiatic sovereignty.[72] The Athenians

69. Herodotus 5.73.2–74.1.

70. It is possible that the Athenians repudiated the pledge of their emissaries only after surviving the attack of Cleomenes and his allies (Herodotus 5.74–78), in which case they perceived no need for an alliance with Persia. (So Thomsen 1972, 125.) Even in this scenario, the Athenians would have acted with an awareness of the meaning of complying with Persian terms.

71. Rivalry between supporters of Cleisthenes and of the Spartans is described by Herodotus 5.70–73. R. Parker 1996, 122–24, comments on the considerable evidence for concerns over propriety and sacrilege in the decades at the turn of the sixth to fifth centuries; he observes (124) that "The nerve-centre of the city's religion was now the democratic council."

72. The dependence of Ionian tyrannies on Darius' kingship is emphasized by Histiaeus of Miletus, on the occasion of Darius' Scythian campaign (Herodotus 4.137). The trial of Miltiades at Athens for tyranny in the Chersonese (ca. 492; Herodotus 6.104) indicates that Athenians were attuned to the disjunction between the Asiatic paradigm for sovereignty and their own.

must have been just as aware as Socles of Corinth was of how such a submission would subvert the established relationships both within their political community and between their community and their gods, the "gods of the Greeks" (as Socles had invoked them). For this was precisely the point in time at which the Spartans proposed to their allies that they reinstate Hippias as tyrant at Athens, and when Socles defeated this proposal by delivering his speech on the horrors of tyranny.[73]

If the connection between tyranny and submission to the sovereignty of Asia was only hypothetical to the Athenians before 506, it was clear and real within a year or two after that date. Herodotus reports that when the Spartans failed to win the support of their Peloponnesian allies for restoring Hippias to tyranny at Athens, Hippias left Sparta and returned to Sigeum, near Troy:[74]

> Once he was back in Asia, Hippias used all possible means to malign the Athenians in the presence of Artaphernes, and did everything he could to get Athens under his and Darius' control. When the Athenians learned what Hippias was doing, they sent messengers to tell the Persians not to listen to Athenian exiles. But Artaphernes told them that if they valued their safety, they had to accept the return of Hippias. The Athenians rejected this demand when it was reported back to them, resolving from that moment to be openly hostile to the Persians.

Hippias had persuaded Artaphernes that he was the legitimate ruler of Athens and that his rulership would be harmonious with the sovereignty of Darius if the Persians would restore him to tyranny at Athens. The legitimacy of Hippias' claim over Athens, Herodotus later reports, was described symbolically as a return to "his own mother."[75] This allusion to the land as the mother of the tyrant was precisely the imagery of legitimate tyranny that a ruler of Sardis would understand.[76] We may be sure that the Athenians understood it too. Their determination to be openly hostile to the Persians implied that they were prepared to oppose Persia militarily if the occasion arose; it also meant that the Athenians were prepared to refute Persian claims in rhetorical terms. Perhaps the most effective way of uniting all Athenians in opposition to Persia, and of attracting other Greeks to their cause, was to reject by all demonstrable means the ritualized tokens of Asiatic tyranny in the

---

73. Herodotus 5.90–93, discussed in chapter 4, with notes 53–62.

74. Herodotus 5.96.

75. Herodotus 6.107.1. On the symbolism of Hippias' dream, see chapter 4, with notes 65–67.

76. On the Mother as the earth at Sardis, see chapter 4 at note 67; chapter 5, with note 94. Herodotus 5.93 attests Hippias' preoccupation with oracular rhetoric; 7.6.3–4 refers to oracles later recited to Xerxes on behalf of the Peisistratids (cf. 6.94). On the relationship of motherhood to tyranny, note the epigram for Archedice daughter of Hippias, boasting that her father, husband, brothers, and sons were tyrants (quoted by Thucydides 6.59.3).

name of the gods of the Greeks. Their commitment was in effect a declaration of war on the gods of tyranny.

## THE IONIAN REVOLT

Not long after their resolution to be openly hostile (*polemioi*) to the Persians, Herodotus tells us, Aristagoras of Miletus arrived at Athens with his appeal to the Athenians to join the Ionian uprising. As Herodotus describes the appeal, after rehearsing the same arguments he had offered to Cleomenes at Sparta (presumably the map of Hecataeus and an appeal to the gods of the Greeks were also parts of his argument at Athens), Aristagoras also pointed out how appropriate it was for the Athenians to aid the Milesians, their own colonists. "So anxious was he to get Athenian aid, that he promised everything that came into his head, until at last he succeeded." "Apparently," Herodotus adds, "it is easier to impose upon a crowd than upon an individual, for Aristagoras, who had failed to impose upon Cleomenes, succeeded with thirty thousand Athenians."[77]

The map of the world made Aristagoras' plea to the Athenians for support appear in different terms than it had at Sparta. The Spartans had reckoned themselves the partners of Lydia in a balance of sovereignty, and now reckoned that they should not overstep their side of that balance. But the Athenians were open to the argument that they had a destiny to fulfill in Asia. As Herodotus notes, the most persuasive part of Aristagoras' argument was his acknowledgment that Athens was the ancestral home of the Milesians. Aristagoras thus affirmed an Athenian perception of their homeland as "the oldest land of Ionia," as Solon had once called it.[78] Where Aristagoras had tried but failed to persuade the Spartans to assert sovereignty over the entire *oikoumenē*, he succeeded in persuading the Athenians to assume leadership over the Ionians who dwelt at the heart of the *oikoumenē*. The centerpiece of his battle plan for winning the sovereign independence of Ionia was to be the capture of Sardis.

To modern commentators, the strategy of the Ionian Revolt that unfolded in the attack on Sardis has seemed daring but ill conceived. Ionian strength was at sea, and was not well suited to carrying on a continental war. Those who have sought to account for events according to purely military objectives have tried to make sense out of a confused passage from Plutarch's *On the Malice of Herodotus* (*Moralia* 861b–c), which describes the attack on Sardis as a strategy for raising a Persian siege of Miletus.[79] But this siege of Miletus

---

77. Herodotus 5.97.2, translated by A. de Sélincourt.
78. Solon fr. 28a (Edmonds *EI*, from Aristotle *Athenian Constitution* 5.2).
79. Grote 1862, vol. 3, 248, adopts this approach; it is followed also by Cary in *CAH*, 1st ed., vol. 4 (1926), 221–22; Balcer 1984, 236–37; and 1995, 178–80; tentatively by Gorman 2001, 140.

followed the approach of the king's fleet in Plutarch's account, which could not have happened as early as 498.[80] It is surely best not to treat Plutarch's jumbled diatribe as evidence equal or superior to Herodotus' account.[81] Herodotus himself provides testimony to the fact that the Ionian Revolt really was ill conceived, in strategic terms. According to his account, sober reflection on the balance of power presented to the war council of the Ionians by Hecataeus himself was summarily dismissed from consideration.[82] Herodotus demonstrates that the Ionians felt that they had a viable grand strategy, and were not merely reacting to Persian threats. But Herodotus never tells us what their plan was, only that it failed.

The grand strategy of the Ionian Revolt must have been easy for the Ionians to apprehend, and must have inspired confidence, to judge by the manner in which it gained widespread popular support among the Athenians and the Greeks of Asia. The march on Sardis itself provides the most direct clue to this strategy, but the role of Miletus at the head of the uprising is also an important element to consider.

A generation earlier, when Cyrus captured Sardis, the Milesians alone of all the Ionians had rushed to offer submission to Persia, obtaining from Cyrus the same terms of submission that the Milesians had observed under the Lydians.[83] Herodotus gives a notable reason for the decision of the Milesians: "They stood apart from the rest of the Ionians," he tells us, "solely because of the weakness of the entire Hellenic race, among whom the Ionians constituted by far the weakest and most insignificant part."[84] The historical context of this observation, at the time of the fall of Sardis to Persia in 547, marks the earliest notice of a theme that was a commonplace by Herodotus' day: Ionia was by nature a rich and productive land that bred weak and complacent people.[85] Another way of viewing this observation is to say that Ionia

---

80. According to Herodotus 5.105–8, Darius had not even given orders for the response to the sack of Sardis until after the Ionian Revolt had spread to Cyprus.

81. Plutarch *Moralia* 861b–c is devoted to impugning Herodotus' judgment on, among other points, the merits of the Eretrian contribution to the uprising, and to this effect he cites Lysanias of Mallus' *History of Eretria* (*FGrHist* 426); but there is serious confusion here, either in Plutarch's judgment or in the tradition of his manuscripts, which show signs of defect at this point. Plutarch's further citation, at *Moralia* 861c–d, of Charon of Lampsacus (= *FGrHist* 262 F 10) in fact confirms the outline of Herodotus' account and does nothing to support Plutarch's account of a siege of Miletus at the outset of the revolt. Although Grote 1862, vol. 3, 248 n. 4, makes use of Plutarch, he notes that "the citation is given there confusedly, so that we cannot make much out of it." Murray 1988, 468, warns of the anachronisms; Hammond 1967, 205 n. 3, outright rejects the use of Plutarch on this matter.

82. Herodotus 5.36.

83. Herodotus 1.141.4.

84. Herodotus 1.143.2.

85. Herodotus' observation of the weakness of Ionia in 1.143.2 is associated with his account (1.142.1) of the excellence of the climate of Ionia. The theme is amplified in the Hip-

was the ideal land for dominion within the *oikoumenē*, and that the Ionians had come to accept their inevitable role as compliant subjects to whoever was their sovereign overlord. Milesian submission to the sovereignty of Alyattes and Croesus was the foundation for this view of Ionia's place in the world. Milesian science justified this view.

Miletus was the center of Ionian science in the areas of cosmology and geography associated with the work of Thales and Anaximander. In the previous chapter, Ionian science was characterized as part of a Lydo-Ionian conceptual system that recognized the unique position of Sardis in the order of the *oikoumenē*. For those who accepted this ideology, the balance of power appeared to be in the hands of the lord of Sardis. Those who did not control the symbols of Sardis were by definition weak. Milesian leadership, therefore, had the highest respect for the power of Sardis, and their view was influential among Ionians and Greeks generally. According to Aelius Aristides, speaking of the outset of the Ionian Revolt: "Up to that time, the Greeks marveled at Sardis, and ranked it with Babylon and the wonders of India."[86] When Sardis was firmly held by the Persians, there was no alternative to submission; "no one dared to march against it," a scholiast to Aristides explains, "because the symbols of Persian sovereignty were there."[87] But when Milesian leadership deemed it possible to pry Sardis from the grasp of the Persians, the balance of power could instantly be reversed. Respect for Milesian science made this possibility plausible, and help from Greeks across the Aegean in 499/8 made such a bold stroke seem bound to succeed. The initial popularity of the Ionian uprising indicates that this ideological strategy was easily understood and widely accepted.

In 499/8 the Ionians along with the Athenians and Eretrians made their plan of attack, identifying the symbols of power at Sardis with power itself. Recognizing this factor, and taking account of the events reported by Herodotus, we can discern the overall plan for the Ionian Revolt. Aristagoras is said to have put down tyranny and promoted equality before law (*isonomia*) at Miletus and throughout Ionia.[88] Such measures required a form of

---

pocratic *Airs, Waters, and Places* 12, and still embraced by Aristotle *Politics* 7.7.2–3, 1327b. The theme has recently been examined by R. Thomas 2000, esp. chapter 3, 75–101.

86. Aristides *Panathenaicus* 94 (121, p. 197 Dindorf).

87. Scholion to Aristides *Panathenaicus* 94 (121.4, Dindorf vol. 3, p. 122): οὐδεὶς γὰρ εἰς αὐτὰς ἐτόλμα στρατεύειν, διὰ τὰ Πέρσου βασίλεια ἐνταυθοῖ εἶναι. The usual rendering of τὰ Πέρσου βασίλεια is "the Persian royal palace." This may be correct, but such a royal establishment amounts to the same thing as "the symbols of Persian sovereignty."

88. Herodotus 5.37.2. Pericles Georges 2000 argues that the overthrow of tyrannies, *tout court*, was the goal of the revolt, and that the Ionians expected that a negotiated settlement with the Persians could have ended the matter peaceably. This plan was upset, Georges argues, by "the sudden arrival of Athenian and Eretrian forces in Asia [which] turned the scale of the sit-

communal government, and the rejection or suppression of the ideological tokens of tyranny. The first consideration must have been met by instituting a common deliberative body of the sort said to have been proposed years earlier by Thales.[89] The second was met by embracing Artemis of Ephesus as a divine protector. Artemis, with her revered seat at Ephesus, would become the champion of sovereignty for the Ionians in Asia as Athena was for the Athenians across the Aegean. Kybebe, the divine consort at Sardis, would be displaced, and the Ionians would defend the virginity of their sovereign goddess by beating down any would-be tyrant who might claim the goddess as a bride.[90] Finally, the status quo ante could be restored to the golden age of Croesus. If the Persians could be driven from Sardis, the Halys River would again become the rightful boundary of a dominion that would now be in Ionian hands.[91] The disaster suffered by Croesus when he had attacked Cyrus would thus be repaired, and the new rulers of Sardis could prepare to meet any future challenge from the Persians with all the resources that Croesus had enjoyed, and with greater wisdom.

The transformation of the former Lydian empire into an Ionian league may well have been a dream entertained by leading Ionians of an earlier generation, during the lifetimes of Thales and Anaximander. The elder son of Alyattes, a man named Pantaleon, had an Ionian mother and had powerful supporters based in the cities of Ionia prior to his defeat and execution by

---

uation, in the Persian's eyes, from local recalcitrance to a war of invasion, and forced the Ionians themselves off the fence" (25). This scenario is implausible on several grounds. It offers no explanation for why the Persians might be induced to accept such changes peaceably, especially after the injuries to Persian interests committed by Aristagoras and his supporters (Herodotus 5.36.4–37.2); it dissociates the diplomatic efforts of Aristagoras (5.38) from the planning and efforts of his supporters (5.36); it fails to explain how the Athenians and Eretrians could have so forcefully upset a delicate (hypothetical) balance in Ionia; most important, it fails to explain why the Athenians and Eretrians felt that an attack on Sardis was the right thing to do.

89. On Thales and the concept of communal deliberative government, see Herodotus 1.170.3; cf. 1.141.4–142 on the relationship between the Panionium meeting place and cosmic centrality of Ionia. Ionian leaders promoting their uprising on Cyprus in 497 speak in the name of the league (or common council) of the Ionians (τὸ κοινόν τῶν Ἰώνων): Herodotus 5.109.3. The standardized electrum coinage issued by several Ionian mints at this time is also evidence for communal government: see Gardner 1918, 91–103; Kraay 1976, 30, 36–39. On the relationship of these matters to the organization of the Ionian Revolt, see Murray 1988, 480–82.

90. On Artemis of Ephesus as a counterpart to Kybebe at Sardis, see chapter 4, with notes 113–18.

91. Accordingly, the easternmost peoples of continental Asia who joined the revolt were the Paeonians living in Phrygia (i.e., on the eastern boundaries of the former Lydian empire): Herodotus 5.98. Note that Aeschylus *Persians* 865 treats the Halys River as a boundary best not crossed. The Delphic oracle to Croesus, as reported by Aristotle *Rhetoric* 3.5.4, specified the Halys as an ominous boundary; Herodotus 1.53.3, 1.72, 75, is more oblique.

his half-brother, Croesus.[92] The Ionians who had hoped that Pantaleon, one of their own, would rule over them, may have become the core supporters of another Lydian, Pactyes, who attempted to throw off the Persian yoke as soon as Cyrus withdrew from Sardis.[93] Two decades later, similar considerations appear to have encouraged the ambitious Polycrates of Samos to trust in the offer of partnership with Oroetes, the satrap of Sardis, to his undoing.[94] At the same time, Peisistratid visions of appropriating Delos and Naxos had directed the collective aspirations of the Athenians toward acquisition of Ionian symbols of power.[95] By the time of Aristagoras' appeal to the Athenians, the Ionian cause had become the antityrannical cause, very much in keeping with Athenian concerns of the moment. Hippias was encouraging Artaphernes to restore him to tyranny at Athens. Symbolic logic may have persuaded the Athenians that if they were to take control of the seat of tyranny at Sardis, and if tyrannies everywhere were dissolved in favor of egalitarian governments as Aristagoras had announced, then the Persians would have no basis for supporting the return of Hippias.

There is good reason to believe, therefore, that the capture of Sardis was planned as both the opening and the crowning achievement of the Ionian uprising against the Persians. Herodotus indicates that the march against Sardis proceeded according to a preconceived plan, and not as a reaction to Persian threats or for lack of anything better to do. After assembling the allied forces at Miletus, Aristagoras appointed commanders and sent the expedition on its way: "The fleet sailed for Ephesus, where the ships were left at Coressus in Ephesian territory; the troops, a strong force, then began their march up county with Ephesian guides. They followed the course of the Caÿster, crossed the ridge of Tmolus, and came down upon Sardis, which they took without opposition."[96] Their march traced precisely the route of a traditional procession from the Temple of Artemis at Ephesus to the shrine of Artemis at Sardis.[97] The sanctity of the mission, not the obscurity of the route, was the reason for securing Ephesian guides.[98] Although Herodotus makes

---

92. On Pantaleon, half-brother and rival to Croesus, see Herodotus 1.92.3–4; Nicolaus of Damascus *FGrHist* 90 F 65; Plutarch *Moralia* 401e. These accounts are summarized by Pedley 1968, 79–80.

93. Herodotus 1.154–161, where Pactyes receives considerable support among Aeolian and Ionian Greeks before the Persian power overwhelms all resistance.

94. Herodotus 3.122–25, discussed in chapter 5, at notes 126–28.

95. See chapter 5, with notes 108–16.

96. Herodotus 5.100, translated by A. de Sélincourt.

97. The traditional procession is attested in the fourth-century Sacrilege Inscription. (See chapter 4, note 114.) The topographical features and ritual significance of this route, particularly in its passage across Mount Tmolus, are discussed by Rose Lou Bengisu 1996, esp. 10–13.

98. Murray 1988, 143, infers that this was an unusual route taken to achieve surprise, hence the need for guides. Balcer supposes that "the majority of Ephesians, however, loyal to their Persian overlords, were unwilling to revolt, but faced with a foreign army in their midst, a few

no mention of music or ceremony, we may suspect that it proceeded to the accompaniment of ritual music like that he describes for Lydian armies, and like that described by Polyaenus for the army of Midas.[99] In any event, the march was a procession of ritual conquest, for its goal was a sacred symbol.[100]

Arriving in sufficient force to seize the lower city of Sardis without opposition, the Ionians were nevertheless unable to capture the acropolis held by Artaphernes and a Persian garrison. Sometime in the course of plundering the town an Ionian soldier set a house on fire, causing a general conflagration throughout the lower town and burning down a sacred grove and, presumably with it, the shrine of Kybebe. Whether or not this was intentional, the Persians certainly interpreted the burning of the shrine of Kybebe as a deliberate act, for it became their justification for burning the temples of Greece. After the abduction of Helen this was arguably the most famous casus belli of classical antiquity.[101]

The Ionians had evidently hoped to drive the Persians out of Sardis and so take from them the tokens of their sovereignty over Asia—Sardis itself, with its shrines, gardens, tumuli, and sacred landmarks. With the burning of the lower city at Sardis, and with it the shrine of Kybebe, some among the Ionians might have believed that their mission was accomplished. In ruins, the lower city with its shrine of Kybebe was no longer a thing of beauty, and perhaps therefore no longer a thing of power. But having left the Persians in possession of Sardis with its ruined sacred places, the Ionians had also left them the most explicit justification for seeking revenge.

These symbolic realities provide the basis for explaining the radical transformation in the Athenian attitude toward the uprising after the failure to

---

perhaps reluctantly guided the army up the Kayster valley across the Tmolus range into Sardis" (1984, 236; cf. 1995, 179). I see no basis for describing the Ephesian role in these terms.

99. On the martial rituals of Midas and the Lydians, see chapter 2 at notes 121–27. For Artemis of Ephesus as a champion of warriors in the time of the Peloponnesian War, see Xenophon *Hellenica* 1.2.6; cf. *Agesilaus* 1.27. Note also the connections between Artemis Orthia, Lydia, and warfare cited in chapter 2, note 127. Herodotus' story (8.65) of the ghost procession from the sanctuary of Demeter at Eleusis, accompanied by sounds of the *Iacchos* song, on the eve of the battle of Salamis provides an example of an analogous martial ritual march.

100. The idea of seizing power by appropriating a sacred symbol is exemplified at Athens by the successive seizures, or attempted seizures, of the Acropolis by Cylon (Herodotus 5.71; Thucydides 1.126), Peisistratus (Herodotus 1.59–60), and Isagoras and Cleomenes (Herodotus 5.72).

101. Herodotus 5.102.1: καὶ Σάρδιες μὲν ἐνεπρήσθησαν, ἐν δὲ αὐτῇσι καὶ ἱρὸν ἐπιχωρίης θεοῦ Κυβήβης τὸ σκηπτόμενοι οἱ Πέρσαι ὕστερον ἀντενεπίμπρασαν τὰ ἐν Ἕλλησι ἱρά. Herodotus reiterates the Persian grievance at 5.105, 6.101.3, and 7.8b; at 5.97.3, Herodotus describes Athenian and Eretrian involvement in the Ionian Revolt as "the beginning of evils" (ἀρχὴ κακῶν), underscoring the importance of this casus belli. Aristotle *Posterior Analytics* 2.11, 94a36–94b7, treats the attack on Sardis as the unprovoked cause of war between Persia and Athens, and an archetype of cause and effect. The epitome of Diodorus 10.25 reports that "the Persians learned to burn shrines from the Greeks, and returned this outrage to those who had committed it first."

take Sardis. While the Ionians of necessity remained committed, and even succeeded in widening the scope of the insurrection considerably over the following year, after the failure at Sardis "the Athenians utterly abandoned the Ionians, and even though Aristagoras sent them many appeals by messenger, they refused to help them."[102] The Athenians were motivated, above all else, by the desire to keep Peisistratid tyranny out of Athens. The failure to take control of Sardis meant that the Ionians had failed to take control of the power of tyranny, and therefore the Athenians would have to seek other means of averting the threat of tyranny from Athens. They, with their Ionian kinsmen, still failed to see that Persian sovereignty was a new and larger power than the tyranny of Asia centered at Sardis. Only Hecataeus, in Herodotus' account, had a true appreciation of this larger power, which was now turning its attention to Athens.

Although the Athenians had no further part in the Ionian Revolt, Herodotus tells us that their participation in the attack on Sardis was seen by the Persians, and by Darius in particular, as a most serious affront to Persian sovereignty. The Ionians, Darius knew, would receive their due punishment; but the Athenians were something new. Taking up his royal armament, the bow and arrow, Darius discharged an arrow into the sky and uttered a vow in the name of Zeus (i.e., Ahuramazda) to punish the Athenians.[103] We might take this story as a bit of dramatic conceit for the benefit of Athenians in Herodotus' audience; but the course of events bears it out. With the sack of Sardis, the Athenians became known to Darius as the chief obstacles to his sovereignty at the juncture of Asia and Europe. Divinities were invoked both as witness and as justification for the actions that followed.

When Herodotus calls the offended deity at Sardis "a local divinity, Kybebe," he emphasizes her connection to this place, but he also obscures her wider associations with sovereignty. These wider associations were a contentious issue, possibly misconstrued at the time of the Ionian Revolt and still not perfectly understood in Herodotus' day. As in his silence on the wider significance of the rites rejected by the Scythians, Herodotus was leaving it to his readers to decide for themselves if the Ionians and their allies deserved any part of the retribution that the Persians vowed to mete out to them.[104] He did so, as we shall see, because the challenge to sovereignty, both worldly and divine, issued by the Ionians against the lords of Asia in 498 had not yet been resolved by the time Herodotus was writing.

102. Herodotus 5.103.1.

103. Herodotus 5.105, recapitulated in 5.108.1. The imagery of the Persian king as archer was most memorably broadcast on the Persian gold darics introduced by Darius.

104. So François Hartog 1988, 244–45, has correctly recognized Herodotus' deliberate avoidance (5.102.1) of acknowledging the identity of Kybebe as related to the apostasy of the Greeks from Persian rule.

### THE HERALDS OF DARIUS

To all but the most piously simple among the Athenians (the sort of people who would later believe that the "wooden walls" of the Acropolis would protect them from the onslaught of Xerxes) it was clear that the attack on Sardis had failed to destroy the power of the Persians in Asia. A new approach was needed to deal with the Persians and their support of Peisistratid tyranny. In 496, just over a year after the withdrawal of the Athenians from Ionia, Hipparchus son of Charmus, probably the grandson of the exiled Hippias and the senior representative of the friends and kin of the Peisistratids still at Athens, was elected eponymous archon.[105] By placing a Peisistratid symbolically at the head of the Athenian state on their own accord, the Athenians were hoping to preempt all Persian claims to the right of reestablishing the Peisistratid tyranny at Athens.[106] The move was probably not expected to placate the Persians, who were still *polemioi* to the Athenians. More likely it was intended to placate the gods—insofar as the Persian demand may have insinuated a divine justification—and to remove the fear that divine will might aid the Persians in their mission to reestablish Peisistratid tyranny.

This move may have calmed Athenian fears for the moment. But the sack of Miletus by the Persians in 494, and with it the destruction of the oracular shrine of Apollo at Didyma, provoked distress and alarm among Athenians over what Herodotus calls "a disaster that the Athenians felt as their own."[107] The expansion of Persian military operations in the Aegean thereafter demonstrated that the gods were not going to keep the Persians at a safe distance from Athens. When Darius and his commanders were ready to move directly against the Athenians, they pressed their demands in a manner that was designed to generate anxiety among the Athenians and their fellow Hellenes over whether any aid and support would be forthcoming from the gods of the Greeks against those who invoked the gods of sovereignty.[108]

---

105. On Hipparchus son of Charmus, see Aristotle *Athenian Constitution* 22.4–6; on his filiation, see Raubitschek 1958, 106–7, and Davies 1971, 451–52, where reasons for regarding him as the grandson of the tyrant Hippias are stronger than the arguments of Thomsen 1972, 21–22, favoring the view that Hipparchus was a brother-in-law of the tyrant Hippias. Meritt 1939, 62–64, argues that the younger Peisistratus, son of Hippias, was archon in 497/6, which would place the election of a Peisistratid immediately after the return of the Athenians from Ionia. (For discussion see ML 11; Thomsen 1972, 126.)

106. The election of Hipparchus has been seen as evidence of a new "policy of appeasement towards the Persians" (so Thomsen 1972, 126).

107. Herodotus 6.21.2 refers to the fact that "the Athenians displayed their great distress at the sack of Miletus in many different ways"; among them, at an unspecified later date, they fined the playwright Phrynichus for reminding them of "the disaster they felt as their own" (οἰκήϊα κακά) when he dramatized the event in a tragedy.

108. Persian sovereignty is invoked in the name of θεοὶ βασιλήϊοι by Cambyses, at Herodotus 3.65.6, and by Histiaeus of Miletus, at Herodotus 5.106.6. For the gods of kingship invoked

In 491 Darius "sent heralds this way and that throughout Greece, with instructions to request earth and water for the king."[109] Herodotus reports that many Greeks honored the request, but some did not.[110] Only in the cases of Athens and Sparta does Herodotus provide any further information about the reception these heralds received, and he provides this information only to explain why Xerxes later did not bother to send heralds to Athens and Sparta as his father had: "At Athens they were thrown into the *barathron*, at Sparta they were pushed into a well—and told that if they wanted earth and water for the king, to get them from there."[111]

The treatment of Darius' heralds at Athens and at Sparta, as told by Herodotus, is so remarkable that some scholars have doubted its historicity, while others pass over the event in silence.[112] Yet the incident is attested by more indications than the plain statement given by Herodotus. Herodotus bears witness to an enduring unease on the part of both Athenians and Spartans over this incident, lasting until the time of the Peloponnesian War:[113]

> Just what disagreeable consequences were suffered by the Athenians for this treatment of the king's messengers, I am unable to say; perhaps it was the destruction of their city and the countryside around it—though I do not myself believe that this happened as a direct result of their crime. The case is clear, however, with respect to the Spartans: upon them fell the anger of Agamem-

---

in Persian texts ("Ahuramazda . . . and also the other gods who exist," among whom is Anahita), see the texts cited above in notes 19, 24–30, and 64. Note especially the correspondence between the domain of Anahita, according to Yasht 5 (quoted at note 29 above), and the control exercised by θεοὶ βασιλήιοι over the fertility of the earth, of women, and of flocks, according to Herodotus 3.65.7.

109. Herodotus 6.48; cf. Herodotus 6.94, 7.32.

110. Herodotus 6.48–49 reports that earth and water were given by "many of the mainlanders and all of the islanders visited by the heralds." Cf. 7.131–32, enumerating those who gave earth and water later to Xerxes.

111. Herodotus 7.133.1, translated by A. de Sélincourt.

112. So, for example, Charles Hignett 1963, 87, calls the incident "probably unhistorical," and Hermann Bengtson 1968, 43, says it "hardly seems plausible." The incident is not mentioned at all in chapters 6–8 covering this era in *CAH*, 1st ed., vol. 4 (1926), by E. M. Walker, G. B. Gray, M. Cary, and A. R. Munro; nor in the otherwise close examination of this period by M. F. McGregor 1940; nor in the voluminous survey of Persian history by Pierre Briant 2002. Gustav Glotz 1925–45, vol. 2, 33, refers guardedly to the execution of Darius' heralds as "la tradition officielle." On the other hand, George Grote 1862, vol. 3, 272–74, recognized the execution of Darius' heralds at Athens and at Sparta as a decisive moment: "The proceeding now before us is of very great importance in the progress of Graecian history. It is the first direct and positive historical manifestation of Hellas as an aggregate body, with Sparta as its chief, and obligations of a certain sort on the part of its members, the neglect or violation of which constitutes a species of treason" (273). Grote's lead has been followed by N. G. L. Hammond 1988, 498 and 500. Louise-Marie Wéry 1966 and Raphael Sealey 1976, each reviewing scholarship on this dispute, have also argued in favor of the historicity of these events.

113. Herodotus 7.133.2–134, modified translation of A. de Sélincourt.

non's herald, Talthybius. There is in Sparta a temple dedicated to Talthybius, and a family—the Talthybiadae—descended from him, which enjoys the sole privilege of holding the office of herald. Now there was a long period after the incident I have mentioned above during which the Spartans were unable to obtain favourable signs from their sacrifices; this caused them deep concern, and they held frequent assemblies at which the question "Is there any Spartan who is willing to die for his country?" was put by the public crier. Two Spartans, Sperthias the son of Aneristus, and Bulis the son of Nicolaus, both men of good family and great wealth, volunteered to offer their lives to Xerxes in atonement for Darius' messengers who had been killed at Sparta.

Sperthias and Bulis were spared by Xerxes, but Herodotus affirms that divine punishment visited the Spartans many years later, during the Peloponnesian War, when the sons of these two Spartans were sent as envoys to Persia, and were intercepted on their way, taken to Athens, summarily executed, and thrown into a pit.[114] On the question of divine retribution suffered by the Athenians, Herodotus prefers not to offer his own opinion, except in the negative. It was a matter in which, as he implies, conflicting opinions were held in his day. Among later sources, Plutarch, Pausanias, and Aelius Aristides each relate the story of the execution of the Persian heralds with slightly different details, indicating that Herodotus' was not the only account of the incident to come down from classical antiquity.

Herodotus, followed by Pausanias and Aelius Aristides, refers to the execution of heralds (*kērykes*), in the plural, and the disposal of their bodies in the *barathron*. Pausanias adds that Miltiades was responsible for the execution of the heralds by the Athenians, meaning that he proposed this drastic measure. As with the affair as a whole, scholars have found reasons to doubt the historicity of Miltiades' alleged part in it.[115] But once we grant that there are no reasons to doubt that the heralds from Darius were treated as Herodotus says they were, then there is no good reason to dismiss Miltiades' role. Recently returned from the Thracian Chersonese and pressed to clear himself from the charge of having exercised tyranny, Miltiades had more

---

114. Herodotus 7.133–37 reports the incidents at Athens and Sparta and the general speculation in later years about their eventual consequences. Thucydides 2.67 confirms Herodotus' account about the eventual fate of the Spartan envoys. Aristophanes' several jokes about throwing scoundrels into the *barathron* (*Knights* 1362, *Clouds* 1450, *Frogs* 574, *Wealth* 431) might have this incident in mind. (Later scholiasts brought up the comparison.) Hammond 1988, 500, points out that these incidents were associated with the Monument of Talthybius at Sparta (Pausanias 3.12.7), giving the story a tangible focus at least as early as the late fifth century.

115. Pausanias 3.12.7; Aristides *On the Four* 184 (p. 247 Dindorf), *Panathenaicus* 99 (122, p. 198 Dindorf). Wéry 1966, 474–75, argues that the assignment of blame to Miltiades was a Spartan story, designed to spread blame to the Athenians, who had (in Wéry's view) actually murdered not the heralds, but only their interpreter. This is not how Herodotus reports the matter, however.

need than almost any other Athenian to prove his uncompromising opposition to tyrannical rule. By leading the condemnation of the heralds in 491,
Miltiades placed his personal allegiance beyond question, and established
the credentials that enabled him to lead the Athenians into battle against
the Persians and against tyranny at Marathon.[116]

Plutarch, on the other hand, associates this event with a famous decree proposed by Themistocles, encouraging modern scholars to conclude that later
sources were casting around for a famous name to associate with an infamous
event, and that neither name deserves credence, especially since Herodotus
is silent in this matter.[117] But Herodotus' silence means not that no such account was known to him—only that he felt it was unnecessary, or would be
indiscreet, to draw attention to such details. Plutarch specifies that the decree
proposed by Themistocles was aimed at the interpreter (*hermēneus*) of the Persian delegation, "because he dared to use the Hellenic language to convey
barbarian commands."[118] Aelius Aristides also speaks of the condemnation and
execution of the interpreter as a memorable act, and attributes it to Themistocles.[119] Aristides points out that a special example was made of the interpreter because he was a Greek and because the Athenians felt that "a colonist
from their city should not become an interpreter for their natural enemy
against the interests of their city and of the Greeks," and so a point was made
of giving this man a separate verdict of condemnation before he was put to
death and thrown into the *barathron* along with the rest of the heralds.[120]

Two separate resolutions, then, are connected with this event, the decision
to execute the heralds, and the decision to execute their Greek interpreter
as well. Each resolution is connected with a famous Athenian statesman. The
first is attributed to Miltiades, who had recently fled from Persian forces on
the frontier of Europe and Asia and returned to Athens, where, in the year
of Darius' heralds, he was elected to the generalship that he held at
Marathon. The second is attributed to Themistocles, who had been archon
in 493/2, when the Athenians were coming to grips with the destruction of

116. Hammond 1988, 500, similarly defends the historicity of Miltiades' role on this occasion. On Miltiades' trial for exercising tyranny in the Chersonese, see Herodotus 6.104. On
his recognized leadership at Marathon, see Herodotus 6.109–10, 132; see also Ostwald 1988,
340. Contrast the allegations surrounding the role of the Alcmaeonidae at the battle of
Marathon: Herodotus 6.121–31.

117. So How and Wells 1912, vol. 2, 179.

118. Plutarch *Themistocles* 6.2.

119. Aristides *On the Four* 184 (p. 247 Dindorf).

120. Aristides *Panathenaicus* 99 (122, p. 198 Dindorf). A scholion to this passage (Dindorf
vol. 3, 125) identifies the interpreter as a Samian, "said by some to be called Mys." Another
scholion (Dindorf vol. 3, 591), explaining the same incident in Aristides *On the Four* 184 (Dindorf p. 247), identifies the interpreter as an Ionian, and gives his name as Lycidas, which is
almost certainly a mistake arising from the account of the execution of Lycidas the Athenian
in Herodotus 9.5.

Miletus at the end of the Ionian Revolt, and who later led the Athenians in resistance to the invasion of Xerxes. These attributions are plausible—Who more likely would have led the Athenian response to the heralds in 491?— and for that very reason also suspect: Who, if one wanted to invent likely names, could be more believable? Credence bears a lighter burden, I find, if we take the accounts of our sources at face value. Miltiades and Themistocles in fact were both playing leading roles in defining the Athenian stand in the face of Persian demands at this very time. As we will see in the following chapter, Herodotus and his contemporaries knew that, along with the memories of their great accomplishments, suspicions of great sacrilege attended the memory of both Miltiades and Themistocles. There is every likelihood that both of them were influential in the deliberations of the Athenian council when a response to Darius' heralds was given.

### THE *MĒTRAGYRTĒS* AT ATHENS

The submission of earth and water required of the Athenians, as discussed earlier in this chapter, was to be an acknowledgment of their place within the *oikoumenē*, and an acknowledgment of the rightful sovereignty over the *oikoumenē* exercised by the lord of Sardis, who was now the Great King of Persia. The practical requirements of submission were not likely to be specified; as Amélie Kuhrt has demonstrated, by submitting earth and water one signified readiness in perpetuity to respond to whatever request the Persian king might make.[121] More important to the occasion was a simple, recognizable, public expression of the concept at issue, wherein political relationships were harmonized with familiar concepts of the nature of the world and the nature of religious authority. The demand for earth and water was such an expression, but the demand still required an argument to justify the concepts that it represented. For all the reasons adduced above, and because Herodotus tells us specifically that Kybebe at Sardis was the publicly announced reason for the Persian reaction against Greece and against Athens in particular, we should expect that the demand for earth and water was justified by a declaration, by a man of religious authority among Darius' heralds, of the omnipotence of Kybebe, known to the Ionians and Athenians as the Mother of the Gods. In the mission of Darius' heralds to Athens we should recognize the historic occasion of the arrival of the *Mētragyrtēs* at Athens.

The heralds must have presented their demand to the Athenian council, where foreign emissaries were customarily heard.[122] The herald who spoke

---

121. Kuhrt 1988, 92, 93, 95–96.

122. The council's role in receiving embassies is well attested later (Rhodes 1972, 43, 54, 57–58), and is implied at this time by the reception of the Spartan king Cleomenes by Isagoras as a leading spokesman of the Athenian council (Herodotus 5.72.1). The council's role in

of Kybebe was most likely a eunuch and priest of the cult of Kybebe at Sardis, a Phrygian either in fact or in accordance with the convention that Phrygia was the original home of her cult. Julian and other late sources clearly regarded the *Mētragyrtēs* who came to Athens as a eunuch, and there is no reason to treat this feature as an anachronism when referring to the early fifth century.[123] Although later sources characterized the spokesman for the Mother of the Gods in derogatory terms as one of her begging priests, a eunuch emissary of Darius was no beggar, but a high court official. Eunuchs as respected men of learning, trusted emissaries, and high officiants of cult are well attested in Anatolia during the Persian period and before.[124] Fifth-century sources refer to a minister of the Mother of the Gods as the *Kybēbos* (*Κυβῆβος*), identifying him specifically as a representative of Kybebe. Simonides, the elegiac poet of the Persian War era, used the word *Kybēbos*, according to the Byzantine scholar and patriarch Photius, who explains this term as what "the Ionians call the *Mētragyrtēs*, who is now also called Gallus."[125] This *Kybēbos* was also known for having been "thrown headfirst," exactly the treatment given to the *Mētragyrtēs* when he was thrown into the *barathron*.[126] The identification of the *Mētragyrtēs* as *Kybēbos* links this man directly with Kybebe, or the Mother of the Gods at Sardis, and the citation by Simonides demonstrates a general awareness, at the time of these events, of the importance of a spokesman for Kybebe.

Another source contemporary to the events we are discussing attests that the Athenians were familiar with eunuchs as spokesmen for Persian sovereignty. Phrynichus, the Attic tragedian whose *Sack of Miletus* was so disturb-

---

defining religious policy is noted by R. Parker 1996, 124 (cited above, note 71). On the archaeological remains of the old Council House in the agora at this time, see Thompson 1937, 127–35; Camp 1986, 52–53; Shear 1993, 418–24; 1995.

123. On the accounts of Julian and other late sources, see chapter 2, with note 10. On the evidence for eunuchs in the archaic cult of Kybebe, Cybele, or the Mother of the Gods, see chapter 4 at note 85.

124. See the discussion in chapter 4, with notes 74–88, and see especially the testimony (cited in chapter 4, notes 83 and 84) to the eunuchs bearing the name and title Megabyzus serving in succession as the high attendant to the cult of Artemis of Ephesus.

125. Photius *Lexicon* s.v. *Κύβηβον· τὸν θεοφόρητον* [codd.: *θεόφραστον*] *·Κρατῖνος Θράτταις· Ἴωνες δὲ τὸν μητραγύρτην καὶ γάλλον νῦν καλουμένον· οὕτως Σιμωνίδης* (= Semonides fr. 36 [West]). Photius' citation of Simonides has long been reassigned by modern editors to Semonides, the iambic poet of the seventh century, on the basis of other fragments demonstrably misattributed in late sources. Recent scholarship, however, has found reason to restore the ancient assignment of some of these fragments to Simonides of Ceos, poet of the era of the Persian Wars (e.g., M. L. West 1974, 179–80; 1996), and such should be the verdict on this citation as well, which has no independent basis for assignment to Semonides.

126. *Etymologicum Magnum* 543.11: *Κυβῆβειν· κυρίως τὸ ἐπὶ κεφαλὴν ῥίπτειν* ("*Kybēbein,* or 'to do the Kybebe thing,' in particular means to throw headfirst"). Cf. Photius *Lexicon* s.v. *Μητρῷον· οἱ δ' Ἀθηναῖοι ἀπέκτειναν αὐτὸν* [sc. *τὸν μητραγύρτην*], *ἐμβαλλόντες εἰς βάραθρον ἐπὶ κεφαλήν* (passage cited and translated in chapter 2 at note 11).

ing to the Athenians, presented a eunuch as the opening speaker in his *Phoenician Women,* a forerunner to Aeschylus' *Persians.*[127] This eunuch, we are told, announced the disaster that had befallen Xerxes' army in a manner that Aeschylus later adapted to his messenger's speech. To an Athenian audience, the laments of this eunuch serving the Persian king would be all the more satisfying in memory of the dire warnings uttered by another such eunuch, just over a decade before. Phrynichus also composed pleasant and memorable choral songs in honor of Pan and the Mountain Mother (μήτηρ ὀρεία), according to Aristophanes.[128] These songs for Pan and the Mother were performed at some time during the years when the threat from Persia was looming. In view of what happened to the Mother's eunuch spokesman in 491 (as argued here), it would have been reassuring for Athenians afterward to think of the Mother of the Gods as in an agreeable mood.

Reassurance was needed after the Athenians had dealt with Darius' messengers, for, as Herodotus indicates, the encounter was disturbing. Later sources describe the *Kybēbos* or *Mētragyrtēs* as possessed by the Mother of the Gods and out of his mind, reporting that he announced that "the Mother is coming in search of her daughter!"[129] Based on the foregoing evidence and discussion, we may venture some conjectures about the message that Darius' spokesman delivered.

Darius' eunuch herald, the *Kybēbos,* will have explained that Kybebe was the earth, Ge; that she was the mother of sovereign Zeus, Rhea; that she was the divine consort and mother of kings, Aphrodite; that she was the bearer of cultivated crops, Demeter; that her daughter, as virgin and as bride, signified the participation of all humankind in the cycles of birth and death that grounded mortal existence on its immortal foundation. He will also have explained that the tokens of these truths lay in Asia, where life, humanity, and bread were first created. There the power of the Mother had been revealed, at the center of the *oikoumenē,* through successive generations of kings whose reverence to the Mother assured the prosperity of all their subjects, and whose tyranny over many nations was legitimized through the sustenance of cultivated grain. There also, Ephesian Artemis, the goddess as nature in harmony with human prosperity, had her ancient seat. Since the time of Croesus, all Ionians had paid tribute to Kybebe at Sardis, and to Ephesian Artemis

127. The synopsis of Phrynichus' *Phoenician Women* is given in the hypothesis to Aeschylus' *Persians* on the authority of the fifth-century literary historian Glaucus of Rhegium.

128. Aristophanes *Birds* 737–52, in which the chorus imitates Phrynichus by name while singing: "I perform sacred tunes for Pan and holy dances for the Mountain Mother" (Πανὶ νόμους ἱεροὺς ἀναφαίνω σεμνά τε μητρὶ χορεύματ' ὀρείᾳ). Pan is associated with the Mother of the Gods also by Pindar, in a fragment of a partheneion (fr. 95 Sandys), and Pan's cult was introduced to Athens at this time (Herodotus 6.105; see R. Parker 1996, 187, on the "truly striking" number of new cults associated with the Persian Wars).

129. Photius *Lexicon* s.v. Κύβηβον and *Suda* s.v. βάραθρον (cited in chapter 2 at note 13).

alongside her. If Athens was truly the motherland of the Ionians, as the Athenians claimed, and if the Athenians were the beneficiaries of these divine gifts, as they manifestly were, then they owed reverence to the seat of divinity at the center of these symbols. In paying it, they would also render obeisance to the king whose power Kybebe upheld, and who defended her, especially after her shrine had recently been treated so outrageously.

All such themes would have been familiar to the Athenians, historically through their contact with Lydia and Ionia, intellectually through the influence of Ionian cosmogonic speculation, and spiritually through the diffusion of mythic, cultic, artistic, and musical themes from Ionia, Lydia, and the East. Familiarity made it difficult for the Athenians to deny these claims. In order to reject the demands made on behalf of Darius, the Athenians would have had to reject the deity in whose name these demands were propounded, and to distance themselves from the universalizing principles in cosmology, theology, and geography that underlay Darius' claim to world sovereignty. In defense of their own independence, the Athenians had to assert the independence of their divinities from those of Asia, and the priority of their own rites of primeval origin.

The Athenian councilors, then, will have denied that Kybebe was in fact Earth, to whom they owed reverence. Kybebe was ἐπιχωρίη, "local," according to the Athenians; she might be a divinity known in Asia, but she was certainly not the same as Rhea, Aphrodite, or Demeter or her daughter. These were distinct. The Mother who was known to Athenians in Eleusinian rites was either Demeter, the mother of Kore, or Rhea, the mother of Demeter, not the Phrygian Mother.[130] Athenians worshipped Aphrodite Pandemos, the goddess who bestowed her blessings on "All the People," and not just on her chosen *tyrannos*.[131] According to a tradition that appears in its fully developed form at about this time, the Athenians themselves were the descendants of autochthonous ancestors, sprung from the thin but hardy soil of Attica, not the rich but enervating soil of Asia.[132] As for the landmarks

---

130. Herodotus 8.65.4 attests the use of "Mother" (μήτηρ) to refer to Demeter. The shrine of the Mother, the Metroön in Agrae, attested as early as the 470s or 460s (*IG* I³ 234, line A 5), is the earliest evidence for a cult place that might have been associated with the Asiatic Mother. This Mother was co-opted into the cult of Eleusinian Demeter, and her shrine became the site of the Lesser Mysteries. Simon 1983, 26–27, argues that the Mother at Agrae was the Asiatic Mother identified as Rhea, who presided over the reconciliation of Demeter to the company of the gods in *Homeric Hymn* 2, *To Demeter* 441–70. The connection of the Lesser Mysteries with the Mother of the Gods is also defended by R. Parker 1996, 188–89 and 194; and by Roller 1999, 175. Robertson 1996 argues that the Mother in Agrae had nothing to do with the Asiatic Mother.

131. On Aphrodite Pandemos, and the Solonic foundation of her cult, see chapter 4, notes 134–35. Note also the prominence of Aphrodite Pandemos on Attic coins of the period ca. 510–480: Simon 1970.

132. Rosivach 1987 argues that the idea of Athenian autochthony was created in the period when the word *autochthōn* is first attested, "viz. in the period between the Persian Wars and the

of divine and human sovereignty and its primeval generation and regeneration, the Athenians could point to their own counterparts of the sacred grove of Kybebe and the Gygaean lake at Sardis. At Athens such landmarks were found in the ancient shrines of Olympian Zeus, Cronus and Rhea, Pythian Apollo, Earth, Dionysus in the Marshes, and Aphrodite in the Gardens, all clustered between the Acropolis and the Ilissus stream.[133] As for Artemis, the Athenians honored Delos in the midst of the Aegean as her birthplace, and likewise that of her brother, Apollo.[134] If the Ionians observed rites of the Apaturia and the Anthesteria in common with the Athenians, it was because the Ionians had brought these customs with them as colonists from Athens, according to the Athenians, and not because these rites were older in Asia.[135]

To close the case, to demonstrate their confidence in their own theology and history, and to silence the heralds, the Athenian councilors had them arrested and put to death.[136] Blasphemy may have been the formal basis of their summary condemnation. The charge against the interpreter, as reported by Plutarch and Aelius Aristides, was that he had "dared to use the Hellenic language to convey barbarian commands."[137] A gulf in language and in ethnic identity between Greeks and barbarians was thereby given a sharp definition. Probably because of this event, the Greek language became

---

middle of the fifth century" (305). For a more discursive analysis, see Loraux 1993, esp. 39–41. Shapiro 1998 surveys monuments illustrating the Athenian myth of autochthony. Note that Thucydides 1.2 supports both the notion of Athenian autochthony and the idea that Attica, in origin, lay outside the *oikoumenē*, precisely because it was not endowed with rich, nurturing soil. Aelius Aristides *Panathenaicus* 113 (126, p. 205 Dindorf) praises the city of Athens as "the first to generate humanity, and the first to discover the means of life" immediately after praising the city for the victory over the Persians at Marathon in 490.

133. See Thucydides 2.15.3–4; Pausanias 1.18–19; Travlos 1971, 291 figure 379. Note that Pausanias attests to the place, by the temenos of Olympian Earth, where the flood of Deucalion (primeval waters) drained away. Also note that in the Anthesteria at Athens, veneration of the dead was combined with the renewal of sovereignty in the Sacred Marriage of Dionysus and the Basilinna, which began at Dionysus' sanctuary in the Marshes (See chapter 1 at notes 88–89, and chapter 4 at notes 29–30.)

134. See chapter 5, note 112.

135. Herodotus 1.147.2 identifies the Apaturia as a common festival of all Ionians who came from Athens. (The exception of Ephesians and Colophonians is discussed below in the chapter 7.) Thucydides 2.15.4 notes the Dionysian rites of the Anthesteria as "just like those that are still observed today by the Ionians who came from Athens."

136. The authority of the Athenian council to make summary decisions without reference to the full assembly was clearly an issue at this early date. Legislation partially preserved in *IG* I³ 105, probably originally composed in the early fifth century, demonstrates a concern to limit the power of the council (see Aristotle *Athenian Constitution* 45.1 on the council's former authority) to impose, among other decisions, the death penalty "without [a resolution of] the full Athenian demos." See the discussions of Ostwald 1986, 31–40; 1988, 327–32.

137. See notes 118–20 above.

a prerequisite for participation in the Mysteries of Eleusinian Demeter.[138] Isocrates gave the strongest expression of this cultural divide, stating that "at the celebration of the Mysteries, the Eumolpidae and the Kerykes [the Athenian sacred "Heralds"], because of our hatred of the Persians, give solemn warning to other barbarians also, even as to men guilty of murder, that they are forever banned from the sacred rites."[139]

The treatment of Darius' heralds in 491 set the precedent of a public sentence of death for irreverent speech. The example would serve to inhibit dealings with the Persians deemed treasonous to Athens and to Greece,[140] to intimidate prominent intellectuals who pressed too far with ideas influenced by Asiatic ideology and Ionian cosmology,[141] and especially to condemn to death those who could be accused of willful disrespect for the sanctity of Demeter's rites.[142] In view of such conditions, we can more readily understand the tactful silences on cultic matters that we have already detected in Herodotus' narrative of the historical interaction of Greeks and barbarians. And we can understand why he was not more explicit in explaining the murder of Darius' heralds. What he did say about it is startling enough: "Just what disagreeable consequences were suffered by the Athenians for this treatment of the king's messengers, I am unable to say; perhaps it was the destruction of their city and the countryside around it." (7.133.2).

## THE LEGACY OF THE *MĒTRAGYRTĒS:* THE ARGUMENT SO FAR

In this and preceding chapters I have developed the argument that the story of the *Mētragyrtēs*, the minister of the Mother of the Gods put to death by the Athenians as told by Julian and other late sources, was in fact part of the

138. The "radical secrecy" of the Eleusinian rituals (Burkert 1985, 276) is otherwise difficult to explain. See Herodotus 8.65.4 on the restriction of the Mysteries to Hellenes.

139. Isocrates 4, *Panegyricus* 157 (translated by G. Norlin), describing the "everlasting wrath" (ἀείμνηστος ὀργή: i.e., toward Asiatics).

140. The precedent was followed in the summary executions in 479 of the Athenian councilor Lycidas and his family (Herodotus 9.5; cf. Isocrates 4, *Panegyricus* 157; Lycurgus *Against Leocrates* 122), and in the summary execution in 430 of Peloponnesian ambassadors intercepted on their way to Asia (Thucydides 2.67).

141. This threat is reflected in the decree attributed to Diopeithes, probably of the 430s, against those "who do not respect divine matters [τοὺς τὰ θεῖα μὴ νομίζοντας] and who teach doctrines about the heavens," said to have been aimed against Anaxagoras: Plutarch *Pericles* 32.1; cf. Xenophon *Memorabilia* 4.7.6; Plato *Apology* 26c–d; see Wallace 1994, 137–38, for cautions about this account of the decree of Diopeithes. According to Diogenes Laertius 2.12, Anaxagoras was put on trial at Athens on charges "not only of impiety, but also of Medism."

142. The condemnation of Alcibiades and those deemed to have profaned the Mysteries in 415 is discussed in chapter 9. Diagoras of Melos was condemned at this time for his views of the Eleusinian rites, views said to be Phrygian in inspiration (Aristophanes *Birds* 1073; cf. Lysias 6, *Against Andocides* 16–17; Wallace 1994, 131–33; above, chapter 2 at note 103).

story of Darius' heralds who came to Athens demanding earth and water, and who were put to death by the Athenians, as told by Herodotus. If the evidence accumulated in support of this argument has seemed persuasive, then the story that Robert Parker has characterized as "obviously not true, . . . or rather, even if it were true, we could not know it to be so" now enters the realm of knowable history.[143] Although Herodotus did not explicitly connect the heralds with Kybebe or the Mother, the present argument supports the conclusion that one of the historians of the age of Alexander the Great, either Anaximenes or Theopompus, did refer to this incident, and connected the foundation of the Metroön at Athens late in the fifth century with atonement for the treatment of "that Phrygian man."[144]

Such a conclusion makes a bold claim about the place of religion at the boundaries of myth and history. We see historical actors shaping religious practices, affirming some and rejecting others. We see the establishment of classical paradigms, and we also see that, over the longer span of Mediterranean history, traditional elements were eventually recast to serve different paradigms of the workings of divine will. In view of these large claims, and in view of the agnostic cautions of careful scholars like Parker, it is reasonable to expect some readers to be uncomfortable about finding so much interpretive space between the lines of Herodotus. Not all will want to count themselves persuaded by the argument to this point.

It will be useful, therefore, to recapitulate the chief points that, in my judgment, compel such a reading of Herodotus and of the events covered in his narrative. The most significant testimony comes from fifth-century sources, some of them contemporary to the events under discussion. Each of these points constitutes an independent datum whose evidentiary value does not rely on any prior argument, aside from the assumption that Herodotus and other fifth-century sources provide a reasonably reliable reflection of contemporary understandings:

1. The burning of Kybebe's shrine at Sardis was the reason why the Persians burned the shrines of the Greeks who refused to submit to them, according to Herodotus.
2. The heralds of Darius who demanded tokens of submission from the Athenians (therefore atonement for the burning of Kybebe's shrine) were thrown into the *barathron* at Athens, according to Herodotus (as later sources say the *Mētragyrtēs* was treated).
3. Herodotus attests to uncertainty about the consequences the Athenians might face for the murder of Darius' heralds in the era of the Peloponnesian War; Athenian playwrights of that era attest a growing concern

143. See chapter 2 at note 15.
144. See the sources and discussion cited in chapter 2, with notes 30 and 31.

about the justifiable wrath of the Mother of the Gods (as is discussed in following chapters).

4. The *Kybēbos*, the "man of Kybebe," was mentioned by Simonides, a poet of the Persian War era, and later by Cratinus, in the era of the Peloponnesian War. (Later sources identify the *Kybēbos* as the *Mētragyrtēs* and the eunuch *Gallus*.)

5. Eunuchs were regularly employed as trusted emissaries of the Persian kings, as Herodotus attests.

6. A eunuch announced the defeat of Xerxes at the opening of Phrynichus' *Phoenician Women*, a work of the Persian War era.

7. Phrynichus was also responsible for choral verses in praise of the Mountain Mother, as Aristophanes recalled.

8. Phrygians, as dramatic stereotypes, were almost synonymous with eunuchs, and were notoriously superstitious, as Euripides and Timotheus attest.

9. Aeschylus presents the chorus of his *Persians* invoking the ghost of Darius by the Phrygian title for a king, *ballēn* (specifically, ἀρχαῖος βαλλήν), confirming that the Greeks readily accepted the conjunction of Persian and Phrygian symbols of sovereignty.

Without the explanation advanced here, many of these data from fifth-century sources remain unrelated and without apparent significance. Should we be content to leave this testimony in obscurity if evidence for wider connections and meanings is at hand? Is it not reasonable to assume that the burning of Kybebe's shrine had consequences that were expressed in terms of her cult? Is it not likely that Simonides' reference to the *Kybēbos* had something to do with a representative of that cult, whose memory made an impression on a broad sector of the Greek public? Once we entertain the possibility that such deductions are reasonable and likely, these data begin to make sense in the context of the stories later told of the *Mētragyrtēs*.

If we ask why Herodotus was not more explicit about the relationships among these events, we must come to terms with his particular historical perspective. Herodotus wrote at a time when Athenian and Persian relations were in a delicate balance. Without foreknowledge of where these relations were leading, he sought to explain why Greeks and Persians had originally gone to war with each other. He was discreet on matters pertaining to religion because divine providence would reveal her hand only in the course of time, and in some matters it was not yet clear to Herodotus if enough time had passed. A century later, as the world was being transformed by Alexander, when the fate of the Persian empire had been sealed, and when the greatness of Athens was past, the mission of the *Mētragyrtēs* was narrated in its historical context. The story told then about the Mother of the Gods, her eunuch minister, and the Athenians was part of the record of a bygone era.

Time and perspective gave the story new focus and meaning, but these were not the wholesale creation of fourth-century historiography.

Even without introducing the *Mētragyrtēs* into the narrative, it is evident that the execution of Darius' emissaries was the decisive moment in determining how the Athenians would position themselves in relation to the empire of Darius and his son Xerxes. This event, in tandem with the simultaneous slaying of Darius' heralds at Sparta, was also the decisive moment in defining a conceptual divide between Europe and Asia. The Greeks were erecting a paradigm for sovereignty that now, more clearly than ever before, stood independent of and in opposition to the sovereignty of Asia. These were the circumstances that crystallized the distinction between Greeks and barbarians, as it came to be understood from the Greek perspective.[145]

The Greeks of Asia, meanwhile, fell into the ambiguous space between these sovereign ideologies that would characterize their position for as long as the Persian empire lasted. When Ionians on both sides of the Aegean were united, as they had been briefly during the Ionian Revolt and would later again be under the Athenian empire, optimism for their place in the Hellenic cause was high. But whenever Asiatic and Hellenic powers confronted each other across the Aegean, the Ionians were powerless, and fell as easy victims to the demands for retribution on one side or the other.

We are now in a position to recognize that these essential oppositions, and the ambiguous ground between them, also found expression in concepts of divinity. The gods of the Greeks now came to be defined according to an ideology of Hellenic sovereignty and freedom opposed to the claims of divine authority advanced by the rulers of Asia. For this reason, any Hellene who wished could be initiated in the Eleusinian Mysteries, but barbarians, and specifically Persians, were excluded.[146] The most conspicuous consequence of rejecting Darius' demands and executing his heralds was, of course, the war with Persia that followed. Now that we can better appreciate the symbolism embedded in the religious dimension of this clash between Europe and Asia, we will be better able to recognize further indications of its effects as Athenians and Persians widened the gulf between them, and then, later in the fifth century, as they moved toward reconciliation. The course of these developments traced in succeeding chapters will lead us to the outcome of the story, when the Athenians eventually did atone for their violence against the Mother of the Gods and her minister, as Julian attests.

145. According to Edith Hall (1989, 16): "The invention of the barbarian in the early years of the fifth century was a response to the need for an alliance against Persian expansionism and the imposition of pro-Persian tyrants." Note also the judgment of George Grote quoted above, note 112.

146. See above at notes 138–39.

# Chapter 7

# Persian Sovereignty and the Gods of the Athenians

The murder of Darius' heralds in 491 marked a critical point in the formation of Greek identity. From that moment on, the movement toward classical forms in both politics and religion became decisive. Considering the inherent diversity within Greek culture, this was not a unitary movement, and in many respects the Athenians stand apart from the rest. But by setting themselves alongside the Spartans in a leading role among Greeks resisting Persian domination, the Athenian example became increasingly influential. Within this movement the distinction between the Hellenic and the Asiatic or barbarian reached its sharpest definition. The earlier archaic age of innocence described in chapter 1, when Greeks had participated easily in the culture of Asiatic tyranny, was now long past. While the Spartans were able to claim that they maintained an ancient and unchanging form of sovereignty that had kept them free from tyranny, the Athenians were defining themselves by the radical rejection of their own recent experience of tyranny. But tyranny, as it has been described in the present study, was more than a political system. Tyranny was implicated in an ideological system with strong expressions in the area of religion, and religious beliefs and practices could not easily be rejected or modified to suit a political agenda.

Moments of crisis can provoke decisive and deliberate change. The murder of the heralds, according to the present argument, was the most conspicuous instance in classical antiquity of a radical rejection of religious belief for the sake of a political agenda. The present chapter considers some of the tensions generated by this drastic measure, and traces the evidence for continuing changes in Athenian religious institutions in the years after 491. The particular focus will be on the relationship between the hallmarks of classical Athenian religion and the symbols of Persian sovereignty. Cults of Artemis, Athena, and Demeter, powerful goddesses with sublimated sexuality, seem to stand in the Athenian consciousness in the stead of the cult of Kybebe, who shared their powers but whose unveiled sexuality (she was Aphrodite to the inhabitants of Asia) was the essence of her bond to tyranny. Delos, and the shrine of Apollo's birth, became the symbolic center of the alliance formed by the Athenians to prosecute the ongoing war against Persia. Ideological concepts embedded in each of these cults underwent changes associated with the end of war between Athens and Persia, at the time of the so-called Peace of Callias, when the construction of the Parthenon began. All these responded, in revealing ways, to the concepts associated with the great goddess of sexuality, sovereignty, and the earth at Sardis.

This chapter begins with an examination of the testimony of Herodotus to the lingering anxiety over the possible consequences of the treatment of Darius' heralds. Public anxiety over the divine displeasure of Mother of the Gods or her surrogates loomed over the men who had leading roles in the execution of Darius' heralds. Relying, in some instances, on sources as late as Plutarch might encourage the view that certain details may have been introduced into these stories many years after the events themselves. Yet fifth-century evidence often confirms Plutarch, and in several important instances Herodotus himself is the source of detailed testimony to the anxieties felt by the Athenians. Moreover, as was pointed out in the final sections of the previous chapter, sources contemporary to the events themselves, namely Simonides and the tragedian Phrynichus, testify to Athenian interests in Kybebe and the Mother of the Gods at the time of the Persian Wars. Conversant with all of these early sources, Plutarch stands in a long tradition of authorities stretching back to Herodotus, and to poets before him, who grappled with the challenge posed to the Athenians most pointedly in 491, the challenge of comprehending the nature of divinity that sustained humanity and legitimized sovereignty on earth.

### THE MOTHER OF THE GODS REJECTED

Herodotus sets his account of the execution of Darius' heralds in an unusual historical perspective. The incidents at Athens and Sparta are not mentioned where we might expect them, in the narrative of Darius' response to the Ionian Revolt and preparation for the Marathon campaign. There Herodotus mentions Darius' decision to send his heralds throughout all of Greece, and later he describes Darius' resolution to conquer those Greeks who refused to submit tokens of earth and water.[1] But the story of the violent rejection of the heralds is told only later, when it is given as the reason why Xerxes omitted Athens and Sparta from the itinerary of the heralds that he in his

---

1. Herodotus 6.48–49.1 and 6.94.

turn sent to Greece shortly before his invasion of 480. So the account, at that point, is retrospective. It serves to remind Herodotus' audience of the connection between cause and consequence, and to emphasize Xerxes' professed role as an agent of retribution.[2]

A yet more striking feature of the perspective of this account of the heralds is that it contains the latest datable event in Herodotus' *Histories*, the capture by the Athenians of Spartan ambassadors, the sons of Sperthias and Bulis, on their way to the Persian king in 430, and the summary execution of these ambassadors at Athens. This, Herodotus tells us, was the ultimate consequence for the Spartans of their part in the murder of Darius' heralds. By this account, Herodotus reminds his listeners that, where divine anger is concerned, the link between cause and consequence cannot be foreseen. He tells this to an audience, his contemporaries, who were prepared to believe that they were witness to the consequences of events that had transpired more than sixty years earlier.

Seen from this perspective, the story of the murder of Darius' heralds has a profound and potentially unsettling message for the Athenians of Herodotus' day. For the consequences of their actions were not yet certainly known. "Perhaps it was the destruction of their city and the countryside around it," Herodotus conjectures, but then he states that this is not his own opinion.[3] Herodotus then describes at length how omens eventually prompted the Spartans to atone for their own outrageous treatment of Darius' heralds by sending Spartans to Susa, to receive whatever punishment the Persians might think fit. Xerxes, who by then had succeeded his father, returned the Spartans unharmed. Herodotus goes on: "This conduct on the part of the Spartans succeeded for a time in allaying the anger of Talthybius. . . . Long afterward, however, during the war between Athens and the Peloponnesians, the Spartans believe that it was aroused again—and this, it seems to me, came about by the most manifest divine intervention [θειότατον φαίνεται γενέσθαι]."[4]

Herodotus then tells how divine retribution visited the sons of the Spartans who had originally been sent to the Persians in atonement. These men, in 430, were apprehended in Thrace while on their way to the Persian court, and were turned over to the Athenians. Thucydides gives a full account of the treatment these emissaries received upon their transport to Athens: the

2. Herodotus' account of the murder of Darius' heralds (7.133–37) is followed by the statement that Xerxes' declared goal was to punish Athens, and by so doing to conquer all of Greece (7.138). Following this, Herodotus offers the opinion that it was Athens that saved all of Greece (7.139). The retrospective force of this entire passage echoes the summary of Athenian deeds given by an Athenian speaker at Sparta on the eve of the Peloponnesian War, as reported by Thucydides 1.73.2–74.

3. Herodotus 7.133.2, quoted in full in chapter 6 at note 113.

4. Herodotus 7.137.1, modified translation of A. de Sélincourt.

Athenians "put them to death that very day, without giving them a trial or hearing the defense that they wished to offer; and they threw their bodies into a pit [ἐς φάραγγα ἐσέβαλον]."[5]

So the Spartans, by their own admission, finally atoned in full for their treatment of Darius' messengers after more than sixty years had passed. But it was clearly still a matter of dispute in Herodotus' day whether or not the Athenians had yet atoned for their own deed.[6] In fact, their summary execution of the Spartan ambassadors to Persia in 430—the year that the plague first struck Athens—must have revived public anxiety about the consequences of their similar treatment of Darius' ambassadors some sixty years earlier. This would seem to account for the rising concern with the Mother of the Gods as a minister of divine vengeance, a concern that becomes discernible in Attic drama from this moment on.[7] There are various indications that events closer to the time of the Persian Wars were also interpreted in light of this anxiety.

### PLACATING ARTEMIS AND HONORING DEMETER

Apprehension among the Athenians about the possible consequences of divine wrath as the result of their treatment of Darius' heralds can be seen in the special devotion that they displayed to the cult of Artemis in the course of the war against the Persians that followed.[8] Before the battle of Marathon, the Athenians vowed to sacrifice a goat to Artemis the Huntress for every Persian killed. After the battle, we are told, they did not have enough goats to fulfill their pledge, so they instituted an annual sacrifice of five hundred goats to Artemis.[9] For victory at Marathon the Athenians are said to have founded a temple to Eucleia (Fair Fame), a deity elsewhere known as Ar-

5. Thucydides 2.67.4. Thucydides reports that ambassadors from Corinth, Tegea, and Argos accompanied the two Spartans and shared their fate on this occasion. Such a summary execution, without trial, indicates that the authority to carry out the death sentence must have come from the council. (See chapter 6, note 136.)

6. Pausanias 3.12.7 states that divine punishment for the murder of the heralds at Athens fell on the family of Miltiades alone. This may have been common opinion in Herodotus' day. Plato *Gorgias* 516d recalls that Miltiades narrowly escaped being thrown into the *barathron* himself, suggesting that his otherwise distinguished memory bore some serious taint.

7. See chapter 2, notes 17–24. Roller 1996, 308, provides a more complete list of the datable references to the Mother of the Gods in fifth-century Attic drama, which range from Euripides' *Cretans*, ca. 430, to his *Bacchae* in 405.

8. The question why Artemis received such attention as a result of the Persian Wars has been raised by Amandry 1967, 274–75, and R. Parker 1996, 155, but not yet satisfactorily answered.

9. Xenophon *Anabasis* 3.2.12; Aristotle *Athenian Constitution* 58.1; Plutarch *Moralia* 862b–c. Aelian *Varia Historia* 2.25 attributes the sacrifice to a vow made by Miltiades. See Simon 1983, 82, on the ceremonies accompanying this sacrifice.

temis, who also received honors after the victory at Plataea.[10] After the battle of Artemisium the Athenians made a thank offering for victory to Artemis Proseoa (Who Faces the Dawn).[11] After the battle of Salamis, Artemis again was the goddess propitiated by the Athenians, at Munychia in Piraeus, and in a sanctuary on Salamis.[12] Another cult associated with Artemis is said to have been established by Themistocles personally, in the name of Aristoboule (She of Best Counsel), about which more will be said below.

The Athenians seem to have been keenly aware that, if they were to scorn the great goddess of Asia in the guise of Sardian Kybebe, they must make special efforts to appease her in another form.[13] It is possible, however, that a more specific anxiety prompted devotions to Artemis. One of Darius' emissaries, perhaps even the spokesman for Kybebe, the *Mētragyrtēs* himself, may have been a Megabyzus, one of the eunuch priests of Ephesian Artemis.[14] If this was so, not only would his murder account for the concern of the Athenians to propitiate Artemis in particular, but it would also explain the unspecified murder alluded to by Herodotus on account of which the Ephesians and the Colophonians in his day no longer celebrated the Apaturia, a festival of kinship observed by the Athenians and all other Ionians.[15] Ephesus had been the launching point for the Ionian attack on Sardis in 498, in which Ephesian guides led the way, so there is no reason to believe that any antagonism between Ephesians and those Ionians who professed loyalty to Athens yet existed. The murder of Darius' heralds provides the most likely circumstance for the opening of this rift, and can explain why the Athenians were especially eager to please Artemis soon after that event.

10. Pausanias 1.14.5, where the proximity of the Temple of Eucleia to the Eleusinion in Athens may be significant; cf. 9.17.1–2; Sophocles *Oedipus Tyrannus* 160–62; Plutarch *Aristides* 20.5–6.

11. Plutarch *Themistocles* 8.2–3; *Moralia* 867f.

12. Munychia: Plutarch *Moralia* 349f; Deubner 1932, 204–7; Simon 1983, 81–82; cf. Simonides *Epigram* 24 (*EG*). On the date of the festival to Artemis Munychia, and its connection to the battle of Salamis, see Badian and Buckler 1975. Artemis on Salamis: Pausanias 1.36.1.

13. See chapter 4, with notes 109–19, on the close connections between Artemis of Ephesus and Kybebe at Sardis.

14. A connection between a Megabyzus of Ephesus and assertive "barbarian" words is indicated by Hesychius' definition of the phrase "Megabyzean words": "Boastful; from the Persian king. Some say they were barbarian words. Some Megabyzi were priests of Artemis, and some were generals of the Persian king" (s.v. Μεγαβύζειοι λόγοι· μεγάλοι· ἀπὸ τοῦ Περσῶν βασιλέως. οἱ δὲ βαρβάρους. καὶ οἱ τῆς Ἀρτέμιδος ἱερεῖς. καὶ οἱ στρατηγοὶ τοῦ Περσῶν βασιλέως Μεγάβυζοι). On the Megabyzi, see chapter 4, with notes 83 and 84.

15. Herodotus 1.147 refers to the Apaturia as a Panionion festival affirming Athenian ancestry, and notes the exception of the Ephesians and the Colophonians κατὰ φόνου τινὰ σκῆψιν. The exceptions have never been explained. The widely attested Ionian month name Apaturion is noted by Trümpy 1997, 10–119, in her study of Ionian calendars. Sources on the Athenian festival of the Apaturia are collected and discussed by Deubner 1932, 231–34; Parke 1977, 88–92; see also Simon 1983, 74–75. The Apaturia festivals attested at Samos and at Troezen are discussed by Nilsson 1906, 463–64.

Demeter was another deity that the Athenians made special efforts to appease after their violent rejection of Darius' heralds. The cult of Demeter at Eleusis had been growing in popularity among the Athenians, to judge by the archaeological and literary evidence, since the Peisistratid era.[16] The *Mētragyrtēs* had evidently used the virtual identity of Kybebe and Demeter, both addressed as Mother, to assert that the Sardian Mother was in fact Demeter in her primal form, at her most venerable seat. This effort to co-opt an Attic institution probably provoked the strict injunction of secrecy regarding the Eleusinian rituals of initiation, as we have already observed, and also the restriction of initiation to Hellenes, nominally excluding barbarians, particularly Persians.[17]

While rejecting the barbarian, the Athenians appear to have embraced the Eleusinian goddess even more closely than before, and to have broadcast more vigorously the claim of Eleusis to be the place where the staff of life was given by the goddess to humanity. Close to 490 a modest precinct on the lower slopes of the Acropolis above the agora belonging to a chthonic deity, presumably Demeter, was substantially enlarged to become the Athenian Eleusinion.[18] In addition to a fine enclosure wall, as excavations have revealed, this Eleusinion was embellished with a temple of Triptolemus.[19] In approximately the same period, in the 480s and following decades, the image of Triptolemus as the missionary of Demeter achieved its greatest popularity as a theme of Attic vase painting.[20] In the rites of Eleusinian Demeter and the mission of Triptolemus, the Athenians were clearly advancing an Athenian, or Attic, alternative to the Sardian paradigm for the spread of civilization and the establishment of the *oikoumenē*.[21]

16. On the transformation of the sanctuary and festivals of Eleusinian Demeter into civic institutions in the sixth century, see Mylonas 1961, 77–105; Boersma 1970, 24–25, 185; Simon 1983, 17–37; Shapiro 1989, 67–83; R. Parker 1996, 97–101. The composition of *Homeric Hymn 2, To Demeter*, is another measure of the rising prominence of Eleusis. It is usually dated ca. 600 B.C.E., although no objective evidence precludes a date closer to 550 B.C.E. See Richardson 1974, 10–11; Janko 1982, 181–83; Clinton 1993, 110–12, who especially points out that the absence of any reference to Athens in the hymn does not necessarily mean that Eleusis was independent of Athens.

17. On the restriction of Eleusinian rites to Hellenes, see chapter 6, with notes 138–39.

18. Pausanias 1.14.1–4 describes as much as his conscience permits of the Eleusinion by the agora. On the archaeology of the City Eleusinion see Miles 1998, esp. 38–40 for the evidence of late sixth-century houses destroyed to make way for the expansion of the sanctuary. Miles dates the commencement of the expansion to ca. 500, but inasmuch as domestic deposits and a well closed by the expansion contain pottery datable to ca. 500–490, it is possible that the expansion took place closer to ca. 490.

19. See Miles 1998, 35–57.

20. Raubitschek and Raubitschek 1982 survey representations of the mission of Triptolemus in Attic art; Shapiro 1989, 76–77, examines the archaic examples, the earliest of which is dated to ca. 540.

21. Shapiro 1989, 77, draws attention to the appearance of a black African and two Amazons on the reverse of a vase of ca. 530 depicting the mission of Triptolemus on the obverse. He appropriately notes that "one wonders if they could here be a shorthand reference to the

Herodotus likewise indicates that the Athenians were anxious to discover signs that Eleusinian Demeter was truly on their side in the conflict with Xerxes. Moreover, in each of the incidents that Herodotus narrates regarding Eleusinian Demeter, he reveals an intensity of personal conviction about the presence of a god's hand that is uncharacteristic of his usually more dispassionate authorial stance. Just as in his speculations about the possible consequences of the crime committed by the Athenians against Darius' heralds, Herodotus shows that he is every bit as anxious as the Athenians to see indications that the court of divine favor has upheld the cause of Athens and of Greece.

After describing the final decision made by Eurybiades and the Greek commanders to stay at Salamis and face the Persian fleet, Herodotus mentions portents and measures taken to secure divine assistance. He gives most attention to a portent that was admittedly not widely known at the time, but that became known through later retellings. This was "a story that used to be told by Dicaeus the son of Theocydes, an Athenian exile," who "used to appeal to Demaratus and others to witness the truth of it."[22] These two men, according to Herodotus, were the sole witnesses to an apparition coming from Eleusis, in the form of a rising dust cloud, as if thirty thousand men were on the march, and the sound of voices singing the mystic *Iacchos* song. This was a phantom of the annual procession "that the Athenians conduct every year for the Mother and the Maiden for those among themselves and the rest of the Greeks who wish to become initiates."[23] Coming from a deserted countryside and eventually dissolving into a cloud that floated toward Salamis, the apparition was a sign that divine vengeance was on the side of the Athenians, and of the Greek fleet at Salamis. This martial and musical procession (specifically of men, ἀνδρῶν τρισμυρίων) in the name of the Mother and the Maiden (τῇ μητρὶ καὶ τῇ κούρῃ), portending destruction to the enemy, was the likeness of the processions of conquest in the name of the Asi-

---

whole of the inhabited earth, the *oikoumenē,* which will receive the benefits of agriculture." Such a universal embrace most likely was the scope of the mission of Triptolemus as envisioned in Peisistratid Athens, but, significantly, neither the *Homeric Hymn to Demeter* nor Herodotus nor any Attic source ever names the *oikoumenē* as the realm of Eleusinian Demeter. Isocrates, for example, never uses the term *oikoumenē* to describe the influence of Athens or Eleusinian Demeter, although he does use the term when speaking of the worldwide influence of the descendants of Heracles (Isocrates 6, *Archidamus* 32). If, as seems likely, this avoidance of the term *oikoumenē* in an Athenian context was deliberate, it must have been because the term was too closely linked to the Asiatic origin of the concept. (See chapter 5.) Triptolemus and Eleusinian Demeter are said to have served the entire *oikoumenē* only in postclassical sources, beginning with Hecataeus of Abdera (*FGrHist* 264 F 25.235–39 = Diodorus 1.29.1) and Timaeus (*FGrHist* 566 F 164.61–70 = Diodorus 5.4.3–4), where Eleusis is made into an intermediate station of Demeter's gift originating either in Egypt or in Sicily.

22. Herodotus 8.65.1 and 6, translated by A. de Sélincourt.
23. Herodotus 8.65.4.

atic Mother that were familiar to the lore and practice of Phrygia and Lydia.[24] But this procession championed the Hellenic cause, and Demaratus knew that Xerxes would recognize its distressing implications, according to Herodotus, if he learned of it.

The patronage of Eleusinian Demeter for the Greek cause was marked by further miracles, as Herodotus attests. At the battle of Plataea, fighting was heaviest in the vicinity of a sanctuary that happened to be dedicated to Eleusinian Demeter (where Mardonius himself, the Persian commander, was killed). At the close of his battle narrative, Herodotus remarks:[25]

> It is a wonder to me how it should have happened that, though the battle was fought close to the sacred grove of Demeter, not a single Persian soldier was found dead upon the sacred soil, or appears ever to have set foot upon it, while round about the sanctuary, on unconsecrated ground, the greatest number were killed. My own view is—if one may have views at all about divine matters [εἴ τι περὶ τῶν θείων πρηγμάτων δοκέειν δεῖ]—that the Goddess herself would not let them in, because they had burnt her sanctuary at Eleusis.

Finally, the patronage of Eleusinian Demeter is extended to Asian soil itself, and made to signify the divine hand giving victory to the Greeks at Mycale. After other significant portents are noted, Herodotus reports that the Persians prepared a defensive position for themselves at Mycale, "where there is a temple sacred to Demeter of Eleusis; the temple was built by Philistus the son of Pasicles when he accompanied Neileus, the son of Codrus, on the expedition for the founding of Miletus."[26] The temple, in other words, was believed to have been founded in the same movement from Attica that had established the ancestral kinship of Ionians with Athenians. As the ensuing battle gets under way, Herodotus interrupts his narrative to report:[27]

> During the advance, a herald's staff was found on the edge of the beach, close to the water, and at the same time a rumour flew through the ranks that the Greeks had beaten Mardonius in Boeotia. Many things make it plain to me that divine matters influence human affairs [δῆλα δὴ πολλοῖσι τεκμηρίοισί ἐστι τὰ θεῖα τῶν πρηγμάτων]—for how else could it be, when the Persian defeat at Mycale was about to take place on the same day as his defeat at Plataea, that a rumour of that kind should reach the Greeks, giving the army greater courage and a fiercer determination to face the risks of battle? It was another odd coincidence that both battles should have been fought near a precinct of Demeter of Eleusis— for, as I have already mentioned, the fighting at Plataea was in the immediate

24. See chapter 2 at notes 121–27.
25. Herodotus 9.65.2, modified translation of A. de Sélincourt. Propitious omens for the Plataean campaign in the name of Eleusinian Demeter are also mentioned at Herodotus 9.19, 57, 62, and 69, in addition to the passage quoted here; see also Plutarch *Aristides* 10.5 and 11.3–8.
26. Herodotus 9.97, translated by A. de Sélincourt.
27. Herodotus 9.100–101, modified translation of A. de Sélincourt.

neighborhood of Demeter's temple; and the same thing was to happen at Mycale. Moreover, the rumour that Pausanias' men had already been victorious
at Plataea was perfectly correct; for Plataea was fought early in the day, but
the action at Mycale did not take place until the evening; and the fact of this
concurrence of dates—the same day of the same month—was proved when
they reckoned back a short time afterwards. Before the report of Plataea
reached them, there was profound misgiving amongst the troops, not so much
on their own account as for the fate of Greece at the hands of Mardonius; but
once the good news came, they moved to the assault with better heart and
quicker pace. And so it was that both sides were eager to come to grips, knowing that the sake for which they were fighting was control of the Hellespont
and the Aegean islands.

By all rational calculation, Herodotus affirms, the Greek cause was divinely
supported. The most convincing proofs that he cites for this support served
to ratify the special sanctity with which the Athenians honored Demeter of
Eleusis. By these proofs the Athenians were reassured, in Herodotus' day as
much as they were a generation earlier, that they enjoyed the favor of the
great Mother of the earth's fertility.

### MILTIADES, THEMISTOCLES, AND THE MOTHER OF THE GODS

Traditions recorded as early as Herodotus describe the fates of the two Athenians, Miltiades and Themistocles, whose names were prominently connected with the decision to impose a death sentence on Darius' heralds. In
both cases, the hand of fate is that of the divine Mother, in one or another
of her guises.

Pausanias reports that Miltiades, the victor at Marathon in 490, had been
responsible for the execution of Darius' heralds at Athens. As a result, the
"wrath of Talthybius," which "left its mark on the Spartan state, in the case
of Athens privately afflicted the house of one man, Miltiades the son of Cimon."[28] Herodotus provides a detailed account of the demise of Miltiades,
and records that he suffered retribution for offenses that he committed
against the Earth Goddesses (χθόνιαι θεαί, referring to Demeter and Kore).

Miltiades died within a few years of his great victory at Marathon, we are
told, from a gangrenous wound received during his failed attempt to capture Paros.[29] Herodotus affirms, on the authority of the Pythia, that Miltiades suffered his miserable end as divine punishment for viewing or handling forbidden sacred objects in the shrine of Demeter Thesmophoros on

28. Pausanias 3.12.7. The historical value of this testimony is discussed in chapter 6 at notes
114–20.

29. The death of Miltiades is reported by Herodotus 6.136, following the account of his
failed siege and its consequences (6.133–35).

the island, which he had done for the express purpose of delivering the town of Paros to its enemies. Discreet as always in such matters, Herodotus does not indicate how Miltiades' violation of the sanctity of Demeter's shrine and its contents was supposed to force Paros to pay tribute to Athens. But when we recall the ritual aspect of the Lydian campaigns against Ionian cities, and recall that Paros was among the islands that had previously offered submission to Darius, we begin to understand the nature of this affair.[30] It would seem that Miltiades, in the company of an attendant of the shrine named by Herodotus, had attempted to appropriate the sacred symbols of Parian prosperity as a preliminary to appropriating that prosperity itself. But the siege failed, so this fact and the subsequent painful death of Miltiades were seen as a sign that he had proceeded improperly in the all-important ritual aspects of his undertaking.[31] Pausanias' authority clearly felt that Miltiades paid this price also for impropriety in the closely related matter of dealing with the heralds of Darius.

Themistocles, according to Plutarch, was responsible, and even won high praise, for the proposal by which the translator who accompanied Darius' emissaries was put to death for daring to use the Hellenic tongue for barbarian demands.[32] It is somewhat ironic, therefore, that Themistocles later learned the Persian tongue and lived out his final years in Asia Minor as a vassal of Artaxerxes.[33] It is still more remarkable that he did so as a devotee of the Mother of the Gods.

Even before his exile, Themistocles had a close relationship with a goddess of divine retribution, identified sometimes with Artemis, and elsewhere with the Mother of the Gods. In his review of the unpopular side of Themistocles, which eventually led to his ostracism, Plutarch reports that Themistocles[34]

> caused distress to most Athenians by building the shrine to Artemis whom he called Aristoboule [She of Best Counsel] because he had offered the best coun-

---

30. Compare Herodotus 7.153, where possession of the sacred objects of the earth goddesses (the same terminology used in 6.134–35) assured tyranny for the family of Gelon of Syracuse (discussed in chapter 2 at notes 128–31). Note also the incident involving the shrine of Demeter Thesmophoros on Aegina (6.91), where eventually divine retribution resulted in a transfer of power. Submission of earth and water by all islanders is reported by Herodotus 6.49.1.

31. Ephorus *FGrHist* 70 F 63 (from Stephanus of Byzantium s.v. Πάρος) reports that Paros was on the point of surrendering when chance events led to the failure of the siege. From this we might suppose that Miltiades had begun to prepare the ceremonial accompaniments for the surrender when he met with unexpected resistance. For a comparable scenario relating tribute to cultic appropriation, see the story about the struggle between Athens and Aegina over the cult of Damia and Auxesia (Herodotus 5.82–88).

32. Plutarch *Themistocles* 6.2; see chapter 6, with notes 118–20.

33. Thucydides 1.138.1; Plutarch *Themistocles* 29.3.

34. Plutarch *Themistocles* 22.1–2.

sel to the city and to the Hellenes. He built the shrine close to his house in Melite, where now the public officers throw out the bodies of those who have been put to death, and where they carry out the garments and the nooses of those who have been executed by hanging.

The "Best Counsel" thus celebrated by Themistocles is usually assumed to be his strategy for victory at Salamis, and therefore to be an unseemly display of personal pride.[35] But the cult was more likely a public institution of about 490 affirming the bold resolution of the Athenians to put to death the offensive emissary of Darius. The only other attested cult of Aristoboule is on Rhodes, where, in front of her image, a condemned prisoner was put to death in the course of an annual festival of Cronus.[36] Aristoboule is the deity of capital punishment, an explanation that also makes sense of the incidental details that Plutarch reports, which otherwise serve as nothing more than a needlessly graphic description of the location of her shrine. Moreover, as Noel Robertson has recently argued, Aristoboule (the only name originally applied to the cult, according to Plutarch) was most probably an epithet of the Mother of the Gods on Rhodes.[37] The establishment of a public cult of Aristoboule, who could be recognized as an avatar for Kybebe (much as the Eumenides were offered cult, as Aeschylus depicts, to placate their wrath as Erinyes) could certainly have caused distress to most Athenians. If this had been done not long after Darius' demands were rejected, then anxiety over this act of arrogance would be nearly at fever pitch a decade later, when Xerxes was on his way to take Athens and destroy its shrines and temples.

The shrine of Artemis (called Aristoboule by Themistocles) that Plutarch identifies in the deme of Melite has been excavated. It is a late fourth-century

35. I, with many others, previously accepted this view (Munn 2000, 24, 326), which is supported by the explicit statement of Plutarch, in *Moralia* 869c–d, that Aristoboule commemorated Themistocles' plan to fight at Salamis. Also accepting this view, Robert Parker rightly asks, "Was it with authorization [of the assembly] that Themistocles founded his offensively vainglorious shrine to 'Artemis Aristoboule'?" (1996, 215–16). Pierre Amandry 1967, 277, recognizing the tendentiousness of Plutarch's account, questions the reliability of his statement there, and suggests that Plutarch was misled by a movement to glorify Themistocles starting in the late fourth century. I now share Amandry's doubts, although the solution I see allows for the late archaic cult of Aristoboule. (See below.) It should be noted that the verb Plutarch uses to describe the effect of this foundation on the Athenians, ἠνίασε, has more the meaning of causing grief or distress than indignation or annoyance. This makes it more likely that there was something distressing about the decision itself rather than merely the fact that Themistocles' self-congratulation was annoying.

36. Porphyry *On Abstinence* 2.54. The judicial and retributive aspects of Aristoboule are confirmed by Artemidorus *Onirocriticon* 2.37: "Aristoboule and Eunomia mean the same as Nemesis."

37. Robertson 1996, 278–81, where he notes (279 n. 170) the suggestion of H. Usener that "Aristoboule" refers to the death sentence.

structure with possible foundations belonging to the early fifth century.[38] In view of the industry that later generations devoted to recovering the relics of the famous Themistocles, it is not improbable that this deme shrine near the executioner's gate was identified as the foundation of Themistocles only much later, when the site of his original dedication to Aristoboule was long forgotten.[39] An alternative candidate for the shrine of Aristoboule that Themistocles dedicated is found in the Athenian agora.

Immediately north of the Council House, remains of a small templelike building have been identified under the Hellenistic Metroön. According to the archaeological evidence, this building was constructed around the beginning of the fifth century (a date of ca. 490 would not be out of line with this evidence), and was destroyed when Xerxes sacked Athens in 480/79, not to be rebuilt thereafter. Largely because of its location under the later Metroön, its excavator, Homer Thompson, conjectured that the building was a shrine to the Mother of the Gods.[40] The present historical interpretation makes it most unlikely that any public shrine of the Mother of the Gods would have been erected at Athens in the early fifth century, but the attested shrine of Aristoboule could well have been erected in this place, beside the Council House, soon after the execution of the heralds. Such a prominent public dedication to Aristoboule would have been an appropriate demonstration of public confidence in the decision. Those who questioned the wisdom of the decision could well have felt ill at ease in the presence of this monument, and may have wished to limit responsibility for it, and the brazen act it commemorated, to Themistocles personally. Some thirty years after Xerxes' sack of the city, following the entente with Persia known as the Peace of Callias, when the Athenians began to reconstruct their ruined temples, there would have been little inclination to revive the memory of the decision to kill Darius' heralds. The shrine in the agora therefore remained an abandoned ruin, and a century later the memory of Themistocles' dedication to Aristoboule was associated with a shrine of Artemis near the place for the disposal of bodies, in Melite.

38. The excavation and the fourth-century inscription identifying the structure as a shrine of Artemis are published by Threpsiades and Vanderpool 1964. See also Amandry 1967, who doubts that the shrine existed in Themistocles' time; Travlos 1971, 121–23, and Wycherley 1978, 189–92, who support the excavators' identification of an original foundation by Themistocles.

39. This is the view of Amandry 1967. The decree of Themistocles discovered and published by Michael Jameson (1960) is prime evidence for the later industry around the reputation of Themistocles, whatever one makes of its historicity; see Habicht 1961, Jameson 1963, and Amandry 1967. Thucydides 1.138.6 and Plutarch *Themistocles* 32.3–5 attest the variety of conflicting accounts about the disposition of Themistocles' remains.

40. On the excavation and identification of this building, see Thompson 1937, 135–40. For other interpretations of these remains, see the summary by R. Parker 1996, 190 n. 139; and most recently the radical interpretation advanced by S. G. Miller 1995 and rejected by T. L. Shear 1995.

Themistocles' devotion to the Mother of the Gods, later associated with Artemis, is more directly attested in his last years in exile. Following his flight to Asia and his appeal for asylum to the Persian king Artaxerxes, Plutarch reports that Themistocles built a temple of the Mother Dindymene at his new home at Magnesia on the Maeander, where he appointed his daughter as her priestess.[41] The temple and his daughter's service as priestess were trappings of tyranny in the Asiatic style, and this was certainly the role in which Themistocles lived out the last years of his life. He issued coins in his own name at Magnesia, bearing an image of Apollo and an eagle, tokens of sovereignty.[42] After his death, the Magnesians honored Themistocles in the manner of a founder or hero, by building a tomb for him in their agora, and it was known to Thucydides.[43] Descendants of Themistocles were honored for centuries at Magnesia. Some of these descendants made a prominent dedication on the Acropolis at Athens, a bronze statue of Artemis Leucophryne, thereby honoring both the memory of Themistocles and the patron goddess of their city, Magnesia.[44]

In view of the endeavor of Athenians to distance themselves from tyranny and its symbols in his day, the example of Themistocles in Asia seems hard to believe. But we cannot dismiss the account of his last years given by Thucydides, the evidence of his own coinage and of his tomb, and the strength and consistency of the traditions about his commitment to the sovereignty of Persia and all of its trappings. These details bear witness to the enduring influence of the traditions of Asiatic sovereignty, and to the full knowledge of them that an Athenian statesman like Themistocles could possess. The same can be said of Miltiades, and his ill-advised involvement in the cult of the Earth Goddesses on Paros. In fact, the very intimacy of these men with

41. Plutarch *Themistocles* 30.1–3 (also Strabo 14.1.40), where the institution is attributed to a dream of the Mother that saved Themistocles' life. Compare Hippias' dream of his own mother (representing his native land) as a portent, frustrated in the event, or his restoration to power (Herodotus 6.107, discussed above in chapter 4 at note 65). Plutarch *Themistocles* 31.1–2 reports that Themistocles discovered in the shrine of the Mother at Sardis a bronze statue of a maiden bearing water (κόρη ὑδροφόρος) that he himself had once dedicated at Athens, which had since been carried away by Xerxes' army. The relationship of this image of a κόρη ὑδροφόρος to Phrygo-Lydian images of the Mother is discussed in chapter 2 at note 115.

42. Kraay 1976, 244 and no. 906; Cahn and Gerin 1988.

43. Thucydides 1.138.5; cf. Plutarch *Themistocles* 32.3. It is noteworthy that the alleged manner of Themistocles' death, by drinking bull's blood (Plutarch *Themistocles* 31.5, Diodorus 11.58.3), is a feature that he has in common with Midas (Strabo 1.3.21).

44. Pausanias 1.26.4. Noting that the Temple of the Mother Dindymene no longer existed in his day, Strabo 14.1.40 praises the Hellenistic Temple of Artemis Leucophryne at Magnesia. The dedication at Athens was probably made no earlier than the late third century B.C.E., when independent Athenian relations with the Greek cities of Asia were again possible after more than half a century of Antigonid domination. See Habicht 1997, 193, for the historical circumstances.

the ideology of Asiatic tyranny makes their roles in the fight against it all the more believable. They knew what they were up against, and they understood the ideological as well as the military terms of the contest.

### · FOUNDING THE LEAGUE AT DELOS

In the course of his account of the second purification of the island of Delos by the Athenians, in 426/5, Thucydides refers to the era of the "great ancient gathering at Delos of Ionians and surrounding islanders, which they celebrated along with their women and children, just as the Ionians now do at Ephesus."[45] As evidence for this gathering, Thucydides quotes from the *Homeric Hymn to Apollo,* taking it for a composition of Homer.[46] Somehow, between the time of Homer and his own day, the customs of a Panionian gathering and festival had lapsed, Thucydides notes, and they had to be revived during the Peloponnesian War. This is a curious perspective, because it implies that Delos was in decline, and its traditional festivities generally neglected, for at least the preceding century and a half, during which (as Thucydides was aware) conspicuous devotions were paid to Apollo at Delos by Peisistratus, Polycrates, Datis, and finally, after the defeat of Xerxes, by the Athenians and their allies.

Thucydides' perspective may reflect a characteristic mode of devotions to Delian Apollo. Delos was a place of inauguration, of starting out, or of restoration to an original, pristine beginning. Purifications, like those carried out by Peisistratus and the later fifth-century Athenians, had this meaning; Polycrates' cosmic anchoring of the island of Delos had this meaning; Datis' lavish sacrifice on his expedition of conquest had this meaning.[47] Inauguration was the essence of Apollo, the young warrior, and the meaning of his birthplace; the restoration of pristine origins was what those who came to Delos sought. These meanings were congenial to the notion that Delos was the center of the world, and that order in some sense emanated from Delos. Whenever, across the span of a century or more, a new order became manifest in the Aegean, rituals at Delos were the most appropriate way to signify the fact..

In 479, the spectacular defeat of Xerxes and the failure of the Persians to enlarge their power across the sea from Asia made Delos, at the center of the sea, a propitious place to observe a new beginning. But for what manner of order in the world? The split that soon emerged between Sparta and Athens over the leadership of the Hellenic cause can in part be explained in terms of their differing outlooks on the significance of Delos at this mo-

45. Thucydides 3.104.3.
46. The balance of scholarship now regards the hymn as a composition of the time of Polycrates: see chapter 5, note 120.
47. On these events, see chapter 5 at notes 108–20 and 139.

mentous point in time. To the Spartans, Delos was the boundary marker of the natural and separate dominions of European Greece and Asia; to the Athenians, it was the central gathering place and link that connected these two parts of the world.

Delos was a distinctive landmark in the final campaign of the war against the Persians in 479, when King Leotychides of Sparta commanded the Hellenic fleet. According to Herodotus, while the fleet was at Aegina, Leotychides was approached by a delegation of Ionians from Chios endeavoring to persuade the Greeks to sail to Ionia in order to put down local tyrannies and to liberate the Greeks of Asia from Persian rule. But, as Herodotus notes,[48]

> it was only with great difficulty that [the Chians] persuaded them to advance as far as Delos, for the Greeks had little experience of what lay beyond, and imagined it to be full of Persian troops and of every sort of danger. As for Samos, it seemed to them as far away as the Pillars of Heracles. The result was that while the Persians were too badly scared to risk sailing west of Samos, the Greeks, in spite of the earnest solicitation of the Chians, did not dare to sail east of Delos. Their mutual fears stood sentry over the intervening area.

In view of the Greek and even Spartan expeditions to Ionia in the previous generation, this characterization of dread of the unknown beyond Delos has seemed a gross exaggeration on Herodotus' part. It has been taken as a reflection of Ionian impatience with Greek, specifically Spartan, hesitation or timidity on this occasion.[49] But the specific terms of this exaggeration suggest that Herodotus is not so much characterizing Ionian contempt as he is revealing Greek doctrine of the day. A growing awareness of the schematic configuration of a world composed of two continents, Europe and Asia, together with the spectacular failure of the sovereign of Asia to expand his power across Europe, encouraged acceptance of the principle that the world east of Delos was as alien to the European Greeks as was the world beyond the Pillars of Heracles. This view of the separate domains of worldly power became a Spartan doctrine. Cleomenes' rejection of the petition of Aristagoras to the Spartans to become champions to the Greeks of Asia marks the inception of this doctrine; Leotychides' resistance to Ionian pleas to sail beyond Delos reveals the established doctrine as a guiding principle of Spartan leadership.

Eventually, after still more Ionian envoys appealed to Leotychides, he was persuaded to sail toward Samos and to engage with the Persian forces that

48. Herodotus 8.132.2–3, translated by A. de Sélincourt.

49. See, e.g., How and Wells 1912, vol. 2, 279, "A dramatic exaggeration. . . . In this *reductio ad absurdum* the author (or his Ionian source) is deriding the timidity of the Greeks and their admiral"; Meiggs 1972, 33, "Herodotus overdramatizes the situation"; R. Thomas 2000, 11, "This reads like a quiet rebuke to mainland Greeks for their ignorance of the Asian side of the Aegean."

by then had withdrawn to Mycale, on the Asiatic mainland. It is noteworthy, however, that Leotychides took this decision only after discovering a suitable omen, according to Herodotus, and only after propitious sacrifices were made by the assembled Greeks on Delos. The importance of these rituals is shown by the fact that a famous seer, Deïphonus son of Euenius, was sent from Corinth to Delos for the occasion; Herodotus gives a lengthy digression to explain the fame that attached to the name of Euenius.[50] By all indications, then, Leotychides was ready to be persuaded, but he required an elaborate ritual to validate his decision to override prevailing doctrine. In this manner, the Greek campaign to liberate Ionia was launched under the auspices of Apollo at Delos, and it was crowned by victory at Mycale, according to Herodotus, through the blessings of Eleusinian Demeter.[51]

No justification, ritual or otherwise, was sufficient to persuade the Spartans to maintain a presence on the shores of Asia. Among the Ionians, only islanders were admitted into the Hellenic alliance under Spartan leadership. The Spartan solution to the problem of defending the Greeks of Asia was a proposal to resettle them in Hellas, on land confiscated from Medizing Greeks, and to leave Ionia to the barbarians. This proposal was vociferously opposed by the Athenians, and was abandoned.[52] Consistently with Spartan policy, in the two years following the victory at Mycale the Spartan regent Pausanias avoided aggression against Persians on Asian soil while leading Greek forces on Cyprus and at Byzantium. At the same time, because Pausanias respected the right of the Persians to rule on Asian soil, he treated Persian sovereignty in Asia with courtly respect. But in so doing he laid himself open to the accusations of Ionians that he was betraying their interests and conspiring with the Persians.[53]

Willingness to accept Persian rule in Asia was the undoing of Spartan leadership, and enabled the Athenians to replace the Spartans in leading the continuing conflict with Persia. Testimony to the nature of this transfer of leadership is remarkably consistent: the Spartans were unwilling to lead, and made no move to prevent the Athenians from taking over the leadership of

50. Herodotus 9.90–96.1. In the *CAH* account of this episode, Barron 1988, 592–93 and 611–12, takes no notice of the rituals and makes no mention of Deïphonus, but makes the suggestion that the arrival at Delos of a sizable portion of the Athenian fleet tipped the balance in Leotychides' decision to attack the Persians. This is plausible, but Herodotus emphasizes other factors.

51. Herodotus 9.97–101, as discussed above at notes 26–27.

52. Herodotus 9.106.

53. On the behavior of Pausanias, and the widespread views that he was on too familiar terms with Xerxes and the Persians, see the account of Thucydides 1.128–35 and the notices of Pausanias by Herodotus 5.32 and 8.3.2, and Thucydides 1.94–95; cf. Plutarch *Aristides* 23; *Cimon* 6. See also the notices of Spartan policy under Pausanias' leadership by Thucydides 1.75.2, 3.10.2–3, 6.76.3.

the Greeks of Ionia and the Aegean.[54] It is now possible to see that this passive decision by the Spartans resulted from a deep conviction on their part that the very nature of the world enjoined them against leading the Greeks of Asia. Delos, to paraphrase Herodotus, was the marker in the middle that instilled fear in them when they contemplated crossing its boundary.

The Athenians clearly felt differently about Ionia, and about the significance of Delos. For them, Delos was the link that joined the two shores of the Aegean and bound them to their Ionian kinsmen. Aeschylus, himself a veteran of the sea battle at Salamis, portrayed the defeat there of Xerxes, in his *Persians,* as a victory brought by "Ionian hands" (563), wrought by "Ares of the Ionians" (950–52), by "Ionian marines" (1011), and by "the courageous Ionian people" (1025), while also showing that Athens was the bastion of independent Ionian strength. In 477, the Athenians formalized their leadership of the collective might of the Ionians through mutual pledges to carry on war against the Persians and by appointing Delos to be their common meeting place and treasury.[55]

Devotion to Delian Apollo was an appropriate marker for the new leadership undertaken by the Athenians especially because it signified, in a well-publicized manner, the difference between the Athenian and the Spartan view of the Hellenic cause. The title that the Athenians gave to their treasurers, the *Hellēnotamiai,* "treasurers of the Greeks," was an indication of the Panhellenic authority that the Athenians were asserting, based on their supremacy at sea. Centered at Delos, this supremacy was held to be, like the island itself, a unique element of nature. Harmony between Athenian leadership and the forces of nature was also demonstrated in the ceremony of allegiance pledged by the followers of the Athenians. Their oaths were pronounced as iron masses were dropped into the sea, signifying that their pledge to follow the Athenians was considered to be as fundamental to the natural order of the world as the weight that would keep the iron under the sea.[56]

In championing the cult of Delian Apollo the Athenians were aligning

---

54. So Thucydides 1.75.2 (Athenian speaking at Sparta), 1.89.2 and 95–96.1 (Thucydides' own voice), 3.10.2 (Mytileneans speaking at Olympia); cf. Xenophon *Hellenica* 6.5.34 (Spartan speaking at Athens); Herodotus 8.3.2; Diodorus 11.46.4–5; Plutarch *Aristides* 23. Aristotle *Athenian Constitution* 23.2 states that when the Athenians took over the leadership, the Spartans were unwilling (whether to lead themselves or to allow the Athenians to lead is unclear, but evidently they did nothing; see Rhodes 1981, 291–92).

55. Thucydides 1.96.2; cf. Isocrates 4, *Panegyricus* 156. The construction of a new temple to Apollo on Delos is associated with the establishment of the common treasury here by the Athenians. This early fifth-century temple was left incomplete in midcentury, and finished only in the late fourth century, a feature that is generally explained by the removal of the treasury to Athens in 454: see Bruneau and Ducat 1966, 84–85; Boersma 1970, 62 and 170 no. 35; on Athenian policy toward Delos and Delian Apollo generally, see R. Parker 1996, 149–51.

56. Aristotle *Athenian Constitution* 23.5; Plutarch *Aristides* 25.1.

themselves not only with the Ionians of the Asiatic coast and the islands of the Aegean, once Polycrates' domain, but potentially with all Greeks and non-Greeks of Asia, Cyprus, the Levant, and Egypt honoring the young god who represented the perpetual renewal of divinely guided sovereignty. Sea power sustained the widening confrontation with Persia in these regions over the quarter-century that followed the foundation of the Delian League, and the influence of Delian Apollo was its justification. The high point of this policy was reached as Delian forces led by Athens gave support to uprisings against Persia on Cyprus and in Egypt during the 450s.

As this policy approached its practical and ideological limits in the years around 450, we find signs that the Athenians were exploring the means of establishing mutually recognized spheres of interest to stabilize relations between the sovereignties exercised by Persia and by Athens. This movement resulted in a settlement known to posterity as the Peace of Callias. The nature of this new understanding deserves some consideration, both because it reveals developing elements of the worldview of the Greeks, particularly the Athenians, and because the agreement was accompanied by a realignment of the balance of devotions in public cult.

## THE PEACE OF CALLIAS

A new equilibrium between Persians and Greeks was identified, in the memory of the following generations of Athenian orators, as the treaty of peace negotiated with Artaxerxes I by Callias son of Hipponicus and finalized sometime between 450 and 448.[57] Despite many references to this agreement in sources as early as the beginning of the fourth century, the historicity of the Peace of Callias, as it is known, has been a notoriously vexed subject in modern scholarship.[58] There is no compelling reason to doubt the historicity of this agreement. The terms attributed to the agreement were appropriate to

57. Herodotus 7.151 mentions negotiations between Callias and Artaxerxes, but omits any clear indication of date or purpose. Diodorus 12.4.5 places the agreement in the archonship of Pedeius (449/8). These and other sources attesting the Peace of Callias are collected by Bengtson *SV* 152 and Fornara 95; see also note 64 below. In modern scholarship on the date, Wade-Gery 1940, 149–50 (= 1958, 227) argues for 450/49; Meiggs 1972, 151, argues for 450; Badian 1993, 48–49, argues for 449/8 as the date of Callias' second negotiation with Persia. (See note 58 below.)

58. Wade-Gery 1940 (reprinted 1958) remains a fundamental study of the Peace of Callias; see also Raubitschek 1964; Meiggs 1972, 129–51; Badian 1993, 1–72; Samons 1998. Badian's argument (2–12) for a treaty under Xerxes immediately after the battle of the Eurymedon allows far too little time for so radical a change in Persian policy; Samons likewise argues against this aspect of Badian's reconstruction. These scholars are among the large majority who support the historicity of the peace negotiated with Artaxerxes I; others argue that the idea of a fifth-century treaty was invented in the fourth century. (See Badian 1993, 187 n. 5, for references.)

the occasion, and at the same time explain why a degree of ambiguity attached to its memory.

A treaty that resolved or suspended a half-century of hostility between Greeks and Persians had to be more than simply an agreement to stop fighting. It had to represent a meeting of minds on issues where previously there had been conflicting claims of sovereignty. According to the elements of sovereignty described in foregoing chapters, the conflict involved clashing assertions of supremacy expressed in geographical terms and justified by divinity. Resolution of conflict, therefore, had to accommodate both Persian and Athenian understandings of the nature of power; of how geography affected these relationships; and, ultimately, of how alternative theological hierarchies could coexist.

Most of the terms of the agreement negotiated between Callias and Artaxerxes, as they were later reported, concerned the geography of power. The theologies justifying the agreement are not explicitly described in connection with the treaty. But there are indications that patterns of religious devotion were the chief media through which the new relationships of power were given expression. A prime indication of the implicit importance of the religious element is the fact that Callias, whose reputation ultimately depended on the outcome of these negotiations, was a hereditary *Kēryx*, "Herald," or officiant of the cult of Eleusinian Demeter.[59] Of all Athenian notions of sanctity that were offended by the demands of Darius, the most profound were those represented by Demeter. It is therefore surely no accident that the primary negotiator of the settlement with Artaxerxes was an Athenian herald and officiant of Demeter's cult at Athens.

The agreement known as the Peace of Callias accommodated two competing notions of sovereignty: the collective sovereignty represented by the Athenians, and the embodied sovereignty of the Persian king. Sovereignty implies perfection, however, and sovereignty compromised is less than perfect, less than absolute, and is therefore no longer truly sovereign. To maintain the integrity of the sovereignty of both parties required the avoidance of certain forms of expression, and, above all, avoidance of the treaty format that was otherwise typical among Greeks: a public display of explicit terms and conditions by which both sides were bound, under oath before gods.[60] By virtue of his claim to supreme sovereignty, Artaxerxes, like his pre-

---

59. On the family of Callias son of Hipponicus, see Xenophon *Hellenica* 6.3.3–6; Andocides 1, *On the Mysteries* 112–31; Davies 1971, 263–65. Note that Aristotle *Rhetoric* 1405a records an exchange of quips between Iphicrates and Callias grandson of Callias about knowing the difference between a *Mētragyrtēs* and a *daidouchos* ("torch bearer," the Eleusinian office held by Callias). On the office and *genos* of the Kerykes, see R. Parker 1996, 300–302.

60. This typical Greek format is well represented among the original documents collected by Bengtson 1962 (*SV*).

decessors and successors, could not be bound by oath to an agreement with any other party except a god.[61] He could, however, indicate terms and conditions that met with his approval.[62] Therefore, as with later and better-attested negotiations and agreements between Greeks and the Persian king, the outcome of negotiations between Callias and Artaxerxes must have been an announcement as to what the king saw fit to allow.[63] The terms and conditions of these arrangements must have become a matter of record at some level, since the Athenians could later cite them as precedent.[64] But it is highly unlikely that the text of any treaty was inscribed for permanent public display at the time of the consummation of Callias' negotiations.

Even if, then, neither side would openly announce concessions made to the other in the name of compromise, such concessions must have been worked out as a matter of practicality. We can see this process of compromise reflected in the terms as they are reported by Diodorus (12.4.5) and other sources, and in those terms we can recognize the key principles according to which each side defined its sovereignty. On the Greek side, these principles can be reduced to two elements: first, they upheld the Greek ideal of maritime supremacy, an ideal formulated in the time of Polycrates and given new expression in the Delian League; second, they upheld the ideal of Ionian autonomy, an ideal that had been stillborn in the Ionian Revolt of 499–494, but revived again through the Delian League. On the Persian side,

61. No Persian king ever renounced the claim to be "Great King, King of Kings, King of countries, King in this earth" or "king in this great earth far and wide" (quoting two texts of Artaxerxes II: Kent 1950, 154 [A²Sa 1], and 155 [A²Hc 1–2]). Cf. the claims to sovereignty made by Darius and Xerxes, cited in chapter 6, note 63.

62. This point is made by V. Martin 1963, criticizing Bengtson 1962 on the subject of Persian-Greek treaties. Appreciation of this point does much to account for the lack of contemporary record of the agreement, and to account for how and why its terms, even its existence, could later become a matter of contentious debate.

63. Diodorus 12.4.4–5 describes the Peace of Callias in just this manner; see Badian 1993, 41–50; Briant 2002, 580–82. On the circuitous diplomacy between Greeks and Persians in the period 412–405, when satraps alternately act on the king's authority and defer to his judgment, see Lewis 1977, 83–135; Badian 1993, 42–45; Munn 2000, 155, 162–64, 175–77, 195–200. Note especially the most famous outcome of such negotiations, the so-called Peace of Antalcidas, or the King's Peace of 386: see Xenophon *Hellenica* 5.1.31, and the discussion of V. Martin 1963 on the manner of expressing the king's agreement to the terms of a settlement.

64. All knowledge of the terms of the Peace of Callias derives from an inscription (known only by report) erected at Athens sometime after 403 describing the agreement that existed between Athens and Darius II, the successor of Artaxerxes I. Andocides 3, *On the Peace with Sparta* 29, refers to the negotiation of perpetual friendship between Athens and Darius, affirming that the agreement made with his predecessor, Artaxerxes I, still obtained. (See Wade-Gery 1940.) Theopompus *FGrHist* 115 F 153 and 154 testifies that the inscription recording the treaty with Darius was in Ionic lettering, the style adopted at Athens in the archonship of Eucleides (403/2); consistent with this information, the earliest references come from Lysias 2, *Epitaphius* 56–57; Plato *Menexenus* 241d–e; Isocrates 4, *Panegyricus* 118 and 120.

the guiding principle was the notion of terrestrial sovereignty inherited in its variant forms from Lydia, Babylon, and Egypt, but in practice now confined to sovereignty over the Asiatic continent, including Cyprus and Egypt, but accommodating Hellenic maritime sovereignty and the political independence of Ionian Greeks.

The resulting compromise in effect revived the domain of the former Lydian kingdom, now chiefly comprising the satrapies of Sardis and Hellespontine Phrygia,[65] as a sort of intermediate zone within which Greek identity and Persian sovereignty could coexist. To the east of the Halys River, once the limit of Croesus' empire, the Persian king recognized no restriction to his exercise of sovereign authority. Within the former Lydian domain, the king's satraps still exercised authority and levied local troops (including Greeks) to protect their interests, but no royal levy such as those led by Cyrus, Darius, and Xerxes was to be brought across the Halys from the east: "The barbarians were prevented from marching with an army beyond the Halys River" (Isocrates 12, *Panathenaicus* 59).[66] Likewise, no Greek expeditionary force was to operate on the king's land: "The Athenians are not to send troops into the territory that the king rules" (Diodorus 12.4.5). The political communities of the Greeks along the Asiatic coast were to be no concern of the king: "The Greek cities of Asia are to be autonomous" (Diodorus 12.4.5); "no tyrant reigned over Greeks, nor was any Greek city enslaved by the barbarians" (Lysias 2, *Epitaphius* 57).[67] The Greeks were allowed to contribute

65. This domain bears comparison to the Phrygian, Lydian, and Ionian sway exercised by Oroetes (chapter 5, note 135), control of which was probably also the goal of the Ionians in 499. (See chapter 6, with notes 88–91.) This domain was much the same as the area later put under the command of Cyrus the Younger (Xenophon *Hellenica* 1.4.3, in this case including the satrapy of Cappadocia: Xenophon *Anabasis* 1.9.7). This was also the domain that later became the Roman province of Asia: see chapter 5, note 8; and cf. Strabo 2.5.24, who defines what came to be called Asia Minor as consisting of "the nations dwelling inside the Halys, . . . all of which alike we call Asia."

66. Isocrates also names the Halys as a boundary to the king's forces in *Oration* 7, *Areopagiticus* 80; Thucydides 1.16 draws attention to the crossing of this boundary by Cyrus the Great. Wade-Gery 1940, 136–43 (= 1958, 214–21) explains the Halys as the boundary for the king's own levy (what he dubs the "Palatine" army), and cites the relevant passages illustrating how satraps in the west managed their military affairs through local levies and mercenary forces. The command exercised by Cyrus the Younger over "the forces that assemble on the Castolus plain" in Lydia (Xenophon *Hellenica* 1.4.3; *Anabasis* 1.9.7), describing his appointment to Sardis in 408/7, reflects this reliance on local levies. Wade-Gery (140, = 218) regards this as evidence of "the final shaking off of the treaty restrictions." On the contrary, I regard this as a description of a local levy, therefore evidence that Darius II still administered his dominions in the west in accordance with the treaty. See also Badian 1993, 53, who notes that "there is no mention, even in our oratorical sources, of any limit on the satrapal forces, and we known that satraps continued to use both native levies and mercenaries (including Greeks) as they saw fit."

67. It is not certain whether the term "autonomy" was actually used in the agreement with Artaxerxes I ca. 450/49: see Ostwald 1982, 25–26; Badian 1993, 51–52. The idea, if not the

to their own common treasury—"We levied tribute from some of those within the king's domain" (Isocrates 4, *Panegyricus* 120)—but the soil of Asia occupied by Greeks still belonged to the king, in consideration of which they owed him tribute: "They continued to pay tribute on the land down to my day at the rate set in the time of Artaphernes" (Herodotus 6.42.2).[68] To assure autonomy for the Greek cities of Asia, "the satraps of the Persians are not to come nearer to the sea than a three day's journey" (Diodorus 12.4.5), a distance corresponding to the march from Sardis to Ephesus.[69] Thus, in principle, the king retained his claim to all of Asia, while the autonomy of the Greeks of Asia, under Athenian leadership, was respected.

Greek supremacy by sea, in the West at least, was tacitly acknowledged. The Athenians liked to recall that the king had to accept limits on his use of the sea. Diodorus (12.4.5) reports the terms in words often echoed by fourth-century sources: "No Persian warship is to sail inside of Phaselis or the Cyanean Rocks."[70] By these terms the Aegean and all waters to the west

word itself, probably was expressed. The term was definitely in current use when the agreement was confirmed with Darius II, probably in 423: see Thucydides 5.18.5 on αὐτονόμους εἶναι in the Peace of Nicias.

68. Tribute assessed by Artaphernes was based specifically on measurement of the χώρη, "land" or "countryside," according to Herodotus 6.42.2. (Cf. Thucydides 8.58.1–4.) The χώρα βασιλέως (king's land) was his productive land, in keeping with the concept of πόλεις discussed in chapter 5. This definition excludes revenue generated from the commerce and industry of Greek towns ("cities," πόλεις), which was the basis of the Athenian tribute (as indicated in Thucydides 8.18.1 in the phrase ἐκ τούτων τῶν πόλεων ὁπόσα Ἀθηναίοις ἐφοίτα χρήματα). De Ste. Croix 1972, 313–14, recognizes that the distinction between πόλις and χώρα, familiar to the administration of Hellenistic monarchies, "may well have made its first formal appearance in the Peace of Callias." Murray 1966, followed by Meiggs 1972, 61–62 (among others), maintains the improbable thesis that tribute was assessed by the Persians but not actually paid for decades. But continued payment to the king is the simplest way of understanding the statement by Thucydides 8.5.5 that, in 412, Tissaphernes was under orders from Darius to exact the tribute due to him from those Greek cities where it had not been paid on account of Athenian interference (most likely in support of the recent rebellion of Pissouthnes and Amorges; cf. Andocides 3, *On the Peace with Sparta* 29). Wade-Gery originally saw the matter in these terms: "The King then was entitled to certain limited revenues from the Greek cities" (1940, 133 = 1958, 212; Wade-Gery later changed his mind, as noted by de Ste. Croix 1972, 310, who subscribes to Murray's thesis).

69. Demosthenes 19, *On the False Embassy* 273, specifies the "the king is not to approach within a day's ride from the sea"; Plutarch *Cimon* 13.4 says that "the king is to keep [one day's] horse ride away from the Greek sea." This is not an alternative boundary to the Halys, but seems rather intended to prevent influence of the king from disrupting the affairs of the Greek cities lying in the direction of the coast from Sardis. (Herodotus 5.54 gives the distance from Sardis to Ephesus.) The injunction probably specified the person of the king, since satraps did in fact move freely in the course of their dealings with the Greek cities. (See Thucydides 1.115.4–5 in 441/0, 3.34 in 427, and 8.35–36 in 412/1).

70. Like Diodorus, Isocrates (above, notes 64 and 66) and Lycurgus *Against Leocrates* 73 place the boundary at Phaselis, on the eastern Lycian coast. Alternatively, Demosthenes and Plutarch (above, note 69) name the nearby Chelidonian Islands as the boundary. The Cyanean

of it became a Greek sea. Of course, the Athenians did not like to recall that they had conceded Cyprus to the king, and just as no Persian fleet would dare to sail along a Greek coast, neither did the Greeks venture to provoke the king by sailing against his strongholds on the Phoenician or Egyptian coasts. An equilibrium had been reached.

The Athenians made the agreement the basis for celebrations of self-affirmation. Enjoying mastery on one element and a firm foundation on the other, the Athenians were not shy about boasting of their prowess on both. An epigram quoted in several later works links the victories that established their new standing to the forces that shaped the earth: "Ever since the sea parted Europe from Asia and grim Ares first stalked the cities of mortals, no fairer deed of earthly men ever occurred on land and sea alike. For these men destroyed many Medes on Cyprus and took a hundred Phoenician ships, filled with men, on the high sea; and Asia grieved greatly over them, struck by both hands with the power of war."[71] So we find land and sea linked in rhetorical and poetic expressions of the power wielded by Athens and her allies in the time of Pericles, under whose rising leadership Callias had negotiated the agreement with Persia.[72] Later generations echoed the rhetoric of this occasion when the pride of Athens was at stake. Early in the Peloponnesian War, Aristophanes parodies the bombastic "Olympian thundering" of a decree moved by Pericles against the Megarians at the beginning of the war with the words: "Let them not remain either on sea or on land!" (*Acharnians* 534). Later generations also recalled this time as the beginning of a new epoch of stability and order in the world: "And so the war against the barbarians was fought out to the end by the whole city on their own behalf, and on behalf of fellow Greeks. There was peace, and our city was held in honor" (Plato *Menexenus* 242a).

---

Rocks, named by Demosthenes, Lycurgus, and Diodorus, lay in the Black Sea just off the approaches to the Bosporus from the east (Herodotus 4.85.1, 89), and so represented a ban against the entry of any Persian ship to the Bosporus from the Asiatic coast of the Black Sea. (Wade-Gery 1940, 135–36 [= 1958, 214], seems to assume that all Persian ships must originate from the direction of Phoenicia, and therefore he needlessly supposes that the naming of this Black Sea boundary is due to some confusion in our sources.)

71. Diodorus 11.62.3. The epigram is also quoted, with small variations, by *Palatine Anthology* 7.296; Aelius Aristides 2, *On the Four* 209; it is attributed to Simonides 45 *EG* (= Edmonds *LG* vol. 2, 386 no. 171). Diodorus and Aristides associate the epigram with Cimon's victories at the Eurymedon in Pamphylia in the 460s, but reference to Cyprus in the version cited by Diodorus, among other considerations, makes it likely that the epigram celebrated Cimon's final campaign and victory at Salamis on Cyprus: see Thucydides 1.112.2–4, Diodorus 12.3–4, and the discussions of Meiggs 1972, 126–28; Badian 1993, 58–60 and 64–66. On the likely conflation of celebrations of this victory at (Cyprian) Salamis with the famous battle of 480, see Badian and Buckler 1975.

72. Alliance between Pericles and the family of Callias in the mid-450s is indicated by the marriage of Hipponicus son of Callias to Pericles' first wife: see Davies 1971, 262–63.

The end of war and the establishment of peace (*eirēnē*) observed here were not commonplace events. Conceptually, this transition marked a change in the human condition, as far as it encompassed the affairs of Greeks and barbarians.[73] Unlike the treaties by which Greek states agreed to put a stop to warfare for a stipulated period of time, this settlement had no limit. When the settlement with Artaxerxes was later reaffirmed with his successor, Darius II, we are told by Andocides (3, *On the Peace With Sparta* 29) that the agreement represented "friendship for all time." Peace in perpetuity is a not a concept expressed in diplomatic language among the Greeks unless we include the next major multilateral treaty between Greeks and Persians, the King's Peace, or Peace of Antalcidas, of 386.[74] The establishment of such an equilibrium with the rulers of Asia, rulers who claimed to be "king in this great earth far and wide,"[75] and who believed that their sovereignty was a manifestation of divine will, was an affirmation of the sovereign grandeur of the Athenians. The supremacy enjoyed by Athenian leadership within its proper domain was now acknowledged by the Persians, by all indications upheld by the gods, and seemed in fact to be part of the natural order of the world.

## HONORING ATHENA ON THE ACROPOLIS

The Athenians marked the transition to a new relationship with Persia by new devotions to the gods most closely associated with their civic identity and sovereignty. Construction of a new *telestērion,* or initiation hall, in the sanctuary of Demeter at Eleusis was one sign of this transition, but the most conspicuous was surely the construction of the Parthenon, which commenced in 447/6.[76] The building of the Parthenon was the logical outcome

73. Cf. Thucydides' description of the Peloponnesian War as "the greatest disturbance among Greeks and a certain part of the barbarians, one might say, extending to the majority of mankind" (1.1.2), which globalizes the affairs of Greeks and barbarians. The term *eirēnē* is used by Herodotus 1.74.2 to describe the treaty on the Halys of 585 (see chapter 5 and notes 29–31), and it was used by Aeschylus *Persians* 768–69 to describe how "during his reign Cyrus establish peace for all friends." These examples, where *eirēnē* emerges from the deeds of sovereign kings, show that *eirēnē* is not used anachronistically in this context by Plato, nor in the so-called Congress Decree cited by Plutarch (discussed below), as has been argued, e.g., by Seager 1969, 136–37.

74. Ryder 1965, 5, observes that "the King's Peace was the first Greek peace treaty known to us which did not include a time-limit." (He does not give consideration to the Peace of Callias.) The King's Peace was not entirely a Greek treaty, which is an important factor when considering why it departs from the typical format of Greek peace treaties.

75. See above, note 61.

76. Commencement of construction on the Parthenon is dated to 447/6 by the evidence of inscribed building accounts; see the summary in ML 59. The relationship between the building program on the Acropolis and the building program at Eleusis is indicated in Plutarch *Pericles* 13.4–5 and in *IG* I³ 32. For reviews of the Periclean building program and Plutarch's

of a change the first outward sign of which was the transfer of the common treasury of the Greeks from Delos to the Athenian Acropolis, probably in 454. Not only was the treasury itself moved from Delos to Athens, but Athena, as the new custodian of the treasury of the *Hellēnotamiai,* now began to receive a regular tithe from the tribute of the allies.[77] Ancient sources reveal that Athena's new perquisite was immediately seen as a sign of Athenian aggrandizement, and it became controversial for that reason.

The transfer of the Delian treasury is usually explained, by reference to a passage from Plutarch, as a sign of anxiety over the security of a treasury in the middle of the Aegean against the danger of Persian aggression. Plutarch mentions this anxiety only rhetorically, however, to make the point that no such fear existed to justify the move. According to Plutarch, Pericles' political opponents "cried out in the assemblies: 'The people has lost its fair fame and is in ill repute because it has removed the public moneys of the Hellenes from Delos into its own keeping, and that the seemliest of all excuses which it had to urge against its accusers, to wit, that out of fear of the Barbarians it took the public funds from that sacred isle and was now guarding them in a stronghold, *of this Pericles had robbed it.*'"[78] The transfer of the Delian treasury and the embellishment of the city with temples like the Parthenon were both, according to critics of Pericles, open signs of sheer arrogance on the part of the Athenians. They were not even disguised by a pretense of necessary caution.

Unjustified arrogance according to one party is pride worthy of celebration according to another. The reason for the transfer of the Delian treasury to the custody of Athena on the Acropolis must have been a widely held view that Athens and the cult of Athena, not Delos and the cult of Apollo, defined the true center of the Ionian world. Such a view would have been more acceptable if it were expressed not by Athenians but by other Ionians, and accordingly we find that the transfer of the treasury was originally proposed to the allies by the Samians.[79] The preeminence of Athens celebrated on this occasion should also mark the high point of the doctrine that recognized

---

account of it (*Pericles* 12–14), see Boersma 1970, 65–81; Hurwit 1999, 157–59 and 310–12. The decision to build the Parthenon is sometimes dated to 450/49 based on the Strasbourg Papyrus, a fragmentary commentary on Demosthenes 22, *Against Androtion;* but the authority is unknown, and the date is based on an emended archon's name, so it is not reliable evidence: see Meiggs 1972, 515–18; excerpts in Fornara 94.

77. Inscribed records of the tithe (ἀπαρχή) to Athena on the Acropolis commence in 454, establishing the date of the transfer: see Meiggs 1972, 109; see also ML 39.

78. Plutarch *Pericles* 12.1–2, translated by B. Perrin, with emphasis added. The boasts of Athenian strength, evident in the epigram quoted above at note 71, would be the most obvious way in which Pericles could be said to have robbed the Athenian demos of a fair pretext for protecting the treasury on the Acropolis.

79. As reported by Plutarch *Aristides* 25.3, citing Theophrastus.

Athens as the only Ionian city of note, as acknowledged by Herodotus.[80] The reality of Athenian power as a force in the world was thereby given a cosmological explanation, and given public acclamation in the name of Athena.

The celebration of Athena on the Acropolis was the fulfillment of a vision of Athenian greatness that had already taken form before the invasion of Xerxes. When Xerxes had burned the temples on the Acropolis, he had destroyed a great temple to Athena under construction on the site of the later Parthenon.[81] The decision to build a new temple as a consequence of new relations with Persia is revealed in a passage from Plutarch's *Life of Pericles*, summarizing a public initiative known to scholarship as the Congress Decree. This was a decree proposed by Pericles calling for a meeting of all Greeks at Athens to discuss the state of affairs left unresolved by the war against the Persians. It was announced almost certainly during the interval of no more than three years between the conclusion of Callias' negotiations with Artaxerxes and the beginning of construction on the Parthenon.[82]

Plutarch (*Pericles* 17) describes the occasion of the Congress Decree as "when the Lacedaemonians began to be annoyed by the increasing power of the Athenians." This emerging annoyance can readily be identified with the confident assertion of Athenian power, enough to make the entire continent of Asia groan when "struck by both hands with the power of war," as declared in the epigram celebrating victories by land and sea at Cyprus, quoted above. Plutarch goes on:[83]

> Pericles, by way of inciting the people to cherish yet loftier thoughts and to deem itself worthy of great achievements, introduced a bill to the effect that all Hellenes wheresoever resident in Europe or in Asia, small and large cities alike, should be invited to send deputies to a council at Athens. This was to deliberate concerning the Hellenic sanctuaries which the Barbarians had burned down, concerning the sacrifices which were due to the gods in the name of Hellas in fulfillment of vows made when they were fighting with the Barbarians, and concerning the sea, that all may sail it fearlessly and keep the peace.

80. Herodotus 1.143.2 notes the belief in the general weakness of Ionians, with the sole exception of Athens. (See chapter 6, with notes 84–85.)

81. The recent reexamination by Manolis Korres of fragments and blocks from the "Older Parthenon" has confirmed that the marble temple under construction on the site of the later Parthenon was destroyed in the fires of Xerxes' sack of the Acropolis in 480: see Korres 1992, 70, 76–77; see also the overviews by Boersma 1970, 38–39, 176; Travlos 1971, 444–45; Hurwit 1999, 132–35.

82. Meiggs 1972, 512–15, summarizes the evidence indicating that the Congress Decree, as reported by Plutarch, derives from a genuine decree of Pericles, probably copied by Craterus. Meiggs gives reasons for accepting the historicity of this decree over the objections raised by Seager 1969, but allows that Seager's arguments establish reasonable grounds for doubt. (Meiggs' views are followed by Hurwit 1999, 57–58.) The evidence presented in this study removes the basis for the doubts that Seager indicates. (See note 73 above.)

83. Plutarch *Pericles* 17.1, translated by B. Perrin.

To summon the Greeks to come and take part in the deliberations for the peace and common welfare of Hellas, twenty messengers were sent in four different directions (to the Greeks of Asia and the islands, to Thrace and the Hellespont, to the Corinthian Gulf and the Peloponnese, and to Euboea and Thessaly). Later Athenian decrees attest the practice of sending announcements to Athenian allies in four directions.[84] In each case, there are variations in how the directions or destinations are defined, but there are always four. The notion of four destinations in Athenian imperial decrees (for which the Congress Decree is the earliest example) suggests the notion of four cardinal points, or the four corners of the earth of Near Eastern tradition, representing the entirety of the earth.[85] Universal scope is certainly in keeping with the spirit of this decree, and with the Athenians' view of their place in the world at this time.[86]

Ambitious vision, in fact, is precisely the quality that Plutarch wished to illustrate in describing this decree of Pericles. For despite the fact that the scheme of Panhellenic convention actually came to nothing "owing to the opposition of the Lacedaemonians," nevertheless Plutarch "cited this incident . . . to demonstrate the man's disposition and the greatness of his thoughts." These qualities of Pericles are nearly exact echoes of the qualities that Herodotus attributes to Polycrates of Samos when describing the latter's ambitious vision to rule the sea.[87] For Pericles and the Athenians, like Poly-

84. Heralds are sent to four destinations (Ionia, the islands, Thrace, and the Hellespont) in the Decree of Thudippus, *IG* I³ 71, lines 4–6 (ML 69, = Fornara 136), and in the Coinage Decree, *IG* I³ 1453, clause 9 (ML 45, = Fornara 97). In the Cleinias Decree, *IG* I³ 34, lines 22–28 (ML 46, = Fornara 98), the same four destinations are to be served by two groups of two messengers. On this feature of the Congress Decree, see Meiggs 1972, 512.

85. On a map of the world as conceived by Anaximander and Hecataeus, moving from Athens in the directions of Asia, Thrace and the Hellespont, Thessaly, and the Peloponnese could indeed be viewed as four cardinal directions. "Four corners of the earth" often describes the extent of Assyrian kingship: e.g., *ANET* 274 (Tiglath-pileser I), 276 (Shalmaneser III), 281 (Adad-nirari III), 297 (Assurbanipal). Four cardinal points define the extent of dominion also in the Hebrew bible: e.g., Genesis 13:14, 28:14; Deuteronomy 3:27; Isaiah 11:12.

86. See Aelius Aristides *Panathenaicus* 14–20 (Dindorf 158–61) for the full expression of this Athenocentric ideology: Athens is at "the midpoint of the whole earth" (16: ἐν μέσῳ τῆς πάσης γῆς), and is "the Acropolis of heaven and the empire of Zeus . . . which in fact is the lot of Athena and a place proper to her deeds and nurslings" (19: τὴν ἀκρόπολιν τοῦ οὐρανοῦ καὶ τὴν τοῦ Διὸς ἀρχὴν ὡς ἀληθῶς γιγνομένην λῆξιν τῆς Ἀθηνᾶς καὶ τῶν ταύτης ἔργων τε καὶ θρεμμάτων τόπον οἰκεῖον, translated by C. A. Behr). This rhetoric is likely to reflect authentic Athenian ideology of the mid-fifth century. (Cf. Herodotus 1.143, 5.77–78.) The cosmology underlying it closely echoes the ideology and symbolism surrounding the Temple of Bel-Marduk at Babylon in the time of Nebuchadnezzar II. (See chapter 5, with notes 104, 105.)

87. Herodotus 3.122 refers to Polycrates' ambitions for πρήγμασι μεγάλοισι. (Cf. Plutarch *Pericles* 17.1 on Pericles' intention of encouraging the Athenian demos ἔτι μᾶλλον μέγα φρονεῖν καὶ μεγάλων αὐτὸν ἀξιοῦν πραγμάτων.) At 3.125, Herodotus concludes that Polycrates died in a manner unworthy of his φρονήματα, and that, aside from the Syracusan tyrants, he was second to none

crates before them, the height of grandiosity was achieved (in the case of Athens), or lost (in the case of Polycrates), when the leader of the Greeks collaborated with the Persian lord of Asia in a plan to divide world sovereignty.

The Congress Decree was, in effect, the publication by Pericles and the Athenians of their settlement of the affairs of the world with Artaxerxes. It was the contemporary record of what later became known as the Peace of Callias, as the terms of the decree reveal. Just as the form of Persian sovereignty did not allow the king to admit compromise with another power, so too did the sovereignty exercised by the Athenians constrain the manner of their announcement of new conditions. Theirs was a collective sovereignty based on the principle that the common will of the Greeks was conveyed through resolutions made under Athenian leadership and endorsed by their allies. Over time, the distinction between an Athenian proposal and its endorsement by loyal allies diminished to the point where the proposal itself was virtually fiat.[88] Therefore, the invitation to deliberate at Athens "concerning the sea, that all might sail it fearlessly and keep the peace" was tantamount to a declaration that the sea was the eminent domain of Athens and that peace must now be observed.[89] By this announcement the Athenians were proclaiming that a state of war no longer existed between Greeks and barbarians, so those Greeks who took to the sea should no longer feel free to plunder the barbarians at will. Whether or not the Spartans and Peloponnesians approved of these developments, and whether or not a Panhellenic conference actually convened, the Athenians and their loyal allies were in a position to enforce these points.

Time and war had changed the conditions that had outraged the Greeks in 480–479. Xerxes, against whom the Athenians had vowed unending war on account of his destruction of Greek shrines and statues,[90] was dead and gone, and Artaxerxes, his son and successor, had indicated his pleasure to relinquish the attempt to repeat his father's and grandfather's ventures. Com-

---

in his μεγαλοπρεπείη. (Cf. Plutarch *Pericles* 17.3 on the φρόνημα καὶ τὴν μεγαλοφροσύνην of Pericles.) Kallet 2003, 127–37, assesses the rhetoric associated with Athenian building programs under Pericles, recognizing in it the ambiguous and contested implications of tyrannical behavior.

88. The peace with Persia and the Congress Decree must figure prominently in the debate, ancient and modern, over when the Delian League became the Athenian empire. These conditions correspond well to the description given by the Mytileneans appealing to Sparta for support of their rebellion from Athens, in 428: "As long as the Athenians led on a basis of equality, we followed them with enthusiasm; but when we observed that they were giving up their hatred of the Mede and were becoming more concerned with the enslavement of their allies, we were no longer without fear" (Thucydides 3.10.4). The same shift in Athenian attitudes is found in the accusations of Pericles' opponents cited above at note 78.

89. On the appropriateness of the word *eirēnē* in the Congress Decree (Plutarch *Pericles* 17.1 and 3) as an announcement of a new condition of world affairs (*pace* Seager 1969), see note 73 above.

90. Herodotus 8.143.2.

mon ritual observance was the most conspicuous manner by which the Athenians could demonstrate that all Greeks were following their lead in observing the new relations with the Persians. The most appropriate ceremony to mark this change in the affairs of the world was to rebuild those shrines and sanctuaries that had lain in ruins since the invasion of Xerxes.[91]

It is no accident that the Athenians celebrated this occasion as they had their victory at Marathon, by commencing a great marble temple to Athena on the Acropolis. Under the leadership of Pericles, the Athenians were at last masters of the forces arrayed against them, and so construction of a great marble temple to Athena Parthenos was begun anew, in 447/6, on a new plan.[92] This glorification of Athena continued a trend, begun in the age of Peisistratus, of honoring Athena as the most appropriate divine patron for the Athenian form of sovereignty.[93]

In view of the intimate association of the city of Athens with the goddess Athena, as she is known to us from classical literature and especially from the monuments of the Acropolis, it is hard to imagine that any other deity could ever have been so honored by the Athenians. We should keep in mind, however, that the Athenians themselves told how Athena won pride of place on the Acropolis only after a close contest with Poseidon, a contest remembered in cult places on the Acropolis and represented on the west pediment of the Parthenon.[94] Furthermore, we should recall that Athena's temple on the Acropolis was never considered the oldest shrine in Athens, nor was it

91. See Hurwit 1999, 141–45, and Ferrari 2002 on the condition of the monuments on the Athenian Acropolis destroyed by the Persians. On the pledge not to rebuild the temples destroyed by the Persians, sworn among the Greek allies before the battle of Plataea according to Diodorus 11.29.3, see Meiggs 1972, 504–7; and Siewert 1972. See also Raubitschek 1964, 158 (= 1991, 9), and Connor 1968, 78–84, for an analysis of the remarks of Theopompus *FGrHist* 115 F 153 on the controversy that later arose over the question of whether or not the Athenians had betrayed their resolve to make war on Persia and not to rebuild the temples destroyed by Xerxes.

92. On the chronological relationship of the Parthenon to its unfinished predecessor, see notes 76 and 81 above. Korres 1997, 225–36, argues persuasively for the presence of a Peisistratid temple on the site of the later Parthenon, and (236–40) for the presence of a poros limestone temple under construction between ca. 510 and 490, construction on which gave way, after 490, to a new plan for a marble temple, the "Older Parthenon," which was never completed.

93. The preeminence of Athena's monuments on the Acropolis began with the construction, shortly before 550, of the first great archaic temple on the Acropolis, presumed to be Athena's by virtue of the new prominence of her festival at that time: see Hurwit 1999, 105–21. Korres 1997, 225–36, places this temple on the site of the later Parthenon.

94. Pausanias 1.24.5 notes "the contest for the land of Poseidon against Athena" depicted on the western (rear) pediment of the Parthenon. The contest was decided either by vote of the twelve gods (Apollodorus *Library* 3.14.1; Ovid *Metamorphoses* 6.70–82) or by vote of the Athenian people (Aelius Aristides *Panathenaicus* 40–44 [169–70 Dindorf]; Varro, in Augustine *City of God* 18.9–10; Hyginus *Fabulae* 164). The depiction of this contest on the Parthenon is discussed by Hurwit 1999, 31–33. Poseidon and Athena were each honored, and the

ever the largest temple laid out in the city: those honors went to Olympian Zeus.[95] The abandonment of the unfinished monumental temple to Olympian Zeus at the end of the Peisistratid period underscores the significance of the increasingly selective focus on Athena. The temple to Zeus was a monument to monarchy (or specifically to tyranny, as Aristotle notes).[96] Fittingly, therefore, it remained unfinished throughout the era of classical democracy at Athens, and was completed only in a later age of monarchs identified with Olympian Zeus. From the era of nascent democracy under Peisistratus until the rise of Hellenistic monarchy, Athenian aspirations to realize and celebrate a novel form of collective sovereignty led them to place Athena, the virgin daughter of Zeus, at the center of their civic rituals.

Beginning in the mid-sixth century, at the time of the organization of the Great Panathenaic festival, Athena was celebrated on the Acropolis as an armed warrior goddess.[97] Her martial reputation, serving her image as protector of the city, was closely associated with her role in the Battle of Gods and Giants. The depiction of Athena in that Gigantomachy became the traditional theme of the peplos woven for the goddess at Athens, and the battle was featured in the pedimental sculptures of the Old Athena Temple of the late sixth century.[98] Striking down earthborn giants as they attempted to overthrow Zeus, Athena distinguished herself as defender and upholder of the kingship of her father, acting in this respect as an upholder of the cosmic order, much as did Apollo. But Athena's service to her father was not a solo role. She was a forefighter (*promachos*) in a common struggle shared with her kin, the divine siblings and children of Zeus. In this respect, the celebration of Athena's role in the Gigantomachy was parallel to the role of the

---

tokens of their contest were preserved in and near the Erechtheum: Herodotus 8.55; Pausanias 1.26.5–6, 27.2; see Hurwit 202–4.

95. Thucydides 2.15.4 names the Temple of Olympian Zeus first among the ancient (ἀρχαῖα) shrines of Athens. Pausanias 1.18.8 reports the Athenian claim that the Temple of Olympian Zeus was founded by Deucalion, and that his grave was nearby. On the remains of the unfinished Peisistratid temple of Olympian Zeus (later completed by Antiochus IV and Hadrian), and an earlier archaic temple under its foundations, see Travlos 1971, 402–3; Wycherley 1978, 155–64.

96. Aristotle *Politics* 1313b, where the Peisistratid temple is listed along with the Pyramids of Egypt, the dedications of the Cypselids, and the works of Polycrates of Samos as τυραννικόν.

97. Before the mid-sixth century, the armed Athena was not typical, as noted by Shapiro 1989, 37: "Representations of Athena on Attic vases earlier than the time of the first Panathenaics are surprisingly few, but all share one striking feature, that the goddess is shown unarmed, even without aegis and gorgoneion." On the emergence of the armed Athena image, see also Ridgway 1992, esp. 127–31.

98. On the Gigantomachy in Attic art, see Shapiro 1989, 38–40, and note his remarks on p. 38: "The earliest Gigantomachies, about 560 or slightly later, all come from the Akropolis, a remarkable correlation of subject matter and findspot which has no parallel in Attic blackfigure." On the theme represented on the peplos, see Simon 1983, 39 and 71; Pinney 1988, 471; Barber 1992, 103 and 117.

Athenians among their Ionian kin and allies, fighting in the forefront for a common cause.[99] Athena represented primacy among kinsmen in collective service to the rightful sovereign order of the cosmos.

The symbolism of Athena at Athens has another parallel to that of Apollo at Delos and associated with Athens from the time of Peisistratus. As noted above, by removing mortal remains from burials around Apollo's sanctuary, Peisistratus assured that the no mortal lineage had an exclusive link with the god. The very nature of Athena as Parthenos, "Virgin," likewise assured that no dynastic lineage could claim the exclusive privilege of sovereignty through descent from the goddess. Athena Parthenos was the eternally virginal, motherless daughter of sovereignty (Zeus). Abiding in the house of Erechtheus at Athens, according to such a traditional authority as the Homeric *Odyssey* (7.78–81), Athena provided the Athenians with an even more perfect counterpart than Apollo to the Asiatic goddess of sovereignty patronized by the Persians. The goddess of Asia in her likenesses—Aphrodite with Anchises; the concubine of King Meles; the mate of Gordius and mother of Midas; Kybele with Attis—was at times a divine nymph and could couple with her chosen mortal in concealed ritual to generate a semidivine king, whose god-given power would be revealed at the right time. Likewise, Zeus or Poseidon or Apollo could consort with mortals to generate godlike heroes destined to dominate their peers. But Athena could engender no such privileged line. Hers were foster children, the Athenians, who all shared her endowments collectively.[100] To her surrogate offspring Athena bestowed her protective love, wisdom, and the power of divine sovereignty that came from Zeus. But she could never endow a line of tyrants with the supreme title of divine birth. This was why the goddess celebrated in such glorious fashion in the Parthenon on the Acropolis was the preeminent symbol of Athenian sovereignty in the age of Pericles.

---

99. Promachos (Forefighter) is the epithet given to armed Athena and associated especially with the most famous bronze statue of Athena on the Acropolis, a statue created by Pheidias at around the time of the commencement of the Parthenon; see Richter 1970, 168–69; Ridgway 1981, 169; 1992, 130–31; Shapiro 1989, 26; Hurwit 1999, 24–25. This statue is identified as a tithe from the spoils of the victory at Marathon (Pausanias 1.28.2), and her martial supremacy is represented, significantly for the mid-fifth-century occasion, by the goddess standing with her arms not in a combat pose, but at rest. Athena the Forefighter as symbol of Athens' protective role at this time is reflected in the rhetoric of the day. According to Plutarch, Pericles defended the appropriation of funds by the Athenians because they were "fighting in the forefront" (προπολεμοῦντες) on behalf of their allies (*Pericles* 12.3).

100. The virgin-maternal relationship between Athena and the Athenians is the touchstone of the essays of Nicole Loraux collected in volumes (1993, 1998, and 2000) organized around the themes of Athenian communal identity, maternity, and autochthony.

# Chapter 8

# Herodotus and the Gods

Preceding chapters have traced tyranny as an ideological system that ordered power relationships, communal identity, worldview, and religion. As the sovereignty of Achaemenid Persia took root in Asia and took the place of Lydia on the horizon of the Greeks, it drew on the ideology of tyranny in all of its aspects, from political to religious, to bring its subjects into harmonious cooperation with its manifest power. Greeks were divided in their response to this mixture of pressure and persuasion. Many elements of communal identity, cosmology, and theology among Greeks were rooted in the ideology of tyranny, and strong tyrannies, such as the Peisistratids at Athens, Polycrates on Samos, and the Deinomenids in Sicily, continued to flourish. But so did efforts to organize communal identity around stable institutions rather than strong personalities, especially at Sparta and at Athens. As both of these states saw their ideological foundations threatened by the aggressive claims of Persian sovereignty, tyranny and its attributes began to acquire the face of odious oppression to Greeks. But the exercise of any form of sovereign power could never be entirely divorced from the symbols associated with tyranny. This was a conundrum that both Sparta and Athens had to face.

Chapter 6 identified the religious terms in which the Athenians, along with the Spartans, rejected obeisance to the sovereign authority of Persia. Chapter 7 followed this perspective through some of the distinctive political and institutional developments that followed the defeat of Xerxes. Throughout, Herodotus has been our primary guide. Herodotus reveals the common awareness of the relationship between systems of power and systems of religious ideology when he quotes Greeks rallying their countrymen against tyranny and against Persia in the name of "the gods of the Greeks," and likewise when he quotes the friends of Persia declaring allegiance to the king in the name of "the gods of sovereignty."[1] These and other expressions of the perceived connections between divine and human affairs in Herodotus' *Histories* bring us, in this chapter, to an examination of Herodotus' depiction of the relationship between religious ideology and political history.

This topic is especially appropriate at this point since, in tracing the evolving relationship between the Mother of the Gods and Athens, we are approaching the point in time and historical perspective from which Herodotus himself viewed the events he was writing about. It becomes increasingly relevant, therefore, to consider the nature of Herodotus' convictions about the role of the gods in historical events, and especially to look for indications of how he himself dealt with the problem of historical perspective when treating matters of religion. For not only is he our primary source in this investigation, but as an active observer and commentator, generating some manner of public discourse on the times in which he lived, Herodotus can be considered also a participant in the events themselves.

## RELIGION IN GREEK HISTORICAL THOUGHT

The truths asserted by religious ideology have a peculiar and problematic relationship to the account of causes and effects rendered in political history. For although they may be of paramount importance to those involved in events, religious truths appear to lack the sense of objective reality that attends the historical discussion of cities, ships, soldiers, resolutions, and deeds. As a result, while gods have a prominent place in the stories of cause and effect told in epic and other genres of poetry, they are withdrawn from the forefront of the accounts of events told by Greek historians, where observable reality remains as the primary domain. The apparent distinction between subjective attitudes toward gods as opposed to objective attitudes toward cities, ships, and soldiers has yielded the impression that, while Greeks generally took issues of piety into serious consideration, Greek historians were not similarly motivated by religious sensibilities. Historians like Herodotus and Thucydides, and political philosophers like Plato and Aristotle, appear to speak from a viewpoint of religious detachment, motivated above all else by a pursuit of intellectible standards of judgment. This detachment we regard as a leading characteristic of Greek intellectual achievement. But it places Greek intellectuals in a problematic and paradoxical relationship to the popular beliefs and attitudes to which they themselves bear witness. Do they participate in these beliefs, or in some sense stand apart from them?

---

1. Note the resolve for battle against Persians urged in the name of θεοὶ Ἑλλήνιοι or Ζεὺς Ἑλλήνιος at Herodotus 5.49.3 (Aristagoras at Sparta), 8.144 and 9.7a (Athenians to the Spartans), and 9.90.2 (Samians to the Spartans). See also chapter 5, note 148, on the expression "the gods of the Greeks," and chapter 6, note 108, on the expression "the gods of sovereignty."

This was, at times, even a contemporary question. (It was the focal point of the trial of Socrates, for instance.) It remains an unresolved question.

From the foregoing chapters we can see that, in Herodotus and other sources, issues of divinity are represented selectively, and we can begin to discern some of the reasons why this should be so. From the era of the Persian Wars onward, participants and contemporary observers generated records of praise in song and oratory, and monuments in stone and bronze, to memorialize the clash of ships and soldiers, the capture of cities, and the will and words of men. Even if these records, tendentious as they no doubt were, were subject to later historical criticism or revisionist interpretation, the events themselves retained a high degree of objective acceptance, because the relations of power that they had established had an evident and enduring presence, and because the events themselves were intelligible in terms of the goals and aspirations of those who had participated in them, and those whose lives were shaped by them.

Not so for the gods. Although signs of their enduring presence and influence were widely recognized, and although they too participated in historical events according to popular belief, no mortal could say how the lives of gods were shaped by the events of this world. Human interaction with the gods depended on the notion that the gods had appetites and aspirations, could be moved to affection or malice, and could feel pride and jealousy, and regret and grief. But how could these causes and their effects be observed and recorded? This was the domain of seers and oraclemongers, some of whom had long careers and estimable reputations as consultants on matters of divinity in public affairs. Their pronouncements, assessing the future on the basis of present signs and prophecies from the past, had something of the quality of historical interpretation. But their judgments were always subject to reassessment in light of later events and shifts in public sentiment, and were far less constrained by objective evidence than were assessments of the deeds and motives of men. Over the long run, the accumulating evidence for the instability of power, especially sovereign power, confronted men with the inscrutability of the gods. To paraphrase Herodotus himself on this point, no historical conclusion was secure until a story reached its end. For mortals, this could be defined as the span of a lifetime. For gods, there was no such point of measure.

The historian's perspective on the human element of his story could be chosen deliberately, according to selected outcomes and meanings, but to account for the divine element was more problematic. From the standpoint of historical inquiry, events may be regarded as objective facts, but from the standpoint of divinity, and of the ability of the human intellect to fathom divinity, events are always contingent. Another way of expressing these circumstances would be to say that, while religious beliefs always play an active role in historical events, they respond to a different historical dynamic than do the events themselves. From a historical perspective, past events have observable outcomes and various levels of closure that religious beliefs cannot have, for the ultimate outcome and closure that validate religious belief must always lie at an indeterminate point in the future. As Herodotus points out, the man who places confidence in his ability to know the future is either a fool or a tyrant. In either case, as Herodotus argues, such a man's attitude toward divinity was out of balance.

The problem of historical perspective described here thus corresponds exactly to the problem of distinguishing human from divine motives that lies at the heart of the Greek rejection of tyranny. For the tyrant claims that his goals are at one with the divine, thereby denying any perspective on ultimate meaning but his own. In the classical period, the Greek project in politics, religion, and philosophical and historical thought was to demonstrate that no man had such a lock on ultimate meaning. Events themselves revealed the structures of meaning, including the goals and aspirations of the gods, which could be assessed only through critical inquiry and by avoiding the delusions of tyranny.

As a result of this relationship between religion, tyranny, and the emergence of critical historical perspective, the Greek historians themselves, starting with Herodotus, show a tendency to abstract religion and the gods from their analyses of events, even while they attest to their importance among the subjects of their narratives. The modern perspective on Greek historiography has often extrapolated this tendency to the extreme of denying that religion and the gods had any significant role in Greek historical thought. Closer inspection reveals that this was not the case.[2] Herodotus' *Histories* bears ample evidence, much of it tacit but some of it quite explicit, that classical Greek historical thought was not only sensitive to the claims of widely held religious beliefs, but was even designed, with selective discretion, to provide historical affirmation of them.

## HERODOTUS AND THE UNNAMED DIVINITY

Near the end of his *Form and Thought in Herodotus* (1966), Henry Immerwahr offers a well-reasoned appraisal of the role Herodotus allows for the gods, or τὸ θεῖον, "the divine," in shaping events: "The importance of the divine in Herodotus is precisely that it guarantees the world order. Therefore the majority of the historical actions in Herodotus are accompanied by some kind

---

2. For contrasting opinions on the role of religion in Herodotus' historical thought, compare Donald Lateiner 1989, 64–67 and 196–205 (who minimizes its influence), and John Gould 1994, 91–98 (who sees religion as more nearly central to Herodotus' thought). Following Gould's lead, Thomas Harrison 2000b and Jon Mikalson 2003 both present substantial studies of the place of religion in Herodotus' *Histories*.

of divine causation, which parallels human motivation, but on a higher plane."[3] In most cases, Herodotus reveals an awareness of this higher plane through the words he attributes to others. So, for example, Herodotus introduces τὸ θεῖον for the first time in his *Histories* in the sermon that Solon the Athenian addresses to King Croesus of Lydia: "I know that divinity is utterly jealous" (ἐπιστάμενόν με τὸ θεῖον πᾶν ἐὸν φθονερόν, 1.32.1). The concept of the mutability of fortune that this passage establishes, as has been widely recognized, is thematic for Herodotus' entire work, and the view expressed in the words of Solon may reasonably be taken as an expression of Herodotus' judgment.[4]

There are, in addition, many instances in which Herodotus makes declarative statements in his own voice regarding the role of τὸ θεῖον, "the divinity," or "divine intervention," or its plural, τὰ θεῖα, "divine matters" (The translations are essentially interchangeable.)[5] Some of the most emphatic of these instances have already been quoted in chapter 7. In one passage quoted there (at note 27), the phrase δῆλα δὴ πολλοῖσι τεκμηρίοισί ἐστι τὰ θεῖα τῶν πρηγμάτων ("Many things make it plain to me that divine matters influence human affairs," 9.100.2) closely echoes Herodotus' asides in his account of the battle of Plataea (δοκέω δέ, εἴ τι περὶ τῶν θείων πρηγμάτων δοκέειν δεῖ, ἡ θεὸς αὐτή . . . ["My own view is—if one may have views at all about divine matters—that the goddess herself . . . ," 9.65.2]) and in his report of the fate of the Spartan ambassadors to Persia who were executed at Athens in 430 (δῆλον ὦν μοι ὅτι θεῖον ἐγένετο τὸ πρῆγμα ["It is clear to me that events transpired through divine intervention," 7.137.2]). In each case, while affirming the effect on historical events of τὸ θεῖον or τὰ θεῖα, Herodotus appears to speak more from the standpoint of an involved participant than as a detached observer. In one of these cases—the execution of the Spartans as the long-deferred retribution for their execution of Darius' heralds—Herodotus

---

3. Immerwahr 1966, 312.

4. Herodotus affirms the view of Solon in his own words at 1.34.1, when he reports that "great nemesis from god seized Croesus" (ἔλαβε ἐκ θεοῦ νέμεσις μεγάλη Κροῖσον). Solon's words are also echoed by other wise advisors in the *Histories*: Amasis to Polycrates at 3.40.2, "I cannot take pleasure at your great good fortune, knowing as I do that divinity is jealous" (ἐμοὶ δὲ αἱ σαὶ μεγάλαι εὐτυχίαι οὐκ ἀρέσκουσι, τὸ θεῖον ἐπισταμένῳ ὡς ἔστι φθονερόν); Artabanus to Xerxes at 7.10e, "It is God's way to bring the lofty low. . . . God in his envy . . . tolerates pride in none but himself" (φιλέει γὰρ ὁ θεὸς τὰ ὑπερέχοντα πάντα κολούειν. . . . ὁ θεὸς φθονήσας . . . οὐ γὰρ ἐᾷ φρονέειν μέγα ὁ θεὸς ἄλλον ἢ ἑωυτόν, translated by A. de Sélincourt); Artabanus to Xerxes at 7.46.4, "God who gave us a taste of this world's sweetness has been jealous in his giving" (ὁ δὲ θεὸς γλυκὺν γεύσας τὸν αἰῶνα φθονερὸς ἐν αὐτῷ εὑρίσκεται ἐών, translated by de Sélincourt). On the thematic nature of Solon's advice to Croesus, see Immerwahr 1966, 154–61, 306–25; Lateiner 1989, 44, 196–205; Gould 1989, 78–81; T. Harrison 2000b, esp. 33–63; Mikalson 2003, 150–51.

5. Linforth 1928, esp. 233–37, lists and discusses the variety of expressions Herodotus uses to indicate the presence of an unnamed, often unknown or unknowable, but nevertheless specific divinity.

actually is speaking from within the circle of involved participants, for he is describing an event of his own day. In two other instances, the expulsion of the Aeginetans in 431 and the earthquake that shook Delos not long before the Peloponnesian War, Herodotus identifies events of his own day as the divinely ordained outcome of circumstances set in motion in the time of the Persian Wars.[6] In these instances, we should note that Herodotus makes some of his strongest statements about the historical impact of the gods on human affairs with contemporary events in mind. Inasmuch as we are inquiring into the impact of religious concerns on the political affairs of Athens at the time of the Persian Wars, and looking for the consequences of these concerns in later years, and especially in the era of the Peloponnesian War, Herodotus' presentation of the historical role of τὸ θεῖον and τὰ θεῖα becomes part of our primary evidence.

Most frequently, Herodotus uses τὸ θεῖον or τὰ θεῖα to indicate divine agency at work in a particular event (as in the examples above).[7] In such cases, τὸ θεῖον and τὰ θεῖα serve along with, and sometimes interchangeably with, such terms as ὁ θεός, ὁ δαίμων, τὸ δαιμόνιον, and their plurals, all of which Herodotus employs to indicate the workings of gods, who sometimes can be named and sometimes cannot.[8] At two points in his *Histories* (2.3.2, 2.65.2), Herodotus uses τὰ θεῖα not to characterize a specific event or circumstance, but to characterize the realm of ideas about the divine in a manner that begins to approach our meaning of the term "religion." Although τὰ θεῖα in this sense is not the manner in which Herodotus most often acknowledges di-

---

6. Herodotus 6.91 refers to the curse (ἄγος) that attached to the Aeginetans for their murder of one of the supporters of Nicodromus, a friend of the Athenians, when he had sought refuge at the shrine of Demeter Thesmophoros. As a result, according to Herodotus, the Aeginetans, "although they tried by sacrifices to expiate the curse, were unable to propitiate the goddess before suffering expulsion from their island." The Aeginetans had brought on this curse in the course of events surrounding their submission of earth and water to Darius ca. 491 (Herodotus 6.49), and the consequences that Herodotus reports actually befell them in 431, when the Athenians expelled them from the island (Thucydides 2.27). At 6.98, Herodotus draws attention to the unique earthquake that shook Delos as a consequence of the Persian landing there in 490. Herodotus does not indicate when, after Datis' departure, the earthquake took place, but his wide temporal framework is indicated in this passage by his characterization of the reigns of Darius, Xerxes, and Artaxerxes. The earthquake at Delos is also reported by Thucydides 2.8.3 among the omens discussed at the outbreak of the Peloponnesian War in 431.

7. Instances of τὸ θεῖον or τὰ θεῖα influencing events in Herodotus' narrative are listed and discussed by Linforth 1928, 233–36; see also T. Harrison 2000b, 176–77; Versnel 2000, 112–29; Mikalson 2003, 131–33; and note 8 below.

8. Particularly instructive is the passage at 7.12–18, where a dream that appears to Xerxes and Artabanus (called an ὄψις, ὄνειρον, and ἐνύπνιον) is said to be θεῖα, τι τοῦ θεοῦ μετέχον, θεῖον, θεοῦ τινος πομπῇ, τὰ θεοῦ πεμπόμενα, and δαιμονίη. Herodotus' terminology for divinities, both named and unnamed, is studied by Linforth 1928; T. Harrison 2000b; 158–81, and Versnel 2000, 112–29—all of whom stress that no fundamental theological distinctions can be recognized in Herodotus' usage.

vinity, these two general references provide a more direct insight into the conceptual framework within which Herodotus understands the historical significance gods and divinity.

Among studies of this meaning of τὰ θεῖα in Herodotus, one of the most perceptive is Ivan Linforth's essay "Herodotus' Avowal of Silence in His Account of Egypt" (1924).[9] In it, Linforth focuses on the meaning of Herodotus' famous disclaimer regarding his account of Egyptian religious customs (2.3.2): "I am not eager to relate what I heard of explanations of τὰ θεῖα, apart from the names of deities, for I consider all people to have equal understanding of such things; whatever I do mention of these matters will be because I am compelled to do so by the course of the narrative."[10] Linforth demonstrates that the meaning of τὰ θεῖα in this passage is not as broad as "religion," nor as narrow as "Mysteries" or "secret rites." Instead, τὰ θεῖα here refers to the understanding of divinity that emerges from "(1) the prevailing conceptions of the nature of the gods, their characters, personalities and attributes and (2) . . . that portion of universal history which preceded the time when the course of human events assumed the human complexion which it wears at the present."[11] In other words, τὰ θεῖα refers to the myth-historical role of the gods in establishing and sustaining the present world order, a role that, to anyone who accepts such accounts, still works its influence along lines set forth in foundation myths.

## RELIGION AND UNIVERSAL HISTORY

As Linforth and others have recognized, Herodotus' professed reticence about discussing τὰ θεῖα does not amount to a uniform dismissal of myth and legend from his *Histories*. Herodotus knows much of what we would call mythology and theology. He treats this knowledge with respect, and he introduces numerous elements of various myths into his wide-ranging view of the past. But Herodotus is clearly selective in his discussion of the mythical past, and Linforth and more recent commentators have not been able to identify Herodotus' criteria for what to admit and what to exclude.[12] At is-

9. Linforth 1924.

10. Herodotus 2.3.2: τὰ μέν νυν θεῖα τῶν ἀπηγημάτων οἶα ἤκουον, οὐκ εἰμὶ πρόθυμος ἐξηγέεσθαι, ἔξω ἢ τὰ οὐνόματα αὐτῶν μοῦνον, νομίζων πάντας ἀνθρώπους ἴσον περὶ αὐτῶν ἐπίστασθαι· τὰ δ᾽ ἂν ἐπιμνησθέω αὐτῶν, ὑπὸ τοῦ λόγου ἐξαναγκαζόμενος ἐπιμνησθήσομαι.

11. Linforth 1924, 273. Mikalson 2003, 144, draws a similar conclusion about the meaning of this and a related passage, Herodotus 2.65.2.

12. Linforth never develops an explanation for what he terms Herodotus' "skepticism" (1924, 286) or "reasonable agnosticism" (1928, 239), and even asks his readers to "waive the question of the rationality of [Herodotus'] fundamental polytheism" (1928, 239). Thomas Harrison has responded to the views of scholars who have simplistically asserted that Herodotus was uninterested in religion, but he offers no explanation for Herodotus' "resigned detach-

sue, as we shall discuss further below, is Herodotus' perspective on the nature of human understanding of τὰ θεῖα. This understanding, in turn, is the basis on which Herodotus articulates the relative unity or diversity of humanity.

Here we may advance the argument by recognizing that Herodotus' reticence serves a consistent purpose. By generally avoiding any discussion of myths about the roles of the gods, particularly foreign gods, in establishing and sustaining the present world order, Herodotus manages to avoid the sensitive issue of evaluating the truth of one tradition as compared to another. Herodotus did not wish to lend authority to any foreign mythology that might challenge the most venerable beliefs about τὰ θεῖα held by the greater portion of his audience. For foreign myths, as we have seen in the previous chapters, support foreign views of the order of the world.

Each of the various theogonies recounted by the different peoples known to Herodotus served to establish its own geography of primal origins, and therefore to privilege one or another set of sacred places, and thus to lend authority to the living custodians of that tradition. When allied with real sovereign power, as in the case of Sardis under Alyattes and Croesus, and later under Darius and Xerxes, such theogonies and sacred traditions (τὰ θεῖα) became virtually indistinguishable from the concept of that sovereign power itself. To the extent that sovereign powers were pitted against each other in real geographic and military terms, so too were their theogonies and sacred traditions.

Yet the world and its gods, as perceived by Herodotus and his peers, manifestly constituted a single coherent system within which various sovereign powers rose and fell. Within this world no one sovereign was all-powerful, and accordingly, no single account of τὰ θεῖα allied to worldly sovereignty could claim a monopoly on truth. A man of reason, like Herodotus, who did not doubt that gods were at work in the world, could only conclude, as he did (2.3.2), that "all people have equal understanding of such things" (i.e., τὰ θεῖα). Were we to allow ourselves to be less tactful than Herodotus, we would say that "all people have an equally defective understanding of such things." And so Aubrey de Sélincourt translates this phrase, and better captures Herodotus' meaning: "I do not think that any one nation knows much more

---

ment" (T. Harrison 2000b, 242, referring to something close to Linforth's "reasonable agnosticism"). Harrison tries to make resignation a virtue when, at the conclusion of his book, he advises his readers to resist the temptation of trying "to draw together the different strands of Herodotus' fatalism into a single synthesis" (240–41). John Gould 1994, 98–106, on the other hand, does offer a unifying explanation for what Herodotus leaves out "when it comes to the interpretation of religion, above all the religion of other cultures" (98). Gould suggests that Herodotus as a Greek lacked the appropriate conceptual framework for discussing "what we might call the differing 'ideologies' or world-views of different religious traditions" (102). The present chapter points to a different explanation, but shares with Gould the premise that Herodotus' religious sensibilities are historically implicated.

about such things than any other." History, as Herodotus expounds it, has shown this to be true.

Historical relationships have much to do with what Herodotus is willing to say about τὰ θεῖα. When he describes peoples who were completely foreign to the Greeks, such as those Scythians who did not dwell within the *oikoumenē*, Herodotus is untroubled about discussing the deeds of the gods in their foundation myths.[13] But in discussing the beliefs and customs of peoples who shared the *oikoumenē* with the Greeks, the issue becomes more delicate. In the case of the Persians, for instance, Herodotus gives only a summary outline of their pantheon and religious customs, chiefly to emphasize how different they are from Greek deities and customs.[14] In the case of the Lydians, Herodotus tells us even less. He describes no pantheon, says nothing about the character of their gods, and tells us next to nothing about their religious customs.[15] This near silence is certainly conditioned by the historical development from a century past, when many Greeks, and Ionians especially, had associated themselves with Lydian sovereignty and had accepted a transparent relationship between their own and Lydian concepts of divinity, until Herodotus' day, when many Greeks were resisting the Persian appropriation of Lydian sovereignty and concepts of divinity. The less said about the theological tangle created by these historical circumstances, Herodotus evidently felt, the better.

Egypt was a special case. Egypt seemed both reassuringly familiar and profoundly different to a Greek like Herodotus. On the one hand, the land, climate, and customs of Egypt were different, even diametrically opposite to

13. Herodotus 4.5–10; so also with foundation legends in which gods are less directly involved: 4.32–35, 110–16.

14. Herodotus 1.131–32.

15. In Linforth's (1926) detailed listing and discussion "Greek Gods and Foreign Gods in Herodotus," no Lydian gods are listed. (See the chart, pp. 6–7; similar results are indicated by T. Harrison 2000b, 208–22, with chart, 210–11.) Given the importance of Lydia in Herodotus' narrative and the wealth of material that Herodotus could have commented on (see the overview of Lydian deities by Hanfmann 1983b), this is a remarkable circumstance. A tendency to speak of Lydian deities as Greek (e.g., Zeus in 1.44; cf. 1.35.2) may be a partial explanation of this apparent silence. (Mikalson 2003, 161–64, traces this tendency when he discusses Herodotus' depiction of "Croesus' Greekness in religious matters.") But in fact the differences between Lydian and Greek deities were as evident to Herodotus as they were between any other ethnic groups. (Note that Croesus identifies Apollo as "the god of the Greeks" at 1.87.4 and 90.2.) Most significant, Lydian Kybebe is one of only three deities, as Linforth 1926, 23, points out, "in whom Herodotus fails to recognize Greek divinities under other names" (the other two being the Thracians Salmoxis and Pleistorus, whose alien nature is echoed by Aristophanes *Birds* 1571–1682, where the incomprehensibility of the Thracian god Triballos is parodied). Linforth comments (24): "It is scarcely to be supposed that Herodotus was not cognizant of the familiar identifications of Kybebe; but the differentiation in the present passage [5.101] springs from the . . . spirit of national consciousness. . . . War not only divides nations but also alienates the gods of one nation from the gods of another."

those of all other peoples, as Herodotus points out (2.35). But as it was an ancient land within the *oikoumenē*, its gods were commensurate with the gods of the *oikoumenē* elsewhere. The great antiquity of Egyptian records meant that the Egyptians had refined their understanding of τὰ θεῖα to a greater degree than most peoples, certainly more than the Greeks. By Herodotus' day, the priority of Egypt in knowledge of τὰ θεῖα was a matter of record among Greeks. The Greeks had learned much from the Egyptians, in Herodotus' estimation, including the names of the gods (by which Herodotus means their individual characteristics).[16]

But Egypt was also the ultimate proof of the imperfect grasp of the human intellect on τὰ θεῖα. For not even the Egyptians, with all their learning and wealth, had been able to avoid falling into a reduced and dependent role in the structures of power in the world of Herodotus' day. Egypt was therefore useful to study and learn from, because of its long history, and safe to discuss, because it posed no threat to the sovereign independence of Greeks. The great antiquity of Egyptian Heracles, for instance, provided the foundation for one of Herodotus' most venturesome chronological statements, relating the Egyptian to the Phoenician and the Greek Heracles (2.42–45).[17] At the end of this deductive tour de force, Herodotus saw fit to add a prayer for divine forbearance: "I hope that both gods and heroes will forgive me for saying what I have on these matters" (2.45.3).

In Herodotus' understanding, the doings of gods and heroes, τὰ θεῖα, are to be found in all periods of the past and present, as witness the accomplishments and sufferings of men. Within the reaches of history, verifiable human accomplishments and sufferings suffice to testify to the influence of τὰ θεῖα. But in probing the depths of the recorded past, in Egypt, Herodotus was reaching to the boundaries of what was humanly verifiable, beyond which only gods and heroes could vouch for the validity of his understanding. In this liminal zone between knowledge and faith, there was a greater chance that Herodotus would stray from the truth, and in so doing might arouse the indignation of τὰ θεῖα. This was why Herodotus prayed for the forbearance of the gods and heroes.

## HERODOTUS' WAY OF KNOWING THE PAST

Reliable knowledge about the nature of power and about the role of divine forces in shaping it, according to Herodotus' understanding, can come only

16. Regarding the names of deities referred to by Herodotus at 2.3.2 and especially at 2.50–53, Linforth 1924, 285–86, has aptly observed that the naming of deities signifies the differentiation of deities—that is, the recognition of the individual traits and characteristics of gods, by whatever name they might be called in whatever language.

17. On the importance of Heracles for Herodotus' universal chronology, see Vannicelli 2001.

from reliable knowledge of the course of past events. In keeping with this principle Herodotus makes his most confident assertions about τὰ θεῖα, as we have noted above, in relation to the best-known events of the recent past. By the same standard, the most distant events, namely the births of gods and their creation of the world order, were subject to the least reliable form of human understanding. For this reason, Herodotus placed little weight on the authority of such accounts, despite the fact that spokesmen for nearly every different ethnic group that he encountered had much to say on the subject.

As has often been observed, in *Histories* 1.5–6 and 3.122.2, Herodotus claims to have a qualitatively richer understanding of events from the time of the reigns of Croesus and Polycrates onward, from roughly the second half of the sixth century, than was available to him for earlier times.[18] Students of Herodotus have generally understood this horizon of historical knowledge in chronological terms, supposing that events as far back as the reign of Croesus, roughly contemporary to the generation of Herodotus' grandfather, were knowable to him because they had not yet faded from popular memory preserved in oral tradition.[19] But there are two problems with this picture of Herodotus' access to the past.

The first problem arises from the indication, best documented in Greek history by Rosalind Thomas, that oral tradition unaided by written texts (and sometimes even with written texts) is notoriously vague and unreliable by the time it reaches back three generations.[20] Those who feel that Herodotus draws on oral and not written sources must imagine specialized remembrancers, hypothetically affiliated with temples, priesthoods, or leading families, to explain the level of detail he conveys.[21] But the general presence of

18. The key passage is 1.5–6, at the outset of *Histories,* where Herodotus declines to speculate about the truth or falsity of Persian or Phoenician accounts of legendary events, but says (in A. de Sélincourt's translation, with emphasis added): "I prefer to rely on *my own knowledge,* and to point out who it was in actual fact that first injured the Greeks, and I will proceed with my history" (1.5.3). Immediately after this, Herodotus names Croesus, and goes on: "This Croesus was the first of the barbarians *that we know of* who reduced some Greeks to tributary status, and made friends with other Greeks" (1.6.2). The passage at 3.122.2, "Polycrates is the first of the Greeks *that we know of* who had designs to rule the sea," is taken as a recapitulation of the chronological principle stated in 1.5–6; see Shimron 1973.

19. Oswyn Murray's essay "Herodotus and Oral History" (1987; reprinted in Luraghi 2001a) has set forth the central questions and problems involved in understanding Herodotus' text in relation to oral tradition. Shimron 1973 argues for the significance of the generation of Herodotus' grandfather as a boundary of reliable oral tradition; Gould 1989, 19–41, reviews indications that Herodotus relies extensively on such orally transmitted stories.

20. See R. Thomas 1989.

21. So, e.g., Felix Jacoby 1949, 161, imagines Herodotus relying on "tellers of tales . . . of some standing" representing leading families at Athens; cf. 169–70. M. I. Finley 1965, 22, is appropriately skeptical about the reliability of unstudied memory generally, and so suggests (28) that oral tradition was preserved by "the noble families in the various communities . . . [and] priests of such shrines as Delphi, Eleusis and Delos. They alone, in most circumstances

such specialized preservers of oral memory remains a hypothesis born of the necessity to explain, according to the theory of oral transmission, the authority that Herodotus reflects. It is becoming increasingly evident that the most articulate remembrancers on which Herodotus drew were actually texts, or, more broadly speaking, the expertise of those who relied on texts (poetry for the most part) to preserve the intricacies of the memorable past.[22] If Herodotus was in fact a compiler of oral traditions, as he is generally described, then they were text-based oral traditions.

This observation helps resolve the second and more serious problem with the supposed horizon of the knowable past set at the time of Croesus—the fact that as soon as Herodotus appears to establish this horizon, he ignores it. Not only does Herodotus immediately shift his narrative in book 1 back to the time of Gyges, four generations before Croesus, but elsewhere too, particularly in his account of Egypt, he reports events of the distant (to us, mythical) past with no regard for any chronologically fixed horizon of secure understanding.[23] Together these factors indicate that Herodotus' criterion for the knowable past relied on something other than the limited range of memory transmitted orally. Stories preserved over two and a half centuries of textually transmitted Greek poetry, for the Greek past, and an immensely richer literate tradition for the Asiatic and Egyptian past, are the obvious mainstays of the accounts told to and heard by Herodotus.[24]

Literary underpinnings, then, can account for the selective details that Herodotus represents in the form of an oral history reaching back many more than three generations before his day, but hardly ever, in his accounts of the

---

at least, had the interest to remember events and incidents which mattered to them." Murray 1987 (in Luraghi 2001a, 27–28) provides reasons to doubt Finley's suggestion that the conveyors of oral tradition can be so specifically circumscribed.

22. The recently published fragments of the Persian War elegies of Simonides have raised a new interest in the textual foundations of Herodotus' *Histories;* see now Boedeker and Sider 2001, and the remarks by Luraghi 2001a, 12–13. Among those who have recently pointed to the evidence that will justify a reappraisal of the orality of Herodotus' sources, see esp. Bertelli 2001, Bowie 2001, and Fowler 2001 among the essays edited by Luraghi 2001a.

23. The generation of Croesus does not correspond to "a firm distinction drawn between human and mythic history" in Herodotus' understanding of the past, as is commonly stated (in this case by Lateiner 1989, 35), for Herodotus provides too many exceptions that would have to be explained away. In this respect I agree with T. Harrison 2000b, 207, where he concludes an analysis of "the limits of knowledge and inquiry" by stating that "the Herodotean conception and rejection of 'myth' are of modern construction, built on sand and held together with wishful thinking." (See also Mikalson 2003, 22.) The imperceptible transition between what modern scholars (but not Herodotus or Thucydides) distinguish as myth and history is the subject of an essay by M. I. Finley 1965.

24. See Bowie 2001 for an overview of the Greek literary tradition, and Vannicelli 2001 for an analysis of Herodotus' interweaving of the Greek with the much older Egyptian documentary tradition.

Greeks, earlier than the beginning of the seventh century.[25] It is noteworthy that Herodotus occasionally even refers to texts, usually poetic and not infrequently oracular texts (e.g., 1.12.2, "Archilochus the Parian, who lived at that time, preserves [Gyges'] memory in iambic trimeter"; 2.23, "I imagine that Homer or some earlier poet made up the name [of Oceanus] and put it in his poetry"; 4.13.1, 14.2, "Aristeas the son of Caÿstrobius, a Proconessian, says in his poetry . . . the poetry now known among the Greeks as the *Arimaspea*"; 4.35.3, " [the Delians] call upon [the Hyperborean maidens Arge and Opis] using the names used in the hymn that Olen the Lycian composed for them, and from [the Delians] the islanders and Ionians have learned to invoke Opis and Arge in song"; 8.77, "when the prophecy of Bacis speaks so clearly, I do not dare doubt it, nor do I admit doubts from others").[26]

Most often, however, Herodotus derives authority simply from what people say, with no hint that any textual authority might lie behind the oral account. This is entirely characteristic of his times. Herodotus wrote for audiences that regarded authoritative information as something spoken and heard in contexts that conveyed collective affirmation (festal hymns, dramatic choruses, public rhetoric, e.g.), even when spoken words came from a text, and what was heard was also what was read.[27] Authority lay with the speaker and the setting, and most often in Herodotus the speaker was a collective voice (the Argives, the Corinthians, the Delphians, etc.),[28] representing the community of those who conveyed and affirmed the given account. In this sense we can accept the importance of textual sources for Herodotus' undertaking, yet we can still understand Herodotus' *Histories* as the product of an oral culture.

If we accept that texts underlie the preservation of most if not all of the elements of the stories of the past that Herodotus tells, then, we must return

25. Stories at both ends of what Rosalind Thomas calls the "floating gap" (Thomas 2001) therefore fall within the range of documented literary tradition (a shorter range among the Greeks, of course, than among the Egyptians; see note 24 above).

26. See also Herodotus 5.90.2 and 7.6.3–4 on the oracles collected by the Peisistratids. In the late fifth century, close to the time when Herodotus wrote, various forms of textual authority were becoming more commonly acknowledged, and in some cases achieving the standing of legal authority at Athens; see Munn 2000, 247–329.

27. This priority of textual authority is evident in the citation of the poetry of Olen in Herodotus 4.35 (quoted in the text above), where Herodotus observes that "the islanders and Ionians have learned to invoke Opis and Arge in song" from the Delians rather than from the poetry of Olen, which Herodotus knows to be the source of the songs sung by the Delians. On hearing the written word, see Munn 2000, 114–18 and 385 n. 45.

28. For a list of such references to collective sources of testimony in Herodotus, see Jacoby 1913, cols. 398–99. On the phenomenon, see Fowler 2001, 98–100; R. Thomas 2001, 205–6; and especially Luraghi 2001b, with his discussion of Herodotus' reliance on the "social surface" (Luraghi 159, with n. 54) of oral history presented as "local knowledge."

to the observation from which we began above, and make of it a question, namely: Why did Herodotus treat events from the time of Croesus as intrinsically more knowable than earlier events? If the availability of a textually transmitted tradition was the sole criterion for secure knowledge of the past, and that tradition was over a century older than Croesus among the Greeks, and far older than that among their Eastern neighbors, then why does Herodotus suggest that the quality of his knowledge about the past changes significantly at about the time of Croesus?

The answer lies not merely in recognizing Herodotus' sources and informants, but in understanding the critical standards according to which he deemed that some of the stories that he heard gave testimony to a past that he could claim to know, whereas others he treated noncommittally as being only what this or that people said. Once we understand the criteria according to which Herodotus asserts his command over the past, we will see why he regards some aspects of τὰ θεῖα to be within the bounds of human understanding, whereas other aspects, especially the theogonies and cosmogonies that define for us the worldviews of different religious traditions, lie outside those bounds.

The qualitative boundary to knowledge that Herodotus associates with Croesus is not primarily chronological in nature. Rather, it has to do with the quality—or even better, the quantity—of the testimonies available to him from that era onwards. Herodotus makes this boundary of knowledge explicit in his account of Egyptian history. At *Histories* 2.147.1, he describes a transition in the knowability of Egyptian history corresponding to the end of an era of kings, Sesostris to Sethus, that immediately preceded the establishment of the Saïte dynasty under Psammetichus I:[29]

> So far, then, my account has relied on what the Egyptians alone say, but now I will report views about this country shared by other people as well as by the Egyptians. This will be supplemented as well by what I personally saw.

This marker is again noted and further explained by Herodotus at *Histories* 2.154.4. Speaking of the Ionians and Carian mercenaries who had helped establish Psammetichus in power, Herodotus says:[30]

> They were the first foreigners to live in Egypt, and it is thanks to their residence there that we Greeks have had some connection with the country, and that is how we have reliable information about Egyptian history from the reign of Psammetichus onward.

---

29. Herodotus 2.147.1, translated by R. Waterfield. Just prior to this passage, framing a short excursus on the antiquity of the gods and what others, including Hecataeus, have to say on this subject, Herodotus also emphasizes his reliance on Egyptian priestly sources up to this time period (2.142.1).

30. Herodotus 2.154.4, translated by R. Waterfield.

Here we have a clear description of the criterion that Herodotus uses to claim that "we have reliable information" (ἐπιστάμεθα ἀτρεκέως). It is the mutually confirming testimony of different peoples (here explicitly different ethnic and linguistic groups). No learned men (λόγιοι), not even the Egyptians whom Herodotus avows to be "by far the most learned [λογιώτατοι] of all peoples I have ever met and questioned,"[31] not even the Egyptian priests with all their records and monuments can provide Herodotus with as reliable (ἀτρεκέως) an account of the past, in his judgment, as the account that he himself forms when he has access to the mutually confirming testimony of different peoples. We might better call this the indisputable account of the past, the past that may be taken as known (as Herodotus says, these are things that "we know" (ἴδμεν) or "we understand" (ἐπιστάμεθα) precisely because everyone who has any basis for holding an opinion on the subject is in agreement.[32]

This boundary of knowledge is therefore a cultural horizon. It is the period in which the Greeks became intimately familiar with the ways of their neighbors. It is, in effect, exactly what we call the "orientalizing" period. The question of precisely how the stories that constituted this body of knowledge about the past were preserved among Greeks and other peoples clearly did not concern Herodotus as much as it does his modern commentators. He generally takes for granted the consequences of practices that we identify with this era among the Greeks: increased trade and contact, the spread of literacy, the proliferating varieties of poetry, and the accumulation of inscribed dedications and monuments. But often enough he cites his sources to show us the basis of the authority that he asserts. The boundary that Herodotus describes in Egypt is chronological in the sense that it corresponds to the ascendancy of the Saïte dynasty, in the first half of the seventh century. This, in fact, is roughly the boundary of the securely knowable past, the *spatium historicum,* as it has been termed, from Herodotus' perspective elsewhere in Asia and in Greece as well. Referring to the dedications of Gyges still to be seen at Delphi (an example of the sort of supplemental observations that Herodotus mentions in his methodological statement regarding Egyptian history), Herodotus reports that "Gyges was the first of the barbarians that we know of [πρῶτος βαρβάρων τῶν ἡμεῖς ἴδμεν] who made dedications at Delphi—after

31. Herodotus 2.77.1, where these "most learned" Egyptians are specifically said to be those who "inhabit the cultivated land of Egypt" (οἳ μὲν περὶ σπειρομένην Αἴγυπτον οἰκέουσι): i.e., those who are within the *oikoumenē.* At 2.3.1, Herodotus identifies the Egyptians of Heliopolis as the λογιώτατοι of the Egyptians, after which he makes his disclaimer that no one really knows more than anyone else about τὰ θεῖα (cited above, note 10).

32. See Shimron 1973 for discussion of the several passages in which Herodotus asserts certain knowledge in terms of what "we know" (ἴδμεν) or "I know" (οἶδα; see note 18 above). Shimron argues for a three-generation limit to the *spatium historicum* so indicated by Herodotus, but must argue in the face of several exceptions to this hypothetical chronological boundary (1.14.3, 1.23.1, e.g.). On ἐπιστάμεθα, see Herodotus 2.154.4 (cited above, note 30).

Midas son of Gordius, king of Phrygia."[33] The iambic poetry of Archilochus, noted among the source citations above, gave Herodotus still more information about Gyges. Gyges was a contemporary and ally of Psammetichus, and the man who sent him the Ionian and Carian mercenaries that marked the beginnings of foreign familiarity with Egypt, according to Herodotus.[34] Gyges, therefore, belongs within Herodotus' knowable past just as much as Croesus does—the amount of detail may have been less in the case of Gyges, but it included reliable (ἀτρεκέως) information.

Herodotus reveals the epistemological criterion according to which he constructs his *Histories* at the very beginning of his work. In his opening chapters, Herodotus cites Persian, Greek, and Phoenician versions of the stories of woman stealing that were the basis of the ancient conflict between Greeks and barbarians. If such a variety of peoples, including even peoples pitted against each other in the struggle for sovereignty, could agree on the broad outlines of an ancient story, then, according to the logic of Herodotus' demonstration, it deserves credence. In this paradigmatic display, Herodotus also illustrates how an ancient story, verified in broad outline, could also be subject to conflicting or unverifiable testimony in detail. Here as elsewhere, Herodotus signals the point at which a widely accepted account gives way to the unverifiable testimony of a single source, or where conflicting accounts must speak for themselves without reconciliation. By indicating that his own credence extends no farther than what is confirmed by multiple authorities, Herodotus establishes credentials for sound judgment that he will later be able to exercise without always revealing the nature of his sources, even sometimes to sustain a judgment that he admittedly offers as his own considered opinion. Time (and, by implication, the duration of memory) did not define a horizon of the knowable past according to Herodotus' method; the mutually reinforcing testimony of respectable sources did so.[35]

We, at our great remove in time and intellectual habits, do not participate in the milieu of widely accepted accounts in the same manner as did Herodotus' primary audience, and so we have not fully appreciated the importance of this opening ἀπόδειξις, or demonstration of method.[36] But we

33. Herodotus 1.14.3. On the dedication of Midas, see chapter 2, note 118. Midas' standing on the threshold of historicity is discussed in the section "The Legacy of Midas" in chapter 2.

34. See chapter 3, note 9.

35. Lateiner 1989, 84–90, lists instances (150 of them) of alternative versions of events or explanations, where Herodotus acknowledges differences of testimony or judgment in his narrative (see also Lateiner's lists of instances where Herodotus admits uncertainty or insufficient information, 69–75), and disagreement with other writers or authorities (104–8; both lists overlapping with that of alternative versions). Jacoby 1913, cols. 392–402, collects and discusses the impressive array of ethnic or local authorities, Greek and non-Greek, that Herodotus consulted.

36. It will be apparent that I see no implicit irony, parody, or disdain in Herodotus 1.1–5. Contrary to what is argued, e.g., by Drews 1973, 88–90, and Lateiner 1989, 38, I do not be-

should recognize that Herodotus' feat, here and throughout his work, was to embrace the diversity of peoples and places around much of the world known to the Greeks, as it was described in the works of Anaximander and especially Hecataeus, and to orchestrate from the monuments and testimonies found in these places a reasonably coherent account of causes and effects spanning peoples, centuries, and continents. The result was a narrative commanding a level of credibility appreciably above that of the hymns of praise, speeches, memorials, and discourses on piety produced for the self-affirmation of a group, such as the citizens of a single city, the subjects of a monarch, or the priesthood of a particular cult, who held an undifferentiated outlook on the world.

Stories dealing with τὰ θεῖα constituted a major class of the testimony available to Herodotus, but they were also the most idiosyncratic and therefore the least amenable to verification from diverse sources ("I do not think that any one nation knows much more about such things than any other"), and so, to the extent that he could, he left them out of consideration. But as Herodotus clearly shows in the examples listed above, wherever confirmed events revealed a pattern that could be only, in his judgment, the hand of divine providence at work, he does indeed draw attention to τὰ θεῖα. Herodotus' Histories thus served to isolate and characterize what was actually knowable about τὰ θεῖα, and in this sense we may regard Herodotus to be not merely attentive, but profoundly concerned with the gods throughout his work.

When we consider the implications of such a perspective for the general character of the historical narrative that Herodotus constructs, we arrive at an understanding that is not inconsistent with the view of those who, with Donald Lateiner, point to indications that Herodotus "stresses human autonomy, . . . presents human and political causes for the events he believes historical," and "generally omits the gods from his own explanations of historical events."[37] But the overall characteristics of the narrative, where cause and effect are explained as the deeds of men, do not efface the explicit meaning of Herodotus' selective statements about divine causation.[38] In fact, by omitting the gods from explanations wherever they are not needed (although

---

lieve that Herodotus' discussion of legendary abductions of women at the opening of his Histories conveys tongue-in-cheek mockery of Hecataeus, or a joke shared with Aristophanes, with no explicit indication whatsoever of what he is up to. Compare Thucydides' frank statements about Agamemnon's army at Troy (1.9–11), and note that, like Herodotus, Thucydides specifically indicates and even names those whose historical judgment he doubts or disdains (the majority of Athenians, 1.20.2; poets and λογογράφοι, 1.21.1 [cf. 6.2.1]; Homer, 1.9.4 and 10.3; Hellanicus, 1.97.2).

37.  Lateiner 1989, 67; see also 196–205 for Lateiner's strong skepticism about Herodotus' interest in religion; cf. the criticisms of Gould 1994, 92–98; and Versnel 2000, 117 n. 96.

38.  As Lateiner would have it when he states (in reference to 7.139.5): "The weight of the narrative overwhelms the pietistic aside" (1989, 209).

still present, as Herodotus states at 7.139.5, "It was the Athenians who—
after the gods—drove back the Persian king"; and as he has Themistocles
observe, at *Histories* 8.60c, "If men do not make reasonable plans, neither
will the god lend support to human designs"), Herodotus makes the force
of his observations of divine intervention all the more convincing to a like-
minded audience.

## THE KNOWLEDGE HERODOTUS SHARED WITH HIS AUDIENCE

For present purposes we must consider the nature of participatory verification that Herodotus expected from a like-minded audience. On occasions
when Herodotus reports the action or effects of a god, or τὰ θεῖα generally,
such as those cited above (at notes 5–8), he often does so without reporting
the corroborating testimony of multiple sources. Nevertheless, even here his
method of verification through multiple authorities is implicitly at work. For
he must expect the authority of his own testimony to be affirmed by the common dispositions within his primary audience. How, then, can we deduce
what his primary audience was?

From the outset, Herodotus defines Greeks and barbarians as his subjects,
and as his sources of authority. In speaking of these peoples, in a sense Herodotus also speaks to them. We could say, then, that Herodotus speaks to
a universal audience, and aims at truths that will be admitted by all of the
peoples he describes. But as a Greek telling a story that begins with what happened to Greeks ("who it was who first committed wrongs against the
Greeks"), and that ends at a peak of Greek triumph over barbarians, it is clear
that the center of Herodotus' audience lay within the Hellenic world. Few
would object to a characterization of Herodotus' audience as chiefly Panhellenic. But this is only a loose description. We could further specify that
his audience lay with those Greeks who were especially interested in the relationship between the two most powerful Greek states at the time of Xerxes'
invasion, Athens and Sparta. These two are the first Greek states to receive
an extended discussion in Herodotus' book 1, when King Croesus looks for
a suitable Greek ally (1.56–68); these two were also the great rivals for supremacy in the Greek world at the time when Herodotus was writing (7.137,
9.73). Herodotus clearly addresses an audience alive to the rivalry between
Athens and Sparta in his day, during the Peloponnesian War, in his famous
judgment of the respective strategies favored by the Spartans and Athenians
at the time of Xerxes' invasion:[39]

> At this point I find myself compelled to express an opinion which I know most
> people will object to; nevertheless, as I believe it to be true, I will not sup-

39. Herodotus 7.139, translated by A. de Sélincourt.

press it. If the Athenians, through fear of the approaching danger, had abandoned their country, or if they had stayed there and submitted to Xerxes, there would have been no attempt to resist the Persians by sea. . . . I cannot myself see what possible use there could have been in fortifying the Isthmus, if the Persians had commanded the sea. In view of this, therefore, one is surely right in saying that Greece was saved by the Athenians. It was the Athenians who held the balance: whichever side they joined was sure to prevail. It was the Athenians, too, who, having chosen that Greece should live and preserve her freedom, roused to battle the other Greek states which had not yet submitted. It was the Athenians who—after the gods—drove back the Persian king. Not even the terrifying warnings of the oracle at Delphi could persuade them to abandon Greece; they stood firm and had the courage to meet the invader.

Athenians would have applauded this statement. It expresses the central justification for Athenian leadership among the Greeks in the aftermath of Xerxes' invasion. Indeed, Thucydides depicts an Athenian speaker casting this very argument—without reference to the gods—in the face of a Peloponnesian assembly just before the outbreak of the great war between these two powers (Thucydides 1.73.2–75.1).[40] By making such a strongly partisan statement, however well founded it appears to be, Herodotus puts all of his credibility into the balance. It is highly significant that he does so in order to advance an Athenian point of view. But is he speaking to Athenians? Do the objections that Herodotus foresees from "most people" mean that he could not be speaking primarily to an Athenian audience?

An Athenian audience was often addressed as if it were a forum for Panhellenic opinion or universal truth. This was a rhetorical conceit that responded to a strong element of Athenian self-representation. Although speakers before Athenian audiences do not often concede that most people hold opposing views, the depiction of an argument overcoming opposing views is a widespread rhetorical stance, found in the Athenian speeches in Thucydides, in Euripides and Aristophanes, as well as in the orators.[41] It is also true that Athenian audiences were anything but unified in their opinions and judgments, especially when it came to formulating Athenian pol-

40. Lysias 2, *Epitaphius* 33–45, elaborates the theme of Herodotus 7.139 before an Athenian audience, and reduces Herodotus' "most people will object" to a rhetorical question (42): "Who among the rest of the Greeks could dispute Athenian resolve?" Isocrates 4, *Panegyricus* 93–99, does the same, ostensibly before a Panhellenic audience.

41. See, e.g., the Periclean funeral oration (esp. 2.37–41) and the Mytilenean debate (3.37–48) in Thucydides; Euripides *Suppliant Women* 399–597. Aristophanes often presents his poetry as good advice in the face of critics (*Acharnians* 628–64, *Knight* 503–50, *Frogs* 675–737, e.g.; and see note 40 above for examples from Lysias and Isocrates). In the interests of philosophy born at Athens, Socrates, in Plato's *Apology*, provides the classical example of a speaker of truths against the opinions of most people.

icy under the stresses of the Peloponnesian War.[42] One of the best ways to win the approval of such an audience was to argue a popular Athenian position as if it were addressed to the jury of Panhellenic opinion. This is precisely what Herodotus does in this passage, and a similar effect can be found elsewhere: for example, where Herodotus states that Athens was the only Ionian state worthy of esteem (1.143.2), or where he states that freedom from tyranny was a fine thing in all respects, since it enabled the Athenians to defeat (and subjugate) their Greek enemies (5.78).[43]

Not only do selected comments seem especially appropriate to an Athenian audience, but Herodotus' entire outlook suits that of Athens and Athenian policy in the late fifth century. Like Herodotus' *Histories,* Athens and its Delian allies were seeking to understand the place of Hellenes in the world at large. For a generation, Pericles had encouraged the Athenians to think of their city as the center of a world empire, which meant that the world, as it was known to the Greeks, was an essential part of Athenian self-awareness.[44] Herodotus' *Histories* was an instrument of that self-awareness, with a boundless curiosity characteristic far more of Athens than of Sparta in his day. Herodotus' purpose, moreover, had much in common with the sophistic mission of his day, wherein intellectuals from all over the Greek world came to Athens to find an audience, and generally avoided Sparta.[45]

Finally, there is the strong tradition that Herodotus read his work to the Athenian council. The reliably attested detail that the orator Anytus proposed an award be given to Herodotus by the Athenians makes it difficult to discount this tradition.[46] For both specific and general reasons, therefore, we should conclude that Herodotus' primary audience was Athenian.

---

42. In Thucydides 2.60–64, Pericles responds directly to Athenian critics and opponents of his war policy, including those who denounce Athenian power as tyranny (2.63.2); Cleon makes a similar argument in 3.37. On the polarity of internal debate reflected in these and related passages, see Raaflaub 2003, 80–81; and Kallet 2003, 120. The subject of internal criticisms of democracy is examined at length by Ober 1998.

43. Apparent counterindications, when Herodotus observes, in effect, "How could the Athenians be so foolish?" (e.g., Peisistratus' second advent to tyranny, 1.60, and Aristagoras' success at persuading the Athenians to join the Ionian Revolt, 5.97), are no counterarguments, for such reproach is also characteristic of rhetoric before Athenian audiences (e.g., Cleon's speech in Thucydides 3.37–40).

44. Dewald 2003, 31, offers a similar judgment: "Herodotus' interest in the structural implications of large empires and the theme of tyrannical despotism throughout the *Histories* may in fact have seemed to many of his audience quite directly, even if tacitly, aimed at contemporary Athens." Internal evidence for Herodotus' relationship to Athens is reviewed by Fornara 1971, 37–58; Ostwald 1991; see also Konstan 1987, Raaflaub 1987, Moles 1996, and Blösel 2001 on thematic resonances.

45. This aspect of the intellectual context of Herodotus' work is examined at length by Rosalind Thomas 2000.

46. The late fourth-century Athenian author Diÿllus is cited by Plutarch *Moralia* 862a–b for the information that Anytus was responsible for proposing the reward given to Herodotus

An Athenian audience would have been especially receptive to Herodotus' most emphatic affirmations of the evidence for divine intervention.[47] Five out of the seven most miraculous or portentous events of the recent past that Herodotus draws attention to involved Athens, Athenian cults, or Athenian interests: the earthquake that shook Delos (6.98), three miracles involving Eleusinian Demeter (8.65; 9.65, 100–101), and the uncertain consequences of the slaying of Darius' heralds (7.133–37); the exceptions are the miraculous repulse of the Persians from Delphi (8.38–39), and the wrath of Talthybius that fell on the Spartans for their part in the slaying of Darius' heralds.[48] For all of these reasons, then, it is reasonable to conclude that Herodotus' views of τὰ θεῖα were framed primarily with an Athenian audience in mind.

This observation gives us a better understanding of why Herodotus generally speaks obliquely and with tact when identifying the indications of divine agency. The open discussion of τὰ θεῖα in a political forum was a delicate matter at Athens in the 420s and 410s. Prominent seers like Diopeithes and Lampon are known to have advised the Athenians, even drafting decrees touching on imperial business and sacred matters.[49] Some men who made their reputations dealing with τὰ θεῖα fell afoul of public esteem, like Diagoras, whose theological speculations were mocked in Aristophanes' *Clouds*, and who, sometime around 415, was publicly condemned for daring to say too much, or the wrong things, about the Mysteries of Demeter.[50] This much is reliably attested. Beyond this, we are told that Ionian-style cosmo-

---

for reading his work at Athens. I have proposed the events of 415 as the historical context for this reading to the Athenian council in Munn 2000, 114–18 and 386 n. 51.

47.  Lateiner 1989, 67, lists passages where Herodotus, in his own voice, "reports divine interference in human affairs": 1.34.1; 2.45.3; 3.108.2; 6.27.1, 98.1; 7.137.2; 8.13, 37–39, 129.3; 9.65.2, 100.2, 101.1. The list is minimal and can be expanded (see, e.g., T. Harrison 2000b, 64–101), but it does include the most prominent instances, among which the passages discussed here (6.98.1; 7.133–37; 8.38–39, 65; 9.65, 100–101) are clearly the most emphatic.

48.  Similarly, the fateful hand of Demeter Thesmophoros on Aegina (Herodotus 6.91) and on Paros (6.134–35) may be seen to be working for the benefit of Attica.

49.  Aristophanes *Birds* 988 names both Diopeithes and Lampon as celebrated seers. Diopeithes is also lampooned in *Knights* 1085, *Wasps* 380; he is the proposer of *IG* I³ 61 (ML 65; Fornara 128), dealing with regulations for Methone and the payment of the tithe to Athena; he is probably the same Diopeithes active in oracular interpretation at the beginning of the fourth century (Xenophon *Hellenica* 3.3.3). On the decree of Diopeithes against impiety (Plutarch *Pericles* 32.1), see below, note 52. Lampon was one of the founders of Thurii (Diodorus 12.10.3–4), associating him in this role with Protagoras (Diogenes Laertius 9.50), and at least indirectly with Herodotus himself (Aristotle *Rhetoric* 3.9.2; Strabo 14.2.16); Plutarch *Pericles* 6.2 associates Lampon with Anaxagoras and Pericles. Lampon proposed the rider to the Eleusinian first-fruits decree (*IG* I³ 78, line 47; ML 73; Fornara 140). Blösel 2001, 187–88, traces a plausible connection between "oracles about Euboea" cited in a decree (*IG* I³ 40, lines 64–66; ML 52; Fornara 103) and Herodotus' discussion of an oracle of Bacis (8.20).

50.  On Diagoras the Melian, see Aristophanes *Clouds* 830, *Birds* 1072, *Frogs* 320; Lysias 6, *Against Andocides* 17. See also the discussion in chapter 2 at notes 103–4.

logical speculation, as expounded in the 430s and 420s by the likes of Protagoras and Anaxagoras, drew public reproach and even political attacks.[51] Plutarch reports that Diopeithes had a decree passed by the Athenians threatening indictment for anyone "who did not respect τὰ θεῖα or who taught doctrines regarding the heavens," and that Anaxagoras was his intended target.[52] In the *Clouds,* Aristophanes makes fun of Socrates for supposedly doing such things. Aristophanes' jests were never far from the serious preoccupations of the Athenians, and this is confirmed by Plato's depiction of Socrates defending himself in court not so much against the formal charges that he faced in 399, but against the prejudices created against him a generation earlier for his supposed involvement in Ionian-style speculation.[53]

Playwrights of this era, it has often been observed, appear to have enjoyed more freedom to discuss, speculate about, and even ridicule matters of divinity and religion.[54] This was perhaps because they were giving words to others, and these words revealed their true wisdom or folly through the course of events acted out by fictive characters on stage. In this manner, the playwrights depicted the inherent tensions felt by all, and preserve a fair reflection of the range of issues that could and did come up for discussion at Athens, in private and in public. But anyone who wrote in his own voice as Herodotus did, asserting what he knew or believed to be true, had to be more circumspect. He was asserting meanings that were relevant to real, current events, not merely setting in motion fictional characters whose deeds could be evaluated in terms of storybook outcomes. If he expected his wisdom to do him credit, he had to recognize also that he could quickly become a scapegoat if events were to show his judgment to be seriously flawed.

For these reasons, and with such examples in mind, we can see why Herodotus was circumspect. His subject led him into the heart of the dispute over sovereignty and divinity that had led to the execution of the *Mētragyrtēs* and his Greek interpreter, along with the rest of Darius' emissaries. Charges of impiety in the affair of the Mysteries would lead to the condemnation and execution of some of Herodotus' own contemporaries in 415. Herodotus could therefore not afford to be explicit in his account of affairs at Athens in which the Mother of the Gods had a role, even if (and perhaps particu-

---

51. See Ostwald 1986, 191–98 and 266–90, on the prevalence of theological and cosmological speculation at Athens in the 430s and especially 420s, and the suspicion with which it was popularly regarded. Dover 1976 (reprinted 1988) examines the later evidence—much of it distorted by the traditions recorded in comedy as well as by the memory of the trial of Socrates— for the alleged trials of many of these intellectuals. See also Wallace 1994.

52. Plutarch *Pericles* 32.1; see Dover 1976 (= 1988, 146–47); Ostwald 1986, 196–97; Wallace 1994, 137–38. See also chapter 6, note 141.

53. Plato *Apology* 18c–19d, 26d.

54. See Yunis 1988 for a discussion of novelty and tradition in the religious views found in Euripidean drama.

larly if) her name and nature were the subjects of frequent discussion at Athens in his day. We can therefore understand why Herodotus professed himself "not eager to relate" the particulars of τὰ θεῖα, even though he must have encountered any number of knowledgeable Greek and non-Greek informants who were happy to discuss such matters openly and at length.

Given his deference to Athenian sensibilities, it is surely significant that Herodotus introduces τὸ θεῖον for the first time in his *Histories* in the lesson that Solon the Athenian addresses to King Croesus of Lydia: "O Croesus, I know that divinity is utterly jealous . . ."[55] Through this thematic episode, and others like it, Herodotus prompts his audience not only to look for shifts of fortune in the course of the history he narrates, but also to recognize these shifts as the effects of τὸ θεῖον. Beginning with the fated fall of Croesus and reaching the climax of the contest between Xerxes and the Greeks, Herodotus indicates in the passages discussed above the most significant instances, in his judgment, of the effects of τὸ θεῖον. He gives unique emphasis, as we have noted, in his discussion of the outcome of the divine anger stirred by the murder of Darius' heralds, where he uses the superlative, θειότατον φαίνεται γενέσθαι (7.137.1): "This, it seems to me, came about by the most manifest divine intervention."

The hand of anonymous divinity, τὸ θεῖον, is thus repeatedly seen in play, according to Herodotus, at decisive moments in the contest to determine the relationship between Greeks, particularly the Athenians, and the lords of Asia. Significantly, he sees Demeter, specifically Eleusinian Demeter, as the most appropriate deity to name on such occasions. It seems fair to say that Herodotus' reticence about naming a divinity in most instances, and his emphasis on the avenging influence of Eleusinian Demeter when he does in fact name a deity, were prompted by his awareness that the whole matter of divine retribution for the murder of Darius' emissaries was coming to a head at the time when he was writing.

## HERODOTUS, THE GODS, AND HISTORY

In the 420s and 410s, thoughtful men were concerned that war, plague, and possibly even the arrogance of the Athenian demos itself might be signs that the gods were working out a punishment for past Athenian misdeeds, among which the condemnation of Darius' emissaries loomed ominously. Herodotus harnessed this theme of divine retribution, and by selective emphasis he showed that the force of τὸ θεῖον had, historically, been on the side of the Greeks. Moreover, he gave the Greeks, and Athenians in particular, priority in the tradition of understanding the ways of τὸ θεῖον, through Solon's advice to Croe-

55. On Solon's advice to Croesus, see above, at note 4.

sus, and he emphasized the fall of Croesus and especially the failure of Xerxes as the greatest proofs of the workings of this force in the affairs of men.

This was a reversal of the roles that had been historically enacted when Darius' messengers warned the Athenians, when their warning was violently rejected, and when Xerxes afterward brought destruction to Athens. At the time Herodotus was writing, Athenians were keenly aware of the historical polarity of warning and destruction. So Sophocles has Oedipus spit back Teiresias' unwelcome words of warning by calling him a *dolios agyrtēs,* "deceitful begging priest" (alluding to the *Mētragyrtēs*),[56] while the audience knew that the begging priest was the wiser of the two. Cratinus staged two comedies that made fun of agitated women; in one he mentioned or depicted an *agersikybēlis,* "beggar of Cybele," and in the other, a *Kybēbos,* "Kybebe-man."[57] In this case it is likely that the Kybebe-man was made fun of, but a joke at his expense would have had punch only if this figure were close to the center of a serious controversy.

In just this manner, Aristophanes places a parody of Lydian and Phrygian ritual warnings at the center of his send-up of a very serious issue, the establishment of universal sovereignty. In the *Birds,* Aristophanes has his protagonist, Peisetaerus, reject a message from Iris warning of destruction brought down by the wrath of Zeus, in the following manner: "Cut out the mumbo-jumbo [παφλάσματα] and listen yourself! Hold still! Look here! Do you think you're spooking some Lydian or Phrygian with words like that? [πότερα Λυδὸν ἢ Φρύγα ταυτὶ λέγουσα μορμολύττεσθαι δοκεῖς;]"[58]

Even in Herodotus' day, an Athenian audience associated the intonement of a warning of cosmically ordained doom with the superstitions of Lydia and Phrygia. Such talk, like the words of oraclemongers and soothsayers consulted by the Athenians before their expedition to Sicily, was in vogue especially when the Athenians, as rulers of the sea, were preparing to move their forces to reconfigure the balance of power in the world.[59] Worries about transgressing the limits set by τὸ θεῖον made the Athenians particularly anxious at such a time, which was why allegations of profaning the Mysteries led to such an uproar. Before this audience, Herodotus' reasoned demonstration of how their greatest successes had been achieved with the support of τὸ θεῖον, a force that had stricken down the proudest lords of Asia, must have seemed timely, wise, and welcome.

---

56. Sophocles *Oedipus Tyrannus* 387–88.

57. See chapter 2, note 22.

58. Aristophanes *Birds* 1243–45. Peisetaerus goes on, using Lydian symbolism, to threaten Zeus by pointing out that his own lightning-bearing eagles will be working against him.

59. On soothsayers and oracle mongers at the time of the Sicilian expedition, see Thucydides 8.1.1; Aristophanes *Birds* 958–90; Plutarch *Nicias* 13.1. Note the references to maps and geographical knowledge (or ignorance) in these same passages (discussed in chapter 5, with notes 144–45).

# Chapter 9

# The Mother of the Gods at Athens

Chapters 6 and 7 presented the argument that the tale of the *Mētragyrtēs,* the wandering priest of the Mother of the Gods, who came to Athens only to be killed by the intolerant Athenians, originated in the execution of Darius' heralds in the first decade of the fifth century. We are now approaching the historical conclusion of the tale of the *Mētragyrtēs,* in the last decade of the fifth century, when the Athenians received the Mother of the Gods and established her cult in their Council House. The present chapter examines these circumstances, and provides a perspective from which it is possible to see how the story of the Mother of the Gods and Athens was remembered more for its legendary qualities, as a story of sacrilege, suffering, and repentance, than for its place in Athenian political history. In this story, in other words, we see myth in the making.

In its historical setting, the eventual acceptance of this foreign deity at Athens can now be recognized as a feature of the evolving relationship between Athens and Lydian and Phrygian Asia. What was once familiar and not entirely foreign to Athenians of the seventh and early sixth century was alienated by the rise of the Persian empire. Through the era of the Persian Wars and the first generation of the Delian League, the Athenians defined themselves, culturally and politically, in ways that emphasized their independence of the customs and institutions associated with Asia, the native land of tyranny and of an ancient ideology of civilized order in the world, the *oikoumenē.* Under these conditions, Athenians rejected the Mother of the Gods, Kýbebe at Sardis, and put to death the heralds who demanded submission to the sovereign order that she represented.

In this chapter we will find that the recognition and acceptance of the Mother of the Gods corresponds to a measured reversal of this trend of cultural relations. After the Peace of Callias had established an equilibrium

between the Athenian and Persian empires, adversaries were gradually transformed into partners. As a sovereign power that claimed legitimate domination over Greeks in Asia as well as in Europe, the Athenians were beginning to reexamine what they had in common with the cultures of barbarian
Asia: Euripides' *Bacchae* reflects this theme of underlying affinity; Herodotus' *Histories* is another expression of this perspective. In this context the Athenians finally recognized the Mother of the Gods, and accepted her as their
own. The eventual establishment of the Mother at Athens, then, is not a simple story of the unfamiliar becoming familiar, or of outlandish rites coming
into vogue. It is part of the story of the Athenian accommodation to the ideology of universal sovereignty.

The arrival of the Mother of the Gods at Athens is also, in a sense, part of
a story of the return of the symbols and attributes of tyranny to Athens. As
the Athenians, in the late fifth century, struggled to secure their sovereignty
from the assaults of the Spartans and their allies, we find signs that the Athenians were increasingly interested in appropriating, or reviving, traditional
symbols of power. The second purification of the island Delos during the
Peloponnesian War is one illustration of this interest. More subtle signs of
this appear in various symbols associated with tyranny. The massive display
of wealth, particularly in the form of the tribute of the allies paraded before
the Athenians and visitors to their city at the time of the Dionysia, calls to
mind the pride of Croesus in displaying his wealth to visitors, as described
by Herodotus.[1] Eroticism in public art, as in the procession of seductive Victories on the balustrade of the Temple of Athena Nike on the Acropolis, calls
to mind the culture of beauty associated with the power of Sardis in the poetry
of Sappho.[2] More explicitly, Athens was described as a "tyrant city" by Pericles, by his successor in leadership, Cleon, and by Aristophanes.[3] Displays of
wealth and surpassing beauty may be taken for a pride in power and success
common to many eras, but the explicit evocation of tyranny at Athens was
more than an incidental figure of speech. The idea of tyranny was in the air
at Athens in the late fifth century.

Tyranny, in the Asiatic mode, invested sovereign power in the single preeminent individual, whereas democratic Athens embodied sovereign authority in the institutions of collective government. Since the time of Solon
the Athenians had made it a matter of law that their state would never cede

1. On the display of tribute, see Aristophanes *Acharnians* 504–6 and Isocrates 8, *On the Peace*
82, with the analyses of Raubitschek 1941; and Meiggs 1972, 433–34.
2. On the new level of eroticism in Athens in the late fifth century, see Stewart 1997, esp.
101–2, where he notes the relation of this trend to the earlier orientalizing images of the Naked
Goddess, and 148–50, with an appraisal of the Nike Balustrade.
3. See the discussion in chapter 1, with notes 13 and 14.

sovereignty to a tyrant.[4] The career of Peisistratus and his sons, labeled a tyranny only after the fact, showed how a skillful leader could finesse the distinction between personal power and the institutions of collective government.[5] The unsurpassed popularity of Pericles, and his strong hand of leadership, suggested to some that he was attempting to do the same.[6] But it was in the final decades of the fifth century that allegations of tyranny became most heated, and came to focus particularly on Pericles' kinsman and protégé Alcibiades. In the career of Alcibiades we find the most conspicuous celebrations of a single preeminent man, the most controversial ambitions of a man who identified his city's success with his own, and the most notorious condemnations of a man for impious acts, and for suspicions that he aspired to tyranny. These attributes and characterizations of Alcibiades are significant here because all indications point to the short-lived triumph of Alcibiades, on his return to Athens from exile in 408, as the occasion on which the Mother of the Gods arrived in Athens.

## ALCIBIADES' TYRANNICAL AMBITIONS

Alcibiades was born at the time when the entente between Persia and Athens was reached, in the mid-fifth century. He was descended from some of the most celebrated lineages at Athens, and was raised as the ward of Pericles after the death in battle of his father, Cleinias. Coming of age as Athens was going to war with the Peloponnesians, Alcibiades moved confidently into the highest social circles at Athens. He married the granddaughter of Callias, the Eleusinian herald and torch bearer who had led the negotiations with Artaxerxes.[7] Birth, education, and family connections thus put Alcibiades at the center of the Periclean vision for Athens and its empire, and he embraced this heritage as a personal mission.

Alcibiades treated political leadership as a birthright that he expected all to acknowledge, not just at Athens but abroad as well.[8] He was known for

4. See Aristotle *Athenian Constitution* 16.10 and the analyses of Ostwald 1955; Rhodes 1981, 220–23; and Gagarin 1981.

5. The constitutional character of Peisistratus' regime is noticed by Herodotus 1.59.6, Thucydides 6.54.5–6, and Aristotle *Athenian Constitution* 14.3 and 16.2.

6. On the comparison of Pericles to a tyrant, and specifically to Peisistratus, see Plutarch *Pericles* 3, 7.1–3, 16.1; and the analysis of Andrewes 1978.

7. On Alcibiades' family connections, see Davies 1971, 9–16.

8. Throughout Thucydides' account of Alcibiades' career, he is characterized as claiming preeminence as his due in his own words, or asserting it through his actions: see Thucydides 5.43.2–3; 6.16, 89; 8.12, 16, 47, 56, 81–82, 88–89.1. Alcibiades' alleged wish to replace Heracles as the progenitor of Spartan kings was the ultimate expression of this ambition: see Athenaeus 12.535b–c and 13.574d (quoting an anonymous comic poet); Plutarch *Alcibiades*

jealously claiming all credit for the successes that attended him. Commentators seize on this trait as reason to denounce the ostentation of Alcibiades, but tend to overlook a larger point: Alcibiades was entirely the creature of the admiration of others. In his youth, he could not have risen so quickly in public affairs without the considerable support of influential elders and peers.[9] At the height of his career, wealthy backers made it possible for Alcibiades to distinguish himself above all others in formal honors of victory, in choral contests at home and especially in his chariot competitions abroad.[10] His victories in the Panhellenic games were unparalleled, as were the celebrations and commemorations of his victories.[11] These events were spectacles, where the prestige of Alcibiades grew through public acclamation in ever widening audiences.

Alcibiades also pursued more private ceremonies of power, where his prestige was manifested to an inner circle of kinsmen and supporters, and where Alcibiades demanded and received pledges of unconditional allegiance.[12] When the doings in these intimate communions became known through rumor and eventually through official inquiry, they embroiled Alcibiades in allegations of sexual perversion, religious profanity, and, ultimately, in the allegation that he was aiming at tyranny.[13] Although much remains unknown and unknowable about the allegations against Alcibiades, the prominence given to his (ill-)reputed sexual liaisons should tell us that these acts themselves were seen as elements of his quest for power, and not just as self-in-

---

23.7, *Lysander* 22.3. The claim was taken seriously when the succession to the Eurypontid kingship at Sparta was in dispute, not long after Alcibiades' death: see Xenophon *Hellenica* 3.3.1–4; Cartledge 1987, 113.

9. See the anecdotes collected by Plutarch *Alcibiades* 3–6. The award of the prize of valor to Alcibiades at his first battle, at Potidaea in 432, attests the sort of favorable regard he received: see Plato *Symposium* 220d–e; Isocrates 16, *On the Team of Horses* 29.

10. The financial backing of Teisias, which enabled Alcibiades' phenomenal show in the chariot races at Olympia in 416, attests the sort of support that he continued to receive: see Isocrates 16, *On the Team of Horses* 1–3, 50; Diodorus 13.74.3–4; Plutarch *Alcibiades* 12.2–3; and the commentary of Davies 1971, 501–3. Cf. Thucydides 6.15.3 on Alcibiades' lifestyle, especially in horse racing, exceeding his means.

11. On the lavish services provided to Alcibiades at Olympia, see [Andocides] 4, *Against Alcibiades* 29–30; Plutarch *Alcibiades* 12.1; and Athenaeus 12.534d. Alcibiades' Olympic victory was celebrated in poetry by Euripides (Plutarch *Alcibiades* 11.2; Athenaeus 1.3e), and by publicly displayed paintings (Plutarch *Alcibiades* 16.5; Athenaeus 12.534d–e; Pausanias 1.22.7).

12. The description of Alcibiades' failed attempt to seduce Socrates, famously put in Alcibiades' own words in Plato's *Symposium*, esp. 217a–219d, is the most explicit testimony to this facet of Alcibiades in private.

13. As Thucydides puts it (6.15.4): "Fearing the enormity of his abnormal comportment regarding his own person, and of his ambition in every single undertaking, the majority became hostile to him in the belief that he was aiming at tyranny" (φοβηθέντες γὰρ αὐτοῦ οἱ πολλοὶ τὸ μέγεθος τῆς τε κατὰ τὸ ἑαυτοῦ σῶμα παρανομίας ἐς τὴν δίαιταν καὶ τῆς διανοίας ὧν καθ᾽ ἓν ἕκαστον ἐν ὅτῳ γίγνοιτο ἔπρασσεν, ὡς τυραννίδος ἐπιθυμοῦντι πολέμιοι καθέστασαν).

dulgent diversions from the more serious business that occupied Alcibiades in sober moments.[14] Alcibiades would hardly have appeared so formidable, and been so feared specifically on account of his private behavior, if those around him did not recognize that his more sensational private acts also portended tyranny.

As a young man, Alcibiades had been initiated into Asiatic customs as part of his introduction to the Ionian aristocracy. Evidence for this comes in the form of the invective against Alcibiades composed by his elder contemporary Antiphon, quoted by Athenaeus for the purpose of illustrating the infamous excesses of the Ionians. Antiphon writes of Alcibiades:[15]

> When you had been presented by your guardians to your parish, they gave you your inheritance and you went off by sea to Abydus, not to recover some debt owing to you or to establish some official connection [προξενία], but by reason of your lack of discipline and depravity of your character, to learn from the women of Abydus the ways of behavior befitting your mentality, so that you could spend the rest of your life putting them into practice.

According to Antiphon, at a point in his life when an honorable young Athenian would begin assuming the responsibilities of citizenship at Athens, Alcibiades began whoring with the women of Abydus, on the Asiatic side of the Hellespont. The orator Lysias adds further details. He is quoted as saying that Alcibiades was taken to the Hellespont by his uncle Axiochus, where "the two of them together married and cohabited with Medontis of Abydus." One of the two men (no one knew which) fathered a daughter on Medon-

---

14. The attested public reaction to the *paranomia* ("abnormality," "perversity") in Alcibiades' personal behavior has given rise to much discussion about how his sensual indulgences came to be read politically. Among recent commentators, James Davidson 1997, 294–301, has argued that it was not so much Alcibiades' likeness to tyrants of old that was objectionable: "Rather, a tyrannical man's desires were already outpacing the resources of a private citizen and forcing him to extremity. He needed to overthrow the system to get himself out of debt. It was not so much a tyranny of aspiration as a tyranny of desperation" (299). David Gribble 1999, 30–89, interweaving the character of Alcibiades with vignettes of Meidias and Timarchus (from Demosthenes 21, *Against Meidias,* and from Aeschines 1, *Against Timarchus,* neither of whom was suspected of aspirations to tyranny), likewise identifies "an excessively luxurious lifestyle" with "the absence of control over desires both physical and political" (53–54). Victoria Wohl 2002, 124–70, also sees the threat of Alcibiades' *paranomia* primarily in terms of sensual excess, but, significantly, she argues that its transgressiveness was not merely self-motivated, arising rather from the reciprocal relationship between public desires and Alcibiades' own disposition to *paranomia.* Wohl thus comes closest to the present argument, recognizing that Alcibiades' sensual behavior, as seen by Athenians, involved the enactment of a public yearning for tyrannical power.

15. Antiphon fr. C 1 (Maidment, = Thalheim *AO* fr. 6; from Athenaeus 12.525b), translated by R. K. Sprague. In Munn 2000, 112–13, I argue that the occasion for the composition of Antiphon's invective was the indictment and anticipated trial of Alcibiades for his role in the profanation of the Mysteries.

tis, and later both men slept with the daughter as well.[16] Antisthenes the Socratic, writing in the generation after Alcibiades, expands the picture of incestuous habits by stating that Alcibiades was so unrestrained that he had intercourse with his own mother, sister, and daughter, "as the Persians do."[17] The Persian custom that Antisthenes alleges was a characteristic of royal courts (at least as far as sisters and daughters were concerned).[18] A man who had intercourse with a woman who turned out to be his own mother was, of course, the archetype of a tyrant.[19] The implication behind these allegations was that Alcibiades was a devotee of the rites of tyranny, a charge that may not be far from the truth.

If the powers of tyranny could be aroused through ritual acts, why not animate them for the benefit of Athens? Much as the city of Athens itself, in this period, cultivated the rites of foreign deities, so too did Alcibiades. Evidence for this comes from the comic playwrights contemporary to Alcibiades. Eupolis, for example, famously lampooned Alcibiades as an initiate to the rites of the Thracian goddess Cotyto in his *Baptae*.[20] Whether the rites of Cotyto had anything to do with tyranny is uncertain, but other ritual exploits of Alcibiades were more explicit. Some of them were matters of comic fantasy, but some were matters of official inquisition.

The most notorious example of Alcibiades' appropriation of power through ritual was his role in the so-called profanation of the Eleusinian Mysteries. In the early spring of 415, Alcibiades presided over a series of secret meetings between his inner circle of followers and the factions of his chief political rivals in order to secure their common goal, the ostracism of the demagogue Hyperbolus. The solemn pledges of communion among the rival factions brought together by Alcibiades, when they later came to public attention, became the basis for the charges that Alcibiades and many of his

16. Lysias fr. 5 (Thalheim *LO* p. 346; from Athenaeus 12.534f–535a, 13.574e).

17. Antisthenes, quoted by Athenaeus 5.220c. Gribble 1999, 76 n. 207, points out that this need not literally refer to Alcibiades' own mother, daughter, and sister; it could refer to Medontis and her daughter. *Dissoi Logoi* DK 90 F 2.15 attests that the idea of intercourse by Persians with their daughters, mothers, and sisters was a rhetorical commonplace at the end of the fifth century.

18. Cambyses the son of Cyrus the Great married his own sisters (Herodotus 3.31). Artaxerxes II married his own daughters (Plutarch *Artaxerxes* 23.3–4, 27.5). Darius III married his sister Stateira (Plutarch *Alexander* 30.2). Archelaus of Macedon gave his daughter in marriage to his son (Aristotle *Politics* 1311b13–15). Mausolus the Carian married his sister Artemisia (Diodorus 16.36.2). On the practice of sibling marriages in Hellenistic monarchies, particularly in Ptolemaic Egypt, see Carney 1987.

19. See chapter 4, with notes 65–67.

20. On Cotyto, see Eupolis *Baptae* fr. 93 (KA); and see KA vol. 5, 332–33, for testimonia linking the satire to Alcibiades. Storey 1990, 20–22, discusses the apocryphal tradition about Alcibiades' reaction to this play. The cult of Cotyto is attested in Thrace, Corinth, and Sicily: see Jameson et al. 1993, 23–27.

peers had desecrated the sacred Mysteries of Demeter. The abuse of a religious ritual was identified as a threat to the democratic community, and as a result, perhaps for the first time since the execution of Darius' heralds, men were condemned to death at Athens for actions construed both as an offense against the Eleusinian deities and as an attempt to subvert the Athenian democracy.[21] Many of those indicted, including Alcibiades himself, escaped into exile before they could be brought to justice at Athens.

In exile Alcibiades became an advisor to the Spartans, not because he had forsaken Athens, as he explained openly on more than one occasion, but because Athens had become corrupted by jealous and small-minded leaders who had to be driven from power before Athens could be set on the right path.[22] An argument like this measured political virtue by a higher standard than simple loyalty to the powers that be. It appealed to a sense of virtue beyond the ken of lesser men, in Alcibiades' estimation, a perspective that resonated with the Spartans' contempt for democracy. It also reinforced Alcibiades' consistent claim that he himself was more capable of achieving high honors than any other Athenian. Alcibiades was inviting the Spartans, and, soon thereafter, the Ionians of Chios, Ephesus, and Miletus, as well as Tissaphernes and the Persians, to involve themselves in his vision of excellence. It was an appealing vision precisely because it was cast in universal terms and did not proceed from parochial, local loyalties. Even though the actual attainment of unity through a shared vision of excellence was elusive, Alcibiades did succeed in persuading many to begin moving toward it with him.

Aristophanes parodies the cosmic dimensions of Alcibiades' grandiose schemes in his *Birds,* where Peisetaerus (= Alcibiades), an exile from Athens, persuades the birds to found a city in the sky, midway between heaven and earth, in order to besiege the gods and gain sovereignty ($\beta \alpha \sigma \iota \lambda \epsilon \acute{\iota} \alpha$). Sovereignty itself is personified as the Queen of Heaven ($\beta \alpha \sigma \acute{\iota} \lambda \epsilon \iota \alpha$, 1634, 1687, 1730, 1753), whom Peisetaerus forces Zeus to surrender in obeisance to the new regime. In the final scene of the play, Peisetaerus marries Queen Sovereignty in a comic Sacred Marriage, thereby consummating his transformation into the all-powerful tyrant ($\tau \acute{\upsilon} \rho \alpha \nu \nu o \varsigma$, 1708; $\pi \acute{\alpha} \nu \tau \alpha$ $\kappa \rho \alpha \tau \acute{\eta} \sigma \alpha \varsigma$, 1752), lord of gods, birds, and men (1706–65). The scheme was a complete send-

---

21. Chief testimony to the affair of the Mysteries and the related desecration of the herms comes from Thucydides 6.27–29, 53, 60–61; Andocides 1, *On the Mysteries* 11–24; and Plutarch *Alcibiades* 19–22. The present account of Alcibiades' actions in the affair of the Mysteries (developed at greater length in Munn 2000, 106–26) argues that they were more purposeful than capricious, as they are often described. (Contrast Murray 1990.)

22. This argument is found in Alcibiades' speech at Sparta (Thucydides 6.92), in his speech to Athenian forces at Samos (Thucydides 8.81.2), and in his speech upon his return to Athens (Xenophon *Hellenica* 1.4.13–16, 20; cf. Plutarch *Alcibiades* 33.2; Diodorus 13.69.1; Justin 5.4.13–18; Nepos 7.6.4). Similar arguments were made posthumously by his son the younger Alcibiades: Isocrates 16, *On the Team of Horses* 4–11, 16–21.

up of the notion of sovereignty proceeding from a carnal union with the (anonymous) divine personification of sovereignty, a notion familiar to Greeks from the example of Lydian tyranny and the Greek tyrannies inspired by it. The play reveals how widely known and even popular Alcibiades' ambitions were at the very time, in early 414, when he was establishing his influence among the Spartans.[23]

## THE SYMBIOTIC SOVEREIGNTY OF GREEKS AND PERSIANS

By 411, Alcibiades had left Sparta and taken up with Tissaphernes, the Persian satrap of Sardis, where he let it be known that he could bring about a mutually beneficial alliance between Athens and Persia.[24] Thucydides presents this scheme as the product of Alcibiades' devious imagination, but in fact Alcibiades' plan was little more than a proposal to restore the status quo between Persia and Athens that had existed at the outbreak of the Peloponnesian War.[25] In explaining Alcibiades' advice to Tissaphernes, Thucydides describes the principles of symbiotic sovereignty that had been the basis of Athenian-Persian relations over the previous generation.

According to Thucydides, Alcibiades encouraged Tissaphernes to use his influence to reestablish a balance of power among Athens, Sparta, and the king, in which open warfare would appear to be an advantage to no party. This would be most easily achieved, Alcibiades advised, by allowing the Athenians and Spartans to wear each other down (Thucydides 8.46.1–2). Once peace through balance was achieved, however, the future lay in closer ties between Persia and Athens. Alcibiades pointed out that the king would find the Athenians to be "the more suitable partners in leadership" (Thucydides 8.46.3). The Spartans were fighting to liberate the Greeks from Athenian rule and would not, according to Alcibiades, be likely to leave the Greeks of Asia under Persian rule. The Athenians, on the other hand, were more interested in dominion by sea, and would more readily join with the Persians to "collaborate in the subordination of the element of the sea to themselves, and all those Greeks who live on the king's land to the king" (Thucydides 8.46.3).

---

23. Although the point has not been generally acknowledged, the identification of Peisetaerus in the *Birds* with a popular image of Alcibiades has gained increasing recognition in recent years; see Vickers 1989, and Henderson 1997, 139–45, who see Alcibiades here in a specifically Athenian context; and Munn 2000, 124–26, where Alcibiades is seen in his wider Hellenic, and even universal context. On the Sacred Marriage in the *Birds*, see chapter 1, with notes 92–96; and see Clark 1998, 20.

24. Thucydides 8.45–49 describes the development of Alcibiades' plan.

25. Note that the Athenians were already courting the active support of Persia at the outbreak of the Peloponnesian War; see Aristophanes *Acharnians* 61–125 and 647–48, and *Knights* 478; Thucydides 4.50.1–2; cf. Andocides 3, *On the Peace* 29. See Raubitschek 1964, 155–57.

Alcibiades' argument epitomized the principles that had been the basis of the Peace of Callias.[26] As with the conditions announced by Pericles in the Congress Decree, Alcibiades' aim was to assure Athenian supremacy on the sea by securing Spartan acquiescence after gaining Persian cooperation.[27] With Athens sovereign over the sea, maritime commerce was in principle subject to Athenian approval, and liable to Athenian taxation. Shortly before the outbreak of the Peloponnesian War, Pericles made this principle the basis of his decree excluding the Megarians from commerce in the harbors controlled by Athens and its allies.[28] Five years prior to the arrival of Alcibiades at the court of Tissaphernes, the remorseless application of this principle had led the Athenians to destroy the Melians, and to attempt to subdue all of Sicily. Only two years earlier the Athenians had quantified this principle, by instituting the *eikostē*, a 5-percent tax on maritime commerce, in place of the *phoros*, or tribute paid to the Delian League.[29] Alcibiades' policy, like Pericles' before him, thus embraced the image of Athens as the tyrant city, wielding absolute authority within its domain, and cooperating in tyranny with the lords of Asia.

In this cause, Alcibiades won over first Tissaphernes at Sardis, then the Athenian fleet at Samos, and finally Pharnabazus, satrap of Hellespontine Phrygia. In 409, by a treaty drawn up at Chalcedon, Pharnabazus was persuaded to conduct a Greek embassy to King Darius II to consummate an agreement along the lines proposed by Alcibiades. This mission, in which representatives from Sparta, Argos, and Syracuse accompanied the Athenians, must have been prepared to discuss a resolution to hostilities among all warring parties.[30] Although this mission eventually ended in failure in just over two years, for a brief period there was reason to anticipate the dawn of a new era of harmonious relations between Greece and Asia.

The vision born in the Treaty of Chalcedon, and set in motion when Pharnabazus received the Greek ambassadors at Cyzicus, in the fall of 409, was intended to resolve what Thucydides calls "the greatest disturbance [*kinēsis*] among Greeks and a certain portion of the barbarians, extending,

26. See chapter 7 at notes 57–75.
27. See chapter 7, with notes 82–89.
28. On the Megarian Decree, see Thucydides 1.139.1–2, and the contrasting assessments of de Ste. Croix 1972, 225–89; and Meiggs 1972, 202–3, 266.
29. Thucydides 7.28.4. Although Thucydides characterizes this as a crisis measure, it was the outcome of a rationalizing trend in Athenian imperial policy under way for some time, also represented in the Coinage Decree (*IG* I³ 1453, = ML 45; Fornara 97; probably to be dated between 425 and 415) and satirized generally in Aristophanes' *Birds* (and specifically in lines 1021–54); see Kallet 2001, 195–226.
30. Xenophon *Hellenica* 1.3.8–13. On the Treaty of Chalcedon, see Munn 2000, 162–64 and 397 n. 32, on the status of the ambassadors; appendix c, pp. 335–39, provides authority for the chronology used here.

one could say, to the majority of humanity" (Thucydides 1.1.2). This has always seemed a rather grandiose characterization of the Peloponnesian War, at least as far as it affected the barbarian world.[31] But we may now recognize the issues that were at stake, and the concepts behind Thucydides' allusive description. The "certain portion of the barbarians" was a reference to the barbarians of Asia, whose fate, as Herodotus emphasized from the outset of his history, was intimately bound up with that of the Greeks of Asia and of Europe. The proper domains of the sovereign of Asia and the sovereign of the sea were at stake. The resolution of the current war among the Greeks and Persians would determine the nature of Hellenic and Asiatic sovereignty over the *oikoumenē*, the settled world, which certainly did embrace a significant portion of humanity.

### THE MOTHER OF THE GODS ACCEPTED

Alcibiades now offered all of Greece and Asia, at least along its seaboard, the prospect of peace through the cooperative efforts of Athenians and Persians. With this vision of the future before them, the time was at hand for the Athenians to reassess their relationship with the deity who embodied tyranny in Asia. Not only was it appropriate to propitiate the Mother of the Gods in order to heal the rift that had opened wide with the execution of Darius' heralds, but it was also appropriate to celebrate her as the hand of divine providence that had revived the fortunes of Athens under the leadership of Alcibiades.

Alcibiades had prepared the way for the propitiation of the Mother of the Gods by paying court to her at Sardis. This can be inferred from a sequence of events described for us by both Xenophon and Plutarch. Following the naval victory over the Spartans at Abydus in the Hellespont, in 411/0, Alcibiades came to Tissaphernes "decked out with gifts of hospitality and friendship, bearing offerings for sovereignty [θεραπεία ἡγεμονική]," whereupon Tissaphernes conducted Alcibiades to Sardis and "confined him [εἶρξεν]" there for thirty days.[32] The description of Alcibiades' arrival as a

---

31. Gomme calls this an exaggeration (1945, 91); Connor calls it excessive (1984, 21). *Kinēsis* is a distinctly abstract manner of describing war, or political disturbance (as in Thucydides 3.75.2; Aristotle *Politics* 1268b25). Its use here suggests that Thucydides locates this war within a philosophical debate over the meaning of stability and change in the order of the world (e.g., Plato *Theaetetus* 180e–181c; *Parmenides* 139a, 162e, referring to the debate over the concepts of motion, rest, and being in Eleatic philosophy).

32. Xenophon *Hellenica* 1.1.9 and Plutarch *Alcibiades* 27.4 both mention the ξένια καὶ δῶρα, while Plutarch adds reference to θεραπεία ἡγεμονική, and emphasizes that the occasion was Alcibiades' self-glorification following the victory at Abydus. The details in Plutarch's account probably come from Duris of Samos, who is cited as the source for similar details about Alcibiades' homecoming in Plutarch *Alcibiades* 32.2.

triumphant victor bearing offerings for sovereignty suggests a ritual of courtship aimed at some notion of sovereignty itself, located at Sardis. The arrest and confinement of Alcibiades at Sardis must be considered a sham, for it is clear that Tissaphernes did not make any real effort to detain Alcibiades indefinitely. His thirty-day confinement, moreover, corresponds to the length of the stay of Cyrus the Younger in the royal compound and *paradeisos* at Celaenae in Phrygia, at the start of his march against his brother just ten years later.[33] The fact that Tissaphernes named his favorite *paradeisos* "Alcibiades," a name that everyone used thereafter, according to Plutarch, establishes a strong association of this place with the Athenian.[34] This garden was certainly a place for rituals of sovereignty, and very likely identical with the Place of Purity of the Lydians, and the sacred grove of Kybebe at Sardis.[35] Alcibiades' confinement at Sardis was most likely devoted to his initiation into the rites of sovereignty endowed by the goddess at Sardis. The fact that Sophocles, one year later, made reverential mention of the Mother at Sardis as "Mountain goddess, all-nourishing Earth, Mother of Zeus himself, who dwells by the great gold-bearing Pactolus, . . . blessed one, enthroned on bull-devouring lions" indicates that, on the eve of Alcibiades' return to Athens, this specific seat of divinity was regarded with high esteem at Athens.[36]

Alcibiades made his triumphant homecoming in 408, less than a year after formalizing his agreement with Pharnabazus at Chalcedon, and two years after winning the great naval victory over the Spartans at Cyzicus that marked the decisive turn in Athenian fortunes. The Mother of the Gods was especially venerated at Cyzicus.[37] Her sacred mountain, Dindymon, overlooking Cyzicus, was the site of a shrine of the Mother of the Gods reputed to have been founded by the Argonauts in thanksgiving for fair weather that allowed them safe onward passage.[38] A storm cloud had masked the approach of the Athenian fleet against Cyzicus in 410, Xenophon notes, and had lifted in time for them to trap the Spartan fleet.[39] This gift of providence to the Athenians, whose commander, Alcibiades, had recently devoted himself to the power of sovereignty at Sardis, must have been widely seen as a sign that the Mother Dindymene was favoring them.

33. Xenophon *Anabasis* 1.2.7–9; see chapter 4, note 10.

34. Plutarch *Alcibiades* 24.5. The location of the *paradeisos* "Alcibiades" is not stated, but that it was at Sardis is a likely inference. A few years later, Cyrus the Younger entertained Lysander in his beautiful *paradeisos* at Sardis: Xenophon *Oeconomicus* 4.20–25.

35. See chapter 4, with notes 16–18.

36. Sophocles *Philoctetes* 392–402, cited in chapter 3 at note 122.

37. See Herodotus 4.76, discussed in chapter 6 at note 53.

38. Apollonius *Argonautica* 1.936–1152; Strabo 1.2.38 (citing Demetrius of Scepsis and Neanthes of Cyzicus), 12.8.11; cf. Pausanias 8.46.4.

39. Xenophon *Hellenica* 1.1.16.

Figure 14. Miniature replica of Agoracritus' statue of the Mother of the Gods enthroned, holding a libation dish and a tympanum, with a recumbent lion on her lap, fourth century B.C.E. (Photo: courtesy of the Allard Pierson Museum, Amsterdam, inv. no. 3986).

It is most probable that the triumphal return of Alcibiades in 408 was the occasion when the old Council House at Athens became the Metroön.[40] On his homeward voyage across the Aegean, Alcibiades made a stop on the island of Paros.[41] It is possible that he made this stop, which Xenophon re-

40. The earliest historical attestation of the Metroön associates it with Alcibiades during his return to Athens in 408: Athenaeus 9.407b–c, quoting Chamaeleon of Pontus (early third century B.C.E.). Doubts about the historicity of this passage expressed by Sickinger 1999, 131–32, are not compelling. On the occasion, see Munn 2000, 170–71.

41. Xenophon *Hellenica* 1.4.11.

ports but does not explain, in order to select the most suitable Parian stone and bring it to Athens along with the celebrated Parian sculptor Agoracritus; or Alcibiades could have made this stop in order to take delivery of the statue that Agoracritus had already prepared for the occasion.[42] The dramatic entrance of Alcibiades' ship into Piraeus, with a purple sail and with the accompaniment of a prize-winning *aulos* player, as reported by Duris of Samos, is more believable if we recognize that he was escorting the Mother herself, in some form, into Athens.[43]

On this occasion, the Mother of the Gods at Athens symbolized harmony between the Athenian and Persian empires.[44] Because she represented the highest priorities of the Athenian state, the Athenian Council House was an appropriate place for her seat. Her installation there was also significant for the reason indicated by Julian: it gave unambiguous proof that the Athenians had formally reversed the effects of the decision, taken in the very same Council House, to reject Darius' demand for obeisance and to put to death his heralds, among them the man (the *Mētragyrtēs* or *Kybēbos,* or *Gallus* as he was later called) who had attempted to explain to the Athenians the nature and meaning of this great goddess. Obeisance was now given—not to an emissary of the Persian king (although Alcibiades himself was close to this role), but to the divine ideal that justified all sovereign power on earth.

Celebration, assertion of power, and expiation of lingering fears were combined in the act of bringing the Mother of the Gods into the Council House. Athenians could read whichever meaning they wished into the occasion. Those who were mindful of the past, as Herodotus was, could hope that this act of conciliation would avert any further disagreeable consequences that might yet strike them in retribution for the murder of the *Mētragyrtēs.* For they could well wonder if they had already paid by "the destruction of their

42. On the attribution of the statue to Agoracritus, see chapter 2, note 27. Olga Palagia 2005, 124–25 and note 56, has identified fragments of a statue base found in the Athenian agora that may have belonged to Agoracritus' statue of the Mother of the Gods; the fragments resemble those of the base of Agoracritus' statue of Nemesis at Rhamnus. That the statue of the Mother was carved from Parian marble is an inference. Agoracritus' statue of Nemesis was carved out of a block of Parian marble that Pausanias 1.33.2 says was brought from Paros by the Persians who landed at Marathon, where they intended to make a trophy out of it. A relief of the Mother of the Gods in the classical marble quarry on Paros could commemorate the quarrying of the stone for Agoracritus' statue from that place. On the relief, see Bodnar 1973; Naumann 1983, 196–202 and plates 28.2, 29.3–4. Cf. Pausanias 8.37.3 on the miraculous revelation of the stone out of which Demophon carved the images of Demeter and Despoina at Lycosura, where the size of these statues is compared to that of the Mother at Athens.

43. Duris' account is recalled in Plutarch *Alcibiades* 32.2–3 and Athenaeus 12.535d.

44. Alain Blomart 2002, 29–31, argues that the celebration of the Mother of the Gods at Athens at this time represented the desire of the Athenians to reinforce their ties to their Asiatic Ionian kinsmen. He does not, however, recognize the links with Persian sovereignty that were also being forged, nor does he recognize the role of Alcibiades.

city and the countryside around it," as Herodotus speculated.[45] Had they been absolved by the plague, or by disaster in Sicily—or would yet more woes be added to their account until they repaid the Mother? The agitated choral hymns of Euripides and Sophocles, and Aristophanes' prayer to Mistress Kybele (δέσποινα Κυβέλη) for health and safety, all testify that the Athenian public as a whole was well aware that such matters were within the domain of the Mother of the Gods.[46] When, therefore, Alcibiades returned to them offering every justification for the public acceptance and celebration of the Mother of the Gods—probably bearing the Mother herself, in some form— we can fully appreciate the widespread joy and enthusiasm that attended the event. Practically the entire city turned out for the occasion, as testified by Xenophon (who witnessed it) and Plutarch (who drew upon other sources, many of them eyewitnesses).[47]

### THE MOTHER OF THE GODS AND THE SOVEREIGNTY OF THE LAWS

The installation of the Mother of the Gods in the old Council House coin-cided with the construction of a new Council House at Athens.[48] The con-struction of a new building was required in order to accommodate a spe-cialized aspect of the work of the council, namely the systematic review of the laws of Athens, which commenced in 411/0. Because of the burden-someness of this ongoing task, a legislative review board of five hundred *nomo-thetai* was appointed to take over this duty of the Council of Five Hundred. The new body of *nomothetai* required a meeting place in which to conduct its work, and so a new meeting place for the regular council was created; the old Council House, now known as the Metroön, or Temple to the Mother of the Gods, was given over to the meetings of the *nomothetai*. This building

45. See chapter 6 at note 113. Indicative of the anxieties of the occasion, Xenophon *Hel-lenica* 1.4.12 draws attention to an ill omen involving the statue of Athena at the time of Al-cibiades' homecoming.

46. Aristophanes *Birds* 874–79; see chapter 7, note 7.

47. Xenophon *Hellenica* 1.4.13–21; Plutarch *Alcibiades* 32–34. Among sources named in this passage, Plutarch cites only the poetry of Critias praising Alcibiades as a contemporary of the events. But others named in the passage (Duris of Samos, Theopompus, Ephorus) and others named elsewhere (Archestratus, Theophrastus) all lived within a century of Alcibiades' life-time and certainly had access to many sources who were contemporary. Among these con-temporary sources, Plutarch cites an impressive selection elsewhere in his biography of Alcib-iades: Antisthenes, Euripides, Hellanicus, Isocrates, Phaeax, Plato, Thucydides, Xenophon, and the comic playwrights Archippus, Aristophanes, Eubulus, Phrynichus, and Plato Comicus. Plutarch makes the point that more intimate details are known of Alcibiades, and known from contemporary sources, than of any of his peers (1.2).

48. Shear 1995, 189, emphasizes this coincidence; see also Sickinger 1999, chapter 4, 93–113.

also became the repository for the officially revised laws and other documents of the state.[49]

If the new Council House was not already built when the Mother of the Gods arrived in Athens in 408, then her arrival would justify the move to accommodate her as well as the *nomothetai* of Athens. For the Mother of the Gods was supremely appropriate to preside not just over the deliberations on the affairs of empire and the sovereignty of the Athenian state, but also over the laws of Athens. Scholars have been hard-put to explain the establishment of the Metroön in the agora.[50] Now it is possible to see that her installation in the old Council House was the culmination of a long process of devotion by the Athenians to an image of law as a maternal force.

The appropriateness of the Mother of the Gods as protectress of the laws can be traced back to her association with Midas. The single feature of the kingship of Midas noted by Herodotus was his administration of justice, as evidenced by his throne of judgment dedicated at Delphi.[51] The ability of Midas resolve civil strife (*stasis*) was the basis of his kingship among the Phrygians, according to the story told to Alexander at Gordium.[52] It was the mother of Midas, the Phrygian Mother of the Gods as the Athenians knew her, who foresaw, founded, and upheld the just kingship of Midas, and it was her cult that "protected [Midas] more effectively than could an armed guard."[53]

The notion of the Mother of Kingship as the Mother of Law was not far from the symbolic logic familiar to Athenians. The idea of law as sovereign is expressed by Pindar, Herodotus, and Plato, among others.[54] At Athens in the time of Pericles and Alcibiades, the sovereign authority of law was commonly identified with the collective will of the Athenian demos.[55] The Mother in the Athenian Council House embodied this idea of law as sovereign, both in its general form and in its Athenian form.

The sovereignty of law at Athens is given memorable expression at the

49. For this explanation of the building of the new Council House, see Munn 2000, esp. 148–50 and 261–75. On the appointment of *nomothetai*, see Thucydides 8.97.2; the decree of Teisamenus quoted by Andocides 1, *On the Mysteries* 84. The association of the *nomothetai* with the Mother of the Gods and the Council House is demonstrated in a decree of the *nomothetai* of 375/4, regulating Athenian silver coinage, that stipulates that counterfeit coinage is "to be sacred to the Mother of the Gods and is to be deposited in the council" (*SEG* 26, no. 72, lines 12–13; Stroud 1974).

50. For references, see chapter 2, notes 36 and 37.

51. Herodotus 1.14.3.

52. Arrian *Anabasis* 2.3.5–6; Justin *Epitome* 2.6.9–10.

53. Justin 11.7.14, quoted and discussed in chapter 2 at note 120.

54. See chapter 1, with notes 6 and 7.

55. See the discussion between Alcibiades and Pericles in Xenophon *Memorabilia* 1.2.41–46. On the equation of law with popular will in this period, see Ostwald 1986, 181–459; Munn 2000, 170–94.

beginning of the fourth century in the dialogue between Socrates and the laws imagined in Plato's *Crito*. There "the laws and community of the city" (οἱ νόμοι καὶ τὸ κοινὸν τῆς πόλεως) express their sovereign authority over all citizens as the irreproachable right of parents to command a child.[56] Although the number and the gender of the speaking laws and community are ambiguous, their relationship to citizens is consistently described in terms of genesis, nurture, guiding wisdom, and supreme authority. They speak as "the native land [πατρίς]," which is "more precious, more venerable, more sacred, and held in greater honor among gods and thoughtful men" than one's own father and mother.[57] Socrates does not speak of the Mother of the Gods, but the terms of his expression here illustrate well the manner in which the generative, fostering, and wise Mother of the Gods, as an analogy for the laws of the land, was envisioned on her throne in the old Council House.

Socrates speaks of the laws of Athens as the laws of a city. But Athens was also mother city to an empire, and the Mother of the Gods was an appropriate emblem of the laws of Athens as the instruments of communal harmony within an empire. In her guise as patron of Asiatic tyranny, she stood for harmony within a community of many nations, made up of disparate parts, but under her tutelage forming a natural unity, as siblings under one mother—the Great Mother.[58] She thus embodied the Asiatic concept of the *oikoumenē* with which the Athenians now allied themselves, so closely akin to the bond of communion represented by the widely shared observance of Demeter Thesmophoros, "Upholder of Ordinances," and especially by the Mysteries of Eleusinian Demeter promulgated by the Athenians.

## THE NAMES OF THE MOTHER

The Mother of the Gods was more than a vision of overarching unity within the *oikoumenē*. She was also the embodiment of various abstractions of the all-encompassing just community. We find her sharing the same attributes in cult and in legend as Adrasteia, Aristoboule, Eunomia, Nemesis, and Themis. Each of these, as concept and as deity, represents an aspect of truth that resides in good customs and laws. Each of them but one, moreover, embodies an aspect of justice that emerges from collective human behavior, and therefore serves as an abstraction of the proceedings of deliberative coun-

56. Plato *Crito* 50a–52a.

57. Plato *Crito* 51a–b. Cf. the more unambiguous depiction of the land of Athens as Mother in *Menexenus* 237b–238b.

58. These are the essential qualities of Basileia, the elder sister of Rhea and Pandora, according to Diodorus (3.57.3). In this myth, Basileia "far exceeded her sisters in prudence and wisdom [σωφροσύνῃ τε καὶ συνέσει]," and she "reared all her brothers, showing them collectively a mother's kindness," and "consequently was given the appellation 'Great Mother,'" and eventually "assumed sovereignty, though still a virgin."

cils and courts of law. The exception is Adrasteia, who is inevitable fate, and therefore represents the inescapability of justice, however administered.

"Wise are those who supplicate Adrasteia," says the chorus in the Aeschylean *Prometheus Bound*,[59] after hearing Prometheus prophesy the fall of Zeus from kingship. Adrasteia, the "Relentless One," was destiny or doom, the fate in store for all, for better or for worse. She had been a nurse of the infant Zeus, at home on Mount Ida.[60] Aeschylus places the ancient cult of Adrasteia in the Asian home of Tantalus, in the "Berecynthan land" that was also home to the Mother of the Gods and to Ephesian Artemis, according to other sources.[61] Adrasteia was also the eponym of a plain and a town in Hellespontine Phrygia, known to Homer.[62]

Several sources report that Adrasteia was the name given to a deity who was commonly identified as Nemesis, sometimes as Artemis, in a cult founded in Hellespontine Phrygia by a certain King Adrastus.[63] This King Adrastus was a native of Hellespontine Phrygia, and not the same as the better-known Adrastus of Sicyon, leader of the Seven against Thebes. Homer knows Adrastus as the name of three different Asiatic heroes, all of whom fought and died for Troy.[64] Like Homer, Herodotus saw Asiatic Adrastus as the archetypal bearer of the doom that not even the mighty can escape. In Herodotus' story, the Phrygian Adrastus, "royal by descent, . . . son of Gordias son of Midas," was himself the agent of Nemesis, in Herodotus' own phrase (ἔλαβε ἐκ θεοῦ νέμεσις μεγάλη Κροῖσον, "great nemesis from god seized Croesus"), when he inadvertently killed Croesus' son Atys.[65] In chapters 4 and 5, we ob-

59. [Aeschylus] *Prometheus Bound* 936.

60. Apollodorus *Library* 1.1.6; Apollonius *Argonautica* 3.132–34.

61. Aeschylus *Niobe* fr. 158.2 (Radt). Mother of the Gods: Agatharchides *FGrHist* 284 F 3 (in [Plutarch] *De Fluviis* 10.4–5). Artemis of Ephesus: Callimachus *Hymn* 3.242–47. See also Strabo 10.3.12, 13.1.13.

62. *Iliad* 2.828; Strabo 13.1.13.

63. Antimachus of Colophon (fr. 53 Wyss, quoted at note 75 below) derives both the toponym and the divinity Adrasteia from a foundation made by King Adrastus in honor of Nemesis. Callisthenes *FGrHist* 124 F 28 (in Strabo 13.1.13) makes the same identifications. Demetrius of Scepsis (in Harpocration s.v. Ἀδράστειαν) says that a certain Adrastus (Ἀδράστου τινός) established Adrasteia as a name for Artemis. Harpocration s.v. Ἀδράστειαν also reports that "some say" that Nemesis got the name Adrasteia from "a certain King Adrastus [παρὰ Ἀδράστου τινὸς βασιλέως], or from Adrastus the son of Talaus" (i.e., the king of Sicyon). See also Strabo 12.8.11; Stephanus of Byzantium s.v. Ἀδράστειαν; scholiast to Apollonius *Argonautica* 1.1129, 1116. These and other sources are cited by Santoro 1973, 4–8. See also the discussion of Farnell 1896, vol. 2, 499–500. Hellenistic inscriptions attest the joint cult of Adresteia and Nemesis on Cos: Sokolowski 1969, nos. 160 and 161. Pausanias 10.37.8 mentions a statue of Adrasteia in a temple of Apollo, Artemis, and Leto at Cirrha, below Delphi.

64. *Iliad* 2.830, 6.37–65, 16.693.

65. Herodotus 1.34–45. The relationship of this story to the sacraments of Lydian kingship and the Sacred Marriage is discussed in chapter 4 at notes 31–41. The role of Nemesis in this passage is discussed below at notes 74–75.

served how the customs of Asia treated the inevitable grief and loss entailed by mortality as an affirmation of a form of communion with the divine, given wide expression in funerary cult. It should not be surprising, therefore, to find that Adrastus was a common personal name among the Lydians, indicating that Adrasteia was seen as a propitious and benevolent deity in Asia.[66] At least two decades before the Mother of the Gods was seated in the Council House, this Adrasteia was honored in cult alongside Thracian Bendis at Athens, so the Athenians were clearly familiar with the great goddess of Asia as the inescapability of justice.[67]

Aristoboule, "She of Best Counsel," we have already encountered in chapter 7, above. She was the goddess of the collective decision that seals doom. Among the gods, Aristoboule represented the collective decision that led to the overthrow of Cronus and the rise of Zeus.[68] Among mortals she represented the divine will within the irrevocable sentence of death, a force that the Athenians saw fit to propitiate soon after their decision to execute the heralds of Darius.[69] We learn from the Lydian Artemidorus of Daldis (second century C.E.) that "Aristoboule and Eunomia mean the same as Nemesis" when they appear in dreams.[70] Eunomia, "Good Laws" (or "Good Customs")," was one of the three Horai, daughters of Zeus and Themis (representing sovereignty and rightful order), whose sisters were Dike, "Justice," and Eirene, "Peace," according to Hesiod.[71] Eunomia and her sister Dike were memorably praised by Solon, as benefactors of Athens, safeguards against the harmful forces of Hubris, "Wanton Violence," and Koros, "Excess."[72]

Nemesis, "Retribution," who "means the same" as Aristoboule and Eunomia, was collective reproach, the consequence of public opinion.[73] When

---

66. Atrastas (Adrastus) occurs as a personal name on inscribed funerary stelae from Sardis ranging in date from the late sixth to the late fourth century: see Hanfmann and Ramage 1978, nos. 17, 234, 240, 242; Zgusta 1964, 111 no. 124; Gusmani *LW* 70; Gusmani 1988, 183–84, 192. Pausanias 7.6.6 cites an inscribed monument to a Lydian of the late fourth century named Adrastus at Sardis.

67. Cult of Bendis and Adrasteia in accounts of Treasurers of Other Gods: *IG* I³ 383, col ii, 142–43 (429/8), and *IG* I³ 369.67–68 (423/2); see R. Parker 1996, 195.

68. A connection between capital punishment and the prevailing order of the universe was the basis of the human sacrifice to Aristoboule made on the occasion of the festival of Cronus. (See chapter 7, note 36.)

69. See chapter 7 at notes 37–40.

70. Artemidorus *Onirocriticon* 2.37.

71. Hesiod *Theogony* 901–3. According to Alcman fr. 66 (Edmonds *LG*), Eunomia is the sister of Tyche and Peitho, all daughters of Promatheia.

72. Solon fr. 4 (Edmonds *EI*), esp. 33–35, quoted by Demosthenes 18, *On the False Embassy* 255; echoed by Pindar *Olympian* 13.6–10. On Eunomia, Dike, and Eirene in archaic poetry and thought, with special reference to the developing meaning of *nomos* at Athens, see Ostwald 1969, 62–75.

73. So Nemesis, either as noun or as the verb νεμεσάω, refers to a sense of scandal and reproach active only in a public setting: see, e.g., *Iliad* 2.233; 3.156–57, 410–12; 6.351; *Odyssey*

men were moved by Nemesis to impose not merely reproach but actual retribution for wrongful behavior, they did so under the guidance of social institutions, and, eventually, by the due processes of law. But the gods could also exact retribution through human agents who were unaware that they were fulfilling a divinely ordained purpose. Omens might give clues to the significance of events in progress, but mortal men could fully recognize the workings of divine purpose only through hindsight. A historical perspective, as Herodotus repeatedly emphasizes, is therefore essential to recognizing the ways of divine retribution. To honor Nemesis in cult was to declare one's acceptance of what destiny had dealt in the past, and of what it yet had in store (with the implication that this very act of piety would encourage destiny to be kind). Herodotus wrote to encourage the Athenians to be mindful of Nemesis in all these respects.

Herodotus links Nemesis to the hand of τὸ θεῖον after his narration of Solon's visit to Sardis, when Croesus has dismissed the Athenian sage as a fool of no account: "After Solon's visit, great nemesis from god seized Croesus, so it seems, because he considered himself the happiest of all men."[74] There follows the story of the death of Atys son of Croesus by the hand of Adrastus the Phrygian, son of Gordias son of Midas. "Great nemesis from god" (ἐκ θεοῦ νέμεσις μεγάλη) in this passage is an ambiguous expression, as a description of divine agency. Considered only in this context, "nemesis" could be taken simply as an abstraction, with no allusion to divinity (but for the phrase "from god"). In view of Herodotus' usual reserve in discussing matters of divine agency, however, we must admit that nemesis the force of divinity here is Nemesis the goddess barely disguised. Herodotus' audience certainly understood her to be the goddess in her guise as the Inevitable, or Adrasteia, the "Relentless One," as we learn from Herodotus' younger contemporaries Antimachus and Plato.

Plato knew Herodotus' story of Croesus (compare *Republic* 566c and Herodotus 1.55), and implicitly refers to the divinity at work in this passage of Herodotus when he invokes the goddess Adrasteia (*Republic* 451a): "I salute Adrasteia in what I am about to say; for, indeed, I believe that involuntary homicide is a lesser fault than to mislead opinion about the honorable, the good, and the just." In Herodotus' story, involuntary homicide was Adrastus' crime. A fragment attributed to Plato's contemporary the poet Antimachus of Colophon makes even more explicit the thread that unites Nemesis, Adrastus, and Adrasteia to Herodotus' story and its Asiatic setting: "There

---

1.119, 263, 350–53; Hesiod *Works and Days* 303; Tyrtaeus 10.26; Plato *Laws* 927c. Stafford 2000, 75–78, defines Nemesis as "indignation aroused by injustice," although I suggest that this is better regarded as a meaning abstracted from the primary sense of public reproach, a sense that Stafford also acknowledges (105 n. 10).

74. Herodotus 1.34.1.

is a certain great goddess Nemesis, who apportioned all these things for the fortunate ones; Adrastus first built her an altar by the stream of the Aesepus River, where she is honored and called Adrasteia."[75] The naming of the great goddess Nemesis (Νέμεσις μεγάλη θεός; cf. Herodotus, ἐκ θεοῦ νέμεσις μεγάλη), the locale in Mysia (where Adrastus inadvertently killed Atys), and the role of the goddess in dealing fate to fortunate ones (μάκαρες, said of gods or kings) all mark the poem as a reflection of the significant relationships dramatized in the story of Adrastus in Herodotus. Herodotus' story further resonates with an Athenian audience mindful of the powers guiding just retribution in the world. In his story, Solon, the Athenian lawgiver, is shown to have had a better understanding of the nature of Nemesis than Croesus, tyrant of Asia. By implication, Solon's laws, which were still in the possession of the Athenians, were attuned to the divine force guiding destiny, and therefore were worth more than all the good fortune of Croesus.

Nemesis as the force establishing the balance between Greece and Asia was especially celebrated at Athens at the time when Herodotus wrote. Sometime in the 420s, the Athenians built a great temple of Nemesis at Rhamnus in Attica, and in it they erected a celebrated statue of the goddess.[76] Figures on the base of this statue illustrated the presentation of Helen to her true mother, Nemesis.[77] Among Athenians, therefore, Nemesis was distinctively conceived as the figurative mother of the Trojan War, the archetype of wars between Greeks and Asiatic barbarians, as Herodotus reminds his readers at the beginning of his *Histories*.[78] The comic poet Cratinus produced a play entitled *Nemesis,* probably in the 420s, jesting on the nemesis of war with Sparta that Pericles had provoked.[79] Nemesis at this time was a reminder to Athenians of the cycles of retribution, especially between Greece and Asia. By making this goddess a fine temple and splendid image, the Athenians

75. Antimachus fr. 53 (Wyss; from Strabo 13.1.13):

> ἔστι δέ τις Νέμεσις μεγάλη θεός, ἣ τάδε πάντα
> πρὸς μακάρων ἔλαχεν· βωμὸν δέ οἱ εἴσατο πρῶτος
> Ἄδρηστος ποταμοῖο παρὰ ῥόον Αἰσήποιο
> ἔνθα τετίμηταί τε καὶ Ἀδρήστεια καλεῖται.

76. On the date of the Temple of Nemesis at Rhamnus, see Basileios Petrakos 1987, 317–18; and Margaret M. Miles 1989, 226–35. It was erected over the ruins of a late sixth-century temple that had been destroyed at the time of the Persian Wars; this late archaic temple replaced an older, early sixth-century temple on the spot: Petrakos 299–305. On the statue of Nemesis by Agoracritus, see Pausanias 1.33.2.

77. Pausanias 1.33.7–8. The identification of Nemesis as the mother of Helen was told in the *Cypria,* fr. 8 (Evelyn-White; = Athenaeus 8.334b). This birth of Helen appears as a variation of the tradition that Helen was the child of Leda; see Apollodorus *Library* 3.10.6–7, where a rationalization of the two versions is presented. Stafford 2000, 78–82, reviews these traditions in the context of the cult at Rhamnus.

78. Herodotus 1.3–4.

79. See Plutarch *Pericles* 3.3.

were expressing the hope that divine retribution was at last at ease and at home in Attica, where she could now promote the harmonious resolution of this ancient conflict.

Themis received honors along with Nemesis in a smaller and older temple adjoining the classical Temple of Nemesis at Rhamnus.[80] Themis, too, was the divine patron of communal harmony, or "Just Order," as Walter Burkert calls her, or "the force that brings and binds men together, . . . the collective conscience, the social sanction," in the words of Jane Harrison.[81] Harrison draws attention to the role of Themis in Homer as convener of deliberative assemblies, showing her to be an embodiment of collective order.[82] Themis so conceived is close in concept to the meaning of the Mother of the Gods in her later establishment in the Athenian Council House.

The wisdom of Themis was not only collective, but was also closely allied with the divine sovereign, Zeus, whose counsel and bed she shares and by whom she bears Eunomia, Dike, and Eirene.[83] Like Nemesis, she collaborated with Zeus in setting in motion the events that led to the Trojan War.[84] Themis is perhaps best known, according to Aeschylus' formulation in the *Eumenides,* as *mantis* at Delphi after her mother, Gaea, Earth.[85] Elsewhere Aeschylean tradition names her "Themis, Earth—she is but one in form though her names are many," as the mother of Prometheus, who delivered a prophecy that enabled Zeus to win kingship over the gods.[86] As mother of Prometheus, Themis was also mother-in-law to Asia, according to a Greek tradition rivaling the Lydian account in Herodotus; according to a tradition attested by Apollodorus, the mother of Prometheus was Asia herself.[87]

The identification of Themis as Asia, or as the Asiatic Mother of the Gods,

80. The Temple of Themis was erected after the Persian destruction of the late archaic Temple of Nemesis and before the classical Temple of Nemesis: see Petrakos 1987, 306–8. The joint cult of Themis and Nemesis is attested in dedicatory inscriptions of the end of the fourth or the early third century: *IG* II² 3109, 3462, 4638; see the discussion of Stafford 2000, 56–60.

81. J. E. Harrison 1927, 485; Burkert 1985, 185.

82. *Iliad* 15.87–99, 20.4–6; *Odyssey* 2.68–69. See also the discussion of the semantics of Themis' name by Stafford 2000, 45–49.

83. See *Homeric Hymn* 23, *To the Son of Cronus, Most High;* Pindar *Hymns* fr. 30 (Bergk, = Sandys p. 514); cf. *Iliad* 15.87–99. See also note 71 above.

84. According to Proclus' summary of the *Cypria* (fr. 1, Evelyn-White 489), "Zeus plans with Themis to start the Trojan War," and does so by inducing strife among Hera, Athena, and Aphrodite.

85. Aeschylus *Eumenides* 1–4; cf. Euripides *Iphigeneia in Tauris* 1259–83; Pausanias 10.5.6. Earth and Themis have altars next to each other at Olympia: Pausanias 5.14.10.

86. [Aeschylus] *Prometheus Bound* 209–10: Θέμις καὶ Γαῖα, πολλῶν ὀνομάτων μορφὴ μία. Themis also saved Zeus' kingship through prophecy by warning him against intercourse with Thetis: Apollodorus *Library* 3.13.5. Note that the divinity in the genealogical position occupied by Themis in the Hesiodic tradition is called Promatheia by Alcman fr. 66 (Edmonds *LG*).

87. Herodotus 4.45.3; Apollodorus *Library* 1.2.2–3. Note the close parallel between Themis, daughter of Uranus and Gaea (or Ge), sister of Hyperion (named next to Rhea in Hesiod

as implied by these theogonic traditions, is demonstrated in the archaic image of the Mother among the battling gods and giants on the north frieze of the Siphnian Treasury at Delphi. In modern scholarship, this figure in the Siphnian Gigantomachy has been commonly called Kybele after her attribute, the lion-drawn chariot in which she rides and with which she strikes.[88] Recently this identification has been emended to Themis on the basis of a corrected reading of the traces of a painted inscription naming the goddess on the frieze.[89] The label should be seen as an amplification, however, and not a change in our understanding of the identity of this figure, who so clearly represents the unstoppable power of the Asiatic Mother as she was known among Ionians and islanders.[90]

In chapter 5, I advanced the suggestion that the Siphnian Treasury at Delphi was part of the program developed by Polycrates of Samos for promoting an Ionian-centered vision of Panhellenism.[91] The appearance of Themis-Kybele in the Gigantomachy frieze, as well as the overall composition of the frieze itself, gives strong support to this suggestion. The cosmic Battle of the Gods and Giants depicted the triumph of divine sovereignty, the rule of Zeus, as an achievement of collective action. In the Siphnian Gigantomachy, the unusual figure of Themis-Kybele assumes a prominent role as a champion of collective cosmic sovereignty, taking a place usually occupied, in Athenian Gigantomachies, by Athena. Themis-Kybele drives a chariot placed so as to give her a prominence equal to Poseidon (also driving a chariot) and second only to Zeus (also driving a chariot) in the center. Athena is present, but her place close to Zeus has been taken by Hera, who is the patron goddess of Samos.[92] The entire effect is consistent with Polycrates' efforts to align

---

*Theogony* 133–35 and Diodorus 5.66.3), and Basileia, also called the Great Mother, who is daughter of Uranus and Ge, sister of Hyperion (named next to Rhea in the so-called Atlantian theogony of Diodorus 3.57.2–3).

88. So, e.g., Vermaseren 1977, 71 and plates 25 and 26; Naumann 1983, 155 and plate 21.2; Watrous 1982, 161–63. The identification has not always been accepted, however; some have thought such a prominent depiction of Kybele in a Greek monument to be uncharacteristic at this early date: see Simon 1984, 6–10.

89. Brinkmann 1985, 101–2, N17, and 123, with n. 165. The identification of this figure as Themis is now generally noticed as a correction of the earlier identification as Kybele: see e.g. Roller 1999, 136 n. 76; Stafford 2000, 48.

90. The prominence of Kybele in Ionian cults of the sixth century is a further indication that the goddess named Themis on the Siphnian frieze at Delphi would have been recognized by contemporary viewers, particularly Ionians, as the Asiatic Kybele or Mother. See Naumann 1983, 117–18; Graf 1985, 107–15, 317–18, 388, 419–20.

91. See chapter 5 at notes 121–23. R. T. Neer 2001, esp. 294–302, has recognized the manner in which the several themes of the sculpture on the Siphnian Treasury endorse the harmony established by communal action.

92. The relationship among the figures on the Siphnian frieze is best appreciated in the reconstruction by Moore 1977. Contrast the Siphnian arrangement with the prominent group-

divine symbols with his ambition to become ruler of the sea and of the coast-lands of Asia.

The goddess labeled "Themis" and displaying the attributes of Kybele on the Siphnian frieze demonstrates that the goddess of Asia, in her role as the upholder of cosmic order, was more readily envisioned as a member of the Olympian pantheon when the earthly foundation of this vision was centered toward the east, in the Ionian Aegean. Themis, in this guise, is in fact Kybele, or the Mother of the Gods, with all that this implies for her links to Asia. The installation of the Mother at Athens, in "a symbolic centre of Athenian political life" (as Robert Parker puts it), betokens a shifting toward the east in the concept of the centering of Athenian dominion.[93]

At Athens and elsewhere on the Greek mainland, Themis shared cult and identity not only with Earth and with Nemesis, but also with Demeter and es-pecially with Aphrodite. On the southern slope of the Acropolis, Pausanias describes a group of associated cults beginning with a temple of Themis, in front of which is a monument of Hippolytus, recalling his fate at the hands of Aphrodite, followed by a cult of Aphrodite Pandemos and Peitho, and cults of Ge Kourotrophos (Earth, Nurturer of the Young) and Demeter Chloe (Green, or Verdant), and he concludes: "You can learn all about their names by conversing with the priests."[94] Elsewhere in Greece, Themis is frequently associated in cult with Aphrodite.[95] This affiliation reveals Themis as an ex-pression of the rightful relationships resulting from the bonds of love pro-moted by Aphrodite. Themis, consort of Zeus, is thus recognizable as another impersonation of the divine Mother, who was knowing prophetess, attractive bride, wife of the all-powerful king, and mother of the attributes of justice.

---

ing of Poseidon (probably) and Athena on either side of Zeus (probably) in the pediment of the Old Temple of Athena on the Acropolis, discussed by Moore 1995, 638–39. Speaking of the Siphnian frieze, Watrous 1982, 162, calls attention to the manner in which "Athena, notably, has been removed from her position, traditional in Attic vase painting, within the central group"; he remarks on the unique placement of Hera, who faces Zeus and turns her back on Athena.

93. R. Parker 1996, 188.

94. Pausanias 1.22.1–3. On Aphrodite Pandemos, see chapter 4, with notes 134 and 135. On Ge Kourotrophos, and the appellative Kourotrophos used of a number of maternal deities, including Hecate, Demeter, and Artemis, see T. H. Price 1978, 106–12. On Demeter Chloe, compare *viridem Cybelen*, "Green Cybele," in Ovid *Fasti* 4.363–64. Cults of Chloe Themis and Ge Themis are also attested at Athens; see Stafford 2000, 61–66.

95. Aphrodite and Themis share a temple at Epidaurus: Pausanias 2.27.5. Temples of Aphrodite and of Themis are side by side at Tanagra: Pausanias 9.22.1. In the agora at Troezen (where Hippolytus and Aphrodite were famous) there was an altar of the Themides: Pausanias 2.31.5. An archaic statue of Themis stood beside the Seasons (*Hōrai*), her daughters, inside the Temple of Hera at Olympia, perhaps gracing the union of Zeus and Hera, whose statues were nearby: Pausanias 5.17.1. Themis is one of the names by which Anchises tentatively addresses Aphrodite herself (immediately after he calls her Aphrodite) in *Homeric Hymn* 5, *To Aphrodite* 94; like Aphrodite herself, Themis is also closely tied to Ares in *Homeric Hymn* 8, *To Ares* 4.

In these respects she was analogous to the bride of Gordius and mother of Midas among the Phrygians, the consort of Anchises among the Dardanians, and the concubine of Meles among the Lydians. In each case she was the source of sovereignty and fertility, and the foundation of orderly society.[96]

The Mother of the Gods in the Metroön at Athens united all such affirmations of a deity of sovereignty from the land of Asia, where the institutions of sovereignty were most ancient. At Athens, sovereignty was most appropriately enshrined in the house of deliberative consultation, which she should guide, and in the house of the laws and ordinances of Athens, which should embody and make her manifest. The very period that saw this rising interest in the Asiatic Mother of the Gods at Athens, culminating in her installation in the Metroön, was also the decisive period in the transformation of the concept of *nomos* into written law, and in the idea of the sovereignty of law in a democratic state.[97] Like the laws themselves, physically present at the Athenian Council, the Mother of the Gods was present as a preserver of the state and guardian of freedom and order. Her arrival was a measure of the earnestness with which Athenians sought to make good their dominion at home and abroad, within Europe and Asia, and within the divine heart of sovereign justice.

## THE MOTHER OF THE GODS IN GREEK HISTORIOGRAPHY

The foregoing account of the arrival of the Mother of the Gods at Athens in 408, and her installation in the Council House that afterward became known as her temple, the Metroön, brings the story of the *Mētragyrtēs* to its conclusion. From a close interweaving of many strands of evidence, the present account emerges as the solution to an old puzzle, what Robert Parker has called "a great puzzle and great paradox at the heart of religious and civic life."[98] A final question remains to be answered before this inquiry is closed: Why, if the Mother of the Gods had such significance in a period that is comparatively well documented, do we have no explicit historical account of her acceptance at Athens? If she or her splendid new cult image arrived, as argued here, with such pomp and circumstance under the sponsorship of Alcibiades, then why did her arrival not become part of the historiographical tradition of that period? The particular occasion and its historical significance provide the strongest clue to the likely answer to this question.

Because the Mother of the Gods was enshrined in the Metroön chiefly as

---

96. A connection between Themis and the Mother of the Gods is also suggested by Borgeaud 1996, 34–35, 54.

97. See Ostwald 1986, esp. 252–55, on the emergent concept of the sovereignty of *nomos* (law); and Munn 2000, esp. 264–72, on the historical context.

98. R. Parker 1996, 188, cited in chapter 2 at note 37.

an embodiment of the greater sovereignty of Athens, her reputation was closely linked to the fate of the Athenian empire. When she finally arrived at Athens, in 408, and was enthroned on the very spot where formerly she had been spurned, the Athenians had less than four years ahead of them in which to enjoy the benefits of empire. The hopeful celebrations of victory, wealth, power, and recovered political stability that attended the arrival of the Mother with her champion Alcibiades in fact lasted little more than a year. By 407 the Athenians were experiencing military setbacks, and Alcibiades was driven into exile for the second time.[99] Zealotry in politics was becoming self-destructive, as Aristophanes lamented in the *Frogs* (esp. 674–737), and was threatening to descend into internecine violence.

It is tempting to see the departure from Athens, at about this time, of poets and literati, the likes of Euripides and Agathon of Athens, and Ionian poets like Timotheus and Choerilus, and a great seer like Diopeithes, as an indication that such learned men feared that the favors of the Mother, or τὸ θεῖον more generally, would not save Athens for long.[100] Herodotus, in laying out the lessons to be learned from past contenders for sovereignty, had given them tacit warning. Certainly, Euripides' parting gift, his *Bacchae*, suggests his awareness that those who happened to be in positions of leadership at the moment might not be capable of recognizing or assessing the dangers closing in on Athens.

By the time of Alcibiades' second and final flight into exile, in 407, the Athenians knew that the grand alliance with Persia promised by Alcibiades was eluding their grasp.[101] King Darius II was approaching the end of his life, and his sons, Cyrus the Younger and the future Artaxerxes II, were po-

---

99. The flight of Alcibiades and related events presaging the fall of the Athenian empire are related by Xenophon *Hellenica* 1.5.16–2.1.32 and Plutarch *Alcibiades* 35–37, and are discussed in Munn 2000, chapters 7–9.

100. Euripides, Agathon, Timotheus, and Choerilus are all reported to have moved to the court of Archelaus of Macedon, most likely before 405. All but Agathon are known to have treated themes of Asiatic sovereignty, the Mother of the Gods, or both in their poetry; it is not improbable that Agathon also treated such themes, since his most famous play, *Antheus*, bears the name of a youth who falls afoul of the transgressive eroticism of the wife of a king of Miletus. (See Parthenius *Erotica* 14.) Significantly, both Timotheus and Choerilus later turn up singing the praises of Lysander and of the Spartan ascendancy in Asia: Plutarch *Lysander* 18.4, *Agesilaus* 14.2; Pausanias 3.12.10. Similarly, Diopeithes, named as the proposer of a decree against impiety at Athens (Plutarch *Pericles* 32.1), who "was well supplied with ancient prophecies, and was thought to be eminently wise in religious matters" (Plutarch *Agesilaus* 3.3), and who was influential among Athenians in the 420s and 410s (Aristophanes *Knights* 1085, *Wasps* 380, *Birds* 988), turns up prophesying kingship among the Spartans in the early 390s: Plutarch *Lysander* 22.5–6, *Agesilaus* 3.3–4.

101. Xenophon *Hellenica* 1.4.1–7 describes the delay of the Athenian-led embassy to Darius for three years, from 409 until 407. Aristophanes *Frogs* 1420–34 depicts the conflict between hope and disappointment that most Athenians felt regarding Alcibiades early in 405.

sitioning themselves to contend for the throne. The young Cyrus, seated at Sardis and in control now of most of the Greek relations of the Persian empire, favored the Spartans. He built up their navy at Ephesus, and by the time Darius died in 405, Cyrus' support enabled their admiral Lysander to destroy the Athenian navy and with it the Athenian empire.

So great a transformation in the balance of power, it seemed to some, could have been brought about only through divine agency. ($\theta\epsilon\hat{\iota}\acute{o}\nu$ $\tau\iota\nu\epsilon\varsigma$ $\dot{\eta}\gamma\acute{\eta}\sigma\alpha\nu\tau o$ $\tau o\hat{\upsilon}\tau o$ $\tau\grave{o}$ $\ddot{\epsilon}\rho\gamma o\nu$, says Plutarch.)[102] For this reason, the destruction that fell on the Athenians at Aegospotami in the Hellespont was widely said to be the fulfillment of a portent, the fall of a meteorite to earth at the site of the decisive battle.[103] Two centuries later, a meteoritic stone venerated as an epiphany of the Mother of the Gods was ceremoniously conveyed from Phrygia to Rome.[104] It is likely that, after the battle that destroyed an empire, some saw the meteor at Aegospotami as a sign of her movement of the affairs of Europe and Asia.

For his manifest role in bringing about this cosmic change, Lysander became "the first man among the Greeks for whom the cities erected altars and performed sacrifices as to a god," according to Duris of Samos.[105] At Samos, where the last elements of Athenian power had been broken by Lysander, the festival of Hera was renamed the Lysandreia in his honor.[106] Until recent finds confirmed the institution of the Lysandreia on Samos in the early fourth century, scholars had been reluctant to accept Duris' account at face value— it seemed too much tinged by the light of the honors later paid to Alexander of Macedon to be fully believable.[107] Now there are no strong grounds

102. Plutarch *Lysander* 11.7, a sentence that closes a summation of Lysander's victory at Aegospotami; cf. Herodotus' affirmations of divine agency at 7.137.2, 9.65.2, and 9.100.2, as discussed in chapter 8.

103. Plutarch *Lysander* 12, referring to the dissertation on meteors by Daïmachus in his treatise *On Piety*, has a long digression on meteors prompted by this portent. The Parian Chronicle, *FGrHist* 239.72, and Pliny *Naturalis Historia* 2.149, record the fall of the meteor in the archonship of Theagenides at Athens, 468/7. As in the long-delayed consequences of the execution of the *Mētragyrtēs*, the murders committed by the Aeginetans, and the passage of Datis causing the earthquake at Delos, all attested by Herodotus (see chapter 8, with note 6), there was a significant interval between the portent and its supposed consequence.

104. The famous stone of Pessinus in Phrygian Galatia, also said to be a meteor, was the form in which the Magna Mater was brought to Rome in 204 B.C.E.: Appian *Hannibal* 7.9.56; Herodian 1.11.1; Ammianus Marcellinus 22.9.5–7; Arnobius *Against the Nations* 7.49; cf. Livy 29.10.4–6; Diodorus 34.33.1–2; Strabo 12.5.3; and see the discussion and scholarship cited by Roller 1999, 263–71.

105. Duris *FGrHist* 76 F 71, cited by Plutarch *Lysander* 18.3.

106. On the Lysandreia at Samos, see Plutarch *Lysander* 18.4–5; Athenaeus 596e; Duris *FGrHist* 76 F 26 and 71.

107. See Habicht 1970, 3–7, and Cartledge 1987, 82–86, who both argue that the evidence favors the conclusion that Lysander received divine honors in his own lifetime; and Badian 1981, 33–38, who argues that his cult was posthumous.

for denying that Lysander was honored as a divine force in his own lifetime. We should conclude that Lysander's glorious deeds were taken as proof that he, like the Asiatic tyrants of old, was favored even by Hera, the consort of Zeus.

As upholder of the sanctity of marriage, Hera could embrace only one who in some sense was Zeus himself.[108] We should conclude that Lysander's celebrated accomplishment reinvigorated the ancient Asiatic paradigm of sovereignty, and that Lysander became Hera's partner in a Sacred Marriage. Such singular developments are easier to understand when we recognize that Lysander, by his victory, had appropriated to his person the trappings of divinely supported sovereignty that Alcibiades had lately been cultivating on behalf of the Athenians.[109] Especially when courting the adulation of the Ionians, Lysander knew as well as did Alcibiades how useful it was to identify himself with the ancient Asiatic paradigm of the mortal lover of the goddess. In this way he demonstrated to the world exactly where sovereignty, for the time being, was invested.

The Athenians had hoped that by embracing the Mother of the Gods, and by conspicuously placing their collective sovereign authority under her protection, they could demonstrate the ascendancy of their empire. The total collapse of this public justification for her cult explains why no historical account of this episode has survived. In the literature and inscriptions of the fourth century, the fact that the Mother of the Gods presided over the council and over the laws of Athens is mentioned often enough; but no surviving source of the period ventures to say why she occupied her privileged seat among the Athenians.[110] If the historical account of the reception of the Mother of the Gods at Athens had any political meaning to Athenians, it was humiliation at the failure of their bid for universal sovereignty. The statue

108. On Hera's prominent role in the Sacred Marriage, representing specifically the drive to sexual union in the consummation of marriage, see Burkert 1985, 108 and 131–34; Clark 1998. On mortal victors momentarily assuming the identity of Zeus, see chapter 1 at note 30.

109. Pausanias 6.3.15 compares the adulation of the Samians first for Alcibiades and later for Lysander, noting that the Ionians had previously dedicated a bronze statue of Alcibiades in the sanctuary of Hera at Samos. Pausanias concludes (6.3.16): "It is ever so: all mankind, like the Ionians, pays court to those who are in power." Note the effects of Lysander's charismatic presence among the Ionians a decade later, when "a great crowd continually followed and paid court to him," and when Lysander appeared to be "conducting himself with more pomp than royalty" (meaning more pomp than befitted the Spartan king Agesilaus); see Xenophon *Hellenica* 3.4.7–8.

110. See the sources collected by Wycherley 1957, 150–60. The chief references are cited and discussed by Sickinger 1999, 106–13. The obscurity of the Mother of the Gods at Athens is reflected in the fact that neither she nor the Metroön is mentioned in Heiner Knell's (2000) study of Athens in the fourth century, despite the fact that he devotes more than fifty pages to the cults and monuments of the agora (63–114; at 109 n. 20 he mistakenly dismisses the association of the Council House with the Metroön as later).

of the Mother of the Gods would have this effect for as long as anyone remembered the story of the *Mētragyrtēs,* the reasons for his death, and the reasons for which the Athenians later reversed their attitude toward the concept that he had represented.

It is surely significant that the earliest known historical account of the foundation of the Metroön "on account of that Phrygian man" came from a work entitled *Philippics,* either by Theopompus or by Anaximenes,[111] that was written after another moment of humiliation for Athens, at the battle of Chaeronea in 338. The story of an earlier humbling of the Athenians could thus be told in the context of this second decisive shift in the balance of political power in the Greek world away from Athens, this time toward the ascendancy of Alexander.

### THE MOTHER OF THE GODS, SPARTAN HEGEMONY, AND WAR

At the end of the fifth century, victory over Athens in war had brought Lysander the Spartan into communion with a great goddess of sovereignty, Hera of Samos. Like Alcibiades before him, Lysander was playing a challenging role, encouraging the adulation of his person as a means of demonstrating success, yet seeking not to exceed his authority as an officer of the Spartan state. It says much of Lysander's tact that he was able to descend from such a celestial height and assume his place within the Spartiate order as adviser to the king he helped make, Agesilaus. Lysander was able to make this transition in part because the Spartans took measures to demonstrate that they, collectively, were graced by the favor of the great goddess of Asia.

The first such indication was the foundation of the Metroön at Olympia. As a consequence of a dispute with Elis, for two decades the Spartans had been excluded from Olympia and from participation in its games.[112] Following the defeat of Athens, the Spartans extended their supremacy over Elis as well, defeating the Eleans in a two-year war (402–401). Soon after their return to Olympia, we may strongly suspect, the Spartans sponsored the foundation of the Metroön in the sanctuary of Zeus and Hera at Olympia, near the monument to Lydian Pelops, the Asiatic forefather of Sparta's Atreid kingship.[113] A shrine to the divine Mother near a great king's tumulus echoed

---

111. According to the scholion to Aeschines 3.187; see chapter 2, with notes 30 and 31. Note the interests of Callisthenes, another historian of Alexander, in the lore of Asia Minor, and of Phrygia in particular; see chapter 2, with notes 55, 105, and 106.

112. See Cartledge 1987, 248–53, on the history and chronology of these events.

113. The foundation of the Metroön at Olympia in the 390s ("kaum später als im ersten Jahrhundert des 4. Jahrhunderts," according to Alfred Mallwitz 1972, 161) places it in the decade of strongest Spartan influence at Olympia. K. Hitzl 1991, 8, cites the evidence confirming Mallwitz's conclusion, which has confuted the tendency of earlier scholarship to date the building later in the fourth century. But Hitzl (9–14) argues that the Metroön was built even earlier, be-

a pattern of ritualized sovereignty that we have observed at Lydian Sardis. At Olympia, such monuments to Atreid sovereignty were powerfully linked with the greatest cult place of Zeus in the Hellenic world.

The second strong indicator that the Spartans, with Lysander's encouragement, were especially mindful of the symbols of sovereignty associated with the Asiatic Mother of the Gods, was the war against Persia that they conducted in Asia Minor between 399 and 394. Here we find Agesilaus, not long after assuming the Eurypontid kingship of Sparta, asserting his Atreid heritage and demonstrating his devotion to the sister of Apollo by sacrificing, as Agamemnon had done, on the altar of Artemis at Aulis before sailing to Asia.[114] Following his arrival at Ephesus, Agesilaus devoted pious attention to Artemis of Ephesus.[115] Agesilaus then commenced a campaign against the domain of Artaxerxes II that ranged from Hellespontine Phrygia to Caria, and from Gordium to Sardis.[116] If his campaign had a strategic purpose, it was to assert his military might over the former Lydian domain west of the Halys River. If it was symbolic, then it was to demonstrate that he himself held sovereign power within the very homeland of the Phrygian Mother. This was a ritual that would demand the attention of all who would later contend for sovereignty over Asia and the *oikoumenē*.

This interpretation of Agesilaus' strategy in Asia sets a number of issues in a new light. Scholars have often remarked that, for one reason or another, Agesilaus fell far short of his announced intention to conquer Asia.[117] When we recognize that "Asia" in this context refers to the original domain of Asia, identical with the extent of the Lydian empire, then it is possible to see that Agesilaus more nearly achieved his true military and symbolic objectives. A measure of the significance of Agesilaus' achievement, moreover, is found in the Persian response to his victory in the battle of Sardis. After that event, Artaxerxes II commanded the execution of the man who was defeated on

---

fore the end of the fifth century, under Elean influence, which seems not as probable as a Spartan scenario in the 390s.

114. Xenophon *Hellenica* 3.4.2–4; Plutarch *Agesilaus* 6.4; Pausanias 3.9.4; see also Munn 2000, 317–18, 327.

115. See Xenophon *Agesilaus* 1.27; note that Xenophon himself, having served in Asia, was a devotee of Artemis of Ephesus, and established her cult not far from Olympia: *Anabasis* 5.3.4–13.

116. On Agesilaus' Asiatic campaigns, see Xenophon *Hellenica* 3.4.5–29, 4.1.1–2.8; *Agesilaus* 1.6–38; Isocrates 4, *Panegyricus*, 144; *Hellenica Oxyrhynchia* 11–14, 21–22 (Bartoletti); Diodorus 14.79–80; Plutarch *Agesilaus* 7–15; Pausanias 3.9.1–12; see Cartledge 1987, 180–202.

117. Xenophon *Agesilaus* 1.8 describes Agesilaus' goal of contending with the Persian king for control of Asia; cf. *Hellenica* 3.4.2; Diodorus 15.31.3. Cawkwell 1976, 66, and Cartledge 1987, 213, understand this to mean that Agesilaus' announced aim was the conquest of the Persian empire; for further discussion of Agesilaus' goals, see Seager 1977; Kelly 1978. Hamilton 1983, 125–26, and Cartledge 1987, 217, regard the limited achievements of Agesilaus' Asiatic campaign as the chief evidence that his strategic thinking was not as effective as his tactical skills.

the plain of Sardis, Tissaphernes, his own brother-in-law and for many years the staunch defender of the authority of Artaxerxes and his father in Asia.[118] Sovereign supremacy could not endure the taint of defeat. Just as Alcibiades had earlier understood, when he fled into exile for the second time, an open defeat—even one of minor strategic importance—signified the loss of the favor of the Mother of the Gods.

The cosmic dimension of the stigma of defeat also explains how Theopompus, in his *Hellenica,* could take the defeat of the Spartan navy at the battle of Cnidus in 394 as the end of the Spartan hegemony and a suitable place to end his Hellenic history.[119] From another perspective this seems an odd terminus, since Spartan hegemony in European Greece endured and even grew stronger in the decade following the defeat at Cnidus. But from the perspective of universal dominion over the sea, the defeat at Cnidus marked the end of a Spartan bid for sovereign supremacy over one of nature's elemental domains, analogous to failures of the ambitions of Polycrates of Samos, of Aristagoras of Miletus and the Ionians, of Darius and Xerxes, and of the Athenians and their Delian League and empire. It marked the end of yet another bid for the undivided favor of the mistress of worldly sovereignty, the Mother of the Gods.

## THE MOTHER OF THE GODS, ATHENIAN HEGEMONY, AND PEACE

The Mother of the Gods at Athens, meanwhile, was still a dynamic concept. Although recollection of the establishment of her cult at Athens may have given rise to painful regrets, the Athenians were ever ready to learn, and to adapt concepts from their past to present circumstances. So it is that while the Spartans were making the Mother of the Gods their champion in war, the Athenians were fashioning the Mother into the archetype of peace.

The concept of peace, as a political relationship, as an ideal, and as a divinity, underwent significant development among the Greeks in the fourth century.[120] This was especially the case at Athens, where, we are told, an altar and sacrifices to Peace were established for the first time in celebration of the peace treaty of 375 between Athens and Sparta, according to which the Athenian claim to rule of the sea (or *hēgemonia:* Isocrates 4, *Panegyricus*

---

118. Xenophon *Hellenica* 3.4.25; see Munn 2000, 326–27.

119. Theopompus *FGrHist* 115 T 13 and 14; cf. F 321 (= Plutarch *Agesilaus* 10.5–6).

120. On the distinctive concept of General Peace (*koinē eirēnē*) in the fourth century, see Ryder 1965. Isocrates 8, *On Peace,* delivered ca. 355 B.C.E., represents a politically contextualized argument for the pursuit of peace as the paramount good, which should replace the pursuit of military hegemony or naval supremacy (ἡγεμονία or ἀρχὴ τῆς θαλάττης, both now equated with the unmitigated evil of tyranny at 91, 114; cf. 64–68, 101–5, 111, 142). On the cult of Peace, particularly at Athens, see Simon 1988, 59–66; Stafford 2000, 173–97.

20) was recognized.[121] Although this development is often viewed as an innovative first step toward the increasingly popular cults of personified abstractions like Tyche (Fortune) in the Hellenistic world, in fact it is very much part of an ancient continuum of naming and honoring the various forms of sovereign benevolence whose history we have sampled in this book. Aware of this history, we can now recognize the role in it played by the Mother of the Gods at Athens, and how her aspect was transformed by Athenians in the fourth century.

The Athenians of the fourth century did not leave their beneficent Mother to languish indoors, as a vestige of their own receded glory. In the generation after her enthronement in their old Council House, they presented her anew to the world as the embodiment of a new vision of divinely favored harmony and order whose home was Athens. For the Mother of the Gods can be recognized in the statue of Eirene (Peace) holding the infant Ploutos, or Wealth, that was erected immediately in front of the Metroön in the agora in 361 or 360 B.C.E.[122]

Eirene, daughter of Themis, was the daughter of the Mother of the Gods by the equation of Themis with the Mother discussed above. Alternatively, Eirene, sister of Dike and Eunomia, could, like each of her sisters and their likeness, Nemesis, literally be the Mother in another form, presenting her new child, Ploutos, to the world.[123] As stated at the outset of chapter 2, the very nature of the Mother is manifold, and her identity is contingent on the

121. For the meaning of this treaty and the institution of sacrifices to Peace, in addition to Isocrates 4.20, see Isocrates 15, *Antidosis* 109–10; Philochorus *FGrHist* 328 F 151; and scholion to Aristophanes *Peace* 1019. On the political conditions of this peace treaty, see Munn 1993, 172–80. For discussion of the cultic institutions, see Stafford 2000, 173–77.

122. The statue of Eirene and Ploutos by Cephisodotus is best represented in the Roman copy now in Munich, Glyptothek no. 219. Pausanias 1.8.2 attests the placement of this statue; 9.16.1 attributes it to Cephisodotus. The nature and placement of the statue is discussed by Knell 2000, 73–80; its direct antecedents and cultic status are discussed by Stafford 2000, 178–89. Opinions about the date of the statue have ranged from 375, when the Athenians dedicated an altar to Eirene (above, note 121), to the occasion of another such treaty in 371, and to the common peace treaty negotiated in 362/1, after the battle of Mantinea in 362. (Knell 76 reviews these possibilities.) Evidence is decidedly in favor of the last of these occasions, both because of the singular nature of that common peace treaty (see below, with note 125), and especially because the statue of Eirene and Ploutos was illustrated on Panathenaic prize amphoras dated to the archonship of Callimedes (360/59), which almost certainly advertise the statue as a recent dedication of the Athenians; see Eschbach 1986, 58–70. Ridgway 1997, 259, endorses this date for the statue group; Simon 1988, 63–64, Knell (76), and Stafford (178–80) are noncommittal.

123. See above at notes 70–71. A Hellenistic naiskos of the Mother of the Gods from the Athenian agora depicts her with a child on her lap in place of her usual lion (T. H. Price 1978, 64–65 and fig. 50), reminding us that this attribute of the Mother signifies her progeny, which in the pursuit of peace would more suitably be a child than a lion. See Price on the Eirene and

Figure 15. Roman copy of
Cephisodotus' statue of Eirene
holding the infant Ploutos, original
circa 360 B.C.E. (Staatliche
Antikensammlungen und Glyptothek, Munich, inv. no. GL 219).

time, place, and circumstances in which she appears.[124] The Athenians in
361 were celebrating the conclusion of a new treaty of peace and reconciliation among Greeks, a common (i.e., general) peace (*koinē eirēnē*) that, for

Ploutos group as part of the tradition of the Kourotrophos (62), and on maternal divinities
with children (6–13, 101–32); see also note 94 above.

    124. See esp. the fragment of the Pythagorean Philolaus (quoted in chapter 2 note 6) equat-
ing the Mother of the Gods with "the fire around the center of the universe" and "the Univer-

the first time in history, did not depend upon the will of the king of Persia.[125] Communal peace was now fully naturalized as a Hellenic concept, and not a consort of the lords of Asia.

The statue of Eirene and Ploutos by Cephisodotus was the embodiment of this concept. And this idea was depicted to Athenians not merely as a loving mother presenting her auspicious son to the world, but also as a mother, the Mother, who has risen from her seat in the Metroön and come forth to make her presentation. Commentators on the surviving replicas of Cephisodotus' statue have remarked at how the artist has depicted his goddess in a style reminiscent of the sculptural forms of the late fifth century.[126] It is highly likely that Cephisodotus sought this effect in order to make his image of Eirene recognizable as the same figure that Agoracritus so memorably depicted on her throne in the Metroön. In this way, the Mother could be seen animating the future for Athens, and not merely reminding them of stillborn hopes of the past.

---

sal Hearth." Note that statues of Eirene (Peace) and Hestia (Hearth) stood in the Prytaneum of Athens, according to Pausanias 1.18.3.

125. See Ryder 1965, 140–44, commenting on Tod 145 (= *SV* 292; Harding 57), a treaty declaring *koinē eirēnē* among Greeks, and carefully distancing the Persian king from its proceedings; see also Diodorus 15.89.1. Marking the end of an era, Xenophon closes his *Hellenica* on the eve of this occasion, with the battle of Mantinea in 362, as did Anaximenes, while Dionysodorus and Anaxis ended theirs in the following year: Diodorus 15.89.3, 95.4.

126. So Ridgway 1997, 260; and Knell 2000, 77; among others. Stewart 1997, 152, suggests that Cephisodotus' statue evoked an "overtly sexual" image of Demeter. The Mother of the Gods, with her ancient kinship to both Aphrodite and Demeter, fits even more closely into this imagery.

# Conclusions

Our original question has now been answered, and now we may say that we know how the Mother of the Gods came to Athens. We know in the sense that the story has been filled out and told from its once-upon-a-time beginnings in Phrygia, traced through places and persons familiar from other stories and histories, and taken to its ever-after ending at Athens. The resulting account has a much deeper context than the simple tale of the *Mētragyrtēs*, the eunuch priest of the Mother of the Gods who attempted to introduce her worship to uncomprehending Athenians. The story of the *Mētragyrtēs* tells that he was put to death by the Athenians, and that they suffered the wrath of the Mother of the Gods until finally, under oracular guidance, they propitiated her wrath and established her cult in their Council House. Significant elements of this story are recognizable in the testimony of classical authors, Herodotus in particular. The story of the *Mētragyrtēs* now has a chronology, spanning from the first to the last decade of the fifth century B.C.E. It involves known actors, such as Darius, Miltiades, Themistocles, and Alcibiades. Above all, from a tale told to demonstrate the power of a divinity and to account for a distinctive facet of Athenian civic religion, the story is now seen also to reflect patterns of authority and obeisance that are attested in other myths, in ritual practices, and in historical accounts.

The recovery of a history of the Mother of the Gods as she was known to the Greeks of the classical era has been the immediate goal and guiding impetus of this book. Pressing forward with such a strongly positivist project has led into an intellectual landscape with some unusual features. The arguments leading to the recovery of the history of the Mother of the Gods and Athens have presented us with a series of transgressive conclusions, where categories of analysis that are usually opposed have converged. So, for example, the story of the *Mētragyrtēs* at Athens, which Robert Parker has called "obviously not true" and a "myth," is now seen to be also quite true and to be history. I say "also" because the demonstration that the story contains a significant element of historical truth does not ipso facto exclude the assertion that the story is a myth, in the sense that it contains a theological message that lies outside the scope of historical analysis.

As suggested at the outset of chapter 9, the exegesis of the story of the Mētragyrtēs and Athens developed here reveals myth in the making. Similarly, as indicated in the closing section of chapter 2, the recollections of King Midas by the Greeks bring us into contact with a historical person remembered as a mythical figure. In chapter 4 I advanced the suggestion that the story of Atys, the tragically dying son of Croesus whose story conforms so much to ancient myths of the dying hero, had its origin in the traditional forms of ritualized lamentation accorded to a historical person. Chapters 6 and 7 set forth the testimonia showing that by Herodotus' day, memory of the murder of Darius' heralds was being merged with the mythical past through the Spartan account of the wrath of Talthybius, and all elements were in place for the story of the Mētragyrtēs and the wrath of the Mother to become the Athenian counterpart to the same historical experience. In each of these instances, we can perceive an emerging account of the past that, from our perspective, almost defies classification as either myth or history.

We should remind ourselves, at this point, that any cognitive dissonance we might feel at the suggestion that myth and history converge in these instances is a consequence of the ill fit of this evidence with the conceptual habits we have constructed for ourselves. The distinction between myth and history, it is true, is said to be a Greek achievement, something made manifest particularly in the work of Herodotus and Thucydides. But it is we who have gone on to argue that myth and history constitute fundamentally separate cognitive categories, concerning essentially different issues (that myth admits gods, for instance, while history does not); they were not so fundamentally distinguished in Greek thought. Herodotus, as discussed in chapter 8, and Thucydides, as discussed in my previous book, The School of History, were endeavoring to distinguish between a past that could be reliably known and a past that was less certain (what poets have embellished in song, and therefore have made more mythical than reliable, as Thucydides says). But these were distinctions within a single, coherent continuum of the past. As both Herodotus and Thucydides demonstrate in the opening chapters of their works, to them the past of myth was every bit as real as the more immediate historical past that they wrote about. It was just a less certain form of reality, more liable to misconception and subject to doubts about the details because there was little independent basis for verifying them.

If, according to this reasoning, there are no absolute, categorical distinctions to be made about ways of knowing the past according to Greek and, more generally, ancient ways of thinking, then we must look at the project of Herodotus and Thucydides from another perspective and ask why they were so concerned about distinguishing levels of certainty about it. The overarching reason for their endeavor, and the motive for all elements of the Greek intellectual achievement that has been signified by the modern categories "rationalism" and "science," was to liberate knowledge from tyranny.

An all-powerful tyrant draws all meanings toward himself, as the center of providence, power, and wisdom, and all the truth and beauty that accompany these beneficent forces. As we may perceive most clearly in the case of Midas and his mother, this force draws all meanings from the past toward a single point, where theology and history, primordial divinity and kingship, humanity and immortality, are telescoped into one. "I am not jealous of the doings of gods," says Archilochus with Gyges in view, "nor do I desire great tyranny." Reverence and revulsion are here expressed at the conjunction of divinity and kingship in the earliest attested Greek comment on tyranny. The same oppositions, expressed in terms of kingship and beauty, are present in the story that Herodotus tells of how Gyges gained tyranny. According to categories that were in the process of being distinguished in classical Greek thought, the tyrant is the ultimate transgressive figure.

The most powerful manifestation of the unitarian force of tyranny is not the tyrant himself, however, but popular adulation for the tyrant, and popular desire for the good things that he represents. This desire is greater than the tyrant himself because it lives on after him, calling for the renewal of tyranny, often in ritualized ways. Tyranny requires—in essence, is—the adulation of the masses, who move together for him to the rhythm of drums and the enthralling strains of reed pipes as they march on the road of conquest, like the armies of Sadyattes and Alyattes in the Maeander valley, just as they dance at night in the ecstasies of the Mother, venerating the generative force that has brought good things to them in this world.

Tyranny remains strong only when it receives such popular affirmation. This is why the meeting of Solon and Croesus at the beginning of Herodotus' *Histories* has such thematic importance: Solon, the wise Athenian, denies Croesus the affirmation that he craves and needs. Herodotus then turns the ritual lamentations over the death of Atys at Croesus' own court into the first demonstration of the fallibility of tyranny, which Croesus' own fate, and later that of Xerxes as well, affirms in larger, far more meaningful ways. The power of tyranny is thus humbled before the testimony of Herodotus' history, where consummate effort is made to disentangle popular distortions from what can be more reliably known about the past.

Herodotus begins his *Histories* by working outward from within the myth-historical parables of Mermnad tyranny, establishing critical space between tyranny and history through his reinterpretation of stories that had earlier been told to support different meanings. Such, I suggest, is the basis for reckoning with the alternative meanings that I have identified, in chapters 3 and

4, for events such as the infatuation of Candaules with his wife, the surrender of Miletus to Alyattes, the lesson in tyranny of Thrasybulus to Periander, and the death of Atys. Herodotus' project, in this respect, was not so much a response to an alien ideology of tyranny as it was part of an ongoing critique of the ideology of tyranny within Greek culture. The critical space he sought to establish between the account of history and the myths of tyranny was not a detached interest in evaluating a remote past. It was an immediate concern with the construction of understandings under way in his own day. It was in his own day (within no more than a decade from the time of his writing, I would argue) that Kybebe, whose shrine at Sardis was destroyed in the Ionian uprising of 498, was received as the Mother of the Gods in the Council House of the Athenians, which became her shrine at Athens, the Metroön. If the sovereign people of the Athenians was now courting the divine patron of tyranny, then they should at least be wise enough, as Solon had been but Croesus had not, to recognize the limits of their own mortal abilities even when they were in harmony with her transcendent powers. They had to learn from history.

Herodotus' project was to establish a critical space around the sovereign claims of tyranny, so that tyranny itself could be seen and understood. This project reflects the Greek interaction with ancient traditions of sovereignty in Asia, and, according to the evidence set forth in chapters 2, 3, and 4, it was very much part of the larger intellectual trend of Greek literature under way already with Hesiod and Homer. As with the themes of Herodotus' *Histories,* the conditions of tyranny—specifically, the intimate relationships between divinity and humanity that tyranny presupposes—are strongly intermingled in the foundation of the Greek literary tradition. And that tradition was by no means entirely critical of the ideology of tyranny.

A tyrant king, such as Midas or Gyges, was the focal point of divine favor, manifested by the reverence for the tyrant's mother as the paramount divine Mother herself, for his consort as the paramount divine nymph ("bride") herself, and for his son as the godlike lion; the tyrant himself, by implication, was like a god, and could be viewed as an embodiment of the sovereign divinity on earth, and a king of the underworld when he passed away. Greek awareness of these relationships, and identification of them with the sovereigns of Asia, is clearly reflected when Herodotus has a native of the Hellespontine region address Xerxes as Zeus (7.56.2), and when Aeschylus depicts the sovereign ghost of Darius rising from the grave at the summons of Atossa, the mother of Xerxes, whom he calls "mother of a god," "consort of a god," and "mistress of this land" (chapter 6).

The Greeks, beginning with Hesiod and Homer, denied none of these premises, but established a critical space between themselves and the sons and mates of gods, first, by assigning such demigods to the bygone age of heroes, and second, by pointing out that even such intimacy with the gods could never endow a living man with infallible sovereignty. The artifice of declaring, as Hesiod did, that the age of heroes had ended was not a declaration that demigods no longer exist, but rather a reminder, like the ruins of Cnossus, Troy, and Mycenae, that no such splendid sovereignty could last forever. So god-engendered kings, in Hesiod's outlook, are reduced to bribe-swallowing *basileis,* subject to the same forces of immortal Dike as are all men, in need of instruction from him whom the Muses love, the god-inspired poet. As to the beneficence of an all-protecting goddess, Hesiod shows, in the figure of Hecate, that she is no royal prerogative, but that all worthy men may supplicate her. Homer shows that not even the god-favored Trojans, whose princes win the affection of Aphrodite herself, and who take the hand of the most desirable woman in the world, can survive against the assembled might and cunning of the Achaeans. Nor can Achaean princes and heroes themselves, even the son of a goddess like Achilles, overcome the bonds of mortality except within the critical space of poetry. Odysseus, in a tale with remarkably countertyrannical implications, travels across the world and even to the underworld and back, in quest not of immortality or paramount kingship, but of a return to his earthly domain and mortal wife, willingly leaving the embraces of immortal nymphs and goddesses in order to achieve his homecoming.

The elaborated myths of epic, the works attributed to Hesiod and Homer, were probably first committed to writing sometime in the space between the reigns of Midas and Gyges: that is, roughly in the first half of the seventh century. We can characterize this as an interval when the great tyrant of the previous generation, Midas, was becoming a fixture of legend, while a new tyrant, Gyges, was assuming the mantle of Midas. If tyranny demanded popular approval to gain the breath of life, so too did the poet's art, and we may note that burgeoning tyranny and epic alike were playing to much the same audiences in the seventh century. The Greek audiences of epic were learning to be skeptical of the pretensions of new tyrants or would-be tyrants who claimed to be demigods. But the influence of Gyges, reaching from Ionia and Caria to Assyria and Egypt, proved impressive and undeniable, and the Greeks of Asia Minor became on the whole willing partners of the Lydians. Archilochus comments on the ostentation of Gyges, and a generation later Alcman and Sappho set the perfection of earthly desires in the splendor of Sardis. The Spartans, in this period, appear to have adapted elements of the ideology of Lydian tyranny to their distinctive form of dual monarchy. Elsewhere in the Peloponnese and at Corinth in particular, tyranny on the Lydian model was imported wholesale, complete with the veneration of Aphrodite as the paramount deity.

Those who embraced tyranny also embraced the theology of tyranny, where the consort and the mother of the tyrant held the key symbolic roles. These roles were, in effect, different aspects of one figure who could be abstracted into a single, transcendent divine entity, the Mother. In addition to being the mother of kingship, the Mother also personified the life-sustaining forces of the earth. Among the Lydians and their subjects, therefore, those who derived their sustenance from the earth owed devotion both to the Mother who provided that sustenance, and to the king who was a living embodiment of the Mother's power on earth. As described in chapter 5, the relationship between Lydian sovereignty and the cultivated, life-sustaining earth was a notion that could be extended to the limits of the settled portions of the earth—the *oikoumenē*. Such a concept, at home among the Ionian subjects of Lydia during the reigns of Alyattes and Croesus, was the impetus for the creation of the first Ionian maps of the world, and for the first endeavors to describe the transcendent forces that governed the world and life in it, represented by the legacy of Thales and especially of Anaximander.

The Lydian empire did not survive the attempt by Croesus to expand its dominion, but it left its justification for worldly sovereignty to Persian conquerors. Some of the Greeks living around the Aegean, the Ionians in particular, who had previously submitted to the sovereignty of the Lydians, were disposed to do the same to the Persians. The symbols of sovereignty centered at Sardis were deeply rooted among them. At the instigation of Aristagoras of Miletus, however, the Ionians and Athenians embraced an idea previously championed by Polycrates of Samos—namely that the symbols of sovereignty could be appropriated by the Ionians collectively, so that they could live within the former domain of Lydia not as subjects of the lords of Sardis, but as sovereigns in their own right. This gave rise to the Ionian Revolt, in which, as discussed in chapter 6, the Ionians mistook the symbolic advantages they gained by attacking Sardis for real power. The power of Darius eventually won out, and this prompted the extension of the Persian demand for submission more widely among the Greeks, and among them especially to Athens. The heralds sent to Athens by Darius made demands for submission in terms that had become customary among the Ionians: submission required an acknowledgment of the supremacy of the Mother of the Gods, whose chief seat was at Sardis, where she was known as Kybebe. The rejection of these demands, and the execution of the heralds who had brought them, was the origin of the story of the *Mētragyrtēs* and his death at Athens.

The rejection of the *Mētragyrtēs,* in 491, was a decisive step in the developing relationship between Athens and Persia. It declared a division between Greeks and Persians that amounted to a division in the cosmology of earthly sovereignty. The Greeks now openly declared that the lord of Asia had no just claim on the lands of Europe. The divinity of earthly fertility among the Greeks, Demeter, embraced all those who sought her favors through her rites of initiation, but Demeter at Eleusis did not embrace barbarians or, in particular, Persians. The rejection of Kybebe, the Asiatic Mother, was a theological division with political consequences (or a political division with theological consequences—the priority of terms is arbitrary), and it influenced geographical concepts as well. The common form of the world map, showing two continents, Europe and Asia, divided by water, was viewed as a determinant feature of the rightful form of power and dominion in the world. Awareness that the map of the world so divided was an oversimplification of real geography took hold only as Greeks became aware that it was unrealistic to expect that sovereignty could be partitioned along such a line. This was a realization achieved among the Greeks in the course of the history of the Athenian empire.

The Spartans, who had joined the Athenians in their unqualified rejection of the demands of Darius and later of Xerxes, actually believed that the division of the world between Europe and Asia was divinely ordained, and that their rightful place in the world did not extend across the waters to Asia. This too was a notion that time and experience would change, but change came to the Spartans only after they began to follow the lead of the Athenians. The Athenians, meanwhile, embraced the problem of championing the liberty of all Ionians, including those inhabiting the shores of Asia. For a generation after the defeat of Xerxes, the Athenians led their Ionian allies in war against Persians, and in support of rebellions against Persian rule on Cyprus and in Egypt, until they had established their unquestioned supremacy at sea and had demonstrated their ability to hold their own along the coastlands of Asia. As a result, by the middle of the fifth century an entente was reached between Athens and Persia. This understanding, later known as the Peace of Callias, defined, most significantly, a zone of overlapping authorities, where the Greek cities of Asia and their commerce were to be of no concern to the Persian king and his satraps, while the cultivated lands that the Greeks of Asia occupied were still subject to the king, and were the basis on which tribute was paid to the king. Although each side declared that its sovereignty was just and, in principle, unbounded, both sides respected their practical limits.

One consequence of this entente was a mutual assimilation of the forms of Persian and Athenian sovereignty. From our perspective, this development is most easily recognized on the Greek side, in the transformation of the Delian League into the Athenian empire, with all of the symbolic and practical manifestations of centralized authority that this implies. Another effect, the consequences of which become apparent among the Athenians within the last third of the fifth century, was an emerging acknowledgment of Kybebe, the Asiatic Mother of the Gods, as a force to be reckoned with.

The Mother of the Gods had been known to Athenians for as long as she was known among the Ionians of Asia. Since the conflict with Darius and Xerxes, however, the Athenians had effaced all public acknowledgment of her as patron of Asiatic sovereignty, and had subsumed her character within various expressions of Demeter, or Aphrodite, or Artemis, or Rhea, or the all-mother, Ge or Gaea, the Earth. She was also present in the form of one or another of the abstracted principles of her power, such as Aristoboule, Themis, or Nemesis.

Formal acknowledgment of the Mother of the Gods at Athens, and the establishment of her cult within the Council House of the Athenians, took place under the combined pressures of desperation and hope that characterized Athenian politics in the last decade of the Athenian empire. After the Sicilian disaster, Athenians and Spartans competed for the cooperation of Persia, which could tip the balance of war in Greece decisively one way or the other. Under the leadership of Alcibiades and through his personal intimacy with the seats of power in Asia, the Athenians became hopeful that their supremacy would be restored. Under these circumstances, in 408 the Athenians enthroned the Mother of the Gods in the Council House, in the very building where her minister, an emissary of Darius, had been condemned to death. The Metroön in the agora was thus established, and from this event the story of the Mother and her minister at Athens eventually developed into the parable of the *Mētragyrtēs*.

This fusion of Athenian and Asiatic ideology brought about under the leadership of Alcibiades was the culmination of a process under way at Athens since the Peace of Callias and the heyday of Pericles. In a larger sense, it was a process already under way in the time of Peisistratus. In fact, the power to attract, consume, and grow more powerful and attractive—the essence of Asiatic tyranny—was a power that from the first ignited the Greek creative imagination in an effort to control, define, or appropriate this irresistible force. Athenian democracy was perhaps the most remarkable product of this interaction. And when Athens had become most powerful and most attractive, it was almost inevitable that the Mother of the Gods would be recognized there.

The Mother of the Gods at Athens was sublime and transcendent sovereignty, embodying passion and wisdom in a figure that stood for both erotic and maternal devotion. She was as real as sovereignty itself. She had a known past, as the nurturer of the sovereigns of Asia. Their greatness was her measure, though their fall was proof of their own fallibility, a mortal failing, not hers. Her story was not measured by the span of human life. If mortal men, as tyrants, had failed, then perhaps an immortal, self-regenerating sovereign body, the Athenian demos, represented by its deliberative council, could endure and grow in wisdom under her guidance.

# BIBLIOGRAPHY

Akurgal, E.

    1961. *Die Kunst Anatoliens.* Berlin.

    1968. *The Art of Greece: Its Origins in the Mediterranean and Near East.* Transl. W. Dynes from the German 1966 edition. New York.

Amandry, P.

    1967. "Thémistocle a Mélitè." In *Charisterion eis Anastasion K. Orlandon,* vol. 4, 265–79. Athens.

Andrewes, A.

    1956. *The Greek Tyrants.* New York.

    1978. "The Opposition to Pericles." *JHS* 98, 1–8.

Aro, S.

    2003. "Art and Architecture." In *The Luwians,* ed. H. C. Melchert, 281–337. Leiden.

Astour, M. C.

    1965. *Hellenosemitica: An Ethnic and Cultural Study in West Semitic Impact on Mycenaean Greece.* Leiden.

Auffarth, C.

    1991. *Der drohende Untergang: "Schöpfung" in Mythos und Ritual im alten Orient und in Griechenland am Beispiel der Odyssee und des Ezechielbuches.* Berlin.

Badian, E.

    1981. "The Deification of Alexander the Great." In *Ancient Macedonian Studies in Honor of Charles F. Edson,* ed. H. J. Dell, 27–71. Thessaloniki.

1993. *From Plataea to Potidaea: Studies in the History and Historiography of the Penta-contaetia.* Baltimore.

Badian, E., and J. Buckler.

1975. "The Wrong Salamis?" *RhM* 118, 226–39.

Bakir, T., and R. Gusmani.

1993. "Graffiti aus Daskyleion." *Kadmos* 32, 135–44.

Balcer, J. M.

1979. "Imperialism and Stasis in Fifth Century B.C. Ionia: A Frontier Redefined." In Bowersock et al. 1979, 261–68.

1984. *Sparda by the Bitter Sea: Imperial Interaction in Western Anatolia.* Chico.

1995. *The Persian Conquest of the Greeks, 545–450 BC.* Xenia 38. Constance.

Baldriga, R.

1997. "Aspetti ideologici della presenza frigia nella tradizione greca sul regno di Lidia." In Gusmani et al. 1997, 279–85.

Balmuth, M. S.

1971. "Remarks on the Appearance of the Earliest Coins." In *Studies Presented to George M. A. Hanfmann,* ed. D. G. Mitten, J. G. Pedley, and J. A. Scott, 1–7. Fogg Art Museum, Harvard University, Monographs in Art and Archaeology 2. Cambridge, Mass.

Balsdon, J. P. V. D.

1950. "The 'Divinity' of Alexander." *Historia* 1, 363–88. [Reprinted in *Alexander the Great: The Main Problems,* ed. G. T. Griffith (Cambridge, 1966), 179–204.]

Bammer, A.

1984. *Das Heiligtum der Artemis von Ephesos.* Graz.

Barber, E. J. W.

1992. "The Peplos of Athens." In *Goddess and Polis: The Panathenaic Festival in Ancient Athens.* ed. J. Neils, 103–17. Hanover, N.H.

Barnett, R. D.

1953. "The Phrygian Rock Façades and the Hittite Monuments." *Bibliotheca Orientalis* 10, 78–82.

1975. "Phrygia and the Peoples of Anatolia in the Iron Age." In *CAH,* 3rd. ed., vol. 2, part 2, 417–42.

Barron, J. P.

1988. "The Liberation of Greece." In *CAH,* 2nd ed., vol. 4, 592–622.

Beaulieu, P.-A.

1989. *The Reign of Nabonidus King of Babylon, 556–539 B.C.* New Haven.

Beekes, R.

2002. "The Prehistory of the Lydians, the Origin of the Etruscans, Troy, and Aeneas." *Bibliotheca Orientalis* 59, cols. 205–41.

2003. "The Origin of Apollo." *JANER* 3, 1–21.

Bengisu, R. L.

.1996. "Lydian Mount Karios." In Lane 1996a, 1–36.

Bengtson, H.

ed., 1962. *Die Staatsverträge des Altertums,* vol. 2, *Die Verträge der griechisch-römischen Welt.* Munich.

1968. *The Greeks and the Persians, from the Sixth to the Fourth Centuries.* Transl. J. Conway from the German 1965 edition. New York.

Benveniste, E.

1966. *Titres et noms propres en iranien ancien.* Paris.

1973. *Indo-European Language and Society.* Transl E. Palmer. London.

Berndt-Ersöz, S.

1998. "Phrygian Rock-Cut Cult Façades: A Study of the Function of the So-Called Shaft Monuments." *AnatStud* 48, 87–112.

Bertelli, l.

2001. "Hecataeus: From Genealogy to Historiography." In Luraghi 2001a, 67–94.

Biers, W. R.

1992. *Art, Artefacts, and Chronology in Classical Archaeology.* London.

Bittel, K.

1970. *Hattusha, the Capital of the Hittites.* Oxford.

1980–83. "Kubaba: B., Ikonographie." *RLA* 6, 261–64.

Blomart, A.

2002. "La Phrygienne et l'Athénien: Quand la Mère des dieux et Apollon Patrôs se recontrent sur l'agora d'Athènes." In *Religions méditerranéennes et orientales de l'antiquité, Actes du colloque des 23–24 avril 1999, Institut des sciences et techniques de l'antiquité (UMR 6048), Université de Franche-Comté à Besançon,* ed. F. Labrique, 21–34. Institut Français de l'Archéologie Orientale, Bibliothèque d'Etude 135. N.p.

Blösel, W.

2001. "The Herodotean Picture of Themistocles: A Mirror of Fifth-Century Athens." In Luraghi 2001a, 179–97.

Blundell, S.

1995. *Women in Ancient Greece.* Cambridge, Mass.

Blundell, S., and M. Williamson, eds.

1998. *The Sacred and the Feminine in Ancient Greece.* London.

Boardman, J.

1972. "Herakles, Peisistratos, and Sons." *RA* 57–72.

1978. *Greek Sculpture: The Archaic Period.* London.

1980. *The Greeks Overseas: Their Early Colonies and Trade.* 2nd ed. London.

1989a. *Athenian Red-Figure Vases: The Classical Period.* London.

1989b. "Herakles, Peisistratos and the Unconvinced." *JHS* 109, 158–59.

Bodnar, E. W.

1973. "A Quarry Relief on the Island of Paros." *Archaeology* 26, 270–77.

Boedeker, D.

1974. *Aphrodite's Entry into Greek Epic.* Mnemosyne Supplement 32. Leiden.

Boedeker, D., and D. Sider, eds.

2001. *The New Simonides: Contexts of Praise and Desire.* Oxford.

Boersma, J. S.

1970. *Athenian Building Policy from 561/0 to 405/4.* Groningen.

Bohringer, F.

1979. "Cultes d'athlètes en Grèce classique: Propos politique, discours mythique." *REA* 81, 5–18.

Borgeaud, P.

1996. *La Mère des dieux: De Cybèle à la Vierge Marie.* N.p.

Börker-Klähn, J.

1997. "Zur Herkunft der Bezeichnung 'Muski.'" In Gusmani et al. 1997, 249–60.

Borthwick, E. K.

1988. "Music and Dance." In *Civilization of the Ancient Mediterranean: Greece and Rome,* ed. M. Grant and R. Kitzinger, vol. 3, 1505–14. New York.

Bowersock, G. W., W. Burkert, and M. C. J. Putnam, eds.

1979. *Arktouros: Hellenic Studies Presented to B. M. W. Knox.* Berlin.

Bowie, E. L.

2001. "Ancestors of Historiography in Early Greek Elegiac and Iambic Poetry?" In Luraghi 2001a, 45–66.

Boyce, M.

1979. *Zoroastrians: Their Religious Beliefs and Practices.* London.

1988. "The Religion of Cyrus the Great." In *Achaemenid History,* vol. 3, *Method and Theory: Proceedings of the London 1985 Achaemenid History Workshop,* ed. A. Kuhrt and H. Sancisi-Weerdenburg, 15–31. Leiden.

Briant, P.

2002. *From Cyrus to Alexander: A History of the Persian Empire.* Transl. P. T. Daniels from the French 1996 edition. Winona Lake, Ind.

Brinkmann, V.

1985. "Namenbeschriften an Friesen des Siphnierschatzhauses." *BCH* 109, 77–130.

Brixhe, C.

1979. "Le nom de Cybèle." *Die Sprache* 25, 40–45.

1994. "Le phrygien." In *Langues indo-européennes,* ed. F. Bader, 165–78. Paris.

Brixhe, C., and T. Drew-Bear.

1997. "Huit inscriptions néo-phrygiennes." In Gusmani et al. 1997, 71–114.

Brixhe, C., and M. Lejeune.

1984. *Corpus des inscriptions paléo-phrygiennes*. 2 vols. Paris.

Brosius, M. 1996. *Women in Ancient Persia, 559–331 BC*. Oxford.

1998. "Artemis Persike and Artemis Anaitis." In *Achaemenid History*, vol. 11, *Studies in Persian History: Essays in Memory of David M. Lewis*. ed. M. Brosius and A. Kuhrt, 227–38. Leiden.

Brouwer, H. H. J.

1978. "The Great Mother and the Good Goddess: The History of an Identification." In *Hommages à Maarten J. Vermaseren*, vol. 1, ed. M. B. de Boer and T. A. Edridge, 142–59. Leiden.

Brumfield, A. C.

1981. *The Attic Festivals to Demeter and Their Relation to the Agricultural Year*. Salem, N.H.

Bruneau, P., and J. Ducat.

1966. *Guide de Délos*. 2nd ed. Paris.

Brunnsåker, S.

1971. *The Tyrant-Slayers of Kritios and Nesiotes: A Critical Study of the Sources and Restorations*. Skrifter Utgivna av Svenska Institutet i Athen 17. Stockholm.

Bryce, T.

1983. "The Arrival of the Goddess Leto in Lycia." *Historia* 32, 1–13.

1998. *The Kingdom of the Hittites*. Oxford.

2003. "History." In *The Luwians*, ed. H. C. Melchert, 27–127. Leiden.

Budin, S. L.

2003a *The Origin of Aphrodite*. Bethesda.

2003b. "*Pallakai*, Prostitutes, and Prophetesses." *CP* 98, 148–59.

Bullough, V. L.

2002. "Eunuchs in History and Society." In Tougher 2002a, 1–17.

Bunbury, E. H.

1883. *A History of Ancient Geography*. 2 vols. 2nd ed., with introduction by W. H. Stahl. London. [Reprint: New York, 1959.]

Burke, B.

2002. "Anatolian Origins of the Gordian Knot Legend." *GRBS* 42, 255–61.

Burkert, W.

1975. "Apellai und Apollon." *RhM* 118, 1–21.

1976. "Das hunderttorige Theben und die Datierung der Ilias." *Wiener Studien* 89, 5–21.

1979a. *Structure and History in Greek Mythology and Ritual.* Sather Classical Lectures 47. Berkeley and Los Angeles.

1979b. "Kynaithos, Polycrates, and the Homeric Hymn to Apollo." In Bowersock et al. 1979, 53–62.

1983. *Homo Necans: The Anthropology of Ancient Greek Sacrificial Ritual and Myth.* Transl. P. Bing from the German 1972 edition. Berkeley and Los Angeles.

1985. *Greek Religion.* Transl. J. Raffan from the German 1977 edition. Cambridge, Mass.

1987. "The Making of Homer in the Sixth Century B.C.: Rhapsodes versus Stesichorus." In *Papers on the Amasis Painter and His World,* 43–62. Malibu.

1992. *The Orientalizing Revolution: Near Eastern Influence on Greek Culture in the Early Archaic Age.* Transl. M. E. Pinder and W. Burkert from the German 1984 edition, revised. Cambridge, Mass.

1994. "Olbia and Apollo of Didyma: A New Oracle Text." In *Apollo: Origins and Influences.* ed. J. Solomon, 49–60. Tucson.

1999. "Die Artemis der Epheser: Wirkungsmacht und Gestalt einer großen Göttin." In Friesinger and Krinzinger 1999, 59–70.

Cahn, H. A.

1950. "Die Löwen des Apollon." *MH* 7, 185–99. [Reprinted in *Klein Schriften zur Münzkunde und Archäologie* (Basel, 1975), 17–32.]

Cahn, H. A., and D. Gerin.

1988. "Themistocles at Magnesia." *NC* 148, 13–20.

Calame, C.

1997. *Choruses of Young Women in Ancient Greece: Their Morphology, Religious and Social Functions.* Transl. J. Orion and D. Collins from the French 1977 edition. Lanham, Md.

Camp, J. M.

1986. *The Athenian Agora: Excavations in the Heart of Classical Athens.* London.

Cargill, J.

1977. "The Nabonidus Chronicle and the Fall of Lydia." *American Journal of Ancient History* 2, 97–116.

Carney, E. D.

1987. "The Reappearance of Royal Sibling Marriage in Ptolemaic Egypt." *Parola del Passato* 42, 420–39.

2000. *Women and Monarchy in Macedonia.* Norman, Okla.

Carrington, P.

1977. "A Heroic Age of Phrygia in Ancient Literature and Art." *AnatStud* 27, 117–26.

Cartledge, P.

1987. *Agesilaus and the Crisis of Sparta,* Baltimore.

Caspari, M. O. B.

1910. "On the *ΓΗΣ ΠΕΡΙΟΔΟΣ* of Hecataeus." *JHS* 30, 236–48.

Cassola, F.

1997. "Rapporti tra greci e frigi al tempo di Mida." In Gusmani et al. 1997, 131–52.

Cawkwell, G. L.

1976. "Agesilaus and Sparta." *CQ* 70, 62–84.

Cerri, G.

1983. "La madre degli dei nell'*Elena* di Euripide: Tragedia e rituale." *Quaderni di Storia* 18, 155–95.

Chantraine, P.

1968–80. *Dictionnaire étymologique de la langue grecque: Histoire des mots.* 4 vols. Paris.

Clark, I.

1998. "The Gamos of Hera." In Blundell and Williamson 1998, 13–26.

Clay, J. S.

1986. "Archilochus and Gyges: An Interpretation of Fr. 23 West." *QUCC* 53, 7–17.

1989. *The Politics of Olympus: Form and Meaning in the Major Homeric Hymns.* Princeton.

1994. "Tendenz and Olympian Propaganda in the *Homeric Hymn to Apollo.* In *Apollo: Origins and Influences,* ed. J. Solomon, 23–36. Tucson.

Clinton, K.

1993. "The Sanctuary of Demeter and Kore at Eleusis." In *Greek Sanctuaries: New Approaches,* ed. N. Marinatos and R. Hägg, 110–24. London.

Cohen, M. E.

1988. *The Canonical Lamentations of Ancient Mesopotamia.* 2 vols. Potomac, Md.

Coldstream, J. N.

1977. *Geometric Greece.* New York.

Cole, S. G.

1980. "New Evidence for the Mysteries of Dionysus." *GRBS* 21, 223–38.

1993. "Procession and Celebration at the Dionysia." In *Theater and Society in the Classical World,* ed. R. Scodel, 25–38. Ann Arbor.

1998. "Domesticating Artemis." In Blundell and Williamson 1998, 27–43.

Connor, W. R.

1968. *Theopompus and Fifth-Century Athens,* Cambridge, Mass.

1977. "Tyrannis Polis." In *Ancient and Modern: Essays in Honor of Gerald F. Else,* ed. J. d'Arms and J. Eadie, 95–109. Ann Arbor.

1984. *Thucydides.* Princeton.

1987. "Tribes, Festivals, and Processions: Civic Ceremonial and Political Manipulation in Ancient Greece." *JHS* 107, 40–50. [Reprinted in *Oxford Readings in Greek Religion,* ed. R. Buxton (Oxford, 2000), 56–75.]

Cook, J. M.

1967. "Two Notes on the Homeric Catalogue." *SMEA* 2, 103–9.

Cook, R. M.

1955. "Thucydides as Archaeologist." *ABSA* 50, 266–70.

Cooper, J. S.

1993. "Sacred Marriage and Popular Cult in Early Mesopotamia." In *Official Cult and Popular Religion in the Ancient Near East,* ed. E. Matsushima, 81–96. Heidelberg.

Cornil, P.

1995. "Une étymologie étrusco-hittite." In *Atti del II Congresso Internazionale di Hittitologia,* ed. O. Carruba, M. Giorgieri, and C. Mora, 81–85. Pavia.

Cosi, D. M.

1980–81. "L'ingresso di Cibele ad Atene e a Roma." *Atti del Centro di Ricerche e Documentazione sull'Antichità Classica* 11, 81–91.

Couprie, D. L.

2003. "The Discovery of Space: Anaximander's Astronomy." In Couprie, Hahn, and Naddaf 2003, 165–254.

Couprie, D. L., R. Hahn, and G. Naddaf.

2003. *Anaximander in Context: New Studies in the Origins of Greek Philosophy.* Albany.

Crane, G.

1988. *Calypso: Backgrounds and Conventions of the Odyssey.* Beiträge zur Klassischen Philologie 191. Frankfurt am Main.

Dalley, S.

1979. "The Treaty of Barga'yah and Herodotus' Mylitta." *RdA* 73, 177–78.

1994. "Nineveh, Babylon and the Hanging Gardens: Cuneiform and Classical Sources Reconciled." *Iraq* 56, 45–58.

Davidson, J.

1997. *Courtesans and Fishcakes: The Consuming Passions of Classical Athens.* New York.

Davies, J. K.

1971. *Athenian Propertied Families, 600–300 B.C.* Oxford.

Deller, K.

1999. "The Assyrian Eunuchs and Their Predecessors." In Watanabe 1999, 95–115.

Detienne, M.

1977. *The Gardens of Adonis: Spices in Greek Mythology.* Transl. J. Lloyd from the French 1972 edition. Princeton. [Reprinted with afterword, 1985.]

Deubner, L.

1932. *Attische Feste.* Berlin. [Reprint: Berlin 1966.]

DeVries, K.

　1980. "Greeks and Phrygians in the Early Iron Age." In *From Athens to Gordion: The Papers of a Memorial Symposium for Rodney S. Young,* 33–49. Philadelphia.

　1990. "The Gordion Excavation Seasons of 1969–1973 and Subsequent Research." *AJA* 94, 371–406.

　2002. "The Throne of Midas?" *AJA* 106, 275.

DeVries, K., et al. [P. I. Kuniholm, G. K. Sams, and M. M. Voigt].

　2003. "New Dates for Iron Age Gordion." *Antiquity* 77, June 2003: http://antiquity.ac.uk.

Dewald, C.

　2003. "Form and Content: The Question of Tyranny in Herodotus." In Morgan 2003, 25–58.

Diakonoff, I. M.

　1977. "On Cybele and Attis in Phrygia and Lydia." *Acta Antiqua Academiae Scientiarum Hungaricae* 25, 333–39.

Dicks, D. R.

　1966. "Solstices, Equinoxes, & the Presocratics." *JHS* 86, 26–40.

Diels, H., and W. Kranz, eds.

　1951–54. *Die Fragmente der Vorsokratiker,* 6th ed. 3 vols. Berlin. [Reprint: Zurich, 1996–98.]

Dillon, M. P. J.

　1999. "Post-Nuptial Sacrifices on Kos (Segre, *ED* 178) and Ancient Greek Marriage Rites." *ZPE* 124, 63–80.

Dodds, E. R.

　1940. "Maenadism in the *Bacchae.*" *Harvard Theological Review* 33, 155–76.

Donlan, W.

　1979. "The Structure of Authority in the *Iliad.*" *Arethusa* 12, 51–70.

Dougherty, C., and L. Kurke, eds.

　1993. *Cultural Poetics and Archaic Greece: Cult, Performance, Politics.* Cambridge.

Dover, K. J.

　1976. "The Freedom of the Intellectual in Greek Society." *Talanta* 7, 24–54. [Reprinted in *The Greeks and Their Legacy: Collected Papers,* vol. 2, *Prose Literature, History, Society, Transmission, Influence* (Oxford, 1988), 65–73.]

　1978. *Greek Homosexuality.* Cambridge, Mass.

Drews, R.

　1973. *The Greek Accounts of Eastern History,* Cambridge, Mass.

　1983. *Basileus: The Evidence for Kingship in Geometric Greece.* New Haven.

　1993. "Myths of Midas and the Phrygian Migration from Europe." *Klio* 75, 9–26.

Dupont-Sommer, A., and L. Robert.

1964. *La déesse de Hiérapolis-Castabala (Cilicie)*. Bibliothèque Archéologique et His-torique de l'Institut Français d'Archéologie d'Istanbul, no. 16. Paris.

Dusinberre, E.

2003. *Aspects of Empire in Achaemenid Sardis*. Cambridge.

Edwards, M. J.

1993. "Cybele among the Philosophers: Pherecydes to Plato." *Eranos* 91, 65–74.

Erskine, A.

2001. *Troy between Greece and Rome: Local Tradition and Imperial Power*. Oxford.

Eschbach, N.

1986. *Statuen auf panathenäischen Preisamphoren des 4. Jhs. v.Chr.* Mainz.

Fadinger, V.

1993. "Griechische Tyrannis und alter Orient." In *Anfänge politischen Denkens in der Antike: Die nahöstlichen Kulturen und die Griechen*, ed. K. Raaflaub and E. Müller-Luckner, 263–316. Munich.

Farnell, L.

1896. *Cults of the Greek States*. Vol. 2. Oxford. [Reprint: Chicago, 1971.]

Fauth, W.

1968. "Gyges und die 'Falken.'" *Hermes* 96, 257–64.

1969. "Kybele." In *Der kleine Pauly: Lexikon der Antike*, vol. 3, cols. 383–89. Stuttgart.

1970. "Zum Motivbestand der platonischen Gygeslegende." *RhM* 113, 1–42.

Fehling, D.

1985. *Die sieben Weisen und die frügriechische Chronologie: Eine traditionsgeschichtliche Studie*. Bern.

Ferrari, G.

2002. "The Ancient Temple on the Acropolis at Athens." *AJA* 106, 11–35.

Ferri, S.

1960. "L'inno omerico a Afrodite e la tribù anatolica degli Otrusi." In *Studi in onore di Luigi Castiglioni*, ed. G. C. Sansoni, vol. 1, 293–307. Florence.

Ferrill, A.

1978. "Herodotus on Tyranny." *Historia* 27, 385–98.

Finley, M. I.

1965. "Myth, Memory, and History." *History and Theory* 4, 281–302. [Reprinted in *The Use and Abuse of History* (New York, 1975), 11–33.]

Fleischer, R.

1973. *Artemis von Ephesos und verwandte Kultstatuen aus Anatolien und Syrien*. Leiden.

1983. "Neues zu kleinasiatischen Kultstatuen." *AA* 81–93.

1999. "Neues zum Kultbild der Artemis vom Ephesos." In Friesinger and Krinzinger 1999, 605–9.

Fol, A., and I. Marazov.

1977. *Thrace and the Thracians.* New York.

Fontenrose, J.

1959. *Python: A Study of Delphic Myth and Its Origins.* Berkeley and Los Angeles.

1968. "The Hero as Athlete." *CSCA* 1, 73–104.

1978. *The Delphic Oracle: Its Responses and Operations, with a Catalogue of Responses.* Berkeley and Los Angeles.

Fornara, C. W.

1971. "Evidence for the Date of Herodotus' Publication." *JHS* 91, 25–34.

Forrer, E.

1932. "Assuva." *RLA* 1, 227. Berlin.

Forrest, W. G.

1957. "Colonization and the Rise of Delphi." *Historia* 6, 160–75.

1963. "Inscriptions of SE Chios." *ABSA* 58, 53–67.

Foucart, P.

1873. *Des associations religieuses chez les grecs: Thiases, éranes, orgéons.* Paris. [Reprint: New York, 1975.]

Fowler, R.

2001. "Early *Historiē* and Literacy." In Luraghi 2001a, 95–115.

Francis, E. D.

1990. *Idea and Image in Fifth-Century Greece.* London.

Frankfort, H.

1948. *Kingship and the Gods: A Study of Ancient Near Eastern Religion as the Integration of Society and Nature.* Chicago.

Frappicini, N.

1987. "L'arrivo di Cibele in Attica." *Parola del Passato* 42, 160–72.

Fredericksmeyer, E. A.

1961. "Alexander, Midas, and the Oracle at Gordium." *CP* 56, 160–68.

Frei, P.

1972. "Der Wagen von Gordion." *MH* 29, 110–23.

Friedrich, P.

1978. *The Meaning of Aphrodite.* Chicago.

Friesinger, H., and F. Krinzinger, eds.

1999. *100 Jahre österreichische Forschungen in Ephesos: Akten des Symposions Wien 1995.* Österreichische Akademie der Wissenschaft, Philosophisch-historische Klasse, Denkschriften 260. Vienna.

Frost, F.

2002. "Solon *Pornoboskos* and Aphrodite Pandemos." *Syllecta Classica* 13, 34–46.

Gabriel, A.

1965. *Phrygie, Exploration archéologique*, vol. 4, *La cité de Midas, architecture*. Institut Français d'Archéologie de Stamboul. Paris.

Gagarin, M.

1981. "The Thesmothetai and the Earliest Athenian Tyranny Law." *TAPA* 111, 71–77.

Gardner, P.

1918. *A History of Ancient Coinage, 700–300 B.C.* Oxford.

Garland. R.

1985. *The Greek Way of Death*. Ithaca.

1992. *Introducing New Gods: The Politics of Athenian Religion*. Ithaca.

Garret, A., and L. Kurke.

1994. "Pudenda Asiae Minoris." *HSCP* 96, 75–83.

Garstang, J., and O. R. Gurney.

1959. *The Geography of the Hittite Empire*. British Institute of Archaeology at Ankara, Publication 5. London.

Geertz, C.

1973. "Religion as a Cultural System." In *The Interpretation of Cultures*, 87–125. N.p. [Reprinted from *Anthropological Approaches to the Study of Religion*, ed. M. Benton (London, 1966), 1–46.]

Gehrke, H.-J.

1998. "Die Geburt der Erdkunde aus dem Geiste der Geometrie: Überlegungen zur Entstehung und zur Frühgeschichte der wissenschaftlichen Geographie bei den Griechen." In *Gattungen wissenschaftlicher Literatur in der Antike*, ed. W. Kullman, J. Althoff, and M. Asper, 163–92. Tübingen.

de la Genière, J.

1986. "Le culte de la Mère des dieux dans le Péloponnèse." *CRAI*, 29–48.

Georges, P.

1994. *Barbarian Asia and the Greek Experience: From the Archaic Period to the Age of Xenophon*. Baltimore.

2000. "Persia and Ionia under Darius: The Revolt Reconsidered." *Historia* 49, 1–39.

Georgiev, V. I.

1981. *Introduction to the History of the Indo-European Languages*. Sofia.

1984. "Lydiaka und lydisch-etruskische Gleichungen," *Linguistique Balkanique* 27, 5–35.

Gernet, L.

1968. *Anthropologie de la grèce antique*. Paris.

Gibbs, S. L.

1976. *Greek and Roman Sundials.* New Haven.

Gisinger, F.

1937. "Oikumene." In *RE,* vol. 17, cols. 2123–74. Stuttgart.

Glotz, G.

1925–45. *Histoire ancienne,* part 2, *Histoire grecque.* 4 vols. Paris

Gomme, A. W.

1945. *A Historical Commentary on Thucydides.* Vol. 1. Oxford.

Goodwin, W. R.

2000. "Paradise." In *Eerdmans Dictionary of the Bible,* ed. D. N. Freedman, A. C. My-
ers, and A. B. Beck, 1008–9. Grand Rapids.

Gorman, V. B.

2001. *Miletos, the Ornament of Ionia: A History of the City to 400 B.C.E.* Ann Arbor.

Gould, J.

1989. *Herodotus.* New York.

1994. "Herodotus on Religion." In *Greek Historiography,* ed. S. Hornblower, 91–106.
Oxford.

de Graaf, F.

1989. "Midas wanax lawagetas." In *Thracians and Mycenaeans,* ed. J. G. P. Best and
N. M. W. De Vries, 153–55. Leiden.

Graf, F.

1984. "The Arrival of Cybele in the Greek East." *Proceedings of the VIIth Congress of
the International Federation of the Societies of Classical Studies,* ed. J. Harmatta, vol.
1, 117–20. Budapest.

1985. *Nordionische Kulte: Religionsgeschichtliche und epigraphische Untersuchungen zu
den Kulten von Chios, Erythrai, Klazomenai und Phokaia.* Bibliotheca Helvetica Ro-
mana 21. Budapest.

Graham, A. J.

1983. *Colony and Mother City in Ancient Greece.* 2nd ed. Chicago.

1998. "The Woman at the Window: Observations on the 'Stele from the Harbour'
of Thasos." *JHS* 118, 22–40.

Graillot, H.

1912. *Le culte de Cybèle, mère des dieux, à Rome et dans l'empire romaine.* Paris.

Grayson, A. K.

1974. "The Empire of Sargon of Akkad." *AfO* 25, 56–64.

1975. *Assyrian and Babylonian Chronicles.* Texts from Cuneiform Sources, vol. 5.
Locust Valley, N.Y.

1991. "Assyria: Tiglath Pileser III to Sargon (744–705 B.C.)." In *CAH,* 2nd ed.,
vol. 3, part 2, 71–102.

1995. "Eunuchs in Power: Their Role in the Assyrian Bureaucracy." In *Festschrift für Wolfram Freiherr von Soden,* Alter Orient und Altes Testament 240, ed. M. Dietrich and O. Loretz, 85–98. Neukirchen-Vluyn.

Gribble, D.

1999. *Alcibiades and Athens: A Study in Literary Presentation.* Oxford.

Griffith, M.

1998. "The King and Eye: The Rule of the Father in Greek Tragedy." *PCPS* 44, 20–84.

Griffiths, A.

1987. "Democedes of Croton: A Greek Doctor at the Court of Darius." In *Achaemenid History,* vol. 2, *The Greek Sources: Proceedings of the Groeningen 1984 Achaemenid History Workshop,* ed. H. Sancisi-Weerdenburg and A. Kuhrt, 37–51. Leiden.

Grote, G.

1862. *A History of Greece.* 2nd ed. 8 vols. London.

Grottanelli, C.

1998. "Faithful Bodies: Ancient Greek Sources on Oriental Eunuchs." In *Self, Soul and Body in Religious Experience,* ed. A. L. Baumgarten, J. Assman, and C. G. Strousma, 404–16. Leiden.

Gruen, E. S.

1990. *Studies in Greek Culture and Roman Policy.* Leiden.

Guarducci, M.

1970. "Cibele in un'epigrafe arcaica di Locri Epizefiri." *Klio* 52, 133–38.

Gurney, O. R.

1958. "Hittite Kingship." In Hooke 1958, 105–21.

1962. "Tammuz Reconsidered: Some Recent Developments." *Journal of Semitic Studies* 7, 147–60.

Gürtekin-Demir, R. G.

2002. "Lydian Painted Pottery at Daskyleion." *AnatStud* 52, 111–43.

Gusmani, R. 1964. *Lydisches Wörterbuch.* Heidelberg.

1969a. "Der lydische Name der Kybele." *Kadmos* 8, 158–61.

1969b. "Isoglossi lessicali greco-ittite." In *Studi linguistici in onore di Vitore Pisani,* vol. 1, 501–14. Brescia.

1971. "Le religioni dell'Asia Minore nel primo millennio a.C." In *Storia delle religioni,* vol. 2, 295–341. Turin.

1975. "Lydiaka." *Oriens Antiquus* 14, 265–74.

1976. "Zum Alter des ionischen Wandele ā › o." In *Studies in Greek, Italic, and Indo-European Linguistics Offered to Leonard R. Palmer on the Occasion of His Seventieth Birthday, June 5, 1976,* ed. A. Morpurgo Davies and W. Meid, 77–82. Innsbruck.

1980–86. *Lydisches Wörterbuch: Ergänzungsband.* 3 fascicles. Heidelberg.

1988. "Anthroponymie in den lydischen Inschriften." In *A Linguistic Happening in Memory of Ben Schwartz: Studies in Anatolian, Italic, and other Indo-European Languages,* ed. Y. Arbeitman, 179–96. Louvain-la-Neuve.

Gusmani, R., M. Salvini, and P. Vannicelli, eds.

1997. *Frigi e frigio: Atti del 1° Simposio Internazionale, Roma, 16–17 ottobre 1995.* Rome.

Güterbock, H. G.

1961. "Hittite Mythology." In *Mythologies of the Ancient World,* ed. S. N. Kramer, 139–79. New York.

Guthrie, W. K. C.

1969. *A History of Greek Philosophy.* Vol. 3, part 1. [Reprinted as *The Sophists* (Cambridge, 1971).]

Haas, V.

1994. *Geschichte der hethitischen Religion.* Handbuch der Orientalistik, Erste Abteilung: Der Nahe und Mittlere Osten, 15. Leiden.

Habicht, C.

1961. "Falsche Urkunden zur Geschichte Athens im Zeitalter der Perserkriege." *Hermes* 89, 1–35.

1970. *Gottmenschentum und griechische Städte.* 2nd ed. Zetemata 14. Munich.

1997. *Athens from Alexander to Antony.* Transl. D. L. Schneider from the German 1995 edition. Cambridge, Mass.

Hack, R. K.

1931. *God in Greek Philosophy to the Time of Socrates.* Princeton.

Hadley, J. M.

2000. *The Cult of Asherah in Ancient Israel and Judah: Evidence for a Hebrew Goddess.* Cambridge.

Hahn, R.

2001. *Anaximander and the Architects. The Contributions of Egyptian and Greek Architectural Technologies to the Origins of Greek Philosophy.* Albany.

Hall, E.

1988. "When Did the Trojans Turn into Phrygians? Alcaeus 42.15." *ZPE* 73, 15–18.

1989. *Inventing the Barbarian: Greek Self-Definition through Tragedy.* Oxford.

Halperin, D. M.

1983. *Before Pastoral: Theocritus and the Ancient Tradition of Bucolic Poetry.* New Haven.

Halpern, B.

2003. "Late Israelite Astronomies and the Early Greeks." In *Symbiosis, Symbolism, and the Power of the Past: Canaan, Ancient Israel, and Their Neighbors from the Late Bronze Age through Roman Palaestina,* ed. W. G. Dever and S. Gitin, 323–52. Winona Lake, Ind.

Hamilton, C. D.

1983. "The Generalship of King Agesilaus of Sparta." *The Ancient World* 8, 119–27.

Hammond, N. G. L.

1967. *A History of Greece to 322 B.C.* 2nd ed. Oxford.

1988. "The Expedition of Datis and Artaphernes." In *CAH*, 2nd ed., vol. 4, 491–517.

Hanfmann, G. M. A.

1975. *From Croesus to Constantine: The Cities of Western Asia Minor and Their Arts in Greek and Roman Times.* Ann Arbor.

1980. "On Lydian Sardis." In *From Athens to Gordion: The Papers of a Memorial Symposium for Rodney S. Young,* 99–131. Philadelphia.

1983a. *Sardis from Prehistoric to Roman Times: Results of the Archaeological Exploration of Sardis, 1958–1975.* Cambridge, Mass.

1983b. "On the Gods of Lydian Sardis." In *Beiträge zur Altertumskunde Kleinasiens: Festschrift für Kurt Bittel,* ed. R. M. Boehmer and H. Hauptmann, 219–31. Mainz.

1987. "The Sacrilege Inscription: The Ethnic, Linguistic, Social and Religious Situation at Sardis at the End of the Persian Era." *Bulletin of the Asia Institute* 1, 1–8.

Hanfmann, G. M. A., and N. H. Ramage.

1978. *Sculpture from Sardis: The Finds through 1975.* Archaeological Exploration of Sardis, Report 2. Cambridge, Mass.

Hanfmann, G. M. A., and J. C. Waldbaum.

1969. "Kybele and Artemis: Two Anatolian Goddesses at Sardis." *Archaeology* 22, 264–69.

Harris, R.

1971. "Gipar." *RLA* 3, 377–79.

Harrison, J. E.

1927. *Themis: A Study of the Social Origins of Greek Religion.* 2nd ed. Cambridge. [Reprint: New York, 1962.]

Harrison, T.

2000a. *The Emptiness of Asia: Aeschylus' Persians and the History of the Fifth Century.* London.

2000b. *Divinity and History: The Religion of Herodotus.* Oxford.

Hartog, F.

1988. *The Mirror of Herodotus: The Representation of the Other in the Writing of History.* Transl. J. Lloyd from the French 1980 edition. Berkeley and Los Angeles.

Haspels, C. H. E.

1971. *The Highlands of Phrygia.* 2 vols. Princeton.

Hawkins, J. D.

1976–80. "Karkamiš." *RLA* 5, 426–46.

1980–83. "Kubaba, A.: Philologisch." *RLA* 6, 257–61.

1981. "Kubaba at Karkamiš and Elsewhere." *AnatStud* 31, 147–76.

1982. "The Neo-Hittite States in Syria and Anatolia." In *CAH,* 2nd ed., vol. 3, part 1, 372–441.

1994a. "Mita." *RLA* 8, 271–73.

1994b. "The End of the Bronze Age in Anatolia: New Light from Recent Discoveries." In *Anatolian Iron Ages 3: Proceedings of the Third Anatolian Iron Age Colloquium, Van, 6–12 August 1990,* ed. A. Çilingiroğlu and D. French, 63–71. Ankara.

1998. "Tarkasnawa King of Mira, 'Tarkondemos', Boğazköy Sealings and Karabel." *AnatStud* 48, 1–31.

2000. *Corpus of Hieroglyphic Luwian Inscription,* vol. 1, *Inscriptions of the Iron Age.* 3 parts. Berlin.

Hawkins, J. D., and A. Morpurgo Davies.

1986. "Studies in Hieroglyphic Luwian." In *KANIŠŠUWAR: A Tribute to Hans G. Güterbock on His Seventy-Fifth Birthday, May 27, 1983,* Oriental Institute Assyriological Studies 23, ed. H. A. Hoffner, Jr., and G. M. Beckman, 69–81. Chicago.

Head, B. V.

1911. *Historia Numorum: A Manual of Greek Numismatics.* 2nd ed., with G. F. Hill, G. MacDonald, and W. Wroth. Oxford.

Heidel, W. A.

1921. "Anaximander's Book: The Earliest Known Geographical Treatise." In *Proceedings of the American Academy of Arts and Sciences,* vol. 56, no. 7, 239–88. [Reprinted in *Selected Papers,* ed. L. Tarán (New York, 1980).]

1937. *The Frame of the Ancient Greek Maps.* American Geographical Society, Research Series, no. 20. New York. [Reprint: New York, 1976.]

Henderson, J.

1997. "Mass versus Elite and the Comic Heroism of Peisetairos." In *The City as Comedy: Society and Representation in Athenian Drama,* ed. G. W. Dobrov, 135–48. Chapel Hill.

2003. "Demos, Demagogue, Tyrant in Attic Old Comedy." In Morgan 2003, 155–79.

Henrichs, A.

1976. "Despoina Kybele." *HSCP* 80, 435–503.

1984. "The Sophists and Hellenistic Religion: Prodicus as the Spiritual Father of the Isis Aretalogies." In *Proceedings of the VIIth Congress of the International Federation of the Societies of Classical Studies,* ed. J. Harmatta, vol. 1,339–53. Budapest.

Heubeck, A.

1954. Review of S. Mazzarino, *Fra oriente e occidente: Ricerche di storia greca arcaica* (Florence, 1947). *Historia* 2, 476–85.

1959. *Lydiaka: Untersuchungen zu Schrift, Sprache und Götternamen der Lyder.* Erlanger Forschungen, series A, vol. 9. Erlangen.

1961. *Praegraeca: Sprachliche Untersuchungen zum vorgriechisch-indogermanischen Substrat.* Erlanger Forschungen 12. Erlangen.

1969. "Lydisch." In *Handbuch der Orientalistik* 1, Abteilung 2, Band 1–2, Abschnitt, Lieferung 2, 397–427. Leiden.

Hignett, C.

1963. *Xerxes' Invasion of Greece.* Oxford.

Hitzl, K.

1991. *Die kaiserzeitliche Statuenausstattung des Metroon.* Olympische Forschungen 19. Berlin.

Hodkinson, S.

1999. "An Agonistic Culture?: Athletic Competition in Archaic and Classical Spartan Society." In *Sparta: New Perspectives,* ed. A. Powell and S. Hodkinson, 147–87. London.

2000. *Property and Wealth in Classical Sparta.* London.

Hooke, S. H., ed.

1958. *Myth, Ritual, and Kingship: Essays on the Theory and Practice of Kingship in the Ancient Near East and in Israel.* Oxford.

Horowitz, W.

1988. "The Babylonian Map of the World." *Iraq* 50, 147–65.

1998. *Mesopotamian Cosmic Geography.* Winona Lake, Ind.

Horsley, G. H. R.

1992. "The Mysteries of Artemis Ephesia in Pisidia: A New Inscribed Relief." *AnatStud* 42, 119–50.

How, W. W., and J. Wells.

1912. *A Commentary on Herodotus.* 2 vols. Oxford.

Hunter, R.

2003. *Theocritus: Encomium of Ptolemy Philadelphus.* Berkeley and Los Angeles.

Hurwit, J. M.

1999. *The Athenian Acropolis: History, Mythology, and Archaeology from the Neolithic Era to the Present.* Cambridge.

Hutter, M.

2003. "Aspects of Luwian Religion." In *The Luwians,* ed. H. C. Melchert, 211–80. Leiden.

Huxley, G. L.

1959. "Titles of Midas." *GRBS* 2, 85–99.

Immerwahr, H. R.

1966. *Form and Thought in Herodotus,* American Philological Association Monograph 23. Cleveland. [Reprint: Chapel Hill, 1986.]

Innocente, L.

 1995. "Stato degli studi frigi." In *Atti del II Congresso Internazionale di Hittitologia,*
 ed. O. Carruba, M. Giorgieri, and C. Mora, , 213–24. Pavia.

Isager, S., and J. E. Skydsgaard.

 1992. *Ancient Greek Agriculture: An Introduction.* London.

Jacobsen, T.

 1970. *Toward the Image of Tammuz and Other Essays on Mesopotamian History and Cul-*
 *ture.* Ed. W. L. Moran. Cambridge, Mass.

 1976. *The Treasures of Darkness: A History of Mesopotamian Religion.* New Haven.

Jacoby, F.

 1912. "Hekataios (3)." In *RE,* vol. 7, cols. 2667–2769. Stuttgart. [Reprinted in
 *Griechische Historiker* (Stuttgart, 1956), 186–237.]

 1913. "Herodotos." In *RE,* Supplement 2, cols. 205–520. Stuttgart. [Reprinted in
 *Griechische Historiker* (Stuttgart, 1956), 7–164.]

 1947. "The First Athenian Prose Writer." *Mnemosyne* 13, 13–64.

 1949. *Atthis: The Local Chronicles of Ancient Athens.* Oxford.

 1959. *Diagoras 'O Ἄθεος.* Abhandlungen der Deutschen Akademie der Wissenschaften zu Berlin, Klasse für Sprachen, Literatur und Kunst, no. 3. Berlin.

Jameson, M. H.

 1960. "A Decree of Themistokles from Troizen." *Hesperia* 29, 198–223.

 1963. "Provisions for Mobilization in the Decree of Themistokles." *Historia* 12,
 395–404.

Jameson, M. H., et al. [D. R. Jordan, and R. D. Kotansky].

 1993. *A Lex Sacra from Selinous.* Greek, Roman and Byzantine Monographs 11.
 Durham, N.C.

Janko, R.

 1982. *Homer, Hesiod and the Hymns: Diachronic Development in Epic Diction.* Cambridge.

Jasink, A. M.

 1998. "*TARWANI-:* A Title for Neo-Hittite Rulers." In *Acts of the IIIrd International*
 *Congress of Hittitology,* ed. S. Alp and A. Süel, 341–56. Ankara.

Jeffery, L. H.

 1976. *Archaic Greece: The City-States c. 700–500 B.C.* New York.

Johnston, S. I.

 1990. *Hekate Soteira: A Study of Hekate's Roles in the Chaldean Oracles and Related Lit-*
 *erature.* Atlanta.

Jones, A. H. M.

 1940. *The Greek City from Alexander to Justinian.* Oxford.

Jonker, G.

1995. *The Topography of Remembrance: The Dead, Tradition and Collective Memory in Mesopotamia.* Studies in the History of Religion 68. Leiden.

Kahn, C. H.

1960. *Anaximander and the Origins of Greek Cosmology.* New York.

Kallet, L.

2001. *Money and the Corrosion of Power in Thucydides: The Sicilian Expedition and Its Aftermath.* Berkeley and Los Angeles.

2003. *"Demos Tyrannos:* Wealth, Power, and Economic Patronage." In Morgan 2003, 117–53.

Kaplan, P.

2002. "The Social Status of the Mercenary in Archaic Greece." In *OIKISTES: Studies in Constitutions, Colonies, and Military Power in the Ancient World Offered in Honor of A. J. Graham,* ed. V. B. Gorman and E. W. Robinson, 229–43. Leiden.

2005. "Dedications to Greek Sanctuaries by Foreign Kings in the Eighth through Sixth Centuries B.C.E." *Historia* 54, 1–24.

Karageorghis, J.

1977. *La grande déesse de Chypre et son culte, à travers l'iconographie de l'époque néolithique au VIème s. a.C.* Maison de l'Orient Méditerranéen, no. 5. Lyon.

Karageorghis, V.

2000. *Ancient Art from Cyprus: The Cesnola Collection in the Metropolitan Museum of Art.* With J. R. Mertens and M. E. Rose. New York.

Kearns, E.

1989. *The Heroes of Attica.* BICS Supplement 57. London.

Keel, O., and C. Uehlinger.

1998. *Gods, Goddesses, and Images of God in Ancient Israel.* Transl. T. H. Trapp from the German 1992 edition. Minneapolis.

Keen, A. G.

1998. *Dynastic Lycia: A Political History of the Lycians and Their Relations with Foreign Powers c. 545–362 B.C.* Leiden.

Kelly, D. H.

1978. "Agesilaus' Strategy in Asia Minor, 396–395 B.C." *LCM* 3, 97–98.

Kent, R. G.

1950. *Old Persian: Grammar, Texts, Lexicon.* New Haven.

Kienitz, F. K.

1953. *Die politische Geschichte Ägyptens vom 7. bis zum 4. Jahrhundert vor der Zeitwende.* Berlin.

Kilian, K.

1988. "The Emergence of *Wanax* Ideology in the Mycenaean Palaces." *OJA* 7, 291–302.

Kirk, G. S., et al. [J. E. Raven, and M. Schofield].

  1983. *The Presocratic Philosophers: A Critical History with a Selection of Texts.* 2nd ed. Cambridge.

Knell, H.

  2000. *Athen im 4. Jahrhundert v. Chr. —Eine Stadt verändert ihr Gesicht: Archäologisch-kulturgeschichtliche Betrachtungen.* Darmstadt.

Knibbe, D.

  1995. "Via Sacra Ephesiaca: New Aspects of the Cult of Artemis Ephesia." In *Ephesos, Metropolis of Asia: An Interdisciplinary Approach to Its Archaeology, Religion, and Culture,* ed. H. Koester, 141–55. Valley Forge.

Kohler, E. L.

  1980. "Cremations of the Middle Phrygian Period at Gordion." In *From Athens to Gordion: The Papers of a Memorial Symposium for Rodney S. Young,* ed. K. DeVries, 65–89. Philadelphia.

  1995. *The Gordion Excavations (1950–1973): Final Reports,* vol. 2, *The Lesser Phrygian Tumuli,* part 1, *The Inhumations.* Philadelphia.

Konstan, D.

  1987. "Persians, Greeks, and Empire." *Arethusa* 20, 59–73.

Korres, M.

  1992. *Vom Penteli zum Parthenon: Werdgang eines Kapitells zwischen Steinbruch und Tempel.* Munich. [English edition: Athens, 1995.]

  1997. "Die Athena-Tempel auf der Akropolis." In *Kult und Kultbauten auf der Akropolis: Internationales Symposion vom 7. bis 9. Juli 1995 in Berlin,* ed. W. Hoepfner, 218–43. Berlin.

Körte, G., and A. Körte.

  1904. *Gordion: Ergebnisse der Ausgrabung im Jahre 1900.* Jahrbuch des Kaiserlich Deutschen Archäologischen Instituts, Supplement 5. Berlin.

Kraay, C. M.

  1976. *Archaic and Classical Greek Coins.* Berkeley and Los Angeles.

Kraft, J. C., et al. [I. Kayan, and H. Brückner].

  2001. "The Geological and Paleogeographical Environs of the Artemision." In Muss 2001, 123–33.

Kramer, S. N.

  1969. *The Sacred Marriage Rite: Aspects of Faith, Myth, and Ritual in Ancient Sumer.* Bloomington.

  1991. "The Death of Ur-Nammu." In *Near Eastern Studies Dedicated to H. I. H. Prince Takahito Mikasa on the Occasion of His Seventy-Fifth Birthday.* Bulletin of the Middle Eastern Culture Center in Japan, vol. 5, ed. M. Mori, H. Ogawa, and M. Yoshikawa, 194–214. Wiesbaden.

Kraus, T.

1960. *Hekate: Studien zu Wesen und Bild der Göttin in Kleinasien und Griechenland.* Heidelberger Kunstgeschichtliche Abhandlungen 5. Heidelberg.

Kuhrt, A.

1988. "Earth and Water." In *Achaemenid History,* vol. 3, *Method and Theory: Proceedings of the London 1985 Achaemenid History Workshop,* ed. A. Kuhrt and H. Sancisi-Weerdenburg, 87–99. Leiden.

Kuhrt, A., and S. Sherwin-White.

1987. "Xerxes' Destruction of Babylonian Temples." In *Achaemenid History,* vol. 2, *The Greek Sources: Proceedings of the Groeningen 1984 Achaemenid History Workshop,* ed. H. Sancisi-Weerdenburg and A. Kuhrt, 69–78. Leiden.

Kurke, L.

1991. *The Traffic in Praise: Pindar and the Poetics of Social Economy.* Ithaca.

1993. "The Economy of Kudos." In Dougherty and Kurke 1993, 131–63.

1999. *Coins, Bodies, Games, and Gold: The Politics of Meaning in Archaic Greece.* Princeton.

Kyrieleis, H.

1993. "The Heraion at Samos." In *Greek Sanctuaries: New Approaches,* ed. N. Marinatos and R. Hägg, 125–53. London.

Labarbe, J.

1971. "L'apparition de la notion de tyrannie dans la Grèce archaïque." *AC* 40, 471–504.

Laidlaw, W. A.

1933. *A History of Delos.* Oxford.

Laminger-Pascher, G.

1989. *Lykaonien und der Phryger.* Sitzungsberichte der Österreichischen Akademie der Wissenschaften 532. Vienna.

Lancellotti, M. G.

2002. *Attis—Between Myth and History: King, Priest and God.* Religions in the Graeco-Roman World 149. Leiden.

Lane, E., ed.

1996a. *Cybele, Attis, and Related Cults: Essays in Memory of M. J. Vermaseren.* Religions in the Graeco-Roman World 131. Leiden.

1996b. "The Name of Cybele's Priests the 'Galloi.'" In Lane 1996a, 117–33.

Lapinkivi, P.

2003. *The Sumerian Sacred Marriage in the Light of Comparative Evidence.* State Archives of Assyria Studies 15. Helsinki.

Laroche, E.

1960. "Koubaba, déesse anatolienne, et la problème des origines de Cybèle." In

*Eléments orienteaux dans la religion grecque ancienne,* Travaux du Centre d'Etudes Supériores Specialisé d'Histoire des Religions, Strasbourg, 113–28. Paris.

Lateiner, D.

1989. *The Historical Method of Herodotus.* Phoenix Supplement 23. Toronto.

Laumonier, A.

1958. *Les cultes indigènes en Carie.* Bibliothèque des Ecoles Françaises d'Athènes et de Rome 188. Paris.

Leicke, G.

1994. *Sex and Eroticism in Mesopotamian Literature.* London.

Lejeune, M.

1969. "A propos de la titulature de Midas." *Athenaeum* 47, 179–92.

Lesky, A.

1966. *A History of Greek Literature.* Transl. J. Willis and C. de Heer from the German 2nd edition, 1963. New York.

Lévy, E.

1984. "Naissance du concept de barbare." *Ktema* 9, 5–14.

Lewis, D. M.

1977. *Sparta and Persia: Lectures Delivered at the University of Cincinnati, Autumn 1977, in Memory of Donald W. Bradeen.* Leiden.

1985. "Persians in Herodotus." In *The Greek Historians, Literature and History: Papers Presented to A. E. Raubitschek,* ed. M. H. Jameson, 101–17. Saratoga, Calif.

LiDonnici, L. R.

1992. "The Images of Artemis Ephesia and Greco-Roman Worship: A Reconsideration." *HTR* 85, 389–416.

Lightfoot, J. L.

2002. "Sacred Eunuchism in the Cult of the Syrian Goddess." In Tougher 2002a, 71–86.

Linforth, I. M.

1924. "Herodotus' Avowal of Silence in His Account of Egypt." *University of California Publications in Classical Philology* 7, 269–92. [Reprinted in Tarán 1987, 21–44.]

1926. "Greek Gods and Foreign Gods in Herodotus." *University of California Publications in Classical Philology* 9, 1–25. [Reprinted in Tarán 1987, 47–71.]

1928. "Named and Unnamed Gods in Herodotus." *University of California Publications in Classical Philology* 9, 201–43. [Reprinted in Tarán 1987, 77–119.]

Llewellyn-Jones, L.

2002. "Eunuchs and the Royal Harem in Achaemenid Persia (559–331 B.C.)." In Tougher 2002a, 19–49.

Lloyd, A. B.

1982. "Nationalist Propaganda in Ptolemaic Egypt." *Historia* 31, 33–55.

Lloyd-Jones, H.

1971. *The Justice of Zeus.* Berkeley and Los Angeles.

Loraux, N.

1986. *The Invention of Athens: The Funeral Oration in the Classical City.* Transl. A. Sheridan from the French 1981 edition. Cambridge, Mass.

1993. *The Children of Athena: Athenian Ideas about Citizenship and the Division between the Sexes.* Transl. C. Levine from the French 2nd edition, 1990. Princeton.

1998. *Mothers in Mourning.* Transl. C. Pache from the French 1990 edition. Ithaca.

2000. *Born of the Earth: Myth and Politics in Athens.* Transl. S. Stewart from the French 1996 edition. Ithaca.

Lubotsky, A.

1997. "New Phrygian Inscription No. 48: Paleographic and Linguistic Comments." In Gusmani et al. 1997, 115–30.

Luraghi, N., ed.

2001a. *The Historian's Craft in the Age of Herodotus.* Oxford.

2001b. "Local Knowledge in Herodotus' *Histories.*" In Luraghi 2001a, 138–60.

MacDowell, D. M.

1978. *The Law in Classical Athens.* London.

Malandra, W. M.

1983. *An Introduction to Ancient Iranian Religion: Readings from the Avesta and Achaemenid Inscriptions.* Minneapolis.

Malkin, I.

1987. *Religion and Colonization in Ancient Greece.* Leiden.

1989. "Delphoi and the Founding of Social Order in Archaic Greece." *Metis* 4, 129–53.

2002. "Exploring the Validity of the Concept of 'Foundation': A Visit to Megara Hyblaia." In *OIKISTES: Studies in Constitutions, Colonies, and Military Power in the Ancient World Offered in Honor of A. J. Graham,* ed. V. B. Gorman and E. W. Robinson, 194–225. Leiden.

Mallwitz, A.

1972. *Olympia und seine Bauten.* Darmstadt.

Mallwitz, A., and H.-V. Herrmann.

1980. *Die Funde aus Olympia: Ergebnisse hundertjähriger Ausgrabungstätigkeit.* Athens.

Marinatos, N.

1993. *Minoan Religion: Ritual, Image, and Symbol.* Columbia, S.C.

2000. *The Goddess and the Warrior: The Naked Goddess and the Mistress of Animals in Early Greek Religion.* London.

Martin, R. P.

1993. "The Seven Sages as Performers of Wisdom." In Dougherty and Kurke 1993, 108–28.

Martin, V.

1963. "Quelques remarques à l'occasion d'une nouvelle édition des *Staatsverträge des Altertums.*" *MH* 20, 230–33.

Masson, O.

1987. "Le sceau paléo-phrygien de *Mane.*" *Kadmos* 26, 109–12.

Matsushima, E.

1987. "Le rituel hiérogamique de Nabū." *Acta Sumerologica* 9, 131–75.

McGlew, J. F.

1993. *Tyranny and Political Culture in Ancient Greece.* Ithaca.

McGregor, M. F.

1940. "The Pro-Persian Party at Athens from 510 to 480 B.C." In *Athenian Studies Presented to W. S. Ferguson,* HSCP Supplement 1, 71–95. Cambridge, Mass.

McLaughlin, B. K.

1985. "Lydian Graves and Burial Customs." PhD diss., University of California, Berkeley.

Meiggs, R.

1972. *The Athenian Empire.* Oxford.

Meiggs, R., and D. M. Lewis, eds.

1969. *A Selection of Greek Historical Inscriptions to the End of the Fifth Century B.C.* Oxford.

Meissner, B.

1925. "Babylonische und griechische Landkarten." *Klio* 19, 97–100.

Melchert, H. C.

1994. "Anatolian." In *Langues indo-européennes,* ed. F. Bader, 121–36. Paris.

ed. 2003. *The Luwians.* Leiden.

Mellink, M. J.

1983. "Comments on a Cult Relief of Kybele from Gordion." In *Beiträge zur Altertumskunde Kleinasiens: Festschrift für Kurt Bittel,* ed. R. M. Boehmer and H. Hauptmann, 349–60. Mainz.

1991. "The Native Kingdoms of Anatolia." In *CAH,* 2nd ed., vol. 3, part 2, 619–65.

1993. "Midas-Stadt." *RLA* 8, 153–56.

Meriggi, P.

1953. "Schizzo della delineazione nominale dell'eteo geroglifico (Continuazione e fine)." *Archivio Glottologico Italiano* 38, 36–57.

Meritt, B. D.

1939. "Greek Inscriptions." *Hesperia* 8, 48–90.

Metcalf, P., and R. Huntington.

1991. *Celebrations of Death: The Anthropology of Mortuary Ritual.* 2nd ed. Cambridge.

Metzger, H., ed.

  1979. *Fouilles de Xanthos,* vol. 6, *La stèle trilingue du Létôon.* Paris.

Mikalson, J. D.

  2003. *Herodotus and Religion in the Persian Wars.* Chapel Hill.

Miles, M. M.

  1989. "A Reconstruction of the Temple of Nemesis at Rhamnous." *Hesperia* 58, 131–249.

  1998. *The Athenian Agora,* vol. 31, *The City Eleusinion.* Princeton.

Miller, A. M.

  1985. *From Delos to Delphi: A Literary Study of the Homeric Hymn to Apollo.* Mnemosyne Supplement 93. Leiden.

Miller, M. C.

  1988. "Midas as the Great King in Attic Fifth-Century Vase Painting." *AntK* 31, 79–89.

  1992. "The Parasol: An Oriental Status-Symbol in Late Archaic and Classical Athens." *JHS* 112, 91–105.

  1995. "Priam, King of Troy." In *The Ages of Homer: A Tribute to Emily Townsend Vermeule,* ed. J. B. Carter and S. P. Morris, 449–65. Austin.

  1997. *Athens and Persia in the Fifth Century BC: A Study in Cultural Receptivity.* Cambridge.

Miller, S. G.

  1995. "Old Metroon and Old Bouleuterion in the Classical Agora of Athens." In *Studies in the Ancient Greek Polis,* Historia Einzelschrift 95, ed. M. H. Hansen and K. Raaflaub, 133–56. Stuttgart.

Mitropoulou, E.

  1996. "The Goddess Cybele in Funerary Banquets and with an Equestrian Hero." In Lane 1996, 135–65.

Moles, J.

  1996. "Herodotus Warns the Athenians." *Papers of the Leeds International Latin Seminar* 9, 259–84.

Mondi, R.

  1990. "Greek and Near Eastern Mythology: Greek Mythic Thought in the Light of the Near East." In *Approaches to Greek Myth,* ed. L. Edmonds, 141–98. Baltimore.

Moore, M. B.

  1977. "The Gigantomachy of the Siphnian Treasury: Reconstruction of the Three Lacunae." In *Etudes delphiques,* BCH Supplement 4, 305–35. Paris.

  1995. "The Central Group in the Gigantomachy of the Old Athena Temple on the Acropolis." *AJA* 99, 633–39.

Morgan, K. A., ed.

  2003. *Popular Tyranny: Sovereignty and Its Discontents in Ancient Greece.* Austin.

Morris, I.

1992. *Death-Ritual and Social Structure in Classical Antiquity.* Cambridge.

1993. "Poetics of Power: The Interpretation of Ritual Action in Archaic Greece." In Dougherty and Kurke 1993, 15–45.

Morris, S. P.

2001a. "The Prehistoric Background of Artemis Ephesia: A Solution to the Enigma of her 'Breasts.'" In Muss 2001, 135–51.

2001b. "Potnia Aswiya: Anatolian Contributions to Greek Religion." In *Potnia— Deities and Religion in the Aegean Bronze Age: Proceedings of the 8th International Aegean Conference, Göteborg, Göteborg University, 12–15 April 2000,* ed. R. Laffineur and R. Hägg, 423–34. Liège.

2003. "Imaginary Kings: Alternatives to Monarchy in Early Greece." In Morgan 2003, 1–24.

Mortley, R.

1996. *The Idea of Universal History from Hellinistic* [sic] *Philosophy to Early Christian Historiography.* Lewiston, N.Y.

Mosshammer, A.

1976. "The Epoch of the Seven Sages." *CSCA* 9, 165–80.

1979. *The Chronicle of Eusebius and the Greek Chronographic Tradition.* Lewisberg.

Munn, M.

1993. *The Defense of Attica: The Dema Wall and the Boiotian War of 378–375 B.C.* Berkeley and Los Angeles.

2000. *The School of History: Athens in the Age of Socrates.* Berkeley and Los Angeles.

Murray, O.

1966. "Ο "ΑΡΧΑΙΟΣ ΔΑΣΜΟΣ." *Historia* 15, 142–56.

1987. "Herodotus and Oral History." In *Achaemenid History,* vol. 2, *The Greek Sources: Proceedings of the Groeningen 1984 Achaemenid History Workshop,* ed. H. Sancisi-Weerdenburg and A. Kuhrt, 93–115. Leiden. [Reprinted in Luraghi 2001a, 16–44.]

1988. "The Ionian Revolt." In *CAH,* 2nd ed., vol. 4, 461–90. Cambridge.

1990. "The Affair of the Mysteries: Democracy and the Drinking Group." In *Sympotica: A Symposium on the Symposion,* ed. O. Murray, 149–61. Oxford.

Muscarella, O. W.

1971. "Phrygian or Lydian?" *JNES* 30, 49–63.

1989. "King Midas of Phrygia and the Greeks." In *Anatolia and the Ancient Near East: Studies in Honor of Tahsin Özgüç,* ed. K. Emre, B. Hrouda, M. Mellink, and N. Özgüç, 333–44. Ankara.

1995. "The Iron Age Background to the Formation of the Phrygian State." *BASOR* 299/300, 91–101.

Muss, U., ed.

   2001. *Der Kosmos der Artemis von Ephesos.* Österreichisches Archäologisches Institut, Sonderschriften, Band 37. Vienna.

Mylonas, G. E.

   1961. *Eleusis and the Eleusinian Mysteries.* Princeton.

Naddaf, G.

   2003. "Anthropogony and Politogony in Anaximander of Miletus." In Couprie et al. 2003, 8–69.

Naumann, F.

   1983. *Die Ikonographie der Kybele in der phrygischen und der griechischen Kunst.* IstMitt Supplement 28. Tübingen.

Neer, R. T.

   2001. "Framing the Gift: The Politics of the Siphnian Treasury at Delphi." *CA* 20, 273–336.

Neugebauer, O.

   1951. *The Exact Sciences in Antiquity.* Acta Historica Scientiarum Naturalium et Medicinalium, University of Copenhagen, vol. 9. Copenhagen.

Neumann, G.

   1988. *Phrygisch und griechisch.* Österreichische Akademie der Wissenschaften, Philosophisch-historische Klasse, Sitzungsberichte, vol. 499. Vienna.

   1999. "Wie haben die Troer im 13. Jahrhundert gesprochen?" *Würzburger Jahrbücher für die Altertumsgeschichte* 23, 15–23.

Nilsson, M. P.

   1906. *Griechische Feste von religiöser Bedeutung.* Leipzig. [Reprint: 1995.]

   1940. *Greek Folk Religion.* New York. [Originally published under the title *Greek Popular Religion* ( Philadelphia, 1961).]

   1955. *Geschichte der griechische Religion.* Vol. 1. 2nd ed. Munich.

Nissinen, M.

   2001. "Akkadian Rituals and Poetry of Divine Love." In *Mythology and Mythologies: Methodological Approaches to Intercultural Influences,* Melammu Symposia 2, ed. R. M. Whiting, 93–136. Helsinki.

Nock, A. D.

   1925. "Eunuchs in Ancient Religion." *Archiv für Religionswissenschaft* 23, 25–33. [Reprinted in Nock 1972, vol. 1, 7–15.]

   1928. "Notes on Ruler-Cult I–IV." *JHS* 48, 21–43. [Reprinted in Nock 1972, vol. 1, 134–59.]

   1957. "Deification and Julian." *JRS* 47, 115–23. [Reprinted in Nock 1972, vol. 2, 833–46.]

   1972. *Essays on Religion and the Ancient World.* Ed. Z. Stewart. 2 vols. Cambridge, Mass.

Noe, S. P.

1950. "Beginnings of the Cistophoric Coinage." *Museum Notes* 4, 29–41.

Nollé, M.

1992. *Denkmäler vom Satrapensitz Daskyleion: Studies zur graeco-persischen Kunst.* Berlin.

Oakley, J. H., and R. H. Sinos.

1993. *The Wedding in Ancient Athens.* Madison.

Ober, J.

1998. *Political Dissent in Democratic Athens: Intellectual Critics of Popular Rule.* Princeton.

Oettinger, N.

1977. "Die Gliederung des anatolischen Sprachgebietes." *Zeitschrift für Vergleichende Sprachforschung* 91, 74–92.

Ogden, D.

2001. *Greek and Roman Necromancy.* Princeton.

Oliver, J. H.

1960. *Demokratia, the Gods, and the Free World.* Baltimore.

Olmstead, A. T.

1948. *History of the Persian Empire.* Chicago.

Oppenheim, A. L.

1964. *Ancient Mesopotamia: Portrait of a Dead Civilization.* Chicago.

1965. "On Royal Gardens in Mesopotamia." *JNES* 24, 328–33.

Orthmann, W.

1971. *Untersuchungen zur späthethitischen Kunst.* Saarbrücker Beiträge zur Altertumskunde 8. Bonn.

Osborne, R.

1996. *Greece in the Making, 1200–479 BC.* London.

Ostwald, M.

1955. "The Athenian Legislation against Tyranny and Subversion." *TAPA* 86, 103–28.

1969. *Nomos and the Beginnings of Athenian Democracy.* Oxford.

1982. *Autonomia: Its Genesis and Early History.* American Philological Association, Classical Studies no. 11. Atlanta.

1986. *From Popular Sovereignty to the Sovereignty of Law: Law, Society, and Politics in Fifth-Century Athens.* Berkeley and Los Angeles.

1988. "The Reforms of the Athenian state by Cleisthenes." In *CAH,* 2nd ed., vol. 4., 303–46. Cambridge.

1991. "Herodotus and Athens." *ICS* 16, 137–48.

Özkaya, V.

   1997. "The Shaft Monuments and the *Taurobolium* among the Phrygians." *Anat-Stud* 47, 89–103.

Pachis, P.

   1996. "'Γαλλαῖον Κυβέλης ὀλόλυγμα' (*Anthol. Palat.* VI, 173): L'élément orgiastique dans le culte de Cybèle." In Lane 1996a, 193–222.

Page, D. L., ed.

   1962. *Poetae Melici Graeci.* Oxford.

Palagia, O., ed.

   2005. *Greek Sculpture: Function, Materials and Techniques in the Archaic and Classical Periods.* Cambridge.

Parke, H. W.

   1946. "Polykrates and Delos." *CQ* 40, 105–8.

   1977. *Festivals of the Athenians.* London.

Parke, H. W., and D. E. W. Wormell.

   1956. *The Delphic Oracle.* 2 vols. Oxford.

Parker, R.

   1995. "Early Orphism." In *The Greek World,* ed. A. Powell, 483–510. London.

   1996. *Athenian Religion: A History.* Oxford.

Parker, V.

   1998. "Τύραννος: The Semantics of a Political Concept from Archilochus to Aristotle." *Hermes* 126, 145–72.

Patai, R.

   1990. *The Hebrew Goddess.* 3rd ed. Detroit.

Pearson, L.

   1939. *Early Ionian Historians.* Oxford.

   1960. *The Lost Historians of Alexander the Great.* American Philological Association, Philological Monograph 20. New York.

Pedley, J. G.

   1968. *Sardis in the Age of Croesus.* Norman, Okla.

Penglase, C.

   1994. *Greek Myths and Mesopotamia: Parallels and Influence in the Homeric Hymns and Hesiod.* London.

Petrakos, B.

   1987. "Τὸ Νεμίσιον τοῦ Ῥαμνοῦντος." In *ΦΙΛΙΑ ΕΠΗ εἰς Γεώργιον Ε. Μυλονάν,* vol. 2, 295–326. Athens.

Pfohl, G.

   1967. *Greek Poems on Stones,* vol. 1, *Epitaphs: From the Seventh to the Fifth Centuries B.C.* Textus Minores 36. Leiden.

Pfuhl, E., and H. Möbius.

1977. *Die ostgriechischen Grabreliefs.* 4 vols. Mainz.

Picard, C.

1922. *Ephèse et Claros: Recherches sur les sanctuaires et les cultes de l'Ionie du nord.* Bibliothèque des Ecoles Françaises d'Athènes et de Rome no. 123. Paris.

Pinney, G. F.

1988. "Pallas and Panathenaea." In *Proceedings of the 3rd Symposium on Ancient Greek and Related Pottery, Copenhagen, August 31–September 4 1987,* ed. J. Christiansen and T. Melander, 465–77. Copenhagen.

Pintore, F.

1983. "Seren, tarwanis, týrannos." In *Studi orientalistici in ricordo di F. Pintore,* ed. O. Carruba, M. Liverani, and C. Zaccagnini, 285–322. Pavia.

Poljakov, F. B.

1989. *Die Inschriften von Tralles und Nysa,* part 1, *Die Inschriften von Tralles.* Inschriften Griechischer Städte aus Kleinasien 36.1, Österreichische Akademie der Wissenschaften, Rheinisch-Westfälische Akademie der Wissenschaft. Bonn.

Pongratz-Leisten, B.

2001. "The Other and the Enemy in the Mesopotamian Conception of the World." In *Mythology and Mythologies: Methodological Approaches to Intercultural Influences.* Melammu Symposia 2, ed. R. M. Whiting, 195–231. Helsinki.

Portefaix, L.

1999. "The Image of Artemis Ephesia: A Symbolic Configuration Related to Her Mysteries?" In Friesinger and Krinzinger 1999, 611–17.

Prag, A. J. N. W.

1989. "Reconstructing King Midas: A First Report." *AnatStud* 39, 159–65.

Prandi, L.

1985. *Callistene: Uno storico tra Aristotele e i re Macedoni.* Milan.

Price, S. R. F.

1984. *Rituals and Power: Roman Imperial Cult in Asia Minor.* Cambridge.

Price, T. H.

1971. "Double and Multiple Representations in Greek Art and Religious Thought." *JHS* 91, 48–69.

1978. *Kourotrophos: Cults and Representations of the Greek Nursing Deities.* Studies of the Dutch Archaeological and Historical Society 8. Leiden.

Raaflaub, K. A.

1979. "Polis Tyrannos: Zur Enstehung einer politischen Metapher." In Bowersock et al. 1979, 238–52.

1985. *Die Entdeckung der Freiheit: Zur historischen Semantik und Gesellschaftsgeschichte eines politischen Grundbegriffes der Griechen.* Vestigia 37. Munich. [Revised English edition, *The Discovery of Freedom in Ancient Greece,* transl. R. Franciscono (Chicago, 2004).]

1987. "Herodotus' Political Thought and the Meaning of History." *Arethusa* 20, 241–48.

2003. "Stick and Glue: The Function of Tyranny in Fifth-Century Athenian Democracy." In Morgan 2003, 59–93.

Radner, K.

2001. "Kompositstatuen vom Typus der Ephesia aus dem vorkroisoszeitlichen Heiligtum: Zur Herstellung und Pflege von Götterstatuen im östlichen Mittelmeerraum und im vorderen Orient im frühen ersten Jahrtausend." In Muss 2001, 233–63.

Ramage, A., and P. Craddock.

2000. *King Croesus' Gold: Excavations at Sardis and the History of Gold Refining.* Archaeological Exploration of Sardis, Monograph 11. Cambridge, Mass.

Ramsay, W. M.

1890. *The Historical Geography of Asia Minor.* Royal Geographical Society, Supplementary Papers, vol. 4. London. [Reprint: Amsterdam, 1962.]

Ratté, C.

1989. "Five Lydian Felines." *AJA* 93, 379–93.

1995. "Not the Tomb of Gyges." *JHS* 114, 157–61.

Raubitschek, A. E.

1941. "Two Notes on Isocrates." *TAPA* 72, 356–64.

1957. "Das Datislied." In *Charites E. Langlotz: Studien zur Altertumswissenschaft,* ed. K. Schauenburg, 234–42. Bonn. [Reprinted in Raubitschek 1991, 146–55.]

1958. "Theophrastos on Ostracism." *Classica et Mediaevelia* 19, 73–109. [Reprinted in Raubitschek 1991, 81–107.]

1964. "The Treaties between Persia and Athens." *GRBS* 5, 151–59. [Reprinted in Raubitschek 1991, 3–10.]

1969. "Das Denkmal-Epigram." In *L'epigramme grecque,* Fondation Hardt, Entretiens sur l'Antiquité Classique, vol. 14, 3–36. Geneva. [Reprinted in Raubitschek 1991, 245–65.]

1991. *The School of Hellas: Essays on Greek History, Archaeology, and Literature.* Ed. D. Obbink and P. A. Vander Waerdt. Oxford.

Raubitschek, A. E., and I. Raubitschek.

1982. "The Mission of Triptolemus." In *Studies in Athenian Architecture, Sculpture and Topography Presented to Homer A. Thompson,* Hesperia Supplement 20, 109–17. [Reprinted in Raubitschek 1991, 229–38.]

Redford, D. B.

1992. *Egypt, Canaan, and Israel in Ancient Times.* Princeton.

Rehak, P., ed.

1995. *The Role of the Ruler in the Prehistoric Aegean: Proceedings of a Panel Discussion Presented at the Annual Meeting of the Archaeological Institute of America, New Orleans, Louisiana, 28 December 1992.* Aegaeum 11. Austin.

Rein, M. J.

1993. "The Cult and Iconography of Lydian Kybele." PhD diss., Harvard University.

1996. "Phrygian Matar: Emergence of an Iconographic Type." In Lane 1996, 223–37.

Reiner, E.

1961. "The Etiological Myth of the 'Seven Sages.'" *Orientalia,* n.s., 30, 1–11.

Renger, J.

1975. "Heilige Hochzeit, A.: Philologisch." *RLA* 3, 251–59.

Rhodes, P. J.

1972. *The Athenian Boule.* Oxford.

1981. *A Commentary on the Aristotelian "Athenaion Politeia."* Oxford.

Richardson, N. J., ed.

1974. *The Homeric Hymn to Demeter.* Oxford.

Richter, G. M. A.

1970. *The Sculpture and Sculptors of the Greeks.* 4th ed. New Haven.

Ridgway, B. S.

1977. *The Archaic Style in Greek Sculpture.* Princeton.

1981. *Fifth-Century Styles in Greek Sculpture.* Princeton.

1992. "Images of Athena on the Akropolis." In *Goddess and Polis: The Panathenaic Festival in Ancient Athens,* ed. J. Neils, 119–42. Hanover, N.H.

1997. *Fourth-Century Styles in Greek Sculpture.* London.

Rives, J. B.

2005. "Phrygian Tales." *GRBS* 45, 223–44.

Robert, L.

1980. "La Mère des Dieux lydienne. *BCH* 106, 359–61.

Robertson, N.

1992. *Festivals and Legends: The Formation of Greek Cities in the Light of Public Ritual.* Phoenix Supplement 31. Toronto.

1996. "The Ancient Mother of the Gods: A Missing Chapter in the History of Greek Religion." In Lane 1996a, 239–304.

Roller, L. E.

1983. "The Legend of Midas." *CA* 2, 299–313.

1984. "Midas and the Gordian Knot." *CA* 3, 256–71.

1991. "The Great Mother at Gordion: The Hellenization of an Anatolian Cult." *JHS* 111, 128–43.

1994a. "Attis on Greek Votive Monuments." *Hesperia* 63, 245–62.

1994b. "The Phrygian Character of Kybele: The Formation of an Iconography and Cult Ethos in the Iron Age." In *Anatolian Iron Ages 3: The Proceedings of The Third Anatolian Iron Ages Colloquium Held at Van, 6–12 August 1990,* ed. A. Çilingiroğlu and D. French, 189–98. Ankara.

1996. "Reflections on the Mother of the Gods in Attic Tragedy." In Lane 1996a, 305–21.

1997. "The Ideology of the Eunuch Priest." *Gender and History* 9, 542–59.

1999. *In Search of God the Mother: The Cult of Anatolian Cybele,* Berkeley and Los Angeles.

Rose, H. J.

1924. "Anchises and Aphrodite." *CQ* 18, 11–16.

1959. "The Evidence for Divine Kings in Greece." In *The Sacral Kingship. Contributions to the Central Theme of the VIIIth International Congress for the History of Religions (Rome, April 1955),* Numen Supplement 4, 372–78. Leiden.

Rosivach, V. J.

1987. "Autochthony and the Athenians." *CQ* 37, 294–305.

1995. "Solon's Brothels." *LCM* 20, 2–3.

Rubio, G.

2001. "Inanna and Dumuzi: A Sumerian Love Story." *JAOS* 121, 268–74.

Ruiz Pérez, A.

1994. "Un oracle relatif à l'introduction du culte de Cybèle à Athènes." *Kernos* 7, 169–77.

Ryder, T. T. B.

1965. *Koine Eirene: General Peace and Local Independence in Ancient Greece.* Oxford.

Sacks, K.

1981. *Polybius on the Writing of History.* University of California Publications in Classical Studies 24. Berkeley and Los Angeles.

Said, E. W.

1978. *Orientalism.* New York.

Saïd, S.

1984. "Grecs et barbares dans les tragédies d'Euripide: La fin des différences." *Ktema* 9, 27–53.

de Ste. Croix, G. E. M.

1972. *The Origins of the Peloponnesian War.* Ithaca.

Sakellariou, M. B.

1958. *La migration grecque en Ionie.* Collection de l'Institut Française d'Athènes 17. Athens.

Samons, L. J., II.

1998. "Kimon, Kallias, and Peace with Persia." *Historia* 47, 129–40.

Sams, G. K.

2000. "Midas of Gordion and the Anatolian Kingdom of Phrygia." In *Civilizations of the Ancient Near East*, ed. J. M. Sasson, with J. Barnes, G. Beckman, and K. S. Rubison, 1147–59. Peabody, Mass.

Santoro, M.

1973. *Epitheta Deorum in Asia Graeca Cultorum ex Auctoribus Graecis et Latinis.* Testi e Documenti per lo Studio dell'Antichità 44. Milan.

Schaber, W.

1982. *Die archaischen Tempel der Artemis von Ephesos: Entwurfsprinzipien und Rekonstruktion.* Schriften aus dem Athenaion der Klassichen Archäologie Salzburg 2. Waldsassen.

Schibli, H. S.

1990. *Pherekydes of Syros.* Oxford.

Scholtz, A.

2003. "Aphrodite Pandemos at Naukratis." *GRBS* 43, 231–42.

Seaford, R.

2003. "Tragic Tyranny." In Morgan 2003, 95–115.

Seager, R.

1969. "The Congress Decree: Some Doubts and a Hypothesis." *Historia* 18, 129–40.

1979. "Agesilaus in Asia: Propaganda and Objectives." *LCM* 2, 183–84.

Sealey, R.

1976. "The Pit and the Well: The Persian Heralds of 491 B.C." *CJ* 72, 13–20.

1984. "On Lawful Concubinage in Athens." *CA* 3, 111–33.

Sefati, Y.

1998. *Love Songs in Sumerian Literature: Critical Edition of the Dumuzi-Inanna Songs.* Bar-Ilan Studies in Near Eastern Languages and Culture. Ramat Gan.

Seiterle, G.

1979. "Artemis, die grosse Göttin von Ephesos." *AntW* 10.3, 3–16.

Seltman, C.

1933. *Greek Coins: A History of Metallic Currency and Coinage down to the Fall of the Hellenistic Kingdoms.* London.

Shapiro, H. A.

1986. "The Attic Deity Basile." *ZPE* 63, 134–36.

1989. *Art and Cult under the Tyrants in Athens.* Mainz.

1998. "Autochthony and the Visual Arts in Fifth-Century Athens." In *Democracy,*

*Empire, and the Arts in Fifth-Century Athens,* ed. D. Boedeker and K. A. Raaflaub, 127–51. Cambridge, Mass.

Shear, T. L., Jr.

1993. "The Persian Destruction of Athens: Evidence from Agora Deposits." *Hesperia* 62, 383–482.

1995. "Bouleuterion, Metroon, and the Archives at Athens." In *Studies in the Ancient Greek Polis,* Historia Einzelschrift 95, ed. M. H. Hansen and K. A. Raaflaub, 157–90. Stuttgart.

Shimron, B.

1973. "Πρῶτος τῶν ἡμεῖς ἴδμεν." *Eranos* 71, 45–51.

Sickinger, J. P.

1999. *Public Records and Archives in Classical Athens.* Chapel Hill.

Siewert, P.

1972. *Der Eid von Plataiai.* Munich.

Simon, E.

1953. *Opfernde Götter.* Berlin.

1970. "Aphrodite Pandemos auf attischen Münzen. *Schweitzerische Numismatische Rundschau* 49, 5–19. [Reprinted in *Ausgewählte Schriften,* vol. 1 (Mainz, 1998), 39–48.]

1983. *Festivals of Attica: An Archaeological Commentary,* Madison.

1984. "Ikonographie und Epigraphik: Zum Bauschmuck des Siphnierschatzhauses in Delphi." *ZPE* 57, 1–21.

1988. *Eirene und Pax: Friedensgöttinnen in der Antike.* Sitzungsberichte der Wissenschaftlichen Gesellschaft an der Johann Wolfgang Goethe–Universität, Frankfurt am Main, vol. 24, no. 3. Stuttgart.

Singer, I.

1983. "Western Anatolia in the Thirteenth Century B.C. according to the Hittite Sources." *AnatStud* 33, 205–17.

Sinos, R. H.

1993. "Divine Selection: Epiphany and Politics in Archaic Greece." In Dougherty and Kurke 1993, 73–91.

Smith, J. O.

1996. "The High Priests of the Temple of Artemis at Ephesus." In Lane 1996a, 323–35.

Smith, J. Z.

1978. *Map Is Not Territory: Studies in the History of Religions.* Studies in Judaism in Late Antiquity, vol. 23. Leiden.

Smith, P. M.

1981a. *Nursling of Mortality: A Study of the Homeric Hymn to Aphrodite.* Studien zur Klassischen Philologie 3. Frankfurt.

1981b. "Aeneiadae as Patrons of *Iliad* XX and of the Homeric *Hymn to Aphrodite.*" *HSCP* 85, 17–58.

Smith, S.

1958. "The Practice of Kingship in Early Semitic Kingdoms." In Hooke 1958, 22–73.

Snell, B.

1938. *Leben und Meinungen der Sieben Weisen.* 4th ed. N.p. [Reprint: Munich, 1971.]

Snodgrass, A. M.

1971. *The Dark Age of Greece: An Archaeological Survey of the Eleventh to the Eighth Centuries BC.* Edinburgh.

Sokolowski, F.

1969. *Lois sacrées des cités grecques.* Paris.

Sourvinou-Inwood, C.

1988. "'Myth' and History: On Herodotus III.48 and 50–53." *Opuscula Atheniensia* 17, 167–82. [Reprinted in Sourvinou-Inwood 1991, 244–84.]

1991. *"Reading" Greek Culture: Texts and Images, Rituals and Myths.* Oxford.

Sparkes, B. A.

1991. *Greek Art.* Greece & Rome, New Surveys in the Classics, no. 22. Oxford.

Speiser, E. A.

1955. "Ancient Mesopotamia." In *The Idea of History in the Ancient Near East,* ed. R. C. Dentan, 35–76. New Haven.

Stafford, E.

2000. *Worshipping Virtues: Personification and the Divine in Ancient Greece.* London.

Starke, F.

1997a. "Sprachen und Schriften in Karkamis." In *Ana šadî Labnāni lū allik—Beiträge zu altorientalischen und mittlemeerischen Kulturen: Festschrift für Wolfgang Röllig,* Alter Orient und Altes Testament 247, ed. B. Pongratz-Leisten, H. Kühne, and P. Xella, 381–95. Neukirchen-Vluyn.

1997b. "Troia im Kontext des historisch-politischen und sprachlichen Umfelds Kleinasiens im 2. Jahrtausend." *Studia Troica* 7, 447–87.

Steinkeller, P.

1999. "On Rulers, Priests and Sacred Marriage: Tracing the Evolution of Early Sumerian Kingship." In Watanabe 1999a, 103–37.

Stern, J.

1989. "Demythologization in Herodotus: 5.92.η." *Eranos* 87, 13–20.

Stevenson, W.

2002. "Eunuchs in Early Christianity." In Tougher 2002a, 123–42.

Stewart, A.

1997. *Art, Desire, and the Body in Ancient Greece.* Cambridge.

Storey, I. C.

1990. "Dating and Re-dating Eupolis." *Phoenix* 44, 1–30.

Stroud, R.

1974. "An Athenian Law on Silver Coinage." *Hesperia* 43, 157–88.

Svenbro, J.

1993. "True Metempsychosis: Lycurgus, Numa and the Tattooed Corpse of Epimenides." In *Phrasikleia: An Anthropology of Reading in Ancient Greece,* transl. J. Lloyd (from the French 1988 edition), 123–44. Ithaca.

Sweet, R. F. G.

1994. "A New Look at the Sacred Marriage in Ancient Mesopotamia." In *Corolla Torontonensis: Studies in Honour of R. M. Smith,* ed. E. Robbins and S. Sandahl, 85–104. Toronto.

Talamo, C.

1979. *La Lidia arcaica: Tradizioni genealogiche ed evoluzione istituzionale.* Bologna.

Talbert, R. J. A., ed.

2000. *Barrington Atlas of the Greek and Roman World.* Princeton.

Taplin, O.

1992. *Homeric Soundings: The Shaping of the Iliad.* Oxford.

Tarán, L., ed.

1987. *Studies in Herodotus and Plato by Ivan M. Linforth.* New York.

Tarn, W. W.

1948. *Alexander the Great,* vol. 2, *Sources and Studies.* Cambridge.

Taylor, M. W.

1991. *The Tyrant Slayers: The Heroic Image in Fifth Century B.C. Athenian Art and Politics.* 2nd ed. Salem, N.H.

Thiemer, H.

1979. *Der Einfluß der Phryger auf die altgriechische Musik.* Orpheus 29. Bonn.

Thomas, C. G.

1976. "The Nature of Mycenaean Kingship." *SMEA* 17, 93–116

Thomas, R.

1989. *Oral Tradition and Written Record in Classical Athens.* Cambridge.

2000. *Herodotus in Context: Ethnography, Science and the Art of Persuasion.* Cambridge.

2001. "Herodotus' *Histories* and the Floating Gap." In Luraghi 2001a, 198–210.

Thompson, H. A.

1937. "Buildings on the West Side of the Agora." *Hesperia* 6, 1–226.

Thomsen, R.

1972. *The Origin of Ostracism: A Synthesis,* Copenhagen.

Thomson, J. O.

1948. *History of Ancient Geography.* Cambridge.

Threpsiades, J., and E. Vanderpool.

1964. "Themistokles' Sanctuary of Artemis Aristoboule." *AD* 19, 26–36.

Tougher, S., ed.

2002a. *Eunuchs in Antiquity and Beyond.* London.

2002b. "In or Out? Origins of Court Eunuchs." In Tougher 2002a, 143–59.

Toye, D. L.

1997. "Pherecydes of Syros: Ancient Theologian and Genealogist." *Mnemosyne* 50, 530–60.

Travlos, J.

1971. *Pictorial Dictionary of Ancient Athens.* New York.

Trümpy, C.

1997. *Untersuchungen zu den altgriechischen Monatsnamen und Monatsfolgen.* Heidelberg.

Van Loon, M. N.

1991. *Anatolia in the Earlier First Millennium* B.C., fasc. 13, *Mesopotamia and the Near East,* section 15, *Iconography of Religions.* Leiden.

Vanderhooft, D. S.

1999. *The Neo-Babylonian Empire and Babylon in the Latter Prophets.* Harvard Semitic Museum Monographs 59. Atlanta.

Vannicelli, P.

1997. "L'esperimento linguistico di Psammetico (Herodot. II 2): C'era una volta il frigio." In Gusmani et al. 1997, 201–17.

2001. "Herodotus' Egypt and the Foundations of Universal History." In Luraghi 2001a, 211–40.

Vassileva, M.

2001. "Further Considerations on the Cult of Kybele." *AnatStud* 51, 51–63.

de Vaux, R.

1961. *Ancient Israel: Social and Religious Institutions.* 2 vols. New York.

Vermaseren, M. J.

1977. *Cybele and Attis: The Myth and Cult.* London.

1982. *Corpus Cultus Cybelae Attidisque,* vol. 2, *Graecia atque Insulae.* Leiden.

1987. *Corpus Cultus Cybelae Attidisque,* vol. 1, *Asia Minor.* Leiden.

Vernant, J.-P.

1988. *Myth and Society in Ancient Greece.* Transl. J. Lloyd. New York. [Originally published in French, 1974.]

Versnel, H. S.

1990. *Inconsistencies in Greek Religion,* vol. 1, *Ter Unus—Isis, Dionysos, Hermes: Three Studies in Henotheism.* Leiden.

1993. *Inconsistencies in Greek and Roman Religion,* vol. 2, *Transition and Reversal in Myth and Ritual.* Leiden.

2000. "Thrice One: Thee Greek Experiments in Oneness." In *One God or Many? Concepts of Divinity in the Ancient World,* ed. B. N. Porter, 79–163. Casco Bay.

Veyne, P.

1988. *Did the Greeks Believe in Their Myths? An Essay on the Constitutive Imagination.* Transl. P. Wissing from the French 1983 edition. Chicago.

Vickers, M.

1989. "Alcibiades on Stage: Aristophanes' *Birds.*" *Historia* 38, 267–99.

Vidal-Naquet, J.-P.

1986. *The Black Hunter: Forms of Thought and Forms of Society in the Greek World.* Transl. A. Szegedy-Maszak from the French 1981 edition. Baltimore.

Wade-Gery, H. T.

1940. "The Peace of Kallias." In *Athenian Studies Presented to W. S. Ferguson.* HSCP Supplement 1, 121–56. Cambridge, Mass. [Reprinted in *Essays in Greek History* (Oxford, 1958), 201–32.]

Waelkens, M.

1986. *Die kleinasiatischen Türsteine: Typologische und epigraphische Untersuchungen der kleinasiatischen Grabreliefs mit Scheintür.* Mainz.

Walcot, P.

1966. *Hesiod and the Near East.* Cardiff.

1967. "The Divinity of the Mycenaean King." *SMEA* 2, 53–62.

Wallace, R. W.

1988. "WALWE and KALI." *JHS* 108, 203–7.

1994. "Private Lives and Public Enemies: Freedom of Thought in Classical Athens." In *Athenian Identity and Civic Ideology,* ed. A. L. Boegehold and A. C. Scafuro, 127–55. Baltimore.

Walls, N. H.

1992. *The Goddess Anat in Ugaritic Myth.* Society of Biblical Literature, Dissertation Series, 135. Atlanta.

Wankel, H.

1977. "Die Bekanntmachung des Todesurteils in der ephesischen Inschrift Inv. 1631." *ZPE* 24, 219–21.

Watanabe, K., ed.

1999a. *Priests and Officials in the Ancient Near East.* Heidelberg.

1999b. "Seals of Neo-Assyrian Officials." In Watanabe 1999a, 313–66.

Watrous, L. V.

   1982. "The Sculptural Program of the Siphnian Treasury at Delphi." *AJA* 86, 159–72.

Weidner, E.

   1952. "Das Reich Sargons von Akkad." *AfO* 16, 1–26.

Welles, C. B.

   1934. *Royal Correspondence in the Hellenistic Period: A Study in Greek Epigraphy.* New Haven.

Wéry, L.-M.

   1966. "Le meurtre des hérauts de Darius en 491 et l'inviolabilité du héraut." *AC* 35, 468–86.

West, D. R.

   1995. *Some Cults of Greek Goddesses and Female Daemons of Oriental Origin.* Alter Orient und Altes Testament 233. Neukirchen-Vluyn.

West, M. L., ed.

   1966. *Hesiod: Theogony.* Oxford.

   1970. "Melica." *CQ* 20, 205–15.

   1971. *Early Greek Philosophy and the Orient.* Oxford.

   1974. *Studies in Greek Elegy and Iambus,* Berlin.

   1988. "The Rise of the Greek Epic." *JHS* 108, 151–72.

   1992. *Ancient Greek Music.* Oxford.

   1996. "Semonides." In *The Oxford Classical Dictionary,* 3rd ed., ed. S. Hornblower and A. Spawforth, 1383. Oxford.

   1997. *The East Face of Helicon: West Asiatic Elements in Greek Poetry and Myth.* Oxford.

West, S.

   1992. "Sesostris' Stelae (Herodotus 2.102–106)." *Historia* 41, 117–20.

von Wilamowitz-Moellendorff, U.

   1903. "Apollon." *Hermes* 38, 575–86.

   1920. *Die Ilias und Homer.* 2nd ed. Berlin

Will, E.

   1960. "Aspects du culte et de la légende de la grande mère dans le monde grec." In *Eléments orientaux dans la religion grecque ancienne,* Travaux du Centre d'Etudes Supériores Specialisé d'Histoire des Religions, Strasbourg, 95–111. Paris.

Winkler, J. J.

   1990. *The Constraints of Desire: The Anthropology of Sex and Gender in Ancient Greece.* London.

Winter, I. J.

   1983. "Carchemish *ŠA KIŠAD PURATTI.*" *AnatStud* 33, 177–97.

Winter, U.

1983. *Frau und Göttin: Exegetische und ikonographische Studien zum weiblichen Gottes-bild im alten Israel und in dessen Umwelt.* Orbis Biblicus et Orientalis 53. Göttingen.

Wiseman, D. J.

1983. "Mesopotamian Gardens." *AnatStud* 33, 137–44.

1984. "Palace and Temple Gardens in the Ancient Near East." In *Monarchies and Socio-Religious Traditions in the Ancient Near East,* Bulletin of the Middle Eastern Culture Center in Japan, vol. 1, ed. T. Mikasa, 37–43. Wiesbaden.

1985. *Nebuchadrezzar and Babylon.* Oxford.

Witt, R.

2002. "The Other Castrati." In Tougher 2002a, 235–60.

Wohl, V.

2002. *Love among the Ruins: The Erotics of Democracy in Classical Athens.* Princeton.

Woodbury, L.

1965. "The Date and Atheism of Diagoras of Melos." *Phoenix* 19, 178–211.

Woodward, A. M.

1956. "The Cistophoric Series and Its Place in the Roman Coinage." In *Essays in Roman Coinage Presented to Harold Mattingly,* ed. R. A. G. Carson and C. H. V. Sutherland, 149–73. Oxford

Woolley, L., and R. D. Barnett.

1952. *Carchemish: Report on the Excavations at Jerablus on Behalf of the British Museum,* part 3, *The Excavations of the Inner Town and the Hittite Inscriptions.* London.

Wright, J. C.

1994. "The Spatial Configuration of Belief: The Archaeology of Mycenaean Religion." In *Placing the Gods: Sanctuaries and Sacred Spaces in Ancient Greece,* ed. S. E. Alcock and R. Osborne, 37–78. Oxford.

Wyatt, N.

1996. *Myths of Power: A Study of Royal Myth and Ideology in Ugaritic and Biblical Tradition.* Ugaritische-Biblische Literatur 13. Münster.

Wycherley, R. E.

1957. *The Athenian Agora,* vol. 3, *Literary and Epigraphical Testimonia.* Princeton.

1978. *The Stones of Athens.* Princeton.

Yalouris, N.

1980. "Astral Representations in the Archaic and Classical Periods and Their Connection to Literary Sources." *AJA* 84, 313–18.

Young, R. S., et al. [K. DeVries, J. F. McClellan, L. E. Kohler, M. J. Mellink, and G. K. Sams].

1981. *The Gordion Excavations (1950–1973): Final Reports,* vol. 1, *Three Great Early Tumuli.* Philadelphia.

Yunis, H.

  1988. *A New Creed: Fundamental Religious Beliefs in the Athenian Polis and Euripidean Drama.* Hypomnemata 91. Göttingen.

Zgusta, L.

  1964. *Kleinasiatische Personennamen.* Prague.

  1982. "Weiteres zum Namen der Kybele." *Die Sprache* 28, 171–72.

281n64, 282n66, 283nn67–68, 285,
325, 341–42
Darius III, 43, 322n18
Dascyleum, 110–11, 136, 144, 215
Dascylus, 110–11
Datis, 210n112, 217, 219, 275, 298n6,
342n103
Davidson, James, 321n14
Deioces, 117n82
Deïphonus, 277
Delos, 48, 166n108, 177, 191, 193, 208–
13, 217, 219, 246, 257, 263, 275–79,
286, 292, 303n21, 305; earthquake at,
217n139, 298, 313, 342n103; League
of, 279, 281, 289n88, 312, 317, 325, 346,
357; purification of, 209–10, 275, 313
Delphi, 25, 32n69, 33, 38, 45–46, 68,
70n58, 88, 117n82, 127n124, 146–48,
151n55, 191–93, 198n75, 199n76, 200,
201n82, 211–13, 303n21, 307, 311, 313,
331, 333n63, 337–38; omphalos at, 193
oracle of, 25n40, 28n50, 38, 48n128, 59,
110–11n62, 147, 191–93, 211, 245n91,
270, 311. *See also* Croesus; Earth; Euripides; Gyges; Midas; oracles
Demaratus, 16n7, 268–69
Demeter, 11, 32, 33n71, 34, 39, 56, 57n4,
58–62, 80n92, 91–92, 108, 125, 133,
138–39, 145, 146n44, 151n55, 157, 190,
191n49, 223–24, 255, 258, 262, 267–71,
277, 298n6, 313, 315, 329n42, 332, 339,
349n126, 356–57; and Artemis, 167,
169n121, 223, 255–56; Chloe, 339; and
Dionysus, 82, 153, 167n116; Eleusinian,
39, 247n99, 256n130, 258, 267–69, 277,
285, 313, 315, 323, 332, 356; and Iasion,
138–39, 140n25; and Kore (Persephone),
32, 56n3, 91–92, 146n44, 255–56, 270;
Mysteries of, 39, 82, 258, 313, 323,
332. *See also Chthonië; daidouchos;* Earth;
Eleusis; *Homeric Hymn; Lamētruś;* Mother
of the Gods; Mysteries; χθόνιαι θεαί
Democritus of Abdera, 82n103, 193n57
Democritus of Ephesus, 166n108
Demodice, 45n118, 73n72, 146
Deo, 59, 108n49, 109n51
Detienne, Marcel, 15, 51n138, 142n33
Deucalion, 133, 206n102, 257n133,
291n95
DeVries, Keith, 88n118, 134n94
Dewald, Carolyn, 18n12, 312n44

Diagoras of Melos, 82, 83n104, 88,
258n142, 313
Diakonoff, Igor M., 121n96, 157n74
Dicks, D. R., 202n87
Didyma, 191n48, 199n76, 249
Dike, 34, 334, 337, 347, 355
Dillon, Matthew, 174n135
Dindyme. *See* Dindymene
Dindymene, 56n2, 73–74, 81, 87n114,
109n51, 121n94, 182, 184, 204, 274, 327
Dindymus. *See* Dindymene
Diogenes Tragicus, 167n115
Dionysius I of Syracuse, 171
Dionysus, 6, 8, 39, 58, 68–69, 81, 82,
91n128, 102, 141, 153, 167n116,
175n137, 176–77, 235, 257; as con-
queror, 235n52; and Midas, 68–69;
as teacher of viticulture, 82. *See also*
Ariadne; Bacchus; *Baki;* Basilinna;
Demeter; Sacred Marriage
Diopeithes, 258n141, 313–14, 341
dirges. *See* funerary cult, and music
Diÿllus, 312n46
Dodds, Eric Robertson, 61n16
Donlan, Walter, 17n9
Dover, Kenneth J., 58n7, 314n51
dreams, 127n125, 154–55, 213, 338n63,
274n41, 298n8, 334. *See also* Artemi-
dorus; omens; oracles; prophecy
Drews, Robert, 17n9, 27n48, 80n91,
90n123, 97n4, 308n36
drums, 63, 96, 116, 168, 236, 328, 353
Dumuzi (Tammuz), 107n45, 132–34, 141, 143
Duris of Samos, 326n32, 329, 330n47, 342.
*See also* Index Locorum
Dusinberre, Elspeth, 223n7, 226n18

eagle, 83–86, 127n125, 190, 274, 316n58
Earth (Gaea), 31–33, 36, 49–50, 56–57, 61,
69, 75, 79, 86–87, 91–92, 125–26, 133–
37, 145–55, 204–206, 220–25, 228n28,
231, 239, 241n76, 255–57, 263, 327, 339,
356, 358; cult of, 32nn65–67, 91, 147–52,
228n28, 232n42, 257, 270–71, 274, 337,
339; at Delphi, 147–48, 337; as Demeter,
56n3, 61, 108n48, 145, 270, 274; Heaven
and, 31, 139n22, 206, 323; Mother of
Zeus, 126, 327; and Themis, 108n48, 337.
*See also* autochthony; *Chthonië;* Demeter;
*Homeric Hymn;* Inanna; maps; Mother of
the Gods; *oikoumenē;* Uranus

# INDEX OF SELECT GREEK TERMS

# INDEX LOCORUM

## GREEK AND LATIN AUTHORS

## GREEK INSCRIPTIONS

| | |
|---|---|
| 136 | 288n84 |
| 140 | 313n49 |

**Harding**

| | |
|---|---|
| 57 | 349n125 |

*IG* I³

| | |
|---|---|
| 32 | 285n76 |
| 34 | 288n84 |
| 40 | 313n49 |
| 61 | 313n49 |
| 71 | 288n84 |
| 78 | 313n49 |
| 105 | 257n136 |
| 131 | 26n42 |
| 234 | 256n130 |
| 369 | 334n67 |
| 383 | 334n67 |
| 1453 | 288n84, 325n29 |

*IG* II²

| | |
|---|---|
| 1013 | 201n84 |
| 1237 | 65n33 |
| 3109 | 337n80 |
| 3462 | 337n80 |
| 4638 | 337n80 |

*IG* IV²

| | |
|---|---|
| 131 | 57n3 |

**ML**

| | |
|---|---|
| 12 | 185n26 |
| 45 | 288n84, 325n29 |
| 46 | 288n84 |
| 52 | 313n49 |
| 59 | 285n76 |
| 65 | 313n49 |
| 69 | 288n84 |
| 73 | 313n49 |

"Sacrilege inscription" (Ephesus)

| | |
|---|---|
| Wankel 1977 | 167n114, 246n97 |

*SEG* vol. 26

| | |
|---|---|
| 72 | 331n49 |

*SIG*³

| | |
|---|---|
| 282 | 159n84 |

**Sokolowski 1969**

| | |
|---|---|
| 160, 161 | 333n63 |

**Tod**

| | |
|---|---|
| 145 | 349n125 |

## HEBREW BIBLE

**Genesis**

| | |
|---|---|
| 2:10–14 | 139n22 |
| 10:2 | 93n132 |
| 13:14 | 288n85 |
| 16 | 101n15 |
| 29:14 | 288n85 |

**Numbers**

| | |
|---|---|
| 10:1–10 | 90n125 |

**Deuteronomy**

| | |
|---|---|
| 3:27 | 288n85 |

**2 Samuel**

| | |
|---|---|
| 6:1–5 | 90n125 |

**1 Chronicles**

| | |
|---|---|
| 1:5 | 93n132 |

**Psalms**

| | |
|---|---|
| 68:1–7, 24–25 | 90n125 |

**Proverbs**

| | |
|---|---|
| 8 | 86n112 |

| | |
|---|---|
| Song of Songs | 137nn15 and 17 |

**Isaiah**

| | |
|---|---|
| 1:29 | 137n17 |
| 11:12 | 288n85 |
| 41:1–5 | 197n73 |
| 44:28, 45:1 | 214n129 |

**Ezekiel**

| | |
|---|---|
| 8:14 | 133n2 |

## IRANIAN TEXTS: AVESTAN

| | |
|---|---|
| Yasht 5, *To Anahita* | 229nn29–30, 250n108 |
| Yasht 10, *To Mithra* | 225n1 |
| Yasna 29 | 239n64 |
| Yasna 38 | 228n28, 231n37 |

|                    |                                  |
|-------------------:|----------------------------------|
|        Compositor: | Integrated Composition Systems   |
|              Text: | 10/13 Baskerville                |
|           Display: | Baskerville                      |
| Printer and binder: | Thomson-Shore, Inc.             |

U. M. W,
Nurturing for Community

# ENCOURAGE ME

Also by Charles Swindoll, available
in Large Print from Walker and Company

*Laugh Again*

*The Grace Awakening*

*Three Steps Forward, Two Steps Back*

*Growing Strong in the Seasons of Life*

# ENCOURAGE ME

Charles R. Swindoll

Walker and Company
New York

Large Print Edition by arrangement with Multnomah Press

Unless otherwise identified, all Scripture quotations are from the *Holy Bible: New International Version*, copyright 1978, by the New York International Bible Society. Used by permission of Zondervan Bible Publishers.

Scripture quotations marked NASV are from the *New American Standard Version* © The Loçkman Foundation 1960, 1962, 1963, 1968, 1971, 1972, 1973, 1975, 1977. Used by permission.

Verses marked TLB are taken from *The Living Bible*, copyright 1971 by Tyndale House Publishers, Wheaton, IL. Used by permission.

Verses marked *Phillips* are taken from J. B. Phillips: *The New Testament in Modern English*, revised edition. © J. B. Phillips 1958, 1960, 1972. Used by permission of Macmillan Publishing Co., Inc.

Library of Congress Cataloging-in-Publication Data
Swindoll, Charles R.
  Encourage me / Charles R. Swindoll.
     p.    cm.
    Reprint. Originally published: Portland, Or. :
    Multnomah Press, © 1982.
    Includes bibliographical references.
    ISBN 0-8027-2593-7 (lg. print.)
    1. Consolation. 2. Large type books. I. Title.
  [BV4905.2.S9 1987]
  248.8'6—dc19                              87-27884
                                             CIP

First Large Print Edition, 1987
Walker and Company
435 Hudson Street
New York, NY 10014

Printed in the United States of America
10 9 8 7 6 5 4 3 2

# CONTENTS

# INTRODUCTION

Encourage me.

Maybe you haven't said it out loud in recent days. But chances are you have shaped the words in the silent hallways of your soul.

Encourage me. *Please.*

Maybe you haven't stopped anyone on the street and said that precise phrase. But if someone who cared enough looked close enough . . . they would see the words written in your frowning face, drooping shoulders, pleading eyes. They would hear the words echo in your unguarded comments and unsuppressed sighs.

If the truth were known, you're craving some encouragement. Looking for it. Longing for it. And probably grieving because you've found it in such short supply.

Am I right? Is that where you've been lately? Hibernating in the den of discouragement? Licking your wounds under some heavy, dark clouds that won't blow away? Thinking seriously about quitting the human race?

If so, you are undoubtedly running shy on

reinforcement and affirmation these days. You are beginning to wonder not *when* relief is coming, but *if* it will ever come, right? Even though you may not feel like reading anything, I really believe these pages will help. I am writing them with people like you in mind . . . people who have begun to question their own words and to doubt their own worth. People who feel riveted to the valley where the sun seldom shines and others seldom care.

That's you, isn't it?

That's also me more often than you might guess. The long shadows of discouragement have often stretched across my path. Those times have been bittersweet—bitter at first, sweet later on. So I understand. I do not write out of sterile theory but out of reality. My pen has been dipped in a deep well. The ink has been dark and often cold. At such times I have struggled with a lack of self worth . . . a common battle waged in the valley.

Please let me slip in at this moment one significant truth: You are still valuable. You count. Yes, you. The "you" inside your skin who has your personality and your appearance. No matter what finally led you to where you are today, you're the one I'd like to talk to for awhile. Even though you feel necessary to no one and noticed by none, I'd still appreciate having a few words with you. Yes, even if you are dirty and guilty.

I have only one goal in mind: to encourage you.

You have become acquainted with disappointments, broken dreams, and disillusionment. Crisis seems to be your closest companion. Like a ten-pound sledge, your heartache has been pounding you dangerously near desperation. Unless I miss my guess, negativism and cynicism have crept in. You see little hope around the corner. As one wag put it, "The light at the end of the tunnel is the headlamp of an oncoming train." You are nodding in agreement, but probably not smiling. Life has become terribly unfunny.

Tired, stumbling, beaten, discouraged friend, take heart! The Lord God can and will lift you up. No pit is so deep that He is not deeper still. No valley so dark that the light of His truth cannot penetrate. In His own inscrutable way, He will use the insight of these few pages to bring back the one ingredient that has spilled out of your life. *Encouragement.*

If you miss it and need it and want it, read on. And oh—if you find it, by all means spread it!

Someone close by may be ready to give up the search.

*Charles R. Swindoll*

# PART ONE

# ENCOURAGE ME, LORD

"I cry tears
to you Lord
tears
because I cannot speak.
Words are lost
among my fears
pain
sorrows
losses
hurts
but tears
You understand
my wordless prayer
You hear.
Lord
wipe away my tears
all tears
not in distant day
but now
here."[1]

—Joseph Bayly

Hear my cry, O God;
listen to my prayer.
From the ends of the earth I call to
you,
I call as my heart grows faint;
lead me to the rock that is higher
than I.

(Psalm 61:1-2)

# SEARCHING FOR SHELTER

Discouragement.

Where does it come from?

Sometimes it feels like a dry, barren wind off a lonely desert. And something inside us begins to wilt.

At other times it feels like a chilling mist. Seeping through our pores, it numbs the spirit and fogs the path before us.

What is it about discouragement that strips our lives of joy and leaves us feeling vulnerable and exposed?

I don't know all the reasons. I don't even know most of the reasons. But I do know one of the reasons: We don't have a refuge. Shelters are hard come by these days . . . you know, people who care enough to listen. Who are good at keeping secrets. And we all need harbors to pull into when we feel weather-worn and blasted by the storm.

I have an old Marine buddy who became a Christian several years after he was discharged from the Corps. When news of his conversion reached me, I was pleasantly surprised. He was one of those guys you'd never picture as being interested in spiritual things. He cursed loudly, drank heavily, fought hard, chased women, loved weapons, and hated chapel service. He was a great marine. But God? They weren't on speaking terms when I bumped around with him.

Then one day we ran into each other. As the conversation turned to his salvation, he frowned, put his hand on my shoulder, and made this admission:

Chuck, the only thing I miss is that old fellowship all the guys in our out-fit used to have down at the slop shoot (Greek for "tavern on base"). Man, we'd sit around, laugh, tell stories, drink a few beers, and really let our hair down. It was great! I just haven't found anything to take the place of that great time we used to enjoy. I ain't got nobody to admit my faults to . . . to have 'em put their arms around me and tell me I'm still okay.

My stomach churned. Not because I was shocked, but because I had to agree. The man needed a refuge . . . someone to hear him out. The incident reminded me of something I read several months ago:

The neighborhood bar is possibly the best counterfeit there is to the fellowship Christ wants to give His church. It's an imitation, dispensing liquor instead of grace, escape rather than reality, but it is a permissive, accepting, and inclusive fellowship. It is unshockable. It is democratic. You can tell people secrets and they usually don't tell others or even want to. The bar flourishes not because most people are alcoholics, but because God has put into the human heart the desire to know and be known, to love and be loved, and so many seek a counterfeit at the price of a few beers.

With all my heart I believe that Christ wants His church to be . . . a fellowship where people can come in and say, "I'm sunk!" "I'm beat!" "I've had it!"[2]

Let me get painfully specific. Where do you turn when the bottom drops out of your life? Or when you face an issue that is em-

barrassing . . . maybe even scandalous.
Like:

> You just discovered your son is a prac-
>    ticing homosexual.
> Your mate is talking separation or di-
>    vorce.
> Your daughter has run away . . . for
>    the fourth time. You are afraid she's
>    pregnant.
> You've lost your job. It's your own
>    fault.
> Financially, you've blown it.
> Your parent is an alcoholic.
> Your wife is having an affair.
> You flunked your entrance exam or you
>    messed up the interview.
> You're in jail because you broke the
>    law.

What do you need when circumstances
puncture your fragile dikes and threaten
to engulf your life with pain and confusion?

You need a shelter. A listener. Someone
who understands.

But to whom do you turn when there's
no one to tell your troubles to? Where do
you find encouragement?

Without preaching, I'd like to call to your attention a man who turned to the living Lord and found in Him a place to rest and repair. His name? David. Cornered, bruised by adversity, and struggling with a low self-esteem, he wrote these words in his journal of woes:

> In you, O LORD, I have taken refuge;
> let me never be put to shame;
> deliver me in your righteousness.
> Turn your ear to me,
> come quickly to my rescue;
> be my rock of refuge,
> a strong fortress to save me.
> (Psalm 31:1-2)

Failing in strength and wounded in spirit, David cries out his need for a "refuge." The Hebrew term speaks of a protective place, a place of safety, security, secrecy. He tells the Lord that He—Jehovah God—became his refuge. In Him the troubled man found encouragement.

Now the question: Why do we need a refuge? As I read on through this psalm, I find three reasons unfolding:

First, because we are in distress and sorrow accompanies us.

Be merciful to me, O LORD, for I am
  in distress;
    my eyes grow weak with sorrow,
    my soul and my body with grief.
My life is consumed by anguish
                     (vv. 9-10a).

Eyes get red from weeping. The heavy
weights of sorrow press down. Depression,
that serpent of despair, slithers silently
through the soul's back door.

Depression is

Debilitating, defeating,
Deepening gloom.

Trudging wearily through
The grocery store,
Unable to make a simple choice,
Or to count out correct change.

Surveying an unbelievably messy
  house,
Piles of laundry,
Work undone, and not being
Able to lift a finger.

10

Doubting that God cares,
Doubting in my prayers,
Doubting He's even there.

Sitting, staring wild-eyed into space,
Desperately wanting out of the
human race.[3]

Heavy! But that's why we need a refuge.
Second, because we are sinful and guilt
accuses us.

My strength fails because of my guilt
    and my bones grow weak (v. 10b).

There is shame between these lines.
Embarrassment. "It's my fault." What
tough words to choke out! "I'm to blame."
An old British minister says it all when
he writes:

This is the bitterest of all—to know
that suffering need not have been; that
it has resulted from indiscretion and
inconsistency; that it is the harvest of
one's own sowing; that the vulture
which feeds on the vitals is a nestling

of one's own rearing. Ah me! This is pain.[4]

Harried and haunted by self-inflicted sorrow, we desperately search for a place to hide. But perhaps the most devastating blow of all is dealt by others.

Third, because we are surrounded by adversaries and misunderstanding assaults us.

> Because of all my enemies,
> I am the utter contempt
> of my neighbors;
> I am a dread to my friends—
> those who see me on the street
> flee from me.
> I am forgotten by them as though
> I were dead;
> I have become like broken pottery.
> For I hear the slander of many;
> there is terror on every side;
> they conspire against me
> and plot to take my life
> (vv. 11-13).

See how the hurting are handled? "Utter contempt . . . a dread . . . those who see me flee from me . . . I am forgotten . . . I hear slander . . . there is terror . . . they conspire against me. . . ." Sound like a page out of your journal?

Tortured by the whisperings of others, we feel like a wounded, bleeding mouse in the paws of a hungry cat. The thought of what people are saying is more than we can bear. Gossip (even its name hisses) gives the final shove as we strive for balance at the ragged edge of despair.

Discouraged people don't need critics. They hurt enough already. They don't need more guilt or piled-on distress. They need encouragement. They need a refuge.

A place to hide and heal.

A willing, caring, available someone. A confidant and comrade-at-arms. Can't find one? Why not share David's shelter? The One he called My Strength, Mighty Rock, Fortress, Stronghold, and High Tower.

David's Refuge never failed. Not even once. And he never regretted the times he dropped his heavy load and ran for cover.

Neither will you.

# YOU ARE IMPORTANT

There is only one YOU.

Think about that. Your face and features, your voice, your style, your background, your characteristics and peculiarities, your abilities, your smile, your walk, your handshake, your manner of expression, your viewpoint . . . everything about you is found in only one individual since man first began—YOU.

How does that make you feel? Frankly, I'm elated!

Dig as deeply as you please in the ancient, dusty archives of *Homo sapiens* and you'll not find another YOU in the whole lot. And that, by the way, did not "just happen"; it was planned that way. Why? Because God wanted you to be YOU, that's why. He designed you to be a unique, distinct, significant person unlike any other individual on the face of the earth, throughout the vast expanse of time. In your case, as in the case of every other human being, the mold was broken, never to be used again, once you entered the flow of mankind.

Listen to David's perspective on that subject:

You made all the delicate, inner parts of my body, and knit them together in my mother's womb. Thank you for making me so wonderfully complex! It is amazing to think about. Your workmanship is marvelous—and how well I know it. You were there while I was being formed in utter seclusion! You saw me before I was born and scheduled each day of my life before I began to breathe. Every day was recorded in your Book!

(Psalm 139:13-16 TLB)

If I read this astounding statement correctly, you were prescribed and then presented to this world exactly as God arranged it. Reflect on that truth, discouraged friend. Read David's words one more time, and don't miss the comment that God is personally involved in the very days and details of your life. Great thought!

In our overly-populated, identity-crisis era, it is easy to forget this. Individuality is played down. We are asked to conform to the "system." Group opinion is considered superior to personal conviction and everything from the college fraternity to the businessman's service club tends to encourage our blending into the mold of the masses.

It's okay to "do your thing" just so long as it is similar to others when they do "their thing." Any other thing is the wrong thing. Hogwash!

This results in what I'd call an "image syndrome," especially among the members of God's family called Christians. There is an "image" the church must maintain. The pastor (and his staff) should "fit the image" in the eyes of the public. So should all those in leadership. Youth programs and mission conferences and evangelistic emphases dare not drift too far from the expected image established back when. Nobody can say exactly when.

Our fellowship must be warm, but filled with clichés. Our love must be expressed, but not without its cool boundaries. The creative, free, and sometimes completely different approach so threatens the keepers of the image syndrome that one wonders how we retain *any* draft of fresh air blown through the windows of flexibility and spontaneity.

My mind lands upon a fig-picker from Tekoa . . . a rough, raw-boned shepherd who was about as subtle as a Mack truck on the Los Angeles-Santa Ana Freeway. He was tactless, unsophisticated, loud, uneducated, and uncooperative. His name was Amos. That was no problem. He was a preacher. That *was* a problem. He didn't fit the image . . . but he refused to let that bother him.

He was called (of all things) to bring the morning messages in the king's sanctuary. And bring them he did. His words penetrated those vaulted ceilings and icy pews like flaming arrows. In his own way, believing firmly in his message, he pounced upon sin like a hen on a june bug . . . and the "image keepers" of Israel told him to be silent, to peddle his doctrine of doom in the backwoods of Judah. His rugged style didn't fit in with the plush, "royal residence" at Bethel (Amos 7:12-13).

Aware of their attempt to strait-jacket his method and restructure his message, Amos replied:

". . . I was neither a prophet nor a prophet's son, but I was a shepherd, and I also took care of sycamore-fig trees. But the LORD took me from tending the flock and said to me, 'Go, prophesy to my people Israel'"

(Amos 7:14-15).

Amos was not about to be something he wasn't! God made him, God called him, and God gave him a message to be communicated in his own, unique way. A Tekoa High dropout had no business trying to sound or look like a Princeton grad.

Do I write to an Amos? You don't "fit the mold"? Is that what sent you down into the valley of discouragement? You don't sound like every other Christian or look like the "standard" saint . . . or act like the majority?

Hallelujah! Don't sweat it, my friend. And don't you dare change just because you're outnumbered. Then you wouldn't be YOU.

What the church needs is a lot more faithful figpickers who have the courage to simply be themselves, regardless. Whoever is responsible for standardizing the ranks of Christians ought to be shot at dawn. In so doing they completely ignored the value of variety, which God planned for His church when He "arranged the parts in the body, every one of them, just as He wanted them to be" (1 Corinthians 12:18).

You are YOU. There is only one YOU. And YOU are important.

Want to start feeling better? Really desire to dispel discouragement? I can say it all in three words:

Start being YOU.

# YOU ARE NOT A NOBODY

We haven't gotten very far, but it's already time for a quiz.

Pull a sheet of scratch paper out of your memory bank and see how well you do with the following questions:

1. Who taught Martin Luther his theology and inspired his translation of the New Testament?
2. Who visited Dwight L. Moody at a shoe store and spoke to him about Christ?
3. Who worked alongside and encouraged Harry Ironside as his associate pastor?
4. Who was the wife of Charles Haddon Spurgeon?
5. Who was the elderly woman who prayed faithfully for Billy Graham for over twenty years?
6. Who financed William Carey's ministry in India?

7. Who refreshed the apostle Paul in that Roman dungeon as he wrote his last letter to Timothy?
8. Who helped Charles Wesley get underway as a composer of hymns?
9. Who found the Dead Sea Scrolls?
10. Who personally taught G. Campbell Morgan, the "peerless expositor," his techniques in the pulpit?
11. Who followed Hudson Taylor and gave the China Inland Mission its remarkable vision and direction?
12. Who discipled George Müller and snatched him as a young man from a sinful lifestyle?
13. Who were the parents of the godly and gifted prophet Daniel?

Okay, how did you do? Over fifty percent? Maybe twenty-five percent? Not quite that good?

Before you excuse your inability to answer the questions by calling the quiz "trivia," better stop and think. Had it not been for those unknown people—those "nobodies"—a huge chunk of church history would be missing. And a lot of lives would have been untouched.

Nobodies.

What a necessary band of men and women . . . servants of the King . . . yet nameless in the kingdom! Men and women who, with silent heroism, yet faithful diligence, relinquish the limelight and live in the shade of public figures.

What was it Jim Elliot, the martyred messenger of the gospel to the Aucas, once called missionaries? Something like a bunch of nobodies trying to exalt Somebody.

But don't mistake anonymous for unnecessary. Otherwise, the whole Body gets crippled . . . even paralyzed . . . or , at best, terribly dizzy as the majority of the members within the Body become diseased with self-pity and discouragement. Face it, friend, the Head of the Body calls the shots. It is His prerogative to publicize some and hide others. Don't ask me why He chooses whom He uses.

If it's His desire to use you as a Melanchthon rather than a Luther . . . or a Kimball rather than a Moody . . . or an Onesiphorus rather than a Paul . . . or a Hoste rather than a Taylor, relax!

Better than that, give God praise! You're among that elite group mentioned in

1 Corinthians 12 as:

> . . . some of the parts that seem weakest and least important are really the most necessary. . . . So God has put the body together in such a way that extra honor and care are given to those parts that might otherwise seem less important (vv. 22, 24, TLB).

If it weren't for the heroic "nobodies," we wouldn't have top-notch officers to give a church its leadership. Or quality sound when everyone shows up to worship. Or janitors who clean when everyone is long gone. Or committees to provide dozens of services behind the scenes. Or mission volunteers who staff offices at home or work in obscurity overseas with only a handful of people. Come to think of it, if it weren't for the faithful "nobodies," you wouldn't even have this book in your hands right now.

Nobodies . . . exalting Somebody.

Are you one? Listen to me! It's the "nobodies" Somebody chooses so carefully. And when He has selected you for that role, He does not consider you a nobody.

Be encouraged!

24

# CALL FOR HELP!

A PRAYER TO BE SAID
WHEN THE WORLD HAS GOTTEN YOU
DOWN, AND YOU FEEL ROTTEN,
AND YOU'RE TOO DOGGONE TIRED
  TO PRAY,
AND YOU'RE IN A BIG HURRY,
AND BESIDES, YOU'RE MAD AT
EVERYBODY. . .
                    help.

There it was. One of those posters. Some are funny. Some are clever. Others beautiful. A few, thought-provoking. This one? Convicting. God really wanted me to get the message. He nudged me at a Christian conference center recently when I first read it in an administrator's office. A few weeks and many miles later He shot me the signal again—I practically ran into the same poster in a friend's office. Then just last week, while moving faster than a speeding bullet through a Portland publishing firm, I came face to face with it *again*. But this time the message broke through my defenses and wrestled me to the mat for the full count.

"My son, slow down. Ease back. Admit your needs."

Such good counsel. But so tough to carry out. Why is that? Why in the world is it such a struggle for us to cry out for assistance?

• Ants do it all the time and look at all *they* achieve.

• In my whole life I have never seen a football game won without substitutions.

• Even the finest of surgeons will arrange for help in extensive or delicate operations.

• Highway patrolmen travel in pairs.

• Through my whole career in the Marine Corps I was drilled to dig a foxhole for two in the event of a battle.

Asking for help is smart. It's also the answer to fatigue and the "I'm indispensable" image. But something keeps us from this wise course of action, and that something is pride. Plain, stubborn unwillingness to admit need. The greatest battle many believers fight today is not with inefficiency, but with superefficiency. It's been bred into us by high-achieving parents, through years of high-pressure competition in school, and by that unyielding inner voice that keeps urging us to "Prove

26

it to 'em! Show 'em you can do it without anyone's help!"

The result, painful though it is to admit, is a life-style of impatience. We become easily irritated—often angry. We work longer hours. Take less time off. Forget how to laugh. Cancel vacations. Allow longer and longer gaps between meaningful times in God's Word. Enjoy fewer and fewer moments in prayer and meditation. And all the while the specter of discouragement looms across our horizon like a dark storm front—threatening to choke out any remaining sunshine.

Say, my friend, it's time to declare it. You are not the Messiah of the twentieth century! There is no way you can keep pushing your life at that pace and expect to stay effective. Analyze yourself any way you please, you are H-U-M-A-N . . . nothing more. So? So slow down. So give yourself a break. So stop trying to cover all the bases and sell popcorn in the stands at the same time. So relax for a change!

Once you've put it in neutral, crack open your Bible to Exodus 18 and read aloud verses 18-27. It's the account of a visit Jethro made to the work place of his son-in-law. A fella by the name of Moses. Old Jethro frowned as he watched Moses flash from one need to another, from one person to another. From early morning until late at night the harried leader of the Israelites was neck-deep in decisions and activities. He must have looked very impressive—eating on the run, ripping from one end of camp to the other, planning appointments, meeting deadlines.

But Jethro wasn't impressed. "What is this thing that you are doing for the people?" he asked. Moses was somewhat defensive (most too-busy people are) as he attempted to justify his ridiculous schedule. Jethro didn't buy the story. Instead, he advised his son-in-law against trying to do everything alone. He reproved him with strong words:

> "The thing that you are doing is not good. You will surely wear out. . ."

The Hebrew term means "to become old, exhausted." In three words, he told Moses to

## CALL FOR HELP

The benefits of shifting and sharing the load? Read verses 22-23 for yourself. "It will be easier for you . . . you will be able to endure." That's interesting, isn't it? God wants our life-style to be easier than most of us realize. We seem to think it's more commendable and "spiritual" to have that tired-blood, overworked-underpaid, I've-really-got-it-tough look. You know, the martyr complex. That strained expression that conveys "I'm working so hard for Jesus" to the public. Maybe they're fooled, but He isn't. The truth of the matter is quite the contrary. That hurried, harried appearance usually means, "I'm too stubborn to slow down" or "I'm too insecure to say 'no'" or "I'm too proud to ask for help."

Since when is a bleeding ulcer a sign of spirituality? Or no time off and a seventy-hour week a mark of efficiency? When will we learn that efficiency is enhanced not by what we accomplish but more often by what we relinquish?

The world beginning to get you down? Feeling rotten? Too tired to pray . . . in too big a hurry? Ticked off at a lot of folks? Let me suggest one of the few four-letter words God loves to hear us shout when we're angry or discouraged:

HELP!

# THE HAMMER, THE FILE, AND THE FURNACE

It was the enraptured Rutherford who said in the midst of very painful trials and heartaches:

Praise God for the hammer, the file, and the furnace!

Let's think about that. The hammer is a useful and handy instrument. It is an essential and helpful tool, if nails are ever to be driven into place. Each blow forces them to bite deeper as the hammer's head pounds and pounds.

But if the nail had feelings and intelligence, it would give us another side of the story. To the nail, the hammer is a brutal, relentless master—an enemy who loves to beat it into submission. That is the nail's view of the hammer. It is correct. Except for one thing. The nail tends to forget that both it and the hammer are held by the same workman. The workman decides whose "head" will be pounded out of sight . . . and which hammer will be used to do the job.

This decision is the sovereign right of the carpenter. Let the nail but remember that it and the hammer are held by the same workman . . . and its resentment will fade as it yields to the carpenter without complaint.

The same analogy holds true for the metal that endures the rasp of the file and the blast of the furnace. If the metal forgets that it and the tools are objects of the same craftsman's care, it will build up hatred and resentment. The metal must keep in mind that the craftsman knows what he's doing . . . and is doing what is best.

Heartaches and disappointments are like the hammer, the file, and the furnace. They come in all shapes and sizes: an unfulfilled romance, a lingering illness, an untimely death, an unachieved goal in life, a broken home or marriage, a severed friendship, a wayward and rebellious child, a personal medical report that advises "immediate surgery," a failing grade at school, a depression that simply won't go away, a habit you can't seem to break. Sometimes heartaches come suddenly . . . other times they appear over the passing of many months, slowly as the erosion of earth.

Do I write to a "nail" that has begun to resent the blows of the hammer? Are you at the brink of despair, thinking that you cannot bear another day of heartache? Is that what's gotten you down?

As difficult as it may be for you to believe this today, the Master knows what He's doing. Your Savior knows your breaking point. The bruising and crushing and melting process is designed to reshape you, not ruin you. Your value is increasing the longer He lingers over you.

A. W. Tozer agrees:

It is doubtful whether God can bless a man greatly until He has hurt him deeply.

Aching friend—stand fast. Like David when calamity caved in, strengthen yourself in the Lord your God (1 Samuel 30:6). God's hand is in your heartache. Yes, it is!

If you weren't important, do you think He would take this long and work this hard on your life? Those whom God uses most effectively have been hammered, filed, and tempered in the furnace of trials and heartache.

# AN ANTIDOTE FOR WEARINESS

It was about twenty years ago that my brother, now on the mission field, introduced a hymn to me I'd not heard before. He loves to play the piano—and plays it beautifully—so he sat at the keyboard and played the simple melody and sang the beloved words of a hymn I have since committed to memory. The melodic strains of this piece often accompany me as I drive or take a walk in solitude or return late from a day of pressure and demands. Actually the hymn is not new; it's an old piece based on an early Greek hymn that dates as far back as the eighth century.

Art thou weary, art thou languid,
Art thou sore distressed?
"Come to me," saith One, "And coming
Be at rest."
Hath He marks to lead me to Him
If He be my Guide?

In His feet and hands are wound-prints
And His side.
Finding, following, keeping, struggling,
Is He sure to bless?
Saints, apostles, prophets, martyrs,
Answer, "Yes."[6]

Surely in the home and heart of some soul who reads this book, there is a silent sigh, a twinge of spiritual fatigue . . . a deep and abiding weariness. It's no wonder! Our pace, the incessant activity, the noise, the interruptions, the deadlines and demands, the daily schedule, and the periodic feelings of failure and futility bombard our beings like the shelling of a beachhead. Our natural tendency is to wave a white flag, shouting, "I give up! I surrender!" This, of course, is the dangerous extreme of being weary—the decision to bail out, to throw in the towel, to give in to discouragement and give up. There is nothing wrong or unnatural with feeling weary, but there is everything wrong with abandoning ship in the midst of the fight.

Growing weary is the consequence of many experiences—none of them bad, but all of them exhausting. To name just a few:

We can be weary of waiting. "I am weary

with my crying; my throat is parched; my eyes fail while I wait for my God" (Psalm 69:3 NASV).

We can be weary of studying and learning. "Of making many books there is no end, and much study wearies the body" (Ecclesiastes 12:12).

We can be weary of fighting the enemy. "He arose and struck the Philistines until his hand was weary and clung to the sword" (2 Samuel 23:10 NASV).

We can be weary of criticism and persecution.

I am weary with my sighing;
Every night I make my bed swim,
I dissolve my couch with my tears.
My eye has wasted away with grief;
It has become old because of all my
adversaries
(Psalm 6:6-7 NASV).

Lots of things are fine in themselves, but our strength has its limits. . . . and before long fatigue cuts our feet out from beneath us. The longer the weariness lingers, the more we face the danger of that weary condition clutching our inner man by the throat and strangling our hope, our motivation, our spark, our optimism, our encouragement.

Like Isaiah, I want to "sustain the weary" with a word of encouragement (Isaiah 50:4). Since our Lord never grows weary, He is able to give strength to the weary—He really is! If you question that, you *must* stop and read Isaiah 40:28-31. Do that right now.

But let's understand that God does not dispense strength and encouragement like a druggist fills your prescription. The Lord doesn't promise to give us something to take so we can handle our weary moments. He promises us Himself. That is all. And that is enough. The Savior says:

"Come to me, all you who are weary and burdened, and I will give you rest. Take my yoke upon you and learn from me, for I am gentle and humble in heart, and you will find rest for your souls. For my yoke is easy and my burden is light" (Matthew 11:28-30).

And Paul writes:

For he himself is our peace. . . (Ephesians 2:14).

In place of our exhaustion and spiritual fatigue, He will give us rest. All He asks is that we come to Him . . . that we spend a while thinking about Him, meditating on Him, talking to Him, listening in silence, occupying ourselves with Him—totally and thoroughly lost in the hiding place of His presence.

> Consider him . . . so that you will not grow weary and lose heart (Hebrews 12:3).

Growing weary, please observe, can result in losing heart.

Art thou weary? Heavy laden? Distressed? Come to the Savior. Come immediately, come repeatedly, come boldly. And be at rest.

When was the last time you came to the Lord, all alone, and gave Him your load of care?

No wonder you're discouraged. You're weary!

Come. Unload. He can handle it.

# "FINAL DESCENT. . . COMMENCE PRAYER"

The following incident took place in 1968 on an airliner bound for New York. It was a routine flight, and normally a boring affair. The kind of flights I like—uneventful. But this one proved to be otherwise.

Descending to our destination, the pilot realized the landing gear refused to engage. He worked the controls back and forth, trying again and again to make the gear lock down into place. No success. He then asked the control tower for instructions as he circled the landing field. Responding to the crisis, airport personnel sprayed the runway with foam as fire trucks and other emergency vehicles moved into position. Disaster was only minutes away.

The passengers, meanwhile, were told of each maneuver in that calm, cheery voice pilots manage to use at times like this. Flight attendants glided about the cabin with an air of cool reserve. Passengers were told to place their heads between their knees and grab their ankles just before impact. It was one of those I-can't-believe-this-is-happening-to-me experiences. There were tears, no doubt, and a few screams of despair. The landing was now seconds away.

Suddenly the pilot announced over the intercom:

> We are beginning our final descent. At this moment, in accordance with International Aviation Codes established at Geneva, it is my obligation to inform you that if you believe in God you should commence prayer.

I'm happy to report that the belly landing occurred without a hitch. No one was injured and, aside from some rather extensive damage to the plane, the airline hardly remembered the incident. In fact, a relative of one of the passengers called the airline the very next day and asked about the prayer rule the pilot had quoted. No one volunteered any information on the subject. Back to that cool reserve, it was simply, "No comment."

Amazing. The only thing that brought out into the open a deep-down "secret rule" was crisis. Pushed to the brink, back to the wall, right up to the wire, all escape routes closed . . . only then does our society crack open a hint of recognition that God just might be there and—"if you believe . . . you should commence prayer."

Reminds me of a dialogue I watched on the tube the other night. The guy being interviewed had "come back alive" from Mount St. Helens with pictures and sound track of his own personal nightmare. A reporter for a local television station, he was in close proximity to the crater when the mountain suddenly rumbled to life, spewing steam and ash miles into the air. The reporter literally ran for his life. With camera rolling and the mike on. The pictures were, of course, blurred and murky, but his voice was something else. Periodically, he'd click on his gear.

He admitted after this was played on the talk show that he only vaguely recalled saying many of those things. It was eerie, almost too personal to be disclosed. He breathed deeply, sobbed several times, panted, and spoke directly to God. No formality, no clichés—just the despairing cry of a creature in a crisis. Things like, "Oh, God, oh, my God . . . help! Help!! . . . Oh, Lord God, get me through. God, I need you, please help me; I don't know where I am"—more sobbing, more rapid breathing, spitting, gagging, coughing, panting—"It's so hot, so dark, help me, God! Please, please, please, please . . . oh, God!"

There's nothing to compare with crisis when it comes to finding out the otherwise hidden truth of the soul. Any soul. We may mask it, ignore it, pass it off with cool sophistication and intellectual denial . . . but take away the cushion of comfort, remove the shield of safety, interject the threat of death without the presence of people to take the panic out of the moment, and it's fairly certain most in the ranks of humanity "commence prayer."

David certainly did. When in "the slimy pit . . . the mud and mire," he testifies that Jehovah heard his cry (Psalm 40:1-2). So did Paul and Silas in that ancient Philippian prison when all seemed hopeless (Acts 16:25-26). It was from "the deep" Jonah cried for help . . . choking on salt water and engulfed by the Mediterranean currents, the prodigal prophet called out in his distress (Jonah 2:1-4). Old King Nebuchadnezzar did, too, fresh off a siege of insanity when he had lost his reason and lived like a wild beast in the open field. That former mental patient "raised his eyes toward heaven" and poured out the feelings of his soul to the Lord God, the very One the king had denied in earlier years (Daniel 4:29-37).

Crisis crushes. And in crushing, it often refines and purifies. You may be discouraged today because the crushing has not yet led to a surrender. I've stood beside too many of the dying, ministered to too many of the broken and bruised to believe that crushing is an end in itself. Unfortunately, however, it usually takes the brutal blows of affliction to soften and penetrate hard hearts. Even though such blows often seem unfair.

Remember Alexander Solzhenitsyn's admission:

> It was only when I lay there on rotting prison straw that I sensed within myself the first stirrings of good. Gradually, it was disclosed to me that the line separating good and evil passes, not through states, nor between

classes, nor between political parties either, but right through all human hearts. So, bless you, prison, for having been in my life.[5]

Those words provide a perfect illustration of the psalmist's instruction:

> Before I was afflicted I went astray,
> but now I obey your word.
> It was good for me to be afflicted
> so that I might learn your decrees
> (Psalm 119:67, 71).

After crises crush sufficiently, God steps in to comfort and teach.

Feel headed for a crash? Engulfed in crisis? Tune in the calm voice of your Pilot.

He knows precisely what He is doing. And bellylandings don't frighten Him one bit.

# PART TWO

# ENCOURAGE . . . ME, LORD?

"One of the highest of human duties is the duty of encouragement. . . . It is easy to laugh at men's ideals; it is easy to pour cold water on their enthusiasm; it is easy to discourage others. The world is full of discouragers. We have a Christian duty to encourage one another. Many a time a word of praise or thanks or appreciation or cheer has kept a man on his feet. Blessed is the man who speaks such a word."[7]

—William Barclay

Now if your experience of Christ's encouragement and love means anything to you, if you have known something of the fellowship of his Spirit, and all that it means in kindness and deep sympathy, do make my best hopes for you come true! Live together in love, as though you had only one mind and one spirit between you. Never act from motives of rivalry or personal vanity, but in humility think more of one another than you do of yourselves. None of you should think only of his own affairs, but each should learn to see things from other people's point of view. Let Christ Jesus be your example as to what your attitude should be.

(Philippians 2:1-5 PHILLIPS)

# TAKE TIME
# TO BE TENDER

Back when I was a kid I got a bellyache that wouldn't go away. It hurt so bad I couldn't stand up straight. Or sit down without increasing the pain. Finally, my folks hauled me over to a big house in West Houston where a doctor lived. He had turned the back section into his office and clinic.

It was a hot, muggy afternoon. I was scared.

The doc decided I needed a quick exam— but he really felt I was suffering from an attack of appendicitis. He had whispered that with certainty under his breath to my mom. I remember the fear that gripped me when I pictured myself having to go to a big, white-brick hospital, be put to sleep, get cut on, then endure having those stitches jerked out.

Looking back, however, I really believe that "quick exam" hurt worse than surgery the next day. The guy was rough, I mean really rough. He poked and thumped and pulled and pushed at me like I was Raggedy

Andy. I was already in pain, but when old Dr. Vice Grip got through, I felt like I had been his personal punching bag. To him, I was nothing more than a ten-year-old specimen of humanity. Male, blond, slight build, ninety-nine-degree temperature, with undetermined abdominal pain—and nauseated.

Never once do I recall his looking at me, listening to me, talking with me, or encouraging me in any way. Although young, I distinctly remember feeling like I bored the man—like case No. 13 that day, appendectomy No. 796 for him in his practice. And if the truth were known, an irritating interruption in his plans for nine holes later that afternoon.

Granted, a ten-year-old with a bellyache is not the greatest challenge for a seasoned physician to face . . . but his insensitivity left a lasting impression. His lack of tender caring canceled out the significance of all those neatly framed diplomas, achievements, and awards plastered across the wall behind his desk. He may have been bright . . . but he was even *more* brutal.

At that painful, terrifying moment of my life, I needed more than credentials. Even as a little kid I needed compassion. A touch of kindness. A gentle, considerate, soft-spoken word of assurance. Something to cushion the blows of the man's cut-and-dried verdict, "This boy needs surgery—meet me at Memorial at five o'clock today." Over and out.

Looking back over thirty-five years, I've learned a valuable lesson: When people are hurting, they need more than an accurate analysis and diagnosis. More than professional advice. More, much more, than a stern, firm turn of a verbal wrench that cinches everything down tight.

Attorneys, doctors, counselors, physical therapists, dentists, fellow ministers, nurses, teachers, disciplers, parents, hear ye, hear ye! Fragile and delicate are the feelings of most who seek our help. They need to sense we are there because we care . . . not just because it's our job. Truth and tact make great bedfellows.

Sound too liberal? Weak? Would it help if you could see that someone like the Apostle Paul embraced this philosophy? He did. Although a brilliant and disciplined man, he was tender.

"You know we never used flattery,
nor did we put on a mask to cover up

greed—God is our witness. We were not looking for praise from men, not from you or anyone else.

"As apostles of Christ we could have been a burden to you, but we were gentle among you, like a mother caring for her little children. We loved you so much that we were delighted to share with you not only the gospel of God but our lives as well, because you had become so dear to us"

(1 Thessalonians 2:5-8).

Someday we shall all be at the receiving end—you can count on it. We shall be the ones in need of affirmation, encouragement, a gentle touch of tenderness. It's like the time-worn counsel of the good doctor Thomas Sydenham, the "English Hippocrates" (1624-1689). Addressing himself to the professionals of his day, Dr. Sydenham wrote:

It becomes every person who purposes to give himself to the care of others, seriously to consider the four following things: First, that he must one day give an account to the Supreme Judge of all the lives entrusted to his care. Second, that all his skill and knowledge and energy, as they have been given him by God, so they should be exercised for His glory and the good of mankind, and not for mere gain or ambition. Third, and not more beautifully than truly, let him reflect that he has undertaken the care of no mean creature; for, in order that he may estimate the value, the greatness of the human race, the only begotten Son of God became himself a man, and thus ennobled it with His divine dignity, and far more than this, died to redeem it. And fourth, that the doctor being himself a mortal human being, should be diligent and tender in relieving his suffering patients, inasmuch as he himself must one day be a like sufferer.[8]

And that applies to ten-year-olds with a bellyache, eighty-year-olds with a backache, anybody with a headache . . . and everybody with a heartache.

# A BRIDGE CALLED CREDIBILITY

March 11, 1942, was a dark, desperate day at Corregidor. The Pacific theater of war was threatening and bleak. One island after another had been buffeted into submission. The enemy was now marching into the Philippines as confident and methodical as the star band in the Rose Bowl parade. Surrender was inevitable. The brilliant and bold soldier, Douglas MacArthur, had only three words for his comrades as he stepped into the escape boat destined for Australia.

**I shall return.**

Upon arriving nine days later in the port of Adelaide, the sixty-two-year-old military statesman closed his remarks with this sentence:

**I came through and I shall return.**

A little over 2½ years later—October 20,

1944, to be exact—he stood once again on Philippine soil after landing safely at Leyte Island. This is what he said:

This is the voice of freedom, General MacArthur speaking. People of the Philippines:

## I have returned!

MacArthur kept his word. His word was as good as his bond. Regardless of the odds against him, including the pressures and power of enemy strategy, he was bound and determined to make his promise good.

This rare breed of man is almost extinct. Whether an executive or an apprentice, a student or a teacher, a blue collar or white, a Christian or pagan—rare indeed are those who keep their word. The prevalence of the problem has caused the coining of terms painfully familiar to us in our era: credibility gap. To say that something is "credible" is to say it is "capable of being believed, trustworthy." To refer to a "gap" in such suggests a "breach or a reason for doubt."

Jurors often have reason to doubt the testimony of a witness on the stand. Parents, likewise, have reason at times to doubt their children's word (and vice versa). Citizens frequently doubt the promises of politicians and the credibility of an employee's word is questioned by the employer. Creditors can no longer believe a debtor's verbal promise to pay and many a mate has ample reason to doubt the word of his or her partner. This is a terrible dilemma! Precious few do what they say they will do without a reminder, a warning, or a threat. Unfortunately, this is true even among Christians.

Listen to what the Scriptures have to say about keeping your word:

> Therefore each of you must put off falsehood and speak truthfully to his neighbor . . .
>
> (Ephesians 4:25).

> And whatever you do, whether in word or deed, do it all in the name of the Lord Jesus . . .
>
> (Colossians 3:17).

> O LORD, who may abide in Thy tent? Who may dwell on Thy holy hill? He who walks with integrity. . .

And speaks truth in his heart.

> (Psalm 15:1-2 NASV).

It is better not to vow than to make a vow and not fulfill it

> (Ecclesiastes 5:5).

When a man . . . takes an oath to obligate himself by a pledge, he must not break his word but must do everything he said

> (Numbers 30:2).

Question: Judging yourself on this matter of keeping your word, are you bridging or widening the credibility gap? Are you encouraging or discouraging others? Let me help you answer that by using four familiar situations.

1. When you reply, "Yes, I'll pray for you"—do you?
2. When you tell someone they can depend on you to help them out—can they?
3. When you say you'll be there at such-and-such a time—are you?
4. When you obligate yourself to pay a debt on time—do you?

Granted, no one's perfect. But if you fail, do you own up to it? Do you quickly admit your failure to the person you promised and refuse to rationalize around it? If you do you are really rare . . . but a person of genuine integrity. And one who is an encouragement and can encourage others.

Do you know something? I know another One who promised He would return. He, too, will keep His word. In fact, He's never broken one promise. There's no credibility gap with Him. He *will* return. I can hardly wait to see His smiling face.

Talk about encouragement!

# STAY IN CIRCULATION

People who encourage people aren't loners, out of touch with humanity, distant and unreachable.

During the reign of Oliver Cromwell, the British government began to run low on silver for coins. Lord Cromwell sent his men on an investigation of the local cathedral to see if they could find any precious metal there. After investigating, they reported:

> The only silver we could find is in the statues of the saints standing in the corners.

To which the radical soldier and statesman of England replied:

> Good! We'll melt down the saints and put them into circulation![9]

Not bad theology for a proper, straitlaced, Lord Protector of the Isles, huh? In a few words the direct order states the essence . . .

the kernel . . . the practical goal of authentic Christianity. Not rows of silver saints, highly polished, frequently dusted, crammed into the corners of elegant cathedrals. Not plaster people cloaked in thin layers of untarnished silver and topped with a metallic halo. But real persons. Melted saints circulating through the mainstream of humanity. Bringing worth and value down where life transpires in the raw. Without the faint aura of stained glass, the electric modulation of the organ, and the familiar comforts of padded pews and dimmed lights. Out where bottom-line theology is top-shelf priority. You know the places:

On campuses where students scrape through the varnish of shallow answers.

In the shop where unbelieving employees test the mettle of everyday Christianity.

At home with a houseful of kids, where "R and R" means Run and Rassle.

In the concrete battlegrounds of sales competition, seasonal conventions, and sexual temptations, where hard-core assaults are made on internal character.

On the hospital bed, when reality never takes a nap.

In the office, where diligence and honesty are forever on the scaffold.

On the team where patience and self-control are X-rayed under pressure.

It's easy to kid ourselves. So easy. The Christian must guard against self-deception. We can begin to consider ourselves martyrs because we are in church twice on Sunday— really sacrificing by investing a few hours on the "day of rest." Listen, my friend, being among the saints is no sacrifice . . . it's a brief, choice privilege. The cost factor occurs on Monday or Tuesday . . . and during the rest of the week. That's when we're "melted down and put into circulation." That's when they go for the jugular. And it is remarkable how that monotonous work-week test discolors many a silver saint. "Sunday religion" may seem sufficient, but it isn't. Deception can easily result in a surprise ending.

Shed a tear for Jimmy Brown
Poor Jimmy is no more.
For what he thought was $H_2O$
Was $H_2SO_4$.

It's the acid grind that takes the toll, isn't it? Maybe that explains why the venerable prophet of God touched a nerve with his probing query:

> If racing with mere men—these men of Anathoth—has wearied you, how will you race against horses, . . . If you stumble and fall on open ground, what will you do in Jordan's jungles?
>
> (Jeremiah 12:5, TLB).

Doing battle in the steaming jungle calls for shock troops in super shape. No rhinestone cowboys can cut it among the swamps and insects of the gross world system. Sunday-go-to-meetin' silver saints in shining armor are simply out of circulation if that's the limit to their faith. Waging wilderness warfare calls for sweat . . . energy . . . keen strategy . . . determination . . . a good supply of ammunition . . . willingness to fight . . . refusal to surrender, even with the elephants tromping on your airhose.

And that is why we must be melted! It's all part of being "in circulation." Those who successfully wage war with silent heroism under relentless secular pleasure—ah, *they* are the saints who know what it means to be melted.

You can opt for an easier path. Sure. You can keep your own record and come out smelling like a rose. Your game plan might look something like this:

Dressed up and drove to church. Check
Walked three blocks in the rain. Check
Got a seat and sat quietly. Check
Sang each verse, smiled appropriately. Check
Gave $5 . . . listened to the sermon. Check
Closed my Bible, prayed, looked pious. Check
Shook hands . . . walked out, quickly forgot. Check

Still a saint? Uh-huh . . . a silver one, in fact. Polished to a high-gloss sheen. Icily regular, cool and casual, consistently present . . . and safely out of circulation. (Another touch-me-not whatnot.)

. . . until the Lord calls for an investigation of the local cathedral.

# THE FINE ART OF
# BLOWING IT

It happens to every one of us. Teachers as well as students. Cops as well as criminals. Bosses as well as secretaries. Parents as well as kids. The diligent as well as the lazy. Not even presidents are immune. Or corporation heads who earn six-figure salaries. The same is true of well-meaning architects and hard-working builders and clear-thinking engineers . . . not to mention pro ball players, politicians, and preachers.

What? Making mistakes, that's what. Doing the wrong thing, usually with the best of motives. And it happens with remarkable regularity.

Let's face it, success is overrated. All of us crave it despite daily proof that man's real genius lies in quite the opposite direction. It's really incompetence that we're all pros at. Which brings me to a basic question that has been burning inside me for months: How come we're so surprised when we see it in others and so devastated when it has occurred in ourselves?

Show me the guy who wrote the rules for perfectionism and I'll guarantee he's a nailbiter with a face full of tics . . . whose wife dreads to see him come home. Furthermore, he forfeits the right to be respected because he's either guilty of not admitting he blew it or he has become an expert at cover-up.

You can do that, you know. Stop and think of ways certain people can keep from coming out and confessing they blew it. Doctors can bury their mistakes. Lawyers' mistakes get shut up in prison—literally. Dentists' mistakes are pulled. Plumbers' mistakes are stopped. Carpenters turn theirs into sawdust. I like what I read in a magazine recently.

> Just in case you find any mistakes in this magazine, please remember they were put there for a purpose. We try to offer something for everyone. Some people are always looking for mistakes and we didn't want to disappoint you!

Hey, there have been some real winners! Back in 1957, Ford bragged about "the car of the decade." The Edsel. Unless you lucked out, the Edsel you bought had a door that wouldn't close, a hood that wouldn't open, a horn that kept getting stuck, paint that peeled, and a transmission that wouldn't fulfill its mission. One business writer likened the Edsel's sales graph to an extremely dangerous ski slope. He added that so far as he knew, there was only one case on record of an Edsel ever being stolen.

And how about that famous tower in Italy? The "leaning tower," almost twenty feet out of perpendicular. The guy that planned that foundation to be only ten feet deep (for a building 179 feet tall) didn't possess the world's largest brain. How would you like to have listed in *your* résumé, "Designed the Leaning Tower of Pisa"?

A friend of mine, realizing how adept I am in this business of blowing it, passed on to me an amazing book (accurate, but funny) entitled *The Incomplete Book of Failures* by Stephen Pile. Appropriately, the book itself had two missing pages when it was printed, so the first thing you read is an apology for the omission—and an erratum slip that provides the two pages.

Among the many wild and crazy reports

are such things as the least successful weather report, the worst computer, the most boring lecture, the worst aircraft, the slowest selling book, the smallest ever audience, the ugliest building ever constructed, the most chaotic wedding ceremony, and some of the worst statements . . . proven wrong by posterity. Some of those statements, for example, were:

"Far too noisy, my dear Mozart. Far too many notes."
—The Emperor Ferdinand after the first performance of *The Marriage of Figaro*

"If Beethoven's Seventh Symphony is not by some means abridged, it will soon fall into disuse."
—Philip Hale, Boston music critic, 1837

"Rembrandt is not to be compared in the painting of character with our extraordinarily gifted English artist Mr. Rippingille."
—John Hunt (1775-1848)

"Flight by machines heavier than air is unpractical and insignificant . . . utterly impossible."
—Simon Newcomb (1835-1909)

"We don't like their sound. Groups of guitars are on their way out."
—Decca Recording Company when turning down the Beatles in 1962.

"You will never amount to very much."
—A Munich schoolmaster to Albert Einstein, aged 10.[10]

And on and on it goes. The only thing we can be thankful for when it comes to blowing it is that nobody keeps a record of ours. Or do they? Or do you with others? Not if you are serious about encouragement.

Come on, ease off. If our perfect Lord is gracious enough to take our worst, our ugliest, our most boring, our least successful, our leaning-tower failures, our Edsel flops, and forgive them, burying them in the depths of the sea, then it's high time we give each other a break.

73

In fact, He promises full acceptance along with full forgiveness in print for all to read . . . without an erratum sheet attached. Isn't that encouraging? Can't we be that type of encourager to one another? After all, imperfection is one of the few things we still have in common. It links us close together in the same family!

So then, whenever one of us blows it and we can't hide it, how about a little support from those who haven't been caught yet?

Oops, correction. How about a lot of support?

# THE HEART OF ENCOURAGEMENT

The heart of the word "cordial" is the word "heart." The heart of "heart" is *kardia,* a Greek term that most often refers to the center of a person's inner life . . . the source or seat of all the forces and functions of our inner being. So when we think about being cordial, we are thinking about something that comes from and affects the very center of life itself. Maybe that's why the dictionary defines "cordial" like this:

> . . . of or relating to the heart: vital, tending to revive, cheer or invigorate, heartfelt, gracious. . . .

That's really a mouthful (or a heartful). In fact, that's worth a few minutes' meditation.

Being cordial literally starts from the heart, as I see it. Its origin begins with the deep-seated belief that the other guy is important, genuinely significant, deserving of my undivided attention and my unrivaled interest, if only for a few seconds. As cordiality is encouraged by such a belief, it then prompts me to be sensitive to that person's feelings.

If a person is uneasy and self-conscious, cordiality alerts me to put him at ease, to help him feel comfortable. If he is shy, cordiality provides a relief. If he is bored and bothered, cordiality stimulates and invigorates him. If he is sad and gloomy, cordiality brings cheer; it revives and rejuvenates him. What a needed and necessary virtue it is!

How do we project cordiality? In answer I suggest at least four basic ingredients:

## 1. A warm smile

Now lest you try, let me warn you against faking this. You don't learn to smile by practicing in front of a mirror. A smile has to be a natural part of your whole person, reflecting a friendliness that is genuine. There is nothing about you more magnetic or attractive than your smile. It will fit most every occasion and communicate volumes to other people.

When a king's face brightens, it means life;
his favor is like a rain cloud in spring
(Proverbs 16:15).

I'm afraid that some long-faced saints would crack their concrete masks if they smiled—I really am! Nothing repels like a frown . . . or attracts like a smile. It's downright contagious.

## 2. A solid handshake

Now I'm something of a specialist when it comes to handshakes. I've experienced about every kind.

Some are bonebreakers—like a cross between King Kong and Goliath (sometimes even from little, elderly ladies!). Others are completely boneless—like a handful of cool seaweed or a glove full of warm pudding. Some handshakes leave you exhausted, some cling like a crab, others turn into a small, curious wrestling match, never wanting to let go.

There are those, however, that are solid, sure, filled with such thoughts as, "Oh, how I appreciate you!" and "My, it's good to be in your presence!" and "Let me assure you of my love and interest!" Those say, "You're terrific!"

Never underestimate the value of this cordial expression. The handshake is one of a rare remaining species threatened with extinction in the family of touch. This is one of the quiet ways you "sharpen the iron" of another with your "iron" (Proverbs 27:17).

### 3. Direct eye contact

Accompanying every handshake and conversation, no matter how brief, ought to be an eyeball-to-eyeball encounter. The eyes reflect deep feelings enclosed in the secret chamber of your soul, which have no other means of release. This allows others to read how you feel about them. Cordiality cannot be expressed indirectly.

### 4. A word of encouragement

Keep this fresh, free from clichés, and to the point. Call his name (or ask for it) and use it as you talk. If time permits, mention something you honestly appreciate about him. Be specific and natural, but do not try to flatter the person. Let your heart be freely felt as your words flow.

> Oil and perfume make the heart glad,
> So a man's counsel is sweet to his
> friend (Proverbs 27:9 NASV).

People who encourage are cordial. Are you?

# DRESS YOUR DREAMS
# IN DENIM

(Some collegians think manual labor is the president of Mexico)... until they graduate. Suddenly, the light dawns. Reality frowns. And that sheltered, brainy, fair-skinned, squint-eyed scholar who has majored in medieval literature and minored in Latin comes of age. He experiences a strange sensation deep within his abdomen two weeks after framing his diploma. Hunger. Remarkable motivation accompanies this feeling.

His attempts at finding employment prove futile. Those places that have an opening don't really need a guy with a master's in medieval lit. They can't even spell it. Who cares if a truck driver understands European poetry from the twelfth century? Or what does it matter if the fella stocking the shelves at Safeway can give you the ninth letter in the Latin alphabet? When it comes to landing a job, most employers are notoriously pragmatic and unsophisticated. They are looking for people who have more than academic, gray wrinkles between their ears. They really couldn't care less about how much a guy or gal knows. What they want is someone who can put to use the knowledge that's been gained, whether the field is geology or accounting, engineering or plumbing, physics or barbering, journalism or welding.

That doesn't just happen. People who are in great demand today are those who can see it in their imaginations—then pull it off. Those who can think—then follow through. Those who dress their daring dreams in practical denim workclothes. That takes a measure of gift, a pinch of skill, and a ton of discipline! Being practical requires that we traffic in reality, staying flexible at the intersections where stop-and-go lights flash. It also demands an understanding of others who are driving so as to avoid collisions.

Another mark of practicality is a constant awareness of time. The life of a practical person is fairly uncomplicated and usually methodical. The practical mind would rather meet a deadline and settle for limited objectives than accomplish the maximum and be late.

The favorite expressions of a practical soul often begin with "what?"

What does the job require?

What do you expect of me?

What is the deadline?

What are the techniques?

Or "how" . . .

How does it work?

How long will it take?

How much does it cost?

How fast can it go?

Dreamers don't mix too well with pragmatists. They irritate each other when they rub together . . . yet both are necessary. Take away the former and you've got a predictable and occasionally dull result. Remove the latter and you've got creative ideas without wheels, slick visions without handles . . . and you go broke trying to get it off the runway.

The Bible is full of men and women who dreamed dreams and saw visions. But they didn't stop there. They had faith, they were people who saw the impossible, and yet their feet were planted on planet earth.

Take Nehemiah. What a man! He had the task of rebuilding the stone wall around Jerusalem. He spent days thinking, praying, observing, dreaming, and planning. But was he ever practical! He organized a mob into work parties . . . he faced criticism realistically . . . he stayed at the task without putting out needless fires . . . he met deadlines . . . and he maintained the budget.

Or take Abigail. What a woman! She was married to a first-class fink, Nabal by name, alias Archie Bunker. Because of his lack of wisdom, his greed, prejudice, and selfishness, he aroused the ire of his employees. They laid plans to kill him. Being a woman of faith, Abigail thought through the plot, prayed, and planned. Then she did a remarkable thing. She catered a meal to those hungry, angry men. Smart gal! Because of her practicality, Nabal's life was saved and an angry band of men was calmed and turned back.

It is the practical person, writes Emerson, who becomes "a vein in times of terror that commands the admiration of the wisest." So true. Amazing thing about the practical person—he may not have the most fun or think the deepest thoughts, but he seldom goes hungry!

Just now finishing school? Looking for a job? Is this the reason you're discouraged? Remember this—dreams are great and visions are fun. But in the final analysis, when the bills come due, they'll be paid by manual labor. Labor . . . hard work forged in the furnace of practicality.

I encourage you . . . get with it. Be practical, that is.

# "THE OPRA AIN'T OVER"

The words were painted in bright red on a banner hung over the wall near the forty-yard line of Texas Stadium, home of the Dallas Cowboys football team, on Sunday afternoon.

The guys in silver and blue were struggling to stay in the race for the playoffs. So a dyed-in-the-wool Cowboy fan decided he would offer some back-home encouragement straight out of his country-western repertoire. He scratched around his garage on Saturday and found some paint, a big brush, and a ruler . . . then splashed those words on a king-size bed sheet for all America to read:

The Opra Ain't Over
'til the Fat Lady Sings.

It was his way of saying, "We're hangin' in there, baby. Don't count us out. We have three games left before anybody can say for sure . . . so we're not givin' up! The opra ain't over!"

Sure is easy to jump to conclusions, isn't it? People who study trends make it their business to manufacture out of their imaginations the proposed (and "inevitable") end result. Pollsters do that, too. After a sampling of three percent of our country, vast and stunning stats are predicted. Our worry increases. We are all informed that so-and-so will, for sure, wind up doing such-and-such. At times it's downright scary. And discouraging.

Every once in awhile it's helpful to remember times when those folks wound up with egg on their faces. Much to our amazement, the incredible often happens.

Like when Wellington whipped Napoleon
Or Truman beat Dewey
And Washington won in the Rose Bowl
Like that time the earthquake didn't hit
And England didn't surrender
And Star Wars didn't grab a fistful of Academy Awards
And Hitler wasn't the anti-Christ
And the communists didn't take over America by 1980
And Muhammad Ali could get beaten.

And a nation could continue on through the disillusionments of Viet Nam, White House and senatorial scandals, assassination attempts, energy crises, and nuclear mishaps.

Yes, at many a turn we have all been tempted to jump to so-called "obvious" conclusions, only to be surprised by a strange curve thrown our way. God is good at that. When He does, it really encourages His people.

Can you recall a few biblical examples?

A wiry teenager, armed with only a sling and a stone, whipped a giant over nine feet tall. Nobody would've predicted that.

With an Egyptian army fast approaching and no possible way to escape, all looked bleak. But not so! Against nature and reversing the pull of gravity, a sea opened up and allowed the Hebrews to walk across.

And how about the vast, "indestructible" wall around Jericho? Who would've ever imagined?

Or that dead-end street at Golgotha miraculously opening back up at an empty tomb three days later?

Or a handful of very human disciples turning the world upside down? Anybody—and I mean anybody—who would have been near enough to have witnessed any one of those predicaments would certainly have said, "Curtains . . . the opra is over!"

A lot of you who read this page are backed up against a set of circumstances that seem to spell T-H-E  E-N-D. All looks almost hopeless. Pretty well finished. Apparently over. Maybe you need to read that again, underlining those words:

seem to . . . almost . . . pretty well . . . apparently.

Your adversary would love for you to assume the worst. He'd enjoy seeing you heave a sigh and resign yourself to depressed feelings that accompany defeat, failure, maximum resentment, and minimum faith. After all, it's fairly obvious you're through. Well . . . since when does "fairly obvious" draw the curtain on the last act? It's been my experience that when God is involved, anything can happen. The One who directed that stone in between Goliath's eyes and split the Red Sea down the middle and leveled that wall around Jericho and brought His Son back from beyond takes delight in mixing up the odds as He alters the obvious and bypasses the inevitable.

The blind songwriter, Fanny Crosby, put it another way:

> Chords that were broken will vibrate once more.[11]

In other words, don't manufacture conclusions. Don't even think in terms of "this is the way things will turn out." Be open. Stay that way. God has a beautiful way of bringing good vibes out of broken chords. When the Lord is in it, anything is possible. In His performances there are dozens of "fat ladies" waiting to sing the finale.

The opra ain't over.

# BE AN ENCOURAGER!

It all comes down to this: A strong commitment to the encouragement of others. But Henry Drummond's remark haunts me at times:

> How many prodigals are kept out of the kingdom of God by the unlovely characters of those who profess to be inside!

Will you allow me, in this closing, private chat with you, to pick out one "unlovely" characteristic frequently found in Christian circles . . . and develop it from a positive point of view? I'm thinking of the lack of encouragement in our relationship with others. It's almost an epidemic!

To illustrate this point, when did *you* last encourage someone else? I firmly believe that an individual is never more Christ-like than when full of compassion for those who are down, needy, discouraged, or forgotten. How terribly essential is our commitment to encouragement!

Woven into the fabric of the book of Acts is the quiet yet penetrating life of a man who is a stranger to most Christians. Barnabas emerged from the island of Cyprus, destined to an abstruse role of "minister of encouragement." In fact, his name means "Son of Encouragement" according to Acts 4:36. In comparison to the brilliant spotlights of this book—Peter, Paul, Silas, James, and Apollos—Barnabas appears as a flickering flame . . . but, oh, how essential his light was. How warm . . . how inviting!

Journey with me through Chapter 4. The young, persecuted assembly at Jerusalem was literally "under the gun." If ever they needed encouragement, it was then. They were backed to the wall and financially stripped. Many were pressed, the needs were desperate. The comforter from Cyprus spontaneously gave all he had. He sold a tract of land and demonstrated that he was living for others by bringing the proceeds to this band of believers (vv. 32-37). That's what we might call **encouragement in finances**.

The next time Barnabas appears, he's at it again! In Chapter 11 the Body is growing and the Word is spreading like a flame. It's too big for the leaders to handle. Assistance is needed: gifted assistance. What does Barnabas do? He searches for and finds Saul of Tarsus (v. 25) who was an outcast because of his former life. Not afraid to stick his neck out for a new Christian who was suspect in the eyes of the public, Barnabas took him by the hand and brought him to Antioch. Before the entire assembly, the "Son of Encouragement" gave his new friend a push into a priority position . . . in fact, it was into the very place where Barnabas himself had been experiencing remarkable blessing as a church leader (vv. 22-23, 26).

Without a thought of jealousy, he later allowed Saul to take the leadership and set the pace for the first missionary journey (Chapter 13). It is interesting to note that the names were soon switched from "Barnabas . . . and Saul" (13:1), to "Paul and Barnabas" (13:42). This is the supreme test. It takes a great person to recognize that a man younger than he has God-given abilities and to encourage him to move ahead with full support. This we might call **encouragement of fellowship and followship**.

The curtain comes down upon Barnabas' life in Chapter 15. Journey 2 is about to begin. He and Paul discuss the possibility of taking John Mark, a young man who earlier had chosen not to encounter the rigors of that first missionary journey (13:13). Can you imagine that discussion?

"No," said Paul. "He failed once . . . he will again!"

"Yes," insisted Barnabas. "He can and will succeed with encouragement."

Paul would not withdraw his no vote. Barnabas stood his ground, believing in the young man's life, in spite of what happened before. Same style as always. You know the outcome (vv. 36-39). Barnabas demonstrated **encouragement in spite of failure**.

Oh, the need for this ministry today! Is there some soul known to you in need of financial encouragement? A student off at school . . . a young couple up against it . . . a divorcee struggling to gain back self-acceptance . . . a forgotten servant of God laboring in an obscure and difficult ministry . . . ? Encourage generously!

Do you know of someone who could and should be promoted to a place of greater usefulness, but is presently in need of your companionship and confidence? Go to bat for him! Stand in his stead . . . give him a boost. He needs your fellowship. How about someone who is better qualified than yourself? You would be amazed at the blessing God would pour out upon you if you'd really back him with "followship."

Then there are the failures. The Lots, the Samsons, the Jonahs, the Demases, the John Marks. Yes, they failed. They blew it. Are you big enough to extend a hand of encouragement and genuine love? Lift up the failure with encouragement. It pays off! It did in John's case. He wrote the Gospel of Mark and ultimately proved to be very useful to Paul's ministry (2 Timothy 4:11b).

To Henry Drummond's indictment, I suggest a solution. A new watchword for our times.

ENCOURAGEMENT!

Shout it out. Pass it around.

# CONCLUSION

You can talk all you want about diamonds or dinosaur teeth or marble-sized pearls. Sure they're rare. Sure they're tough to find. You've got to tunnel under mountains, excavate ancient lakebeds, or dive to murky depths in mysterious lagoons.

But I submit that encouragement —genuine, warm-hearted, Christ-inspired encouragement—is an even more precious commodity than these. And infinitely more valuable.

Encouragement is awesome. Think about it: It has the capacity to lift a man's or woman's shoulders. To spark the flicker of a smile on the face of a discouraged child. To breathe fresh fire into the fading embers of a smoldering dream. To actually change the course of another human being's day . . . or week . . . or life.

That, my friend, is no small thing. But it doesn't stop there. Consistent, timely encouragement has the staggering magnetic power to draw an immortal soul to the God of hope. The One whose name is Wonderful Counselor.

Is it easy? Not on your life. It takes courage, tough-minded courage, to trust God, to believe in ourselves, and to reach a hand to others. But what a beautiful way to live. I know of no one more needed, more valuable, more Christ-like, than the person who is committed to encouragement. In spite of others' actions. Regardless of others' attitudes. It is the musical watchword that takes the grind out of living—encouragement.

Those of you who are living with Christ in your life will not be able to maintain this encouraging lifestyle unless the Spirit of God is given the controls and freedom to live His life through you. God gave us His Spirit so that He might come alongside and encourage us day after day. Please release yourself to Him so that you, in turn, can release yourself to others.

Those of you who do not claim to know Christ personally cannot expect to enter into the depths of these thoughts unless you turn, by faith, to the Son of God, Jesus our Lord. Only then can you receive the encouragement God promises His people. And only then can you give to others the kind of lasting encouragement that will not only ease hurts, but also change lives.

When David was "greatly distressed" (1 Samuel 30:6 KJV), nose-to-nose with death and heart-deep in discouragement, Scripture tells us that he "encouraged himself in the LORD his God."

David's Refuge is available to you . . . right now. No waiting. No appointment necessary.

And the Encourager is in.

# NOTES

1. From *Psalms of My Life* by Joseph Bayly, copyright 1969 by Tyndale House Publishers, Wheaton, Ill. Used by permission.
2. Bruce Larsen and Keith Miller, *The Edge of Adventure* (Waco, Tex.: Word Books, 1974), p. 156.
3. Dorothy Hsu, *Mending* (Elgin, Ill.: David C. Cook Publishing Co., 1979). Used by permission.
4. F. B. Meyer, *Christianity in Isaiah* (Grand Rapids: Zondervan Publishing House, 1950), p. 9.
5. Alexander Solzhenitsyn, *The Gulag Archipelago,* quoted in Philip Yancey, *Where Is God When It Hurts?* (Grand Rapids: Zondervan Publishing House, 1977), p. 51.
6. Henry W. Baker, "Art Thou Weary, Art Thou Languid?"
7. William Barclay, The Letter to the Hebrews, *The Daily Study Bible* (Edinburgh: The St. Andrew Press, 1955), pp. 137-138.
8. Reprinted by permission from the Christian Medical Society Journal, Vol. XII Number

2 1981. The Christian Medical Society is a fellowship of Christian physicians and dentists representing Jesus Christ in and through medicine and dentistry.

9. Richard H. Seume, *Shoes for the Road* (Chicago: Moody Press, 1974), p. 117.
10. Stephen Pile, *The Incomplete Book of Failures* (New York: E. P. Dutton, 1979), pp. 165-167.
11. Fanny Crosby, "Rescue the Perishing."

Among the titles available are:

**On the Anvil**
Max Lucado

**The Jesus I Never Knew**
Philip Yancey

**Lord, Teach Me to Pray**
Kay Arthur

**The Knowledge of the Holy**
A. W. Tozer

**Where Is God When It Hurts?**
Philip Yancey

**The Pursuit of Holiness**
Jerry Bridges

**Six Hours One Friday**
Max Lucado

**Heaven: Your Real Home**
Joni Eareckson Tada

**What Happens to Good People
When Bad Things Happen**
Robert A. Schuller

**I Am with You Always**
G. Scott Sparrow

**Strength to Love**
Martin Luther King Jr.

**And the Angels Were Silent**
Max Lucado

**Apples of Gold**
Jo Petty

**The Best of Catherine Marshall**
Edited by Leonard LeSourd

**Book of Hours**
Elizabeth Yates

**Brush of an Angel's Wing**
Charlie W. Shedd

**Finding God**
Larry Crabb

**A Gathering of Hope**
Helen Hayes

**Getting Through the Night**
Eugenia Price

**God Came Near**
Max Lucado

**Golden Treasury of Psalms and Prayers**
Edna Beilenson

**Good Morning, Holy Spirit**
Benny Hinn

**The Grace Awakening**
Charles Swindoll

**The Greatest Salesman in the World**
Og Mandino

**The Greatest Story Ever Told**
Fulton Oursler

**The Guideposts Christmas Treasury**

**Hinds' Feet on High Places**
Hannah Hurnard

**Hope and Faith for Tough Times**
Robert Schuller

**Hope for the Troubled Heart**
Billy Graham

**Laugh Again**
Charles Swindoll

**Love Is a Gentle Stranger**
June Masters Bacher

**Love's Silent Song**
June Masters Bacher

**Lydia**
Lois Henderson

**More Than a Carpenter**
Josh McDowell

**No Wonder They Call Him the Savior**
Max Lucado

**The Power of Positive Thinking**
Norman Vincent Peale

**Prayers and Promises for Every Day**
Corrie ten Boom

**The Source of My Strength**
Charles Stanley

**Three Steps Forward, Two Steps Back**
Charles Swindoll

**To Help You Through the Hurting**
Marjorie Holmes

**To Mother With Love**
Helen Steiner Rice

**A Treasury of Christmas Classics**

**The Wonderful Spirit-Filled Life**
Charles Stanley